SOON, ONE MORNING

SOON,
ONE MORNING

NEW WRITING
BY AMERICAN NEGROES
1940-1962

SELECTED AND EDITED, WITH AN INTRODUCTION
AND BIOGRAPHICAL NOTES, BY

HERBERT HILL

19 63

NEW YORK   ALFRED · A · KNOPF

ACKNOWLEDGMENTS

"Letters from a Journey" by James Baldwin, together with "A Note on the Baldwin Letters" by Robert P. Mills, appeared in *Harper's Magazine,* May 1963. "The Seventh Day," reprinted from *Go Tell It on the Mountain* by James Baldwin. Copyright 1952, 1953 by James Baldwin. Used with the permission of the publishers, The Dial Press, Inc. "Helen" from *Maud Martha* by Gwendolyn Brooks. Copyright 1953 by Gwendolyn Brooks Blakely. Reprinted by permission of Harper & Row, Publishers. "The Mother," "A Song in the Front Yard," "When You Have Forgotten Sunday: The Love Story," and "The Sundays of Satin-Legs Smith" from *A Street in Bronzeville* by Gwendolyn Brooks. Copyright 1944 by Gwendolyn Brooks Blakely. Reprinted by permission of Harper & Row, Publishers. The selection from *Annie Allen* by Gwendolyn Brooks. Copyright 1949 by Gwendolyn Brooks Blakely. Reprinted by permission of Harper & Row, Publishers. Selections from *Beetlecreek* by William Demby, published 1950 by Rinehart and Company, Inc., New York. Copyright 1950 by William Demby. Reprinted by permission of the author. The selection from *A Touch of Innocence,* © 1959 by Katherine Dunham. Reprinted by permission of Harcourt, Brace & World, Inc. The selection from *Lonely Crusade* by Chester Himes, by permission of Alfred A. Knopf, Inc. Copyright 1947 by Chester Himes. The selection from *I Wonder as I Wander* by Langston Hughes, published by Rinehart and Company, Inc., New York. Copyright © 1956 by Langston Hughes. Reprinted by permission of Harold Ober Associates, Inc. Translations by Langston Hughes of "She Left Herself One Evening" by Léon Damas, "Flute Players" by Jean Joseph Rabéarivelo, and "Epigram" by Armand Lanusse, from *The Langston Hughes Reader* by Langston Hughes, published by George Braziller, Inc., New York. Copyright © 1958 by Langston Hughes. Reprinted by permission of Harold Ober Associates, Inc. "Dream Boogie," "Parade," "Children's Rhymes," "Night Funeral in Harlem" from *Selected Poems* by Langston Hughes, by permission of Alfred A. Knopf, Inc., New York. Copyright 1951, © 1959 by Langston Hughes. "Blues in Stereo," "Ask Your Mama," and "Jazztet Muted" from *Ask Your Mama* by Langston Hughes, by permission of Alfred A. Knopf, Inc., New York. Copyright © 1959, 1961 by Langston Hughes. "Rock, Church" from *Something in Common and Other Stories* by Langston Hughes. Copyright © 1963 by Langston Hughes. Reprinted by permission of Hill and Wang, Inc. "Lenox Avenue Mural, Harlem" (appearing here as "Harlem") and "Same in Blues" from *Montage of a Dream Deferred* by Langston Hughes, published by Holt, Rinehart and Winston, Inc., New York. Copyright 1951 by Langston Hughes. Reprinted by permission of Harold Ober Associates, Inc. The selection from *Proud Shoes* by Pauli Murray. Copyright © 1956 by Pauli Murray. Reprinted by permission of Harper & Row, Publishers. The selections from *The Living Is Easy* by Dorothy West are reprinted by permission of and arrangement with Houghton Mifflin Company, the authorized publishers. Copyright 1948 by Dorothy West. The epigraphs are quoted from "Yet Do I Marvel" in *Color* by Countee Cullen, copyright 1925 by Harper & Row, Publishers, by permission of the publishers; and from "O Black and Unknown Bards" in *St. Peter Relates an Incident* by James Weldon Johnson, copyright 1935 by James Weldon Johnson, by permission of The Viking Press.

L. C. catalog card number: 62-15567

THIS IS A BORZOI BOOK
PUBLISHED BY ALFRED A. KNOPF, INC.

FIRST EDITION

TO THE MEMORY

OF

RICHARD WRIGHT

Inscrutable His ways are, and immune
To catechism by a mind too strewn
With petty cares to slightly understand
What awful brain compels His awful hand.
Yet do I marvel at this curious thing:
To make a poet black, and bid him sing!

—COUNTEE CULLEN

———

O black and unknown bards of long ago,
How came your lips to touch the sacred fire?
How, in your darkness, did you come to know
The power and beauty of the minstrel's lyre?

—JAMES WELDON JOHNSON

ACKNOWLEDGMENTS

I AM indebted to many persons for their assistance in making this book possible. I wish to express my appreciation especially to Mr. Saunders Redding, of Hampton Institute, for sharing with me his valuable insights and for his many helpful suggestions; to Mr. Langston Hughes for his encouragement and for his help; and to Mr. Ralph Ellison, who so generously shared his time and wisdom with me. I wish also to express my appreciation to Mr. Arthur B. Spingarn, the distinguished president of the National Association for the Advancement of Colored People, who is the foremost collector of Negro literature in the United States, for his warm encouragement and many kindnesses; to Mr. James Baldwin for his valuable suggestions; to Mr. James W. Ivy, editor of *The Crisis* magazine, who assisted me in a variety of ways, as did Miss Era Bell Thompson, of Johnson Publications, Chicago, and Professor Owen Dodson, of Howard University, Washington, D.C. My thanks also to Dr. Nathan A. Scott, of the University of Chicago; Arna Bontemps, of Fisk University; and Robert Mills, of the General Artists Corporation.

I am indebted to Mr. Paul R. Reynolds, who for more than twenty years was Richard Wright's literary agent and who placed at my disposal valuable documents and manuscripts; to Mrs. Dorothy Porter, curator of the Arthur B. Spingarn Collection at Howard University, who gave to me the personal kindness and warm encouragement that she has given to a generation of scholars working in the field of Negro literature and history.

I wish to note my gratitude to Mrs. Muriel S. Outlaw, who painstakingly typed the manuscript of this book in all of its several revisions and assisted me in the extensive correspondence that this work required.

The idea for this book was born during long talks with Richard

Wright in Paris in the summer of 1960, just a few months before his untimely death. Mr. Wright had planned to write an essay for this volume to be called "Twenty Years of Negro Writing after *Native Son*," and had begun work on this at the time of his death. The dedication of this book to his memory is a small token of my respect and affection for this courageous man who had become a legend in his own time. My very special appreciation to Mrs. Ellen Wright, who made available to me the unfinished manuscripts of her late husband's work.

I must express my appreciation to Mr. Harold Strauss, of Alfred A. Knopf, Inc., who, in addition to giving his professional assistance, frequently gave me the encouragement and advice of a friend.

CONTENTS

Introduction / HERBERT HILL   3

SECTION I: ESSAYS

A Picnic with Sinclair Lewis / HORACE R. CAYTON   21
Letters from a Journey / JAMES BALDWIN   36
The Alien Land of Richard Wright / SAUNDERS REDDING   48
The Dilemma of the American Negro Scholar / JOHN HOPE
    FRANKLIN   60
Hide My Face?—On Pan-Africanism and Negritude / ST.
    CLAIR DRAKE   77
Moscow Movie From *"I Wonder as I Wander"* / LANG-
    STON HUGHES   106

SECTION II: FICTION

Five Episodes / RICHARD WRIGHT   139
Miss Muriel / ANN PETRY   165
From "Lonely Crusade" / CHESTER HIMES   210
Rock, Church / LANGSTON HUGHES   231
Out of the Hospital and Under the Bar / RALPH ELLISON   242
From "Proud Shoes" / PAULI MURRAY   291
The Life of Lincoln West / GWENDOLYN BROOKS   316
Helen From *"Maud Martha"* / GWENDOLYN BROOKS   320
From "The System of Dante's Hell" / LEROI JONES   323
    THE CHRISTIANS
    THE RAPE

Come Home Early, Chile / OWEN DODSON 337

Singing Dinah's Song / FRANK LONDON BROWN 348

The Creek From *"A Touch of Innocence"* / KATHERINE DUNHAM 355

Rat Joiner Routs the Klan / TED POSTON 378

The Almost White Boy / WILLARD MOTLEY 389

The Seventh Day From *"Go Tell It on the Mountain"* / JAMES BALDWIN 401

From *"Beetlecreek"* / WILLIAM DEMBY 452

From *"The Living Is Easy"* / DOROTHY WEST 480

From *"Thunder at Dawn"* / BENJAMIN A. BROWN 503

The Beach Umbrella / CYRUS COLTER 530

SECTION III: POEMS

From *"A Street in Bronzeville"* / GWENDOLYN BROOKS 557
THE MOTHER
A SONG IN THE FRONT YARD
WHEN YOU HAVE FORGOTTEN SUNDAY: THE LOVE STORY
THE SUNDAYS OF SATIN-LEGS SMITH

From *"Annie Allen"* / GWENDOLYN BROOKS 565
FIVE POEMS

Abraham Lincoln of Rock Spring Farm / M. B. TOLSON 571

Veracruz / ROBERT HAYDEN 578

Full Moon / ROBERT HAYDEN 581

Picnic: The Liberated / M. CARL HOLMAN 582

Three Brown Girls Singing / M. CARL HOLMAN 585

Mr. Z / M. CARL HOLMAN 586

From *"Ask Your Mama: 12 Moods for Jazz"* / LANGSTON HUGHES 587
BLUES IN STEREO
ASK YOUR MAMA
JAZZTET MUTED

From *"Montage of a Dream Deferred"* / LANGSTON HUGHES 593
DREAM BOOGIE
PARADE

xiii

CONTENTS

CHILDREN'S RHYMES
NIGHT FUNERAL IN HARLEM
HARLEM
SAME IN BLUES

Translations from the French / LANGSTON HUGHES   603

EPIGRAM / ARMAND LANUSSE (Louisiana)
SHE LEFT HERSELF ONE EVENING / LÉON DAMAS (French Guiana)
FLUTE PLAYERS / JEAN JOSEPH RABÉARIVELO (Madagascar)

To a Brown Girl / OSSIE DAVIS   607

Charlie Parker: The Human Condition / LEROI JONES   609

From *"Preface to a Twenty Volume Suicide Note"* / LEROI JONES   611

THE INSIDIOUS DR. FU MAN CHU
THE NEW SHERIFF
THE TURNCOAT

To Satch (or American Gothic) / PAUL VESEY   614

From *"Ivory Tusks"* / PAUL VESEY   616

A MOMENT PLEASE

SOON, ONE MORNING

INTRODUCTION

BY HERBERT HILL

THE GREATER PART of contemporary American Negro writing is characterized by a determination to break through the limits of racial parochialism into the whole range of the modern writer's preoccupations. Though the Negro world frequently remains their emotional home, Negro writers in a variety of ways have abandoned the literature of simple and unrelieved protest, and have made the creative act their first consideration. They continue to confront American society as Negroes, but increasingly without the conflict between social and literary aspirations that marked the work of Negro authors in the past. Now most often they use the concepts of "Negro" and "race" as universal symbols in a new concern with the problems of individual consciousness, identity, and alienation.

Negro authors, in dealing with the reality of American life, have, of course, been unable to escape an awareness of the racial situation, especially one that fundamentally changes so very little. Now, however, this awareness is being transmuted brilliantly and powerfully into literature. Until recently Negro writing was, with a few important exceptions, mainly interesting as sociology, but today the individual Negro artist is asserting his vision and his creative imagination.

Alfred Kazin recently commented that "all that's good in American writing, American art, comes out of the profound confrontation of social facts. It was true of *Moby Dick*, of *Leaves of Grass*. It comes out of what I consider to be the driving force behind all things, which is human hunger, human desire.

"Only it's a question, of course, not of how much you desire or how bad you feel, but how artistically you can realize your desires.

"Among the best of the contemporary Negro writers, their work and their art represents a realization of their experience and social intelligence. Without this social awareness, their social intelligence, there would be no literature, there would be no art."

Of course, the writer must know what he is attacking, what he is saying no to and why. Ultimately, there is literature and culture and in the final sense this is what will count for the artist.

Today the Negro artist, as he enters into the main stream of contemporary literature, feels a new strength and refuses to be limited to racial protest or to the conventional Negro themes of the past. Self-pity and dreary rage are clearly no longer enough. As the Negro writer moves beyond anger, he develops a new concern for the writer's craft for literary discipline and control, and seeks an involvement in the larger world of art and ideology.

Thus Saunders Redding has expressed this determination in a passage in his book *On Being a Negro in America:* "I want to get on to other things. . . . The obligations imposed by race on the average educated or talented Negro . . . are vast and become at last onerous. I am tired of giving up my creative initiative to these demands." And the gifted Ralph Ellison, commenting on fiction by Negro authors, has written that "people who want to write sociology shouldn't write novels."

Two decades ago, however, the transition had barely begun. The publication in 1940 of Richard Wright's *Native Son* represented a significant moment in the history of the Negro novel in America. Wright drew upon an earlier tradition of naturalism in American writing, and within it created a dramatic novel of protest, with political overtones, which reached a vast audience at home and abroad, and later, as a play and motion picture, exerted a compelling influence on a generation of Negro writers.

If Stephen Crane and Frank Norris and Theodore Dreiser were, as V. L. Parrington observed, "the intellectual children of the nineties, and their art was a reflection of that sober period of American disillusion," then one must regard the "social protest" and "proletarian literature" writers of the 1930's as the "intellectual children" of the crisis of the world order which erupted in 1914, and their art as a reflection of the economic depression that brought collapse and disintegration to American society.

A major characteristic of the naturalistic novels of Dreiser is the rendering of characters that are determined and controlled by economic and social forces. Environment is everything, and man is to be understood as a social creature created by a milieu which is all-pervasive.

The writers of the radical novels of the thirties, continuing in this tradition but now involved in a political movement that proclaimed "art as a class weapon in the class war," were not simply concerned with the effects of environment upon individuals, as an earlier generation of American novelists had been, but consciously launched an attack upon the capitalist system, which, it was alleged, was directly responsible for the brutal exploitation and misery of the workers.

White writers of the "proletarian literature" school frequently dealt with racial themes, and Negro characters were often sentimentally or heroically depicted in novels about the "class struggle." Among these were Scott Nearing's *Free-Born* (1932), Myra Page's *Gathering Storm* (1932), Grace Lumpkin's *A Sign for Cain* (1935), and Josephine Johnson's novels, *Now in November* (1934), *Winter Orchard* (1935), and *Jordanstown* (1937). Negro writers were also affected by the experience of the depression, which was deeply felt by the entire Negro community, and some Negro novelists during this period, such as William Attaway in his novels *Let Me Breathe Thunder* (1939) and *Blood on the Forge* (1941), wrote what are essentially proletarian novels with a Negro rather than a white cast of characters.

Essentially, the framework for *Native Son*, one of the important novels in contemporary American literature, is to be found in its implicit assumption that the social order is directly responsible for the degradation of the Negro, that American society produces conditions that distort and destroy individual human beings who are part of an oppressed group. The character in the book who functions as Wright's spokesman states of Negroes that "taken collectively, they are not simply twelve million people; in reality, they constitute a separate nation, shunted, stripped and held captive within this nation, devoid of political, social, economic and property rights."

Although *Native Son* is basically a novel of protest, Richard Wright went beyond the attack on environment and injustice to a powerful symbolic rendering of the narrative material that is frequently a comment on the action itself.

In a tone of horror and anguish, through a rich use of metaphor and a continuous weaving of symbols into a story line that involves the reader in monstrous events, Wright creates an atmosphere in which everything is of "the extreme situation." And here the literary and artistic creativity of the author clearly differentiates it from other "problem novels" of the period.

Wright's spokesman in *Native Son* tells us, in describing the main character in the book, that he murdered

without thinking, without plan, without conscious motive. But, after he murdered, he accepted the crime. And that's the important thing. It was the first full act of his life; it was the most meaningful, exciting and stirring thing that had ever happened to him. He accepted it because it made him free, gave him the possibility of choice, of action, the opportunity to act and to feel that his actions carried weight. . . .

Let me tell you more. Before this trial the newspapers and the prosecution said that this boy had committed other crimes. It is true. He is guilty of numerous crimes. But search until the day of judgment, and you will find not one shred of evidence of them. He has murdered many times, but there are no corpses. Let me explain. This Negro boy's entire attitude toward life is a *crime!* The hate and fear which we have inspired in him, woven by our civilization into the very structure of his consciousness, into his blood and bones, into the hourly functioning of his personality, have become the justification of his existence.

Every time he comes in contact with us, he kills! It is a physiological and psychological reaction, embedded in his being. Every thought he thinks is potential murder. . . . Every desire, every dream, no matter how intimate or personal, is a plot or a conspiracy. Every hope is a plan for insurrection. Every glance of the eye is a threat. *His very existence is a crime.* . . .

Nathan A. Scott, of the University of Chicago, has observed that *Native Son* is, "paradoxically, controlled by precisely the assumptions about Negro life that elicited its rage, for the astonishing thing that it finally does is to offer a depraved and inhuman beast as the comprehensive archetypal image of the American Negro. The imagination that we meet here is extremist and melodramatic, feeding on the horrific themes of alienation and violence and abysmal fear, and its single occupation is with the racial tragedy. But many writers of great distinction have had what was two hundred years ago called a 'ruling passion,' and it does indeed seem to be very much a part of the kind of brilliance and assertiveness that we associate with major art: so that Mr. Wright should have had his ruling passion is not something that we shall hold against him: but what was unfortunate in him was his utter defenselessness before it."

After the appearance of Wright's *Native Son* and the poignant autobiographical *Black Boy* in 1945, and the publication of such novels as Chester Himes's *If He Hollers Let Him Go* (1945) and *The Street*, by Ann Petry (1946), the fake exoticism of Negro writing vanished, as did the idealized folksiness of tales about quaint and simple colored people.

In classic naturalistic fashion, Negro authors after Wright— such as Himes, Ann Petry, William Gardner Smith, and others— turned their attention to the corrosive effects of the urban slum and, with varying degrees of success, joined the tradition of social protest with the Negro's demands for racial equality and justice.

Thus, during the 1940's, Negro authors were writing "problem novels." Among these were William Gardner Smith's *Last of the Conquerors*, C. R. Offord's *The White Face*, George Wylie Henderson's *Jule*, Ann Petry's *The Street*, Chester Himes's *If He Hollers Let Him Go* and *Lonely Crusade*, Willard Motley's *Knock on Any Door*, Curtis Lucas's *Third Ward Newark*, and Willard Savoy's *Alien Land*. As the development of the creative imagination became the first concern of the Negro writer, the great variety and richness of individual talent became increasingly apparent and a significant shift away from the novel of protest occurred.

In 1950, William Demby's *Beetlecreek* was published, a novel with existentialist overtones in which not only Negro society but all of American culture is sharply condemned for being empty and destructive. Also in 1950, *Stranger and Alone*, Saunders Redding's trenchant depiction of the philistinism and corruption of life in a Negro college was published. A year later, Owen Dodson's *Boy at the Window* appeared—a delicate and lyrical treatment of adolescent sorrow. Earlier novels that foreshadowed this development were Ann Petry's *Country Place*, a sensitive examination of white society and the tension between small towns and big cities, and Dorothy West's *The Living Is Easy*, a sharp and bitter novel highly critical of the Negro middle class. In 1954 *Youngblood*, by John Oliver Killens, appeared. This work, concerned with the life and culture of a Negro community in the Deep South, was Killens's first published novel. He was to enjoy a greater success with his later book, *And Then We Heard the Thunder*, published in 1963.

In 1952, *Invisible Man*, by Ralph Ellison, won the National Book Award. This novel is indeed a magnificent contribution to American letters. It contains brilliantly and powerfully written episodes in which race is used symbolically. In *Invisible Man* Ellison evokes a world which perhaps only an American Negro can fully apprehend, a lunatic, febrile world where love and hate, pity and cruelty, are brutally intermingled. Ellison's work utterly transcends the traditional preoccupations of the Negro writer; ultimately he is concerned not with race but with man.

Clearly, Dostoyevsky's *Letters from the Underworld* engaged the imagination of both Ellison and Wright. Several years before the publication of *Invisible Man*, Wright had written a compelling short story called "The Man Who Lived Underground." Both these writers were drawn to the morbidly fascinating world of Dostoyevsky, not simply because their own characters are the helpless prey of a vast, senseless social order which destroys its victim, but, more importantly, because of their great concern with meaning, with identity, and with the necessity to remain sane in a society where the individual personality is denied and the world appears devoid of meaning. The work of Wright and Ellison suggests that perhaps the art of the grotesque, of fantasy, corresponds closely to the experience of the Negro in the United States, and perhaps that is why some Negro writers have been drawn to the imagery of Dostoyevsky and sense the value of the absurd and the grotesque in the works of Kafka and Joyce.

Invisible Man was one of the most significant American novels of the past two decades, and certainly is the most important novel yet written by an American Negro. For Ralph Ellison, race and the Negro's experience are part of his creative imagination, and in using this material he makes universal what is racial and regional.

In 1953, James Baldwin's *Go Tell It on the Mountain* was published, followed in 1956 by *Giovanni's Room* and in 1962 by *Another Country*. In these novels, as well as in Baldwin's two collections of essays, *Notes from a Native Son* and *Nobody Knows My Name*, he manifests a unique sensibility and intelligence. In his own words, Baldwin is concerned with "the depthless alienation from oneself and one's people—this is the sum of the American experience."

In the work of both Ellison and Baldwin, the Negro's color, his identity, or, rather, his "invisibility," are used poetically and symbolically to communicate the dilemma of all men who are denied dignity and purpose in the contemporary world. Their work demonstrates a new literary sensibility that distinguishes their writing from the work of most Negro authors of the past.

Wright's *Native Son* (1940) came years after the naturalism of Dreiser, and Willard Motley's *Knock on Any Door* (1947) came years after Farrell's *Studs Lonigan*. But now Ralph Ellison and James Baldwin have created their own literary forms; they are not derivative of the writers of a generation ago; they are, in fact, of the *avant-garde* and they are influencing the younger writers now beginning their careers. It is in this development that we can perceive the crucially altered role of the Negro writer in contemporary American literature.

Negro writing in America has a long history. It begins with *A Narrative of Uncommon Sufferings*, by Britton Hamon, published in 1760, and with Jupiter Hammon, a writer of both prose and poetry, whose first work appeared later in the same year. He was soon followed by Phillis Wheatley, a Massachusetts slave, who was given special privileges by the rather unusual Wheatley family and encouraged to write poetry, for which she had a talent rare for that period. Phillis Wheatley's *Poems on Various Subjects, Religious and Moral* was published in 1773. In 1829, another book of poems appeared, *The Hope of Liberty*, by George Moses Horton, who was freed late in life, as Phillis Wheatley had been.

In the North during this early period, a number of free Negroes were active as writers and journalists in the anti-slavery cause. Their articles and stories frequently appeared in the abolitionist newspaper *Freedom's Journal*, the first Negro newspaper in the

United States, which began publishing in 1818. In 1853, James Whitfield, among those whose work often appeared in *Freedom's Journal,* published his *America and Other Poems.* Whitfield wrote:

> *America it is to thee*
> *Thou boasted land of liberty*
> *It is to thee I raise my song*
> *thou land of blood, and crime, and wrong.*

The first novels written by an American Negro were *Clotel, or the President's Daughter* (1853) and *My Southern Home* (1880), by William Wells Brown, who also wrote other novels and a play, *The Escape* (1858). Brown, who was active in the abolitionist movement, was a serious writer, and after the Civil War he produced several ambitious historical and narrative works which achieved a rather large circulation at the time. He was the first American Negro who devoted his life to literature and the first to earn his living as a writer.

The writings of Frederick Douglass, especially *My Bondage and My Freedom, Narrative of the Life of Frederick Douglass,* and *Life and Times,* are among the most important slave narratives of their period and have genuine literary merit. *Poems on Miscellaneous Subjects,* by Frances E. W. Harper, appeared in 1854 and was followed by *Moses, a Story of the Nile* in 1869. Her *Sketches of Southern Life* was published in 1873, and later she wrote a final volume of poetry entitled *The Sparrows Fall and Other Poems.* Mrs. Harper frequently wrote for the *Anglo-African Magazine,* a Negro publication wihch published articles on cultural matters as well as on social and political issues; in 1892 her novel *Iola Leroy, or Shadows Uplifted* was published. Alberry A. Whiteman's book of poetry, *Not a Man and Yet a Man,* was published in 1877. Other volumes of his work appeared between the 1870's and 1900. Other works written by Negroes during this period were essentially abolitionist novels. Among the most prominent of these was *The Garies and Their Friends* (1857), by Frank Webb. One of the most remarkable works of this period is the fascinating *Journal* of Charlotte Forten, written between the years 1854 and 1864.

In the novels written by Negro authors after 1890, there occurs a significant change in subject matter, one that Robert Bone describes as "a shift in theme from attacks upon slavery to attacks upon caste." In these novels the principal characters are usually light enough in color to "pass," handsome, worthy, and cultivated, yet suffering from the stigma of membership in what American society regards as an inferior caste. Thus was born a tradition that stretches from J. McHenry Jones's *Hearts of Gold* (1896) to the novels of Walter White, Jessie Fauset, and Nella Larsen in the 1930's.

Typical of Miss Fauset's novels is *There Is Confusion* (1924), which deals with the problems of upper-class Negroes. In *Plum Bun* (1929) Miss Fauset continued her characterization of well-bred Negroes who cross the color line as a protest against white society and depicted the obsession with distinctions of caste and color within Negro society. This theme was repeated in Miss Fauset's *The Chinaberry Tree* (1931), in which the main characters are cultivated, respectable Negroes in the professions who are victims of racial restrictions.

Nella Larsen's *Quicksand* (1928) and *Passing* (1929) are also in this vein. Walter White's *Flight* (1926) is set among the Negro bourgeoisie of Atlanta and is concerned with the conflicts and torments of Negroes who leave their racial group and seek acceptance in white society. White's first novel, *The Fire in the Flint* (1924), which dealt with the lynching of Negroes, was a remarkable success and anticipated later novels dealing with racial violence.

An early folk tradition based mainly upon Southern rural material has been richly exploited by several generations of Negro writers—as in the dialect stories and poems of Daniel Webster Davis, Paul Lawrence Dunbar, and others. The best and most sophisticated writer in this genre was James Weldon Johnson, as he shows in "God's Trombones" (1927). Johnson, however, is best remembered for his only novel, *The Autobiography of an Ex-Coloured Man*," first published anonymously in 1912 and reprinted many times since. Among Johnson's other works are *Black Manhattan*, the autobiographical *Along This Way*, and a collection of poetry, *St. Peter Relates an Incident*.

One of the most interesting writers of the past who did not belong to the sociological or protest school of Negro writing was Charles Waddell Chesnutt, who, at the turn of the century, revealed a fine literary talent. Chesnutt was a writer of originality, aware of style and literary tradition, and had a profound insight into Southern life. Chesnutt's writing was far beyond the literary fashion and taste of his time. In such imaginative and original novels as *House Behind the Cedars, The Marrow of Tradition,* and *The Colonel's Dream,* as well as in the short stories he contributed to *The Atlantic Monthly* and other publications, Chesnutt eschewed the puerile romanticism of Thomas Nelson Page, Thomas Dixon, and other popular writers of his day. One must also note the work of W. E. B. Du Bois, who, early in his long career, wrote two novels, *Quest of the Silver Fleece* (1911) and *Dark Princess* (1928). For all their inherent interest, these two novels and the later trilogy, *The Black Flame* (the first volume of which, *The Ordeal of Mansart,* appeared in 1957), are generally regarded as literary failures. Du Bois demonstrated greater literary talent in *The Souls of Black Folk* (1903) and in his autobiographical work, *Dusk of Dawn* (1940).

During the 1920's, when the novels of Jessie Fauset, Nella Larsen, and Walter White were fascinating white and Negro readers alike, another group of Negro writers, known as the "Harlem School," was creating the so-called "Negro Renaissance" and deriding the pretensions, subject matter, and genteel style of the older group.

In 1925, *The New Negro,* a volume of writings by Negro authors edited by Alain Locke, appeared. Langston Hughes, in describing the "New Negro" movement, wrote: "We younger Negro artists now intend to express our individual dark-skinned selves without fear or shame." There were many young and talented writers who participated in the "New Negro" movement of the 1920's and early 1930's. Among these were Claude McKay, Zora Neale Hurston, Walter Turpin, Eric Walrond, and Wallace Thurman. George Schuyler's *Black No More* (1931), Arna Bontemps's *God Sends Sundays* (1931), and Rudolph Fisher's *The Walls of Jericho* (1928) were typical of this period and aroused considerable interest at the time.

Claude McKay's books—such as *Home to Harlem,* a national best seller in 1928, and *Banjo* (1929)—were an expression of the spirit and temper of this group, whose subject matter was often the Negro lumpen world and the life of the colored working class. This material shocked and offended the sensibilities of the more conservative Negro intellectuals such as Du Bois, who in a review for *The Crisis* magazine in 1928 stated that McKay's *Home to Harlem* "for the most part nauseated me, and after the dirtier parts of its filth I feel distinctly like taking a bath." In his third volume of fiction, *Gingertown* (1932), McKay told more stories of Harlem's "low life." This was followed in 1933 by a novel set in Jamaica, *Banana Bottom*, and an autobiographical travel book, *A Long Way from Home* (1937).

In *A Long Way from Home* McKay relates his rather unusual experiences in revolutionary Russia, in several African countries, in France and Germany, and in England with the Fabian Society, as well as his personal encounters with Leon Trotsky, George Bernard Shaw, Frank Harris, and H. G. Wells, among others.

Born on the island of Jamaica, Claude McKay was a highly gifted writer whose work had a significant effect upon many young Negro intellectuals and writers in New York during the 1920's and 1930's. He came to the United States at an early age, and after studying at Tuskegee Institute and the Kansas State College of Agriculture, he traveled extensively as a seaman and later became Max Eastman's assistant on the influential *Liberator* magazine.

In 1911 his first volume of poetry, *Songs of Jamaica*, was published; a second book of poetry, *Constab' Ballads*, was published in London in 1912; and a final volume of selected verse was brought out in 1953, with an introduction by John Dewey and a biographical note by Max Eastman.

One of McKay's poems, "If We Must Die," written in 1919, achieved wide popularity. His other books were *Harlem Shadows* (1922), and *Harlem: Negro Metropolis* (1940). Claude McKay was a prolific and versatile writer who was concerned with literature and ideology and who received serious attention from the intellectual community of his time.

One of the major figures of the Negro Renaissance was the highly talented poet Countee Cullen, who wrote a novel, *One Way to Heaven* (1932), which is quite different from the works of Claude McKay and the other writers of the Harlem School in that it is primarily concerned with respectable churchgoing folks and presents a satiric portrayal of Negroes with social pretensions and their equally absurd white acquaintances.

Wallace Thurman was among the young Negro intellectuals who were drawn to Harlem during the 1920's. Thurman came to New York from the University of Southern California, and in addition to writing and editing for the Negro *avant-garde* periodicals *Fire* and *Harlem*, he wrote two novels, *The Blacker the Berry* (1929) and *Infants of the Spring* (1932). Thurman's work is characterized by scathing, brutal satire and criticism of the intellectuals of the Negro Renaissance. The setting of *Infants of the Spring* is a place called "Niggeratti Manor," which is populated with bizarre characters who inhabit a colored bohemia.

The most important writer of the Negro Renaissance was Jean Toomer, a poet and short-story writer whose major work, *Cane*, was published in 1923. *Cane* is written in an unusual style, a mixture of prose and poetry, sensuous, and with a strange mysterious atmosphere, rich with fantasy and subtle suggestions.

In his foreword to *Cane*, Waldo Frank wrote: "A poet has arisen among our American youth who has known how to turn the essence and materials of his Southland into the essence and materials of Literature . . . This is a first book in more ways than one. It is a harbinger of the South's literary maturity; of its emergence from the obsession put upon its mind by the unending racial crisis. It marks the dawn of direct and unafraid creation. And, as the initial work of a man of 27, it is the harbinger of a literary force of whose incalculable future I believe no reader of this book will doubt." Among the other distinguished literary figures who hailed *Cane* were Paul Rosenfeld and Alfred Kreymborg.

However, the promise of *Cane* was never realized, for Jean Toomer rejected the world of literature and turned his back upon possible greatness; eventually he himself vanished.

Today very little is known of Jean Toomer. He has published almost nothing since 1923. Some of his short stories appeared in the second and third editions of *The American Caravan* and a poem, "Blue Meridian," appeared in *New American Caravan of 1936*, but virtually nothing else of importance has been published.

It has long been rumored that Toomer, a light-skinned Negro, had "crossed the color line." In discussing this possibility, Arna Bontemps has written: "Jean Toomer stepped out of American letters; despite the richness of his thought and his gift of expression, he ceased to be a writer . . . While he may have escaped its strictures and inconveniences in his personal life, he did not get away from the racial problem in any real sense. His dilemmas and frustrations as a writer are equally the dilemmas and frustrations of the Negro writers who have since attracted attention. The fact that most of them have not been provided with his invisible cloak makes little difference. He is their representative man. He stands as their prototype."

This comment by Arna Bontemps calls attention to the special problems Negro authors face in finding an audience and getting published. In the past Negro writers failed to use what Henry James called the "angle of vision," because of their need to secure an audience of white readers, the only audience in fact that existed. Thus they attempted to exploit those elements in Negro life that would interest white readers. In the 1920's, Langston Hughes has said, "the Negro was in vogue." During this period there was little difference between such white writers as Julia Peterkin and Roark Bradford, who dealt with Negro themes, and Negro writers themselves. Both stressed exoticism, sensuality, Negro humor and dialect material.

Today most Negro writers no longer try to please their white audiences and no longer try to propagandize for "the race." There is also a new courageousness which might be described simply as telling the truth. This is expressed in frequent harsh criticism of Negro life and in self-exposure; at the same time the Negro writers of today show no reluctance to deal with the private terrors and absurdities of the white man's situation, as in Demby's *Beetlecreek*, Petry's *Country Place*, Paule Marshall's short story "Brooklyn," or the novels of Willard Motley. Thus a greater richness and diversity characterizes the work of the contemporary Negro writer, and their creative imagination now responds more distinctly as an individual reaction to the Negro's social experience.

In this regard there is another significant break with the past, for one of the important developments in contemporary Negro

writing is the new treatment of the Negro peasant, who in the
past was usually dismissed as a simpleton or buffoon but who is
now frequently used as a symbol of high comic-tragic irony. Ralph
Ellison, who has so brilliantly utilized the Southern Negro peasant
and his folklore in *Invisible Man*, has attributed this to the influence of William Faulkner, who in his own way frequently used
Southern Negro folk material, which Ellison goes on to describe
as "one of the great unused folklores." Both Ellison and Faulkner
in their different and separate ways have transformed the material
of the Southern Negro peasant into literature, and have thus made
it accessible to those far removed from the world of the rural
Negro in the American South.

Langston Hughes has used the same folk material, but in relation to the life of the Southern Negro now living in the big
cities of the North. For almost forty years Hughes has been
prodigiously creative and has worked with virtually every literary
form, including novels, short stories, essays, opera librettos, popular
ballads and blues, musical comedies, gospel plays, historical pag-
eants, and children's verse and stories. He is, of course, best known
for his poetry, which first appeared in book form in 1926 with the
publication of *The Weary Blues*, which led Carl Van Vechten to
describe him at that time as "The Negro Poet Laureate." Since
The Weary Blues Hughes has published several other volumes of
poetry and must be regarded as a major American poet.

With his prolific imagination and sensitive ear, Hughes has
raised to the level of art the material of the blues and the jazz
idiom as well as the songs of the gospel singers and the "shouts"
of the rural South. He has also transformed into literature the
folklore and the cadences of speech of the urban Negro. It is important to note, however, that Hughes has frequently transcended
the limitations of folk material, and has worked in pure verse
forms to great effect. This is also true of some of his stories, which
are really not quite as naïve as they might appear to be.

One of the most gifted and imaginative of the Negro poets in
the United States is Sterling Brown, who has had a long and distinguished career as teacher, critic, and poet. Among his published
works are a volume of poetry, *Southern Road* (1932), *The Negro
in American Fiction* (1938), and *Negro Poetry and Drama* (1938).

His poetry appears in many collections, and he was an editor of
The Negro Caravan (1941).

James Weldon Johnson, in his introduction to *Southern Road,*
stated that in his poetry Sterling Brown had "dug down into the
deep mine of Negro folk poetry. He found the unfailing sources
from which sprang the Negro folk epics and ballads such as 'Stag-
olee,' 'John Henry,' 'Casey Jones,' 'Long Gone John' and others. . . .
He has made more than mere transcriptions of folk poetry, and he
has done more than bring to it mere artistry; he has deepened its
meaning and multiplied its implications."

Gwendolyn Brooks is widely regarded as one of the important
American poets of this period. Miss Brooks won the Pulitzer
Prize for Poetry in 1950 and is the author of four books of poetry,
*The Bean Eaters, Annie Allen, A Street in Bronzeville, Bronze-
ville Boys and Girls,* and a novel, *Maud Martha.*

Poetry magazine, in summing up the work of Gwendolyn Brooks,
stated: ". . . she shows a capacity to marry the special quality of
her racial experience with the best attainments of our contemporary
poetry tradition. Such compounding of resources out of varied
stocks and traditions is the great hope of American art." Harvey
Curtis Webster concluded his article on the poetry of Gwendolyn
Brooks in *The Nation* by saying: "She is a very good poet, the
only superlative I dare use in our time of misusage; compared not
to other Negro poets or to other women poets but to the best
of modern poets, she ranks high."

Miss Brooks has a unique gift for imagery and lyricism which
permits her to work with great effect in the modern idiom, and in
prose and poetry as well as in the ballad form. In her sonnets
especially, there is a fragile quality, tender and poignant, that is
unusual for a contemporary poet, and at other times Miss Brooks
has written poetry that, in the words of Peter Viereck, "laughs
and cries and dances, poetry . . . that throws back its head and
sings aloud."

An analysis of the history of Negro writing indicates three main
tendencies: a strong folk tradition, racial protest, first during the
anti-slavery struggle and again in modern times, and now the most
recent development, which might be described as the emergence
of an aesthetic tradition.

The works of Ralph Ellison and James Baldwin, of Hughes and Brooks, of Ann Petry and others, are an indication of the richness and diversity in the writing of American Negroes. Today, the Negro writer is not "in vogue" as he was during the 1920's, and increasingly the work of the Negro author must be judged in terms of literature. Ralph Ellison won the National Book Award, but not as a Negro novelist; Gwendolyn Brooks won a Pulitzer Prize, but not as a Negro poet; and Langston Hughes was admitted into the National Institute of Arts and Letters as an *American* writer. They received this recognition for the worth of their work as literature and for their contribution to American letters, and this is, of course, the only basis for judgment. A profound disservice is done to the Negro writer, now and in the future, if any criteria are invoked except those of art and literature.

The purpose of this book, beyond giving pleasure to its readers, is to display the range of contemporary writing by American Negroes in the light of these criteria.

SECTION I

—

ESSAYS

Horace R. Cayton

Mr. Cayton writes: "I hope that my piece on Sinclair Lewis is not construed as a racially-inspired criticism of this famous and gifted man of American letters. For his time and period, Red Lewis was a good guy. He was driven by his abiding hate, which grew out of both his real and imagined rejection from middle-class society, and used every weapon to fight this enemy. In *Kingsblood Royal* he used the Negro. Later in life when his alienation became intolerable he tried desperately to get some human warmth from his Negro servants, for he could purchase their services. In his despair he could not realize that Negroes had changed, and was unaware of the more fundamental fact that affection, love, and kindness cannot be purchased. All Red had to work with then was money.

"If there is a lesson to be learned from this writer's life it is that rejection creates hate, and hate, alienation; and that alienation is a form of death. The Negro in America has refused to accept rejection, and is denying alienation and defeating death in a manner in such sharp contrast to the fate of Red Lewis."

"A Picnic with Sinclair Lewis" is published here for the first time and will be part of an autobiographical memoir Horace Cayton is now writing. He is the co-author, with George S. Mitchell, of *Black Workers and the New Unions*, published in 1935, and

collaborated with St. Clair Drake on *Black Metropolis,* which won
the Anisfield-Wolf Award in 1945. The New York Public Library
named *Black Metropolis* as the outstanding book on race relations
for that year.

Mr. Cayton was born in Seattle, Washington. He has been a
Fellow of the Julius Rosenwald Fund; research assistant in Studies
in Geriatric Mental Illness at the Langley Porter Clinic, San
Francisco; special assistant to the Commissioner of Welfare, New
York City; and director of the Parkway Community House,
Chicago.

After graduation from the University of Washington, Horace
Cayton pursued graduate studies at the University of Chicago and
New York University and took special training at the Institute for
Psychoanalysis in psychiatry and the social sciences. He has held
teaching positions at Fisk University, the College of the City of
New York, and the University of Chicago.

Mr. Cayton's essays on mental illness, race relations, and religion have been included in several important studies, and his
articles have appeared in *The New Republic, The Nation, Holiday,*
and the *American Journal of Sociology.* He has reviewed books
in the fields of literature and the social sciences for *The New
York Times, The Nation, The New Republic,* the Chicago
Tribune, the Chicago *Sun-Times,* the *American Journal of Sociology,* and for twenty years was a columnist for the Pittsburgh
Courier.

A PICNIC WITH SINCLAIR LEWIS

BY HORACE R. CAYTON

When *Kingsblood Royal* by Sinclair Lewis first came out, I was
complimented to see that my name was mentioned in the book.
It was just a casual mention; my name was among a few authors
one of the characters suggested reading. I reviewed the book
favorably although I realized it was not one of Mr. Lewis' best
works. The fact that a man of his stature was on the right side of

the Negro question was too important for me to subject the book to intense literary criticism. When I finished the review, I sent it to Mr. Lewis and thanked him for mentioning me in the book. He replied by return mail, inviting me to visit him if I were ever in the neighborhood of Williamstown, Massachusetts. Later that year I went to Yaddo, a retreat for writers in Saratoga Springs, New York. Again, I wrote Lewis and it was arranged for me to visit him at his estate, Thorvale Farm.

The Lewis estate was large and lovely. His spacious and comfortable house stood on a hill overlooking a beautiful valley. In addition to the main house, there were a couple of small cottages for servants and guests, a large swimming pool, a tennis court, and a farm. The establishment was run by three Negro servants.

Joseph, the chauffeur and cook, was about thirty or thirty-five, a competent, pleasant, and rather sophisticated man Lewis had found in New Orleans. Joseph was fond of "the old man," as he sometimes called the writer. He was very loyal to his employer and told me on one occasion that Lewis had put him in his will. He knew that he had a good job and did his work well. I never got the feeling that he was sly or cunning, but he was something of an "Uncle Tom," though a very high-class one. I suspected that he had a better education than he let on. From conversations I had with him, I gathered that Joseph did not always intend to be a servant; he was going to see this stint with Lewis through and then with his inheritance move on to a life more to his taste.

Alma was the maid, and Wilson, her husband, the gardener-handy man. They had one small child. Alma was a light-colored, plump, and attractive creole from Louisiana, in her late twenties or early thirties. She seemed to dominate the quiet, easygoing Wilson. She outwardly accepted her position, kept her place, did her work, and demanded and received respect. I got some insight into her character the first day I arrived. Lewis and Joseph had met me at the train some little distance from Williamstown. When we got to the house, I stopped downstairs for a cup of coffee and Joseph took my bags up to my room. When I finally went up to my room, Alma had unpacked for me and taken my soiled clothes to be washed. She greeted me when I walked into the room: "Mr. Cayton," she said, "I am Alma." But she was young and attractive, and I didn't want to treat her just as a servant; I wanted her to know that I recognized that we were both Negroes. "What is your last name?" I inquired. "Alma will do," she stated simply. She let me know that I was a guest and should stay in my place and she would stay in hers. And that set the tone of my relationship with all of the servants.

There was one more member of the household, Barnaby Conrad, Lewis' secretary. He was an extremely charming and talented young man who had just returned from Spain, where he had been a bullfighter, and was now engaged in writing his first novel. He was more of a companion than secretary to Lewis and, as far as I saw, his only obligation was to play chess with the writer after supper. Barney, who was so gifted in so many ways, was a poor chess player and hated it. He was delighted when I began to take his place in the after-supper games, and although I was a poor player too, I managed to win about two games out of three. Everyone liked Barney. Lewis was helping him with his book, although Barney was a little afraid of him. The servants looked on him as a special friend.

Lewis was the master of his household—the complete master. I never heard him reprimand anyone or issue an order, but his control was absolute. Joseph might have been responsible for the efficient running of the household, but he was not some sort of old retainer who really dominated the master; although I never heard him take orders, he must have received sharp and definite instructions about all details. I seldom saw Alma around the house, but evidence of her work was ever present. Wilson kept up the grounds and served the meals on Joseph's day off. Apparently he knew what to do and did it well, as I never saw Lewis talking with him. Meals were served on time—eight o'clock for breakfast, one o'clock for lunch, and seven o'clock for dinner—and were announced by a large gong near the head of the stairs in the living room. I was warned by Barney that everyone was expected to be on time. The household followed Lewis' routine; people fitted into his mold. He was a stubborn man, set in his ways; while living in his home one conformed to his pattern of life.

That it was important and necessary to Lewis for people to follow his pattern of life became evident to me the second day of my visit. Right after lunch he customarily took a nap. The first day, after we had finished eating and had talked for about a half hour, he suggested that we go to our rooms and rest for a while. It had been a welcome suggestion, as I was tired from my trip. The second day, taking it for granted that the routine had been firmly established, he announced that it was time to lie down for a while. Then followed what turned out to be a contest of wills between Lewis and myself.

"I don't think I'll nap today, Red" (he had insisted that I call him Red an hour after I had met him and he called me by my first name), I stated innocently. "Perhaps I'll go down and see the farm."

"You'll feel much better after a little rest," he answered, seemingly solicitous of my well-being.

"Oh, I'm not a bit tired," I replied. "How do I get to the farm?"

"I still think you should rest," he insisted, not answering my question.

It then occurred to me that he might not want me to see the farm, so I changed my tactics. "Perhaps I'll take a walk up the stream instead," I ventured.

"That is a beautiful walk, Horace," Red observed, "but it's much nicer when it's cooler, in the afternoon. Why don't you rest for an hour or so and then take your walk?"

It would have been much easier at this point to have just gone to my room and read for an hour to please him. He had been extremely pleasant and had put himself out to make my stay as enjoyable as possible. But I felt pushed; I didn't feel that I should give in on the question of how I should spend my time if it did not interfere with the household routine.

"I don't want to rest, Red," I stated. "I'll find something to do."

With that I left the table, went to my room, put on my swimming suit, and went to the pool. I lay by the side of the pool for a couple of hours sleeping, reading, and thinking. I was a little annoyed at the scene at the luncheon table, but after a while I forgot it. In the latter part of the afternoon, I saw Lewis coming down the rather steep hill from the house at an awkward old man's pace. When he sat down next to me, he was as pleasant as ever. After a bit he said, "About that nap business, Horace, forgive me. I'm just an old bastard always trying to run people's lives. It's one of my faults."

Life at Thorvale Farm was extremely pleasant for me. The food that Joseph prepared was excellent and the weather perfect. Lewis was one of the most delightful conversationalists I have ever known. He knew something about everything; he talked on any subject well and on some brilliantly. At first, of course, it was the Negro question. He knew a number of the great Negro leaders and artists and commented on them with wise insight and occasionally a bit of malice; he was far from a Negrophile. He was pleased that *Kingsblood* had annoyed many people. He was extremely proud of the fact that a film of one of his books, *Arrowsmith*, had pictured a Negro in a dignified way at a time when Hollywood was making clowns of them. He described in detail the scene from *Arrowsmith* in which the protagonist addressed a doctor who had been fighting the plague; the doctor's back had been to the screen, and when he turned, the startled audience saw that he was black. Lewis seemed sympathetic to the Negro cause, like many other liberals of that period, except that he knew more about it and had written on the subject. But he didn't want to be thought of as the savior of the Negro race just because he had written *Kingsblood*; he was a writer, not a politician or reformer, he informed me. After a while we dropped the subject and our conversations ranged all over the field of contemporary life in America.

One thing that surprised me was that he did little talking about literature. It may have been that he thought that as a sociologist I was not interested in literature or was not particularly well informed. When I would attempt to discuss some contemporary novel, he would make some remark about the author and drop the subject. He made no reference to his own work except to date some event by a book he was working on at the time. In a sense he seemed defensive about his current position in American letters. When I had first arrived from Yaddo, he asked me half curiously and half disdainfully what the young writers there were thinking about. I am sure that he really wanted to know if they thought of him and, if so, what they thought of him. If I had had to answer truthfully, it would have been embarrassing. The avant-garde who came to Yaddo were concerned with Kafka, Catholicism and communism, Hemingway, Faulkner, and Robert Penn Warren, but not Lewis. When I had told a group of them that I was visiting Lewis, he was dismissed as a journalist, dated and commercial. But he talked about other things in the most delightful and interesting manner; sometimes I forgot that he was a great world-famed author as we sat and joked at the table or as I beat him at chess.

There was one area of thought, however, where he was unsure, uninformed, and I dare say frightened. That was the subject of psychoanalysis. Every writer I had known had taken Freud for granted, so much for granted that many had not bothered to read or understand him. Psychoanalysis had become part of the mass thinking of the country, maybe in vulgar and bastardized form, but it was even being accepted by the motion pictures. I was filled with the subject. As a sociologist, I had of course read Freud, but now I was more immediately and more urgently involved, as I was being psychoanalyzed. I had given Lewis a copy of an essay on the psychology of the Negro in which I attempted to combine some of the concepts of sociology and psychoanalysis in an attack on the problem. I was more interested and proud of this little essay than I was of the book Lewis had in mind when he mentioned my name in *Kingsblood* and I was extremely anxious to talk with him about it.

I skirted the subject on several occasions; it is hard to come right out and ask a man what he thinks about something you have written after you have given it to him to read. Lewis seemed to avoid the subject. One day when we were sitting in the sun out in a field, I broached the subject directly. Carried away, I developed for him my ideas about the unconscious feelings of both love and hate which the American Negro feels toward the strong white man, and the variety of ways, consciously and unconsciously, in which many white men use the Negro to fill the unrealized, empty areas of their existence. It was an approach, I informed Lewis, which would help to explain the adolescent posturing and the casual cruelty of many whites toward Negroes; the irrational fear and hatred of the prejudiced whites and the emotional defense of the liberal whites, which was sometimes equally irrational.

Lewis let me finish, but I could see that he was either uncomfortable or bored. "I guess there is a lot in what you say, Horace," he said after a moment. "I read your essay and thought it was good." Then: "Let's get back to the house." I was hurt, and felt that I hadn't made myself clear, for I was sure that what I had said deserved more consideration than he was giving it. I started in again to try to elucidate further, but looked up to see him already headed toward the house. We never mentioned the matter again.

I had not stayed at Thorvale Farm long before I began to realize that my friend was a lonely man. There were almost no visitors, only three during my stay: the mother of a young girl who had lived with him and left him, his agent, and Ida Kay, a young woman who ran a bookstore in Williamstown. Of course, I reasoned, a famous man might want to isolate himself so he could work. That was understandable. But why had he invited me, a stranger, and become so friendly with me in such a short length of time if he wanted privacy? Moreover, he sought me out nearly every day at the pool for conversation and had hinted at an impossible plan for me to live in one of his cottages so I could write. This wealthy, famous author seemed to be without a friend, lonesome and hungry for company. It was puzzling.

One day when I came down for breakfast Lewis was beaming. Before I sat down he said, "Lana and Spencer are coming for dinner tomorrow."

"Good," I replied. Then on second thought I asked, "Who are Lana and Spencer?" They were the movie stars who had had leading roles in a film made from one of his books.

The next day I allowed myself plenty of time to dress for the occasion. Dinner was scheduled for eight, but the guests were expected late in the afternoon. At seven Lewis and I were sitting on the terrace waiting. We talked casually for a while but I could see that he was impatient. At seven-thirty he mentioned the guests for the first time that evening: "I guess they got held up on the road," he said. We continued to talk, but less freely, while another half hour passed. Again he mentioned the coming of the guests: "They will phone any minute to tell me they are having traffic difficulties, I guess." The atmosphere was a bit strained, so

I made some excuse and went to the kitchen and asked Joseph for a drink; Lewis was not drinking at the time and had not offered me a drink, but I could always get one from Joseph. Joseph was sitting in the kitchen reading a magazine. When he had fixed my drink, he returned to his seat and I perched myself on a high stool near him.

"I wonder why the guests are so late," I inquired.

"They aren't coming," he replied. "They won't be here at all." Then he decided to let himself go and it was the only time he criticized Lewis in front of me. "They aren't coming because they have gotten what they want from the old man. Oh, he was king pin when we were in Hollywood talking about the picture; he had something to do with the casting, I guess. But they got their parts and they don't need him now."

"But it's a dirty trick if they don't," I said.

"It's to be expected," Joseph replied. "He can't help it but it's really the old man's fault. You just can't order people around; expect them to always come to you and not give anything in return. He can give things but not himself. They probably expected to come but got with people and just didn't."

A little later Lewis gave in and said that we might as well eat. It was a miserable meal and we didn't play chess afterwards. In my room I picked up an anthology of stories and there was one in it by Lewis. Turning to the back of the book, I found short sketches of the authors. In reading the one on Lewis, I realized emotionally for the first time since I had been there that I was in the home of a great writer; the first American to win the Nobel award, a man who had coined words—"Babbitt," "Main Street"—for our English language. What had happened that such a person could be stood up by a couple of movie personalities and feel it so keenly?

It took me a longer time to find out how deep Lewis' sense of rejection was and how bitter he felt about it. We were at the breakfast table and the author was in one of his more quiet moods. Joseph had brought our second cup of coffee and I was preparing to drink mine and go for a walk. Without any sort of preparation, Lewis looked directly at me and said, "I know how it feels to be a nigger, Horace."

I looked up startled, then turned to see if Joseph had heard. We had not been talking about the Negro question for some time and I was surprised that he had suddenly returned to it. Then there was that little red surge of emotion that always springs up in me when someone, no matter how friendly, uses the word "nigger."

"When I was in England," he continued, apparently without giving a thought to my possible reaction, "I was taken up by society. I was a middle western hick to them, I guess, crude and uncultured. At first I felt complimented to be courted by the literary figures, the rich, cultured upper class. Even the nobility. Then I realized that they looked upon me as if I were a freak, an ape that had been taught clever tricks. How to ride a bicycle. But still an ape. Then I felt like a nigger. For whatever a Negro might achieve in America there are white men who still look on him as an educated ape."

On the second of July, Lewis announced that we should celebrate the Fourth with a picnic. It was a welcome suggestion, for as pleasant as my stay had been, some new faces would be exciting. The morning of the Fourth, Joseph was busy getting out hampers and fixing food.

"Oh, the picnic," I said, "I'd almost forgotten it. Who is going?"

"Just the people in the house," he replied.

I didn't understand immediately. Barney had gone on a trip to New York, and there was only Lewis and myself. I had hoped that he would have invited some neighbors. "Just the two of us?" I inquired.

"No, the servants, too," Joseph answered without looking up.

Having the servants was all right with me. I had grown to like them. But what about Lewis? He had kept them, as far as I could see, at a distance. I had never seen the writer talk to Alma, and although Barney and I had slipped up to her cottage for a drink, around the house she was reserved and distant, even with me. Wilson didn't speak to Lewis unless he was spoken to. The formality of the house tended to draw a sharp line between master and servant, for Lewis, in dealing with his help, was more aristocratic than democratic. Just what kind of picnic could it turn out to be?

I had further misgivings when he stated at the table, "It will be a sort of a family affair." The people Lewis was referring to, Alma, Wilson, and Joseph, were a younger and newer type of servant, not old family retainers. They liked and respected their employer, but I was sure, from what I knew of them, that they would not welcome a family picnic with the old man.

It took two cars to transport us and the food and equipment to a grove of trees near the swimming pool, where the picnic was to be held. Lewis and I rode in his big, roomy car with Joseph driving. Wilson followed with the jeep. Alma walked. It was a beautiful day, and at noon, when we arrived, the sun was hot. The shade of the grove was welcome and before us stretched the long, spring-fed pool. The setting was perfect.

Everything went well at first, when there were things to do. Joseph took charge of the food and started the fire in the grill. Wilson was carrying and hauling from the jeep. Lewis, Alma, and I sat at the table and watched. Alma looking strange and attractive without her uniform, in a printed-cotton summer dress. Lewis made a big thing of treating Alma, the only woman among four men, with solicitous attention, almost with chivalry. There were a few jokes about Joseph's ability to cook outside, and we all laughed too much. Joseph seemed pleased and smiled, but said nothing. Wilson made innumerable trips to the car, examined the shrubbery, and then finally took a seat at the far end of the table.

Alma had not uttered a word after greeting us when we had first come to the grove. She was pleasant, but withdrawn. I tried to figure out whether she was nervous or perhaps frightened; after all, she was from the South. I felt sure that she must be resentful at this command performance; this once-a-year exhibition of democracy which was an invasion of her privacy. Or was she silent because she was confused and didn't know how to act? And for that matter none of us could fall back on etiquette to help us in this break in caste and class lines. It was all up to Lewis, who had insisted on this little fake drama of domestic life. He was busy for a while telling a slightly malicious story of some picnic he had been to in his youth. I laughed and Alma smiled.

When Joseph served us the delicious steaks, there was another flurry of activity. Alma heaped our plates with a tossed salad,

Wilson got coffee, and there was a passing of salt, pepper, rolls, and butter. We settled down to eat, and in the silence which followed, again the burden of establishing conversation fell on Lewis. He spoke directly and exclusively to Alma.

"We picked a good day for the picnic, didn't we, Alma?"

"Yes, Mr. Lewis."

"I think it is nice to get together once in a while, don't you?"

"Yes, Mr. Lewis."

"I've come to hate most holidays, Alma. Christmas, New Year's, and the rest, but the Fourth of July isn't so bad. At least you can get out in the open."

"Yes, Mr. Lewis."

She looked at Lewis attentively and smiled pleasantly each time she said "Yes, Mr. Lewis." But she didn't unbend from her role of the good servant. I knew she could be different, for with Barney and me she had been warm and fun-loving, although even on those occasions quiet and a bit dignified. She seemed to accept being on the picnic as a part of her job, but it was work for which she had little training or taste. Lewis kept on with his interrogation.

"This is a beautiful part of the country, isn't it?"

"Yes, Mr. Lewis."

I took my steak sandwich and walked over to the pool out of earshot. I was confused and offended; just what was the idea of this silly business? I wondered. The great Sinclair Lewis, who had kept his servants at an aristocratic distance, forcing a one-sided conversation with his uncomfortable Negro maid. The idea crossed my mind that he was trying to humiliate me in some way, but I quickly dismissed it. Then was he trying to prove that he really believed in racial equality as he had written in *Kingsblood*? I wasn't sure, but certainly this was a ludicrous way to demonstrate it. I became indignant for Alma. Why had he subjected this woman to such a trying ordeal when it was clear that she would much rather be at home with her husband and child? Had the whole thing been just for his own amusement? To satisfy some cruel urge to see the woman squirm? Why hadn't he invited some of his neighbors rather than impose on these simple people?

My back was turned and I was lost in thought, so I didn't see Lewis when he joined me at the pool.

"It didn't come off, did it?" he stated sharply.

"No, Red, it didn't."

"Horace, you see why I have to have a colored mammy, can't you?" he stated rather than asked.

"I don't know," I answered. "I'm confused."

We sat around the pool for a while trying to make conversation, then gave up. The caravan drove back to the house. The picnic had lasted for a little more than an hour.

That night in my room, I thought about the picnic and Lewis' curious statement, for I was disturbed and couldn't sleep. I was annoyed about the mammy business; in spite of our frank and friendly talks, I felt he had presumed a bit on our relationship. No Negro likes black-mammy talk, and for Lewis to think of Alma, who was at least thirty years his junior, as a mammy was ridiculous. But, I thought, I must have been taking the whole thing too seriously; Lewis' remark, the picnic, and Alma's discomfort. But still all of it indicated something about Lewis' attitude toward race, and that was important for me to know.

I reread *Kingsblood Royal* that night, and having met Lewis, I saw it as a different book. Yes, some of my white liberal friends in Chicago had been right; it was a poor book. It had an improbable plot and the characters were stereotyped caricatures. Lewis had learned a lot about Negro life, knew important names, happenings, and the general tenor of the Negro's existence in America. But he had not penetrated much beneath the surface— a surface open to any competent observer. And more, he had sentimentalized Negroes and made villains of the middle-class whites. In no sense did the book give a new and richer insight into the complex problem of race in the United States. It was an attack, a diatribe against the people Lewis had been fighting in so many of his books, for most of his life—the Babbits, the citizens of Main Street.

And what about his attitude toward Negroes? I speculated. Did Lewis have any real respect or regard for Negroes or had he used them as another weapon with which to wage his private war against the society which he would not or could not accept? In the book I had just read, how he ridiculed Kingsblood's wife, who wanted to make their spirited Negro maid a sweet and trusting member of the Yuletide family group! He had made the wife say to the young servant, "The tree is just as much for you as it is for us, of course." How could this literary genius fall into the same trap he had so acidly depicted in his novel?

A more charitable line of thought developed in my mind. This man was lonely beyond belief. For reasons I could never know, or even guess, he had isolated himself beyond recall from society; not only from the middle class he had attacked but from literary people, his peers. Within him there was a consuming rage for warmth, for devotion, for someone who would love him and care for him. But it must be, in his fear of tenderness, someone he could control. And who else could better fit this fantasy than the Negro? Isolated on his hilltop mansion, at that period of his life, Lewis had need for his Negro servants in his lifelong struggle to find an at-homeness with people.

It has been fourteen years since the picnic, but I find the memory of it still vivid in my mind. Lewis died tragically and alone; not even his paid secretary was with him when the end came. He had traveled endlessly and aimlessly in Europe, cut off from old friends and unable to make new relationships. The pattern of his existence which I had observed in Williamstown was never broken; his search for human warmth acceptable to his peculiar demands was never rewarded.

After Lewis left for Europe, Alma and Wilson remained at Thorvale as caretakers. Thorvale (ironically enough, for Lewis hated organized religion) was sold to the Carmelite Fathers as a retreat. Alma is there now as the cook. Wilson is working for an electric company. Judy, their only child, attends the local high school. They live in the same white cottage on the grounds they occupied when I knew them.

Joseph is dead. It was true that he was in Lewis' will; I had never completely believed it when he had first told me. But the terms of the will were designed to keep him in a position of gentle bondage. Joseph was to receive one-sixteenth of the estate, certainly a generous sum, if he was in Lewis' service or in a position of a retainer at the time of the author's death. But it just didn't work out in Joseph's favor. Shortly after my visit to Thorvale Farm, the woman I had met there, the mother of the young girl Lewis loved and failed to win, became a member of the household, a companion housekeeper, and usurped some of Joseph's duties and authority. She accompanied the writer on one of his trips to Europe. Joseph was in charge of the luggage when they sailed and two of her bags were lost in the confusion. Joseph was discharged by letter. He wrote and begged Lewis to reconsider. Lewis' reply contained one word—fired.

Part of Sinclair Lewis' estate was left to the National Association for the Advancement of Colored People and the Urban League.

James Baldwin

In his review of the essays of James Baldwin, Alfred Kazin observed that Baldwin's first collection, *Notes of a Native Son*, "is one of the two or three best books ever written about the Negro in America, and it is the work of an original literary talent who operates with as much power in the essay form as I've ever seen."

Of Baldwin's second collection of essays, *Nobody Knows My Name: More Notes of a Native Son*, Kazin commented as follows: "The extraordinary thing about these essays is that he can give voice to all his insights and longings and despairs without losing control—indeed, without ever missing his chance to dig in deeper. Speaking now with the moral authority of the future, now with the bitterness of Harlem, now with the sophistication of the perennial American abroad, now with the toughness of the adventurer who knows the slums and messes of Paris, now as the dopester on Gide's marriage, now as the literary celebrity moving in the company of other celebrities, he somehow manages never to enjoy things so well that he will get heedless, never suffers so constantly that he will lose himself. He is bitter yet radiantly intelligent as he seizes the endless implications in the oppression of man by man, of race by race. To be James Baldwin is to touch on so many hidden places in Europe, America, the Negro, the white man—to be forced to understand so much!"

In addition to his essays, James Baldwin is the author of three novels, *Go Tell It on the Mountain*, *Giovanni's Room*, and *Another Country*. (See also pages 401–2.)

A NOTE ON
THE BALDWIN LETTERS

BY ROBERT P. MILLS

One advantage of being James Baldwin's literary agent, as well as his friend, is that business matters oblige him to keep more or less continually in touch as he wanders here and there in the world—his friends are so numerous that he cannot possibly write any letters but those which must be written immediately. The observations which follow were all included in communications sent back to New York during a trip motivated largely by an invitation from William Shawn, editor of *The New Yorker*, to write a series of articles, and from his publishers, The Dial Press, to write a book based on the same trip.

When Mr. Baldwin left this country in September 1961, he was very close to the end of *Another Country*, a novel he had been working on for some five years, and in the middle of a long and difficult-to-write essay called "Down at the Cross," about religion and the Muslim movement. He took Paula, his charming teen-age sister, with him as far as Paris and left her there with friends, not fully realizing that he had taken her from "a ghetto to a developing *plastique* battleground." Then he proceeded, as a guest of the government, to Israel, which he looked upon as a sort of gateway to Africa. *Another Country* refused to be finished on the way, and it had to be finished before Africa, so he went ahead of schedule to Turkey, where friends offered refuge. By the time that work was done, time was pressing in—he had accepted an invitation from Grove Press to be a judge in the awarding of the Prix International des Editeurs, which meant he had to be in Mallorca by April 30, and there were other things that had to be done before then.

The pressures and pains of being a writer are clearly not easy to bear—as Mr. Baldwin specifically points out in his reference to my nine-year-old son, Freddie, some of whose stories he had read shortly before his departure—but perhaps not quite as agonizing as these extracts might imply. When Mr. Baldwin read his words over on his return to this country, his first comment was that he had not really been *that* gloomy all the time he was gone. This is not altogether surprising; it would be difficult, I should think, to be so penetrating about the problems of man living with man without possessing an abundant, even zestful sense of the enduring nature of life.

LETTERS FROM A JOURNEY

BY JAMES BALDWIN

Paris
September 15, 1961

I feel very strange and naked, but I guess that's good. Appetite seems to be returning, and I'm able to work. And Paris is still beautiful, in spite of its danger and sorrow and age.

Pray for me.

Israel, October 5

This is almost the only night I've had since I got here when it's been possible to write letters. Being a guest of the government really involves becoming an extremely well cared for parcel post package. But the visit seems, so far, to have been a great success: Israel and I seem to like each other. I've been trying, as usual, to do too many things at once and I've been keeping a diary of sorts of things as they happen—places I've been, people I've talked to— every night, when I come home. But I come home late and I get up early (the phone rings, and it's the hotel manager informing me that "my" car has arrived)—and off I and the government go—tomorrow morning, for example, to the Negev and the Dead Sea. I am always worried about wearing out my welcome, and imagined I'd be gone by now: but no, they keep saying, Please don't hurry. Still, I'm leaving Monday morning.

I must say, it's rather nice to be in a situation in which I haven't got to count and juggle and sweat and be responsible for a million things that I'm absolutely unequipped to do. All I'm expected to do is observe, and, hopefully, to write about that which I've observed. This is not going to be easy; and yet, since this trip is clearly my prologue to Africa, it has become very important to me to assess what Israel makes me feel. In a curious way, since it really *does* function as a homeland, however beleaguered, you can't walk five minutes without finding yourself at a border, can't talk to anyone for five minutes without being reminded first of the mandate (British) then of the war—and of course the entire Arab situation, outside the country, and, above all, within, cause one to take a view of human life and right and wrong almost as stony as the land in which I presently find myself—well, to bring this thoroughly undisciplined sentence to a halt, the fact that Israel *is* a homeland for so many Jews (there are great faces here, in a way the whole world is here) causes me to feel my own homelessness more keenly than ever. (People say: "Where are you from?" And it causes me a tiny and resentful effort to say: "New York"— what did *I* ever do to deserve so ghastly a birthplace? and their faces fall.) But just because my homelessness is so inescapably brought home to me, it begins, in some odd way, not only to be bearable, but to be a positive opportunity. It must be, must be made to be. My bones know, somehow, something of what waits for me in Africa. That is one of the reasons I have dawdled so long—I'm afraid. And, of course, I am playing it my own way, edging myself into it: it would be nice to be able to dream about Africa, but once I have been there, I will not be able to dream anymore. The truth is, that there is something unutterably painful about the end of oppression—not that it *has* ended yet, on a black-white basis, I mean, but it *is* ending—and one flinches from the responsibility, which we all now face, of judging black people solely as people. Oh, well. I think of the poor Negroes of the US who identify themselves with Africa, or imagine that they identify

themselves with Africa—and on what basis? It would seem to be
clear, but it is not: Africa has been black a long time but American Negroes did not identify themselves with Africa until Africa
became identified with power. This says something about poor
human nature which indeed one would rather not be forced to
see—enough of this. And, at the same time, the continuing situation of the black people of this world, my awareness of the bland-
ness with which white people commit and deny and defend their
crimes fills me with pain and rage. Well. This promises to be an
extremely valuable journey.

Israel, October 8

Stood on a hill in Jerusalem today, looking over the border: the
Arab-Israeli border. There is really something frightening about
it. There is something insane about it, something which breaks the
heart. I've been wandering up and down Israel for a couple of
weeks now, have stayed in a kibbutz near the Gaza strip, have
been in an art colony near Haifa, wandered through bazaars; and
indeed all of this, all I have seen, is Jewish—if you like. But it is
really the Middle East, it has that spice and stink and violence and
beauty; and it is not Jewish so much as it is Semitic; and I am
very struck by the realization that the Semites were nomads and
this is still, somehow, the atmosphere of the entire country. What
is a Jew? An old question, I know, but it presents itself to one
with great force once one is in this country. Jehovah, Christ, and
Allah all came out of this rocky soil, this fragile handkerchief at
the gate of the Middle East. And the people—the Jews—of this
beleaguered little country are united, as far as I can tell, by two
things only (and perhaps "united" is too strong a word). One
is the experience of the last World War and the memory of the
six million—which is to say that they are united by the evil that
is in the world, that evil which has victimized them so savagely
and so long. But is this enough to make a personality, to make an
identity, to make a religion? (And *what*, precisely, is a religion?
And how dreary, how disturbing, to find oneself asking, now,
questions which one supposed had been answered forever!) But
one is forced to ask these kindergarten questions because the only
other thing which unites the Jew here is the resurrection of the

Hebrew language. The most religious—or, in any case, the most orthodox—people here are the Yemenites, who are also the most lively, and who seem to produce the only artists—well, that is not quite true; but it is almost true; they produce the only artists who can be said to be working out of the Jewish or Semitic or nomadic past. They are also at the bottom of the social ladder, coming from the most primitive conditions—having been, in fact, only yesterday transported from the 12th century. Well. In spite of the fact that the nation of Israel cannot afford, and is far too intelligent, to encourage any form of social discrimination, the fact remains that there is a tremendous gap between a Jew from Russia or France or England or Australia and a Jew but lately arrived from the desert. Is the resurrection of the language enough to bridge this gap? And one cannot help asking—I cannot help asking—if it is really desirable to resurrect the Jewish religion. I mean, the Jews themselves do not believe in it any more: it was simply one of the techniques of their survival—in the desert. Lord, I don't know. One cannot but respect the energy and the courage of this handful of people; but one can't but suspect that a vast amount of political cynicism, on the part of the English and the Americans, went into the creation of this state; and I personally cannot help but be saddened by the creation, at this late date, of yet another nation—it seems to me that we need fewer nations, not more: the blood that has been spilled for various flags makes me ill. Perhaps I would not feel this way if I were not on my way to Africa: what conundrums await one there! Or perhaps I would not feel this way if I were not helplessly and painfully—most painfully—ambivalent concerning the status of the Arabs here. I cannot blame them for feeling dispossessed; and in a literal way, they have been. Furthermore, the Jews, who are surrounded by forty million hostile Muslims, are forced to control the very movements of Arabs within the state of Israel. One cannot blame the Jews for this necessity; one cannot blame the Arabs for resenting it. I would—indeed, in my own situation in America, I do, and it has cost me—costs me—a great and continuing effort not to hate the people who are responsible for the societal effort to limit and diminish me.

Someone said to me the other day that the real trouble between

Arabs and Jews has to do with the fact that their idea of a nation
—the Arab idea, the Jewish idea—is essentially religious. For the
word "religious," I read "tribal." Is it not possible to hope that
we can begin, at long last, to transcend the tribe? But I will think
about this more another day. Whether I want to or not.

Anyway—Jerusalem, God knows (!), *is* golden when the sun is
shining on all that yellow stone. What a blue sky. What a beautiful
city—you remember that song? *Oh, what a beautiful city!* Well,
that's the way Jerusalem makes one feel. I stood today in the upper
room, the room where Christ and his disciples had the last supper,
and I thought of Mahalia and Marian Anderson and *Go Down,
Moses* and of my father and of that other song my father loved
to sing, *I want to be ready To walk in Jerusalem, Just like John.*
And here I am, far from ready, in one of the homelands which
has given me my identity and on my way to another. To ask oneself "What is a Jew?" is also, for me, to ask myself "What is a
black man?" And what, in the name of heaven, *is* an American
Negro? I have a gloomy feeling that I won't find any answers in
Africa, only more questions.

Turkey, October 20

In great haste, far from my own desk. A virus, Mid-eastern, &
trouble, account for my silence. News from Paris bad, Algerian
situation unutterable; & Paula, especially as my sister, much too
close to it, & frightened. ("Fear," she says, "is an awful thing.")
Well. More of this in a real letter.

I have an awful feeling that I've only moved Paula from a
ghetto to a developing *plastique* battleground.

But have been working, steadily, just the same, & will send a
batch of stuff, finally, including contracts, before I finally leave
here.

Hold on, hold on. Don't be mad at me, if you are, this is a
fearful passage.

Turkey, November 20

I am seeing Kenyatta's daughter sometime this week—she is in
town; and this encounter, along with the news of the famine in

Kenya, may take me out of here at a moment's notice. But I hope not, it would be extremely awkward for me now. I'm barrelling ahead with the book, because I want the book in NY before I go to Africa. I dare not predict, again, the time that it will take; but I'm very close to the end.

I am also working on "Down at the Cross." It's my hope that God will be good and that it won't take too long to hammer into its final shape. For I also want *that* in NY before I leave here— I particularly want it to be finished before I try to deal with Africa. The Israeli notes are still disorganized, and the Israeli story—for reasons which have nothing to do with the Israeli character, really —is fairly disheartening. But I must do it. And I am also pre- paring an essay on Turkey. With these last two, I can only hope to have everything down, and up to date, before I take off.

My actor friend's military duties have taken him to the Turkish Siberia, and I'm staying with his sister and brother-in-law. I had meant to move to a hotel, but they all considered this to be an insult. They're very nice people. There's something very sweet, for me, and moving and rare in feeling their impulse to make life as easy as possible for me, so that I can work. I've gained a little weight here and this is taken, apparently, as an enormous justifica- tion for Turkey's existence. Well, I exaggerate, of course,—but life *has* been, after my prolonged storm, very restful here. The only trouble is that you do not know how you can possibly repay such people. Perhaps it is important to learn that there are some people who don't think of payment—time, perhaps, for me to learn how to take. If you don't learn how to take, you soon forget how to give.

Best to Anne, Alison, Freddie, you. I hope Freddie's having some hard, second thoughts about that business of being a writer. But he sounded pretty definite. Your trials with me, dear friend, may prove to be but a weak rehearsal for what's coming .

Love. Write.

Turkey, December

I've just cabled you to send money to me here, so I can get out, and money to meet me in Paris. I thought I had explained to you—but perhaps I didn't, I've been so goddamn swamped and upset—that I am going, now, Saturday, from Paris to Dakar and Brazzaville. I have temporarily eliminated Kenya mainly because I wanted to have my novel finished before I went to Africa (have you received it and have you read it? anxiety is eating me up); and then because Kenyatta seemed never to be in Kenya; and finally because Turkish currency regulations do not allow one to buy traveller's checks *or* take any money out of Turkey; so that I would have had to arrange to stop somewhere else, anyway. I first thought Athens, and then decided on Paris—at first because I thought Paula was still there, and now because I'm indescribably weary and depressed and weary of new places. Mary will be in Paris, I'll spend the holidays with her, and take off at the beginning of the year. I'll be there a month, and be in NY in February. I'll certainly turn in one, possibly two, of the NYorker articles, and return to Africa in the spring and finish up their assignment in the summer. Then, back to NY, and the play. (Kazan and I are in correspondence, he'll be in Athens next month, but I, alas, will not be.)

This is one of the reasons I jumped at the Grove Press invitation: it gives me a deadline to get out of NY. For I must say, my dear Bob—though I am perhaps excessively melancholy today— one thing which this strange and lonely journey has made me feel even more strongly is that it's much better for me to try to stay out of the US as much as possible. I really *do* find American life intolerable and, more than that, personally menacing. I know that I will never be able to expatriate myself again—but I also somehow know that the incessant strain and terror—for me—of continued living there will prove, finally, to be more than I can stand. This, like all such decisions, is wholly private and unanswerable, probably irrevocable and probably irrational—whatever that last word may mean. What it comes to is that I am already fearfully menaced—within—by my vision and am under the obligation to minimize my dangers. It is one thing to try to become articulate where you are, relatively speaking, left alone to do so and quite another to make this attempt in a setting where the terrors of other people so corroborate your own. I think that I must really reconcile myself to being a transatlantic commuter—and turn to my advantage, and not impossibly the advantage of others, the fact that I am a stranger everywhere. For the fact won't change. In order for me to make peace with American life, as it is now lived, I would have to surrender any attempt to come to terms with my own. And this surrender would mean my death.

In fact, I'm probably suffering from a species of post-natal depression. Something very weird happens to you when a book is over, you feel old and useless, and all that effort, which you can't, anyway, remember, seems to have come to nothing. But I'll feel less grim, probably, when I write you again, from Paris, and I'm pushing ahead with the essay and will get it to you before I leave for Dakar.

Loche-les-Bains, February, 1962

Got to Paris, late, as you know, and began tracking down debts and possessions—no easy matter—with the intention of leaving almost at once.

Anyway, partly because I was running around Paris without a winter coat, I came down with the grippe, which rapidly developed into a heavy and painful bronchitis—I thought it was pleurisy, and had visions of pneumonia. The doctor filled me with drugs and told me that, fantastically enough, there was nothing seriously wrong with me, except the bronchitis, but that I was terribly run down and ought not go on to Africa in my exhausted state. I was glad enough to hear this, in a way, I was certainly tired and sad; and so I came here, to the mountains, to the village where I finished my first novel, ten years ago. And Lucien, very much as he did then, came up with me to help me get settled—and has now gone back on the road (he is a salesman) to feed *his* robins.

So. I meant to write you sooner, but at first I simply could not get myself together enough to do it, and then couldn't stay awake long enough: the French notion of medicine is to knock you out. Then, when I got to the mountains, all I did was sleep—the mountain air, I guess. I feel much better now, ready to start again —though I also feel very still and sad.

This is not quite the tone I meant to strike when writing you, for I know that you tend to worry about me, but it seems to be the only tone I can manage—but please do not worry, everything is much better now. And in fact, Paris was the only really bad spot and that might not have been so bad if I had not fallen ill. Though, in another way, I think that that might have been lucky.

I am again reworking the interminable "Down at the Cross," and will send it off to you as soon as I've sent the rewrites to Jim. You'll see, I imagine, when you read it, why it has been so hard to do, and it probably also illuminates some of the unsettling apprehensions which have so complicated this journey.

Which brings us to the third point: I've kept, as I've told you, a kind of incoherent, blow by blow account of this trip, and I intend, before I leave the mountains, to get at least the Israeli section out to you, so that you can send it to Shawn. Again, I think that this will make clearer than any of my letters can, how complex, once I got to Israel, the whole idea of Africa became. It became clear to me at once that I could not hope to manage that confrontation with an exhibition, merely, of journalistic skill. I could only deal with it in an extremely, even dangerously personal way, and try to make the reader ask his own questions and make his own assessments. And this sorrow, if I may call it that, was deepened in Turkey, where the whole sombre question of America's role in the world today stared at me in a new and inescapable way; and the question of America's role brings up, of course, the question of what the role of the American Negro is, or can be. Well. I suppose the Israeli piece will cause some people to think I'm anti-Semitic, and God knows what the reaction to the Turkish chapter will be. But they are part of the African book, they must be.

As for Africa, I'd rather like your advice at this point. I, personally, would like to go from here to Dakar at the end of this month—Dakar and Brazzaville—and stay down there until I meet Grove Press in Mallorca at the end of April. In May, I have a tentative rendezvous to meet Elia Kazan in Greece—I saw him just before he left Paris. My own idea was to finish the play during May and June, so that he can take it back with him to New York; and then return to Africa, Ghana, Nigeria, and Kenya, and return to New York in the Fall. Once I get to Africa, I imagine that I will be extremely busy, particularly with students, and I don't want to stint: it has taken me so long to get there!

The only problem, as far as I can see, involves the American lectures. As you know, I don't have any very clear idea of what that schedule was; but it's my impression that the only firm commitment was for Monterey College, sometime in April. If need be, I can fly back for that, since Grove Press, in any case, will fly me out. What do you think? I don't see that there's any great need for me to be home for *Country*'s publication—though I am willing to listen, of course. Finally, though, I must say, I simply dread facing the tigerish Negro press if I return to America without having visited the land which they so abruptly are proud to claim as home. The more particularly as neither *Another Country* nor my report on Africa is likely to please them at all.

This trip has had the effect of opening something in me which I must pursue, and I do not think that I can do that and be a Negro leader, too. And, in any case, my whole attitude toward the fact of color undergoes several melancholy changes: I don't know where they will lead me, but I must buy the time to find out. There is a very grim secret hidden in the fact that so many of the people one hoped to rescue could not be rescued because the prison of color had become their hiding place. I don't know what this means, for me, for us, for the world, for the future of Africa— I don't yet know what color means in Africa (but I *will* know). Life has the effect of forcing you to act on your premises—the only key I can find to my spectacular recklessness—and I have said for years that color does not matter. I am now beginning to feel that it does not matter *at all*, that it masks something else which *does* matter: but this suspicion changes, for me, the entire nature of reality.

Ah. Bear with me, dear friend. I make my journeys by a radar I must trust, and must pursue and bear my discoveries in the best way I can. I know it's hard on everybody's nerves, and it's certainly hard on mine, but I'm not being frivolous and it is done out of love.

Write me, quickly, please, the morale is wildly fluctuating, I'm always afraid, and I'm pregnant with some strange monster.

Saunders Redding

IN COMMENTING on his work, Saunders Redding recalls "In my senior year at Brown University I had a story published in *transition*, which Eugene Jolas was editing in France at the time. The story was called "Delaware Coon," and when, three years later, I showed it to my father, he hit the ceiling. The idea of a son of his traducing the Negro race, etc., etc. Some people think I still traduce the Negro race. My defense is a simple one, for all its boastful tone: I'm devoted to Truth, and if I tell the truth about people who happen to be Negro people, it is not because I wish to malign the race: it is only because the truth about Negro people seems the most important truth the American democracy needs to learn."

Saunders Redding, who was graduated from Brown University (Ph.B., M.A.), is currently Johnson Professor of Literature and Creative Writing at Hampton Institute, Hampton, Virginia. He has been a visiting professor of English at Brown University (1949–50), where he conducted a graduate course on the Negro in American Literature and an undergraduate course in Creative Writing; Rosenfeld Lecturer at Grinnell College (Iowa); and a visiting lecturer at Bowdoin College (Maine), Hamilton College (New York), Lake Forest College (Illinois), and the University of Virginia.

His first book, *To Make a Poet Black*, was published in 1939, and in 1940 he was named a Rockefeller Foundation Fellow and traveled throughout the Southern states. This journey resulted in his second book, *No Day of Triumph*, which won the Mayflower Award "for distinguished writing" in 1944. Appointed a Guggenheim Fellow that same year, Redding devoted the next six years to teaching and to writing a novel, *Stranger and Alone* (1950), *They Came in Chains* (1950, The Peoples of America Series), and *On Being Negro in America* (1951). When *On Being a Negro in America* was reissued in 1962, William L. Shirer wrote that Mr. Redding "has set down with restrained bitterness, great dignity and sensitive insight what it is like to be a Negro in the United States . . . eloquent, passionately written."

In 1952, the U. S. State Department asked Redding to go to India, where he spent several months lecturing in India's universities and holding informal discussions with Indian intellectual and political figures, and in 1955 his book *An American in India* was published. To the Mainstream of America Series he contributed *The Lonesome Road* (1958), a history of the Negro in America. Again appointed a Guggenheim Fellow in 1959, he has since been working on another book, scheduled for publication in 1964.

He is a member of the editorial board of the *American Scholar*, the publication of the Phi Beta Kappa honorary society. His articles have appeared in *The Atlantic*, *Harper's*, *American Mercury*, *Antioch Review*, *The American Scholar*, and other publications.

Mr. Redding wrote "The Alien Land of Richard Wright" especially for this collection.

THE ALIEN LAND OF
RICHARD WRIGHT

BY SAUNDERS REDDING

1

The dedication of Richard Wright's posthumous book, *Eight Men*, is more than a curious anomaly. It is an irony. It is addressed to friends in France, "whose kindness made me feel at home in an alien land," and the irony has greater poignancy because the author did not intend it. Wright lacked the ironic cast of mind and heart. Except in intimate privacy and on those rare occasions when he was at ease with his friends, when he was often gay, he had no sport with mockery, especially if it was turned against himself. He had no eye for fun; no ear or tongue for jest. In public— and his books were public—he took the world and all men as he took himself, with grim seriousness.

So the dedication of *Eight Men* was gravely meant as an expression of gratitude to a people who ranked him with the greats of modern fiction, and in this sense it means what it says. But in a more important sense it does not. For if Richard Wright was at home in the "alien land" where he had lived for nearly fifteen years, how could he have written (in *White Man, Listen!*) near the close of those years, "I am a rootless man"? At home and rootless? Surely both were not true. "But," he went on, "I am neither psychologically distraught nor in any wise particularly perturbed because of it." Without exception, directly or by implication, his published works refute him. No modern writer of comparable gifts and reputation has been so mistaken in his judgment of himself, nor understood and valued the sources of his spirit less.

Wright the novelist was first and last an American novelist. He was not at home in France. He never absorbed, nor ever was absorbed in, the strange environment, the Gallic atmosphere. He saw the *mise en scène*, but did not comprehend it, nor did he have the writer's sense of being in it. He was no cosmopolite, like Henry James. France was for him what it had been for Joyce—a friendly lodging and a refuge, a comfortable convenience, a place to hang his hat. But not a home.

One proof is in the fact that he never wrote about it. He could not. His passions were not there; they were involved elsewhere. The one thing French that caught him was existentialism, and this held him disingenuously and only long enough for him to write his one unqualifiedly bad novel, *The Outsider*. And this was an American novel—that is, it was a novel about an American Negro—and in its dedication the word "alien" crops up again: "For Rachel, my daughter who was born on alien soil." He had lived in France for nine years when he wrote that, and in that ninth year, thinking that the Gold Coast, "the ancestral home of millions of American Negroes," would be less alien, he went there. But Africa was not home. *Black Power*, the book he wrote about it, is a plain statement of the fact.

Indeed, he was nearer home in Spain. There he "felt most keenly . . . the needless, unnatural, and utterly barbarous nature of the psychological suffering . . ." because "I am an American Negro with a background of psychological suffering." What drew his attention was, he said, "the undeniable and uncanny psychological affinities that they [Spanish Protestants] held in common with American Negroes." And, finally, there is that dedication of *White Man, Listen!* to those "who seek desperately for a home for their hearts."

2

Wright's heart's home, his mind's tether, was in America. It is not the America of the motion pictures, or of the novels of Thomas Wolfe, J. P. Marquand, and John O'Hara, or of the histories of Allan Nevins and Samuel Eliot Morison. It is the America that only Negroes know. It is a ghetto of the soul, a boundary of the mind, a confine of the heart. There is no cause for wonder in the fact that Wright sought escape from it and tried to reject it. Other Negro writers have done so, and some are still doing it. There are various ways. Some pretend there is no such America. Some who, like Jean Toomer, are fair enough to pass, go into the white race. Some turn to fantasy, as Countee Cullen and William Braithwaite did. Others—William Demby, William Gardner Smith, Chester Himes, and James Baldwin—like Wright, expatriate themselves for longer or shorter times in Italy, Switzerland, Spain, or France. But no matter how it is done, escape is a commitment to self-abnegation, and the moment the Negro writer, or any other writer, so commits himself he begins to flag as a creative artist. He turns precious and arty; honesty deserts him; dedication wilts; passion chills.

America has not yet changed to the extent that a Negro writer can deny, effectively suppress, or truly escape what Wright himself defined as the "inevitable race consciousness which three hundred years of Jim Crow living has burned into the Negro's heart." He cannot escape the supra-consciousness of what living in America has made him. If the pathos of man is that he yearns to be whole, hungers for fulfillment, and strives for a sense of community with others, it is the particular tragedy of the Negro in America that no success gratifies the yearning, that great fame does not feed the hunger, and that the wealth of Croesus does not abate the struggle to be free, whole and *naturally* absorbed in the cultural oneness of his native land. "The fact of separation from the culture of his native land," Wright wrote a few years back, "has . . . sunk into the Negro's heart. The Negro loves his land, but that land rejects him." He is always apart. He is, God help him, always alone. "I know America," Wright wrote.

It is a bitter knowledge, but it sustained his great honesty and integrity as a writer. Insofar as he used it to appeal to the cognitive side of man's being, as he did in *Twelve Million Black Voices*, sections of *White Man, Listen!* and in various essays, he followed in the tradition of more provincial Negro writers, whose sole effort was to destroy the prevailing racial stereotypes with battering-rams of facts. This is an honorable tradition, and Wright, too, learned from the sociologists, the academic psychologists, and the social activists. But Wright was no one's disciple. He quickened the tradition with his own passionate vitality; he glorified it with his skill for appealing to the connotative and affective side of man's being. He transmuted his knowledge into *Uncle Tom's Children, Native Son,* and *Black Boy*—into art that was, as

Dorothy Canfield Fisher said, "honest, dreadful, heartbreaking."

And, indeed, this was the sum of his creative power. He was no dedicated craftsman, like Hemingway; no novelist-philosopher, like Sartre and Camus; no brilliant stylistic innovator, like Joyce and Faulkner. His talent was to smite the conscience—and to smite the conscience of both white and black Americans. Whites read him and lamented, "Is this what our democracy has done?" Negroes read him and quavered, "Is this us?"

Negroes, as Wright remarked, "possessed deep-seated resistances against the Negro problem being presented, even verbally, in all its hideous fullness, in all the totality of its meaning." They did not want to believe what other Negro writers—Du Bois, for instance, and Rayford Logan and Charles S. Johnson—had been for years telling them in academic terms, and by implication, and also sometimes by imaginative inversion. They did not want to believe that they were as helpless, as outraged, as despairing, as violent, and as hate-ridden as Wright depicted them. But they were. They did not want to believe that the America that they loved had bred these pollutions of oppression into their blood and bone. But it had. "Is this us? And is this our America?" It was.

As Richard Wright saw it, redemption lay in revolution; so he became a Communist. He was, he said, at about the time of the publication of *Native Son*, a "card-bearing" member of the Party. He gave his reasons. American democracy isolated him because he was a Negro: the Communist Party offered "the first sustained relationships of my life." He was amazed and immensely gratified to learn "that there did exist in this world an organized search for the truth of the lives of the oppressed and the isolated." He joined the search, he was a member of the revolution because he thought that Negro experience could find "a home, a functioning value and a role" in communism's radical position.

"If you possess enough courage to speak out what you are," Wright wrote, "you will find that you are not alone." He had enough courage, and he spoke out; and this courageous speaking out, it should be remarked, was the only literary creed—it was certainly no aesthetic theory!—he ever went by. Like his mother's face when he once surprised her staring at a particularly lurid cartoon, Wright reflected what he felt in the dark places of his soul—disgust and anger, shame and fear. And these combined with innate honesty to form the main elements of Richard Wright's extraordinary literary power.

He struck with that power in his first published work, *Uncle Tom's Children,* a collection of four *nouvelles.* Three of these are about lynching, and the fourth, "Fire and Cloud," is about revolution, purification, and deliverance, and it ends in exhortation: "Freedom belongs to the strong!" Each is a violent and brutal and shockingly undisguised, *unliterary* comment, not on life, but on a way of having to live and of being forced to live in ignorance, fear, and shame. In his first book Wright is preoccupied with—is, indeed, already beginning to be obsessed by—"the disinherited, the dispossessed," and in Big Boy of the lead story, "Big Boy Leaves Home," he has already created the prototype of all his heroes, who were ever to be angry, bitter, vengeful, violently hurling themselves against the walls that barred them from a life that they knew was a better life than theirs, belonging to people no better than themselves. They knew this from the movies, the picture magazines, and the screaming headlines in the daily press. But while white people were no better, they were different—so different as to seem to Bigger Thomas (*Native Son*) not people at all, but "a sort of great natural force, like a stormy sky looming overhead, or like a deep swirling river stretching suddenly at one's feet in the dark" threatening a death to which one could react "only in fear and shame."

These were Wright's own dominant, empirical emotions. He did not have to create them for his fictional purposes. They were the very substance of his childhood, youth, and manhood, until he moved abroad. He tells us in *Black Boy,* his autobiography, that he learned at an early age "the reality—a Negro's reality—of the white world. . . . I was tense each moment. . . . I did not suspect that the tension I had begun to feel would lift itself into the passion of my life. . . . I was always to be conscious of it, brood over it, carry it in my heart, live with it, sleep with it, fight with it." In a way more direct than is true of most important modern authors of fiction, Wright's heroes were in naked honesty himself, and not imaginary creations that served merely to express his complicated personality.

This is not to say, however, that their adventures and their characterizing quirks and habits, their whims of thought and the compulsive violence of their behavior, were also Wright's. Not by any means. These were the fancied and observed externalizations of what such hero-personalities would do and say and outwardly be—personalities which, unlike Wright's own, were not guided by a moral intelligence, an active social sense, or ethical thought. The tragedy of Wright's heroes is that they lack this direction, and the blunt point of Wright's fiction is that American society denies them the opportunity to acquire it. Speaking in defense of Bigger Thomas, the lawyer of *Native Son* spoke for all Wright's heroes: "Excluded from, and unassimilated in our society, yet longing to gratify impulses akin to our own but denied the objects and channels evolved through long centuries for their socialized expression, every sunrise and sunset make him guilty of subversive actions."

But if the characterizing externalizations are the measure of Wright's imagination, the structure of his heroes' personalities, the patterns of their emotions, and the types of their dreams are the measure of Wright's honesty and of his self-knowledge as a Negro. It is inconceivable that Wright's essay "How Bigger Was Born" is true in fact. It is true only—and the "only" implies no derogation—in spirit. Though the essay declares it, it is hardly to be taken literally or literally believed that Wright conceived of Bigger Thomas as sometimes Negro and sometimes white. This is an elastic rationalization to justify what the author himself then embraced as a saving *modus vivendi:* the united front of the Communist line—the people's movement, the brotherhood of the oppressed. Bigger Thomas was Negro all the time. And so, of course, was Richard Wright. He made this clear, after he left the Party, in what is probably his most brilliant essay.

This neglected essay—the introduction to a book entitled *Black Metropolis*—is of far greater importance than any one citation indicates. Whether by accident or design, the essay discloses the *central stream* of Wright's entire development both as man and as writer. It reveals the sources of his thoughts and feelings. It takes us into the matrix of his creative conceptions.

He read William James early, at fifteen or sixteen. He got to read him by a subterfuge which involved a denial of his selfhood, and while this was certainly a part of the matter, the greater part was that he found objective philosophical confirmation of what experience had already taught him—that "the lives of the dispossessed are not real to white people." On more than one occasion he had been treated as if he did not exist as a sensate being. As a hotel bellboy in a Southern town he had been summoned to rooms where naked white women lolled about unmoved by any sense of shame at his presence, because "blacks were not considered human beings anyway. . . . I was a non-man, something that knew vaguely that it was human but felt that it was not. . . . I felt doubly cast out."

Then he read James, and James was later supported by the professional social psychologists. It is revealing to quote the passage that Wright quotes: "No more fiendish punishment could be devised . . . than that one should be turned loose in society and remain absolutely unnoticed by the members thereof. If no one turned around when we entered, answered when we spoke, or minded what we did, but if every person we met 'cut us dead,' and acted as if we were non-existent things, a kind of rage and impotent despair would ere long well up in us, from which the cruelest bodily tortures would be a relief; for these would make us feel that, however bad might be our plight, we had not sunk to such a depth as to be unworthy of attention at all."

This is the ground of all Wright's works, fiction and non-fiction. It is the thought, the theme, and the dramatic design. The passage revealed, as it were, him to himself. It is scarcely to be doubted that from the moment he read it, groping through it toward the knowledge of its empirical truth and listening to its mournful echoes in the still locked chambers of his soul, Wright became a man with a message and a mission. Long before he wrote White Man, Listen! the message was addressed to a white audience, and the mission was to bring awareness to that audience and perhaps thereby to save the world.

Both the message and the mission were particularized by Richard Wright's conception of a world where men "still cling to the emotional basis of life that the [old] feudal order gave them," and by his supra-consciousness of being Negro in that world. Translated into creative terms, this necessitated the rendering of Negro life with greater circumstantiality than had ever before been attempted. Oh, what psychological detail, what analysis of external influences, what precise attention to physical minutiae! He was in the naturalistic tradition, but without the naturalistic writer's aesthetic theories, abstract knowledge, and controls. Wright put everything in to arouse an audience which he hoped would be white, as principally it was. Only rarely did he write for Negroes, and only then when he was pressed, and then only on political subjects. He reasoned that Negroes already knew the particulars of what it was to have "uncertainty as a way of life" and "of living within the vivid present moment and letting the meaning of that moment suffice as a rationale for life and death." But whites did not know, so he had to tell them—in the rage of Silas (in "Long Black Song"), in the weakness of Mann (in "Down by the Riverside"), in the despair of Bigger, and in the words of Bigger's Communist lawyer:

"I plead with you to see a mode of *life* in our midst, a mode of life stunted and distorted, but possessing its own laws and claims, an existence of men growing out of the soil prepared by the collective but blind will of a hundred million people. I beg you to recognize human life draped in a form and guise alien to ours, but springing from a soil plowed and sown by our own hands. I ask you recognize the laws and processes flowing from such a condition, understand them, seek to change them. If we do none of these, then we should not pretend horror or surprise when thwarted life expresses itself in fear and hate and crime.

"This is life, new and strange. . . . We have kept our eyes turned from it. This is life lived in cramped limits and expressing itself not in terms of our good and bad, but in terms of its own fulfillment. Men are men and life is life, and we must deal with them as they are; and if we want to change them, we must deal with them in the form in which they exist and have their being."

Listen, white folks!

3

Wright's books sold more than a million copies here at home, so there were those who listened, and many of them must have felt as Dorothy Canfield Fisher felt. Still it changed little. What

Wright had seen as a possible agent of change, the American Communist Party, disappointed him. He held on for a while, and he remained happy that he had written those stories in which he had "assigned a role of honor and glory" to the Party, but his commitment of faith crumbled. His rejection of the Party early in the war years was only a gesture, for the Party had already rejected him. After the war, when change still did not come, he rejected America.

This, however, was more than a gesture: it was an action of the greatest consequences. Life in France, in Paris, where he went to live, in some ways fulfilled him as a social being. The freedom was good. The "strangeness" was good. The reputation his books had earned him with the French and among Europeans generally was good to savor. He and his family could live where they wished and go where they wanted without the old uncertainties, the fears. It was all good. "I do not expect ever again to live in the States," he said in the spring of 1959.

But what was good for him as a social being was bad for his work. He had taken his Negroness with him, but he could not take with him the America that bred and fed his consciousness of Negroness. Perhaps he sought to nourish that consciousness by a kind of forced feeding. He read the American press assiduously, and particularly the American Negro press. He kept up a voluminous correspondence with American friends. He made friends with French Africans—Negroes—in Paris, who conceived, edited, and largely wrote the Negro quarterly publication *Présence Africaine*. He helped them to found the Society of African Culture and was instrumental in establishing an American branch of the Society. But none of these activities was enough. All of them together were not.

When *The Long Dream* was published in 1958, what was happening to Richard Wright—what, indeed, had already happened —seemed obvious to his American readers. The Fishbelly of that book was Big Boy of "Big Boy Leaves Home"; he was the preacher's son of "Fire and Cloud"; and he was Bigger Thomas of *Native Son*—except that now he was an anachronism. The limitations of mood, the restricted inventiveness, and the congeneric characterizations that defined Wright's work were no longer projective of the small, new realities and the big, new *Weltansicht* of the only place and people that could ever be Wright's home. Angry scorn alternating with bleak despair was no longer enough. Violence and brutal physical degradation were still a part of the new reality, but they were no longer all of it. Cowardice, self-abasement, and unmitigated suffering do not now highlight the drama and furnish the big dramatic scenes. *The Outsider* (1956) seemed rather silly; and one is not surprised that the best stories in his posthumous *Eight Men* were written before he left the States.

In going to live abroad Richard Wright had cut the roots that once sustained him; the tight-wound emotional core came unwound; the creative center dissolved; his memory of what Negro life in America *was* lost its relevance to what Negro life in America *is*—and is becoming. The people and the events of his latest books are not true. While Wright remained honest, he was honest only to the memory of things past, to passions spent, to moods gone vapid, and too often these moods found expression in vaporous language:

He peered out of his window and saw vast, wheeling populations of ruled stars swarming in the convened congresses of the skies anchored amidst nations of space and he prayed wordlessly that a bright, bursting tyrant of living sun would soon lay down its golden laws to loosen the locked regions of his heart and cast the shadow of his dream athwart the stretches of time.

Richard Wright had forgotten the tough American idiom. He had been gone from home too long. But he had already earned the right to be judged by his best, and that best was in the moral stance from which he never wavered, and in his courage as a writer, and in his honesty as a man.

John Hope Franklin

JOHN HOPE FRANKLIN was born in Oklahoma. In 1935 he received a B.A. (*magna cum laude*) from Fisk University. He did graduate work in history at Harvard University, where he was awarded the M.A. and Ph.D. degrees in 1936 and 1941, respectively. While at Harvard he held the Edward Austin Fellowship from the University and a fellowship from the Julius Rosenwald Fund.

Professor Franklin has taught at Fisk University, North Carolina College at Durham, and Howard University. In 1956 he became a professor and chairman of the Department of History at Brooklyn College. He has also served as visiting professor at Harvard University, the University of Wisconsin, Cornell University, the University of California at Berkeley, and the University of Hawaii. Abroad he has served twice as professor at the Salzburg Seminar in American Studies in Austria, was a visiting lecturer at the Seminar in American Studies at Cambridge University in England, and has lectured in many German cities. He has participated in forums and discussion groups in several European countries, as well as at the Tenth International Congress of Historical Sciences in Rome. In 1957 he represented the American Council of Learned Societies at the centennial observances at the Universities of Calcutta, Madras, and Bombay. In 1960 he was Fulbright Professor at several Australian universities.

His first book, *The Free Negro in North Carolina, 1790–1860,* was published in 1943. In 1947 he brought out *The Civil War Diary of James T. Ayers,* and his well-known *From Slavery to Freedom: A History of American Negroes,* a revised edition of which appeared in 1956. Also in 1956 the Belknap Press published his book *The Militant South.* In the fall of 1961 his edition of Tourgée's *A Fool's Errand* was published by the John Harvard Library. His most recent book, *Reconstruction after the Civil War,* was published in 1961 in the University of Chicago's American Civilization Series. Professor Franklin has contributed articles to leading journals in the United States and in Europe. For fifteen years he has served on the editorial board of the *Journal of Negro History.* From 1958 to 1961 he was on the executive committee of the Mississippi Valley Historical Association, and in December 1958 he was elected to the Council of the American Historical Association, on which he currently serves as chairman of the executive committee.

"The Dilemma of the American Negro Scholar" was written for this volume at the request of the editor. According to Dr. Franklin, the essay "examines the role of the Negro scholar in the historical context of the difficulties that any American intellectual experiences. There has always been the tendency to deprecate the role of the American scholar, and Negroes in that group have usually been disregarded altogether. The Negro scholar, in search of areas in which he could be effective and, at the same time, strike at the tangled web of prejudice, has frequently turned to Negro studies—Negro history, sociology, anthropology, literature, etc. While he has done much to establish this as a respectable, even popular field, he has had to struggle against the temptation to be polemical and passionate in the cause of justice. The struggle is a continuing one and constitutes the Negro scholar's major dilemma."

THE DILEMMA OF THE AMERICAN NEGRO SCHOLAR

BY JOHN HOPE FRANKLIN

The problems of the scholar who belongs to a particular group, ethnic or otherwise, must be considered in the context of the general problem of the scholar in the United States. In America the scholar's role in the community and the nation has always been limited. Indeed, his role has been rather carefully defined by the history of the country. Questions have often been raised about the effective use of the scholar in a society whose fundamental preoccupation has been with problems that have had little or nothing to do with the life of the mind. Intellectual prowess and mental acumen, it was argued almost from the beginning, could make no substantial contribution to the tasks of clearing the forests, cutting pathways to the frontier, and making a living in the wilderness. The intellectual life was reserved for those whose task it was to preserve and promote the moral and religious life of the community. In the early days of the nation there was a widespread feeling, moreover, that these aspects of life could be kept separate from the other aspects. Meanwhile, the rest of the community could live in blissful ignorance, with little or no concern for the great world of scholarship and learning that might be flourishing as far away as London and Paris or as close as the nearest county seat.

This was a mere fiction, but Americans liked to believe in it. In the final analysis, however, those who devoted themselves to intellectual pursuits became forces in the community in spite of the community itself. The lack of respect for learning or the lack of concern for it melted before the exigencies of conflict, when ideological justifications and rationalizations were needed for actions that had already been taken. Thus, when the patriots were fighting for independence, the scholars came to the rescue of the polemicists and agitators, and Locke and Hume and Dickinson and Jefferson became household words among groups considerably larger than those who could be described as learned. It was at this juncture that the peculiar ambivalence that was to characterize American attitudes became evident. On the one hand, there was little regard, if not downright contempt, for the scholar and the serious thinker. On the other hand, there was the acknowledged need for the talents and resources of the man who was devoted to the intellectual life; and there was a willingness to call upon him to strengthen the hand of those who had decided upon a particular course of action.

There has always been some acknowledgment, from that day to this, of the importance of the role of the scholar and intellectual in American life. Too often it has been begrudgingly conceded and too often the pervasive influence of scholarship in policy making and decision making is wholly unrecognized. We have been inclined to discount this influence and to insist that theorizing is the pastime of less practical-minded people. As for ourselves, we move, we act, we get things done, we have no time for indulging in the fantasies that emanate from the ivory tower. We do not seem to care that for this attitude we may be branded unintellectual or even anti-intellectual. We prefer to be known and recognized as practical-minded, down-to-earth. After all, our constitution is a practical, workable document. Our economy reflects our hardheaded approach to exploiting our resources and developing effective and efficient means of production. Even our social order and our institutions are evidence of our pragmatic orientation. I would suspect, however, that the more generous and broad-minded among us would recognize the fact that an untold amount of scholarship went into the writing of our constitution; that theoretical scientists as well as technicians and businessmen helped to make our economy what it has become; and that many scholarly hands contributed to the formulation of our social order and the institutions of which we boast.

The point is that, whether he wanted to or not, the American scholar has been drawn irresistibly into the main stream of American life, and has contributed his knowledge and his ingenuity to the solution of the major problems that the country has faced. Jonathan Edwards's *Freedom of the Will*, with all its scholarship, good and bad, was primarily an effort to preserve the unity of the older religious institutions in the face of powerful currents of change. Thomas Jefferson was a close student of eighteenth-century political theory, but the most significant manifestation of his scholarship in this area is to be found in the Declaration of Independence, whose practical-mindedness can hardly be surpassed. Even Ralph Waldo Emerson's *American Scholar*, while embodying some remarkable generalizations about the intellectual resources and powers of mankind, was in truth a declaration of American intellectual independence, calling the American scholar to arms in the war against ignorance and in behalf of the integrity of American intellectual life.

In recent years the story has been essentially the same. It was Woodrow Wilson, the former professor at Princeton, testing his theories of congressional government while President of the United States. It was James MacGregor Burns, of Williams College, adding scholarship and a new dimension to the traditional campaign biography with his life of John F. Kennedy. It was John Kenneth Galbraith descending from the insulation of a Harvard economics chair to make searching and stimulating observations on the industrial and business community of the nation. If these and scores of other scholars were faced with dilemmas—of whether to satisfy themselves in attacking the theoretical problems of their fields or to grapple with the fundamental problems of mankind— they resolved them fearlessly and unequivocally by applying their disciplines to the tasks from which they felt that they could not escape. In that way they gave meaning, substance, and significance to American scholarship.

It is in such a setting and context that we must examine the position of the American Negro scholar. The dilemmas and problems of the Negro scholar are numerous and complex. He has been forced, first of all, to establish his claim to being a scholar, and he has had somehow to seek recognition in the general world of scholarship. This has not been an easy or simple task, for, at the very time when American scholarship in general was making its claim to recognition, it was denying that Negroes were capable of being scholars. Few Americans, even those who advocated a measure of political equality, subscribed to the view that Negroes—any Negroes—had the ability to think either abstractly or concretely or to assimilate ideas that had been formulated by others. As late as the closing years of the nineteenth century it was difficult to find any white persons in the labor or business community, in the pulpit or on the platform, in the field of letters or in the field of scholarship, who thought it possible that a Negro could join the select company of scholars in America.

The Negro, then, first of all had to struggle against the forces and personalities in American life that insisted that he could never rise in the intellectual sphere. Thomas Nelson Page, the champion of the plantation tradition and the defender of the superiority of the white race, insisted that "the Negro has not progressed, not because he was a slave, but because he does not possess the faculties to raise himself above slavery. He has not yet exhibited the qualities of any race which has advanced civilization or shown capacity to be greatly advanced." In 1895, a future President of the United States, Theodore Roosevelt, argued that "a perfectly stupid race can never rise to a very high plane; the Negro, for instance, has been kept down as much by lack of intellectual development as anything else." If one were to thumb through the pages of the most respectable journals of the early years of this century—*Atlantic, Harper's, Scribner's, Century, North American Review*—he would find the same spirit pervading the articles published there. Industrial and vocational education, they contended, was peculiarly suitable for the Negro. Negroes, they argued, were childish, simple, irresponsible, and mentally inferior. It was the same wherever one looked.

The Negro who aspired to be a scholar in the closing years of the nineteenth century and the opening years of this century must have experienced the most shattering and disturbing sensations as he looked about him in an attempt to discover one indication of confidence, one expression of faith in him and his abilities. If he doubted himself, it would be understandable, for he had been brainwashed, completely and almost irrevocably, by assertions of Caucasian superiority, endorsements of social Darwinism, with its justifications for the degradation of the Negro, and political and legal maneuverings that lowered the Negro still further on the social and intellectual scale. But the aspiring Negro scholar did not doubt himself, and he turned on his detractors with all the resources he could summon in the effort to refute those who claimed he was inferior. In 1888, a Negro, William T. Alexander, published a whole volume to support the claim that the Negro was the intellectual equal of others. "By the closest analysis of the blood of each race," he argued with eloquence, and futility, considering the times, "the slightest difference cannot be detected; and so, in the aspirations of the mind, or the impulses of the heart, we are all one common family, with nothing but the development of the mind through the channel of education to raise one man, or one people above another. . . . So far as noble characteristics are concerned, the colored race possess those traits to fully as great a degree as do the white."

Alexander and numerous contemporaries of his had faced their dilemma, and they had made their choice. They *had* to combat the contentions of Negro inferiority. They *had* to demonstrate that Negroes were capable of assimilating ideas and of contributing to mankind's store of knowledge. They made their argument simply and directly. It was as though whites had said they could not count, and Negroes then counted from one to ten to prove that they could. There were subtle, more sophisticated ways of proving their mental acumen, but if Negroes thought of them, they must have been convinced that such methods would have no effect on those whose arguments were not based on fact or reason in the first place.

It must have been a most unrewarding experience for the Negro scholar to answer those who said that he was inferior by declaring: "I am indeed *not inferior*." For such a dialogue left little or no time for the pursuit of knowledge as one really desired to pursue it. Imagine, if you can, what it meant to a competent Negro student of Greek literature, W. H. Crogman, to desert his chosen field and write a book entitled *The Progress of a Race*. Think of the frustration of the distinguished Negro physician C. V. Roman, who abandoned his medical research and practice, temporarily at least, to write *The Negro in American Civilization*. What must have been the feeling of the Negro student of English literature Benjamin Brawley, who forsook his field to write *The Negro Genius* and other works that underscored the intellectual powers of the Negro? How much poorer is the field of the biological sciences because an extremely able and well-trained Negro scientist, Julian Lewis, felt compelled to spend years of his productive life writing a book entitled *The Biology of the Negro?*

Many Negro scholars, moreover, never entered any of the standard branches of learning. Perhaps they would have been chemists, geologists, essayists, critics, musicologists, sociologists, historians. But they never were. From the moment of their intellectual awakening they were drawn inexorably, irresistibly into the field that became known as Negro studies. Here they were insulated from the assaults of the white scholars, who could be as vicious and as intolerant in their attacks and in their attitudes as the out-and-out racists were. Here, too, they would work relatively unmolested in a field where they could meet, head on, the assaults of those who would malign them and their race. In a sense, they could establish not only a professional standing by dealing objectively and in a scholarly fashion with the problems related to them and their race, but also the value and integrity of the field of Negro studies itself, which they had brought into being.

The careers of three Negro scholars—W. E. B. Du Bois, Carter G. Woodson, and Alain L. Locke—epitomize the history of Negro scholarship in the first half of the twentieth century. All three were carefully trained and held degrees of doctor of philosophy from Harvard University. After writing a doctoral dissertation that became Volume I in the Harvard Historical Studies, Du Bois moved on from his path-breaking work on the suppression of the African slave trade to a series of studies that not only treated many aspects of the Negro problem but also covered a number of areas in the social sciences and the humanities. He produced *The Philadelphia Negro*, a modern sociological study: he was the editor of the Atlanta University *Studies of the Negro Problem*, called a pioneering work in the field of the social sciences; he wrote *The Souls of Black Folk*, a critique of approaches to the solution of the race problem, *Black Folk Then and Now*, a history of the Negro in Africa and the New World, *Black Reconstruction*, a study of the Negro's part in the years following the Civil War, and literally dozens of other works. In his ninety-fourth year, he has recently completed an epic three-volume novel of the Negro,

The Ordeal of Mansard, and is now planning an encyclopedia of the Negro.

Woodson's first scholarly work, *The Disruption of Virginia,* was a rather general study. He soon settled down to a systematic study of the Negro, however. Successively, he produced his *Education of the Negro Prior to 1860,* his studies of the free Negro, his *Century of Negro Migration, The History of the Negro Church, The Negro in Our History, African Background Outlined,* and many others. In 1915 he organized the Association for the Study of Negro Life and History, and shortly thereafter became editor of the *Journal of Negro History,* which today is one of the major historical publications in the United States.

Alain Locke's career was, in several important respects, different from that of Du Bois and Woodson. He was an honor graduate of Harvard College, where he was elected to Phi Beta Kappa. He was a Rhodes Scholar at Oxford and later studied at the University of Berlin. Trained in philosophy, he soon became involved in the literary activity that was later called "The Negro Renaissance." Although he maintained his interest in the theory of value and cultural pluralism, he became a powerful force in articulating the position and aspirations of the new Negro. Thus, his *The New Negro: An Interpretation, The Negro in Art,* and *Plays of Negro Life* eclipsed his "Values and Imperatives," "Ethics and Culture," and "Three Corollaries of Cultural Relativism." After 1925 he never gave very much attention to purely philosophical problems.

Under the shadow and influence of these three figures and others, there emerged a large number of Negro scholars who devoted themselves almost exclusively to the study of some aspect of the Negro. Soon recognized fields emerged: the history of the Negro, the anthropology of the Negro, the sociology of the Negro, the poetry of the Negro, the Negro novel, the Negro short story, and so on.

In moving forthrightly in this direction, what had the Negro scholar done? He had, alas, made an institution of the field of Negro studies. He had become the victim of segregation in the field of scholarship in the same way that Negroes in other fields had become victims of segregation. There were the Negro press, the Negro church, Negro business, Negro education, and now

Negro scholarship. Unhappily, Negro scholars had to face a situation, not entirely their own creation, in the perpetuation of which their stake was very real indeed. In the field of American scholarship, it was all they had. It grew in respectability not only because the impeccable scholarship of many of the Negroes commanded it, but also because many of the whites conceded that Negroes had peculiar talents that fitted them to study themselves and their problems. To the extent that this concession was made, it defeated a basic principle of scholarship—namely, that given the materials and techniques of scholarship and given the mental capacity, any person could engage in the study of any particular field.

This was a tragedy. Negro scholarship had foundered on the rocks of racism. It had been devoured by principles of separatism, of segregation. It had become the victim of the view that there was some "mystique" about Negro studies, similar to the view that there was some "mystique" about Negro spirituals which required that a person possess a black skin in order to sing them. This was not scholarship; it was folklore, it was voodoo.

The Negro scholar can hardly be held responsible for this sad turn of events. He had acted in good faith, and had proceeded in the best traditions of American scholarship. American scholarship had always been pragmatic, always firmly based on need. Du Bois and Woodson and Locke were in the same tradition as Jonathan Edwards and Thomas Jefferson. Here was a vast field that was unexplored. Here was an urgent need to explore it in order to complete the picture of American life and institutions. Here was an opportunity to bring to bear on a problem the best and most competent resources that could be commandeered. That the field was the Negro and that the resources were also Negroes are typical irrelevancies of which objective scholarship can take no cognizance. One wonders what would have happened had there been no Du Bois, no Woodson, no Locke, just as one wonders what would have happened had there been no Jonathan Edwards, no Thomas Jefferson. Du Bois could have moved toward imperial or colonial history or toward literary criticism; and Woodson could have moved toward political history or economic geography. Locke could have become a leading authority in values and aesthetics.

Perhaps they would have been accepted in the main stream of American scholarship; perhaps not. Their dilemma lay before them, and their choice is evident. It is not for us to say that American scholarship suffered as a result of the choice they made. We *can* say, however, that it is tragic indeed, and a commentary on the condition of American society, that these Negro scholars felt *compelled* to make the choice they did make. Had conditions been different, had they been free Americans functioning in a free intellectual and social climate, they might well have made another choice. Nothing, however, can degrade or successfully detract from the contributions they made, once they had chosen.

There were other Negro scholars, however, who did not take the road to Negro studies, who preferred to make their mark, if they were to make one at all, in what may be termed the main stream of American scholarship. When W. S. Scarborough graduated from Oberlin in 1875 with a degree in Greek and Latin, it was widely thought that the only suitable pursuit for Negroes was in the area of vocational studies. Scarborough neither followed such a course nor yielded to the temptation to become a student of Negro life. In 1881 he published his *First Lessons in Greek*, and several years later he brought out his *Birds of Aristophanes: A Theory of Interpretation*. Then he translated the twenty-first and twenty-second books of Livy, published other works in Latin and Greek, and became a competent student of Sanskrit, Gothic, Lithuanian, and Old Slavonic. But there was no place for him in American scholarly circles, not even at the predominantly Negro Howard University, where the white members of the Board of Trustees took the position that the chair in classical languages could be filled only by a Caucasian. Three generations later, the fate of William A. Hinton, one of America's most distinguished syphilologists, whose discoveries revolutionized the techniques for the detection and cure of dread social diseases, was almost the same. Despite his signal accomplishments, Harvard University Medical School kept him on for many years as a non-teaching clinical instructor. Not until he neared retirement and not until the position of the Negro in American society had significantly changed after World War II was Hinton elevated to a professorial rank. Scarborough and Hinton wore down their knuckles rapping at the door of the main stream of American scholarship. Whenever the door was opened, it was done grudgingly and the opening was so slight that it was still almost impossible to enter.

The wide gap that separates the white world from the Negro world in this country has not been bridged by the work of scholarship, black or white. Indeed, the world of scholarship has, for the most part, remained almost as partitioned as other worlds. The Negro scholars that have become a part of the general world of American scholarship can still be counted on the fingers of a few hands. The number of Negro scholars on the faculties of non-Negro American colleges and universities is still pitifully small. The lines of communication between the two worlds are few and are sparingly used. Thus, the world of scholarship in America is a mirror of the state of race relations generally. Perhaps the world of scholarship is a step or two ahead of the general community; but the vigor and the pragmatism that characterize the American approach to other problems are missing in this all-important area. The Negro scholar is in a position not unlike that of Ralph Ellison's Invisible Man; he is a "fantasy," as James Baldwin puts it, "in the mind of the republic." When he is remembered at all he is all too often an afterthought. When his work is recognized it is usually pointed to as the work of a Negro. He is a competent *Negro* sociologist, an able *Negro* economist, an outstanding *Negro* historian. Such recognition is as much the product of the racist mentality as the Negro rest rooms in the Montgomery airport are. It was this knowledge of racism in American scholarship, this feeling of isolation, that fifty years ago drew from Du Bois this comment: "I sit with Shakespeare and he winces not. Across the color line I move arm in arm with Balzac and Dumas, where smiling men and welcoming women glide in gilded halls. From out the caves of evening that swing between the strong-limbed earth and the tracery of the stars, I summon Aristotle and Aurelius and what soul I will, and they come all graciously with no scorn nor condescension. So, wed with Truth, I dwell above the Veil. Is this the life you grudge us, O knightly America? Is this the life you long to change into the dull red hideousness of Georgia? Are you so afraid lest peering from this high Pisgah, between Philistine and Amalekite, we sight the Promised Land?"

The path of the scholar is at best a lonely one. In his search for truth he must be the judge of his findings and he must live with his conclusions. The world of the Negro scholar is indescribably lonely; and he must, somehow, pursue truth down that lonely path while, at the same time, making certain that his conclusions are sanctioned by universal standards developed and maintained by those who frequently do not even recognize him. Imagine the plight of a Negro historian trying to do research in archives in the South operated by people who cannot conceive that a Negro has the capacity to use the materials there. I well recall my first visit to the State Department of Archives and History in North Carolina, which was presided over by a man with a Ph.D. in history from Yale. My arrival created a panic and an emergency among the administrators that was, itself, an incident of historic proportions. The archivist frankly informed me that I was the first Negro who had sought to use the facilities there; and as the architect who designed the building had not anticipated such a situation, my use of the manuscripts and other materials would have to be postponed for several days, during which time one of the exhibition rooms would be converted to a reading room for me. This was shocking enough, but not as crudely amusing as the time when the woman head of the Archives in Alabama told me that *she* was shocked to discover that despite the fact that I was a "Harvard nigger" (those are her words) I had somehow retained the capacity to be courteous to a Southern lady. She ascribed it all to my Tennessee "seasoning" before going into the land of the Yankee!

Many years later, in 1951, while working at the Library of Congress, one my closest friends, a white historian, came by my study room one Friday afternoon and asked me to lunch with him the following day. I reminded him that since the following day would be a Saturday, the Supreme Court restaurant would be closed, and there was no other place in the vicinity where we could eat together. (This was before the decision in the Thompson restaurant case in April 1953, which opened Washington restaurants to all well-behaved persons.) My friend pointed out that he knew I spent Saturdays at the Library, and he wondered what I did for food on those days. I told him that I seldom missed a Saturday of research and writing at the Library of Congress, but that my program for that day was a bit different from other days. On Saturdays, I told him, I ate a huge late breakfast at home and then brought a piece of fruit or candy to the Library, which I would eat at the lunch hour. Then, when I could bear the hunger no longer during the afternoon, I would leave and go home to an early dinner. His only remark was that he doubted very much whether, if he were a Negro, he would be a scholar, if it required sacrifices such as this and if life was as inconvenient as it appeared. I assured him that for a Negro scholar searching for truth, the search for food in the city of Washington was one of the *minor* inconveniences.

These incidents point up not only the distress caused by physical inconveniences but also the dilemma of the scholar who, first of all, would persevere in remaining some kind of a scholar and, secondly, would remain true to the rigid requirements of equanimity, dispassion, and objectivity. To the first dilemma, the true scholar who is a Negro has no more choice than the Negro who is a true painter, musician, novelist. If he is committed to the world of scholarship, as a critic, sociologist, economist, historian, he *must* pursue truth in his field; he *must*, as it were, ply his trade. For scholarship involves a dedication and a commitment as truly as does any other pursuit in the life of the mind. If one tried to escape, as my white historian friend declares that he would, he would be haunted by the urge to fulfill his aspirations in the field of his choice; and he would be satisfied in no other pursuit. If he could indeed become satisfied by running away from his field, it is certain that there was no commitment and dedication in the first place. Thus, the true scholar who is a Negro has no real choice but to remain in his field, to "stick to his knitting," to persevere.

But in the face of forces that deny him membership in the main stream of American scholarship and that suggest that he is unable to perform creditably, the task of remaining calm and objective is indeed a formidable one. There is always the temptation to pollute his scholarship with polemics, diatribes, arguments. This is especially true if the area of his interests touches on the great questions in which he is personally involved as a Negro. If he yields to this attractive temptation, he can by one act destroy his effectiveness and disqualify himself as a true and worthy scholar. He should know that by maintaining the highest standards of scholarship he not only becomes worthy but also sets an example that many of his contemporaries who claim to be the arbiters in the field do not themselves follow.

It is, of course, asking too much of the Negro scholar to demand that he remain impervious and insensitive to the forces that seek to destroy his dignity and self-respect. He must, therefore, be permitted to function as vigorously as his energies and resources permit, in order to elevate himself and those of his group to a position where they will be accepted and respected in the American social order. This involves a recognition of the difference between scholarship and advocacy. On the one hand, the Negro scholar must use his scholarship to correct the findings of pseudo psychologists and sociologists regarding Negro intelligence, Negro traits, and the alleged Negro propensity for crime. He must rewrite the history of this country and correct the misrepresentations and falsifications in connection with the Negro's role in our history. He must provide the social engineers with the facts of the Negro ghetto, the overt and the subtle discriminations inflicted on the Negro in almost every aspect of his existence, the uses and misuses of political and economic power to keep the Negro in a subordinate position in American life. There is also a place for advocacy, so long as the Negro scholar understands the difference. Recognizing the importance of the use of objective data in the passionate advocacy of the rectification of injustice, the Negro can assume this additional role for his own sake and for the sake of the community. When I wrote the first working paper to be used in the briefs of the National Association for the Advancement of Colored People in their school desegregation arguments, I was flattered when the chief counsel, Thurgood Marshall, told me that the paper sounded very much like a lawyer's brief. I had deliberately transformed the objective data provided by historical research into an urgent plea for justice; and I hoped that my scholarship did not suffer.

When such an opportunity does not present itself, there is still another way to keep one's scholarly work from being polluted by passion—namely, by blowing off steam in literary efforts. A few examples will suffice: Several years ago, while waiting in the segregated Atlanta railway station, I was so mortified and touched by the barbaric treatment of Negro passengers by railway officials and city policemen that I immediately sat down and wrote a piece called "DP's in Atlanta," in which I drew some comparisons between the treatment of these Negroes and the treatment of displaced refugees in Nazi-occupied countries during World War II. After that, I was able to go out to Atlanta University and give the series of lectures that I had been invited to deliver.

On another occasion I had a further opportunity to engage in some writing that was not particularly a scholarly effort; at the same time, it did not seem necessary to deny its authorship. In 1959, I was invited to give the Lincoln sesquicentennial lecture for the Chicago Historical Society. En route I went into the diner for my evening meal just before the crowd arrived. I thus had a choice seat, at a table for four. Soon the diner was filled and a long line of people were waiting at the entrance—singly and in groups of twos and fours. They all declined to join me, and I sat in splendid isolation for the better part of an hour. As places became vacant near me they took their seats, and I was able to hear their orders to the waiters as well as their conversations with their new companions. When I returned to my compartment, I wrote a short piece called "They All Ordered Fish." You see, it was Ash Wednesday, and these Christian ladies and gentlemen were beginning their forty days of commemoration of the agony of their Lord, Jesus Christ. Neither "DP's in Atlanta" nor "They All Ordered Fish" has ever been published. They remain in the uncollected papers of a Negro scholar who has faced his share of dilemmas.

I suspect that such a repression of one's true feelings would not be satisfying to some, and it may even be lacking in courage. I do not commend it; I merely confess it. It is doubtless a temporary escape from the painful experience of facing the dilemma and making the choice that every Negro scholar must sooner or later make. For the major choice for the Negro scholar is whether he should turn his back on the world, concede that he is the Invisible Man, and lick the wounds that come from cruel isolation, or whether he should use his training, talents, and resources to beat down the barriers that keep him out of the main stream of American life and scholarship. The posing of the question, it seems, provides the setting for the answer. I have said that the American scholar has been drawn irresistibly into the main stream of American life, and has contributed his knowledge and ingenuity to the solution of the major problems his country has faced. I now assert that the proper choice for the American Negro scholar is to use his knowledge and ingenuity, his resources and talents, to combat the forces that isolate him and his people and, like the true patriot that he is, to contribute to the solution of the problems that all Americans face in common.

This is not a new and awesome prospect for the Negro. He has had to fight for the right to assist in the defense of his country when his country was locked in mortal struggle with its enemies. He has had to fight for the right to discharge his obligations as a voting citizen. He has had to fight for the right to live in a community in order to help improve that community. It is the same wherever one looks—in education, employment, recreation, scholarship. It is, therefore, a goodly company the American Negro scholar joins as he chooses to make of the course he pursues a battleground for truth *and* justice. On the one hand, he joins those of his own color who seek to make democracy work. On the other hand, he joins his intellectual kinsmen of whatever race in the worthy task of utilizing the intellectual resources of the country for its own improvement. A happier choice could hardly be made. A happier prospect for success, even in the face of untold difficulties, could hardly be contemplated.

St. Clair Drake

ST. CLAIR DRAKE is professor of sociology at Roosevelt University, Chicago, and senior lecturer in sociology at the University of Ghana. He is co-author, with Horace Cayton, of *Black Metropolis*, one of the most important sociological studies of the American Negro community, a revised edition of which appeared in 1962. Professor Drake has contributed to many professional journals in the United States and abroad.

Of this essay Professor Drake has written: "A new political vocabulary has arisen in modern Africa. It contains words such as 'negritude,' 'Pan-Africanism,' 'African Personality,' 'African Socialism.' These verbal symbols are a part of the African Revolution. They carry rich meanings for the Africans who coined and use them. They form the focus for debate and dialogue; they serve to interpret and structure social actions; some of them take on the quality of myth. This essay discusses the origins of two of these terms and the cluster of ideas associated with them, and explores their relevance to contemporary American Negro thought and action."

"Hide My Face" was written especially for this collection.

HIDE MY FACE?

On Pan-Africanism and Negritude

BY ST. CLAIR DRAKE

I run to the rocks to hide my face;
The rocks cried out, No hiding place,
There's no hiding place down here.
—A SPIRITUAL

The end of the Second World War marked the beginning of the liberation of Africa and of racial integration in the United States. Although there is no causal connection between these two momentous developments, they are interrelated and they influence each other. That they occurred at approximately the same time has profound implications for Negro Americans, all of whom are aware that they are "of African descent." In America, this "African descent" is considered to be the only really socially relevant fact about Negroes, and some states actually define a Negro as "anyone with an ascertainable trace of Negro blood." Whether those who are defined as "American Negroes" like it or not, history and the peculiar evaluations of American society have linked them with the fate of Africa and its peoples. This is a reality to which Negroes in the United States have always had to adjust.

In 1925, the distinguished American Negro literary critic Alain Locke presented an anthology to the public which bore the title *The New Negro*. The poets, essayists, and writers of fiction whose works appeared in the volume were participants in what came to be called the "Negro Renaissance," that remarkable outburst of literary creativity which followed the First World War. The dominant theme in the work of all these writers was "the Negro experience." The intellectual vanguard of ten million Negro Americans were expressing the moods and wishes, the aspirations and frustrations, the joy as well as the anger, of their ethnic group. They were also revealing their own sensitive reactions to reality, and laying bare the distinctive configurations of ideas and emotions which each had elaborated in order to cope with reality. For some of them, Africa was a part of this reality.

Alain Locke in his own essay, "The Negro's Americanism," dissociated himself from those who saw extensive evidence of African cultural survivals in the United States, insisting that "what there is today in Harlem distinct from the white culture that surrounds it is, as far as I am able to see, merely a remnant from the peasant days in the South. Of the African culture not a trace." But he did not mean by this that he was unconcerned with Africa or African culture. African art was one of his consuming interests.

The two most talented of the "New Negro" poets, Langston Hughes and Countee Cullen, felt impelled to speak of a sense of "kinship" with Africa. Langston Hughes's confrontation of the African reality was composed of bewilderment tinged with nostalgia, as these lines from "Afro-American Fragment" suggest:

> So long,
> So far away
> Is Africa. . . .
> Through some vast mist of race
> There comes the song
> I do not understand . . .

Apparently Langston Hughes could not bring himself to accept the kind of "understanding" which his fellow troubadour, a white man, Vachel Lindsay, had achieved. He too had heard the song "Boomlay, boomlay, boomlay, BOOM." Lindsay was so sure *he* understood that he gave his poem "The Congo" a subtitle, "A Study of the Negro Race." The poetic "study" was divided into three parts: "Their Basic Savagery," "Their Irrepressible High Spirits," and "The Hope of Their Religion." Vachel Lindsay had no doubts about the origin of the gusto which expressed itself in drunken table pounding by

> Fat black bucks in a wine-barrel room,
> Barrel house kings with feet unstable.

They had inherited the wild emotions of "tattooed cannibals." He could plainly see "the Congo creeping through the black," and this "insight" also explained to him why

> Wild crap shooters with a whoop and a call
> Danced the juba in their gambling hall. . . .
> Guyed the policemen and laughed them down . . .

These American Negroes were simply blood kinsmen of "cake walk princes . . . fat as shotes" cavorting in the jungle, and putting "the skull-faced lean witch doctors" to rout with their exhuberant dancing. Both Africans and American Negroes such as these were under the spell of "Mumbo Jumbo, God of the Congo," the god who will "hoodoo you."

But Vachel Lindsay also saw a vision of hope for Negroes, in Africa and America:

> A good old Negro in the slums of the town
> Preached at a sister for her velvet gown,
> Howled at a brother for his low down ways. . . .
> And the people all repented a thousand strong
> From their stupor and savagery and sin and wrong.

So Mumbo Jumbo died in the jungle, and "pioneer angels cleared the way for a Congo paradise . . . a singing wind swept the Negro nation . . . and redeemed were the forests, the beasts, and the men . . ."

Such eschatological anthropology was widely shared by Americans during the early years of the century, offensive as it may sound to modern ears. Both the image of African savagery and the implications of inherited African traits repelled many American Negroes, while others accepted the image, believed in the myths, and worked for the specific variety of "redemption" about which Vachel Lindsay wrote. The "New Negro" had to come to terms with the image and the popular Negro reaction to it.

Langston Hughes did not reject identification with Africa because he saw it as a derogation. He sought, rather, for the deeper understanding that comes from knowledge and empathy.

Countee Cullen, too, chose to grapple with the African reality and America's distortion of it. In his long, rich, image-laden poem "Heritage," Africa emerges as a romantic land of "wild, barbaric birds, Goading massive jungle herds," a land of supple cats and slithering silvery snakes. Mumbo Jumbo was present too, for Cullen found "Quaint, outlandish heathen gods, Black men fashion out of rods." Africa was, to him, the setting for a D. H.

Lawrence paradise where "Young forest lovers lie, Plighting troth beneath the sky."

Vachel Lindsay's evangelical Puritanism led him to reject Africa until it should have been "redeemed." Cullen not only accepts it as it is, but also rejects the vision of "redemption." He even expresses regret that he and other American Negroes have been subjected to such "redemption," for he sees them as having been symbolically castrated in the process:

> My conversion came high-priced,
> I belong to Jesus Christ. . . .
> Lamb of God although I speak
> With my mouth thus, in my heart
> Do I play a double part. . . .
> Wishing he I served were black . . . ?
> Not yet has my heart or head
> In the least way realized
> They and I are civilized.

Cullen bemoans the fact that Christianity has forced him to "Quench my pride and cool my blood." This romantic, neo-pagan response to Africa was probably as shocking to most middle-class Negroes as Vachel Lindsay's was repulsive. The significant thing is that Countee Cullen felt he *had* to respond to Africa.

Langston Hughes heard "the song" through "some vast mist of race," and said frankly, "I do not understand." Countee Cullen, however, reported that he too felt "the Congo creeping through the black," or, as he phrased it, "The unremittent beat Of cruel padded feet Walking through my body's street." And like the feet in Thompson's "Hound of Heaven," they beat with "majestic instancy," and made him cry out, "Ever must I twist and squirm, Writhing like a baited worm." Cullen, in this mood, felt that American culture was stifling what the African poet Senghor would call his *negritude*. Cullen began his poem with a query:

> What is Africa to me
> Copper sun or scarlet sea,
> Jungle star or jungle track,
> Strong bronzed men, or regal black,
> Women from whose loins I sprang
> When the birds of Eden sang?

> One three centuries removed
> From the scenes his fathers loved,
> Spicy grove, cinnamon tree,
> What is Africa to me?

In 1951, Akinsola Akiwowo, a Nigerian student studying in the United States wrote "Song in a Strange Land," which appeared in *Phylon*, a quarterly published by Atlanta University. His artistry is not so polished as that of either Langston Hughes or Countee Cullen, but the sentiments are significant:

> *Shall I sing your song, Africa,*
> *In this strange land of hate and love?*
> *Shall I sing to them whose forebears*
> *Were torn away from you long ago?*
> *For they know you not, but believe*
> *All the strange and gory stories*
> *They oft have read and seen in films:*
> *Apes, thick jungles, and men with spears,*
> *And nude women with pancake lips.*
> *They have not seen how, what, you are;*
> *That long estrangement shuts their eyes . . .*
> *Some say you are a thing of shame!*
>
> .   .   .
>
> *But fill our hearts, Africa's sons,*
> *With holy untiring zest to work,*
> *And ask no rest till She is free*
> *And great with true greatness from Thee.*
> *Then make them see again, dear Lord;*
> *Open their ears, unleash their tongues*
> *And make them see, hear, proclaim*
> *What they now refuse to apprehend!*

Since "Song in a Strange Land" was sung, "holy untiring zest" has brought results. In 1961 African states were sitting in the United Nations. A new image of Africa was in the making.

The struggle for independence and for national development is something all American Negroes can understand and it is a phenomenon with which they can all identify.

The wheel has come full circle, for when the Governor General of Nigeria was inaugurated, Langston Hughes was among the honored guests. (He had been a schoolmate of Governor Azikiwe at Lincoln University.) The Governor ended his address by quoting Hughes's poem of optimism, "Dawn." Meanwhile, Langston Hughes had been hearing songs from Africa which he could understand. He had never abandoned the effort to understand. So he compiled an anthology, *An African Treasury: Articles, Essays, Stories, Poems by Black Africans*. Having understood, he was now taking it upon himself to interpret, and in the introduction to this volume he wrote:

When I first began to gather this material, the term *negritude*— currently popular with African writers, especially poets influenced by Senghor—had not come into common use. But there was in most of the writing that reached me an accent of Africanness—blackness, if you will—not unlike the racial consciousness found in the work of American Negro writers a quarter of a century ago. The Harlem writers of that period, however, had to search for their folk roots. The African writer has these roots right at hand. . . . Evident in most African writing, of course, is a pride in country, which underlies everything that is thought and spoken south of the Sahara today. It is an African pride with a character all its own, which owes allegiance neither to West nor East but to its newly emerging self. . . . Perhaps the phrase that best sums up this swelling pride and fierce insistence on individual identity is *African Personality*. . . . While it is a personality necessarily—and happily—as varied as the people of Africa, it is founded on a common bond, a common yearning . . . 'Come back, Africa!'

Cultural Pan-Africanism

The term "negritude" was first used by the Haitian poet Aimé Césaire and by the Senegalese scholar-poet Léopold Senghor. The American Negro scholar Samuel Allen has pointed out in his essay "Tendencies in African Poetry":

The term is not amenable to easy definition. . . . It represents in one sense the Negro African poet's endeavor to recover for his race a normal self-pride, a lost confidence in himself, a world in which he again has a sense of identity and a significant role.

But, in another dimension, the term denotes the assumption that there are impulses, traits, and conceptions of the world which are

characteristic of Negroes everywhere. To Senghor, these include
"softness" and a non-mechanical approach to men and things,
"spirituality," and a direct but symbol-laden approach to sexuality.
Senghor sees negritude as that quality of life in Harlem which
"softens" the hardness of New York. And he recognizes it in the
American soldiers on the streets of Paris, to whom he speaks as
follows:

Behind your strong face, I did not recognize you.
Yet I had only to touch the warmth of your dark hand—
        my name is Africa!
And I discovered lost laughter again, and heard old
        voices, and the roaring rapids of the Congo

                    .   .   .

Oh black brothers, warriors whose mouths are
        singing flowers—
Delight of living when winter is over—
You I salute as messengers of peace!

   Allen points out that many American Negro intellectuals are

inclined to feel that to affirm the rights and dignity of the Negro as
a man among men is one, and a valid, thing but to acclaim a specific
quality or a complex of traits or attitudes as peculiarly Negro . . . is
distinctly another matter and smacks of the racism American social
scientists have patiently been attempting to erase.

   However, he notes that, in fact, negritude has a dialectical dimension, that it involves what Jean-Paul Sartre calls in his *Black
Orpheus* anti-racist racism; it accentuates differentness in order to
win respect and abolish differences. Those who assert their negritude most vigorously have never isolated themselves from the main
stream of French intellectual and political life and are "deeply
aware that man, ultimately, is man and that his race is an attribute,
only, of his more basic membership in the human community."
One suspects that, had he lived to know them, Countee Cullen
would have felt very much at home with "the poets of negritude."
Langston Hughes, on the other hand, displays a depth of understanding but does not seem to have been caught up in the mystique
of either negritude or the "African Personality."

Whatever one may think of the concept of negritude in its relation to modern social science, or as it applies to American Negroes, it is important to realize that it serves the function of reinforcing the self-esteem of an emergent Africa, and of investing the struggle for African liberation with meanings that transcend the continent—a struggle believed to benefit people of African descent everywhere. And it is significant, too, that those who developed the concept of negritude have been profoundly influenced by the "Negro experience" in America. The Haitian intellectuals of the early 1920's were influenced by the Negro Renaissance in the United States, and a most distinguished member of their ranks, Dr. Jean Price Mars, influenced Senghor, who in his essay "Que Sais-Je?" has written:

Studying at the Sorbonne, I began to reflect upon the problem of a cultural renaissance in Black Africa, and I was searching—all of us were searching for a "sponsorship" which could guarantee the success of the enterprise. At the end of my quest it was inevitable that I would find Alain Locke and Jean Price Mars.

In 1947 an African intellectual from Senegal, Alioune Diop, established the magazine *Présence Africaine* in Paris, under the sponsorship of such patrons as Sartre, Camus, and Paul Rivet, as a medium for self-expression by Negroes everywhere. Richard Wright, the American Negro novelist, was a member of the sponsoring group. In 1956 the Society of African Culture, which had arisen to give organized expression to the objectives of *Présence Africaine*, convened the First International Congress of Negro Writers and Artists in Paris. A number of American Negroes accepted an invitation to attend, and as a result, an *American* Society of African Culture came into being.

When the poet-philosopher of negritude, Léopold Senghor, visited the United States in 1962 in his role as President of Senegal, the American President arranged a literary luncheon in his honor at the White House. In his introduction, President Kennedy referred to the 16,000,000 American Negroes as a bridge between the United States and Africa. Senghor, in turn, payed tribute to the poets of the American Negro Renaissance of the twenties as an early source of inspiration for him and his fellow intellectuals in Paris. Both men seemed to assume that something other than the color of the skin forms an enduring—and desirable—bond between Africans and Negroes in the United States. So long as white Americans and Africans act upon such an assumption, Negro American intellectuals will be forced to participate in what their Continental counterparts refer to as a "dialogue," an effort to discover what the "something" is. "What is Africa to me?" becomes an inescapable question.

The French-speaking "poets of negritude" feel that the bond between New World Negroes and Africans lies in the persistence of certain African behavior patterns and approaches to life which have survived in the New World. Senghor is very explicit about this when he speaks of *"the sense of communion, the gift of myth-making, the gift of rhythm"* as "the essential elements of negritude which you will find indelibly stamped on all the works and activities of the black man . . ." To him there is a Negro *élan,* the "active abandon of the African Negro toward the object" which is not only very real but is also a much-to-be-desired trait. He is convinced, furthermore, that Negroes differ fundamentally from white men in that "European reason is analytic through utilization; Negro reason is intuitive through participation." He even insists that "emotion is Negroid," and complains that he has been "wrongly reproached" for saying so, adding, "I do not see how one can account otherwise for our characteristics, for this negritude, which is the 'ensemble of cultural values of the black world' including the Americas, and which Sartre defines as 'a certain emotional attitude in respect to the world.'" As Sartre and Senghor see it, this Negro ethos expresses itself in various forms of art and ritual as well as in customs and institutions. It finds its purest expression, of course, in Negro-African cultures, but it is also evident in various aspects of Afro-Cuban, Afro-Brazilian, Afro-Haitian, and Afro-American cultural and social life. According to this view, where Negroes from Africa have been subjected to the influences of other cultures, they have borrowed and blended, rephrased and reinterpreted, but the end product always bears the stamp of negritude. (Senghor would probably cite the "swinging" of Anglo-Saxon hymn tunes in American Negro churches or the embroidering of Bible stories as vivid examples.) When groups or individuals try to suppress their negritude—and they can do so—they become "inauthentic Negroes, carbon copies of white men. They also thereby deprive the World Culture of the fructifying stimulus of 'Negro emotion.'"

In a paper prepared for the Second Congress of Negro writers and Artists, which met in Rome in 1959, Senghor presented an erudite and eloquent defense of his belief that the African tropical environment has, through the centuries, produced a human being with a special type of nervous and glandular system, "a being with open senses, permeable to all solicitations, even to the very waves of nature, without intermediary filtrants—I do not say without gaps—between subject and object. A thinking man to be sure, but first of all a man sensitive to forms and colors and especially to odors, sounds and rhythms." Such men are not confined to Africa. He writes:

What strikes me concerning Negroes in America is the permanence of non-physical but psychic traits of the African Negro, despite the mixture and despite the new environment. Some may try to explain this by segregation. To be sure, segregation explains partially the permanence of psychic traits, particularly the gift of emotion, but it does not explain all, especially not with Negroes of Latin America, where segregation is less real.

Certain of the reality of negritude and convinced that the African environment has produced it, Senghor falls back upon heredity for an explanation of both its tenacious persistence and the manner in which it changes. Speaking to a group of students at Oxford in 1962, he made an attempt to explain why negritude becomes diluted and attenuated when Negroes come in contact with other cultures, and revealed a Lamarckian view of inheritance in his comment that "as certain biologists point out, the psychological mutations brought about by education are incorporated in our genes and are transmitted by heredity." Thus, the negritude of New World Negroes has been changed through contact with a dominant culture (and by miscegenation), while the existence of negritude in Africa has been, and is, threatened by political and cultural imperialism.

It is not clear to what degree the so-called "apostles of negritude" agree with Senghor in detail, but all of them feel that the primary task of Negro intellectuals everywhere is to express negritude, proudly and without shame or apology, and to protect their cultures and literary and artistic traditions from being denigrated and disintegrated by bearers of "Western" culture (whether capitalist or communist). They feel that negritude should be cherished and cultivated and that enrichment from contact with other cultures should be carefully controlled. Negro Americans are summoned to participate along with Africans and West Indians in this historic task.

Most American Negro intellectuals have declined the invitation, although they have not broken off the dialogue. They feel that they have heard all of this before from the lips of enemies and patronizing white friends, and from Negro romantic primitivists of the twenties, such as Countee Cullen, as well as from less sophisticated members of their own group. It is disquieting to hear it now from a cultivated French-African savant. The concept of negritude elaborated by Senghor conjures up the ghost of Vachel Lindsay. It evokes unpleasant memories of Southern orators warning against the powerfulness of Negro blood that "always tells." It is a reminder of all the preachers—black and white (including Arnold Toynbee)—who espouse a peculiar kind of black messianism in which Negroes are said to have a mission to teach white men how to abjure materialistic goals and to demonstrate that patience and long-suffering are higher virtues than the iniquitous struggle for power. It presents an image of a kind of man they do not want to be, for they have no desire for "intuitive reason" in the place of "analytical reason." It rejects those values of the Western world which they have learned to prize —critical rationality, success in controlling the natural environment, Aristotle's Law of Measure, and, above all, individuality. It confuses race and culture, cause and effect, in a fashion they have learned to avoid. Senghor's voice seems to resound with echoes of Marcus Garvey, Mr. Mohammed, and Senator Bilbo. But above all, most Negro intellectuals reject this concept of negritude not only because they consider it undesirable but because they feel that it substitutes mysticism for science and ignores reality as they see it.

Yet, of the essential ingredients of negritude—a sense of communion, the gift of myth-making, and the gift of rhythm—they cannot deny their prevalence in the character structure and institutional expressions of thousands of American Negroes. Church services and political rallies, dancing and drama, as well as the songs and sagas of work and play and worship, are suffused with these characteristics. But modern social science has shown us that the presence of such traits has nothing to do with the inheritance of a special kind of nervous system or with inborn emotionality. In fact, there is nothing uniquely African about this particular combination of traits. They are to be found among peasant and tribal peoples everywhere. They are characteristic of what anthropologists call "folk societies." And until recently, most American Negroes were folk—rural and unsophisticated. Admittedly, the specific cultural forms through which these traits manifested themselves were, in the beginning, African; and African survivals are today perhaps more prevalent than many American Negroes wish to admit (although less widespread than some enthusiastic anthropologists would have us believe). No one denies that Negro American life has developed a "flavor" all its own. But it is Negro American not African. Even those who emphasize the presence of African survivals in American Negro life, such as Melville J. Herskovits in his *Myth of the Negro Past*, are careful to stress the fact that the culture of Negroes in the United States is Afro-American and not African, and that heredity has nothing to do with the retention of Africanisms.

Such African survivals as do exist, as well as a folk "sense of communion" and tendencies toward "myth-making," are rapidly disappearing as Negroes become predominantly urban and as participation in America's mass culture obliterates the ethos of the folk. Prosaic disenchantment and routine decorum are important earmarks of the constantly growing Negro middle-class, which has, moreover, set complete integration into American society as its goal. A "sense of communion" and the habit of "myth-making" still persist in lower-class churches in America, but as Senghor himself states, these are really characteristics of peasant societies. They will exist for decades to come in Africa and the West Indies, but in America, where Negroes are a numerical minority and share the values of the larger society, the processes of mobility and secularization are inexorable and irreversible. Negritude as Senghor

defines it could not continue to persist in the United States even
if all of the intellectuals desired it to do so.

One folk trait—"the gift of rhythm"—does persist, however,
though not for the reasons Senghor would adduce. Rhythm is a
salable commodity. It is marketed by members of jazz bands as
well as by athletes of the Harlem Globetrotters variety. But it is
a "gift" that has been acquired in large measure by the white
Benny Goodmans in competition with the black Louis Arm-
strongs. It is probable that this aspect of negritude, expressed
through music and dance, will persist in urban areas as well as
rural, among white people as well as black. And insofar as it is
not tied up with beliefs that "that's why darkies were born," it
will be approved and treasured. But Langston Hughes's note of
warning always sounds in the background:

> Because my mouth is wide with laughter
> And my feet are gay with song
> You do not know I suffer
> I've held my pain too long.

Although African cultural survivals and the folk character of
American Negro life will become more and more attenuated, it is
likely that an appreciation for African cultures and cultural
products on the part of American Negroes will increase. Growing
numbers of American Negroes, of all social levels, are learning to
look at African art without laughing at the techniques of distortion or being puzzled by its stylization. They are beginning to face
the bare bosoms and wild leaps of African concert artists without
embarrassment and shame. They feel less threatened personally
by the sight of sweating black bodies gyrating in magic rituals on
screen and stage. They are beginning to feel that African cultural
phenomena are not a "reflection upon the Negro race." Such
transformations in attitude are taking place, in part, because of a
growing awareness that white people of importance and influence
think of African cultural products as important, beautiful, and
acceptable. Negro American intellectuals can, perhaps, help to
provide a more meaningful basis for acceptance.

But however much Negro Americans come to appreciate African
cultures for what they are, it is likely that they will continue to

think of the African folk and their products as different, non-Western, exotic, strange—as *African*. Some will come to understand what negritude means to the African intellectual, but they will not feel that it has any reference to them. They will identify but not emulate and will admire and appreciate without any desire to imitate. (And very, very few will feel the call to "return 'home.'") A few artists and intellectuals will "cash in" on the growing interest in Africa, but most will have more immediate American concerns to engage their time and attention. As familiarity with and appreciation of the poets of negritude grow among Negro Americans, they will feel a real sense of identity with the French-African poet Demas, who sings:

> The white man killed my father
> My father was proud—
> The white man seduced my mother
> My mother was beautiful—
> The white man burnt my brother
> Beneath the noonday sun—
> My brother was strong
> His hands red with black blood—
> The white man turned to me
> And in a conqueror's voice said,
> "Hey boy, a chair, a napkin, a drink."

Every American Negro will know what this poet is talking about. They will also understand what makes Demas write:

> Give me back my black dolls
> To disperse the image of pallid wenches, vendors of love
>   going and coming
>   on the boulevard of my boredom

But such words will have no personal significance except for those who have known a type of interracial sexual experience that is still rare in America. They will even understand the psychology of rejection which appears in Aimé Césaire's poem which exalts black people as

> . . . those who have never invented anything
> They abandon themselves possessed to the essence of all things
> Ignoring surfaces but possessed by the movement of all things.

But here American Negroes will begin to pull back emotionally. They are not prepared to glorify "those who have never invented anything"; they will be inclined to dismiss such sentiments as a "sour-grapes mechanism" which American Negroes no longer feel that mature sophisticated people should use. And they are likely to comment cynically that "Africans will sing another tune as soon as they have the sense of power that comes from independence and factories and dams." The mysticism and surrealism of Césaire is likely to leave them cold except for the enjoyment of words superbly handled:

> My negritude is not a rock, its deafness
> hurled against the clamor of the day
>
> .   .   .
>
> It plunges into the red flesh of the earth
> It plunges into the burning flesh of the sky
> It pierces the opaque prostration by its upright patience

Lovers of *avant-garde* poetry will enjoy Césaire and perhaps allow themselves to wish for a moment that they too had been born in a setting that could produce such an impassioned affirmation of identity.

In a sense the African writer stands today where the American Negro writer stood in the twenties. Now Sartre's *Black Orpheus* has overtones that echo what Carl Van Vechten used to say. This is nothing for Africans to be ashamed of or apologetic about, for the black man of letters has to go through this experience in a white man's world. But American Negroes have already passed through it. As Africans shake off colonial controls and confront the white world as political equals, as Negro poetry and fiction become more abundant, the concept of negritude itself will change. For instance, we already find Senghor in his Oxford address saying:

Today our negritude no longer expresses itself in opposition to European values, but as a complement to them. Henceforth its militants will be concerned, as I have often said, not to be assimilated but to assimilate. They will use European values to arouse the slumbering values of negritude which they will bring as their contribution to the Civilization of the Universal.

As Senghor begins to think in these terms he is led to emphasize a dimension of negritude quite different from discussions of nervous systems and genes and the inheritance of acquired characteristics—negritude viewed as *myth.*

In defending his concept he reminded his English audience that all men live by myths. "For what are Free Enterprise, Democracy, Communism, but myths around which hundreds of millions of men and women organize their lives? Negritude itself is a myth (I am not using the word in any pejorative sense), but a living dynamic one, which evolves with its circumstances into a form of humanism . . . it welcomes the complementary values of Europe and the white man, and indeed of all other races and continents. But it welcomes them in order to fertilize and reinvigorate its own values, which it then offers for the construction of a civilization which shall embrace all mankind." He himself has been working all along to weave Marxism and Catholicism into the fabric of negritude in order to produce an ideology of "African Socialism." Presumably negritude as myth can stand on its own feet without the prop of belief in the inheritance of acquired characteristics—as a body of belief about the nature of African society and its worth, including the cultural products of African society which have survived here and there in the New World.

Intellectuals are continuously involved in the process of making and remaking myths to replace those elaborated by the folk. American Negro intellectuals do not reject the dialogue with their African and West Indian counterparts as the process of remaking the myth goes on. They have the obligation, however, to submit the myth of negritude to ruthless critical analysis as a part of their contribution to the process. There is some evidence, for instance, that Senghor misunderstands some of the findings of modern science as well as the nature of race relations in the United States. For instance he writes:

The Negro is quite different. American psychotechnicians have already confirmed that his reflexes are more natural, better adapted. That explains his utilization in industry and in the technical services of the armed forces in a higher percentage than that which he represents in the population of the United States of America.

What American Negroes know to be pseudo science in the service of those who are looking for rationalizations for segregation and discrimination is interpreted by Senghor as welcome fact! And he explains the consequences of a caste system in industry and in the armed services as a recognition of the Negro's anatomical uniqueness! This lack of familiarity with the natural and social sciences is prevalent to a surprising extent among British and Continental men of letters, but for African and West Indian writers to emulate them and to perpetuate their errors is a disservice to "the race" which they so passionately profess to defend and to advance.

Yet, if purged of its antiquated notions of biology and instinctual psychology, the concept of negritude has value in focusing our attention upon the cultural survivals and subtle African orientations which may still exist among us. It encourages serious consideration of African cultures and frees us from prejudices and distortions to which we have all been subjected. It opens up whole new vistas of appreciation for the great contributions which Africa has made to the stream of world culture. The myth of negritude—the belief that black men have developed cultures of worth, and that although these cultures may be different from those of the West they have values which all can appreciate and share—has important morale-building functions. It can give confidence to the masses in the West Indies and America, as well as in Africa, who smart under the stigma of their blackness and of being of African descent, although the intellectuals hardly need such a crutch.

Equally important is a recognition that *American* Negroes are involved in a struggle to become fully integrated into the nation and culture of their birth. This fight for equal rights does not mean that they deny their African heritage. It does, however, pose problems quite different from those faced in the West Indies and Africa, where dignity and equality are to be sought in a creative nationalism which leads toward sovereign states and federations of states. There is no danger that American Negroes will forget that they are Negroes, for no matter how much one may wish to be a Negro *American,* society forces him to see himself as an American *Negro.*

French-speaking African and West Indian writers have developed the concept of negritude as an ideology and a program to give meaning to their literary efforts. In its emphasis upon mystique, it is peculiarly French. Perhaps it is more than language which draws American Negro intellectuals closer to English-speaking writers and artists in Africa and the West Indies. They have no "program," no mystique, no ideology. They simply write and dance and sing and argue to express what they loosely and half-jokingly refer as as the African Personality.

In this era of African liberation, the myth of negritude should be, and probably will be subordinated to the broader myth of "Pan-African solidarity," viewed as the attempt to unite all Africans irrespective of race, creed, and color into some kind of functioning cohesive political unit. But negritude will live as an important subsidiary myth in the Pan-African movement, emphasizing that black Africans, West Indians, and Negro Americans *are* one people because they all suffer from the world's low estimation of Negroidness, blackness, African origins. They are bound together by memories of past suffering and by the hope of future triumphs. The success of one fragment of the dispersed peoples of African descent reflects credit upon all; the failure of one injures the reputations of all the rest. It is this common fate, not genes, which binds them together and reinforces the struggle against racism. It was the Negro folk in America who produced the spiritual "Walk Together, Children, Don't Ya Get Weary, There's a Great Camp Meeting in the Promised Land."

While preparations were being made in 1921 for the Second Pan-African Congress in London, a new and colorful leader burst upon the Harlem scene—the Honorable Marcus Aurelius Garvey, D.C.L., as he styled himself, a self-educated, eloquent, and fanatically zealous Jamaican who had come to the United States in 1915 to study Booker T. Wshington's program and leadership. He had remained to organize his own Universal Negro Improvement Association with a doctrine of "Africa for the Africans," Black Zionism for picked cadres of New World Negroes, and racial solidarity for the rest so that they could carry on mutually beneficial trade with Africa through an African Communities League and the Black Star Line.

Garvey began to build up a following as the war ended, and on August 1, 1920, the First International Convention of the U.N.I.A. met in Harlem with evangelical fervor. A motto was proclaimed: "One God! One Aim! One Destiny." The U.N.I.A welcomed everyone who desired "to work for the general uplift of the Negro peoples of the world." As the movement grew Garvey became the "Provisional President of Africa." The African Orthodox Church was organized with a black hierarchy and gave its blessings to the idea of a black God, a black Jesus, a black Madonna, and black angels. (Garvey gave Countee Cullen the black God he yearned for, but the poet could not accept Him on U.N.I.A. terms.)

The Universal African Legion rode on horseback in Harlem parades, the forerunners of the shock troops who would someday, at Garvey's call, hurl the white men into the sea, as "400,000,000 black men" rose under the banner of the red, black, and green. The Black Eagle Flying Corps marched in their uniforms, awaiting the day when the movement would supply them with planes to scourge those who had ravished "the Motherland." The Universal Black Cross Nurses studied first aid so they could give succor to black bodies everywhere. Pioneers were selected to begin what Garvey called Africa's "redemption." The uniforms, the parades, the speeches, the promises, and the hopes drew hundreds of thousands of urban Negroes to the Garvey movement in the immediate postwar years. How many actually dreamed of emigrating we shall never know.

There was a tone of superiority and condescension in the New World Negroes' U.N.I.A. manifesto, but the "Beloved and Scattered Millions," schooled as they were in church and lodge, knew no other idiom in which to speak:

To establish a universal confraternity among the race; to promote the spirit of love and pride; to reclaim the fallen; to administer to and assist the needy; to assist in civilizing the backward tribes of Africa; to assist in the development of independent Negro nations and communities; to establish a central nation for the race; to establish commissaries or agencies in the principal countries of the world for the representation of all Negroes; to promote a conscientious spiritual worship among the native tribes of Africa; to establish universities, colleges, academies, schools for the racial education and culture of the people; to work for better conditions among Negroes everywhere.

Garvey's collected speeches appeared in the *Philosophy and Opinions of Marcus Garvey*. Passionate in their espousal of black nationalism, they made such an impact upon Nkrumah when he was a student in America that he cites them as one of the primary sources of his "inspiration" as a developing nationalist leader.

The American Communist Party was founded the same year that Garvey called his first convention, and the Negro members of the Party received orders to bore from within and try to capture both the Garvey movement and the National Association for the Advancement of Colored People, which was founded in 1909. The N.A.A.C.P., the Pan-African movement, and the Communist Party were alike in one respect. They were all led by intellectuals whose problem was how to make contact with the masses. Garvey had no such problem, and while his movement grew apace in American cities and in the West Indies, another type of popular leader was emerging in Africa.

Just before the Second Pan-African Congress met in Brussels to chide the Belgians, a half-educated carpenter in the Congo, Simon Kimbangu, announced that he was "touched by the grace of God on the 18th March, 1921." His followers announced that the world would end in October, and fire from heaven would wipe out all white men. Some Kimbanquist preachers, however, declared that American Negroes would soon be coming to deliver their Congo brothers from white oppression. Kimbangu was immediately jailed, but the movement spread. (In 1958 eighteen years after Kimbangu's death, Belgian authorities in the Congo arrested over 3,000 Kimbanquists.) Similar "prophet movements" arose in the twenties in Kenya, the Rhodesias, and South Africa.

During 1923 the Garvey movement grew rapidly. Negotiations were proceeding for land in Liberia for the establishment of a colony. Steamships were being purchased for the Black Star Line. The ingathering of the exiles seemed about to begin. All the while, Du Bois and other Negro leaders were denouncing Garvey as a menace and a fraud and warning the Negro public against supporting him. But in 1924 a mission left for Liberia to complete arrangements for the settlement. Then, under pressure from

Britain and France and fearful of Garvey's pretensions, Liberia suddenly broke off all negotiations. The Black Star Line ran into financial difficulties. The U.N.I.A. was facing the beginning of the end.

Although the Garvey movement was heading for disaster in the United States, its influence was spreading in Africa. In 1920, the President of the newly organized Congress of British West Africa said in his inaugural address that he had heard of the U.N.I.A. and charged his members to draw inspiration from it, and to be ready to welcome their "brothers" from overseas to share in the wealth of the country and to help in developing it. Nigerians slept on the beaches at Calabar with bonfires burning to light the ships of "Moses Garvey" in for the landfall. And Kadalie, leading the most powerful social movement South Africa had ever seen, said he had been profoundly influenced by Garveyism. George Padmore, a West Indian ex-Communist, in *Pan Africanism or Communism?* has called attention to the fact that

In certain places the punishment for being seen with a *Negro World* [the U.N.I.A. paper] was five years at hard labor, and in French Dahomey it was life imprisonment. It was suppressed in such places as Trinidad, British Guiana, Barbados, etc., in the West Indies and all French, Italian, Portuguese, Belgian, and some of the British colonies in Africa.

Thomas Hodgkin, in his *Nationalism in Colonial Africa*, notes that "the impact of Garveyism can be traced in British and French West Africa as well as in South Africa, particularly during the period of unrest and revolt immediately following the First World War"; referring to the growth of African independent churches, he writes:

Probably the most important single outside stimulus was the American-born Garvey movement, in which the strands of Ethiopianism and Pan Africanism were closely interwoven. Marcus Garvey . . . was successful in spreading the idea of Independent African churches as an instrument of African liberation.

About 1935 the African separatist churches among the Kikuyu in Kenya brought in one of Garvey's bishops to train and ordain preachers. It was this group of churches and their affiliated schools that formed part of the seedbed from which the Mau Mau eventually grew.

But in 1925, the year of the publication of *The New Negro*, the Garvey bubble burst. The Provisional President of Africa was sent to a federal prison, convicted of using the mails to defraud. As the gates closed upon him, he promised that if he died he would return in the wind and the rain to trouble the white man and lead the black man to victory. Garvey was an embarrassment to Negro intellectuals. (It is significant that none has ever chosen to write a biography of him.) But all of them concede that black folks were given a sense of pride and worth as a result of his efforts.

Du Bois convened his Fourth (and last) Pan-African Congress in 1927, in New York. Most of the 220 delegates represented American Negro women's organizations, but representatives of ten foreign countries were also present, including Chief Amoah II from the Gold Coast. It was in this year, too, that President Harding pardoned Garvey and deported him to Jamaica.

Garvey blamed the leaders of the N.A.A.C.P., the Communists, and the Jews for his downfall rather than his own business ineptitude and overweening arrogance. His charges were, of course, absurd. The Communists, on the other hand, after their failure to infiltrate the Garvey movement, denounced it. The Sixth Congress of the Communist International in 1928 made a slashing attack upon the movement in a formal ideological statement:

> Garveyism, which formerly was the ideology of the masses, like Gandhism, has become a hindrance to the revolutionization of the Negro masses. Originally advocating social equality for Negroes, Garveyism subsequently developed into a peculiar form of Negro "Zionism" which instead of fighting American imperialism advanced the slogan: "Back to Africa!" This dangerous ideology, which bears not a single genuine democratic trait, and which toys with the aristocratic attributes of a non-existent "Negro kingdom," must be strongly resisted, for it is not a help but a hindrance to the mass Negro struggle for liberation against American imperialism.

George Padmore, writing in *Pan Africanism or Communism?* in 1955, claims that

Had the Communists succeeded in capturing the Garvey movement and in gaining control of other black nationalist groups, specially selected Negro militants were to have been recruited and trained in Moscow as cadres for colonial work in Africa.

Padmore was himself a leader in the colonial section of the Communist International during the period of which he writes. In 1935 he broke with the Communists, and went to London, where he organized the International African Service Bureau and the Pan-African Federation.

By the time the Second World War erupted, Padmore had developed a distinctive Pan-African theory, namely, that only Africans could liberate Africa, and that only "Pan-African Socialism" could prevent an eventual Communist takeover there. Kwame Nkrumah joined the small group of nationalists around Padmore in 1943, and the two of them, together with Jomo Kenyatta, did the preparatory political work for the Fifth Pan-African Congress.

When the Sixth Pan-African Congress (the All African Peoples Conference organized by Padmore and Nkrumah) met in Ghana in 1958, Nkrumah began his speech to the final session with these words:

We are happy to see so many of our brothers and sisters from the New World here today. Before many of us were conscious of our own degradation, it was the New World Negroes who raised the banner of African liberation. Two names I must mention, Marcus Garvey and W. E. B. Du Bois.

New Images in the Making

Both Countee Cullen and the church-oriented segment of the American Negro population shared Vachel Lindsay's widely accepted image of Africa. But whereas the Negro poet made a virtue of African "primitivism," the Christians deplored it. Negro Christians differed from white Christians, however, in their appraisal of what were, to them, the undesirable aspects of contemporary African reality. They saw Africa in a larger time perspective. They visualized a Golden Age in the remote past, before the present state of affairs had come to pass, as well as an Africa to be "redeemed" in the future. Du Bois, Garvey, and the Communists, too, were convinced that Africa would be "redeemed," but not in a religious sense. The Communists looked forward to the classless society that would emerge from a revolution led by New World Negroes. Garvey had an apocalyptic vision of a united Africa functioning as a powerful equal in the comity of nations. In his view, too, Negroes would play a messianic role. Some kind of African Socialism lay in the future, as Du Bois and Padmore conceived it, but African leaders would make their own revolution, with New World Negroes operating only as catalytic agents. Some Africans were influenced by all the varieties of "redemption" which emanated from the New World, but history did not assign a decisive role to any of them.

The African leaders who breached the bastions of colonialism in the 1950's and 1960's elaborated their own ideas of Pan-Africanism, negritude, and the "African Personality," ideas which reflect the influences of Marxism and Western democratic thought, but also acknowledge some intellectual indebtedness to New World Negro intellectuals and leaders. But the product is their own, based upon a fierce and passionate conviction that Africans alone must determine the goals and the strategies of their own liberation and development. It is this African "pride" that Hughes came eventually to understand. Du Bois understands it, too, but feels that the Communist world is more likely to respect it than is the West. The relation of New World Negroes to contemporary Africa is now in the process of redefinition.

For a very small group of American Negroes, the New Africa will offer a refuge from the race prejudice of the present or the integration of the future, but latter-day Garveyism is likely to have a very limited appeal. The African states will probably welcome the few exiles who want to be gathered in so long as they become peaceful and industrious citizens. There will not be, however, any campaigns urging them to "come home."

For a somewhat larger group, Africa will offer a focus for meaningful social action. It has served this function in the past for members of missionary societies. It does so today for a growing number of American Negroes who are interested in cementing intercultural ties or doing research. A "cult of Africa" has always existed within the Negro community. It will probably grow in size, and will include a mutually incompatible group of devotees ranging from Harlem's fanatical black nationalists who heckle at United Nations meetings, through middle-class families that specialize in entertaining African dignitaries, to members of the American Society for African Culture. Varied groups of Africans are beginning to cherish their relationships with these segments of the Afro-American world. Thoughtful American Negroes are aware of some of the dangers inherent in this type of close identification with Africa. Tendencies to gloss over, and even to suppress, the less favorable aspects of African life will appear. Temptations to claim a monopoly of understanding Africa will manifest themselves. There may even be sharp conflicts of loyalty if some African states veer away sharply from the West. There is also the risk of isolation from white friends and colleagues, although this has not happened to French-African intellectuals who emphasize their negritude. Despite the dangers, some American Negroes will continue to feel that the rewards of a close identification with Africa are worth the risks.

Increasing numbers of American Negroes, too, are likely to find careers in Africa with American church, government, or business institutions. African attitudes toward them, will, no doubt, always be a mixture of pride at seeing successful Negroes occupying high places and some measure of apprehension, wariness, and resentfulness over Negroes allowing themselves to be "used" by the white man in his contact with Africans. But insofar as Negroes are not involved in the exploitation of Africans or in attempts to frustrate their national aspirations, Pan-African sentiments of friendliness are likely to override antagonism. The fortunes of Negroes who represent the American government abroad, however, can be expected to vary with the twists and turns of both African and American foreign policy. As for missionaries, the "African Personality" is certain to reject any among them, whether they be black or white, who stand in the way of the development of Africa's own brand of Christianity or try to control Africa's churches.

For most American Negroes, however, Africa is likely to remain the far-off but inescapable fact that it has always been. It will become less and less a source of embarrassment, however, as the image of successful nations replaces that of "savages." Leaders cut in the heroic mold of Kenyatta and Lumumba will continue to stir the imagination and provide symbols of protest and courage with which American Negroes can identify, but there will be no ever-present sense of involvement with Africa. Feelings of shame and rejection, however, are likely to give way to pride over specific persons and events. At the same time, any attempts to suggest that they are Africans and not Americans will certainly be resisted. They will be interested in Africa, but not especially "concerned," and the idea that American Negroes have any mission to "redeem" Africa, in either a religious or a secular sense, will disappear.

When the executive secretary of the N.A.A.C.P., in welcoming Nkrumah to America, spoke of the "blood tie," everyone knew that he was using the term in a symbolic and metaphorical sense, that he was talking about historical experiences and sentiments which bind American Negroes to the peoples of Africa. "Blood" will continue to function as a most inadequate verbal symbol for something else, and American Negro intellectuals must accept it as one of their never-ending duties to explain to less highly trained Americans, as well as to many of their European and African counterparts, that insofar as they accept the idea of negritude (as either a present reality or a convenient myth), they speak of qualities which have survived by virtue of the toughness of a culture, not through the immutability of genes.

As the processes of integration in the United States proceed at an accelerated pace, many Negroes may find themselves wishing to cling to certain aspects of Negro life in America which seem to them rich, familiar, and warm, despite the fact that they will, at the same time, demand all of their civil rights. This is in no way inconsistent with the pluralistic conception of American society which is gaining popularity in some quarters. But, in any event, full integration into American life is a long way off, and amalgamation is even further away. There will be Negro Americans and a "Negro community" in America for many, many years to come. Their white fellow Americans are not going to let Negro Americans forget that they are of African descent even if they want to. Negro Americans will continue to confront the question: "What is Africa to me?" Seeing integration opening up before them, many will be inclined to answer: "Nothing!" Others will give Langston Hughes's answer of the 1920's—"So long, so far away"—and for them the song will be, forever, the song they cannot understand.

For others, however, because of the African friends they have made, or because they wish to be identified with the process of "poetic justice" now working itself out, or because of sentiments which became deeply imbedded in their youth, or because they smart under the continued impact of deprecatory definitions placed upon their own physical Negroidness, Africa will function as a "spiritual homeland." They will share the feelings which made a Nigerian who had studied in America, Mboni Ojike, write a book entitled *I Have Two Countries*. There is nothing "un-American" about this, for such identification has its parallel among the Poles and the Irish, the Jews and the Swedes, and numerous other groups who keep alive both memories and contacts with an "ancestral homeland."

Perhaps the most significant impact which the New Africa and America's changing image of it will have may be the reassurance it will give in regard to the capacity and worth of "blackness." Seeing successful and forceful Africans winning the respect of white Americans—people like Senghor and Azikiwe—will bolster the self-esteem of many American Negroes. For darker and more Negroid individuals whose self-esteem is frequently threatened by the derogatory appraisals which American aesthetic standards place upon their physical traits, the New Africa will have the same tonic effect that the Garvey moment had—an acceptance of their own physical image. There will be no need, however, for fantasy symbols such as black angels and Madonnas, for attractive black airline hostesses and African beauty queens competing in international contests, as well as the artists and the diplomats, will exist in reality.

Many American Negroes will feel no need for the psychological support that comes from identification with the New Africa. For those Negroes who do feel the need for "roots," however, the New Africa will, no doubt, excite emotions similar to those which stirred Jean Toomer, the American Negro poet of the "Renaissance," when he came to terms with his Southern background, and sang:

Oh land and soil, red soil and sweet gum tree,
So scant of grass, so profligate of pines
Now just before an epoch's sun declines,
Thy son, in time, I have returned to thee,
Thy son in time I have returned to thee. . . .

Langston Hughes

JAMES LANGSTON HUGHES was born in 1902 in Joplin, Missouri, but he has lived most of his adult life in Harlem. He graduated from Central High School in Cleveland and studied at Columbia College in New York and Lincoln University in Pennsylvania, from which he graduated in 1929.

Mr. Hughes has written more than thirty books, in addition to six opera librettos, approximately twenty produced plays, thousands of newspaper and magazine articles and stories, and more than fifty songs, ballads, and translations.

Langston Hughes is often called the "O. Henry of Harlem." He says: "I am greatly influenced by the blues and the Gospel songs and by the urban folk material of contemporary Negro life." He has lectured extensively and given many poetry readings in the United States and abroad.

"Moscow Movie" is taken from Mr. Hughes's autobiography, *I Wonder as I Wander*, published in 1956.

MOSCOW MOVIE

From *I Wonder as I Wander*

BY LANGSTON HUGHES

Banner at the Border

Driving as fast as I could from coast to coast, I got to New York just in time to pick up my ticket, say goodbye to Harlem, and head for the North German Lloyd, loaded down with bags, baggage, books, a typewriter, a victrola, and a big box of Louis Armstrong, Bessie Smith, Duke Ellington, and Ethel Waters records. I was the last passenger up the gangplank, missing all the friends who had come to see me off, for when I arrived visitors had been put ashore.

Crossing the Atlantic on the *Bremen*, it was wonderful weather. My first two days aboard, I did nothing but sleep. After almost nine months of continuous travel, lecturing from Baltimore to Bakers-field, Miami to Seattle, then a breakneck trip by Ford across the whole country, I was pretty tired. The boat was full of young people, and when I did wake up, the voyage was fun. I practiced German, studied Russian, played deck games, and danced.

I had not known most of the group going to make the Moscow movie. When I became acquainted with them on board, it turned out that the majority were not actors at all, as I had supposed they would be. Of the twenty-two Negroes headed for Moscow, most were youthful intellectuals—recent college graduates curious about the Soviet Union—or youngsters anxious to see Europe, but whose feet had never set foot on any stage and whose faces had never been before a motion-picture camera. There were only two professional theater people in the group. The one really seasoned actor accompanying us was Wayland Rudd, and the other Thespian was Sylvia Garner, who had played a minor role in *Scarlet Sister Mary*, having been one of the few Negroes in that "Negro" drama as performed by Ethel Barrymore, Estelle Winwood, and other whites in blackface. These two professionals were also the only really mature people in our group, everyone else being well under thirty and some hardly out of their teens. There were no middle-aged or elderly folks, should there be such roles in the film we were to make. It turned out, however, that as yet no one had seen the scenario, or even knew the story. But that worried none of us. It was fun to be traveling. Besides, at home, jobs were hard to get and wages were low.

Among these young Negroes were an art student just out of Hampton, a teacher, a girl elocutionist from Seattle, three would-be writers other than myself, a very pretty divorcee who traveled on alimony, a female swimming instructor, and various clerks and stenographers—all distinctly from the white-collar or student classes. Although we had heard that the film was to be about workers, there was not a single worker—in the laboring sense—except perhaps the leader of the group (the one Communist Party member, so far as I knew), and he did not look much like a worker. But, at least, he had not been to college, and had no connection with the arts. That most of our group were not actors seems to have been due to the fact that very few professional theater people were willing to pay their own fares to travel all the way to Russia to sign contracts they had never seen. Only a band of eager, adventurous young students, teachers, writers, and would-be actors were willing to do that, looking forward to the fun and wonder of a foreign land as much as to film-making. There were a few among them who said they wanted to get away from American race prejudice forever, being filled up with Jim Crow. These hoped to remain abroad. But most of the twenty-two simply thought they had found an exciting way to spend the summer. An exciting summer it turned out to be, too.

When we got to Berlin, we ran into the first of our experiences with the famous Russian red tape: permission for our visas had not been okayed. In fact, it seemed the Russian Consulate had not been alerted to our coming at all, so it would have to cable Moscow to find out if an American Negro group really had been invited to the Soviet Union to work in a film. In Berlin, Negroes were received at hotels without question, so we settled down to await visas. We ate in any restaurant we could afford. In the German capital, I could not help but remember my recent experiences in the South with restaurants that served whites only, and auto camps all across America that refused to rent me a cabin in which to sleep. Nevertheless, in spite of racial freedom, Berlin seemed to me a wretched city. Its beautiful buildings and wide avenues in the center of the town were ringed with gray slums.

Our hotel was near one of the big railroad stations. There I put a coin into what I thought was a candy-bar machine, but a package of prophylactics came out instead. The streets nearby teemed with prostitutes, pimps, panderers and vendors of dirty pictures. Some of the young men in our group got acquainted for the first time with what Americans in the pre-Kinsey era termed "perversions." Unusual sex pleasures from beautiful girls were openly offered in no uncertain phraseology on every corner and at pathetically low prices. Some of the young men, not having much money, bargained rather sharply to satisfy their curiosity as cheaply as possible. Data was exchanged in the hotel lobby.

"Man, do you know what a girl just offered to do for me for a quarter—a blonde, too."

"Aw, fellow, you'd be cheated at that rate. See the chick outside the door? She does what you're talking about for fifteen cents—or a pack of Camels."

The pathos and poverty of Berlin's low-priced market in bodies depressed me. As a seaman I had been in many ports and had spent a year in Paris working on Rue Pigalle, but I had not seen anywhere people so desperate as these walkers of the night streets in Berlin. The only amusing incident I remember about my stay there occurred in the Haus Vaterland, a big amusement center of bars, restaurants, and dancing halls in the center of town. Among its attractions was a Wild West Bar on the lower floor, and a Turkish Coffee House with red hassocks and rich rugs on an upper floor. There thick muddy black coffee was served in graceful brass pots with long spouts. A blackamoor in baggy velvet trousers, gold embroidered jacket, and a red fez poured coffee. He looked like a Nubian slave from Cairo, and it did not occur to us to try to talk to him. But as he poured our coffee, he overheard us speaking English. He almost dropped the pot as he cried, "I'm sure glad to see some of my folks!" He was from Harlem. "Say, what's doing on Lenox Avenue?"

All of a sudden one day, our Soviet visas came through. The Russian Consulate phoned our various hotels, saying the visas were ready and that we must leave on the afternoon boat train for Stettin. At the time of the phone call, I was looking at paintings in a museum. I was almost left behind, for when I reached the hotel, the others had departed for the Consulate to pick up their visas, and from there had gone on to the railroad station. I rushed my baggage, books, typewriter, records, and victrola into a cab and headed for the Consulate. There, for once, with dispatch (so many things are done in slow motion in the Soviet orbit) my passport was stamped, and I sped for the station. On the way, my taxi ran into a delivery boy on a bicycle. The police had to take down names and numbers and inspect the taxi license. I barely made the train, throwing my bags, boxes, and records in the windows to my anxious companions, and leaping on as it was pulling out.

At Stettin we went directly aboard a Swedish boat—beautiful, very clean and spotlessly white outside and in. I have never seen such a white boat. And all the other people were white, too. We were the only dark passengers. But voyagers and crew were so cordial and friendly to us that we might well have been royal guests. The trip across the Baltic to Helsinki was almost like a fairy-tale journey on a boat filled with amiable people. The only thing they neglected—being Scandinavians, I guess they did not know—was to tell us about *smörgasbord*. Nobody told us that all the creamed potatoes, smoked ham, sardines, salads, sturgeon, hot dumplings, stuffed rolls, and other beautiful things to eat, spread buffet style on a long white table in the big white dining room preceding dinner, were not intended for dinner. So, at our first meal, we made the mistake which many foreign travelers in Scandinavia make—while everybody else waited for us to finish, we ate our fill of these wonderful foods intended merely for appetizers. Then dinner was served.

It was June and the time of the "white nights." The further north we got, the longer the days became. On reaching Finland, it was daylight at midnight. Helsinki was a plainly pleasant town with music and dancing in the parks in the long white twilights. The people were friendly there, too. They did not seem to look

upon Negroes as curiosities—not even twenty-two together—
though some Finns had never before seen so many colored folks,
and some had never seen any.

In Helsinki, we stayed overnight and the next day we took a
train headed for the land of John Reed's *Ten Days That Shook the
World,* the land where race prejudice was reported taboo, the land
of the Soviets. At the border were young soldiers with a red star
on their caps. Spread high in the air across the railroad tracks,
there was a banner: WORKERS OF THE WORLD UNITE. When the train
stopped beneath this banner for passports to be checked, a few
of the young black men and women left the train to touch their
hands to Soviet soil, lift the new earth in their palms, and kiss it.

Scenario in Russian

In Moscow we were quartered in the Grand Hotel, a block from
the Kremlin, in the heart of the capital. It had enormous rooms
with huge pre-Tsarist beds, heavy drapes at the windows, and deep
rugs on the floors. It had a big dark dining room with plenty to
eat in the way of ground meats and cabbage, caviar, and sometimes fowl, but not much variety. Most of the guests at the
Grand seemed to be upper-echelon Russians—industrial plant
managers and political personages, checking in for a few days then
gone—with whom we never became acquainted.

Most of the tourists then coming to Russia were housed at the
New Moscow or the National. And sometimes a few Americans
stayed at the Metropol, but that aristocratic old hotel seemed to
be reserved largely for important political visitors from lands other
than the U.S.A., ballet dancers, and beautiful but mysterious
girls whom some said were secret-service agents. At any rate, the
Metropol seemed to be the only hotel in Moscow with any bar-
stool girls about. It was also the only hotel with a jazz band, and
pretty woman available with whom to dance.

"All spies," said some of the fellows in our group, who found
the Metropol an agreeable but expensive hangout. "Spies who
can't be seduced."

"Spies or not, they sure look good to me," said others. "And
dance!"

"I'm teaching one to lindy-hop," declared one of our fellows on his second day in town, "and she can out-lindy me already. They sure got some fine dancing spies in this town!"

I never found out exactly what was the function of the young Russian beauties at the Metropol. They definitely were not prostitutes, as are many such bar-stool lovelies in other European cities. Prostitutes in Russia were few and far between, since the Russian women, like everybody else, had jobs. Anyhow, the Russians said, prostitution was not "sovietski"—meaning it just wasn't the proper thing to do. "Ne sovietski" was a phrase one heard often. If somebody pushed too brusquely into a bus or streetcar, others would turn around and say, "Citizen, that's not sovietski." If two men got into a brawl in the street, the police would say, "Stop! Ne sovietski!" If a child snatched another's candy away, the mother would scold, "Ne sovietski!" Any form of rudeness or misbehavior might be characterized as not being "sovietski," in other words, not worthy of a Soviet citizen.

Of all the big cities in the world where I've been, the Muscovites seemed to me to be the politest of peoples to strangers. But perhaps that was because we were Negroes and, at that time, with the Scottsboro Case on world-wide trial in the papers everywhere, and especially in Russia, folks went out of their way there to show us courtesy. On a crowded bus, nine times out of ten, some Russian would say, "Negrochanski tovarish—Negro comrade—take my seat!"

On the streets queuing up for newspapers, for cigarettes, or soft drinks, often folks in the line would say, "Let the Negro comrade go forward." If you demurred, they would insist, "Please! Visitor to the front." Ordinary citizens seemed to feel that they were all official hosts of Moscow.

The first thirty days or so in Moscow were all *free days*, because the scenario had not yet been completed. Our actors, therefore, were at leisure, although being paid for the time. The contracts had been signed a few days after we arrived. But mine, a special contract as a writer, was held up a week or so while it was being drawn in detail. When it was finally handed to me in triplicate at the studio, it was entirely in Russian. I said, "I can't read a word of it, and I won't sign something I can't read."

The officials of Meschrabpom Films assured me it was all right
—"*Horashaw!*"

"That may be," I said, "but I will sign only a contract I can
read, in English. I have just come from California, where I heard
about people signing contracts in Hollywood which they had not
read carefully, and—"

"Don't mention Hollywood in the same breath with the film
industry of the Workers' Socialist Soviet Republics," shouted the
Meschrabpom executive with whom I was dealing. "That citadel of
capitalist escapism—Hollywood! Bah!"

"Don't yell at me," I said. "I'll go right back home to New
York and never sign your contract."

So I went back to the hotel, leaving the documents on his desk.
A week later English copies were sent me, and I signed them—at
a salary which, in terms of Russian buying power, was about a
hundred times a week as much as I had ever made anywhere
else. I had paid my own fare to Moscow, as had each of the
others in our group. On my way across the United States, I had
left several hundred dollars with my mother in Cleveland to help
on her expenses while I was in Europe. Meschrabpom Films re-
funded all travel expenses to us in dollars once we had gotten to
Moscow, and I held on to mine to use on the return trip home.

In looking back at the saga of the twenty-two American
Negroes who spent their own money to go several thousand miles
to make a picture with no contracts in front, and, on the other
hand, looking at a film concern that would bring to its studios
such a group without exercising any sort of selectivity beforehand,
I am amazed at the naïveté shown on both sides. But I must say
there was never any temporizing regarding work or money. We
arrived in Moscow ready to work, and we were promptly paid all
monies due. Nevertheless, our expedition ended in an international
scandal and front-page headlines around the world, with varying
degrees of truth in the news stories, depending on the politics of
the home paper or its Moscow correspondent.

The script of the film we were to make consisted of an enormous
number of pages when I first saw it—entirely in Russian! Just like
my contract, it had to be translated. This took two or three weeks.
Meanwhile, all of us "Negro-worker-comrades," as Muscovites

called us, were almost nightly guests of one or another of the great theaters, the Moscow Art Theater, the Vakhtangov, the Meyerhold, the Kamerny, or the Opera, where we saw wonderful performances and met their distinguished actors. There was sightseeing by day, or nude bathing in the Park of Rest and Culture on the banks of the Moscow River. Finally, after weeks of shows, parties, and pleasure, I received an English version of the scenario and retired to my room in the Grand Hotel to read it.

At first I was astonished at what I read. Then I laughed until I cried. And I wasn't crying really because the script was in places so mistaken and so funny. I was crying because the writer meant well, but knew so little about his subject, and the result was a pathetic hodgepodge of good intentions and faulty facts. With his heart in the right place, the writer's concern for racial freedom and decency had tripped so completely on the stumps of ignorance that his work had fallen as flat as did Don Quixote's valor when good intentions led that slightly demented knight to do battle with heknew-not-what.

Although the scenario concerned America, it was written by a famous Russian writer *who had never been in America*. At that time, only a very few books about contemporary Negro life in our country had been translated into Russian. These the scenarist had studied, and from them he had put together what he thought was a highly dramatic story of labor and race relations in the United States. But the end result was a script improbable to the point of ludicrousness. It was so interwoven with major and minor impossibilities and improbabilities that it would have seemed like a burlesque on the screen. At times that night as I read, I could not keep from laughing out loud, to the astonishment of my two roommates, lying at that moment half asleep in their beds, dreaming about being movie actors. But the situation really wasn't funny when I started thinking about my companions and the others from Harlem who'd come so far to perform in a film. But, not wishing to upset them immediately, I said nothing about the absurd script, since I had no idea what position the studio might take concerning my report on it.

I simply took the scenario back to the Meschrabpom officials the next morning to tell them that, in my opinion, no plausible film could possibly be made from it since, in general, the script was so mistakenly conceived that it was beyond revision.

"It is just simply *not true* to American life," I said.

"But," they countered indignantly, "it's been approved by the Comintern."

The Comintern was, I knew, the top committee of the Communist Party concerned with international affairs.

"I'm sorry," I said, "but the Comintern must know very little about the United States."

"For example?" barked the Meschrabpom officials.

To convince them, I went through the scenario with the studio heads page by page, scene by scene, pointing out the minor nuances that were off tangent here, the major errors of factual possibility there, and in some spots the unintentional portrayal of what amounted to complete fantasy—the kind of fantasy that any European *merely* reading cursorily about the race problem in America, but knowing nothing of it at first hand, might easily conjure up. I made it clear that one could hardly blame the scenarist who had had, evidently, very meager facts available with which to work.

Having red-penciled all of the errors, I said, "Now what is left from which to make a picture?"

The Russians are in general a talkative people, very argumentative and often hard to convince. I had to go over and over it all again, not only with the first officials that day, but several other sets of officials in the studio on subsequent days. They in turn, no doubt, checked with their political higher-ups. These political higher-ups, so I heard, months later, fired about half of the studio executive staff for permitting the mistakes of the scenario to happen in the first place. Meanwhile, as the days went by, nothing was said to the cast concerning the script difficulties. I left up to the studio official announcement of its problems. So our twenty-one actors continued to enjoy the pleasures of Moscow, although most of them began to be a bit restive and a little bored.

The film in English was to have been called *Black and White*. Its locale was Birmingham, Alabama. Its heroes and heroines were Negro workers. The men were stokers in the steel mills, the women domestics in wealthy homes. The white leading role was that of a progressive labor organizer, presumably a member of a union like the incipient CIO, who wanted Negroes and whites to be organized fraternally together. Its villains were the reactionary white bosses of the steel mills and the absentee owners, Northern capitalists, who aroused the poor white Southern workers against both the union and the Negroes. Its general outline was plausible enough, but almost *all* of its details were wrong and its accents misplaced.

There was, for example, an important scene intending to show how a poor but beautiful colored girl might be seduced by a wealthy young white man in Alabama. The girl was pictured serving a party in the home of the director of the steel mill, whose son became entranced by their lovely dark-skinned servant. This hot-blooded white aristocrat, when the music started, simply came up to the beautiful Southern colored girl passing drinks and said gently, "Honey, put down your tray; come, let's dance."

In Russia, old Russia of the Tsars or Soviet Russia, in a gay mood, master and maid quite naturally might dance together in public without much being made of it. But *never* in Birmingham, if the master is white and the maid colored—not even now in this democratic era of integration.

Later, to show what the scenarist imagined to be the delusions of the possibilities of capitalism in the minds of Negroes wealthy enough to have escaped from the working class, and to indicate how, nevertheless, such Negro capitalists because of race must eventually ally themselves with the workers, the scenario had some fabulously wealthy colored men portrayed as owning their own radio studios and broadcasting towers in Birmingham. When, at the film's climax, a mob of poor white workers have been falsely aroused against their fellow Negro workers, and the white union organizer has been stoned out of town, a great race riot breaks out in which the poor whites attack both rich and poor Negroes alike, stoning them and bombing their homes. Then it is that the rich Negroes rush to their radio station and start broadcasting to the North for help. Who comes to their rescue? Not the Northern white liberals or philanthropists, who simply shake their heads and say, "These things take time, education, patience." It is the white workers of the industrial North, already unionized and strong, who jump into their cars and buses and head straight for Alabama to save their Negro brothers. These pages of the scenario presented a kind of trade-union version of the Civil War all over again, intended as a great sweeping panorama of contemporary labor battles in America. It would have looked wonderful on the screen, so well do the Russians handle crowds in films. Imagine the white workers of the North clashing with the Southern mobs of Birmingham on the road outside the city, the red fire of the steel mills in the background, and the militant Negroes eventually emerging from slums and cabins to help with it all! But it just couldn't be true. It was not even plausible fantasy—being both ahead of and far behind the times.

"All I can see to do for this film," I said, "is to start over and get a new one, based on reality, not imagination."

"Will you write it?" the Russian executives asked me.

"I couldn't," I said. "I've never lived in the South, never worked in a steel mill, and I know almost nothing about unions or labor relations. For this kind of film you need somebody who knows a great deal about what he is writing. The only thing I know anything at all about in this script are the work songs and spirituals—and of those there is already a good selection."

"We'll keep the songs," said the officials, "and get a new scenario. The cast can start rehearsing the music immediately."

So that is what partially happened. The following week, after a month of leisure, our twenty-two Negroes—including myself—started rehearsing songs. The first rehearsal of the music was funnier than anything in the script. The director, who had been especially imported from abroad for this film, was a young German named Karl Yunghans, who spoke neither Russian nor English well, so he had to work with us mostly through an interpreter. Yunghans had been brought from Berlin for this Negro film because he had successfully directed a recent African travelogue. Like the scenarist, Yunghans had never been in the United States and had never known any Negroes other than Africans. He knew nothing at all about race relations in Alabama, or labor unions, North, South, or European. He was an artist. But he was an eager and ambitious young man, very worried about the current delays in his picture, and most anxious to begin to create in cinema what Meschrabpom intended to be the first great Negro-white film ever made in the world. An enormous budget, millions of rubles, had been allotted to its making. Money was no problem. Yunghans had been in Russia several months now, waiting to begin. Meanwhile he had married one of the prettiest women in Moscow, a simple girl with the blondest of blonde hair and the bluest of blue eyes. She was a little doll of an actress, quite unspoiled, whom he hoped to take back to Germany with him and develop into a star. But Yunghans nearly became a nervous wreck after that first singing rehearsal—because almost none of the Negroes in our group could sing.

Europeans, as well as Americans, seem to be victims of that old cliché that all Negroes just naturally sing—without effort. Other than two or three, the twenty-two of us who had come to Russia could hardly carry a tune. Being mostly Northerners, only a few of us had ever heard a spiritual outside a concert hall, or a work song other than "Water Boy" in a night club. I had traversed the South once, but many of our group had never crossed the Mason-Dixon line. They had but little feeling for folk rhythms, and no liking for the idiom. Being city people, college-trained, they were too intellectual for such old-time songs, which to them smacked of bandannas and stereotypes. However, in order to become movie stars, they were willing to *try* to learn "All God's Chillun Got Shoes," "Didn't My Lord Deliver Daniel?" or the "Hammer Song." But if you can't carry a tune, and have no rhythmical sense for singing in the folk style either, you cannot learn to do so quickly. The discordant sounds that arose from that first rehearsal in Moscow failed to fool even a European. *These Negroes simply could not sing spirituals*—or anything else.

The woman who had performed with Ethel Barrymore saved the day for all of us. Sylvia had a good voice, and she knew many of the old songs, having once been a Baptist choir singer. So at the first rehearsal she sang all the songs in the script herself. To keep the young German director from being too depressed, she also gave an entire folk-song concert herself that afternoon in the big barren studio room. And she made many of the younger Negroes there, who had never before appreciated the beauty of the songs of their grandparents, suddenly aware of the power of

"Nobody Knows de Trouble I've Seen," "Swing Low, Sweet Chariot," and "Go Down, Moses." But Sylvia was a moody woman. At later rehearsals, when she didn't feel like singing, she wouldn't. Besides, she said, the others threw her off key if they chimed in, and this upset her.

Sylvia was a large woman who had gone into the theater in the days of the shimmy-sha-wobble and the eagle-rock, which she could dance with gusto. Sergei Eisenstein, after *Potemkin* at the height of his fame as a film director, gave a party for us shortly after our arrival in Moscow, and Sylvia sang. Late in the evening there was general dancing, during which Sylvia tried to teach a staid old professor of semantics from the University of Moscow to shimmy. This dignified professor was a very stiff man and not really able to shake like jelly on a plate. But he liked Sylvia's warm teaching so well that he became her constant escort, squiring her to all the intellectual affairs of Moscow. And Sylvia became an American folk-song star on the Moscow radio—except that in doing spirituals they wouldn't let her sing "God," "Lord," or "Jesus" on the air.

At that time in Moscow, although some churches were open and one occasionally saw a cassocked priest on the street, there was an official anti-religious campaign under way. The radio belonged to the Soviet state, so religious songs were taboo on the air. An exception was made, however, of the spirituals—as examples of great Negro folk art—with the provision that when these songs were sung, the words "God," "Lord," "Christ," and "Jesus" were not to be used.

When Sylvia announced that she had been signed to give a series of programs on the Moscow radio, all of us wondered how she would get around this edict, so we got into the habit of never missing one of her programs, just to see what surprises would pop out. Often for the Deity, Sylvia would substitute whatever word came into her head, usually something relating to religion, but sometimes not, if the Christian word in the text caught her unawares. For example, an old spiritual like "My Lord, What a Morning" might emerge simply as, "My Soul, What a Morning." But one day, "My God is so high, you can't get over Him, you can't get under Him," came out as "Old mike is so high, I can't get over it, I can't get under it! Oh, this mike is so high! Hallelujah!"

One day Sylvia said, "Them Russians don't understand English, and I'm tired of faking. I'm gonna get God into my program today."

"How?" we asked.

"Just wait and see," she said.

All of us had our ears glued to the radio receivers in the Grand Hotel when Sylvia came on the air that night. She opened with "Oh, rise and shine and give God the glory." Only what she actually sang was:

> Rise and shine
> And give Dog the glory! Glory!
> Rise and shine!
> Give Dog the glory . . .

"Ah-ha!" we said with glee when Sylvia got back to the hotel, "you didn't get away with it, did you?"

"What do you mean, I didn't get away with it?" cried Sylvia. "God was in my songs tonight."

"Where?" I asked.

"Where He ought to be," said Sylvia. "What is d-o-g but 'God' spelled backwards?"

The Mammy of Moscow

Among the crowd of Russian actors and writers who greeted us at the station when we arrived in Moscow, there were also four Negroes: a very African-looking boy named Bob, a singer called Madam Arle-Titz, a young man named Robinson who was a technician, and Emma Harris. Of the four, Emma is the one nobody can forget. She was a "character." Everybody in Moscow knew Emma, and Emma knew everybody. Stalin, I am sure, was aware of her presence in the capital. Emma was perhaps sixty, very dark, very talkative, and very much alive. She had been an actress, and wherever she was, she had the ability to hold center stage. As our train came slowly to a stop in Moscow that morning, the first person we heard on the platform was Emma.

"Bless God! Lord! I'm sure glad to see some Negroes!" she cried. "Welcome! Welcome! Welcome!"

It seemed she had been wanting to see a sizable number of Negroes for a long, long time. Emma was from Dixie, and she had been in Moscow almost forty years. Since I am always hankering to see more and more Negroes myself, right off I took a liking to Emma.

All of us on the train were glad to see her. Emma made us feel at home. For the next few weeks, while we waited for the studio to start filming, "Let's go see Emma" was the phrase heard most often among us. When we didn't go to see Emma, Emma came to see us. She was a frequent visitor at the Grand Hotel. Official guides were assigned to our group by the theatrical unions and our film studio—but what the guides did not show us, Emma could, including the after-hour spots of Moscow. As old as she was, she liked to stay up all night, and she had incredible energy. Yet, in the middle of the capital of the Workers' Republics, Emma did not work. And, although freedom of speech was felt to be lacking in the U.S.S.R., Emma said anything she wanted to say. It was Emma who first told us the joke about the man who saw a swimmer drowning in the Moscow River. The man jumped in and pulled the wretch out. When the rescued one was revived, the man asked, "Who is it that I have saved?"

The rescued answered, "Stalin."

Whereupon the man cried, "Oh, my God, how unfortunate!" and jumped into the river himself.

Emma had little use for the Soviet system as compared to Tsarist days. Nevertheless, she was a featured speaker at all of the big Scottsboro rallies then being held in Moscow on behalf of the unfortunate boys under sentence of death in faraway Alabama. Emma could make a fiery speech in Russian, denouncing American lynch law, then come off the platform and sigh, "I wish I was back home."

Emma said she was from Kentucky, but her last stopping place in the United States had been Brooklyn. She had come to Europe at the turn of the century with a theatrical troupe. In Russia she had attracted the attention of a Grand Duke, and there Emma had remained all these years, growing, as she claimed, ever more homesick for Dixie. Naturally, when the Tsar fell, the Duke fell too. Emma was left with a mansion in Moscow. The Soviets cut up her mansion into a dozen apartments, but permitted her a sizable flat on the first floor, where she lived quite comfortably. Emma said she made her living as a translator, but I never observed her at work, never found her without the time to cook a feast, serve a drink, or talk. She had some of the best food in Moscow. Her table was the only one in Russia on which I ever saw an apple pie or, in a private home, a whole roast turkey. Yet she had only an ordinary citizen's ration card. But Emma knew all about black markets—and speakeasies. In a city where almost nothing was open after midnight, Emma could always find a place to buy a drink. One night she took me, at two A.M., to a cellar den, where vodka and brandy were only a little more expensive than at regulation cafés during legal hours. And the customers in the sub-rosa joint looked just like speakeasy patrons around the world. They all knew Emma and she knew them and, before dawn came, everybody got slightly bleary-eyed.

"I'm like a cat with nine lives, honey," Emma said. "I always land on my feet—been doing it all my life wherever I am. These Bolsheviks ain't gonna kill me."

At the enormous Scottsboro benefits, indoors or out, Emma would be introduced to a cheering audience as "our own beloved Negro comrade, Emma, who before she came to the Soviet motherland, knew the stinging lash of race hatred in her native America." Emma must have been in her early teens when she joined up with a show to leave Dixie. But she could denounce race prejudice in no uncertain terms, in long sentences, in fluent Russian, without taking a breath. At the end of her speech, she would hail the workers of the world, the Soviet Union, and Stalin, in traditional form, eyes blazing in her dark face, and walk off the platform to bravos. Had she been in a play, she would have taken a half-dozen bows after each speech.

"They ought to turn them colored boys loose," she would say, for Emma was truly moved at the plight of the youngsters in Kilby Prison. Her Scottsboro speeches came from the heart. But she had not been home for so long herself that she had lost all personal consciousness of color. When some of the members of our movie group told her that, were she to return to the land of color lines, she would not like it, she did not believe us. She honestly wanted to come back to America. "Things ain't what they used to be here since these sovietskis come in," she said. "Why, I used to have me six servants and a boot boy. Now, best I can do is one old baba older'n me, part time."

It was Emma who first told us that summer that there was a famine in the Ukraine, where, she said, the peasants had refused to harvest the grain. Living in the Grand Hotel and eating well, or accepting Emma's black-market hospitality, I never would have known there was hunger a few hundred miles south of Moscow. But Emma said, "Why, down around Kharkov, people's so hungry they are slicing hams off each other's butts and eating them. That's no lie! A Russian I know just come from there; he told me folks is turned into cannibals."

Emma lived near one of the large Moscow railroad stations, so she met friends coming and going. She first told us about the many railroad wrecks that later that year were openly played up in the Soviet papers as an urgent problem to be remedied. Emma would say, "Man, last night there was a wreck right in the depot—one train going out, another coming in, both on the same track. These thick-headed comrades don't know how to run no trains. Bang! Fifty people smashed-up-kilt in the railroad yard. Ambulances been going by my door all night long."

Not a word of these frequent catastrophes would appear as news in the Moscow papers. But sometimes journalists in a position to know confirmed Emma's tales. Since the Soviet papers concerned themselves mostly with details of the Five-Year Plan or decrees on collective farming, Emma would often say, "I ain't read about a good murder in no paper here in years. And these train wrecks you *never* read about, but they sure upset my nerves. Don't you think we need a little of this here Georgia brandy?"

The Georgia she referred to being in the Caucasus, not Dixie, Emma would pull out a bottle, almost always of a quality that few in Moscow could afford. Perhaps it was a gift from some foreign diplomat, she might explain casually, or from an American newspaperman with access to the *valuta* shops. Emma was a great favorite with the American colony in Moscow—of the right more than the left. The white Southerners especially loved her. Affectionately—and not at all derisively from their viewpoint—they

called her "the Mammy of Moscow." Often to her they brought
their excess food rations for a private feast, with the result that
Emma's pantry was always full. She knew many styles of cuisine,
having traveled all over Europe in her dancing days, and so could
make anything from corn pudding to Hungarian goulash. But for
her Southern friends Emma would cook corn bread and greens,
spoon bread, also barbecued spareribs, if she could find any.

Emma had been in Russia long enough to know how to find
almost anything. What she could not purchase in the regular food
stores (which had little), she could locate on the open market, or
else beg or borrow from some embassy, ballet dancer, or privileged
foreign resident. Her friends were many, and her guests of varied
sorts and character. For the dyed-in-the-wool leftist among the
Americans in Moscow, Emma was too much of a "mammy," although they tolerated her. But the Russians of all classes seemed
to accept her wholeheartedly. And the nonpolitical foreigners loved
her. She was always a good hostess, jolly and full of humor—train
wrecks or not. Certainly Emma added a big dash of color all her
own to the grayness of Moscow.

Negroes in the U.S.S.R.

Other than the colored students said to be in residence at the
Lenin School (the official Communist Party School for foreign
students, which visitors never saw), there were in 1932 to my
knowledge, not more than a half-dozen American Negroes in Moscow, with the exception of our movie group. Paul Robeson came
later in concert, also Marian Anderson, and I believe Roland
Hayes. Some years before, long before my arrival, the Jamaican
poet Claude McKay had turned anti-Soviet and had gone to live
in France, so his name was hardly mentioned when I was in Russia
and his books were no longer on sale. What few Negroes there
were in Moscow, of course, were conspicuous wherever they went,
attracting friendly curiosity if very dark, and sometimes startling a
peasant fresh from the country who had never seen a black face
before.

The slender spectacled brownskin young technician named Robinson was well liked and was elected by his fellow factory workers
to the Moscow City Soviet. Robinson invited me to a performance

of *Eugene Onegin* at the Bolshoi Opera House, to which tickets were very hard to get. Being a worker in heavy industry, he could secure priority seats, so as his guest I sat in the orchestra of one of the great theaters of the world and saw a lavish production based on Pushkin's famous poem.

Pushkin, a descendant of "the Negro of Peter the Great," is adored in Russia and his mulatto heritage was constantly played up in the press when I was there. His *Onegin* and *Boris Goudunov* are standard in all Soviet schools. In the very heart of Moscow where the main trolley lines meet, there is a statue of Pushkin.

The professional actors in our group were by no means the first colored Thespians to visit Russia. Ida Forsyne had danced the cake-walk in Moscow at the turn of the century, and Abbie Mitchell and Georgette Harvey had had great popularity in St. Petersburg in Tsarist days. As far back as 1858, as the Moor in Shakespeare's *Othello*, the New York Negro actor Ira Aldridge had created a sensation.

Russia, both before and after the Revolution, had a fondness for Negro artists, but after the Soviets came to power, not very many had been there. The reception accorded us twenty-two Negroes who came to make a movie—and whom the Muscovites took to be artists—could not have been more cordial had we been a Theatre Guild company starring the Lunts. The newspapers hailed our arrival with front-page stories and pictures. We were interviewed by press and radio. The leading theaters extended us invitations to dress rehearsals and performances. Bids to concerts, cultural events, receptions, and parties were more than we could accept.

Although Negroes of African descent in Russia are few, there are millions of Asiatic peoples in the Soviet Union, so brownskins in Moscow were no rarity when we arrived to make our film. But, while we were there, the twenty-two colored folks from Harlem were lionized no end and at cultural gatherings we were always introduced as "representatives of the great Negro people."

Conscious of being wholeheartedly admired, we solemnly decided at one of our first group meetings in the Grand Hotel shortly after our arrival, that we must all do our best to "uphold the honor of our race" while in Russia, and behave ourselves at all times in public. We did pretty well, I think; but occasionally somebody kicked over a bucket, to the embarrassment of most of the others. Then the leader would call a group meeting, speeches would be made, and the culprit chided for "disgracing the race" —usually by being a little too drunk at the Metropol bar. But occasionally something of more serious nature happened.

About a month after our arrival one of the girls in our group attempted suicide in a very unorthodox manner. Affairs of the heart having become complicated, as she later explained from a hospital bed, she came home one night to the Grand Hotel and put two bottles on her night table. One was a bottle of red wine, the other was a bottle of potassium formaldehyde, also red. She then put on her best lace nightgown, got into her enormous canopied bed, and pondered whether to drink the wine and get drunk, or drink the potassium formaldehyde and die. When she thought of her beloved from Harlem with the Russian girl who had taken her place, she reached out and got the poisoned solution, turned the bottle up to her lips, and drank. Fortunately, when it began to burn her stomach, she screamed, not once but half a dozen times. In fact, she screamed so loud that everybody in the hotel came running to see what was the matter. She was taken to the hospital and saved. A few days later she was back rehearsing spirituals with us. But the other girls declared that she, a Negro, had "disgraced the race," creating all that excitement in the Grand Hotel.

White Sands of Odessa

Perhaps if we had been at work making a film, the near tragedy of the suicide attempt might not have occurred. But by then we had seen most of the sights of Moscow, so there was little left to do except to go to shows, parties, Emma's house, or the Metropol Bar. Folks were becoming bored. Few took the trouble to try to learn Russian, although a teacher was available. The days were long, and at night public places closed down too early to exhaust the energies of a group of lively Harlemites. One of the boys took up with a female truck driver, very buxom, hale, hearty, and wholesome. But the others kidded him so about going with a truck driver that he ceased being seen with her near the Grand Hotel. Another of our intended actors somehow got his dates crossed, for, at exactly the same moment one evening, two Soviet girls, not acquainted with each other, showed up at the hotel and asked to see him. The desk clerk rang his room, but before the fellow answered, the girls had begun to pull each other's hair out. When the young man arrived on the scene, he did his best to stop them, but the episode of hair-pulling spread all over Moscow. This deplorable incident, too, was considered at a group meeting to be a "disgrace to the race."

"We need to be at work," our leader said. "Singing spirituals every other day is not enough. Idleness is demoralizing!"

Vainly he tried to get from the studio some schedule as to when actual filming would begin, but without success. I, as a writer, could get no information either, beyond "We're still considering the problems of the scenario."

Meanwhile, the director of the film, Yunghans, busied himself with the producing staff in casting the white roles. Only one white role was of any real importance to the plot, that of the labor organizer who endangered his life by attempting to organize Negroes and whites together in the South. For the part of this labor leader, an American dancer, John Bovington, had been chosen. When Mr. Bovington showed up at the studio, we did not think he looked like a labor organizer. He was of the school of modern interpretive dancing where every gesture has a meaning, a flow, a nuance. Our film was to be done in a naturalistic, not a stylized manner, so we were a bit puzzled at this selection for a worker's role.

After rehearsal, at supper with Yunghans and his charming blue-eyed wife, Yunghans asked, "Vot ist matter? Bovington nich look like American worker?"

I explained that American labor organizers, in the public mind at least, were rough-and-tumble guys, not esthetic looking. Yunghans argued that he had been politically informed by Meschrabpom that *progressive* American organizers were very intelligent. I granted that they might be intelligent. But since in our film the man was to be portrayed organizing the steel industry, a tough field, he at least should look a little like a worker, and not walk like a dancer.

As Yunghans' wife made coffee after dinner, he and I went to sit on the balcony of their tall apartment house, the lights of Moscow in the darkness below. The young German was very distressed.

After months of waiting to begin his first major picture, here he was with actors who had never acted, Negroes who could not sing, no scenario—and for his leading man, his worker-hero-labor organizer, a dancer! So much time being wasted, so slow, these Russians, so much red tape! In broken English, poor French, and voluble German, Karl poured out his troubles on my shoulder. At the studio he was afraid to complain too loudly, to make too much fuss, because when he married one of Russia's prettiest young actresses, he had been promised permission to take her back to Germany with him. He was afraid this permission might not be forthcoming if he got in bad with the Soviet film-makers. But what can a man do? You can't make a film from nothing—and with nobody. Such stupidities drive an artist crazy.

In English, scanty French, and bad German, I sympathized with Karl. But I also said quite plainly that I did not believe either of us would ever see a film called *Black and White*. Then, almost immediately, I was sorry I'd said it. I could see that if the picture were not made, Yunghans would be even more disappointed than the young Negroes who had come all the way from Harlem to work in it. After all, film-making was his profession. He was young and ambitious. This was to have been his great opportunity. To the twenty-two of us from Harlem, it was partly a lark, a summer jaunt, plus a brief escape from the color lines back home. Only two or three of the Negroes were thinking seriously of a career in films. Most of them intended to get their master's degrees in college and go into a profession. But Yunghans had come to Moscow to make a great picture. Now, with an absurd scenario, tone-deaf Negroes, and for a labor organizer, a dancer! His voice shook as he spoke of it. His world was going to pieces. I was glad when his wife came out on the balcony with the coffee, for I have never known what to do in the presence of heartbreak.

A few days later an order came from the Meschrabpom Studio that all twenty-two of us were to be transported that weekend to Odessa. We were told that portions of our picture would be filmed shortly on the Black Sea, where the cotton fields of the South could be simulated. At the prospect of a change, we were all delighted. We proceeded to pack with alacrity, but we did not leave on schedule. Several days passed before the matter of tickets and train accommodations were worked out by the studio. Meanwhile some of us, at the invitation of the American journalist Anna Louise Strong, attended a dance recital by John Bovington. Its main feature was a dance composition called *The Ascent of Man* which pictured Primeval Man emerging from the primal ooze to become MAN, with capital letters, in all his physical glory. This dance had originally been done naked. Moscow, although permitting nude bathing in the Park of Rest and Culture, did not condone nudity on the stage. So the night I saw him perform, Primeval Man possessed a loincloth.

Circulating among the Americans in Moscow there were a number of amusing stories about John Bovington, who, like Isadora Duncan, had come to Russia seeking artistic freedom, only to find that he would be required to put on clothes when dancing. And he was a *nature* dancer, not a ballet dancer. He believed in the natural grace of the human body, not its distortion by toe-stands or the acrobatics of the entrechat. One of the stories about him was that he lived entirely on raw vegetables, fruits, and nuts. He and his wife, Jeannie, were among the early American nudists. Another story about them was to the effect that once, in California, they had been invited to dance at an afternoon tea given by Charles Erskine Scott Wood and his wife, Sara Bard Field, at Los Gatos. Pedaling down from San Francisco to present *The Ascent of Man,* imagining themselves Adam and Eve in primal guise, within the gates of the estate the Bovingtons dismounted from their bikes, removed their clothing, and proceeded to ride up to the door of Los Gatos unencumbered by raiment. The astonished butler, struck dumb, was unable to question their entry. Sara Bard Field and the Colonel, though surprised, did not bat an eye. The Bovingtons were presented to the guests as young dancers who would show how flesh emerged from the slime to become MAN and WOMAN.

A space was cleared before the stone fireplace and the dance began flat on the floor. But just as man wriggled upward to the point where he walked on his hands, and was about to become half human, somebody laughed. At this affront, Bovington leaped like Tarzan to the mantelpiece and sat there, glaring at the offender. People thought this a part of the dance at first, as both he and his wife froze into postures of contemplation. Finally, when nothing more happened, someone asked if the program was over, and if they might all have a drink. No answer on Bovington's part. He simply sat like Rodin's Thinker on the shelf above the fireplace. It took a great deal of persuasion on Colonel Wood's part to persuade the dancers to continue *The Ascent of Man*.

When I met John Bovington in Moscow, his wife, Jeannie, had divorced him to marry the famous Russian playwright Afinogenev. Without her lovely presence, *The Ascent of Man* was not as thrilling as I imagine it had once been. Nevertheless, Bovington still gave an impressive performance alone. When we met at the studio, it turned out he had never seen the scenario of the picture he was to make. No one had seen the scenario other than Karl Yunghans, myself, the studio executives, and, I presume, the Comintern. My copy had been taken from me for revisions. As to whether the script would be entirely rewritten or not, no official would commit himself. My guess was that the whole matter was undergoing political consideration at the Comintern, and that nothing creatively was being done on it.

When the members of our group asked me what was happening, all I could say was, "Certain changes still have to be made in the script."

"They certainly take their time," was the opinion of the Negroes, "but we should worry."

All of us were being paid regularly, wined and dined overmuch, and had the whole theater world of Moscow for our enjoyment. Nevertheless, we were glad to board a train for the Black Sea. On the way south, stopping at Kiev, we heard there was a Negro resident, so we immediately expressed our desire to meet him. Since we were only there overnight, it took quite a lot of doing on the part of our translator-guides to locate him. But finally he was found and brought to our hotel late in the evening to meet us. I have never seen a more astonished human being, for this Negro in Kiev had probably never seen a black face before, other than his own in the mirror. At the sight of twenty-two Negroes all at once, he was struck dumb. His language was Ukrainian, not Russian, and he was probably of Abkhasian descent from the small colony of former Turkish slaves on the Black Sea. Somehow, during the turbulent years of the Revolution he had gotten tossed onto the streets of Kiev, where eventually he became a fireman, riding a big truck through the streets of the city whenever a blaze broke out. He looked to be about thirty, tall, dark, and rather handsome, but not at all talkative. In fact, he looked as if he were afraid of us and as soon as he politely could, the Negro excused himself and disappeared.

In Odessa we were housed in a charming hotel near the sea, where an electric fountain fell in varicolored spray at dinner in an open-air patio. Odessa was a deluxe Soviet resort for higher-echelon workers, and its hotels were very beautiful. I had never stayed in such hotels in my own country since, as a rule, Negroes were not then permitted to do so. Besides, I had never had enough money for such fine living in America.

At that time Piscator was working on a picture laid in Holland, and a whole Dutch village had been built for him on a plateau just outside Odessa. And not far from our hotel were the famous white steps to the sea where Potemkin had been filmed. The water front that served as background for portions of this famous film was within walking distance. And there were wonderful beaches all about. There were no signs of any sets constructed as yet for our film, and neither the director nor any of the studio executives had come to the Black Sea with us. We were completely on our own, and did as we pleased, so most of the day we spent in the warm sun at the beaches with crowds of Russians, all in their best bathing suits, since at Odessa it was not considered chic to bathe nude as did the Muscovites on the Moscow River.

By this time, the influence of our group leadership was at a low ebb. The Negro in charge had so often tried to present an optimistic picture as to the date for the making of our film, but weeks had gone by and as yet nothing encouraging had happened. The group had begun to split up into cliques and factions. One faction had begun to feel that the Soviets were deliberately giving them the run-around. So why go out of their way to please the Russians anyhow? As to bathing nude in Odessa, why not? With such wide and wonderful beaches, one faction reasoned, nude bathing made much more sense there than it did on the crowded banks of the Moscow River, where a person might dive under the water only to come up accidentally among the opposite sex a few feet away. The result of this reasoning was that, in spite of the pleas of our group leader, that summer thousands of astonished citizens from all over the Soviet Union, dressed in their best bathing suits, would suddenly see streaking down the Odessa sands a dark amazon pursued by two or three of the darkest, tallest, and most giraffe-like males they had even seen—all as naked as birds and as frolicsome as Virginia hounds, diving like porpoises into the surf, or playing leapfrog nude all over the place.

The Bitter End

As guests of the Theatrical Trade Unions we were invited on a pleasure cruise of the Black Sea, a gay and pleasant trip around the Crimean Peninsula to Sebastapol, Yalta, Gagri, Sochi, Sukhum, and down the coast almost to Turkey. One of the members of our group had been left behind in Moscow, hospitalized with a minor ailment, so he was not with us on the cruise nor had he reached Odessa when on our return we went back to the hotel where the illuminated fountain played. More days of sunshine and sea bathing followed, but still there was no word of a filming schedule. Then suddenly one morning our entire group was rounded up posthaste for an urgent meeting. Our missing member had just arrived from Moscow with important news. When we were all assembled, the young man arose gravely, faced us for a moment in silence, then solemnly announced, "Comrades, we've been screwed!"

From his pocket he pulled a recent copy of the Paris *Herald Tribune* with a dispatch to the effect that our film had been canceled. "And they didn't even have the courtesy to tell us," he cried. "I got up out of my sickbed and went to the studio to check this—*Black and White* is abandoned."

The story had been given to the newspapers a week before any of the cast learned about it. Later the studio claimed that since we were on a cruise, we could not be reached when the decision was made. The day after we got the news, one of the Meschrabpom executives arrived in Odessa to inform us officially that there would be no picture, but that we would be paid in full for the duration of our contracts, and that transportation via London, Paris, or Berlin back to the United States would be available whenever we wished to depart. Relative to the future we were offered three choices: exit visas at any time, an extended tour of the Soviet Union before leaving, or work in the Soviet Union for any who desired to remain permanently. All of us were invited to stay in Russia as long as we wished.

No Negroes went bathing on the Odessa beaches that day. Instead, hell broke loose. Hysterics took place. Some of the girls really wanted desperately to be movie actresses. Others in the group claimed the whole Negro race had been betrayed by Stalin. Some said the insidious hand of American race prejudice had a part in it all—that Jim Crow's dark shadow had fallen on Moscow, and that Wall Street and the Kremlin now conspired together never to let the world see in films what it was like to be a downtrodden Negro in America. From morn to midnight factional group meetings were interrupted only long enough to eat. Almost everyone had a different opinion. There was a general agreement on only one thing— that we should return to Moscow immediately for a showdown with the film company. As soon as accommodations could be arranged, we entrained for the capital, leaving the white sands of Odessa behind us.

We got back to Moscow to find the city filled with late summer visitors, and all the hotels crowded to capacity. A great many English and American tourists were there spending foreign money, so they were given preference as to rooms. There was no space at the Grand Hotel. Finally Meschrabpom was able to get us accommodations at a small hostel directly in front of the main gate of the Kremlin. It was called the Mininskaya. Distinctly third-rate, it had no dining room, and no private baths. Very minor officials from the provinces seemed to constitute its guests. But its location was fascinating, just a few hundred yards down the hill from St. Basil's Church, between the Moscow River and Lenin's Tomb, and right across the street from the big gate through which the sleek cars of Voroshilov and Stalin sped past the Kremlin walls. I liked the Mininskaya better than I did the Grand. It seemed much more like an integral part of Russia to me.

Violent dissensions split our group asunder. Tempers flared.

Some contended that all of us were merely being used as pawns in a game of international politics. Because Washington's recognition of Russia was rumored in the offing, not only our film, some said, but the cause of Negro rights was being sacrificed to curry American favor. Two members of our group claimed that Colonel Raymond Robbins had urged them weeks ago, over drinks in the Metropol Bar, to withdraw from the cast of a motion picture which, in the colonel's opinion, would be a black mark against the United States. Colonel Robbins was said to have been sent to Russia as a negotiator concerning future diplomatic relations between the two countries.

Certainly newspapers all over the world reported the canceled *Black and White*. The New York *Herald Tribune* story read in part:

NEGROES ADRIFT IN "UNCLE TOM'S" RUSSIAN CABIN
Harlem Expeditionary Unit Is Stranded in Moscow

Moscow, Aug. 11—A sensation has been caused in the American colony here by the sudden collapse of the Meschrabpom project to produce a motion picture depicting "the exploitation of the Negro in America from the days of slavery to the present." As a result of this collapse the future of twenty-two American Negroes, including Langston Hughes, novelist and poet, who was brought here from New York two months ago to play the principal role in the film, is uncertain. . . . The correspondent understands that the Soviet authorities suppressed the film for fear that its appearance would prejudice American opinion against the Soviet Union. Since the occupation of Manchuria by Japan the Soviet authorities more than ever have been eager for a re-approachment with the United States as a means, among other things, of strengthening the position of the USSR in the Far East.

Another American newspaper said:

. . . It was persistently rumored among Americans in Moscow that the film would never be produced. It was known that many influential Americans were actively working against the project. Foremost among these was Colonel Hugh Cooper, builder of the recently constructed Dnieperstroi Dam, the largest engineering feat of its kind in the world. Cooper is reputed to be the one foreigner who has free access to the offices of Joseph Stalin. . . . Upon hearing of the project, he hastened to Moscow for a conference with Stalin. Finding the Soviet

Dictator out of the city, the engineer secured an interview with V. M. Molotov, chairman of the Council of People's Commissars. Those Russians and Americans close to the source of information in Moscow insist that the film was ordered off within twenty-four hours after this interview.

Some of the newspapers at home certainly made the physical situation of our group in Moscow seem much worse than it really was. One representative of a leading American news service cabled to New York—and the world—stories to the effect that all of us were stranded, starving in Moscow, unfed, unpaid, and destitute. He knew better, for he saw some of us spending money daily at the Metropol Bar or lunching in its expensive dining room. But the papers for which he wrote were anti-Negro and anti-Soviet, so when we showed him the clippings after they reached us by air, he simply grinned. It was the first time I realized that a big-name correspondent would deliberately lie to conform to an editorial policy. We were neither stranded, unpaid, nor destitute and he knew it. But the result of his stories was a flood of frantic cables from relatives in America, worried about our fate.

The Meschrabpom officials finally informed the group officially that the scenario was inadequate. They said it was unfortunately not worthy of the kind of picture they had hoped to make. They also indicated politely that the Negro actors were not *quite* what they had expected, either—which did not soothe tempers any. But most of our group brushed these explanations off simply as false excuses to cancel the film. About half of our group leaned strongly to the contention that its cancellation was a betrayal of the Negro in exchange for diplomatic relations with Washington. I stated in a group meeting that, in any case, no decent film could have been made from the scenario, and had we made that particular film, all of us would have been ashamed of it in the end. Whereupon, one of the members of the group arose to call me a *Communist* Uncle Tom. He solemnly stated that my books in the United States had never amounted to much, so for that reason I had come to the Soviet Union to build a new literary career. And he closed his speech by terming me an opportunistic son-of-a-bitch. I arose to call him a similar name—so the meeting broke up in general vituperations. But later we laughed about it, made up, and from then on everybody jokingly called all of our meetings "son-of-a-bitch meetings."

As to what to do about the situation—since it seemed impossible to gain immediate access to Stalin as some wished—we argued loud and long in the Mininskaya Hotel. Sometimes during our discussion, across the street beyond the Kremlin walls, we would hear Stalin's guards at rifle practice.

Someone would say, "Hear that? They just shot another Russian."

Somebody else would joke, "Shsss-ss-s! I found a dictaphone behind the radiator this morning. Do *you* want to be liquidated?"

After several days it was agreed by unanimous vote that we would present our case to the Comintern, which was said to be, next to the Kremlin itself, the last word on international affairs. So a delegation, including myself, was chosen to go to the Comintern. There we were received by several old Bolsheviks sitting at a long table in a gloomy room. Some of our delegation arose and denounced Meschrabpom, Communism, and "the Soviet betrayal of the Negro race" in no uncertain terms. I took the position that it was regrettable no film was to be produced, but since the script had been so mistakenly conceived, it seemed to me wise to make none. However, I hoped that at some future date a picture dramatizing race relations sympathetically—in a way which, up to that time, Hollywood had not chosen to do—might be brought to completion. Gravely, we were thanked for our statements, and told that the Comintern would take the whole matter under immediate consideration and give it the most serious attention. So far as I know, however, no such picture as *Black and White* has yet been made in the U.S.S.R.—or anywhere else in the world. The problems of organized labor and race in the Deep South are still to be brought to the screen.

SECTION II

FICTION

SECTION II

Richard Wright

RICHARD WRIGHT, who was to become one of the important figures in contemporary American literature and the most prominent Negro writer of his time, was born September 4, 1908, on a plantation near Natchez, Mississippi, and spent his youth in Memphis, Tennessee.

At the age of nineteen he went to Chicago, where he worked as a street cleaner, dishwasher, post-office clerk, porter, and at other jobs, all this while writing in fictional form about his childhood in the South and his experiences in Chicago.

In 1937, Richard Wright joined the Federal Writers Project, and his first book of four novellas, *Uncle Tom's Children*, was published in 1938 and won the annual *Story* magazine award. In 1939 he received a Guggenheim Fellowship.

The publication of *Native Son* in 1940 was to make him world-famous. This was followed, in 1945, by the autobiographical *Black Boy*. His other novels were *The Outsider* (1953), *Savage Holiday* (1954), and *The Long Dream* (1958). A collection of Wright's short stories entitled *Eight Men* was published in 1961. His five non-fiction books are *Twelve Million Black Voices* (1941), *Black Power* (1954), *The Color Curtain* (1956), *Pagan Spain* (1957), and *White Man, Listen* (1957).

In 1950, together with other distinguished writers who had

broken with communism, he contributed an important essay to the volume *The God That Failed.*

Richard Wright's articles have appeared in major publications throughout the world, and his short stories are included in several anthologies. His books have been translated into many languages and are frequently reissued in various countries throughout the world.

On November 28, 1960, Richard Wright died in Paris at the age of fifty-two.

The following episodes are taken from the last, unfinished novel by Richard Wright and appear here in print for the first time.

FIVE EPISODES
FROM AN UNFINISHED NOVEL
BY RICHARD WRIGHT

Episode I

When he awakened the next afternoon, he did not know where he was. He lifted himself and glared suspiciously about the room, the effort making his eyes blur and his head ache. He sank to the pillow, tasting his thick, bitter tongue, feeling his head as big as the room. "I drank too much," he groaned contritely. To ease the constriction in his throat, he edged to the white lip of sink and pursed his lips to the faucet and winced as cold water cascaded into his feverish stomach. He straightened, fighting against retching, wanting to curse or cry. Sweat broke on his skin and he lay down again. He slept.

He was roused by a soft knocking. The door cracked and a white woman's face peered from behind the jamb. He stiffened, filled with alarm.

"*Bonjour, monsieur. Etes-vous malade? Voulez-vous votre petit déjeuner?*"

He shut his eyes; he did not understand and did not care. The door closed and a few moments later the woman brought him *confiture, café au lait, beurre,* and *croissants* on a tray.

"*Tâchez de manger un peu,*" she urged, glancing at the half-empty bottle on the floor.

"*Merci,*" he mumbled as she left. It took him an hour to eat the food, but it made him feel better. Then he leaped from bed, grabbed his trousers, and felt his wallet. Yeah, he still had his money. He opened the window and breathed sun-warmed, humid air. Three flights below the cobblestoned street clanged with traffic. To his right, past a line of gray-white buildings, he glimpsed a teeming boulevard. Ought he go out? He took an experimental step on watery legs. No. He lay down again and was soon snoring.

His recuperating was the beginning of a week of lassitude of indecision. Mme Couteau, the proprietor of the Prinspol Hôtel, sent him to a nearby café whose waiters spoke a bit of English, and for several days he lived on sandwiches and coffee. He went for occasional walks, but the city's physical aspect intimidated him. Once he ventured upon the Champs-Elysées and saw an American movie, but it depressed him. "Hell, I'm doing just what I did in America," he accused himself. But, slowly, things were happening in him; he could eat now in café's surrounded by white Frenchmen, Americans, and Germans without tension. And he marveled at how good it felt to relax. "I've been toting a hundred-pound sack of potatoes on my back all my life and it's goddamned good to get rid of it," he told himself. What elated him about Paris was the number of Africans, Chinese, and Indonesians swarming the streets. After he had learned the names of a few *apéritifs,* he sat for longs hours on café terraces covertly eyeing black Africans escorting blondes on their arms, and he would steal glances at white Americans, wondering at their degree of fury. "Jesus, if *Africans* can do that, *I* ought to be able to go to town," he told himself. Yet he did nothing. Exiled, he lived on his silent island, moping about cafés, speaking only to waiters. Fishbelly was crushed, scared, lost. Lacking words to make known even his needs, he went to bed that Saturday night full of tense doubt. Were there other American Negroes in Paris? "No reason to be scared," he told himself. "I can do what I want, go where I please." Yet anxiety quivered at the core of him.

He awakened Sunday morning, stripped, and gave himself a cat bath at the sink. Then he combed his artificially straightened hair, dampened it, scooped out of a jar labeled "Conk" a walnut-sized dose of a potent, sticky chemical, and massaged it into the roots of his hair. He now brushed the lame strands and pressed tightly over them the knotted top of a woman's nylon stocking. After his hair had dried, it would cling to his skull in a solid, glistening black cap.

He dressed with womanly fastidiousness, donning nylon underwear, a pale-green nylon shirt, a pearl-gray Dacron suit, and a mauve necktie, then shod his feet in light-tan suede shoes. The tip of a white silk handkerchief peeped shyly from his upper left-hand coat pocket. The snap brim of a dark-gray felt hat, the speckled orange-and-black band of which sported a red feather, almost hid his right eye. Who in all Paris was as immaculately clad as he? Yet he perceived a fatal flaw, about which he was powerless: his color. Well, he had been assured that he had no need to brood over his skin tint in France. With a cigarette slanting from his lips, he weighed his face in the wardrobe's cloudy mirror, frowning, for he found his image displeasing. Turning his back, he surveyed himself over his shoulder. No. That face was too much like all the other ordinary black faces that white folks saw each day. He held still, trying to imagine a black face which he, if he were white, would respect, like, accept. He stood sideways and examined his profile. No. Angled like that, he resembled a criminal; no white man would trust such a face. But what kind of black face did white people like? A kind one? No. People trample on kind faces. An intelligent one? No. An intelligent black would most likely be branded as uppity. He sighed; maybe white folks didn't like any kind of a black face. His body grew weak and he sank upon the bed, feeling futile, unrelated to anything or anybody. "Why in hell did I ever come to France anyway?" he asked himself aloud. He brooded vacantly for a few moments, then lowered his eyes to his new suede shoes and the sharp crease in his Dacron trousers. His clothes were beautiful, well made. Slowly, his spirits began to rise. Who could contest his stylishness? Did he not embody civilization, the advertisements in all the big magazines? Heartened, he stood, fronted the mirror again, lowered his head, staring straight before him, lending his face a touch of the baleful, the dashing, like the heroes he had seen in movies. Yeah, that was undoubtedly his *best* face. Snuffing out his cigarette, he opened the door, descended highly polished stairs, swung into the street, heading toward Boul' Mich', where he hoped to pick up a stray French girl. At the

Place de la Sorbonne he halted, seeing a huge crowd of students waving banners and hearing a chant: "RIDGWAY, GO HOME! RIDGWAY, GO HOME!"

His lips tautened into a smile and he grunted under his breath: "These French sure love politics."

He joined the line of massed, watching people. Blue-capped policemen stood at the curb, truncheons ready. Among the demonstrators was a pretty girl. *"She* can do better than that," he said, appraising her bosom, her long shapely legs. The demonstrators streamed past, and he saw a French boy nudging his companion with his elbow and pointing at him.

"Quel chapeau!" the French boy yelled.

Fishbelly froze. Were they making fun of him? Five-hundred-odd faces turned to look and a good-natured laugh floated from the marching crowd. Even the policemen studied him, smiling. What was happening? Why were they laughing at him? Then a lilting cadence sang in his ears: "QUEL CHAPEAU! QUEL CHAPEAU!"

What were they saying? That they were deriding him was certain. A policeman came to him and asked pleasantly: *"Etes-vous américain, monsieur?"*

"Yeah. *Oui,*" he answered.

The crowd swirled boldly about him now, pointing, chanting loudly: "QUEL CHAPEAU AMERICAIN! QUEL CHAPEAU AMERICAIN!"

Aw, they were making fun of his hat! He shrank, wanting to run. But no. Smile back at them. Wave. The chant grew faster, almost hysterical. "QUEL CHAPEAU! QUEL CHAPEAU AMERICAIN!"

A policeman gently lifted his outlandish hat from his head and pushed it significantly into his hand.

"Voilà," the policeman murmured kindly.

The crowd cheered lustily.

Disconcerted, shamed, Fishbelly moved timidly off, holding his gaudy hat close to his body. But, to his dismay, the crowd followed, chanting: "QUEL CHAPEAU AMERICAIN! QUEL CHAPEAU AMERICAIN!"

Panic-stricken, he ran, his mind teeming with visions of a

possible lynching. No. They were laughing. Heart pounding, he sprinted toward his hotel, trying to secrete the hat under his arm, hearing the mob screaming with delight. He reached the rue Monsieur le Prince and was in sight of his hotel. To his rear the swarming mob was blocking traffic and hurling deafening yells: "QUEL CHAPEAU AMERICAIN! QUEL CHAPEAU AMERICAIN!"

Even the police were laughing now. He remembered that white policemen in the Deep South acted like that when a Negro was being chased by lynch mobs and, though laughter was ringing in his ears, he felt about to faint: a vast black curtain was billowing toward his eyes; he was losing awareness of his arms, legs, feet. Mme. Couteau stood in the hotel door. Chest heaving, face wet, he confronted her. She grinned compassionately and his sensations of fainting faded.

"*Vite, allez dans votre chambre!*" she cried.

He did not understand her, but he took the stairs four at a time and, unlocking his door, barged in and made fast the bolt. He listened, panting. The mob's roar continued: "QUEL CHAPEAU AMERICAIN! QUEL CHAPEAU AMERICAIN!"

There came a pounding at his door.

"*Monsieur Feesh, ouvrez la porte!*" Mme Couteau called.

He cracked the door a timid inch, hearing a storm of shouts.

"*Monsieur Feesh*, let us in, *s'il vous plaît!*"

That was the voice of Micky, the night porter. He opened the door wide and Mme Couteau, followed by Micky, waddled in and stood laughing.

"*Vous êtes fou!*" she gasped. "*Donnez-leur votre chapeau et ils s'en iront.*"

"Give the hat," Micky said.

Fishbelly drew forth his hat, ashamed now of its speckled orange-and-black band, of its blazing red feather. Meekly, he extended it to Mme Couteau.

"*Bon!*" Mme Couteau exclaimed, taking the hat and going to the window, which she flung open. The mob's strident screams poured in.

"QUEL CHAPEAU AMERICAIN! QUEL CHAPEAU AMERICAIN!"

Mme Couteau waved the hat and the shouts swelled like joyous thunder. The street was a churning sea of craning faces and flailing arms.

"LE CHAPEAU! LE CHAPEAU!" the mob railed frenziedly. Mme Couteau threw the hat down and Fishbelly saw the mob scrambling for it. The clamor died and a strange kind of admiration registered in the uplifted eyes.

"*Voilà*," Mme Couteau said, turning and facing Fishbelly with arched eyebrows. "*C'est tout ce qu'ils voulaient.*" She walked from the room, grinning.

Fishbelly watched the mob flow away down the street, holding his hat aloft, venting that hypnotic cadence: "QUEL CHAPEAU AMERICAIN! QUEL CHAPEAU AMERICAIN!"

Their voices faded as they flooded onto the boulevard St-Germain. He sighed, still trembling.

"*Monsieur*, you are hero," Micky grunted, smiling, moving through the door.

Misty-eyed, Fishbelly tried to grin. The street was empty now, but he still caught faint echoes of the chanting in the distance. Rattled, he shut the window and sat upon his bed for a long time. Well, he was going out, mob or no mob. But he would wear other clothes. He changed into slacks and T shirt. When he passed the hotel desk, Mme Couteau smiled tolerantly, asking: "*Ça va?*"

"*Ça va*," he mumbled guiltily.

When he ventured forth this time, no one noticed him and he felt normal. The names of French dishes still troubled him, but he knew of a little restaurant where he could have a *table d'hôte* menu. He was more modest now; he was not hankering for a French whore. He wanted to eat.

Episode II

Entering Imbert's restaurant on the rue Casimir-Delavigne, he found every table taken and he took his place inside the door in a short queue to wait his turn. The restaurant was a family business operated by jolly, bustling, rotund Mme Imbert and her pretty daughter, who served the table. M. Imbert, who could be seen manipulating pots and pans on a sizzling stove through a window-like rear wall, was a beefy, red-faced man wearing a white chef's cap and apron. Knowing his ignorance of the language, the Imberts were always kind to Fishbelly and made him feel at home.

The queue dwindled until only Fishbelly stood. Mme Imbert tossed him a smile, then stared critically at an old woman who, dressed in threadbare black, lingered unaccountably at her table even though she had long since finished her lunch. The old woman was nervous, restless, peering about as if searching for something upon the floor. Mme Imbert shrugged, signaling to Fishbelly to be patient. He smiled, wondering why the old woman was dallying so.

A quarter hour later the old woman still fidgeted, casting anxious glances into nearby corners and under the table. Aw, she's loony, Fishbelly told himself. Mme Imbert compressed her lips, bent to the old woman, and spoke urgently, pointing to him. The old woman jerked her head disdainfully and began a loud, expostulating complaint. Bet she's prejudiced! Another client, a white American, entered and queued directly behind Fishbelly.

"Sort of full today," the man commented.

"Looks like it," Fishbelly hummed warily.

Mme Imbert and the old woman flared in loud, angry argument, with Mme Imbert gesturing indignantly toward the door and the old woman obstinately shaking her head and hammering her palm upon the table.

"*Madame, allez-vous en!*" Mme Imbert finally shouted.

"*Non! Laissez-moi!*" the old woman croaked in a lisp.

The customers paused in their eating and grew silent.

"Tsk, tsk." The man behind Fishbelly clucked his tongue.

"What's happening?" Fishbelly asked.

"That old woman claims that Mme Imbert did not give her her change," the man explained.

Aw, so there was nothing racial after all. The exchange between Mme Imbert and the old woman grew violent, causing M. Imbert to crane his neck through the serving window. The fracas now exploded in screams, and M. Imbert, his face flaming red, stormed from the kitchen and towered over the old woman.

"*Madame, je vous en prie!*" he shouted. "*Allez-vous en!*"

"*Non!*" the old woman shrieked. "*J'y suis! J'y reste!*"

"Bon! Vous l'avez bien cherché!" M. Imbert roared, seizing the old woman's arm and jerking her resisting body from the table.

"Nous vous avons déjà donné votre monnaie, madame, et, si vou n'êtes pas satisfaite, allez à la police!" Mme Imbert cried. Fishbelly stepped to one side as M. Imbert shoved the old woman onto the sidewalk and slammed the door. But the old scarecrow crept back to the entrance, sobbing, peering toward the table from which she had been torn, gesturing forlornly, knotting her bony fingers in agony.

With lifted palms Mme Imbert explained to her clients what had happened while her husband trudged back to the kitchen. Fishbelly felt sorry for the old woman. Maybe she's just forgetful. He had a mind to run after her and give her some money when Mme Imbert took his arm and led him to the table.

"Asseyez-vous, Monsieur Feesh. Je regrette que vous ayez été tellement derangé," Mme Imbert murmured.

"Merci." He was self-conscious because everybody was staring at him.

Fishbelly began to munch his hors d'oeuvres, feeling certain that something other than money had been agitating the old woman. Why had she stared so intently at the floor? He glanced in the direction that the old woman had looked. Oh, God! He stopped chewing and a cold sensation crept down his spine. In a dim corner, near a leg of the table, was a ghostly, disembodied, Cheshire Cat-like grin glaring up at him. He drew in his breath, laying aside his knife and fork. What's that? He bent forward, squinting. Lord in heaven! *It was a gleaming set of false teeth!* The old woman had lost her teeth and, ashamed of admitting it or asking for help in finding them, had pretended that she had mislaid her change! She had hoped that her staring into corners would be interpreted as her looking for her money. Poor woman. . . . Maybe she can't buy another set of teeth. Brimming with compassion, he resolved to find the woman and give her her teeth. Using his napkin, he leaned and gingerly snared the ivory-colored grin, wrapped it delicately, rose, crossed to Mme Imbert, parted the napkin folds and displayed the deathlike grin in his palm. He pointed to the corner where he had found them, then to the door, indicating that the old woman had lost them. Mme Imbert took a backward step and, clasping her hands to her face, exclaimed: "*Mon Dieu!*"

Fishbelly pantomimed his desire to find the woman and restore her lost property, and Mme Imbert nodded sorrowfully. Excited by his errand of mercy, he hurried into the street, forgetting his hunger, scanning the passers-by, clutching the napkin-shrouded teeth. Now, where could she be? She was poor and it was a safe bet that she was either walking or taking the subway. Yeah, the Carrefour de l'Odéon. . . . But when he reached the intersection, she was not in sight. He ran to the subway entrance and looked vainly around. Hell. He felt like a fool standing in the middle of the sidewalk holding a set of false teeth wrapped in a napkin. He was about to toss the bundle into the gutter when he saw the old woman coming slowly forward, her eyes red from weeping, her withered cheeks hollow from lack of teeth, her fingers writhing.

"*Madame!*" Fishbelly called in a whisper, advancing.

The old woman glanced blankly at him and walked on.

"*Madame!*" He spoke with gentle urgency, touching her skinny arm, extended his hand under her nose, the napkin folds falling away and revealing the grinning teeth in his fingers.

The old woman stopped, her shrunken lips parting, then she lifted dazed eyes to Fishbelly's face as a crowd began to collect.

"*Voilà*," he announced. "You left 'em in the restaurant."

Swarming people jostled him, craning their necks. The old woman's doughlike face flushed red and her eyes suddenly blazed. She stepped close to Fishbelly, then paused in indecision; next came an abruptly brutal gesture; she snatched the laughing teeth with her left hand, and with her right sent a stinging slap against his mouth.

"What?" Shocked, Fishbelly staggered back.

An excited jabbering broke out around him. The old woman spun and fled to the bottom of the subway steps, stopped, flicked her hand to her mouth, inserted her teeth, then glared angrily back up at him. Hurriedly she paid her fare, then darted from sight toward a train platform.

Bewildered, he still clutched the napkin; he balled it nervously in his hand, aware of murmuring faces. At the sight of an approaching policeman, he flung the napkin to the gutter and walked off, afraid to look back. Goddamn! I was a fool to bother about her damned teeth. He slowed, filled with contrite marveling. The angry shame that had flashed in the old woman's eyes had not been unfamiliar. Yeah. . . . He had felt that same shame a million times in his life, shame for things that one ought not be ashamed of, shame that made one even more ashamed when one realized that one was helpless to fight against it. Goddammit, how could I know she'd feel like that? His lips still burned from the slap, but the heat was more from force of shame than the weight of the blow.

He was no longer hungry. In fact, he never went back to Imbert's as long as he remained in Paris, for that restaurant had become contaminated with the memory of a shame that he was ashamed to remember. He knew what the woman had felt, but, intimidated by the magnitude of the shame, he wanted to forget it.

Yeah, he'd get a sandwich and a cup of coffee. The hell with that woman. The hell with everybody!

Episode III

As they laughed, a thirtyish, ragged black man shuffled to the table and looked timidly at Ned. His clothes were crumpled, as though he had slept in gutters for weeks. The fly of his filthy trousers was held together by a rusty safety pin, and, though it was warm, an oversized, dirt-streaked gabardine was wrapped around his body. His glassy, bulbous eyes glinted redly in the morning sun. Is he drunk? Fishbelly asked himself.

"Hi, Ned," the man said diffidently.

"Hi, Woodie. Sit down," Ned said.

"Want to speak to you a minute," the man said, sliding into a chair.

"Sure. What's on your mind, Woodie?" Ned asked.

"Lots of things," Woodie mumbled, as though one lifetime was too short to relate them all. "Er . . . Ned, you know, I've made some more discoveries about those Egyptians."

"Yeees," Ned sang, concealing boredom.

"Ned, they were really *black*," Woodie said with sudden passion.

The joints of Fishbelly's bones went weak. Good God! Here, in faraway Paris, he was listening to a new version of Sam's father's proud black nationalism. Way down in Mississippi he used to collect rent from Sam's father and he used to listen to tall tales of the glory of the black man in history.

"So what?" Fishbelly cut jeeringly at Woodie. "Suppose the Egyptians *were* black, what does that get you? Soon's a nigger gets a little education, he gets sick of being black and he buys a big bucket of tar and a brush and he starts back in the Garden of Eden and slaps that tarbrush on God's face, Adam's face, Eve's face, Moses' face, and right on down to Jesus Christ's face. And when he gets through making all history black, what has he got but a bill to pay for the bucket, the tar, and the brush? After that, he hasn't got money enough to buy a pot to pee in."

Woodie's glassy, red eyes veered toward Fishbelly and his lips curled scornfully. Without honoring Fishbelly with one word, he turned back to Ned.

"Some people should have enough politeness to speak only when they're spoken to," Woodie sneered with icy disdain.

"Meaning *me?*" Fishbelly asked, bristling.

"Ned," Woodie intoned softly, ignoring Fishbelly, "there's something terribly important I want to ask you."

"Shoot, Woodie." Ned pretended eagerness.

Woodie glanced suspiciously at Fishbelly, then at the other people on the terrace.

"You can say what you want." Ned encouraged the hesitant Woodie.

"Just want to make sure the wrong people don't hear me," Woodie whispered. He leaned forward and asked: "These satellites, do you think that one of 'em is *near* this earth?"

Fishbelly started. Ned blinked, cleared his throat, then began cautiously: "Well, there's been a lot of rumors of satellite launchings. But it's all still in the talk stage. Mostly science-fiction stuff. I'd suspect that the military powers of several nations are working on it, but we'd not know anything about a satellite until one was put in orbit and announced."

Woodie was forgivingly patient. "You don't get my meaning."

"Maybe I don't," Ned agreed. "Just what *do* you mean?"

"I'm not talking about man-made satellites," Woodie said mysteriously.

"Hunh?" Ned cleared his throat again. "Er, what satellites are you talking about, Woodie?"

"The ones in our solar system," Woodie whispered. "Mars, Venus . . . You know."

"Er . . . well, I think that all the planets are still in their respective orbits," Ned said with safe assurance.

Woodie expressed grave doubt. "I'm not so sure."

"Have you observed anything wrong lately in the solar system?" Ned asked with stiff lips.

"Something's happening," Woodie confided.

"What?" Fishbelly asked, leaning forward.

Woodie sighed, avoiding Ned's and Fishbelly's eyes.

"There is a thing called gravitation," Woodie stated. "You admit that, don't you?"

"They told me about it at school," Ned conceded. "And I've not encountered anything since to make me doubt it."

Woodie spoke with academic persuasion. "Newton discovered gravitation when he saw an apple fall from a tree."

"Yes," Ned said. "I'm listening."

"Now, the only thing that could lessen gravity would be a slowing down of the rotation of the earth, wouldn't it?" Woodie asked, his glassy eyes glowing fearfully, the tiny veins in them looking like red lightning.

"Guess you're right there," Ned assented slowly.

"But there's no direct evidence of that," Woodie pointed out brightly.

"Th-that's true," Ned agreed.

"I've checked," Woodie said. "The day's still twenty-four hours long."

"Yeah. My watch more or less indicates that," Ned concurred.

"But something *is* happening to this earth, something more delicate, sensitive," Woodie declared.

"What?" Ned asked.

"There is a slight lessening of gravity; my *feet* feel it," Woodie informed them.

"Oh, really? In what way?" Fishbelly asked.

"It's obvious," Woodie said, amazed, slightly angered that Ned and Fishbelly did not grasp his point. "There's gravity hunh? Well, when I *walk*, I feel a lessening of it."

"Er . . . how, Woodie?" Ned wanted to know.

Woodie cited final proof. "My feet feel *light*. When I walk, I don't need much strength. I almost float, fly. The earth's not holding me as tightly as before."

"Goddamn, nigger," Fishbelly spat. "You're just *hungry*."

"How long have you been feeling this?" Ned asked, giving Fishbelly a restraining kick under the table.

"For a week or so," Woodie confided. "It started slowly. But now I feel it each step I take. You'll feel it too, if you watch out for it."

"Er . . . Woodie, just what satellite do you think is near the earth? Which one is causing this?" Ned asked.

Woodie grew suddenly modest, tugging nervously at the frayed, blackened collar of his shredded shirt.

"Ned, I don't *know*," Woodie confessed. His face was an image of despair. "I'm reasoning inductively. One mustn't be too hasty in these matters, you know."

"I agree. Now, does *anybody* know what satellite's causing this lightfootedness of yours?" Ned inquired.

"I bet it's those goddamned white folks," Fishbelly stated, his voice charged with intentional sadism.

"*You* got it! You *see* it!" Woodie chanted with gleeful excitement, pointing at Fishbelly.

"And they're keeping it from *us*," Fishbelly said, brutally repressing a smile.

"They're trying to control the solar system." Woodie leaped to embrace the interpretation.

"Have you met any of the whites who know about this?" Ned asked.

"No. They're covering it up. I can't find 'em," Woodie confessed. "But I'm hunting 'em down. There's a secret meeting of scientists at Versailles. I want to float along out there and do some snooping, see?" Woodie glanced apprehensively about. "Say, Ned, can you let me have five hundred francs to get there?"

"Here's a thousand," Fishbelly said, tossing Woodie a bill. "And when you find 'em, you let me know. I want to be *in* on this."

As he took the bill, Woodie's face smiled and softened.

"I didn't expect this kind of racial solidarity from you," he said. "Want to help me find 'em?"

"Er . . . no. I got a date. But tell Ned and he'll tell me and . . ."

"Look!" Woodie exclaimed, rising. "See how I walk? I hardly touch the earth!"

He marched abruptly off, his legs jerking a little as he moved. Neither Ned nor Fishbelly spoke for a moment.

"Last week he was talking about going to London," Ned said. "And I dissuaded 'im."

"Why did he want to go to London?"

"To talk to the Royal College of Scientists," Ned said. "But I knew that the British would know what he was talking about and they'd put 'im straightway in a padded cell. The French think we're all crazy anyhow and so they leave 'im alone."

"Oh, but the French'll get 'im, Ned," Fishbelly said.

"Why?"

"That guy's *gone, long gone.*"

"Yes, he's crazy, but you can't touch 'im here."

"Why?"

"He hasn't bothered anybody."

"Do we have to wait for 'im to *bother* somebody?"

"Yep."

"Why?"

"You can't deprive people of their rights under French law," Ned said.

"But he's going to do something soon," Fishbelly served notice. "Has he the *right* to bother you or me?"

"Let's hope it won't be you or me," Ned sighed.

"But where'd he get that crazy idea about the sun, the moon, the stars . . . ?"

"Fish, that boy's suffering what is known as 'subjective ideas of reference,'" Ned explained.

"Hunh?"

"Well, it's like this. What's happening is deep down in you, too complicated for you to grasp; it's a tangled knot of hot emotions. Your emotions are hurting you and you feel innocent, so you feel that somebody or something must be hurting you. You look around to find out what it is. You see nothing. But you say: 'There *must* be something!' Woodie thinks that it's the stars."

"And the white people control the stars?"

"Right. That's his delusion," Ned said.

"How in hell did he get messed up like that, Ned?"

"Woodie was one of the most brilliant law students in the Sorbonne," Ned related. "He got his degree. He's been here for five years and he's scared to death of going home. He knows that he has to face racism. He's stayed on and on; each time he gets money enough to go, he panics, sweats, and can't move. Now the embassy's sending 'im home. The closer the date of his departure comes, the more he's convinced that something's happening. . . ."

"That a satellite's near the earth?"

"Right. And something *is* happening. It's happening to *him*. He's near a breakdown."

"God, Ned, you scare me."

"I hope it won't happen to you, Fish," Ned mumbled with a smile.

"Ned," Fishbelly protested with a guilty start, "I don't deal in highfalutin stuff like stars, law, satellites . . ."

"Just teasing you, Fish." Ned grinned. "You've got your feet on the ground and you're dealing in stuff that can't go wrong. You're one of the sanest American Negroes over here."

"Gee, Ned, thanks," Fishbelly sighed. "You had me scared there for a moment."

They sat lazing in the sun. Fishbelly was a bit sleepy, but not enough to want to go to bed. He watched traffic flowing past, noting now and then a shapely woman tipping by.

Episode IV

To the right, from around the corner of the rue de Vaugirard, came a thin, well-dressed black woman whose bony, deeply powdered, angular face showed a white grin as she recognized Ned.

"Who's she?" Fishbelly asked.

"Wait. I'll tell you," Ned said. "Hello, Irene."

"Oh, hello, Ned! How are you?" the black scarecrow croaked in cracked soprano. High-strung, seemingly slightly hysterical, she bent forward and shook hands with both Ned and Fishbelly. "I'm in a hurry. Got to see some people. Good-by." She suddenly gave a motiveless guffaw, waved a pink palm, and stalked off on sticklike legs sheathed in rose-colored nylon.

"Ha-ha!" Fishbelly's laugh rolled when the woman was out of earshot.

"What's so funny?" Ned asked.

"She's a walking corpse," Fishbelly commented, recalling the dead black woman he had seen in his father's undertaking establishment in Mississippi.

"She'll outlive you, I bet," Ned wagered.

"Yeah? What's her racket?"

"It's no racket," Ned said. "It's a philosophy. She's the most successful American Negro woman in all Paris."

"Yeah? What does she do?"

"She begs for a living."

"What do you mean?"

"She begs, professionally."

"You're kidding. She didn't ask you for anything."

"No. She's an artistic beggar and she practices her craft among rich white Americans. Her name's Irene Stout. You're too young to remember her. She was quite a gal back in Harlem during the twenties. She was an actress, playing mostly bit parts on Broadway. Like all the rest, she fretted at being limited in her life because of her race and color. Right after the war, she got the crazy idea, at the age of fifty, of coming to Paris, learning French, and going on the stage. It was plumb wild. She came here, but she couldn't, didn't fit in. Her command of the language never got beyond the elementary. She could find no work. She was dead broke, nearly starving. I helped her a few times. Then she disappeared. I thought she'd gone home. But no. One day I got a letter from her. She was in the American Hospital, ill. That is, she said that she was ill. I suspect that she went to the hospital because she couldn't pay her hotel bill. In her letter, she'd asked me for money. I sent her ten dollars. But, Fish, I was not the only one to whom Irene wrote asking for money. Lying in that hospital on her bed, with pen, ink, and paper at her side, she wrote to almost every white American of any consequence in Paris, asking for money. And she got it. One of her letters fell into my hands." Ned paused, pulled out his wallet, and extracted a tattered, folded sheet of faded paper. "Here, Fish, read this and you'll understand the white man's heart. Irene did. She's got over four million francs in the bank, in cash, and . . ."

"Four million?"

"That's right."

"But how'd she get that much money?"

"By begging. Read the letter. It's all in there."

"This is one of the letters she wrote asking for money?"

"That's it."

Fishbelly lowered his eyes and read:

Dear Mr. Green:

I'm sending this letter to the best and finest white man I know. Now, Mr. Green, you don't know me but I know you. You are from Helena, Arkansas, and all of my kin folks are from that wonderful region. Now, Mr. Green, I guess you must be asking yourself who I am to be taking up your precious time like this by writing you a letter. Well, I'm Irene, an old Christian colored woman who spent all of her life working for good white folks. And I never regret a day or an hour of being in their service.

Mr. Green, I'm sick and I done got dead broke and stranded over here when I came to work for some dirty no-good foreigners who left me high and dry, something that my good white folks back at home would never do. Now, I'm sick and alone and in the hospital with nobody to give me a good thought. These folks are taking good care of me, treating me all right, according to their lights, but, Mr. Green, I know in my soul that this foreign medicine they're giving me won't ever make me get well. I know the kind of medicine I need, but I have no friends here to give it to me. I know what I need; I need the good old sweet ground of them United States under my old black feet again. I need God's only country. I need to breathe fresh, wonderful air that blows only in America. I need the food I'm used to, like cornbread, buttermilk, fatback, molasses, collard greens, spareribs, mush, and things like that. But I can't get them things over here. These folks never heard of them.

So I'm asking a good white man to help a good old colored woman who had done lost her way to get back home. Just send me money enough for any old kind of ticket. And anything you send me will get you a heart-felt prayer straight to God. And if I live long enough, I'm going to pay you back, so be sure to put your home address in the letter with the money. Mr. Green, don't let a poor honest old colored woman who has served good white folks all her life die here in a strange country. The Lord will bless you for what you do for me. Oh, if I could only eat some good old chitterlings and watermelon once more before I die! Won't you help me, Mr. Green? I'm asking you to do me this little favor with tears in my eyes and let me see my wide, beautiful, wonderful country again.

Your humble servant,

IRENE STOUT

Fishbelly lifted his eyes and stared at Ned.

"Ned, is this a joke?" he asked.

"No. It's a valid, sentimental document written by a cynical black woman," Ned explained.

"Mr. Green *sent* her the money?"

"Yeah. Two hundred dollars."

"To ship a poor old darky woman home?"

"That's right."

"But she didn't go home?"

"No. While Irene was in the hospital, she wrote over a thousand letters like that . . ."

"And they all sent money?"

"Most of 'em."

"Did you see any of the letters the white folks wrote her?"

"No. She'd never let me see 'em. But I'll bet they were real lulus. Irene told me that some of them actually made her break down and cry."

"Gosh, I wish I could work that on a really big scale," Fishbelly pined.

"Not a chance, Fish," Ned said. "You haven't got the touch. Well, Irene changed all of those dollars into francs on the black market and banked 'em. She left that hospital an independent woman. Now, I met Mr. Green quite by accident and he started telling me how he loved colored folks. To prove how much he loves us, he showed me that letter and told me that he'd sent Irene two hundred dollars. All the recommendation he needed was to phone the hospital and find out if Irene was really there. He asked me if he were not a benefactor of the colored race and I told him: 'Yes. May I keep this letter?' He let me keep it."

"Ha-ha! Does Irene know that you've got this letter?"

"Yes. One day I showed it to her."

"Oh, boy! I bet she was ashamed."

"Ashamed? Proud, rather. She laughed till she cried. And now, every time I see her, she bursts into a big laugh at how she manipulates the foolish racial sensibilities of white folks."

"Goddamn, Ned, that woman's *hard*."

"No. She's bitter, but completely happy about it."

"So she became an actress after all."

"And, boy, what an actress! She's still writing letters and collecting money. She won't tell me what pitch she's using now. In fact, she's on her way somewhere this minute to collect some money."

"Did the hospital doctors ever suspect anything?"

"No. They think that their medicine cured her."

Episode V

Fishbelly mused, smiling, idly scratching his chin, slumped limply, pensively in his chair, his eyelids drooping against the waxing might of the mroning sun. Traffic rolled rumblingly past over cobblestones; a just-felt, balmy wind gently agitated the leaves of the treees. The Parisian landscape was alluring, fragile, caressing. Far down the rue de Tournon, Fishbelly picked out a short Negro striding briskly forward amid a throng of whites.

"Fish, here comes a guy you really ought to know about," Ned said.

"Yeah? Who is he?"

"Jimmy Whitfield."

"What does he do?"

"He operates the white market."

"What's that?"

"Jimmy's a streamlined, twentieth-century pimp," Ned informed him.

"Yeah? What's he got I haven't got?"

"A technique that's original."

"When somebody can tell me how to make money out of

women, I shut my mouth and listen," Fishbelly said. "What does he do to 'em?"

"Jimmy steams women," Ned said, chuckling.

"Steams 'em? What's *that?*"

"Jimmy specializes in loving women for money and he calls it steaming 'em," Ned explained. "He operates according to plan. When you consider where he started from and how far he's gone, he's a success. Jimmy tells me that it's work like any other, exacting, delicate. He knows his trade. The only thing that worries me about 'im is that he might well work himself to death to keep from doing an honest day's work."

Jimmy Whitfield, black, sprucely dressed, grinning, sauntered up and exclaimed with a fat smile: "Hi, Ned. Want to see you, man!"

"How are you, Jimmy? Everything all right?"

"Yeah, man. Everything's under control."

"Jimmy, Fish," Ned introduced them.

"Glad to meet you."

"Same here," Fishbelly said, shaking Jimmy's hand.

Jimmy pulled two ten-thousand-franc notes out of his pocket and handed them to Ned.

"This squares us up, don't it?" Jimmy asked.

"Right. Thanks, Jimmy," Ned said. "Sure you can spare this?"

"Sure, man. The chick I got now's rolling in dough," Jimmy bragged, prancing. "Buying a car soon."

"Eating well, Jimmy?" Ned asked slyly. "You need plenty of proteins in your profession."

"Ha-ha!" Jimmy laughed. "Eating high on the hog these days. Got to blow now. See you all." Jimmy moved off, grinning.

Ned sat looking philosophically at the two bank notes.

"He pays his debts," Fishbelly observed.

"This isn't payment of a debt. It's part payment of a legal fee."

"You practice law here?"

"Not exactly, not officially," Ned said. "But I do give legal advice."

"Was Jimmy in trouble?"

"Yeah. Bad." Ned laughed softly. "Maybe I oughtn't talk about it. But I helped Jimmy more as a friend than as a lawyer. Come to think of it, Fish, Jimmy's story might help you here in Paris, might make you realize how far you are beyond the protection or hurt of French law.

"Jimmy's from Harlem. His father died when he was fifteen and his mother reared 'im when she wasn't busy in white folks' kitchens. Jimmy wasn't bright or bad, just average, a bit on the dull side. But he was bright enough to be race-conscious; they all are. They'd have to be half dead not to be. Jimmy lived from hand to mouth, roaming the streets, spurning school for life, not liking the way he lived. It wasn't that Jimmy condemned his environment; there just wasn't enough money in that sordid environment to go around. And Jimmy wanted more money than Harlem opportunities would let 'im earn.

"One day, at one of those Leftish, progressive parties, Jimmy met a dissatisfied middle-class housewife. He slept with her and he was surprised when she paid him. Jimmy then asked himself what in hell had he been doing all of his life till that time. He quickly took the hint and turned what he had accidentally discovered into an intentional, wholesale business. He became a sexual technician, limiting his practice to frigid white women. Discounting a certain amount of sexual bragging to which most men are prone, Jimmy was extra good at his trade, not because he was a greatly endowed lover, but mainly because of hidden drives behind his sexual impulses. A repressed racial animus aided his intra-sheet activities, spurring him to rouse the most sexually repressed white girl. He became popular, widely sought-after.

"But it wasn't until Jimmy moved his operations from Harlem to Greenwich Village that he came into his own. He began to specialize in girl students from rich families. Intuition helped him to spot those girls who had been led to believe that sex was bad, that the sexual function was for reproduction only, that only animals enjoyed sex. Jimmy's genius could smell such sexual repression in any girl a mile off. He took a small apartment and carried his gal victims there; if they could get a steady stream of money from Mama and Papa, he'd love 'em so hard and regularly that they'd soon do anything on earth for 'im, and, in the end, they'd move in with 'im, bringing their mink coats, their expensive cameras, their FM pickups, de luxe art books, jewelry, etc. Otherwise, he dropped 'em.

"Then, one day, when the gal was at school, he'd move out, taking everything, selling it, pocketing the money, and vanishing. Strangely enough, the girls whom he had swindled and abandoned had emotional reactions that aided and abetted Jimmy's sexual raids. They felt guilty and uncertain. And, of course, Jimmy would have told them about the racial problem, awakened their sympathies, and they'd be deeply hesitant about hurting him, reporting him to the police. How could they admit that they'd been duped by a black boy with whom they'd been sleeping and to whom they'd given money?

"Stunned, shedding a few bitter tears, the girls would keep a stiff upper lip. Jimmy had a foolproof system and knew it. He now had money, women. He dressed so cutely that he looked curious. His tastes in food and drink became cosmopolitan. He even read books in his spare time. He was redeeming his blighted racial pride by inflicting upon the womanhood of the race that had scorned him that part of his body that that race had condemned. Yet, two problems plagued Jimmy: the money was not coming in fast enough, and he was finding that his work was not as easy as he had first thought. It was a race between time and the flesh, and, justly, Jimmy feared that time would vanquish the flesh.

"Being honest with himself, Jimmy knew that his physical performances had begun to slip, just a bit. So he concentrated upon victims a little older, victims who could lay their hands upon more money. It worked even better than with the girl students. Jimmy took up with the divorced wife of a steel magnate. He steamed her, cleaned her out, and she took it, not daring to utter a word to the police.

"Then Jimmy made his first serious blunder. Instead of continuing with older women, he chanced upon another young girl, rich and of good family. He gave her the works. But this gal had spunk. She swallowed her racial pride and went to the police and told her story, charging Jimmy with theft. The police were, of course, most happy to oblige her and they arrested Jimmy. He admitted everything and returned the stolen goods. Here luck enters the picture. The police, after weighing the factors of the case, advised the girl not to press the charge, telling her that the resulting publicity would mar her for life. She assented readily, for, deep in her heart, she loved Jimmy. The law sent Jimmy away with a stiff warning, the whole case being regarded as a lovers' tiff.

"Broke, shaken, casting about for another victim, Jimmy found that the pining wife of the steel magnate was willing to forgive him and take him back, but this time on a new basis. She proposed marriage, pointing out that they could live abroad, that her income was more than enough for the both of them. To make sure that the woman wouldn't welch on 'im, Jimmy made her pregnant, married her, and sailed for France. Jimmy was certain that they were going to live happily ever after.

"But the little rich gal whom he'd wronged, upon hearing of this, got furious. She now hated Jimmy because she'd loved 'im, and was determined to hurt 'im. She went straight to the French Embassy and informed the officials that Jimmy was a criminal. The word was flashed to Paris. The French police gave Jimmy twenty-four hours to get out of France, despite the fact that he was now the father of a bouncing, brown French baby boy.

"It was at this moment that I heard of the case. On the morning of the day of his expulsion, Jimmy came to me with his story. At first he swore that he was being persecuted on racial grounds, but, after I'd pumped 'im for three solid hours, he confessed why the police were chasing 'im, and said: 'Ned, we're black and you know how we got to live.' He wanted desperately to remain in France. But his was a bleak case and the only remedies that I could counsel were drastic ones. I told 'im I would help 'im if he had the courage to follow my instructions to the letter. In despair, he promised.

"I told Jimmy to take a brick, hide it under his coat, and go to the rue de la Paix and stand in front of the richest jewelry store that he could find. Now, Jimmy was supposed to be expelled at four o'clock in the afternoon; he went to the rue de la Paix at one o'clock. He stood there in front of the window of that jewelry store, looking at diamonds, rings, pearls, precious stones, etc. Then he did as I told him to do: he took out his brick and hurled it through the plate glass! When the sound of that shattering glass died, silence took hold of that street. The owners of the store came scurrying out, terrified, looking at their smashed window. Alarms rang. People gathered and gaped. No one touched a thing. No one was in flight. The police came running, blowing their whistles. People began to suspect one another, looking at one another. Masses of diamonds glittered within reach. But the shattered window was not pilfered. Fish, it was electric, stupefying. I was watching the whole drama from across the street. No one knew what to do.

" '*Qui a fait ça?*' the policemen asked of the crowd.

"Jimmy did not answer, for the question had not been directed at him. In fact, no one suspected him. And when he saw that no one was pointing a finger of guilt at him, he said: '*Je . . .*' He was so excited that he was forgetting his French grammar. '*C'est moi, monsieur,*' he said proudly, smiling.

" '*M-mais . . . pourquoi?*' the police demanded.

" '*Monsieur, j'aime la France,*' he told them loudly.

"He was arrested, of course, but ever so reluctantly. The French are paralyzed when things go contrary to their logic. When they took Jimmy into custody, they were sure that they were making a mistake. But Jimmy stuck to his tale. He was put in a cell. He was not expelled from France that day.

"Now, Fish, I told Jimmy to smash that window of the jewelry store so that he could be accused of breaking French law. Until he had committed that crime, he was outside of the pale of French law. But, when he shattered that window, French law stepped in and recognized him, placed him under its scrutiny, and, in a way, under its negative protection; in short, Jimmy was brought within the scope of French civilization. I had explained all this to Jimmy and coached him how to act.

"He told the police the truth. The case was so curious that it leaked into the press. Racial organizations rushed to Jimmy's aid. Under my guidance, Jimmy had performed the first free act of his life.

"Overnight he became an odd sort of hero. After serving a sentence of six months, he was freed and given a card of identity. French law now protects him. Jimmy redeemed his criminality by telling why he broke the window. I charged him fifty thousand francs for that advice; not that I needed the money, but he would not have followed my instructions had I not charged him something. This twenty thousand francs is the last payment of my fee."

"What's Jimmy doing now?" Fishbelly asked.

"He's left the wife of the steel magnate. He got bored with her. He's taking to steaming young girls again," Ned related wearily. "But he's promised that he'd break no more windows. He gave me his word on that. Ha-ha!" Ned snorted. "He'll keep that word. Breaking windows is not Jimmy's line."

Ann Petry

Born and raised in Old Saybrook, Connecticut, Miss Petry studied pharmacy at the University of Connecticut and later worked in the family drugstore. After her marriage in 1928 she moved to New York, where she was a reporter for Harlem newspapers and worked for several social agencies concerned with urban slum conditions. Out of this experience came her first novel, *The Street*, published in 1946, which was written on a Houghton Mifflin Literary Fellowship.

Miss Petry's second novel, *Country Place* (1947), was recognized as a serious literary achievement in the tradition of *Spoon River* and *Winesburg, Ohio*. This was followed in 1953 by *The Narrows*, a novel whose setting is a small New England town containing a Negro section known as "The Narrows." She has also written a biography of Harriet Tubman, the Negro abolitionist, and a children's book, *The Drugstore Cat*.

Miss Petry's short stories have appeared in *Foley's Best American Short Stories of 1946*, in *The Crisis* magazine, and in *Phylon*. Miss Petry has also written a novella, *In Dark Confusion*, based on the Harlem riot of 1943.

Miss Muriel, a complete novella, has its first publication here and contains material that will appear in a larger work now in progress.

MISS MURIEL

BY ANN PETRY

Almost every day, Ruth Davis and I walk home from school together, We walk very slowly because we like to talk to each other
and we don't get much chance in school or after school either.
We are very much alike. We are both twelve years old and we are
freshmen in high school and we never study—well, not very much,
because we learn faster than the rest of the class. We laugh about
the same things and we are curious about the same things. We
even wear our hair in the same style—thick braids halfway down
our backs. We are not alike in one respect. She is white and I am
colored.

Yesterday when we reached the building that houses my father's
drugstore, we sat down on the front steps—long wooden steps
that go all the way across the front of the building. Ruth said,
"I wish I lived here," and patted the steps though they are very
splintery.

Aunt Sophronia must have heard our voices, because she came
to the door and said, "I left my shoes at the shoemaker's this
morning. Please go and get them for me," and she handed me a
little cardboard ticket with a number on it.

"You want to come with me, Ruth?"

"I've got to go home. I'm sure my aunt will have things for me
to do. Just like your aunt." She smiled at Aunt Sophronia.

I walked part way home with Ruth and then turned back and
went up Petticoat Lane toward the shoemaker's shop. Mr. Bemish,
the shoemaker, is a little man with gray hair. He has a glass eye.
This eye is not the same color as his own eye. It is a deeper gray.
If I stand too close to him I get a squeamish feeling because one
eye moves in its socket and the other eye does not.

Mr. Bemish and I are friends. I am always taking shoes to his
shop to be repaired. We do not own a horse and buggy and so
we walk a great deal. In fact, there is a family rule that we must

walk any distance under three miles. As a result, our shoes are in constant need of repair, the soles and heels have to be replaced, and we always seem to be in need of shoelaces. Quite often I snag the uppers on the bull briars in the woods and then the tears have to be stitched.

When I went to get Aunt Sophronia's shoes, Mr. Bemish was sitting near the window. It is a big window and he has a very nice view of the street. He had on his leather apron and his eyeglasses. His glasses are small and they have steel rims. He was sewing a shoe and he had a long length of waxed linen thread in his needle. He waxes the thread himself.

I handed him the ticket and he got up from his workbench to get the shoes. I saw that he had separated them from the other shoes. These are Aunt Sophronia's store shoes. They had been polished so that they shone like patent leather. They lay alone, near the front of the table where he keeps the shoes he has repaired. He leaned toward me and I moved away from him. I did not like being so close to his glass eye.

"The lady who brought these shoes in. Who is she?"

I looked at him and raised one eyebrow. It has taken me two months of constant practice in front of a mirror to master the art of lifting one eyebrow.

Mr. Bemish said, "What's the matter with you? Didn't you hear what I said? Who was that lady who brought these shoes in?"

I moved further away from him. He didn't know it but I was imitating Dottle Smith, my favorite person in all the world. Dottle tells the most wonderful stories and he can act and recite poetry. He visits our family every summer. Anyway, I bowed to Mr. Bemish and I bowed to an imaginary group of people seated somewhere on my right and I said, "Gentlemen, be seated. Mr. Bones, who was that lady I saw you with last night?" I lowered the pitch of my voice and said, "That wasn't no lady. That was my *wife*."

"Girlie—"

"Why do you keep calling me 'girlie'? I have a name."

"I cannot remember people's names. I'm too old. I've told you that before."

"How old are you, Mr. Bemish?"

"None of your business," he said pettishly. "Who—"

"Well, I only asked in order to decide whether to agree with you that you're old enough to be forgetful. Does the past seem more real to you than the present?"

Mr. Bemish scowled his annoyance. "The town is full of children," he said. "It's the children who bring the shoes in and come and get them after I've fixed them. They run the errands. All those children look just alike to me. I can't remember their names. I don't even try. I don't plan to clutter up my mind with a lot of children's names. I don't see the same children that often. So I call the boys 'boy,' and I call the girls 'girlie.' I've told you this before. What's the matter with you today?"

"It's spring and the church green is filled with robins looking for worms. Don't you sometimes wish you were a robin looking for a worm?"

He sighed. "Now tell me, who was that lady that brought these shoes in?"

"My Aunt Sophronia."

"Sophronia?" he said. "What a funny name. And she's your aunt?"

"Yes."

"Does she live with you?"

Mr. Bemish's cat mewed at the door and I let her in. She is a very handsome creature, gray, with white feet, and really lovely fur. "May-a-ling, May-a-ling," I said, patting her, "where have you been?" I always have the feeling that if I wait, if I persist, she will answer me. She is a very intelligent cat and very responsive.

"Does your aunt live with you?"

"Yes."

"Has she been living with you very long?"

"About six months, I guess. She's a druggist."

"You mean she knows about medicine?"

"Yes, just like my father. They run the store together."

Mr. Bemish thrust his hands in Aunt Sophronia's shoes and held them up, studying them. Then he made the shoes walk along the edge of the table, in a mincing kind of walk, a caricature of the way a woman walks.

"She has small feet, hasn't she?"

"No." I tried to sound like my mother when she disapproves of something.

He flushed and wrapped the shoes in newspaper, making a very neat bundle.

"Is she married?"

"Who? Aunt Sophronia? No. She's not married."

Mr. Bemish took his cookie crock off the shelf. He lives in the shop. Against one wall he has a kitchen stove, a big black iron stove with nickel fenders and a tea kettle on it, and there is a black iron sink with a pump right near the stove. He cooks his meals himself, he bakes bread, and usually there is a stew bubbling in a pot on the stove. In winter the windows of his little shop frost over, so that I cannot see in and he cannot see out. He draws his red curtains just after dusk and lights his lamps, and the windows look pink because of the frost and the red curtains and the light shining from behind them.

Sometimes he forgets to draw the curtains that separate his sleeping quarters from the rest of the shop and I can see his bed. It is a brass bed. He evidently polishes it, because it shines like gold. It has a very intricate design on the headboard and the foot-board. He has a little piece of flowered carpet in front of his bed. I can see his white china pot under the bed. A dark suit and some shirts hang on hooks on the wall. There is a chest of drawers with a small mirror in a gold frame over it, and a washbowl and pitcher on a washstand. The washbowl and pitcher are white with pink rosebuds painted on them.

Mr. Bemish offered me a cookie from the big stoneware crock. "Have a cookie, girlie."

He makes big thick molasses cookies. I ate three of them without stopping. I was hungry and did not know it. I ate the fourth cookie very slowly and I talked to Mr. Bemish as I ate it.

"I don't think my Aunt Sophronia will ever get married."

"Why not?"

"Well, I never heard of a lady druggist before and I don't know who a lady druggist would marry. Would she marry another druggist? There aren't any around here anywhere except my father and certainly she couldn't marry him. He's already married to my mother."

"She looks like a gypsy," Mr. Bemish said dreamily.

"You mean my Aunt Sophronia?"

Mr. Bemish nodded.

"She does not. She looks like my mother and my Aunt Ellen. And my father and Uncle Johno say they look like Egyptian queens."

They are not very tall and they move quickly and their skins are brown and very smooth and their eyes are big and black and they stand up very straight. They are not alike though. My mother is business-minded. She likes to buy and sell things. She is a chiropodist and a hairdresser. Life sometimes seems full of other people's hair and their toenails. She makes a hair tonic and sells it to her customers. She designs luncheon sets and banquet cloths and guest towels and sells them. Aunt Ellen and Uncle Johno provide culture. Aunt Ellen lectures at schools and colleges. She plays Bach and Beethoven on the piano and organ. She writes articles for newspapers and magazines.

I do not know very much about Aunt Sophronia. She works in the store. She fills prescriptions. She does embroidery. She reads a lot. She doesn't play the piano. She is very neat. The men who come in the store look at her out of the corner of their eyes. Even though she wears her hair skinned tight back from her forehead, and wears very plain clothes, dresses with long, tight sleeves and high necks, she still looks like—well, like an Egyptian queen. She is young but she seems very quiet and sober.

Mr. Bemish offered me another cookie. "I'll eat it on my way home to keep my strength up. Thank you very much," I said primly.

When I gave the shoes to Aunt Sophronia, I said, "Mr. Bemish thinks you look like a gypsy."

My mother frowned. "Did he tell you to repeat that?"

"No, he didn't. But I thought it was an interesting statement."

"I wish you wouldn't repeat the things you hear. It just causes trouble. Now every time I look at Mr. Bemish I'll wonder about him—"

"What will you wonder—I mean—"

She said I must go and practice my music lesson and ignored my question. I wonder how old I will be before I can ask questions of an adult and receive honest answers to the questions. My family always finds something for me to do. Are they not using their power as adults to give orders in order to evade the questions?

That evening, about five o'clock, Mr. Bemish came in the store. I was sitting on the bench in the front. It is a very old bench. The customers sit there while they wait for their prescriptions to be filled. The wood is a beautiful color. It is a deep, reddish brown.

Mr. Bemish sat down beside me on the bench. His presence irritated me. He kept moving his hand up and down the arms of the bench, up and down, in a quick, nervous movement. It is as though he thought he had an awl in his hand, and he is going in and out making holes in leather and then sewing, slipping a needle in and out, as he mends a saddle or a pair of boots.

My father looked at him over the top of his glasses and said, "Well, Bemish, what can I do for you?"

"Nothing. Nothing at all. I just stopped in to pass the time of day, to see how you all were—" His voice trailed away, softly.

He comes every evening. I find this very annoying. Quite often I have to squeeze myself onto the bench. Pritchett, the sexton of the Congregational church—stout, red-faced, smelling of whiskey —rings the bell for a service at seven o'clock and then he, too, sits in the front of the store, watching the customers as they come and go until closing time. He eyed Mr. Bemish rather doubtfully at first, but then ignored him. When the sexton and Mr. Bemish were on the bench, there was just room enough for me to squeeze in between them. I didn't especially mind the sexton, because he usually went to sleep, nodding and dozing until it was time to close the store. But Mr. Bemish doesn't sit still—and the movement of his hands is distracting.

My mother finally spoke to my father about Mr. Bemish. They were standing in the back room. "Why does Mr. Bemish sit out there in the store so much?" she asked.

"Nothin' else to do."

She shook her head. "I think he's interested in Sophronia. He keeps looking around for someone."

My father laughed out loud. "That dried-up old white man?"

The laughter of my father is a wonderful sound—if you know

anything about music you know he sings tenor and you know he sings in the Italian fashion with an open throat and you begin to smile, and if he laughs long enough, you laugh too, because you can't help it.

"Bemish?" he said. And he laughed so hard that he had to lean against the doorjamb in order to keep his balance.

Every night right after supper, Mr. Bemish sits in the store rubbing the arm of the bench with that quick, jerking motion of his hand, nodding to people who come in, sometimes talking to them, but mostly just sitting.

Two weeks later I walked past his shop. He came to the door and called me. "Girlie," he said, beckoning.

"Yes, Mr. Bemish?"

"Is your aunt with the peculiar name still here—that is, in town, living with you?"

"Yes, she is, Mr. Bemish."

"Don't she ever go in the drugstore?"

"Not after five o'clock, Mr. Bemish. My father doesn't approve of ladies working at night. At night we act just like other people's families. We sit around the table in the dining room and talk, and we play checkers, and we read and we—"

"Yes, yes," he said impatiently. "But don't your aunt ever go anywhere at night?"

"I don't think so. I go to bed early."

"Do you think—" And he shook his head. "Never mind, girlie, never mind," and he sighed. "Here—I just made up a fresh batch of those big cookies you like so well."

I walked down Petticoat Lane toward the drugstore eating one of Mr. Bemish's thick molasses cookies. I wished I had taken time to tell him how cozy our downstairs parlor is in the winter. We have turkey-red curtains at the windows too, and we pull the window shades and draw the curtains, and there is a very thick rug on the floor and it is a small room, so the rug completely covers the floor. The piano is in there and an old-fashioned sofa with a carved mahogany frame and a very handsome round stove and it is warm in winter; and in the summer when the windows are open, you can look right out into the back yard and smell the flowers and feel the cool air that comes from the garden.

The next afternoon, Mr. Bemish came in the drugstore about quarter past three. It was a cold, windy afternoon. I had just come from school and there was a big mug of hot cocoa for me. Aunt Sophronia had it ready and waiting for me in the back room. I had just tasted the first spoonful; it was much too hot to gulp down, and I leaned way over and blew on it gently, and inhaled the rich, chocolatey smell of it. I heard my aunt say, "Why, Mr. Bemish, what are you doing out at this hour?"

"I thought I'd like an ice-cream soda." Mr. Bemish's voice sounded breathless, lighter in weight, and the pitch was lower than normal.

I peeked out at him. He was sitting near the fountain in one of the ice-cream parlor chairs. He looked very stiff and prim and neater than usual. He seems to have flattened his hair closer to his skull. This makes his head appear smaller. He was holding his head a little to one side. He looked like a bird but I cannot decide what bird—perhaps a chickadee. He drank the soda neatly and daintily. He kept looking at Aunt Sophronia.

He comes every day now, in the middle of the afternoon. He should have been in his shop busily repairing shoes or making boots, or making stews and cookies. Instead, he is in our store, and his light-gray eye, the one good eye, travels busily over Aunt Sophronia. His ears seem to waggle when he hears her voice, and he has taken to giggling in a very silly fashion.

He always arrives about the same time. Sometimes I sit in one of the ice-cream-parlor chairs and talk to him. He smells faintly of leather, and of shoe polish, and of wax, and of dead flowers. It was quite a while before I could place that other smell—dead flowers. Each day he stays a little longer than he stayed the day before.

I have noticed that my father narrows his eyes a little when he looks at Mr. Bemish. I heard him say to my mother, "I don't like it. I don't want to tell him not to come in here. But I don't like it—an old white man in here every afternoon looking at Sophronia and licking his chops—well, I just don't like it."

Aunt Sophronia took a sudden interest in the garden. In the afternoon, after school, I help her set out plants and sow seed. Our yard is filled with flowers in the summer; and we have a

vegetable garden that in some ways is as beautiful as the flowers
—it is so neat and precise-looking. We keep chickens so that we
can have fresh eggs. And we raise a pig and have him butchered
in the fall.

When the weather is bad and we cannot work in the garden,
Aunt Sophronia and I clean house. I do not like to clean house
but I do like to sort out the contents of other people's bureau
drawers. We started setting Aunt Sophronia's bureau in order. She
showed me a picture of her graduating class from Pharmacy
College. She was the only girl in a class of boys. She was colored
and the boys were white. I did not say anything about this difference in color and neither did she. But I did try to find out what it
was like to be the only member of the female sex in a class filled
with males.

"Didn't you feel funny with all those boys?"

"They were very nice boys."

"Oh, I'm sure they were. But didn't you feel funny being the
only girl with so many young men?"

"No. I never let them get overly friendly and we got along very
well."

I looked at the picture and then I looked at her and said, "You
are beautiful."

She put the picture back in her top drawer. She keeps her
treasures in there. She has a collar made of real lace, and a pair
of very long white kid gloces, and a necklace made of gold nuggets
from Colorado that a friend of my mother's left to Aunt
Sophronia in her will. The gloves and the collar smell like our
garden in August when the flowers are in full bloom and the sun
is shining on them.

Sometimes I forget that Aunt Sophronia is an adult and that
she belongs in the enemy camp, and I make the mistake of saying
what I have been thinking.

I leaned against the bureau and looked down into the drawer, at
the picture, and said, "You know, this picture reminds me of the
night last summer when there was a female moth, one of those
huge night moths, on the inside of the screen door, and all the
male moths for miles around came and clung on the outside of

the screen, making their wings flutter, and you know, they didn't
make any sound but it was kind of scary. Weren't you—"

Aunt Sophronia closed the drawer with a hard push. "You get
a broom and a dustpan and begin to sweep in the hall," she said.

On Saturday morning, after I finished washing the breakfast
dishes and scrubbing the kitchen floor, I paid a call on Mr. Bemish.
He is cleaning his house, too. He has taken down the red curtains
that hung at the windows all winter, and the red curtains that
hung in front of his bed, separating his sleeping quarters from the
rest of his shop, and he was washing these curtains in a big tub
at the side of his house. He was making a terrific splashing and
the soapsuds were pale pink. He had his sleeves rolled up. His arms
are very white and stringy-looking.

"Too much red for summer, girlie. I've got to get out the green
summer ones."

He hung them on the line and poured the wash water out on
the ground. It was pink.

"Your curtains ran, didn't they?" I looked at a little pink puddle
left on top of a stone. "If you keep washing them, they'll be pink
instead of red."

His own eye, the real eye, moved away from me, and there was
something secret, and rather sly, about his expression. He said, "I
haven't seen your aunt in the store lately. Where is she?"

"She's been busy fixing the garden and cleaning the house.
Everybody seems to be cleaning house."

"As soon as I get my green curtains put up, I'm going to ask
your aunt to come have tea."

"Where would she have tea with you?"

"In my shop."

I shook my head. "Aunt Sophronia does not drink tea in people's
bedrooms and you have only that one room for your shop and
there's a bed in it and it would be just like—"

"I would like to have her look at some old jewelry that I have
and I thought she might have tea."

"Mr. Bemish," I said, "do you like my Aunt Sophronia?"

"Now, girlie," he said, and he tittered. "Well, now, do you think
your aunt likes me?"

"Not especially. Not any more than anybody else. I think you're

too old for her and besides, well, you're white and I don't think
she would be very much interested in an old white man, do you?"

He frowned and said, "You go home. You're a very rude girl."

"You asked me what I thought, Mr. Bemish. I don't see why you
get mad when I tell you what I think. You did ask me, Mr.
Bemish."

I followed him inside his shop. He settled himself near the
window and started to work on a man's boot. It needed a new sole
and he cut the sole out of leather. I looked out the front window.
There is always enough breeze to make his sign move back and
forth; it makes a sighing noise. In the winter if there's a wind, the
sign seems to groan because it moves back and forth quickly.
There is a high-laced shoe painted on the sign. The shoe must once
have been a deep, dark red, but it has weathered to a soft rose
color.

Mr. Bemish is my friend and I wanted to indicate that I am still
fond of him though I disapprove of his interest in Aunt Sophronia.
I searched for some topic that would indicate that I enjoy talking
to him.

I said, "Why don't you have a picture of a man's boot on your
sign?"

"I prefer ladies' shoes. More delicate, more graceful—" He made
an airy gesture with his awl and simpered.

I went home and I told Aunt Sophronia that Mr. Bemish is
going to ask her to have tea with him.

"Will you go?"

"Of course not," she said impatiently.

Aunt Sophronia did not have tea with Mr. Bemish. He sees
her so rarely in the store that he finally came in search of her.

It is summer now and the Wheeling Inn is open for the season.
The great houses along the waterfront are occupied by their rich
owners. We are all very busy. At night after the store is closed,
we sit in the back yard. On those warm June nights, the fireflies come out, and there is a kind of soft summer light, composed
of moonlight and starlight. The grass is thick underfoot and the
air is sweet. Almost every night my mother and my father and
Aunt Sophronia and I, and sometimes Aunt Ellen and Uncle

Johno, sit there in the quiet and in the sweetness and in that curious soft light.

Last night when we were sitting there, Mr. Bemish came around the side of the house. There was something tentative in the way he came towards us. I had been lying on the grass and I sat up straight, wondering what they would do and what they would say.

He sidled across the lawn. He didn't speak until he was practically upon us. My mother was sitting in the hammock under the cherry tree, rocking gently back and forth, and she didn't see him until he spoke. He said, "Good evening." He sounded as though he was asking a question.

We all looked at him. I hoped that someone would say: What are you doing in our back yard, our private place, our especially private place? You are an intruder, go back to your waxed thread and your awl, go back to your horse and your cat. Nobody said anything.

He stood there for a while, waiting, hesitant, and then he bowed and sat down, cross-legged, on the grass, near Aunt Sophronia. She was sitting on one of the benches. And he sat so close to her that her skirt was resting on one of his trouser legs. I kept watching him. One of his hands reached toward her skirt and he gently fingered the fabric. Either she felt this or the motion attracted her attention, because she moved away from him, and gathered her skirt about her, and then stood up and said, "The air is making me sleepy. Good night."

The next afternoon I took a pair of my father's shoes to Mr. Bemish to have the heels fixed. My father wears high-laced black shoes. I left them on Mr. Bemish's work table.

"You can get them tomorrow."

I did not look right at him. I leaned over and patted May-a-ling. "She has such a lovely name, Mr. Bemish. It seems to me a name especially suited for a cat."

Mr. Bemish looked at me over the top of his little steel-rimmed glasses. "You've got a nice back yard," he said.

"I don't think you should have been in it."

"Why not?" he asked sharply. "Did anybody say that I shouldn't have been in it?"

"No. But the front part of the building, the part where the

drugstore is, belongs to everybody. The back part of the building, and upstairs in the building, and the yard are ours. The yard is a private part of our lives. You don't belong in it. You're not a part of our family."

"But I'd like to be a part of your family."

"You can't get to be a part of other people's families. You have to be born into a family. The family part of our lives is just for us. Besides, you don't seem to understand that you're the wrong color, Mr. Bemish."

He didn't answer this. He got up and got his cookie crock and silently offered me a cookie.

After I returned from the shoeshop, I sat on the wooden steps that run across the front of the drugstore. I was trying to decide how I really feel about Mr. Bemish. I always sit at the far end of the steps with my back against the tight-board fence. It is a very good place from which to observe the street, the front of the store, the church green. People walk past me not noticing that I am there. Sometimes their conversations are very unusual. I can see a long way down the path that bisects the green. It is a dirt path and not too straight. The only straight paths in town are those in front of the homes of people who have gardeners.

From where I sat I could see a man approaching. He was strolling down the path that crosses the church green. This is a most unusual way for a man to walk in Wheeling in the summer. It is during the summer that the year-round residents earn their living. They mow lawns, and cut hedges, and weed gardens, and generally look after the summer people. Able-bodied men in Wheeling walked fast in summer.

This tall, broad-shouldered man was strolling down the path. He was wearing a white suit, the pants quite tight in the leg, and he had his hands in his hip pockets, and a stiff straw hat, a boater, on the back of his head.

I sat up very straight when I discovered that this was a very dark colored man. I could not imagine where he came from. He could not possibly be a butler or a waiter even if he wanted to and spent a whole lifetime in trying. He would never be able to walk properly—he would always swagger, and who ever heard of a swaggering butler or a waiter who strolled around a table?

As he came nearer, I saw that he had a beard, an untidy shaggy beard like the beard of a goat. His hair was long and shaggy and rough-looking too. Though he was tall, with wide shoulders, the thick rough hair on his head and the goat's beard made his head and face look too big, out of proportion to his body.

When he saw me, he came straight toward me. He bent over me, smiling, and I moved back away from him, pressing against the fence. His eyes alarmed me. Whenever I think about his eyes, I close mine, trying to shut his out. They are reddish brown and they look hot, and having looked into them, I cannot seem to look away. I have never seen anyone with eyes that color or with that strange quality, whatever it is. I described them as looking "hot," but that's not possible. It must be that they are the color of something that I associate with fire or heat. I do not know what it is.

"You lost?" he said.

"No. Are you?"

"Yup. All us colored folks is lost." He said this in a husky, unmusical voice, and turned away and went in the store.

I went in the store, too. If this unusual-looking man with the goat's beard got into a discussion of "all us colored folks is lost" with my father, I wanted to hear it.

My father said, "How-de-do?" and he made it a question.

The bearded man nodded and said, "The druggist in?"

"I'm the druggist."

"This your store?"

"That's right."

"Nice place you got here. You been here long?"

My father grunted. I waited for him to make the next move in the game we called Stanley and Livingstone. All colored strangers who came into our store were Livingstones—and it was up to the members of our family to find out which lost Mr. Livingstone or which lost Mrs. Livingstone we had encountered in the wilds of the all-white town of Wheeling. When you live in a town where there aren't any other colored people, naturally you're curious when another colored person shows up.

I sat down in the front of the store and waited for my father to find out which Mr. David Livingstone he was talking to and what he was doing in our town. But my father looked at him with no expression on his face and said, "And what did you want?"

The man with the goat's beard fished in the pocket of his tight white pants. In order to do this, he thrust his leg forward a little to ease the strain on the fabric, and thus he gave the impression that he was pawing the ground. He handed my father a piece of paper.

"I got a prescription for a lotion—"

"It'll take a few minutes," my father said, and went in the back room.

The bearded man came and sat beside me.

"Do you live here in Wheeling?" I asked.

"I work at the Inn. I'm the piano player."

"You play the piano?"

"And sing. I'm the whole orchestra. I play for the dinner hour. I play for all those nice rich white folks to dance at night. I'll be here all summer."

"You will?"

"That's right. And I've never seen a deader town."

"What's your name?"

"Chink."

"Mr. Chink—"

"No," he said, and stood up. "Chink is my first name. Chink Johnson."

Mr. Johnson is a restless kind of man. He keeps moving around even when he is sitting still, moving his feet, his hands, his head. He crosses his legs, uncrosses them, clasps his hands together, unclasps them.

"Why are you having a prescription filled?"

"Hand lotion. I use it for my hands."

My father came out of the back room, wrapped up a bottle, said, "Here you are."

Chink Johnson paid him, said good-by to me, and I said, "Good-by, Chink."

"What's his name?"

"Chink Johnson. He plays the piano at the Inn."

Chink Johnson seems to me a very interesting and unusual man. To my surprise, my father did not mention our newest Mr.

Livingstone to the family. He said nothing about him at all. Neither did I.

Yet he comes in the drugstore fairly often. He buys cigarettes and throat lozenges. Sometimes he drives over from the Inn in a borrowed horse and carriage. Sometimes he walks over. My father has very little to say to him.

He doesn't linger in the store, because my father's manner is designed to discourage him from lingering or hanging around. But he does seem to be looking for something. He looks past the door of the prescription room, and on hot afternoons, the door in the very back is open and you can see our yard, with its beautiful little flower gardens, and he looks out into the yard, seems to search it. When he leaves he looks at the house, examining it. It is as though he is trying to see around a corner, see through the walls, because some sixth sense has told him that there exists on the premises something that will interest him, and if he looks hard enough, he will find it.

My mother finally caught a glimpse of him as he went out the front door. She saw what I saw—the goat's beard in silhouette, the forward thrust of his head, the thick shaggy hair—because we were standing in the prescription room looking toward the door.

"Who was that?" she asked, her voice sharp.

"That's the piano player at the Inn," my father said.

"You've never mentioned him. What is his name?"

"Jones," my father said.

I started to correct him but I was afraid to interrupt him because he started talking fast and in a very loud voice. "Lightfoot Jones," he said. "Shake Jones. Barrelhouse Jones." He started tapping on the glass case in front of him. I have never heard him do this before. He sings in the Congregational church choir. He has a pure, lyric tenor voice, and he sings all the tenor solos, the "Sanctus," "The Heavens Are Telling." You can tell from his speaking voice that he sings. He is always humming or singing or whistling. There he was with a pencil in his hand, tapping out a most peculiar rhythm on the glass of a showcase.

"Shake Jones," he repeated. "Rhythm in his feet. Rhythm in his blood. Rhythm in his feet. Rhythm in his blood. Beats out his life, beats out his lungs, beats out his liver, on a piano," and he began a different and louder rhythm with his foot. "On a pi-an-o. On a pi-an-o. On a pi—"

"Samuel, what is the matter with you? What are you talking about?"

"I'm talkin' about Tremblin' Shakefoot Jones. The piano player. The piano player who can't sit still, and comes in here lookin' around and lookin' around, prancin' and stampin' his hoofs, and sniffin' the air. Just like a stallion who smells a mare—a stallion who—"

"Samuel! How can you talk that way in front of this child?"

My father was silent.

I said, "His name is Chink Johnson."

My father roared, terrible in his anger, "His name is Duke. His name is Bubber. His name is Count, is Maharajah, is King of Lions. I don't give a good goddamn what he calls himself. I don't want him and his restless feet hangin' around. He can let his long feet slap somebody else's floor. But not mine. Not here—"

He glared at me and glared at my mother. His fury silenced us. At that moment his eyes were red-brown just like Chink Jones, no, Johnson. He is shorter, he has no beard, but he had at that moment a strong resemblance to Chink.

I added to his fury. I said, "You look just like Chink Johnson."

He said, "Ah!!! . . ." He was so angry I could not understand one word he said. I went out the front door, and across the street, and sat on the church steps and watched the world go by and listened to the faint hum it made as it went around and around.

I saw Mr. Bemish go in the drugstore. He stayed a long time. That gave me a certain pleasure because I knew he had come to eat his ice-cream soda, mouthful by mouthful, from one of our long-handled ice-cream-soda spoons, and to look at Aunt Sophronia as he nibbled at the ice cream. He looks at her out of the corners of his eyes, stealing sly little glances at her. I knew that Aunt Sophronia would not be in the store until much later and that he was wasting his time. It was my father's birthday and Aunt Sophronia was in the kitchen baking a great big cake for him.

If Mr. Bemish had known this, he might have dropped in on the birthday celebration, even though he hadn't been invited. After all, he had sidled into our back yard without being invited and our yard is completely enclosed by a tight-board fence, and there is a gate that you have to open to get in the yard, so that entering our yard is like walking into our living room. It is a very private place. Mr. Bemish is the only person that I know of who has come into our yard without being invited, and he keeps coming, too.

After Mr. Bemish left the store, I crossed the street and sat outside on the store steps. It was hot. It was very quiet. Old Lady Chimble crossed the church green carrying a black silk umbrella, and she opened it and used it as a sunshade. A boy went by on a bicycle. Frances Jackins (we called her Aunt Frank), the colored cook in the boardinghouse across the street, hurried across the street carrying something in a basket. She is always cross and usually drunk. She drinks gin. Mother says this is what has made Aunt Frank's lips look as though they were turned inside out and she says this is called a "gin lip." They are bright red, almost like a red gash across the dark skin of her face. I want very much to ask Aunt Frank about this—how it feels, when it happened, etc.—and someday I will, but I have not as yet had a suitable opportunity. When she is drunk, she cannot give a sensible answer to a sensible question, and when she is sober, or partially sober, she is very irritable and constantly finds fault with me. She is absolutely no relation to us; it is just that my mother got in the habit of calling her "Aunt" Frank many years ago and so we all call her that. Because I am young, she tries to boss me and to order me around, and she calls me "Miss" in a very unpleasant, sarcastic way.

She is a very good cook when she is sober. But when she is drunk, she burns everything, and she is always staggering across the street and stumbling up our back steps, with bread pans filled with dough which would not rise because she has forgotten the yeast, and with burned cakes and pies and burned hams and roasts of beef. When she burns things, they are not just scorched; they are blackened and hardened until they are like charcoal.

Almost every night she scratches at our back door. I have sharper hearing than everybody else; I can hear people walking around the side of the house and no one else has heard them—anyway, I always hear her first. I open the door suddenly and very fast, and she almost falls into the kitchen and stands there swaying, and fouling our kitchen with the sweetish smell of gin and the dank and musty odor of her clothes.

She always has a dip of snuff under her upper lip and she talks around this obstruction, so that her voice is peculiar. She speaks quickly to keep the snuff in place, and sometimes she pauses and works her upper lip, obviously geting the snuff in some special spot. When she comes to the back door at night, she puts the basket of ruined food just inside the door, on the floor, and says to my mother, "Here, Mar-tha, throw this away. Throw it a-way for me. Give it to the hens. Feed it to the pig—"

She turns all two-syllable words into two separate one-syllable words. She doesn't say "Martha" all in one piece. She separates it, so that it becomes "Mar-tha"; she doesn't say "away," but "a-way." It is a very jerky kind of speech.

I am always given the job of burying the stuff in the backyard, way down in the back. I dig a hole and throw the blackened mess into it and then cover it with lime to hasten decomposition and discourage skunks and dogs.

Sometimes I hide behind the fence and yell at her on her way back across the street:

> Ole Aunt Frankie
> Black as tar
> Tried to get to heaven
> In a 'lectric car.
> Car got stalled in an underpass,
> Threw Aunt Frankie right on her ass.

Whenever I singsong this rhyme at her, she invariably tries to climb over the fence, a furious drunken old woman, threatening me with the man's umbrella that she carries. I should think she would remember from past performances that she cannot possibly reach me. But she always tries. After several futile efforts, she gives up and goes back to the boardinghouse across the street. A lot of old maids and widows live there. No gentlemen. Just ladies. They spend their spare time rocking on the front porch, and playing whist, and looking over at the drugstore. Aunt Frank spends her spare time in the kitchen of the boardinghouse, rocking and emptying bottle after bottle of gin.

But on the day of my father's birthday, she was sober; at least, she walked as though she were. She had a basket on her arm with a white napkin covering its contents. I decided she must have made something special for my father's supper. She went in the drugstore, and when she came out, she didn't have the basket. She saw me sitting on the steps but she ignored me.

Aunt Sophronia came and stood in the window. She had washed the glass globes that we keep filled with blue, red, and yellow liquid. She was wearing a dark skirt and a white blouse. Her hair was no longer skinned tight back from her forehead; it was curling around her forehead, perhaps because she had been working in the garden, bending over, and the hairpins that usually hold it so tightly in place had worked themselves loose. She didn't look real. The sun was shining in the window and it reflected the lights from the jars of colored water back on her face and her figure, and she looked golden and rose-colored and lavender and it was though there was a rainbow moving in the window.

Chink Johnson drove up in his borrowed horse and carriage. He stood and talked to me and then started to go in the store, saw Aunt Sophronia, and stood still. He took a deep breath. I could hear him. He took off the stiff straw hat that he wore way back on his head and bowed to her. She nodded, as though she really didn't want to, and turned away and acted as though she were very busy.

He grabbed my arm and actually pinched it.

"What are you doin'?" I said angrily. "What is the matter with you? Let go my arm."

"Shut up," he said impatiently, pinching harder. His fingers felt as though they were made of iron. "Who is that?"

I pried his fingers loose and rubbed my arm. "Where?"

"In the window. Who is that girl in the window?"

"That's my Aunt Sophronia."

"Your aunt? Your aunt?"

"Yes."

He went in the store. One moment he was standing beside me and the next moment he had practically leaped inside the store.

I went in too. He was leaning in the window, saying "Wouldn't you like to go for a walk with me this Sunday?" She shook her head. "Well, couldn't you go for a ride with me? I'll call for you—"

Aunt Sophronia said, "I work every day."

"Every day?" he said. "But that's not possible. Nobody works every day. I'll be back tomorrow—"

And he was gone. Aunt Sophronia looked startled. She didn't look angry, just sort of surprised.

I said, "Tomorrow and tomorrow and tomorrow—" And I thought, well, she's got two suitors now. There's this Shake Jones Livingstone, otherwise known as Chink Johnson, and there's Mr. Bemish. I do not think I would pick either one. Mr. Bemish is too old even though he is my friend. I think of Chink Johnson as my friend too, but I do not think he would make a good husband. I tried to decide why I do not approve of him as a husband for Aunt Sophronia. I think it is because Aunt Sophronia is a lady and Chink Johnson is—well—he is not a gentleman.

That night at supper we celebrated my father's birthday. At that hour nobody much came in the store. Pickett, the sexton, sat on the bench in the front and if anybody came in and wanted my father, he'd come to the back door and holler for him.

There was a white tablecloth on the big, oak dining-room table, and we used my mother's best Haviland china and the sterling-silver knives and forks with the rose pattern, and there was a pile of packages by my father's plate, and there were candles on the cake and we had ice cream for dessert. My old enemy, Aunt Frank, had delivered Parker House rolls for his birthday and had made him a milk-panful of rice pudding, because my father has always said that when he dies he hopes it will be because he drowns in a sea composed of rice pudding, that he could eat his weight in rice pudding, that he could eat rice pudding morning, noon, and night. Aunt Frank must have been sober when she made the pudding, for it was creamy and delicious and I ate two helpings of it right along with my ice cream.

I kept waiting for Aunt Sophronia to say something about Chink Johnson. He is a very unusual-looking man and we've never had a customer, colored or white, with that kind of beard. She did not mention him. Neither did I. My father has never mentioned him —at least not at the table. I wonder if my father hopes he will vanish. Perhaps they are afraid he will become a part of the family circle if they mention him.

Chink Johnson has become a part of the family circle and he used the same method that Mr. Bemish used. He just walked into the yard and into the house. I was upstairs, and I happened to look out of the window, and there was Chink Johnson walking up the street. He opened our gate, walked around the side of the house and into our back yard. I hurried to the back of the house and looked out the window and saw him open the screen door and go into the kitchen. He didn't knock on the door either, he just walked in.

For the longest time I didn't hear a sound. I listened and listened. I must have stood still for fifteen minutes. Then I heard someone playing our piano. I knew it must be Chink Johnson because this was not the kind of music anyone in our house would have been playing. I ran downstairs. My mother had been in the cellar, and she came running up out of the cellar, and my father came hurrying over from the drugstore. We all stood and looked and looked.

Chink was sitting at our piano. He had a cigarette dangling from his lower lip, and the smoke from the cigarette was like a cloud—a blue-gray, hazy kind of cloud around his face, his eyes, his beard—so that you could only catch glimpses of them through the smoke. He was playing some kind of fast, discordant-sounding music and he was slapping the floor with one of his long feet and he was slapping the keys with his long fingers.

Aunt Sophronia was leaning against the piano looking down at him. He did not use music when he played, and he never once looked at the keyboard, he just kept looking right into Aunt Sophronia's eyes. I thought my father would tell Chink to go slap somebody else's floor with his long feet, but my mother gave him one of those now-don't-say-a-word looks and he glared at Chink and went back to the drugstore.

Chink stayed a long time, he played the piano, he sang, or rather I guess you would say he talked to the music. It is a very peculiar kind of musical performance. He plays some chords, a whole series of them, and he makes peculiar changes in the chords as he plays, and then he says the words of a song—he doesn't really sing, but his voice does change in pitch to, in a sense, match the chords he is playing, and he does talk to a kind of rhythm which also matches the chords. I sat down beside him and watched what he was doing, and listened to the words he said, and though it is not exactly music as I am accustomed to hearing it, I found it very interesting. He told me that what he does with those songs is known as the "talkin' blues." Only he said *"talkin'"* and he made "blues" sound like it was two separate words, not just a two-syllable word, but two distinct words.

I have been trying to play the piano the way he does but I get nothing but terrible sounds. I pretend that I am blind and keep my eyes closed all the time while I feel for chords. He must have a special gift for this because it is an extremely difficult thing that he is doing and I don't know whether I will ever be able to do it. He has a much better ear for music than I have.

Chink Johnson comes to see Aunt Sophronia almost every day. Sometimes when I look out in the back yard, Mr. Bemish is out there too. He always sits on the ground, and at his age, I should think it might give him rheumatism. He must be a very brave little man or else his love for Aunt Sophronia has given him great courage. I say this because Chink Johnson is very rude to Mr. Bemish and he stares at him with a dreadfully cruel look on his face. If I were small and slender and old like Mr. Bemish, I would not sit in the same yard with a much bigger, much younger man who obviously did not want me there.

I have thought a great deal about Mr. Bemish. I like him. He is truly a friend. But I do not think he should be interested in Aunt Sophronia—at least not in a loving kind of way. The thing that bothers me is that I honestly cannot decide whether I object to him as a suitor for her because he is white or because he is old. Sometimes I think it is for both reasons. I am fairly certain it isn't just because he's old. This bothers me. If my objections to him are because he's white (and that's what I told him, but I often say things that I know people do not want to hear and that they particularly do not want to hear from someone very much younger than they are), then I have been trained on the subject of race just as I have been "trained" to be a Christian. I know how

I was trained to be a Christian—Sunday school, prayers, etc. I do not know exactly how I've been "trained" on the subject of race. Then why do I feel like this about Mr. Bemish?

Shortly after I wrote that, I stopped puzzling about Mr. Bemish because summer officially started—at least for me. It is true that school had been out for a long time, and we are wearing our summer clothes, and the yard is filled with flowers—but summer never really gets under way for me until Dottle Smith comes for his yearly visit.

Dottle and Uncle Johno went to school together. They look sort of alike. They are big men and they are so light in color they look like white men. But something in them (Dottle says that it is a "cultivated and developed and carefully nourished hatred of white men") will not permit them to pass for white. Dottle teaches English and elocution and dramatics at a school for colored people in Georgia, and he gives lectures and readings during the summer to augment his income. Uncle Johno is the chief fund-raising agent for a colored school in Louisiana.

I believe that my attitude towards Mr. Bemish stems from Dottle Smith. And Johno. They are both what my father calls race-conscious. When they travel on trains in the South, they ride in Jim Crow coaches until the conductor threatens to have them arrested unless they sit in the sections of the train reserved for whites. They are always being put out of the colored sections of waiting rooms, and warned out of the colored sections of towns, and being refused lodgings in colored rooming houses on the grounds that they would be a source of embarrassment—nobody would be able to figure out why a white man wanted to live with colored people, and they would be suspected of being spies, but of what kind or to what purpose, they have never been able to determine.

I have just reread what I have written here, and I find that I've left out the reason why I am writing so much about Dottle. Yesterday afternoon when I came back from an errand, there was a large, heavy-looking bag—leather, but it was shaped like a carpet-bag—near the bench where the customers sit when they wait for prescriptions. I recognized it immediately. I have seen that bag every summer for as far back as I can remember. I wondered if

Dottle had come alone this time or if he had a friend with him. Sometimes he brings a young man with him. These young men look very much alike—they are always slender, rather shy, have big dark eyes and very smooth skin just about the color of bamboo.

I looked at Dottle's big battered old bag sitting on the floor near the bench, and I could almost see him, with his long curly hair, and I could hear him reciting poetry in his rich, buttery voice. He can quote all the great speeches from *Hamlet*, *Macbeth*, *Richard II*, and he can recite the sonnets.

I loved him. He was lively and funny and unexpected. Sometimes he would grab my braid and shout in his best Shakespearean voice, "Seize on her Furies, take her to your torments!"

I looked at Dottle's battered bag and I said to my father, "Is he alone? Or has he got one of those pretty boys with him?"

My father looked at me over the top of his glasses. "Alone."

"How come he to leave his bag here?"

"Well, the Ecckles aren't home. Ellen's gone on vacation—"

"Why does Aunt Ellen always go on vacation when Dottle comes?"

My father ignored this and went on talking. "Johno's gone to Albany collecting money for the school."

"Where is Dottle now?"

"I'm right here, sugar," and Dottle Smith opened the screen door and came in. He looked bigger than he had the summer before. He hugged me. He smelled faintly of lavender.

"You went and grew, honey," he said, and took off his hat and bowed. It was a wide-brimmed panama, and he had on a starched white shirt, and a flowing Byronic kind of black tie, and I looked at him with absolute delight. He was being a Southern "cunnel" and he was such an actor—I thought I could see lace at his wrists, hear mockingbirds sing, see a white-columned mansion, hear hoofbeats in the distance, and hear a long line of slaves, suitably clad as footmen and coachmen and butlers and housemen, murmur, Yess, massah, Yes, massah. It was all there in his voice.

"Why, in another couple years I'll be recitin' poetry to you. How's your momma? This summer I'll have to teach you how to talk. These Yankah teachers you've got all talk through their noses. They got you doin' the same thing—"

For two whole days I forgot about Chink Johnson and Mr. Bemish and Aunt Sophronia. Dottle liked to go fishing and crabbing; he liked to play whist; and he could tell the most marvelous stories and act them out.

The very next day Dottle and Uncle Johno and I went crabbing. We set out early in the morning with our nets and our fishing lines and the rotten meat we used for bait, and our lunch and thermos bottles with lemonade in them. It was a two-mile walk from where we lived to the creek where we caught crabs.

There was a bridge across the creek, an old wooden bridge. Some of the planks were missing. We stood on this bridge or sat on it and threw our lines in the water. Once in a great while a horse and wagon would drive across and set the planks to vibrating. Johno and Dottle would hop off the bridge. But I stayed on and held to the railing. The bridge trembled under my feet, and the horse and wagon would thunder across, and the driver usually waved and hollered, "I gotta go fast or we'll all fall in."

The water in the creek was so clear I could see big crabs lurking way down on the bottom; I could see little pieces of white shells and beautiful stones. We didn't talk much while we were crabbing. Sometimes I lay flat on my stomach on the bridge and looked down into the water, watching the little eddies and whirlpools that formed after I threw my line in.

Before we ate our lunch, we went wading in the creek. Johno and Dottle rolled up the legs of their pants, and their legs were so white I wondered if they were that white all over, and if they were, how they could be colored. We sat on the bank of the creek and ate our lunch. Afterwards Dottle and Johno told stories, wonderful stories in which animals talk, and there are haunted houses and ghosts and demons, and old colored preachers who believe in heaven and hell.

They always started off the same way. Dottle said to Johno, "Mr. Bones, be seated."

Though I have heard some of these stories many, many times, Dottle and Johno never tell them exactly the same. They change their gestures, they vary their facial expressions and the pitch of their voices.

Dottle almost always tells the story about the colored man who goes in a store in a small town in the South and asks for Muriel cigars. The white man who owns the store says (and here Johno becomes an outraged Southern white man), "Nigger, what's the matter with you? Don't you see that picture of that beautiful white woman on the front of this box? When you ask for them cigars, you say *Miss* Muriel cigars!"

Though Uncle Johno is a good storyteller, he is not as good, not as funny or as dramatic as Dottle. When I listen to Dottle I can see the old colored preacher who spent the night in a haunted house. I see him approaching the house, the wind blowing his coat-tails, and finally he takes refuge inside because of the violence of the storm. He lights a fire in the fireplace and sits down by it and rubs his hands together, warming them. As he sits there, he hears heavy footsteps coming down the stairs (and Dottle makes his hand go thump, thump, thump on the bank of the creek) and the biggest cat the old man has ever seen comes in and sits down, looks at the old preacher, looks around, and says, "Has Martin got here yet?" The old man is too startled and too nervous to answer. He hears heavy footsteps again—thump, thump, thump. And a second cat, much bigger than the first one, comes in, and sits down right next to the old preacher. Both cats stare at him, and then the second cat says to the first cat, "Has Martin got here yet?" and the first cat shakes his head. There is something so speculative in their glance that the old man gets more and more uneasy. He wonders if they are deciding to eat him. The wind howls in the chimney, puffs of smoke blow back into the room. Then another and bigger cat thumps down the stairs. Finally there are six enormous cats, three on each side of him. Each one of these cats has asked the same question of the others—"Martin got here yet?" A stair-shaking tread begins at the top of the stairs, the cats all look at each other, and the old man grabs his hat, and says to the assembled cats, "You tell Martin ah been here but ah've gone."

I clapped when Dottle finished this story. I looked around think-ing how glad I am he is here and what a wonderful place this is to listen to stories. The sun is warm but there is a breeze and it blows through the long marsh grass which borders the creek. The grass moves, seems to wave. Gulls fly high overhead. The only sound is the occasional cry of a gull and the lapping of water against the piling of the bridge.

Johno tells the next story. It is about an old colored preacher and a rabbit. The old man tries to outrun an overfriendly and very talkative rabbit. The rabbit keeps increasing in size. The old man runs away from him and the rabbit catches up with him. Each time the rabbit says, "That was some run we had, wasn't it, brother?" Finally the old man runs until he feels as though his lungs are going to burst and his legs will turn to rubber, and he looks back and doesn't see the rabbit anywhere in sight. He sits down on a stone to rest and catch his breath. He has just seated himself when he discovers the rabbit sitting right beside him, smiling. The rabbit is now the same size as the preacher. the rabbit rolls his eyes and lisps, "That wath thome run we had, wathn't it?" The old man stood up, got ready to run again, and said, "Yes, that was some run we had, brother, but"—he took a deep breath—"you ain't *seen* no runnin' yet."

After they finished telling stories, we all took naps. Dottle and Johno were wearing old straw hats, wide-brimmed panamas with crooked, floppy brims. Dottle had attached a piece of mosquito netting to his, and it hung down across his shoulders. From the back he looked like a woman who was wearing a veil.

When we woke up it was late in the afternoon and time to start for home. I ran part of the way. Then I sat down by the side of the road, in the shade, and waited until they caught up with me.

Dottle said, "Sugar, what are you in such a hurry for?"

I said, laughing, "Miss Muriel, you tell Martin I been here but I've gone and that he ain't *seen* no runnin' yet."

I got home first. Chink Johnson was in the store. When Dottle and Johno arrived, I introduced Chink to my uncles, Johno and Dottle. They didn't seem much impressed with each other. Johno nodded and Dottle smiled and left. Chink watched Dottle as he went toward the back room. Dottle has a very fat bottom and he sort of sways from side to side as he walks.

Chink said, "He seems kind of ladylike. He related on your mother's side?"

"He's not related at all. He's an old friend of Uncle Johno's.

They went to school together. In Atlanta, Georgia." I sounded very condescending. "Do you know where that is?"

"Yeah. Nigger, read this. Nigger, don't let sundown catch you here. Nigger, if you can't read this, run anyway. If you can't run— then vanish. Just vanish out. I know the place. I came from there."

My father was standing outside on the walk talking to Aunt Frank, so I felt at liberty to speak freely and I said, "Nigger, what are you talkin' about you want Muriel cigars. You see this picture of this beautiful red-headed white woman, nigger, you say *Miss* Muriel."

Chink stood up and he was frowning and his voice was harsh. "Little girl, don't you talk that way. I talk that way if I feel like it but don't you ever talk that way."

I felt as though I had been betrayed. One moment he was my friend and we were speaking as equals and the next moment, without warning, he is an adult who is scolding me in a loud, harsh voice. I was furious and I could feel tears welling up in my eyes. This made me angrier. I couldn't seem to control my weeping. Recently, and I do not know how it happened, whenever I am furiously angry, I begin to cry.

Chink leaned over and put his hand under my chin, lifted my face, saw the tears, and he kissed my cheek. His beard was rough and scratchy. He smelled like the pine woods, and I could see pine needles in his hair and in his beard, and I wondered if he and Aunt Sophronia had been in the woods.

"Sugar," he said gently, "I don't like that Miss Muriel story. It ought to be told the other way around. A colored man should be tellin' a white man, 'White man, you see this picture of this beautiful colored woman? *White* man, you say *Miss* Muriel!'"

He went out of the store through the back room into the yard just as though he were a member of the family. It hadn't taken him very long to reach this position. Almost every afternoon he goes for a walk with Aunt Sophronia. I watch them when they leave the store. He walks so close to her that he seems to surround her, and he has his head bent so that his face is close to hers. Once I met them strolling up Petticoat Lane, his dark face so close to hers that his goat's beard was touching her smooth brown cheek.

My mother used to watch them too, as they walked side by side on the dirt path that led to the woods—miles and miles of woods. Sometimes he must have said things that Aunt Sophronia didn't like, because she would turn her head sharply away from him.

I decided that once you got used to his beard and the peculiar color and slant of his eyes, why you could say he had an interesting face. I do not know what it is about his eyes that makes me think of heat. But I know what color they are. They are the color of petrified wood after it's been polished, it's a red brown, and that's what his eyes are like.

I like the way he plays the piano, though I do not like his voice. I cannot get my mother to talk about him. My father grunts when I mention Chink's name and scowls so ferociously that it is obvious he does not like him.

I tried to find out what Aunt Sophronia thought of him. Later in the day I found her in the store alone and I said, "Do you like Chink Johnson?"

She said, "Run along and do the supper dishes."

"But do you?"

"Don't ask personal questions," she said, and her face and neck flushed.

She must have liked him though. She not only went walking with him in the afternoon, but on Sunday mornings he went to church with her. He wore a white linen suit and that same stiff straw hat way back on his head. He brought her presents—a tall bottle of violet Eau de Cologne, a bunch of Parma violets made of silk, but they looked real. On Sundays, Aunt Sophronia wore the violets pinned at her waist and they made her look elegant, like a picture in a book.

I said, "Oh, you look beautiful."

My mother said, dryly, "Very stylish."

We all crossed the street together on Sunday mornings. They went to church. I went to Sunday school. Sunday school was out first and I waited for them to come down the church steps. Aunt Sophronia came down the church steps and he would be so close behind her that he might have been dancing with her and matching his leg movements to hers. Suddenly he was in front of her and down on the path before she was and he turned and held out his hand. Even there on the sidewalk he wasn't standing still. It is as though his feet and his hands are more closely connected to his heart, to his central nervous system, than is true of other people, so that during every waking moment he moves, tapping his foot on the floor, tapping his fingers on a railing, on somebody's arm, on a table top. I wondered if he kept moving like that when he was asleep, tapping quarter notes with his foot, playing eighth notes with his right hand, half notes with his left hand. He attacked a piano when he played, violated it—violate a piano? I thought, violate Aunt Sophronia?

He stood on the dirt path and held out his hand to Aunt Sophronia, smiling, helping her down the church steps.

"Get your prayers said, sugar?" he said to me.

"Yes. I said one for you and one for the family. Aunt Sophronia, you smell delicious. Like violets—"

"She does, doesn't she?"

We walked across the street to the drugstore, hand in hand. Chink was in the middle and he held one of my hands and one of Aunt Sophronia's. He stays for dinner on Sundays. And on Sunday nights we close the store early and we all sat in the back yard, where it is cool. Mr. Bemish joined us in the yard. At dusk the fireflies come out, and then as the darkness deepens, bats swoop aorund us. Aunt Sophronia says "Oooooh!" and holds on to her head, afraid one might get entangled in her hair.

Dottle took out one of his big white handkerchiefs and tied it around his head, and said in his richest, most buttery voice, " 'One of the nocturnal or crepuscular flying mammals constituting the order Chiroptera.' "

Dottle sprawled in a chair and recited poetry or told long stories about the South—stories that sometimes had so much of fear and terror and horror in them that we shivered even though the air was warm. Chink didn't spend the evening. He sat in one of the lawn chairs, tapping on the arm with his long, flexible fingers, and then left. Mr. Bemish always stays until we go in for the night. He takes no part in the conversation, but sits on the ground, huddled near Aunt Sophronia's skirts. Once when a bat swooped quite close, Aunt Sophronia clutched his arm.

Sometimes Dottle recites whole acts from *Macbeth* or *Hamlet* or all of the Song of Solomon, or sometimes he recited the loveliest of Shakespeare's sonnets. We forget the bats swooping over our heads, ignore the mosquitoes that sting our ankles and our legs, and sit mesmerized while he declaims, "Shall I compare thee to a summer's day?"

The summer is going faster and faster—perhaps because of the presence of Aunt Sophronia's suitors. I don't suppose Dottle is really a suitor, but he goes through the motions. He picks little bouquets for her—bachelor buttons and candytuft—and leaves them on the kitchen table. He always calls her "Miss Sophronia." If we are outdoors and she comes out to sit in the yard, he leaps to his feet, and bows and says, "Wait, wait. Befo' you sit on that bench, let me wipe it off," and he pulls out an enormous linen handkerchief and wipes off the bench. He is always bowing and kissing her hand.

By the middle of August it was very hot. My father had the store painted, and when the blinds were taken down, the painter found whole families of bats clinging together in back of the blinds. Evidently they lived there. I couldn't get hold of one, although I tried. They were the most peculiar-looking creatures. They looked almost like a person who wears glasses all the time and then suddenly goes without them, and they have a kind of peering look.

Chink Johnson is always in our house or in the store or in the yard or going for walks with Aunt Sophronia. Whenever he is not violating the piano at the Inn, he is with Aunt Sophronia—

He taught her how to dance—in the back yard, without any music, just his counting and clapping his hands. His feet made no sound on our thick grass. On two different sunny afternoons, he gave her dancing lessons, and on the third afternoon, he had her dancing. She was laughing and she was lively-looking and she looked young. He persuaded her to take off her shoes and she danced in her bare feet. Fortunately, nobody knows this but me.

He took her fishing. When they came back, she was quite sunburned but her eyes were shining as though they held the reflected light from the sun shining on water.

Just in that one short summer he seemed to take on all kinds of guises—fisherman, dancer, singer, churchgoer, even delivery boy.

One morning someone knocked at the back door and there was

Chink Johnson with our grocery order, saying to my Aunt Sophronia, "Here's your meat, ma'am, and your vegetables," touching his hat, bowing, unloading the crate of groceries, and then sitting down at the kitchen table as though he owned it, drinking a cup of coffee that no one had offered him, just pouring it out of the enamel pot that stays on the stove, finding cream and sugar himself, and sitting there with his legs thrust way out in front of him, and those terribly tight pants he wears looking as though they were painted on his thighs.

Sometimes when he sits in our kitchen, he laughs. His laughter is not merry. When my father laughs, the sound makes you laugh, even when you don't know what he is laughing about.

When Chink Johnson laughs, I look away from him. The sound hurts my ears. It is like the ugly squawk of some big bird that you have disturbed in the woods and it flies right into your face, pecking at your eyes.

It has been a very interesting summer. I have begun to refer to it in the past tense because there isn't much left of a summer by the middle of August. On Thursday afternoon, Aunt Sophronia and I saw that other ladies liked Chink Johnson too.

Thursday afternoon is traditionally maids' day off and Chink Johnson drove the maids from the Inn into town, in a wagon, late in the day. He stopped in front of the store with a wagon full of girls in long skirts, giggling, leaning against him, a kind of panting excitement in that wagon, their arms around him; they whispered to him, they were seized by fits of laughter, shrieks of laughter.

They came in the store and bought hairnets and hairpins and shampoo and Vaseline and hair tonics and cough medicines and court plaster and a great many items that they did not need because it was a pleasure to be spending money, and to be free of the tyranny of the housekeepers' demands—or so my mother said —some young and attractive, some not so young, about ten of them.

Aunt Sophronia was in the store and she waited on them, studying them. Every once in a while one would go to the door, and yell, "We'll be out in a minute, Chink. Just a little while!" and wave at him and throw kisses at him.

Then they were gone, all at once, piling into the wagon, long full skirts in disarray. One of them sat in Chink's lap, laughing, looking up into his face, and saying, "Let's go in the woods. Chink take us in the woods. I'll help drive."

Aunt Sophronia and I stood in the doorway and watched them as they drove off, going towards the pine woods. The wagon seemed to be filled with wide skirts, and ruffled petticoats, all suddenly upended because Chink said, "Giddup, there!" and hit the horse with the whip, cracked it over the horse's ears, and the horse started off as though he were a race horse.

It was late when they went past the store, going home. Sitting in the back yard, we could hear the horse racing, and the girls squealing and laughing, and Chink singing a ribald song, about "Strollin', and Strollin.'"

Dottle stopped right in the middle of a poem and Mr. Bemish straightened up so that he was not quite so close to Aunt Sophronia's skirts. It was like having Chink Johnson right there in the back yard with us, the rough, atonal voice, the red-brown eyes that looked hot, literally hot, as though if you touched them you would have to withdraw your fingers immediately because they would be scorched or singed or burned, the jutting beard, the restless feet and hands.

We sat absolutely still. We could hear the rattling of the wagon, the clop-clop of the horses hoofs and above it the laughter of the girls, and dominating that sound, Chink Johnson's voice lifted in song. Even after they were so far away we could not possibly hear them, these sounds seemed to linger in the air, faint, far-off.

It was a warm night, brilliant with light from the moon. I pictured the girls as sitting on top of Chink, all around him, on his arms, in his lap, on his shoulders, and I thought the prettiest one should be perched on his head.

Dottle lit a cigar and puffed out clouds of bluish smoke and said, "I never heard the mating call of the male so clearly sounded on a summer's night." He laughed so hard that he had to get out one of his big handkerchiefs and dab at his eyes with it.

Aunt Sophronia got up from the bench so fast that she brushed against Mr. Bemish, almost knocking him over. He lost his balance and regained it only because he supported himself with one hand on the ground. She must have known that she had very nearly upset him but she went marching toward the house, her back very straight and her head up in the air, and she never once looked back.

Dottle said, "Have I offended her?"

My mother said, "It's late. It's time we went in."

Mr. Bemish must have gone home when we went in the house, but he was back in the yard so early the next morning he might just as well have spent the night. Dottle and I were standing in the kitchen, looking down the back yard. He was drinking coffee out of a mug and I was eating a piece of bread and butter. Our back yard is a pretty sight on a summer morning. It is filled with flowers, and birds are singing, and the air is very cool, and there is a special smell, a summer smell compounded of grass and dew on the grass and flowers, and the suggestion of heat to come later in the day.

We looked out the door and there was Mr. Bemish down on his knees in front of Aunt Sophronia. She was sitting on the bench and she looked horrified and she seemed to have been in the act of trying to stop him, one hand extended in a thrusting-away motion. I thought: His pants legs will be very damp because there's still dew on the grass, and how did he get here so early, and did he know that she would be sitting on the bench almost before sunup?

"Ah, girlie, girlie!" he said, on his knees in our back yard, kneeling on our thick, soft grass. "Will you marry me?"

"No!"

"Is it," he said, "because I am old?" and his voice went straight up in pitch just like a scale. "I'm not old. I'm not old. Why, I can still jump up in the air and click my heels together three times!"

And he did. He got up off his knees and he jumped up, straight up, and clicked his heels together three times, and landed on the grass, and there was just a slight thumping sound when he landed.

Aunt Sophronia said, "Mr. Bemish, Mr. Bemish. Don't do that —don't do that—go away, go home—" And she ran toward the house and he started after her and then he saw us standing in the door, watching him, and he stood still. He shouted after her, "I'll

put on my best coat and my best hat and you won't know me—
I'll be back—and you won't know me—"

Dottle glared at him through the screen door and said, "You
old fool—you old fool—"

Mr. Bemish hurried around the side of the house, pretending
that he hadn't heard him.

I did not know when Mr. Bemish would be back, wearing his
best coat and his best hat, but I certainly wanted to see him and,
if possible, to witness his next performance. I decided that whenever Aunt Sophronia was in the store, I'd be in the store too.

When my father went to eat his dinner at twelve-thirty, Aunt
Sophronia looked after the store. There weren't many people who
came in at that hour; it was the dinner hour and Aunt Sophronia
sat in the prescription room, with the door open, and read the
morning newspaper. There was an old wooden chair, by the
window, in the prescription room. It had a faded painting across
the back, a wooden seat and back and arms. It was a very comfortable chair if you sat up straight, and Aunt Sophronia sat up
very straight. She could look out of the window and see the
church green, see the path that went up Petticoat Lane toward
the pine woods, and she commanded a view of the interior of the
store.

I don't think she saw Mr. Bemish when he entered. If she had,
she would have gotten out of the chair immediately to wait on
him. But she was reading the newspaper, and he came in very
quietly. He was wearing a cutaway coat that was too long, and a
pair of striped trousers, and he was carrying a silk hat in his hand,
a collapsed silk hat. He stopped inside the door and put the hat in
shape and then placed it carefully on his head. He looked like a
circus clown who is making fun of the ringmaster, mocking him,
making his costume look silly.

Mr. Bemish went straight through the store, and stood in front
of Aunt Sophronia, and he jumped straight up in the air, like
a dancer, and clicked his heels together three times. The bottles
on the shelves rattled and the back room was filled with a pinging
sound.

"Oh, my goodness," Aunt Sophronia said, frowning. "Oh, my
goodness, don't jump like that." And she stood up.

My father came in through the back door and he said, "What's going on in here? What's going on in here?"

Mr. Bemish said, "I was just showing Miss Sophronia that I can still jump up in the air and click my heels together three times before I come back down again."

My father made a noise that sounded like "Boooooh!" but wasn't quite, and Mr. Bemish retreated, talking very fast. "I had asked Miss Sophronia if she would marry me and she said no, and I thought perhaps it was because she thinks I'm too old and not stylish enough and so I got dressed up and I was showing her I could still jump—"

"Get out of here! Get out of here! Get out of here!"

My father's voice kept rising and increasing in volume, and his face looked as though he were about to burst. It seemed to darken and to swell, to get bigger.

Aunt Sophronia said, "Oh, you mustn't talk to him like that—"

My father was moving toward Mr. Bemish, and Mr. Bemish was retreating, retreating, and finally he turned and ran out of the store and ran up Petticoat Lane with his long coattails flapping about his legs.

My father said, "I shouldn't have let him hang around here all these months. I can't leave this store for five minutes that I don't find one of these no-goods hangin' around when I come back. Not one of 'em worth the powder and shot to blow 'em to hell and back. That piano player pawin' the ground and this old white man jumpin' up in the air, and that friend of Johno's, that poet or whatever he is, all he needs are some starched petticoats and a bonnet and he'd make a woman—he's practically one now—and he's tee-heein' around, and if they were all put together in one piece, it still wouldn't be a whole man." My father shook his fist in the air and glared at Aunt Sophronia.

"I guess it's all my fault—" Aunt Sophronia sounded choked-up and funny.

My father said, "No, no, no, I didn't mean that," and patted her arm. "It's all perfectly natural. It's just that we're the only colored people living in this little bit of town and there aren't any fine young colored men around, only this tramp piano player, and every time I look at him I can hear him playing some rags and see a whole line of big-bosomed women done up in sequined dresses

standin' over him, moanin' about wantin' somebody to turn their
dampers down, and I can see poker games and crap games and—"

My mother came in through the back room. She said, "Samuel,
why are you talking about gambling games?"

"I was trying to explain to Sophy how I feel about that piano
player."

To my surprise, my mother said, "Has Sophronia asked you how
you feel about Mr. Johnson?"

When my father shook his head, she said, "Then I don't think
there is any reason for you to say anything about him. I need you
in the garden. I want you to move one of my peonies."

I wonder what my mother would say if she knew how my father
chased little Mr. Bemish out of his store. I wonder if Mr. Bemish
will ever come back.

Mr. Bemish did come back. He came back the following Sunday. We were all in the store, Aunt Sophronia, and Dottle, and
Chink and I.

Mr. Bemish sidled in through the door. He looked as though
he expected someone to jump out at him and yell "Go home!"
But he came in anyway and he sat down beside me on the bench
near the front of the store.

Chink was leaning on the cigar case, talking to Aunt Sophronia,
his face very close to hers. I couldn't hear what he was saying, but
he seemed to be trying to persuade her to do something, go for
a walk, or something, and she was obviously refusing, politely but
definitely. Dottle was standing near the back of the store, watching
Chink.

Aunt Frank opened the store door, and she stood in the doorway holding the screen door open. She has a cross, sharp way of
speaking, very fast, and very unpleasant. She saw me and she said,
"Where's Mar-tha?"

I wasn't expecting to see Aunt Frank in the store at that hour
and I was so surprised that I didn't answer her.

"What's the mat-ter with you? Cat got your tongue? Didn't
you hear what I said? Where's your moth-er?"

"She's over on the other side of the building, in the kitchen.
She's having coffee with my father."

She scowled at Chink. "How long's that bearded man been in
here talkin' to Sophy?"

Chink turned around and looked toward Aunt Frank. Aunt Sophronia started toward her, moving very fast out from behind the cigar case, saying, "Can I get something for you?"

As Aunt Frank stood there holding the door open, a whole flight of bats came in the store. I say a "flight" because I don't know what else to call a large-sized group of bats. They swooped down and up in a blind, fast flight.

Aunt Frank shrieked, "Ahhh! My hair, watch out for your hair! Ahhhhhh!" and stood up on the bench, and held her black fusty skirts close about her and then pulled them over her head. I decided she had confused mice and bats, that the technique for getting rid of mice was to stand on a chair and clutch one's skirts around one, that is, if you were a lady and pretended to be afraid of mice. I did learn that Aunt Frank was wearing carpet slippers made of dark-gray felt, black cotton stockings, and under the outside layer of skirts there seemed to be a great many layers of black petticoats.

Dottle ran into the back room and held the door tightly shut. There is a glass in the door and he could look out at the rest of us as we dodged the bats. I could see his large white face, and long hair, and I supposed he was as frightened as Aunt Frank that bats would get entangled in his hair, because he squealed, all the rich, buttery quality gone from his voice, just a high-pitched squealing.

Aunt Frank cautiously lowered the outer skirt, fumbled in a pocket, and took out a bottle, not a big bottle, but about the size of an eight-ounce cough-medicine bottle, and she took two or three swigs from it, recorked it, and then re-covered her head.

Chink grabbed a newspaper and slapped at the bats as they circled. "Gotcha. Hi-hi-gotcha—hi-hi-gotcha—hi-hi!" and he folded the newspaper and belted them as they swished past him.

Mr. Bemish stared. I decided that he'd lived with bats and spiders and mice, well, not lived with perhaps, but was so accustomed to them that he could not understand why they should cause all this noise and confusion and fear. He ignored the bats entirely and went to the rescue of his lady love. He clasped Aunt Sophronia to his bosom, covering her head with his hands and arms and he kept murmuring comforting words. "Now, now. I won't let anything hurt you. Nothing can harm you." He took a deep breath and said, quite distinctly, "I love you, my darling. I love you, love you—"

Aunt Sophronia seemed to nestle in his arms, to cuddle closer to him, to lean harder every time a bat swooped past them.

Father came through the back room—he had to wrestle Dottle out of the way before he could get through the door—and he very sensibly held the screen door open, and what with the impetus offered by Chink's folded newspaper, the bats swooped outside.

It was really very exciting while it lasted, what with all the shrieks and the swift movement of the bats. When I began to really look around, the first thing I noticed was that Aunt Sophronia was still huddled in the protective arms of Mr. Bemish. Dottle came out of the back room with his mouth pursed and his cheeks were puffed out a little and I wouldn't have been surprised if he had hissed at Mr. Bemish. He and Chink headed straight towards Mr. Bemish. They are very tall men and Mr. Bemish is short and slender, and as they converged on him, one from the rear and the other from the side, he looked smaller and older than ever.

Aunt Sophronia stepped away from Mr. Bemish. She moved toward Chink. One side of her face was red where it had been pressed hard against the wool of Mr. Bemish's coat.

All of a sudden my father's hand was resting on one of Chink's shoulders. He has large, heavy hands and his hand seemed to have descended suddenly and with great weight. He said, "You'll not start any trouble in my store."

Aunt Frank said, "Bats! Bats!" She indicated that my father was to help her down from the bench. She climbed down awkwardly, holding on to him. "Worse than bats," she said, and she made a wide all-inclusive gesture that took in Chink and Dottle and Mr. Bemish. "Where's Mar-tha?" she demanded. "She still in the kitchen?"

My father nodded. He held the door open for Mr. Bemish, and Mr. Bemish scuttled out. Dottle and Chink went out too.

I found a dead bat on the floor and sat down on the bench at the front of the store to examine it. It had a very unpleasant smell. But it was such an interesting creature that I ignored the odor. It had rather large, pointed ears that I thought were quite charming. It had very sharp little claws. I could see why the ladies had screamed and covered their heads, because if those claws got entangled in their long hair, someone would have had to cut their hair to get a bat out of it. Aunt Frank's hair isn't long; it is like a sheep's wool, tight-curled and close to the skin or scalp. But I suppose a bat's sharp little claws and peculiar wings snarled up in that might create more of a problem than it would if caught in longer and less tightly curled hair.

The wings of the bat were webbed like the feet of ducks with a thin membranelike tissue that was attached to the body, reaching from the front legs or arms to the back legs and attached to the sides. The body was small in comparison to the wide sweep of those curious wings. I stretched its wings out and they looked like the inside of an opened umbrella, and I couldn't help admiring them. I began to think of all the things I'd heard said about bats, "blind as a bat," and the word "batty" meaning crazy, and I tried to figure out why "batty," probably because a bat's behavior didn't make sense to a human being—its fast, erratic flight would look senseless.

Then Aunt Frank's voice sounded right in my ear, and her horrible breath was in my nose, and she smelled worse than the bat. She said, "You throw that nasty thing away. You throw that nasty thing away."

I thrust the dead bat straight at her black and wrinkled face. "Look out," I yelled. "It'll suck your blood. It's still alive. Look out!"

She jumped away, absolutely furious. "You little vixen," she said, and squealed just like a pig. Then she saw my mother standing in the door of the prescription room. "Mar-tha," she commanded, "you come here and make her throw this nasty thing away. Make her throw it away. She's settin' here playin' with a dead bat."

My mother said, "If you want to look at the bat, take it outside or take it in the back room. You can't keep a dead bat here in the drugstore."

"This can't hurt her. It's dead."

She interrupted me. "Many people are afraid of bats. It doesn't make any difference whether the bats are dead or alive—they are still afraid of them."

I went outside and sat on the front steps and waited. There was a full moon and the light from it made the street and the houses and the church look as though they had been whitewashed. I put the bat beside me on the step. I was going to wait for Aunt Frank, and when she came out of the store and started down the steps, I was going to put the dead stinking bat in one of the big pockets in her skirt—the pocket where she kept her bottle of gin. And when she got home and reached for a drink, I hoped she would discover, encounter, touch with her bony fingers, the corpse of "one of the nocturnal or crepuscular flying mammals constituting the order Chiroptera" as a token of my affection.

I must have waited there on the steps for two hours. My father began putting out the lights in the store. I stayed right there, anticipating the moment when my ancient enemy, Aunt Frank, would come stumbling around the side of the building.

And then—one moment I was sitting on the splintery front steps of the store, and the next moment I was running up Petticoat Lane, going just as fast as I could, because it had suddenly occurred to me that Chink Johnson and Dottle Smith had gone out of the drugstore right behind Mr. Bemish and they hadn't returned.

By the time I reached Mr. Bemish's shop, I was panting. I couldn't catch my breath.

Mr. Bemish's wagon was drawn up close to the side of the shop. The horse was hitched to it. Mr. Bemish was loading the headboard of his beautiful brass bed on the wagon. He was obviously moving—leaving town, at night. He walked in a peculiar fashion as though he were lame. He was panting too, and making hiccuping noises like someone who has been crying a long time, so long that no real sound comes out, just a kind of hiccuping noise due to the contractions of the throat muscles and the heaving of the chest.

As I stood there, he got the headboard on the wagon, and then he struggled with his mattress, and then the springs, and then he brought out his cobbler's bench.

Dottle and Chink stood watching him, just like two guards or two sheriffs. None of us said anything.

I finally sat down on the enormous millstone that served as

Mr. Bemish's front step. I sat way off to one side where I wouldn't interefere with his comings and goings.

May-a-ling, his cat, rubbed against me and then came and sat in my lap, with her back to me, facing towards Mr. Bemish.

It didn't take him very long to empty the shop of his belongings. I couldn't help thinking that if we ever moved, it would take us days to pack all the books and the pictures and the china, and all our clothes and furniture. We all collected things. Aunt Sophronia did beautiful embroidery and she collected embroidered fabrics, and mother collected old dishes and old furniture, and my father collected old glass bottles and old mortars, and they all collected books, and then all the rooms had furniture and there were all kinds of cooking pots. No one of us would ever get all of our belongings in one wagon.

Mr. Bemish came out of the shop and walked all around the little building with that peculiar stiff-legged gait. Apparently the only item he'd overlooked was his garden bench. He had trouble getting it in the wagon, and I dumped May-a-ling on the ground and went to help him.

One of Dottle's meaty hands gripped my braid. "He can manage."

I twisted away from him. "He's just a little old man and he's my friend and I'm going to help him."

Chink said, "Leave her alone."

Dottle let go of my hair. I helped put the bench in the wagon, and then went inside the shop with him, and helped him carry out the few items that were left. Each time I went inside the shop with Mr. Bemish I asked him questions. We both whispered.

"Where are you going, Mr. Bemish?"

"Massachusetts."

"Why?"

He didn't answer. His hiccups got worse.

I waited until we'd taken down the green summer curtains and carefully folded them, and put them in the little trunk that held some of his clothes, and put his broom and his dustpan and his tall kitchen cooking stool on the wagon, before I repeated my question. His hiccups had quieted down.

"Why are you leaving, Mr. Bemish?" I whispered.

"They were going to sew me up."

"Sew you up. Did you say—sew you up?"

"Yes."

"Where?" I said, staring at him, thinking: sew up? Sew up what —eyes, nostrils, mouth, ears, rectum? "They were trying to scare you, Mr. Bemish. Nobody would sew up a person, a human being, unless it was a surgeon—after an operation—"

He shook his head. "No," he whispered. "I thought so too, but—no, they meant it—with my own waxed thread—"

"Did they—"

"Hush! Hush!"

We used this little piece of flowered carpet to wrap his wash-bowl and pitcher in and then put the whole bulky package it made on the wagon. We went back inside to make sure that we hadn't forgotten anything. The inside of his shop looked very small and shabby and lonely. There wasn't anything left except his stove and he obviously couldn't take that. It was a very big, handsome stove and he kept it quite shiny and clean.

"Can you keep a secret?" he whispered, standing quite close to me. He smelled old and dusty and withered like dried flowers.

I nodded.

He handed me a small velvet bag. "Hide it, girlie," he whispered. "It's some old jewelry that belonged to my mother. Give it to Miss Sophronia at Christmas from me." He patted my arm.

We went outside and he took down the sign with the lady's high-laced shoe painted on it, and put it on the wagon seat. He climbed in the wagon, picked up the reins.

"May-a-ling, May-a-ling," he called. It was the most musical sound I have ever heard used to call a cat. She answered him instantly. She mewed and jumped up on the wagon seat beside him. He clucked to the horse and they were off.

I waited not only until they were out of sight, but until I could no longer hear the creak of the wagon wheels and the clop-clop of the horses hoofs, and then I turned and ran.

Chink said, "Wait a minute—"

Dottle said, "You don't understand—"

I stopped running just long enough to shout at them, "You both stink. You stink like dead bats. You and your goddamn Miss Muriel—"

Chester Himes

CHESTER HIMES was born in Jefferson City, Missouri, in 1909, attended public schools in Cleveland, Ohio, and after a brief period at Ohio State University, held a variety of jobs, including industrial worker, hotel bellhop, and bartender.

In 1934, his first published short story appeared in *Esquire*, and in 1938 he joined the Ohio Writers Project, in which he wrote a history of Cleveland for the W.P.A. Guide Series.

Mr. Himes received a Rosenwald Fellowship in 1944, and a year later his first novel, *If He Hollers Let Him Go*, was published. Among his other books are *Lonely Crusade* (1947), *Cast the First Stone* (1953), and *The Third Generation* (1954). These novels enjoyed an international success and were published in France, Norway, Sweden, Denmark, and England. His popular detective stories have also been translated into several languages.

The following story is an episode from *Lonely Crusade*, which in its French edition was selected by French critics as one of the five best novels by Americans published in France in 1952.

Mr. Himes makes his home in Paris.

From *Lonely Crusade*

BY CHESTER HIMES

At the end of the working day that Saturday, Luther invited Lee to a party at his house. "Bring your old lady, man, we gonna have a time."

"Oh, we seldom go out any more—" Lee broke off because he could not bring himself to add "together."

"I tells you what, you brings your old lady to dinner and just stay on," Luther said persistently. "The party begins right after anyway."

"Well—I'll see what Ruth has to say." It would be a change, he thought.

Leaving Luther in the car parked before his house, he went in alone to speak to Ruth. But she did not want to come.

"You always objected when I wanted to go to some Communist affair," she reminded him.

"But that was different," he said. "*I'm* using *them*."

"So was I."

"No, you weren't! You weren't doing anything but running around with them, agitating and having a fine time."

"Why, Lee, that isn't so. You know, yourself—"

"Oh, let's don't argue," he cut in. "Do you want to go or don't you?"

"You make everything so hard," she answered, but when he turned and started off, she reluctantly said: "Oh, all right, I'll go."

But the spontaneity was gone. As he stood there a moment before replying, his head seemed to swell almost to bursting with a resentment underscored with bitter fury. Why couldn't she just say yes for once without always pointing out his inconsistencies? Why did his slightest request have to bring on this bickering? Did she think he was an idiot, incapable of judgment? But to her he merely said: "Never mind, I'll go alone," and went out of the house and left her.

On the long drive out to Hollywood the fury left but the re-sentment kept riding him. With a stumbling preoccupation he followed Luther up the stairway over a garage into an incredibly disarranged room of lush, low divans, loud-colored sofas, and oil paintings. In opposite corners sat a black-faced doll with huge red lips and a white-faced doll with golden hair, facing across a white brick fireplace that smoked lazily. Four shaded lamps turned on against the early dusk shed a diffused green light over the Bohemian scene, stirring within Lee's mind the first faint traces of aversion.

"Caliban?" A voice throaty with sex greeted them from the kitchen along with the smell of cooking food.

"Me, baby," Luther called.

A middle-aged, horse-faced woman with burning eyes and a thin, wide mouth came into the room.

"Mollie, Lee," Luther introduced. "This my old lady, man. Ain't she fine?"

In the queer green light her hair was bright orange and her skin an enbalmed white. Her short, chubby feet, white on top and blackish on the bottom with purple painted nails, were bare. And her soft, sagging body, which seemingly had reached satiety in years long past, was clad only in dirty green satin pajamas. There was an abandon in both her manner and appearance that was slightly obscene. She looked at Lee and began laughing.

"So this is Lee?"

"Oh—you've heard of me?" Lee stammered self-consciously.

"Should I have?" she asked, laughing with her lips while her bright blue eyes appraised him with a predacious stare.

"Oh, well no, that is— Well, you said: 'So this is Lee,' and I thought—"

Now her laughter came in gales. "It's the Continental manner."

Luther sat on a divan, took off his shoes and socks, and flexed his big, splayed feet, which were black on top and whitish on the bottom. "What you got to eat, old lady?" he asked.

"I call him Caliban," she said to Lee. "Don't you think he's marvelous?"

"Well, er, I don't know what—"

"Oh, don't bother," she cut him off.

"As Marx would say," Luther said, "a misdirected intent."

Laughingly Mollie returned to the kitchen, her buttocks jiggling loosely in the pajamas.

Kicking a sofa to one side, Luther crossed the room and stacked Sibelius's First Symphony on the record player. Against the symphonic music, he was grotesque, with his long, black, muscle-roped arms swinging from the white T-shirted, convex slope of his shoulders like an ape's. The impulse to laugh welled up in Lee but Luther's appearance of absorption in the music quelled it.

"You like that?" Lee asked.

"I likes it," Luther replied solemnly. "No culture too high for the proletariat."

Lee could not decide whether he was being kidded or not. Luther continued to appear absorbed. Then Mollie returned to the room with a tray of vodka highballs and turned off the record player.

"Enough culture for one day, my Caliban," she said, then lifted her glass. "To F.D.R."

"To Joe Stalin," Luther said.

"To the three component parts of Marxism," Lee said slyly. He caught the quick glances exchanged between Mollie and Luther and grinned to himself.

But Mollie only said: "This calls for another," and when she had refilled the glasses, moved Lee's coat and pulled Lee down on the divan beside her.

"Well, what do you think about it?" she asked brightly, looking him slowly over with a disrobing, half-laughing interest.

"Er, about what?"

"Oh, anything. The war, politics, Marx, or Freud."

"Oh, well—I'm not distinguished for my thinking."

"Nor is my Caliban. But he doesn't let that stop him from expounding on Marx and other of his gods."

"I'm not a parlor pink," Luther said (giving her a flat, muddy look. "Sucking around the party 'cause I'm scared there might be a revolution and I'll lose my little income."

"You're converted," she jibed.

"Not converted—convinced! After the war people like you'll be running back to your fascist friends."

"I was a Marxist abroad long before it became popular over here."

"You don't act like it."

Sitting erect, she took the pins from her hair, plied her fingers through it, and let it cascade down about her neck and shoulders. Then she cooed: "Come to me, my intellectual Caliban, my strong, black apostle with the pygmy brain; come to me and make love to me, my dark, designing commissar."

"Body Marxist!" Luther said, turning his back to her.

"Then be an American Negro," she said laughingly, "and refill our glasses while I talk to Lee."

"And make love to 'im too," he muttered.

"At least give us time," she murmured. "Lee might prefer women of his own race."

"Well—yes," he said.

"Such insolence! Such bourgeois puritanism! Let's eat and forget it."

Holding to an arm of each, she steered them into the kitchen. When they had seated themselves, Luther said to Mollie: "Say the blessing."

"She knows I'm not a Communist," Lee said.

Mollie laughed. They washed down the meat balls and spaghetti with a concoction of Rhine wine and vodka, which enhanced the taste of garlic in the sauce. Luther took off his T-shirt and suggested to Lee: "Take off your coat and tie, man. Your shirt, too. It's hot in here."

"What are we to have, a wrestling match between my two dark gladiators?" Mollie asked delightedly.

"I just b'lieves in being comfortable," Luther said.

"Oh, I'm quite comfortable," Lee declared.

"You are so beautiful, my Caliban, so unsullied and undomesticated. You remind me of a baboon I saw in the Paris zoo." She was laughing outside and all down inside where the effect of the drinks was concentrating the heat of passion in her.

"That's why you likes me."

"I like you because you are black."

"I know you likes me 'cause I'm black."

"Why else do I like you?"

"No, Mama, we got company."

She turned to Lee. "Isn't he marvelous?" Then she began feeling the muscles in Lee's arms as if she had just discovered them. "You are marvelous, too. A man of thin, dark tempered steel."

"All dark mens is tempered steel to you," Luther said sarcastically.

"You, my darling Caliban, are more than just steel. You are bone and steel. You are fire and bone and steel. What do you call those things that make all the noise in the street?"

"A garbage truck," Lee suggested helpfully.

"Aw, man, she mean an air hammer," Luther said sheepishly.

"You know what I mean, you air hammer, you."

"We're shocking Lee, Mama. He don't go for all this stuff."

"Oh, I'm doing fine," Lee averred drunkenly.

"Do you see that nigger?" Mollie finally asked. "That nigger does something to me."

"You drunk, Mama," Luther said levelly. "If you warn't I'd slap you 'way from this table."

"I'm a white woman, and you're a nigger from Mississippi. You wouldn't dare touch me. You lived in Mississippi too long."

"Now quit showing off, Mama," he warned. "You know I lived in Frisco too. That's the sheet you gots to bleach."

"What did you do in Frisco, as you call it, that was so important?"

"I had a fine time and you know it."

She turned to Lee, laughing. "Let me tell you about my Caliban in San Francisco—"

Lee remembered only the part about Luther sunning on the beach, exercising his right as an American citizen and a member of the Communist Party, when a blond, skinny, predatory, oversexed white woman stopped to admire him, picked him up, took him home, fed him, and slept with him.

After that day, Luther quit his job on W.P.A. and moved into her mansion, Mollie related, and under her supervision he began writing illiterate stories about his boyhood in Mississippi. She joined the Communist Party to be near him always, and informed the party officials about Luther's beautiful soul. How exquisitely sensitive he was underneath his Negroid exterior, how noble and courageous, yet retaining the purity of the primitive, the unspoiled, uncluttered originality of the aboriginal—

"Now, Mama, you laying it on too thick," Luther interrupted her.

"And didn't I take you away from her?" she asked.

"Must have. You got me."

She took him by the hand and led him from the table. Without excuse or apology, they crossed the green-lighted living room into the bedroom beyond and closed the door. Presently the sound of laughter came from within. Lee served himself another drink, speculating as to the cause for laughter now.

From unionism to Communism to sensualism, he thought with drunken cleverness. But was that not man's spiral to man's own humanism? For were not these two the appointed apostles of Marx and macrogenitals? And who was he, Lee Gordon, to make fun? What did he, Lee Gordon, believe in? Nothing! Lee Gordon did not even believe in salaciousness, which would have at least procured him a white woman in the last stages of debauchery and a green-lighted living room on the Roman order, he told himself.

He awoke to find himself stretched upon the bedroom couch, dressed except for coat and shoes. From the other room came the sound of many voices. Jumping to his feet, he fought down the impulse to escape through the window and began a frantic search for his coat and shoes, throwing aside the bedding and disarranging the room. He could not tell how long he had slept or what had happened during the interim, which was the thing that worried him. Finally finding the missing garments before his eyes, he fled to the bathroom, where he sloshed cold water over his face until his sense of panic left.

A swift, engulfing fear of self-abasement sobered him. He scoured his memory until he had provided himself with a fragile absolution. But it was with considerable aversion that he put on his coat and went hesitatingly into the living room.

In the weird green light, frantic people in defiant garb created the illusion of a costume ball. But the workers had come as workers, proudly—the Negroes as Negroes, apologetically—the Jews as Jews, defiantly. Only the two Mexican girls had come in costume —they had come as Castilian Spanish.

The self-styled Marxists of Los Angeles were having their hour, Each drink served across the table blocking the kitchen doorway meant another dollar for Russian aid. Russia was being aided while the guests were becoming hilarious, argumentative, indignant, or belligerent, as was their bent.

Nothing said in the babbling flow of words was intelligible. And had it been so, had each shouted word presented the answer to man's eternal seeking, the import would have been lost on Lee Gordon. For Lee was troubled in mind and heavy in heart, hot but he could not sweat. His thoughts were on his wife now, and he was but little short of hating her. If she had come, her presence would have maintained some semblance of decorum, for not even a white woman as depraved as Mollie would want a Negro woman to witness her abandon with Negro men, he told himself. He would not have become drunk. And even if he had, he could have at least retained his self-respect so he would not now feel as depraved as those other two.

Seeing him, Mollie came over quickly and asked with an air of concern: "How do you feel now?"

"Oh, all right," he muttered, avoiding her gaze.

Now debonair in a dramatic red dress, she seemed to have forgotten the episode. She laughed and felt the muscles of his arms.

"And you will do your bit for Russia too," she said sardonically.

"Well—yes—"

"I'm sure you will." She patted him on the cheek, laughing, and moved on.

And later Luther came over, his snowy-white turtle-neck sweater accenting the blackness of his skin. "Hey, man, how you doing?"

"Oh, all right. Have a drink."

"You have one on me, man."

They had their drink. Someone called Luther away. The girl on the other side of the table said precisely: "That will be two dollars."

"Well I— Well yes—"

He wondered if they knew that he was not a Communist. Maybe a Communist had some way of identifying another Communist— as a Jew can identify another Jew, or a Negro, another Negro. Maybe a Communist could smell another Communist—the proletarian pungency or the Stalinist scent. The thought stirred a laugh in him.

A white girl passing turned a brightly painted smile. "Is it personal or can we all share in it?"

"Oh, it's for the masses," he assured her. "I was just thinking about the Stalinist scent."

"What?"

"If a Communist could smell another Communist."

The smile went off. She looked at him a moment longer with hostile curiosity, then went to the table, jerking her head toward him. "Where did they find that?"

The girl selling the drinks shook her head.

After that no one said anything to him or included him in what they were saying. And he had thought Communists were supposed to pounce on a single male Negro. But times had changed, he told himself. Now, there's a war, didn't you know? Or rather the Communist twist, there's a war against fascism.

A defensiveness grew within him. They could not reject him any more than he could reject them. He bought another drink, staring into its amber depths as into a crystal ball, listening to the tinkle of the ice. And his thoughts went back to where for eight long years they had always ended and begun—Ruth!

During the time she had worked at Western Talkie, he had spent a week in San Francisco looking for a job. While he was there he had received a letter from her. He did not know how many times he had read that letter since, because it was the only letter he had ever received from her, and now the words of it came easily to his memory.

"A little while ago a book entitled *You Might Like Socialism* fell into my hands and I read it to the delight of all my Leftist socialist-minded friends, who had persistently not given me up in spite of the fact that they labeled me as an ignoramus who dares live in America as a member of the most oppressed group without joining forces with them in their fight for freedom. My own efforts they say are silly, ineffectual, and even a bit ridiculous. They tell me that unless I awaken very soon I will be living in a world bowed down in slavery forevermore by international fascism.

"Realizing my ignorance I admitted that I would like to learn more about this international fascism and I am greeted with sneers and shouts. They all speak at once denouncing everything.

"They point out eagerly that I am a social worker trained for my job and have to accept work for a time as an industrial worker. They become very bitter and accuse me of trying to evade the issue. They ask me what I know of the Marxian Scientific Formula and want to know sarcastically if I am not aware of a great class struggle going on of which I am a part and parcel. They look quite wild and apoplectic.

"They point their fingers in my face and ask me, answering their own questions: 'You are black, aren't you?' Sometimes, when I am worn out mentally and physically, I say facetiously: 'I'm brown,' and they pounce wildly on me with: 'If you have one per cent black blood you're a nigger.' They sit back triumphantly after such a statement as though to say: 'There you are.'

"What they apparently cant' see is that I like being a Negro regardless of what color I am; that I like being an American even more so and that I wouldn't exchange this democracy I live in for all the Utopias they can possibly picture—"

That was crazy, silly, contradictory! he thought. But so like her. For a moment he felt a smother of tenderness for her, remembering all the pleasant passionate things that had happened between them. All of a sudden from some passing woman he caught a faint essence of perfume that reminded him of her standing in her black lace nightgown on their wedding night, rubbing lotion over her face and arms and spraying perfume on her lips and ear lobes and over her firm young breasts and all down her round slender body so she would smell sweet when she came to him in bed. He filled with a compelling desire for her. His eyes clouded with a film of tears and he remained rigid for a long time, his hand grasping the empty glass in a death grip. His love for her was so intense he could feel it like a separate life throughout his body.

A voice in front of him said: "If we don't get a second front the worst is yet to come."

When Lee Gordon came out of it, he did not see the stubby, bald-headed man in front of him. He saw Ruth as he had left her, critical, cold, apart, a long way off. Still without seeing the man, he said evenly: "Goddamn a second front!"

And then he stepped over to the table and said: "Make it a double this time."

A big white man in a dark gray suit, also buying a drink, braved Lee's tight, black scowl. "I'm Ed Jones, I work for a newspaper."

It required a moment for Lee to get the handle to his voice. "I'm Lee Gordon, I work for a union." Then suddenly he grinned and felt better.

"Good. I belong to a union—and work for it, too."

"Well, I—" He started to say that he was not a member of the union but said instead: "I am strictly for the union men."

Ed looked at him curiously. "At least we don't say grace to the wrong people."

Now Lee looked at Ed curiously. But before he could reply, a pleasant-faced young man with a Boston accent and crew haircut, dressed as a college student, spoke up with a smile: "We don't say grace—period."

"Why?" Lee asked, yielding to the impulse to bait the both of them.

"There is no one to say grace to," Ed replied seriously.

"We have not yet discarded the great god Money."

"But we are discarding it."

"And quickly at this moment," Lee said, noting his empty glass.

The young man laughed and bought them drinks. "What is money but a means for its own discard?" he stated more than asked.

"I might point out that religion and materialism are much the same," Lee said.

"How is that?"

"There is no proof for either unless one believes. I wonder how many of you Marxists realize that it is your belief, and not Marx's proof, that has established the truth of materialism."

"But Marx did not establish the truth of materialism, no more than did we," a fourth voice said. "He merely employed the dialectical conception of it to demonstrate the cycle of capitalism."

Lee looked down at the stubby, bald-headed Jew who had made the remark concerning the second front. "To me the two are the same—Marx and materialism," he replied.

"To you, yes. But you will admit the danger of drawing any conclusion from a lack of information?" the stubby Jew asked equably.

"I admit nothing," Lee snapped. "I said—"

"By the way, my name's Don Cabot," the young man with the Boston accent interrupted quickly.

"Lee Gordon," Lee replied shortly.

"I'm Abe Rosenberg," the stubby Jew said. "But they all call me Rosie."

"Lee, dialectical materialism proves itself," Ed argued doggedly. "Which religion does not do. We see the truth of dialectical materialism in our daily lives, in each step of progress we make. Man discovers nothing, learns nothing—he reflects. Matter changes, develops, progresses, but we think only of the change, the development, the progress of man. But every scientist knows that man could not develop if matter were unchangeable.

"While on the other hand, religion is static. We cannot see the truth of religion; we can only believe it. And we can only believe it so long as it serves its purpose. Man is not embodied in religion —religion is embodied in man. There is no religion that man, in his reflection of materialistic progression, cannot outgrow and overthrow—in fact, has not already outgrown."

"You make it sound as logical as Lenin did, I admit," Lee replied. "But you can not convince me that the masses in Russia are converted to the philosophy of dialectics, or that they know themselves to be reflections of materialistic change. I say the majority of the peasant in Russia have just swapped the Greek Orthodox faith for the Communist faith."

"To be sure," Rosie agreed, spreading his hands. "That only illustrates the truth of dialectical materialism. Are not the masses of Russia reflecting change? Do they have to know it? Or even believe it?"

"As long as they are it, eh?" Lee asked.

"What have you against the Soviet Union?" Rosie challenged.

"The people have no freedom."

"The people have more freedom than any people in the world. Do you have freedom here?"

"We have more than they."

"Pfui! There can be no such thing as freedom in a capitalistic society. They say we have a free press. Pfui! We have the most controlled press in the world today. First of all, it takes a million dollars to buy a small newspaper. Is that free?"

"It is freer than having a big newspaper and having what goes into it dictated to you."

"Are you so naïve as to believe that the contents of an American newspaper are not dictated by the overlords?"

"Not to the extent the contents of the Russian newspapers are dictated by Joe Stalin."

"Pfui! There are no dictators in Russia. The people dictate—all the people. Do all the people in America vote?"

"Why ask me that?"

"Because you, of all people, should know. Freedom! What is freedom?"

"According to Martin Dies it is anti-people," someone said.

"According to Father Coughlin it is anti-Semitism."

"To Hitler, it is anti-everything."

Several laughed.

Lee quoted with drunken memory: "According to Karl Marx, 'Freedom is the appreciation of necessity.'"

There was a moment of startled silence.

"Hear! Hear!" a broad-shouldered man with coarse, lumpy features called from the center of the room. "May I have your attention, please."

"Mike! . . . Mike! . . ." The name ran through the crowd.

"The young man is right," Mike stated. "Freedom is the appreciation of necessity. That is why I am here. We must be informed of the necessities. The necessity of aiding our great ally Russia, who is now valiantly fighting our battles for us—"

From one side of the room came a spontaneous cheer.

"You don't have to cheer me," Mike declared. "All of you know what I am saying. You all know it is the truth. What I am talking about is the necessity of knowledge, the necessity of news from the battle fronts that is not falsified to serve imperialistic ends, the necessity of a free press bringing you true and correct information. I am referring to the *Daily World*. We need money to bring you news coverage of the world during this most important period in the history of mankind. You know that. We need money to compete with the imperialistic press. Our goal is to raise three hundred and fifty thousand dollars. Now I am going to ask for a collection of ten-dollar bills. I want nothing but tens—" He smiled indulgently. "Last night I was to a party in Beverly Hills where I collected nothing but hundreds. Now come on, folks. Don't rush. Nothing but tens—"

Several people went forward with ingratiating smiles. Next Mike called for fives, then ones. Then he passed his hat around and took a silver collection.

No sooner had he departed than someone else appeared and took up a collection for a second front.

"I don't mind so much being pressured out of my money," Lee complained to Rosie, "but what good can it do? You can't force the United States to open a second front."

"But we can let the people know the necessity of it. And the people will know who are their enemies and who are their friends."

"Well, what is the necessity of it? Let me know."

"Our frontiers are no longer on the Atlantic Ocean. They are in Russia."

Another Jew joined the conversation. "Russia must be saved!"

"For who? You Jews? Lee asked harshly.

"You a Negro and you say that?"

"I say that because I am a Negro. Russia is no haven for me. Not even an ideological defense."

"How is it any more an ideological defense to the Jew than to you. You are human too, aren't you?"

"Not in this country. And this is where I have to live and die. I don't see any collection being taken up to fight the Negro problem."

"The Negro problem is indivisible from the problem of the masses. You have no special problem. And Russia is the only nation in the world where human rights are placed above property rights. As long as Russia stands, the masses will have hope."

"Not the Negro in America. Our only hope is here, where Russian influence will never mean a thing."

"You know nothing of the international implications of this war—"

"And I don't care!"

"If it were not for Russia this would be an imperialistic war—"

"All I know is that now is the time to fight the Negro problem and what are you Communists doing but—" Lee broke off to stare at the label on the package of tobacco from which Rosie filled his pipe. "Nigger Hair," it read.

"Good tobacco?" Lee asked.

Rosie's expression did not change. "Cheap. We got the U. S. Tobacco Company to stop using this label, then we bought up the stock at a discount for personal use."

"You shouldn't feel badly about your hair," consoled a woman who had noticed the label. "We can't all have beautiful hair. And it doesn't take a thing away from your character."

"After all, it's what dialectical materialism gave to me," Lee said evenly.

"There's a great deal of anti-Semitism going on right now too," the woman continued.

"Well—yes. How many Jews were there lynched in America last year?"

"Why, I never heard of any Jew being lynched in America."

"There were six Negroes lynched last year in the first year of this war against fascism." He turned to Rosie. "And no Jews. Yet you say the problem is indivisible from the problem of the masses. Lynching alone would divide it."

Rosie shook his head. "I'm worried about you, Lee."

"Oh, sure," Lee drawled. "Now I suppose I'm confused—which is the next charge you Communists make."

"Confused, yes. But that's not what worries me."

"What worries you is that you don't have the answer—"

Someone tugged at his arm. He turned and scowled down at a small, elderly Jewish man with a tired, seamed face and kindly eyes.

"I have something to show you," the old man said.

"Some other time—"

"No, now," the old man insisted. "You must see this now."

"But what is it? I don't want to read anything—"

"Come, let us go into the other room where—"

"No!"

"Yes, you must!" The old man gripped him by the sleeve.

Lee allowed himself to be ushered into the bedroom, where he

was forced gently but firmly into the chair while the old man extracted the small precious package from his inside pocket and began
unwrapping it.

"Look!" he commanded.

It was a vague, blurred picture of a naked Negro but Lee's
drunken vision would not focus immediately upon it. "Look, Pops
—Mister—"

"Goldman."

"Look, Mr. Goldman, what is it? A Negro ballet dancer?" Was
that what this old man wanted him to see?

Leaning close, the old man whispered in his ear, "It is the picture
of a lynching."

Shock went through Lee like veins of gall. He struggled to his
feet, fighting down the taste of nausea. "No!" he shouted. "No,
goddammit! You goddamed fool!" He was moving toward the
door. It was like escaping.

The discussion had now touched upon the double standard. Lee
headed toward it with a sense of seeking cover. Someone was saying: "There are no such things as male and female personalities.
There is only one personality—the human personality."

He swerved toward the bar. But Don called him back: "What
do you think, Lee?"

"What do I think about what?"

"The equality of sexes that exists today in the Soviet Union?"

"Where they have community nurseries with competent in-
structors for the children," a woman supplemented.

"I like the home," Lee said.

"We all like the home. The home still exists. But the old
patriarchal institution of home life where it is regarded as the
center of culture is outdated."

"I like women who are women," Lee went on. "I like to sleep
with them and take care of them. I don't want any woman taking
care of me or even competing with me." He realized suddenly that
he was getting very drunk.

"My, my, such a big strong man," the woman murmured.

"Let's have some music, Luther!" someone called.

Lee found himself at the bar again. A jive record filled the room
with a boogie beat and some of the younger Marxists began jitter-

bugging. Soon an argument ensued as to the correct manner of executing the steps. A young man stated authoritatively that it was done by the entire body.

"It's not! It's in the knees!" shrieked a young woman's excited voice.

Lee turned to look at the speaker. She was a medium-sized girl showing small, pointed breasts in a tight yellow sweater. Her hips were too broad even in the dark blue skirt. And the saddle-leather loafers made her legs seem too large and her ankles too thick. From the neck down she was any girl Lee might see anywhere. But there was something in her face, the zestful mobility of finely cut, sensitive features framed by brown wind-blown hair, that was arresting—more than just the vitality of large brown eyes, the irresistible challenge of a candid mouth. There was an unconscious maternalism that seemed to come from within, as if she not only mothered the meek, but had given birth to them.

Lee was at that stage of drunkenness where the mind is a tricky thing. For he did not realize how long he had stared at her with an intense concentration until the recording had played to the end and, surprisingly, he found himself crossing the room to light the cigarette in her hand.

"Thank you," she said courteously, without coyness, and seemingly without curiosity.

Erskine Hawkins blew the room full of high trumpet notes and they found themselves doing something like a jitterbug waltz to the beat of "Don't Cry, Baby." Lee found her young in his arms but stiff with what seemed an inner reserve.

"If you ride out the beats, the breaks will catch you," he told her.

"I do it from the knees," she persisted.

He laughed indulgently. "That's as good a way as any."

The dance finished and she went to someone else. Then Mollie took Lee for a dance and they did her special crawl. Between laughs she said: "Everybody is for you, dear."

"In what way?"

"In every way."

"They don't act like it."

"You must co-operate."

"I am co-operating."

"That is what I am saying. They are all for you."

He shook his head to clear it. "I must be getting drunk."

Next he danced with a tall, willowy, dark-haired woman who seemed inexpressibly beautiful.

"Last year at this time I weighed two hundred pounds," she informed him.

"You did? What do you weigh now?"

"One hundred and twenty-two pounds."

"That's remarkable."

"You shouldn't worry so about the Negro problem. The Negro is a nation, you know."

"No, I didn't know."

"It is. Are you familiar with Marx's Scientific Formula?"

"Not very."

"You should read it. I'm one of Smitty's secretaries, you know."

"You are? Maybe I'll be seeing you."

"Watch out for Mollie. She's a fink. They won't have her in the Party."

"No? Why?"

"Oh, she's a capitalist stooge. Ando she doesn't work. Don't you know who she is?"

"No, I don't."

"Her husband is a big Hollywood producer."

"Oh, is that so?"

His next dance was with Mollie again.

"What was Sophia saying about me?"

"Who is Sophia?"

"The cow you were dancing with."

"She said you were rich."

Mollie laughed. "They are a jealous bunch of bitches."

"What's the pretty girl's name?"

"You can't mean Jackie?"

"Maybe not. The girl in the yellow sweater."

"That's Jackie. Stay away from her. She's bait."

"That's kinda hard to believe."

"Then take her home. But we may as well be realistic about it. Use a prophylactic."

"Thank you. But I will use dialectics instead."

When he went to buy another drink he was told the whisky was all gone and there was only rum left. Behind him someone proposed a toast to Stalin.

"I will take a shot of rum to drink to Stalin," Lee said to the girl selling drinks.

Several others came up and bought rum to drink to Stalin. Then someone proposed a toast to Roosevelt. Lee and the others refilled to drink to Roosevelt. Twelve Russian heroes were toasted next by name, but Lee could not toast more than three of them, whose names he soon forgot.

After that he found himself out in the kitchen solemnly telling Don that when a Negro raped a white woman, that was a crime, but when a white man raped a Negro woman, that was a joke.

"Speaking of jokes, I will bet you that I can give a dirtier toast than you, Lee," Don challenged.

"Go ahead, it's a bet."

"Here's to two old whores out on the block—"

"One white and one colored," Lee cut in.

"An interracial meeting," Don laughed.

Lee started to say "a Communist get-together" but thought better of it.

Ed came into the kitchen on the tail end of it and remarked seriously: "You know, I will be happy when the day comes when a white man can kick a Negro in the ass without being called a nigger-hater."

"I agree with you," Lee replied solemnly. "And I will be glad when the day comes when a Negro can kick a white man in the ass without being called a frustrated homicidal maniac."

"I will buy you comrades a drink," Don said.

"The man's a capitalist," Ed observed.

"Don't call me a capitalist. A capitalist is a man who panders for his mother, rapes his children, and buys bonds. I'm a Communist."

"Then what is a Communist?" Lee asked.

"A Communist is a person with the head of a capitalist, the heart of a capitalist, the soul of a capitalist, and no money," Ed replied.

Silently they turned to the girl selling drinks and had three rounds of rum. Then Lee staggered into the bathroom and was sick for a long time. When he turned to leave he found that he could not stand. On his hands and knees he crawled through the back hall and out onto the back stoop.

It was raining. He sat in the rain and the water soaked through his clothes and felt cool and clean on his head and face and refreshing to the heat of his skin. Lights in the movie stars' mansions way up in the Hollywood Hills looked like little stars in the darkness— "And the stars shone down over the lot of man—" Some half-remembered line from some forgotten book.

In the cold, clean rain his thoughts cleared and his mind took him back to a party in New York. He had run into an old Los Angeles acquaintance, Al Roberts, in the Hotel Theresa. Al had said: "Let's go up to Mamie's."

"Where's that?"

"Up at 940."

"Is she having a party?"

"She's always having a party."

"Oh, like that. Look, Al, I'm broke."

"You don't need any money. She gives her liquor away. Got an old man making good money and she spends it."

They went up to St. Nicholas Avenue on the bus and climbed to the top floor of an apartment house. A fat, light-complexioned woman with black hair and sleepy eyes, clad in flaming red lounging pajamas, let them into an apartment filled with people getting drunk.

"Mamie, this is Lee. He's a home boy."

She had murmured something incoherently. As Lee was to learn before he left, incoherence was her only charm. He had wandered about and met the people. There had been as many white persons present as there had Negroes, but the whites were inconseqential while most of the Negroes were people of importance who held high positions and were known throughout the nation as leaders of their race. But he had listened in vain for anyone, white or Negro, to make a single statement that had any meaning whatsoever. The Negroes were being niggers in a very sophisticated manner as tribute to their white liberal friends. And the whites were enjoying the Negroes' tribute as only white liberals can.

It would have had some meaning to Lee if the purpose of the party had been sex. A prelude for adultery, or even suicide. But there at Mamie's, sex had been but a vulgar joke. And drinking for drinking only, like tonight—as it had always been, it seemed.

Now as he began to sober up, before the dull aching remorse of hangover settled in, he wondered about this drunkenness. As an aphrodisiac, it would have meaning, yes—or for digestion, as he had heard the Italians drank—or for verse, as the French did. But everywhere he had ever been in America, drinking was for getting drunk, as an anodyne for some great hurt, or for oblivion.

And this was one thing they could not hang on the nigger, he thought with sharp disdain. The nigger loved his watermelon, even though the white folks ate most of them. And the nigger loved his chicken—what little the white folks left. But everybody got drunk —nigger, white man, gentile, Jew.

Maybe the Communists knew something after all. In a nation where so many millions of people kept getting drunk for drunkenness, there must be something deeply wrong. Some gnawing dissatisfaction was too great to endure, because they were not only Negroes and they were not only Communists.

And then he thought, as his sharp sardonic thoughts turned inward: "I ought to go back and have another drink."

Langston Hughes

"Rock, Church" is an original short story published here for the first time. (See the note on Langston Hughes, page 106.)

ROCK, CHURCH

by LANGSTON HUGHES

Elder William Jones was one of them rock-church preachers who know how to make the spirit rise and the soul get right. Sometimes in the pulpit he used to start talking real slow, and you'd think his sermon warn't gonna be nothing, but by the time he got through, the walls of the building would be almost rent, the doors busted open, and the benches turned over from pure shouting on the part of the brothers and sisters.

He were a great preacher, was Reverend William Jones. But he warn't satisfied—he wanted to be greater than he was. He wanted to be another Billy Graham or a Aimee McPherson or a resurrected Reverend Becton. And that's what brought about his downfall—ambition!

Now, Reverend Jones had been for nearly a year the pastor of one of them little colored churches in the back alleys of St. Louis that are open every night in the week for preaching, singing, and praying, where sisters come to shake tambourines, shout, sing gospel songs, and get happy while the Reverend presents the Word.

Elder Jones always opened his part of the services with "In His Hand," his theme song, and he always closed his services with the same. Now, the rhythm of "In His Hand" was such that once it got to swinging, you couldn't help but move your arms or feet or both, and since the Reverend always took up collection at the beginning and ending of his sermons, the dancing movement of the crowd at such times was always toward the collection table— which was exactly where the Elder wanted it to be.

> *In His hand!*
> *In His hand!*
> *I'm safe and sound*
> *I'll be bound—*
> *Settin' in Jesus' hand!*

"Come one! Come all! Come, my Lambs," Elder Jones would shout, "and put it down for Jesus!"

Poor old washerladies, big fat cooks, long lean truck drivers, and heavy-set roustabouts would come up and lay their money down, two times every evening for Elder Jones.

That minister was getting rich right there in that St. Louis alley.

> *In His hand!*
> *In His hand!*
> *I'll have you know*
> *I'm white as snow—*
> *Settin' in Jesus' hand!*

With the piano just a-going, tambourines a-flying, and people shouting right on up to the altar.

"Rock, church, rock!" Elder Jones would cry at such intensely lucrative moments.

But he were too ambitious. He wouldn't let well enough alone. He wanted to be a big shot and panic Harlem, gas Detroit, sew up Chicago, then move on to Hollywood. He warn't satisfied with just St. Louis.

So he got to thinking now what can I do to get everybody excited, to get everybody talking about my church, to get the streets outside crowded and my name known all over, even unto the far reaches of the nation? Now, what can I do?

Billy Sunday had a sawdust trail, so he had heard. Reverend Becton had two valets in the pulpit with him as he cast off garment after garment in the heat of preaching, and used up dozens of white handkerchiefs every evening wiping his brow while calling on the Lord to come. Meanwhile, the Angel of Angelus Temple had just kept on getting married and divorced and making the front pages of everybody's newspapers.

"I got to be news, too, in my day and time," mused Elder Jones. "This town's too small for me! I want the world to hear my name!"

Now, as I've said before, Elder Jones was a good preacher— and a good-looking preacher, too. He could cry real loud and moan real deep, and he could move the sisters as no other black preacher on this side of town had ever moved them before. Besides, in his youth, as a sinner, he had done a little light hustling around Memphis and Vicksburg—so he knew just how to appeal to the feminine nature.

Since his recent sojourn in St. Louis, Elder Jones had been looking for a special female Lamb to shelter in his private fold. Out of all the sisters in his church, he had finally chosen Sister Maggie Bradford. Not that Sister Maggie was pretty. No, far from it. But Sister Maggie was well fed, brownskin, good-natured, fat, and *prosperous*. She owned four two-family houses that she rented out, upstairs and down, so she made a good living. Besides, she had sweet and loving ways as well as the interest of her pastor at heart.

Elder Jones confided his personal ambitions to said Sister Bradford one morning when he woke up to find her by his side.

"I want to branch out, Maggie," he said. "I want to be a really big man! Now, what can I do to get the 'tention of the world on me? I mean in a religious way?"

They thought and they thought. Since it was a Fourth of July morning, and Sister Maggie didn't have to go collect rents, they just lay there and thought.

Finally, Sister Maggie said, "Bill Jones, you know something I ain't never forgot that I seed as a child? There was a preacher down in Mississippi named old man Eubanks who one time got himself dead and buried and then rose from the dead. Now, I ain't never forgot that. Neither has nobody else in that part of the Delta. That's something mem'rable. Why don't you do something like that?"

"How did he do it, Sister Maggie?"

"He ain't never told nobody how he do it, Brother Bill. He say it were the Grace of God, that's all."

"It might a-been," said Elder Jones. "It might a-been."

He lay there and thought awhile longer. By and by, he said, "But, honey, I'm gonna do something better'n that. I'm gonna be nailed on a cross."

"Do, Jesus!" said Sister Maggie Bradford. "Jones, you's a mess!"

Now, the Elder, in order to pull off his intended miracle, had, of necessity, to take somebody else into his confidence, so he picked out Brother Hicks, his chief deacon, one of the main pillars of the church long before Jones came as pastor.

It was too bad, though, that Jones never knew that Brother Hicks (more familiarly known as Bulldog) used to be in love with Sister Bradford. Sister Bradford neglected to tell the new Reverend about any of her former sweethearts. So how was Elder Jones to know that some of them still coveted her, and were envious of him in their hearts?

"Hicks," whispered Elder Jones in telling his chief deacon of his plan to die on the cross and then come back to life, "that miracle will make me the greatest minister in the world. No doubt about it! When I get to be world-renowned, Bulldog, and go traveling about the firmament, I'll take you with me as my chief deacon. You shall be my right hand, and Sister Maggie Bradford shall be my left. Amen!"

"I hear you," said Brother Hicks. "I hope it comes true."

But if Elder Jones had looked closely, he would have seen an evil light in his deacon's eyes.

"It will come true," said Elder Jones, "if you keep your mouth shut and follow out my instructions—exactly as I lay 'em down to you. I trust you, so listen! You know and I know that I ain't gonna *really* die. Neither is I *really* gonna be nailed. That's why I wants you to help me. I wants you to have me a great big cross made, higher than the altar—so high I has to have a stepladder to get up to it to be nailed thereon, and you to nail me. The higher the better, so's they won't see the straps—'cause I'm gonna be tied on by straps, you hear. The light'll be rose-colored so they can't see the straps. Now, here you come and do the nailin'—nobody else but you. Put them nails *between* my fingers and toes, not through 'em—*between*—and don't nail too deep. Leave the heads kinder stickin' out. You get the jibe?"

"I get the jibe," said Brother Bulldog Hicks.

"Then you and me'll stay right on there in the church all night and all day till the next night when the people come back to see me rise. Ever so often, you can let me down to rest a little bit. But as long as I'm on the cross, I play off like I'm dead, particularly when reporters come around. On Monday night—Hallelujah! I will rise, and take up collection!"

"Amen!" said Brother Hicks.

Well, you couldn't get a-near the church on the night that Reverend Jones had had it announced by press, by radio, and by word of mouth that he would be crucified *dead*, stay dead, and rise. Negroes came from all over St. Louis, East St. Louis, and mighty nigh everywhere else to be present at the witnessing of the miracle. Lots of 'em didn't believe in Reverend Jones, but lots of 'em *did*. Sometimes false prophets can bamboozle you so you can't tell yonder from whiter—and that's the way Jones had the crowd.

The church was packed and jammed. Not a seat to be found and tears were flowing (from sorrowing sisters' eyes) long before the Elder even approached the cross which, made out of new lumber right straight from the sawmill, loomed up behind the pulpit. In the rose-colored lights, with big paper lilies that Sister Bradford had made decorating its head and foot, the cross looked mighty pretty.

Elder Jones preached a mighty sermon that night and, hot as it was, there was plenty of leaping and jumping and shouting in that crowded church. It looked like the walls would fall. Then when he got through preaching, Elder Jones made a solemn announcement. As he termed it, for a night and a day, his last pronouncement.

"Church! Tonight, as I have told the world, I'm gonna die. I'm gonna be nailed to this cross and let the breath pass from me. But tomorrow, Monday night, August the twenty-first, at twelve p.m., I am coming back to life. Amen! After twenty-four hours on the cross, Hallelujah! And all the city of St. Louis can be saved—if they will just come out to see me. Now, before I mounts the steps to the cross, let us sing for the last time 'In His Hand'— 'cause I tell you, that's where I am! As we sing, let everybody come forward to the collection table and help this church before I go. Give largely!"

The piano tinkled, the tambourines rang, hands clapped. Elder Jones and his children sang:

> *In His hand!*
> *In His hand!*
> *You'll never stray*
> *Down the Devil's way—*
> *Settin' in Jesus' hand!*
>
> *Oh, in His hand!*
> *In His hand!*
> *Though I may die*
> *I'll mount on high—*
> *Settin' in Jesus' hand!*

"Let us pray." And while every back was bowed in prayer, the Elder went up the stepladder to the cross. Brother Hicks followed with the hammer and nails. Sister Bradford wailed at the top of her voice. Woe filled the Amen Corner. Emotion rocked the church.

Folks outside was saying all up and down the streets, "Lawd, I wish we could have got in. Listen yonder at that noise! I wonder what *is* going on!"

Elder Jones was about to make himself famous—that's what was going on. And all would have went well had it not been for Brother Hicks—a two-faced rascal. Somehow that night the devil got into Bulldog Hicks and took full possession.

The truth of the matter is that Hicks got to thinking about Sister Maggie Bradford, and how Reverend Jones had worked up to be her No. 1 man. That made him mad. The old green snake of jealousy began to coil around his heart, right there in the meeting, right there on the steps of the cross, at the very high point of the ceremonies. Lord, have Mercy!

Hicks had the hammer in one hand and his other hand was full of nails as he mounted the ladder behind his pastor. He was going up to nail Elder Jones on that sawmill cross.

"While I'm nailin', I might as well nail him right," Hicks thought. "A low-down klinker—comin' here out of Mississippi to take my woman away from me! He'll never know the pleasure of my help in none o' his schemes to out-Divine Father! No, sir!"

Elder Jones had himself all fixed up with a system of straps round his waist, round his shoulder blades, and round his wrists and ankles, hidden under his long black coat. These straps fastened in hooks on the back of the cross, out of sight of the audience, so he could just hang up there all sad and sorrowful-looking, and make out like he was being nailed. Brother Bulldog Hicks was to plant the nails *between* his fingers and toes. Hallelujah! Rock, church, rock!

Excitement was intense.

All went well, until the nailing began. Elder Jones removed his shoes and socks, in his bare black feet, bade farewell to his weeping congregation. As he leaned back against the cross and allowed Brother Hicks to compose him there, the crowd began to moan. But it was when Hicks placed the first nail between Elder Jones's toes that they become hysterical. Sister Bradford outyelled them all.

Hicks placed that first nail between the big toe and the next toe of the left foot and began to hammer. The foot was well strapped down, so the Elder couldn't move it. The closer the head of the nail got to his toes, the harder Hicks struck it. Finally the hammer collided with Elder Jones's foot, *bam* against his big toe.

"Aw-oh!" he moaned under his breath. "Go easy, man!"

"Have mercy," shouted the brothers and sisters of the church. "Have mercy on our Elder!"

Once more the hammer struck his toe. But the all too human sound of his surprised and agonized "Ouch!" was lost in the tumult of the shouting church.

"Bulldog, I say, go easy," hissed the Elder. "This *ain't* real."

Brother Hicks desisted, a grim smile on his face. Then he turned his attention to the right foot. There he placed another nail between the toes, and began to hammer. Again, as the nail went into the wood, he showed no signs of stopping when the hammer reached the foot. He just kept on landing cruel, metallic blows on the Elder's bare toenails until the preacher howled with pain, no longer able to keep back a sudden hair-raising cry. The sweat popped out on his forehead and dripped down on his shirt.

At first the Elder thought, naturally, that it was just a slip of the hammer on the deacon's part. Then he thought the man must have gone crazy—like the rest of the audience. Then it hurt him so bad he didn't know what he thought—so he just hollered, "Aw-ooo-oo-o!"

It was a good thing the church was full of noise, or they would have heard a strange dialogue.

"My God, Hicks, what are you doing?" the Elder cried, staring wildly at his deacon on the ladder.

"I'm nailin' you to the cross, Jones! And man, I'm *really* nailin'."

"Aw-oow-ow! Don't you know you're hurting me? I told you *not* to nail so hard!"

But the deacon was unruffled.

"Who'd you say's gonna be your right hand, when you get down from here and start your travelings?" Hicks asked.

"You, brother," the sweating Elder cried.

"And who'd you say was gonna be your left hand?"

"Sister Maggie Bradford," moaned Elder Jones from the cross.

"Naw, she ain't," said Brother Hicks, whereupon he struck the Reverend's toe a really righteous blow.

"Lord, help me!" cried the tortured minister. The weeping congregation echoed his cry. It was certainly real. The Elder *was* being crucified!

Brother Bulldog Hicks took two more steps up the ladder, preparing to nail the hands. With his evil face right in front of Elder Jones, he hissed: "I'll teach you nappy-headed jack-leg

ministers to come to St. Louis and think you all can walk away
with any woman you's a mind to. I'm gonna teach you to leave
my women alone. Here—here's a nail!"

Brother Hicks placed a great big spike right in the palm of
Elder Jones's left hand. He was just about to drive it in when
the frightened Reverend let out a scream that could be heard two
blocks away. At the same time, he began to struggle to get down.
Jones tried to bust the straps, but they was too strong for him.

If he could just get one foot loose to kick Brother Bulldog
Hicks!

Hicks lifted the hammer to let go when the Reverend's second
yell, this time, was loud enough to be heard in East St. Louis.
It burst like a bomb above the shouts of the crowd—and it had
its effect. Suddenly the congregation was quiet. Everybody knew
that was no way for a dying man to yell.

Sister Bradford realized that something had gone wrong, so
she began to chant the song her beloved pastor had told her to
chant at the propitious moment after the nailing was done. Now,
even though the nailing was not done, Sister Bradford thought
she had better sing:

> *Elder Jones will rise again,*
> *Elder Jones will rise again,*
> *Rise again, rise again!*
> *Elder Jones will rise again,*
> *Yes, my Lawd!*

But nobody took up the refrain to help her carry it on. Everybody was too interested in what was happening in front of them,
so Sister Bradford's voice just died out.

Meanwhile, Brother Hicks lifted the hammer again, but Elder
Jones spat right in his face. He not only spat, but suddenly called
his deacon a name unworthy of man or beast. Then he let out
another frightful yell and, in mortal anguish, called, "Sister Maggie
Bradford, lemme down from here! I say, come and get . . . me . . .
down . . . *from here!"*

Those in the church that had not already stopped moaning and
shouting, did so at once. You could have heard a pin drop. Folks
were petrified.

Brother Hicks stood on the ladder glaring with satisfaction at

Reverend Jones, his hammer still raised. Under his breath, the panting Elder dared him to nail another nail, and threatened to kill him stone-dead with a forty-four if he did.

"Just lemme get loose from here, and I'll fight you like a natural man," he gasped, twisting and turning like a tree in a storm.

"Come down, then," yelled Hicks, right out loud from the ladder. "Come on down! As sure as water runs, Jones, I'll show you up for what you is—a woman-chasing, no-good, low-down faker! I'll beat you to a batter with my bare hands!"

"Lawd, have mercy!" cried the church.

Jones almost broke a blood bessel trying to get loose from his cross.

"Sister Maggie, come and lemme down," he pleaded, sweat streaming from his face.

But Sister Bradford was covered with confusion. In fact, she was petrified. What could have gone wrong for the Elder to call on her like this in public in the very midst of the thing that was to bring him famous-glory and make them all rich preaching throughout the land with her at his side? Sister Bradford's head was in a whirl, her heart was in her mouth.

"Elder Jones, you means you really wants to get down?" she asked weakly from her seat in the Amen Corner.

"Yes," said the Elder, "can't you hear? I done called on you twenty times to let me down!"

At this point, Brother Hicks gave the foot nails one more good hammering. The words that came from the cross were nobody's business.

In a twinkling, Sister Bradford was at Jones's side. Realizing at last that the devil must've done got into Hicks (like it used to sometimes in the days when she knowed him), she went to the aid of her battered Elder, grabbed the foot of the ladder, and sent Hicks sprawling across the pulpit.

"You'll never crucify my Elder," she cried, "not for real." Energetically, she began to cut the straps away that bound the Reverend. Soon poor Jones slid to the floor, his feet too sore from the hammer's blows to even stand on them without help.

"Just lemme get at Hicks," was all Reverend Jones could gasp.

"He knowed I didn't want them nails that close." In the dead silence that took possession of the church, everybody heard him moan, "Lawd, lemme get at Hicks," as he hobbled away on the protecting arm of Sister Maggie.

"Stand back, Bulldog," Sister Maggie said to the deacon, "and let your pastor pass. Soon as he's able, he'll flatten you out like a shadder—but now, I'm in charge. Stand back, I say, and let him pass!"

Hicks stood back. The crowd murmured. The minister made his exit.

Thus ended the ambitious career of Elder William Jones. He never did pastor in St. Louis any more. Neither did he fight Hicks. He just snuck away.

Ralph Ellison

RALPH ELLISON was born in 1914 in Oklahoma City and educated in its public schools. He later attended Tuskegee Institute, where he studied music with the hope of becoming a professional musician. Mr. Ellison participated in the Federal Writers Project in New York and also wrote short stories, articles, and book reviews for various magazines.

For *Invisible Man*, published in 1952, Mr. Ellison received the National Book Award for the best American novel of that year. In his acceptance speech he stated that he rejected "the rather rigid concepts of reality," and he speaks of "the rich babble of idiomatic expression around me, a language full of imagery and gesture and rhetorical canniness." In describing his work he says, "I was forced to conceive of a novel unburdened by the narrow naturalism which has led after so many triumphs to the final and unrelieved despair which marks so much of our current fiction."

Ralph Ellison received a Rosenwald Fellowship, the Russwurm Award, the National Newspaper Publishers Award, the Prix de Rome, and the American Academy of Arts and Letters Fellowship to the American Academy in Rome, 1955–57.

He has taught at Bard College and the University of Chicago and was visiting lecturer at the Salzburg Seminar in American Studies in 1954. He has lectured at Bennington, Princeton, Harvard, Fisk, Tuskegee, Rutgers, Wabash, Antioch, and Boston College and in Germany, England, Italy, Spain, Mexico, and several Far Eastern countries.

He has written for *The Antioch Review, The Reporter, Horizon, Common Ground, Saturday Review,* and other publications.

"Out of the Hospital and Under the Bar" is published here for the first time.

AUTHOR'S NOTE

The following narrative formed a part of the original version of a novel called *Invisible Man,* and it marked an attempt to get the hero of that memoir out of the hospital into the world of Harlem. It was Mary's world, the world of the urbanized (or partially urbanized), Negro folk, and I found it quite pleasurable to discover, during those expansive days of composition before the necessities of publication became a reality, that it was Mary, a woman of the folk, who helped release the hero from the machine. I was quite sorry that considerations of space made it necessary that I reconceive the development.

I am pleased for Mary's sake to see this version in print. She deserved more space in the novel and would, I think, have made it a better book. . . .

Reading it now, almost ten years after it was put aside, I have the feeling that it stands on its own if only as one of those pieces of writing which consists mainly of one damned thing after another sheerly happening. If I am right, then it is still in tune with our times and an amusing *riff* on the old theme of "Ain't Life the Damndest?"—with the added advantage that it's happening to the hero (who is something of a liar, if you ask me) and not the reader.

For those who would care to fit it back into *Invisible Man* let them start at the point where the explosion occurs in the paint factory, substitute the following happenings, and leave them once the hero is living in Mary's hope.

For those who desire more than the sheer narrative ride, who hunger and thirst for "meaning," let them imagine what this country would be without its Marys. Let them imagine, indeed, what the American Negro would be without the Marys of our ever-expanding Harlems. Better still, since fiction is always a collaboration between writer and reader, let them take this proffered middle, this *agon*, this passion, and supply their own beginning, and if an ending, a moral, or a perception is needed, let them supply their own. For me, of course, the narrative *is* the meaning.

Chicago
December 1961

OUT OF THE HOSPITAL
AND UNDER THE BAR

BY RALPH ELLISON

When I awakened she stood looking down. Her newly straightened hair gleamed glossily in the intense light, her blue uniform freshly ironed and stiffly starched. Seeing me awake she shook her head and grinned. I tensed, expecting a trick. But not this time. Instead, she tried seriously to communicate with me. Her mood was solemn, and I was almost sure that I understood some of her shouted questions. But just as I had been unable to put my own ideas into words, now I could not put the movements of her lips into definite patterns. Who was she anyway? Why this feeling that I had known her for a long time? Whatever it was she was saying seemed very serious and it included both of us. I watched her, puzzled. Her question was escaping me. She threw up her hands, "Shucks!" she said.

"Shucks!" She froze, her eyes looking into the case, studying something I could not see. What's happening? Was this another trick? She was as still as a mountain. Will she spit upon the lid again? I thought with disgust. My mind overflowed with forebodings of danger. My mouth grew dry. Yet above me she stood as still as before—until, drawn by some almost imperceptible movement of her hands, I saw the whorls of her fingertips pressing worn and fish-belly white now from her blood-draining pressure upon the lids, her worn fingers arching back to palms I could not see.

She drummed upon the glass making a series of light padding sounds, her eyes lost in abstraction. It stopped abruptly, her fingers darting out of my range of vision, disappearing completely. I could not see them about her face, which still leaned over my case; nor below, where through the glass side, I saw her harsh blue uniform. They had to be somewhere along the chromium upper edge of the case where the lid joined the side. Then with a start, I saw them darting along the side of the case. A grating sound began. What on earth! Was she insane? She was twisting the bolts! Visions of calamity flashed through my head. I was in a panic. Suddenly I no longer wanted to be freed. What if she was opening the case too soon? Before my treatment was complete? Suppose she turned the wrong bolts and set the machinery in motion? A strange animal sound filled the case. I tugged at the arm straps, both afraid and furious, seeing her calm and controlled above me as though freeing people from intricate machines was a usual thing. "Stop it! Stop it!" I thought, tugging vainly at the straps. For though I wanted release, I was frightened lest it should come through this ignorant, unscientific old woman. Where was the doctor? Why didn't somebody come? The grating of bolts continued. She frowned, saying "Shhhh, shhhh!" and the animal sounds ceased. Straightening, she looked in with deep conspiratorial expression as she spread her arms along the edge of the lid and lifted. "No," I thought, pressing against the bottom of the case, "oh no!" I held my breath waiting for the flash of short-circuited wires, the blasting shock into oblivion, waiting an eternity, it seemed, but nothing happened. The lid failed to budge. Not even a charge of static flashed over me.

"Shucks!" her lips made.

I shut my eyes as she set herself, lifting. There came a small quick sound, then a click. I looked up. A wave of nausea struck me. There, beneath the lid and inches above my head protruded her work-swollen fingers. I felt an irrational desire to retch as I watched them strain with the heavy lid. My eyes were drawn to their scarred, leather-brown texture, the smooth polish of the knuckles. Suddenly I saw them straighten and work in the air, like the legs of an obscene insect rolled upon its back. The fingertips turned alternately white and pink as she tried to bring back circulation. I was seized by a savage impulse to bite them. But my head could not raise that far. A new sound arose! I had started to moan, when before my eyes the lid now raised a few inches, brought a rush of ether-laden air, and my stomach heaved. The air set off a thermostatic device inside the machine which, as I saw the lid come trembling down, clicked off. A mixture of relief and despair flooded over me as I saw an expression of pain grip her features. Sweat popped upon her forehead, her fingers were caught beneath the lid. Her face glowed up with pain. The rasping of tense breathing came to me. I saw her face set in determined lines as, with the heavy lid still knifing into her fingers, she studied the side of the case. Abruptly I saw her jaws snap shut, the muscles of her throat, roping out as she lifted, the lid rising a tortuous fraction and halting in precarious balance as she sent her right hand sliding swiftly along the edge of the case, giving a sudden twist. I saw a shiny bolt flip between the side of the case and the lid, landing with a faint click. Amazed, I saw her pull her fingers free, then turn quickly to the other end of the case. Another bolt fell into place, and I saw her step back, holding her fingers and breathing heavily. The strange outside air rushed upon me, making me suddenly light-headed. A turmoil of emotions filled me.

"How's that?" she said, peering in through the crack. "I knowed I could get that doggone thing open if I tried. How you feeling?"

I stared dumbly into her bright eyes.

"Well you could be sociable," she said. "How come you don't say nothing? Is you all right?"

I looked into her face, feeling things begin to rush inside of me. A single drop of blood showed on a fingertip that rested upon the edge of the case. "Like dark red wine," I thought light-headedly, her voice was strangely familiar. Who was she? A lost relative, a member of my forgotten family come to the North leaving no forwarding address? An aunt whom I didn't know? Hell no, she's crazy, I thought, realizing what she had done. She *must* be crazy. Why doesn't someone come? But for the slight sighing moan of the machine, it was quiet. Time itself seemed to move to the dragging moans of the mechanism, punctuated by her rasping breath. Far back within me, crouching on the bottom of the case, I waited for an explosion, feeling that an outrageous crime had been committed—for which I would be sacrificed. A furious resentment grew within me.

"Say, son!" she said. "Is you a dummy or something? You look intelligent, so how come you don't say something? Why these white folks got you in this iron straight-jacket?"

A ringing set up in my ears.

Her eyes swept the machine and as she soothed her mashed fingers she snickered, "You must be awful strong for them to have to put you under all this pile of pnk. *Awful* strong. Who they think you is, Jack the Bear or John Henry or somebody like that? . . . Say something, fool!"

Something seemed to give way. "You, you, you! . . ." I shouted angrily, a vile name fighting for expression, and stopped short, surprised. I still had a voice! I could talk! My eyes filled with uncontrollable tears. My anger faded. I looked at her and she seemed to understand.

"Well, at least you can talk," she said. "How you feel?"

"Fine," I whispered hoarsely, "I feel fine."

"What's supposed to be wrong with you?"

"I don't remember, but I'm all right now."

"What you mean you don't remember? You in there, ain't you? Now when *I* was in the hospital I had a tumor. They damn near took out all my works—all but the important ones, that is," she added coyly. "So don't come telling me you don't remember."

"But, I don't," I said. "I've forgotten nearly everything!"

"You *what?*"

"That's right, my memory's gone. I've lost it."

"Shucks, boy, I ain't one of them doctors. You don't have to tell me that stuff. How long you been from down home?"

"I don't remember," I said, "but I don't think it's been long."

She grinned through the crack knowingly. "You must have left in a hurry. Yeah, a heap leaves in a hurry, you know. But you ain't fooling me. I heard them nurses talking 'bout you. They say they

even got one of the psychiatristses and a socialist or sociologist or
something looking at you all the time."

"A psychiatrist!"

"Sho. I was in here cleaning one day when they come in and I
liked to laughed myself sick seeing them write you all them questions when a fool could see you couldn't answer through all that
glass anyway. And I says to myself, that there is the gamest young
scamp I most ever seen, laying up there making a fool outa them
doctors. He ain't no more sick than I am!"

I tried to piece it together. "How long have I been here?" I
asked.

"Eight or nine days—say, don't you want something to eat?"

"Eat?"

"Yeah," she said, straightening and looking around. "They don't
never feed nobody enough in this place."

Then stooping to the crack again she said, "I be back in a
minute. You don't have to worry 'bout the nurse, she won't be
looking in here for a while, cause she's off with her intern boy
friend. Be right back."

She moved away. I heard a door open and close. So old friendly
face was a psychiatrist. Perhaps I *was* crazy, crazy in my private
room. All by myself. "Food." My stomach growled. Breathing the
outside air seemed to have given me a sharp appetite. This old
Mary, she'd probably get me confined to this machine for months
and months—and get herself fired. Who was she and why had
she bothered?

"Here," she said, her bright eyes peeping through the cracked
lid. "All I could find was some kind of canned meat, but it's got
some good ole pork in it and that's what a down-home boy like
you needs."

Saliva welled from the wall of my mouth as I saw the trimmed
sandwich bread appear near the crack. "Here," she said. Then we
both realized that I could not reach it.

"You'd think it was enough for them to have you in that thing,"
she scolded, "but here they have to tie your hands as well. Let's
see . . ." she said, trying to reach beneath the lid to release my
arm. The space was too narrow.

She shook her head. "Guess I'll have to feed you myself," she said. "Open your mouth."

"What?"

"I say open your mouth . . . Lord, here I is feeding another baby. A big ole rusty baby!"

I saw her break off a piece of the sandwich and push her fingers beneath the lid. I didn't like the idea.

"Aw here, boy!" she snapped, tossing the bit of sandwich. For a moment it balanced beneath my nose—long enough for me to catch its odor and snap it up viciously. It was delicious; strange and yet familiar in my mouth. So delicious that I swallowed my anger with the bread and waited eagerly for the next morsel. She sat beside me, looking through with a pleased expression—as though actually feeding a baby.

I could taste the sweet starch of the bread ball and the meat spreading beneath the motion of my teeth. As soon as I swallowed she dropped in another.

"Just look at him eat," she said. "I bet ain't nothing wrong with you a few square meals won't cure. And maybe you a little lonesome too. That's it, you need some company. But I bet you that's all."

I continued to chew, thinking, "No, it isn't all." I wasn't lonesome for people, because I didn't remember anyone. If anything, I was lonesome for my lost name—whatever it was. Suppose it's Cootie Brown! I thought, or "Dobby Hicks" or "Mr. I. P. Freely"?

"Son, you was fooling about forgetting your name, warn't you?" she said as though reading my mind.

"No, I've really forgotten it."

"Well, what you going to do when they send you to the other hospital?"

"*Other* hospital?"

"Sho. They suppose to transfer you. I heard them saying something about it the other day."

Looking into her eyes shining through the cracked lid I felt myself slipping into a bottomless hole. I was sure that I was not asleep, yet it was as though I dreamed.

"They intends to watch you a while," she was saying. "They wants to study your case."

"I've got to get out of here," I said. "I've got to get out right away."

"Boy, you can't go nowhere," she said, her voice rising. "You too weak."

"I'm not weak," I said.

"Sho, you weak. You ain't had no exercise."

"I'm not weak," I insisted. "It's just that my hands are strapped."

She looked at me. "That's right."

"Sure, that's why I seem to be weak. If my hands were freed, I'd show you."

She hesitated. "You don't have to worry right away," she said. "They ain't going to transfer you until sometime next week."

"Are you sure?"

"That's right."

"I've got to get out of here," I said.

"Son, you sho you ain't in some kind of trouble?"

"Trouble?"

"You can tell me," she said, her voice kindly.

"I think so," I said, "I must be. But I can't remember what I did."

"Shucks, there you go lying to me agin!"

"But you're wrong. I'm telling the truth."

She shook her head in silent disbelief.

"Look," I said, "these people might kill me. Nobody knows me. They can do anything they want with me and no one would say a word."

I began to cough, my throat was dry. It became violent.

"Wait, I'll get you some water," she said. "I be back in a second."

I had to get away, how would I do it? If only she'd release my hands! Perhaps then I could think much better. I had to leave, for I feared that now that I was becoming adjusted to this machine, they planned to place me in one that was smaller—more severe. I'd probably be killed next time. If only she'd release my arms, I thought as she appeared with a glass of water.

"Here." She pushed the glass toward the crack and discovering that it was too narrow I had an idea.

"How you get your water?" she asked.

"Through a tube they stick through the lid," I said.

"I don't see no tube. . . . Wonder where they keep it."

"I don't know," I said, pretending to go into a fit of coughing. She looked around hastily, then attempted to push the glass of water into the case. I continued coughing.

"I'll have to open this thing wider," she said fretfully, leaving to get rid of the glass and returning to lift upon the lid. It didn't budge. I coughed more violently, gasping for breath. She lifted again.

"Hurry please," I gasped between coughs. But it was too heavy. After a moment she stopped, breathing tiredly, looking into my distorted face. I had actually started myself to coughing now. For a minute it got completely out of hand, sending great gusts of saliva spraying against the glass.

"Loosen my arm," I managed to gasp, "I'll help you lift it . . ."

Without a word she began to squeeze her arm into the case. "Where is the strap?"

"Here, under the sheet," I sputtered.

"There here's the tightest place I ever tried to get into," she said. Now I could see her forearm groping down the inside of the case. Then her fingers touched my shoulder.

"That's it!" I shouted eagerly.

"I know it," she said between grunts. "You suppose to be coughing, ain't you?"

And I was taken with such an urgent desire to laugh that in suppressing it, I began coughing again.

"All right, all right, I'll have you loose in a second. I thought you was trying to jive old Mary."

"NO, no," I gasped, feeling her loosening the strap that bound my left arm. Suddenly I heard the sound of metal striking against glass.

"There it is," she said, standing up.

Still coughing, I tried to lift my arm. Swift arrow flights of needling pain shot from my wrist to my shoulder, as when a newly mended limb is first removed from its cast. I stopped for a moment.

"Here," she said, "let's get you some water in there before you start coughing again."

"My arm feels strange," I said.

"Sho, it feels strange. You ain't been using it."

I flexed my fingers, clinched them, tried again, vainly. A great sense of impotence took me. I couldn't lift my arm. I looked at it lying beside me, feeling a profound emptiness. It was as though the bone had been removed and my arm become a flabby grey mass of atrophying flesh. I moved my fingers, watching them respond sluggishly. A feeling of a complete drainage and shame grew within me.

"Come on, son," she said, waiting with her hands upon the lid, prepared to lift it further. I wanted to turn my face away.

"What's the matter?"

"I can't," I said.

"You cain't what?"

"I can't raise my arm."

"You just ain't trying. Stop being such a sissy and come on."

"I've tried. It's too weak to raise."

"You'd better hurry," she said with impatience. "I ain't got much more time before the nurse comes back."

"Something's happened to it," I said, gritting my teeth and straining. "Look, I'm really trying."

I began to sweat from the effort, the muscles of my shoulder ached, but the arm lay rubbery at my side.

She shook her head. "I ain't *never* seen no man in the shape you in. . . . Why don't you tell me what you done for them to put you in this thing, so I can help you?"

"But I don't know," I said.

Without a word she reached for one of the bolts that propped the lid. "I got to go," she said, "I cain't help nobody who don't trust me. . . ."

"Wait," I said, filling with a dread of being left alone with the knowledge of my weakness.

"I got no time," she said coldly.

"Please, I'll tell you what I did," I begged, sparring desperately.

"I ain't interested no more," she said, tugging at the bolt.

"Please."

"Naw! You been lying to me all the time."

"I'm sorry," I said, "I was afraid."

"Tell that lie to the white folks; they the ones what wants to believe it. . . . You young Negroes is pass being afraid. . . ."

"But I *was* afraid."

"I got to go," she said, attacking the last bolt. "You young'ns ain't never scaird o' nothing."

"Stay just a minute," I pleaded. "I had to do it. . . ."

"You had to do what? . . . Naw, don't bother me, boy, I told you I got to go. Tell me next time."

"But I had to get him . . ."

"I got to go . . . Get who?" she asked, her eyes narrowing.

"The man."

"What man?"

"He was white . . ."

"A white man, boy?"

"Yes," I said, desperately talking at random. "He had a loaf of bread . . ."

"Some bread, yeah? . . ."

"And he had a bottle . . ."

"Uh huh, and what else he have?" she said shrewdly.

"He had something that looked like a microscope," I said, remembering the instruments pointed at me by the physicians.

"Yes . . . and just as I was going past an alley he tried to stop me . . ."

"Good God! What you do then?"

"Well, he said something that I couldn't understand and then he started after me . . ."

"No he didn't!"

"Yes, he did," I said, watching her closely. "He came after me with the microscope as though he meant to hit me with it . . ."

"He did? And then what happen?"

"Well, when I saw him coming toward me I got scared and hollered, 'Don't come any closer. Don't come any closer—' "

"And the fool kept coming?"

"That's right. . . ."

And what you do then?"

"I saw a bottle on the ground and stooped and picked it up . . ."

"An' what he do then? He keep on coming?"

"No," I said, suddenly gripped by a feeling that I was relating an actual happening, something that had occurred sometime, somewhere, in my past. "He didn't keep coming, he stopped in his tracks and looked up and down the street. I was in the dark and I could see the freckles on the side of his face that was in the light. And he said, 'Look at me, black boy, what kind of man am I?'"

"What kinda man he was?" she said, frowning.

"Yes. And I . . ."

"And what you tell him?"

"I said, 'You're a white man, sir,' and his eyes got bright and he started laughing and said, 'That's right, but what *other* kind of man am I?'

"I didn't know. So I had to tell him I didn't know. And that made him angry.

"He said, 'Don't play dumb, boy. You nigger boys always try to play dumb!'

"'But I'm telling the truth, sir,' I said. And he said, 'All right, all right, so I'm a white man, and what are you?'"

"And what you say then, boy?" she asked.

"I said, 'I'm colored, sir,' but it seemed to make him very angry. . . . His face changed while I was looking at it fast."

"Yeah, he wanted you to call yourself a nigger. How he look, how he look, son?"

"I couldn't see all of it because he was in the shadow of the street light . . . standing in a kind of half light. . . . But his face got tight and started to quiver like he had a tic."

"Go on, boy," she said.

"Well, he became very angry and said, 'That's right, you're a black, stinking, low-down nigger bastard that's probably got the syph and I'm white and you're supposed to do whatever I say, understand . . . ?'"

"And what'd you say?"

"Nothing . . ."

"You ought to have hit the old thing with that bottle. . . . These white folks . . . It oughta been me!"

"I was thinking about trying to run past him, when all at once he jammed his hand in his pocket and brought out a big roll of bills. He said, 'Now, nigger, I want you to stand still while I put this twenty-dollar bill in your pocket.' And I looked at him, and saw that the side of his mouth was twitching and his voice was shaky. I had never heard a man's voice sound like that . . .'"

"What happen, boy?"

"He said, 'See, this is a real twenty-dollar bill. You can have it,' and I said, 'No, thank you, sir, I'm on my way to work.' He looked at me and said softly, 'Please don't be like that, boy.' 'I'm sorry, sir,' I said, 'but I've got to be going . . .'"

She looked dubious, her head to one side. "Boy, you ain't lying to me, is you?" she asked.

"I'm not lying. He said, 'Nigger, do you want to get in trouble?'

"I said, 'No, sir, I always try to keep out of trouble.'

"'You're not keeping out of trouble now,' he said, 'real trouble. I don't believe I ever saw a nigger boy get himself in trouble as fast as you are with me.'

"'No, sir, I don't want to get into trouble with anybody, sir.'

"'Well, if you don't come on and take the money—'

"'No, sir, I'm afraid.'

"'What are you afraid of?'

"'I don't know—I think it's because I didn't do anything to earn it, sir.'

"'You will, you will,' he said, looking at me and starting to laugh again. 'You don't have to worry about that. That's my worry. Nigger,' he said in a hard voice, 'I'm asking you again, what kinda man am I?'

"'You're a white man, sir,' I said.

"'Is that all you can say?'

"'Yes, sir.'

"He seemed to think about it a moment. 'Well, didn't your mammy teach you better than to disobey a white man?'

"'Yes, sir, she taught me.'

"'And don't you know I can have you taken care of? . . .'"

"Good God, boy, what'd you do then?" she interrupted.

"I look at him and thought about fighting him. I thought about trying to run past him, too. He was only a small, slender man, nice-looking in the face that had been beaten up a lot. I said, 'Yes, sir, but I haven't done anything . . .'

"He said, 'You don't *have* to do anything, you know that.'

" 'Yes, sir, I know it.'

" 'All I have to do is step into the diner up there on the corner and speak to the truck drivers, and what'd you do? I wouldn't want to have to do that,' he said.

"I was very worried, so I asked him: 'Please, can't you wait until Saturday, sir. I'll have plenty of time on Saturday, and I always come right past here . . .'

" 'Oh, no,' he said. 'You won't pull that one on me. I know that one. Once before one of you tried to do that. Some of you nigger boys try to be smart. I'm on to you. Now why don't you stop arguing and take the money? I bet you never had a twenty-dollar bill in your whole life, did you?'

" 'No, sir.'

" 'Well, you're going to have this one. Hold still,' he said and started towards me . . ."

"He still have that what-you-ma-call-it in his hand?"

"The microscope? Yes . . ."

"And what you do?"

"That's when I did it."

"Did what, boy?"

"I didn't know what else to do. He kept coming up on me and I tried to tell him not to do it, but he kept on coming and I decided to run past him, and he said, 'You want to be smart? You can have this microscope, too. I won't be needing it any more.' And by then he had rolled the money into a little wad like a spit-ball, rolling it slowly between his fingers. He said, 'It won't take but a minute,' and then he reached out and touched me and I swung the bottle at him and ran. . . ."

"You hit him, boy?"

"I think so. . . ."

"You kill him? You think you killed him?" she asked excitedly.

"I ran, I've been running ever since."

"You run a long ways, didn't you, son?"

"Yes," I said.

"And hopped them freight trains and everything."

"I don't want to talk about it," I said. "I've got to get out of here. Can't you see why I have to get out?"

"Yeah," she said, looking at me with dead seriousness. "I see

it now. You probably killed him, or hurt him bad, and they looking for you. . . . I tell you what, it's too late to do anything right
now 'cause it's time for me to go and that nurse'll be coming in
here. . . ."

"You can't help me?"

"Yeah, but not tonight. You stay here like nothing happen until
I get backed tomorrow and I'll help you git outa here."

"But they might transfer me," I protested.

"No they won't. They don't aim to do that till next week. You
just have to be patient awhile. Besides, you oughta told me the
truth when I first ask you."

And before I could protest further she proceeded to lower the
lid and bolt it, and I felt a profound loneliness take hold of me.
When she was done, she stood above me looking in. Suddenly she
gestured frantically toward the case. With despair I discovered
that she had forgotten to cover my naked arm, lying impotent
and partly exposed beside me. Above me she made frantic signs,
but my muscles couldn't respond. She gestured furiously—only to
stop off, listening, and leave hurriedly, her face full of dismay. I
seemed to boil inside. I would be discovered. She had rushed away
as though someone was coming. I looked at my arm, trying with
all my will to make it respond. It was as though it betrayed me of
a separate will. I had thought all that need be done to free myself
was to have my arms released, but now I was as far from freedom
as before, perhaps farther. A sharp, helpless anger formed within
me as I stuggled, squirming like a pinioned worm, seeing the
sheet dank, clinging, as though plastered to me. Soon I was bathed
in sweat. If only I could turn on my side! . . . or my stomach!
Why hadn't old Mary been a nurse, a technician, a doctor? Or a
lawyer with a writ of *habeas corpus?* Then instead of getting me
into a worse predicament than before she might have given me
some real assistance. I froze.

Under the strain my ears had grown extremely sensitive, for
when she entered the room I heard her through the walls of the
soundproof case. It's all over, I thought, it's all over now. She
loomed, framed in empty space, above my head, holding a bottle
of rubbing alcohol. She looked strange, her face highly flushed, as
though delicately bruised or stung by peach fuzz, her lipstick

badly blurred. I stared. She seemed to look straight at me, but not to see me. She's daydreaming, I thought with a sense of wonder. She seemed lost in some delicious dream. I waited to see her plummet the instant she saw the obscene nakedness of my arm. I steeled myself, waiting for the cry of alarm, already hearing the excited arrival of the technicians and physicians. But she hardly noticed me! I watched her make inscriptions upon my chart as though in a delightful fog. Was she baiting me, trying to give me a false sense of security before sounding the alarm? Maybe she's afraid and plans to call the others when she's safely out of the room. . . . If only the case were open, I thought, I could plead with her or frighten her with threats. Finishing with the charts now she raised her hand lovingly to the light and, with her fingers curved delicately, gazed with admiration upon the flashing of a fiery stone. It was amazing. She seemed to fall into a trance, smiling dreamily into the flashing fire as upon some bright inward happening; then closing her eyes, she turned her head languidly from side to side—a movement of sweet swooning surrender; like a spellbound dancer, or a child dizzy with turning, she took a swirling step toward the case, gliding as in a dream-waltz, her mouth upturned invitingly, to receive an invisible kiss. What on earth? I thought. She was transformed! Before my eyes she had become the heroine of a thousand colorful picture ads, motion picture reels. I could not believe I saw the same plain face. It was lovely, and absurd; the loveliness peeping out of the absurdity, and she seemingly aware of it, carried away with the image of herself reflected in the flashing jewel. For a moment she was still, her flushed face smiling as though listening to an inner voice, then as though dancing a pantomime of tenderness and delicacy, she caressingly adjusted the pressure control of the machine and left wide-eyed without detecting that anything about me was changed.

I fought against the descending pressures filled with a feeling that I had seen something forbidden, something which would get me destroyed even though I didn't understand its meaning. I would have to get free of the machine before the doctors discovered that I had seen. . . .

Suddenly I was clearly awake, as though plunged into an icy pool. Two physicians stood above me, one with a microscope-like instrument focusing its twin eyes with a deadly stare into the case. I stole a look at my exposed arm and watched: My body ached with rigidity. But strangely they seemed unaware of it. They concentrated upon the instrument (one focusing, the other making notes) and I waited for it to tell them what their eyes ignored. But still, with the lenses directed full upon me from a point less than four feet away, nothing happened. I became uneasy. Why didn't they say something? Didn't they see that my arm was free? Yet they made no move. I waited, filled with a sense of angry indignation. They were deliberately ignoring me! Deliberately filling me with suspense. Secretly they were laughing at me! These peckerwoods! My anger grew. I had succeeded in partly freeing myself, something I was sure they were against, and now they ignored me. It was insulting! I felt myself filling with silent rage as I realized that I really was no freer than before—simply because *they* refused to acknowledge my freedom. Yes, and if they should consider me free, if they had only the faintest hallucination of it, then even though I remained in the case with only one arm unstrapped, I would indeed be free. It was crystal clear. These bastards! They had me locked in their eyes like a tadpole in a jug. Looking at the sparkling lenses, the polished cylinders, the smooth forehead topped by blond hair, the calm cheeks . . . I became so angry that I experienced the strange sensation of clenching my fist. There it was, a knuckled ball beside me. I looked up hastily expecting them to look alarmed. Instead they merely became a bit more active with their instruments. Nobody bothered to notice the bare arm, the clenched fist. Defeated, I closed my eyes, trying to shut them out.

My thoughts turned to old Mary. Where had she gone? I grew resentful that by meddling, she had partly freed me and rendered me more insecure. And yet, for all my resentment, I wished for her. I imagined her returning subtly transformed into a young pink nurse; one trained in the intricacies of the machine; but who yet, for some nameless reason, was interested in helping me escape. Yes, she'd come and open the case, bearing with her a clean light smell that was neither the odor of ether nor disinfectant. And I would be set completely free and my impotent arms and legs would be strong and well and I would take her away with me—

where, I didn't know. What was the weather outside? I wondered.
Was it fall or winter, or some unnamed season in between winter
and spring? Oh, well it wouldn't happen like that. Not if they
had noticed my arm, without giving a sign. Old Mary wouldn't
return in *any* form. Perhaps she was already fired never to return
again. It was up to me, I had to get free of the case and find my
way to the street. But what if the rest of my body was as naked as
my arm. Even that wouldn't stop me, I'd walk into the street
naked. I'd find clothes somewhere out there. . . .

But how would I walk? If my legs were as weak as my arm I'd
fall on my face. Still I'd have to risk it. Then once again I heard
the tinkling of keys and looked up to see old Mary. I was so relieved to see her that tears formed in my eyes. This time she
wasted no time trying to communicate through the glass, but
unbolted the case and started lifting the lid. And in the excitement I forgot my impotent arm and discovered myself helping
her from the inside.

"You laying in there gitting strong," she said. "Last time I was
here you couldn't do nothing but eat." She winked.

"You were gone a long time."

"You think I wasn't coming back?"

"I was worried."

"I had to send home to get something for you. It took longer
than I thought."

"What did you send for?"

"Just a little something to give you some strength."

"Something for me to *take?*"

"Sho, just a little home remedy, something I got from my
mama."

Was she kidding again? "You have a mother?" I said.

"Sure, haven't you? Everybody got a mother."

"Of course, but I thought . . ."

"I know, you think I'm too old to have a mama still living. But
I have. The Lawd willing, Mama's gonna be 104 years old on her
next birthday. And her hearing's good and she don't need no
glasses *and* her teeth's better'n mine."

"She must be a remarkable woman."

"Us think she is," she said. "She's a smart woman too. Useta sing alto, grow the best crops in the county, and right now she knows more about roots and herbs and midwifery and things than anybody you ever seen. Here," she said, "take this and swaller it."

I saw her removing something from her apron pocket. "That's what I sent to Mama to get. It'll make you strong. Go on, eat it."

I stared at the substance. It was green, like balled grape leaves that had dried without fading. . . .

"Go on, boy."

I looked at it. I wanted both to reject and accept it. I was fascinated. Around the outer leaf the ribs spread tree-shaped, with the root and uppermost branches beginning inside the ball and ending there. . . . "*What's the matter, boy, you scared?*" I distrusted it, yet I had to draw strength from some source. . . . Fearfully, I put it into my mouth and bit it in half, swallowing part and holding the rest between my teeth

"You swaller it?"

I bowed my head.

"How's it?" she said.

"All right." As dry as it seemed, it went down smoothly, a bittersweet taste that suddenly seemed to set my throat aflame.

"Ah," I began. "Aaaaah!"

"Hush, boy! Keep your mouth shut!"

I wanted to vomit, but already it was burning my stomach.

"You're trying to kill me. . . ."

"Kill you? Fool, that's going to make you strong. . . ."

". . . Get the nurse. . . ."

". . . Sho, if you want to stay in that junk pile. . . ."

"Then give me some water. . . ."

"No water. You be all right in a minute. Don't you know ain't no medicine any good unless it's hard to take? You ought to know that. . . ."

I writhed. Drops of scalding sweat seemed to pop out over my scalp, my eyes went out of focus, distorting her image, my skin flamed. I thought I was going to die.

"That's some good stuff," she said. "You'll be all right now. That stuff'll make a baby strong. Now less see, you better stay at my house. The address ——. You remember it, you hear me. But first we gotta get you out."

"What was that stuff?" I said.

"Never mind. You don't have to worry, we been knowing about it a long time. Least Mama is, and her mama's mama knowed about it. . . ."

"But what is it?"

"Look, boy, ain't no use in your asking me, 'cause I done tole you all I'm going to. It's in you now, so let's think about getting you out of there."

"O.K. I think I can help you with the lid."

"Sho, but the problem is to get you out of the building, and I can't go along with you. That you got to do by yourself. Maybe we better wait till next week. . . ."

"No, I've got to go *tonight!*"

"But liable to get caught. . . ."

"I don't care, I'll have to take the chance."

"Huh, looks like the herb is working. You sho you want to try? All right, all I can do is help you open the lid and then you have ta go for yourself. You might make it, but I don't know. Lucky this here's the third floor." Suddenly I saw her turn. "Oh my Lord, they calling me. . . ."

"Mary, the lid!" I called as she started for the door.

"I be right back," she hissed, her hand on the knob.

"Then turn off the lights!"

As she opened the door I saw her hand dart at the wall and the room went black. "Mary!" The voice was cut off by the shutting door. She was gone and I was aware of my pounding heart.

It had to be now, alone. I raised my head to the cracked lid, listening. Silence. My eyes pressed against a total blackness, without form. An absolute, ether-drenched blackness that poured into my lungs as my mind cursed the voice that had called old Mary away. I would have to do it alone. Go out there alone. But first I had to get from the inside. I rested, my hands exploring the inside of the case.

Beneath the sheet swathing my body I found the electrodes strapped over my navel and my spine. I tugged at the first, hearing a motor click sinisterly in the bowels of the case and, snatching my hands away, it stopped. I would leave it until later. The straps that bound my legs were easy—smooth leather linked with a simple metal buckle. But there were still the two binding my ankles, too far to reach until the lid was further raised. Resting, I planned my next move. I would escape now, before old Mary changed her mind, or became afraid and turned me in. It had to be now. Beyond the door lay a hall, the first problem was to get there. After that I wouldn't think. With my back pressing the bottom I moved my palms upward against the glass and pushed. The smooth hardness of the lid slanted steeply to my right. I pushed upward, my soft muscles seeming to stiffen and burn inwardly as my arms extended and slid toward the outer edge like an impersonal tool. The lid rose slightly. Now, now! With a burst of energy I strained upward, raising it. My hands grew hot with friction, rubbing against the glass. It was stubborn. My arms ached. My ears rang. A wave of nausea boiled up within me, bringing a green bittersweet taste; the rest of the old woman's medicine had dissolved beneath my tongue. I swallowed it down, tasting fire. It seemed to act directly upon my muscles, giving me new strength. I felt the heavy lid swinging like a stone now, smoothly silent in the benevolent blackness. And all the time I was listening, praying a crazy prayer: "Lord, give me the strength of Jack-the-Bear," grunting and straining against the lid.

> *Jack the rabbit*
> *Jack the Bear,*
> *Lift it, lift it,*
> *Just a hair . . .*

Make poetry of it, sing it—no, they might hear. *Sing a song in silence. Sing a song of silence in a strange land. Jack it up, bear it in the dark. It's heavy as the world.* With my arms straight above me now, numbing aches lost in the metal and glass, and the glass and metal inseparable from the blackness, I listened for footsteps beyond the door, expecting the intrusion of the hated light, the swish of a starched uniform, then pushed again. Suddenly there was a click. I felt the slanting plane become perpendicular, the weight left my hands. The lid had clicked back upon its hinges. Hesitantly I sat up, feeling the sheet drop from my back into the case. My body was wet. The ringing in my ears increased swiftly in volume, then faded. There was a silence punctuated by my breathing. For an instant it seemed I had struggled through a dream. I needed to see, if only there were some kind of *black* light present. . . . My body shuddered, then tensed with a swift insistent urge. Rising to my knees I braced myself against the side of the case, feeling the nodes come with me and becoming aware of the danger of electrocution at the instant. I could hear the dull splattering below, seeing it arching downward with a faintly phosphorescent glowing. I held on. At last it ended. I was disgusted, yet amused; for I would have to step in it on my way out. It's your River Jordan, you have to cross over it, I thought. Still kneeling I went after the node, again hearing the machinery click on and whirr. I'd have to hurry before they noticed the fluctuation of the current and came to make an inspection. Releasing it, I searched into the case. The rest of the cord was folded neatly beneath the sheet. I tugged it violently, hearing the machinery whirr up. Enraged, I dropped it cursing, then stopped, petrified by a sudden loud sound outside the door. I seemed to wait a hundred years, the cord tight around my hand. The knob clicked, then silence. Have they come in? But they couldn't, there was no flash of light. But what if the hall lights had been killed? I leaned against the case listening, the tension tearing at my nerves. Something heavy struck again.

"All right," I whispered in a rage. "Why don't you do something? Come and get me! Say something!"

Silence.

"Let's not play games—come on and get me. I'm sick and tired of lying at the bottom of this piece of nickle-plated junk, I'm climbing out! . . ."

I listened, seeming to hear my own voice echoing around the walls.

"Listen, I've learned to control it. Hear that sound? I started it with my finger. Now get away from that door so I can get through. . . ."

Silence.

"Get away from that door," I said, giving voice to something I had felt for a long time. "Do I have to make you a speech? All right, Lincoln freed the slaves and I'm getting out! Say amen! You didn't cure me, you took my energy. That's it, you probably have a hospital full of us, using our energy to run your stupid machinery! What do you care about my name? How'd you get us in here, anyway? With a cold pork chop and a loaf of bread? With a black snake whip, with handcuffs and a log chain? You see, I'm leaving, I'm remembering. Lincoln freed the slaves, I remember that. He freed the field niggers, and the house niggers and the stud niggers; the red niggers and the white niggers, and the yellow niggers and the blue niggers—and I'm freeing me. . . . I'm climbing out. . . ."

Suddenly I seemed to plunge into space, then thudded against the damp floor; and still falling inside of me, falling through a blacker darkness than that in which I sprawled, striking out wildly with my fists expecting them to reach out and grab me. But no hand fell. I lay still. Were they teasing me? I swept my arm in a circle, through emptiness. I crawled a step. Still empty. I whipped the slack cord about in the dark, hearing a dry smacking sound. Had they left in the swift interval of my fall? Had I been unconscious? "No," I said aloud, listening and trying to calm myself, "there was no one; you imagined it all." And lucky too, for I must have sounded insane even though it was a relief to get it out. I crawled again, then something was holding me back. Turning, my hand struck the cord, making it twang like a bass viol. I gave it a sharp tug, and again, this time hearing the creak of rolling wheels, the machine! This wouldn't do.

I tried to stand, feeling the blood rushing dizzily from my head. What had she given me? A strange sensation, to stand; blackness seemed to swirl about me like ink awhirl in a bowl. Now I found the belt that held the nodes in place. It seemed endless, part of my flesh. I snatched the front cord until my hand ached. If only I knew where it entered the machine, I thought, going back. Forcing my thumbs beneath the elastic web of the belt, I tried to slip it down around my hips and it was as though I tried to peel off my flesh. Suddenly in a flash of out-of-focus memory I remembered standing with a string leading from one of my teeth to a doorknob. I headed for the door, pulling the machine behind me.

Slow going, as against the steady pressure of a current. Suddenly a flash of red fire filled my head, and I struck out, feeling a pain in my hand. It was the wall. Reaching the wall, I shuffled sideways, an inch at a time, until my hands found a break in the surface, then down the cool panel to the knob, egg-smooth and silent as I turned it cautiously. With my ear against the door, it seemed as though the surface had come alive with the roar of invisible tides; the muffled and rhythmical thunder of remote machinery. Voices, other sounds, washed underneath, creating a near sub-aural harmony. But still no footsteps. Hurriedly I wrapped the length of the rear cord around the knob, tightening it, then I was turning and falling face forward, stiff as a man of stone, feeling the darkness plunging above me as though falling from a great height. Then jerking taut for a moment I slanted at a dangerous angle, then something snapped loudly and I lay upon the labyrinthine pattern of the floor, drawing upon my nerve to touch the node. It had snapped completely. The belt had given way! I was free of both. Only fine cat whiskers of wire brushed beneath my finger. Crawling excitedly back to the door I pulled myself erect and listened. There was a furor in the depths of the building, like the country choir which I had known somewhere rendering Handel's *Messiah:*

> *Hallelujah—Boom!   Hallelujah—Bong!*
> *Hallelujah—Crash!*
> *He's risen—Smash!*

And suddenly I was certain someone was coming! So I would stand behind the door and slip out unseen. Let them come now and I'm free, I thought, just open the door. . . . A sound arose outside the door, moved on. My heart beat madly. I stood hating the men who had shanghaied me into the machine. Waiting. It became quiet now! Cautiously I turned the knob. A flash of light struck my eyes and I stood blinded and exposed, feeling the air upon my naked body. Then I could see the long, white, disinfected corridor, brightly lighted and empty. Far ahead it turned off. Back of me was a similar emptiness. I started to move and blacked out. But now I found myself crawling down the corridor, trying to rise, stumbling, crawling again, moving past several doors before getting a grip on myself and trying to stand. Pressing against the smooth surface of the wall, I pushed erect and proceeded, holding on to the wall, lurching fearfully to the turn in the corridor which lay ahead.

Reaching the turn I looked back. The cord lay curled upon the labyrinthine pattern of the floor, like a trampled snake. But already I was trying to remember old Mary's address and falling to my knees to better control my legs. Rounding the curve I came to an operating table, its rubber-tired wheels turned inward toward the wall. The corridor was quiet, empty. Gripping a table leg I raised myself, seeing the outline of a form, covered with white. Who sleeps with his head beneath the sheet? As of their own volition, my hands reached out, seizing one white enameled leg. Then the other, as though remembering the principle of some forgotten stroller or kiddie-car. Trying to pull myself upright, I felt the table begin to move—in a circle! I held on trying to guide it away from the wall, my knees knocking against the floor as I tried to stand; trying to guide it back in the other direction as it circled back towards the room from which I'd escaped. But each attempt to stand sent it ahead, wobbling crazily back down the corridor. Stop, you bastard. . . . Why . . . why doesn't he protest? I wonder with swift dread. . . . Stop! Stop! I whisper fiercely, addressing it. And as though in answer the table rolled to a stop. Disarranging the sheet as I pulled upright, I looked into a face, a youth's face. The cheeks were drawn, the eyes closed as though in sleep. I wanted to run but the face held me, as though by some hypnotic spell cast by the eyes beneath the puckered lids. I couldn't move. My eyes refused to look away. I could not turn—until back down the corridor I could hear the sliding of metal gates: an elevator. Holding to the table I opened the door to my old room, and started the table into the darkness, half-stumbling. I felt my foot press upon the discarded cord and it clinging to me for a step and dropping off. The table rolled forward and stopped. I tugged at it desperately, feeling it give suddenly and shoot me backwards. Hard metal pressed into my back: the machine. It was like a dream. I started back toward the door, still holding on to the table, but laughing softly—a muted hysteria that stopped suddenly as my hand found the door; then I was holding my breath, half-expecting, half-hoping, to hear him breathing behind me. All was silence, suspense, vacuum and blackness. "Why'd you let them kill you?" I whispered crazily. Perhaps he had been confined to a machine just as I. Too bad, and I'd better get out of here before they put me back beneath the lid. . . . I started back to the door on wobbly legs, remembering the table. It would be useful. I was swinging it around, broadside to the case, hearing the clink of metal against metal as I pressed it close. But the case was too high, and there was only one thing to do. Nausea washed over me as my hands came in contact with cool flesh. For a moment I started to turn away, then one hand finding the neck and the other slipping beneath the curved spine, I pushed it gently, feeling it come up as though weightless rolling toward the case. If only I could see! I pushed again. Something plunked lightly against the bottom of the case; and with a heave I sent it over the side into the machine. "Get in there, you bastard!" I whispered with sudden anger. "I should shut the lid on you. . . ." How easy it would be now if he had been dressed. I could walk forth into the street fully clothed. Starting away, something stopped the table. My hands groped about. It was a leg, caught in the sheet. Lifting it clear I pushed the table out into the corridor. Looking back, as I shut the door I saw it dangling as though broken in the flash of light.

The corridor was empty, quiet. Where had they gone? Who had it been? Were there machines behind all the doors? With each step my legs seemed to grow stronger. I passed the spot where I found the table, holding it firmly now, careful not to bump the walls. My eyes swept the ceiling, the shut doors. Were they watching from some hidden peepsight in the ceiling? Testing me like a rat in a maze? Let them! I'd show them how intelligent a rat could be. . . . Why didn't I meet someone? Around the curve now, the corridor swept ahead, bringing a wave of indistinct sound. I picked up speed, almost running. Nameless voices from the past seemed to whisper warnings. A new alertness grew. My throat burned with outrage. Tense sensations crackled the length of my spine, in my crouch. Then I saw the elevator shaft and stopped. Was it exit or trap? There was no time to decide. Already it groaned with movement. I swung around, hesitating. Where could I hide? The well-lighted corridors stretched away for thirty feet in three directions, then curved—too far to race before being seen. Back of me, a wall set with a small high window. And now the shaft filled with light and the car was stopping. And as the gate swung open I swung the table around and ran it close. Almost upsetting a small blonde, who carried a covered tray, who, imaculate in her uniform, gave a startled "Oh, my God!"

"Between you and me, it's hot as hell back there," I said, noticing the gleaming breast-pin, the glint of pearly teeth.

"Oh . . . oh yes," she said. "Yes, yes . . ."

"And it's even hotter downstairs," I said, shoving the table inside. She stood petrified and I pushed her gently as I closed the door. "Better watch your tray," I said. . . . Then I was dropping beneath her, hearing the shrill stab of her scream. The car dropped past lighted floors on which, through the glass door, I could see uniformed men and women caught grotesquely in mid-gesture, the precise contortions of the modern dance. All the floors were occupied. My one chance was to make for the basement, the one place that I was sure the car would stop. I shoved the handle toward the extreme position marked "B," feeling the nerves twitch in my legs as I dropped, seeming to hear the little nurse's scream falling featherlike upon me. The car landed with a thud, throwing me to my knees and bouncing as though preparing to spring above. Yanking the control I felt it settle and I broke from the car.

I faced two gloomy corridors, hesitating an instant, then ran for the dimmest, the left, plunging through an atmosphere heavy with medicine, machinery, food, seeing the passage narrowing but afraid to retreat. Then I ran smack against the cart. My hands shooting out landed upon heated metal, jostling the cart and releasing a cloud of steam, as I tried to see the man behind its wavering strands.

"Hy, man," he said. "Look like you're in a hurry." Then the steam was thinning and I could see his white suit in the dim light.

"I didn't see you . . ." I said.

"You were in a hurry. Even so, you think you'll ever get rich?"

"Rich . . . ?" I said through the veil of steam as my mind weighed his question formally, without curiosity. . . . "In here?"

"Sure—step around there, daddy, so I can get past you. . . . Sometimes I think a dope fiend dreamed up this here basement. It's crowded as a barrel of snakes. I say, you think you'll be in the money?"

"Not soon. . . ."

"Shucks, man, you can't tell," he said, beginning to move. "You might dream you up a good one. . . ."

"Dream? It's a nightmare," I said, my voice growing loud, angry as his broad back bent over the handles and he started to push away. "A nightmare," I repeated, my voice rising.

"Shucks, man," he said laughing over his shoulder. "You dream you up a right good nightmare, you liable to break the bank. . . ."

I watched him go still laughing. What if he sounds the alarm? I backed several steps, then turned and ran, his laughter behind me. Voices arose around a passage to the right. Ahead there was light, a dim bulb by which I could see a door marked "Engine Room." I ran for it, thinking, "There will be men, lights. Kill the lights, your only chance is in darkness. . . ."

It opened easily. A wave of bright heat and vibration struck my body. It was a huge room. My teeth chattered as to my right I saw a large man reading at a table, his head down, unaware. I stood paralyzed with alertness, my back arched with tension, my eyes sweeping past three huge engines to the far blank wall set with a small door far to the rear, and seeing on the left stretching behind him a series of furnaces and back around, looking for the switch panel, thinking, "It's got to be here, it's got to . . ." and seeing him look up, his calm freezing into rigid surprise as I yelled desperately, "Where's the switch?" His mouth moved silently, his eyes widening. . . .

"The switch, hurry!" I called.

"Switch?" his mouth said through the machine noise. Then his arm raised, pointing, extending; my eyes following. And there it was attached to pipes cemented into the floor. I ran over, watching him start amazed, beginning to stand, seeing the question looming in his eyes as I gained the bakelite panel and yanked for the largest switch, hearing him yell, "Hey," his voice shrill, disjointed and dreamlike as I saw the room still bright despite the switch in my hand, and now seeing his astonishment changing to indignation as I broke another switch and another, sending blue sparks flying and still the light; and reaching now for a brace of smaller switches and seeing him start forward, as now, at last, one part of the room and then the other fell black. For an instant I was still. His voice was growing more distinct, in the swiftly dying roar of the room, draw- ing closer, seeming to advance out of the slowing hum of the dyna- mos. Gaging my direction by the intensity of the heat upon my body, I ran to my right, remembering the small door far across the room, running past the furnaces, veering away from the heat and feeling the shock as he ran against me. Going down then, hearing him yelling, and me crawling and getting to my feet and leaping back as he scrambled on the floor. Upright now, I danced my in- decision, pivoting this way and that, then remembering and bearing again for the floor. "Hey, hey!" his voice came, and I seemed to race on a treadmill until a crack of intense red light leaped suddenly through to the back of my skull. I had hit the wall, grabbing my head and rolling, feeling my shoulder strike cool metal and beating upon it frantically with my fists. It was the door. I pushed it, grabbing for the handle, shaking it, hearing a popping sound. The man yelled again. Then came a crash. I looked back, seeing space flash out of the blackness as the far door burst open. Several men loomed in the rectangle of light, poised like dancers at the climax of a powerful leap. . . . "He's back there!" a voice cried and they shot into the darkness. I lunged. The metal scraped against my shoulder like a rasp, as at my back the huge loping rhythm of an engine whirled into motion beneath the sound of men's yells and rapid footfalls. Again I lunged, this time it gave, opening outwardly, a seldom used door. I squeezed my body through and plunged into another blackness. It was swiftly cold, dank. I shot along on a level, the floor bouncing roughly against my feet, feeling as though falling endlessly into a black shaft through which damp currents sped upward against me. But no shaft at all, I saw now in a dim filtering of sourceless light, but a storage cellar of indeterminate size. And behind me they had found the door.

"This way," someone yelled, then in a sudden whirlpool of flicker- ing light I could see a narrow passage winding through a jumble of packing cases. Behind me, moving down an incline I could see a group of wavering flashlights; then the men above them, their faces skull-like in the shadows shooting from below. I backed a step and stumbled, hearing a large object crash to the floor. Something looked out of the darkness ahead. For a second beams of light boiled around me, then I tripped and went to my knees, thinking, they have me, they have me! But still I crawled, scrambling, feeling rough wood tearing at my sides and hearing the men come close as I stopped still, listening. They breathed heavily, whispered, stepping softly. Even with their lights they moved slower than I. But hardly had they passed when they returned. More cautiously now, the flashlights crawling over packing cases . . . watching their white-clad legs and thinking, "All right now, it's time you stopped this dreaming. . . ."

"I tell you he kept going," someone said.

"Then where'd he go?"

"How do I know? He certainly didn't walk through us and go back into the engine room. . . ."

"Come on, let's see how far we can go up this way." They moved off. Then, "Shhhh, listen!" I heard, my heart in my mouth now, as somewhere close by a furious struggle began. It went in a circle, a desperate lunging scramble that banged here and there against something for a second, then trailed drily off building in my mind a series of bright sounds scratching rapidly upon the wall of darkness.

"There he goes!"

"Get him this time, understand? We've got to get him!"

I heard them go. "It was a rat," I thought. "They're chasing a rat! Or maybe only a mouse." Perhaps the rat went in the true direction of escape. . . . I got up. I'd have to take the other direction, the rat and I were caught in different mazes. I'd have to find my own way out. The men were still going away from me. If only the rat keeps running, doesn't double back on his trail!

"I hear him up there," a voice called as I moved out into the passageway, thinking, "Sure, up there, maybe two miles. Get after him—"

At first the ether fumes seemed part of the underground air, then the light focused into my eyes, blinding me.

"All right, boy, I've got you cornered. Don't move!"

I crouched, muscles aching with tension, whispering, "No, no . . . !"

"Oh, but yes," the voice said, the light wavering in my eyes as he moved forward, a step at a time. "Oh, yes."

I lowered my head seeing some sort of garment stretched between his hands and I thought, "It's—! He's got a strait-jacket!"

"You might as well come quietly," he said, his nervous laugh hollow in the low cellar. "Here, put this on, you're ill. You'll catch pneumonia in this dampness. . . ."

"No, no," I repeated, recording the nuances of his voice as though hearing it played on a sluggish phonograph and feeling my fear flowing to contempt, thinking, "He's unsure. Unsure . . . !"

"It's for your own good, you'll be released when its time. . . . You're still ill, very ill, you know. . . ."

I saw him still shuffling forward. "You're ill," he repeated.

"Maybe you're the one . . ." I whispered, stalling for time.

He stopped shuffling.

"Ha! Ha! See, you have a sense of humor. You boys always show a sense of humor when you're improving. A few weeks more . . . and you'll . . . be . . . released—"

I could see the gleam of his white buttons now and suddenly I feinted to rush past him, seeing the flashlight beam streak to the ceiling, revealing his white-swathed body crouching before me, his irises dilated like a cat's.

"Don't try that, boy. I can play rough. Why not be a good patient? In time you'll be properly released. . . ."

"Come and get me," I whispered. "I'm already released."

"Oh, I'm going to get you, boy," he said, the cautious ease coming back into his voice. "But why not come peacefully? Why have a setback?"

"Sure," I whispered, "only come on. . . ."

"Here, let me put this around you. . . ."

"What?"

"A robe, you'll be more comfortable. . . ."

"Will it fit? I'm fastidious about my clothes. . . ."

"Oh, it'll fit perfectly . . . My, but you're a character, ha! ha! . . . It'll fit, all right, it's endlessly adjustable. Here, let me show you." Again he inched forward.

"Toss it," I said.

"Sure, sure," he said. "Sure . . ."

I saw his head come forward, the light flashing downward, causing his eyes to gleam for an instant as he lunged toward me —then the shock. I grabbed, feeling the rough canvas brush my arm and him grappling for me, his grip like steel. Slipping off, I jabbed, my fist going deep. He grunted and I hammered him, feeling him burst away, grunting, his head dropping down, and I was already running furiously. But in the same spot, my high-driving knees drumming fiercely against him, making a sound like a boy dragging a stick along a picket dence. He was down, the flash rolling crazily upon the floor, throwing a hot, bright light against a wall as I shot out of the corner and was past, hearing him begin to yell.

It was tortuous going. I felt my way swiftly. I found the up-turned case and felt along in the direction from which the men had returned. He yelled, his words growing more articulate all the time. I moved, afraid to run because of the unseen objects, yet moving as fast as possible. Far behind and to my right I could hear the men following the rat. "Keep on, boys," I thought. "You'll flush him soon." I went around something cold and smooth be-neath the dust, following its long smooth lines until it curved away, then touching here and there the rough surface of a wall. "This way, this way!" he yelled behind me. Suddenly I was amused, remembering how my fist had sunk in. And I was conscious of being somehow different. It was not only that I had forgotten my name, or that I had been processed in the machine, or even that I had taken Mary's medicine—but something internal. My thoughts seemed to be the thoughts of another. Im-pressions flashed through my mind, too fleeting and secretly mean-ingful to have been my own—whoever I was. And yet somehow they were. It was as though I had become capable of new powers of understanding. Perhaps I was insane. But it wasn't so simple. . . .

His voice was stronger now. And far behind a door slammed and I ran again. Ahead it was brightening. A new light grew to my left and I entered a larger room, a kind of storage section, filled with old medical cabinets, stools, bathtubs—all dappled with spots of light filtering down from what looked like a sidewalk studded with thick glass discs. I could feel the damp descend. A cobweb clung to my face. I brushed it away, moving, listening. . . . The sound arose far ahead, a roar, like a roll on an out-of-tune tympany, approached me, setting up a shrill vibration within the dark, beneath which I heard the sound of footsteps and plunged wildly to my left. I felt myself going over, landing against something that creaked and groaned, filling by nose and mouth with dust. Rooting, scrambling, listening, I found myself in a kneeling position on what seemed to be an ancient leather couch. I gripped it, strangling a sneeze and hearing it going over me, passing me, rumbling above the passage like thunder echoing in high clouds.

"We lost him again," a voice said. "There's just too much down here that we don't know about. . . ."

They were close by, but I couldn't see them! I pressed against the dried leather feeling cornered, helpless.

"But I tell you he's up here somewhere. I had him cornered, he didn't come past you so he has to be up here. . . ."

"It's a matter for the police," another voice said.

"But, Doctor . . ."

"Why would he think of coming down *here*?"

"Probably some buried memory guided him. Perhaps this storage basement corresponds to the structure of his mind. . . ."

"He's down here, that's certain, and I think it's our job and not that of the police to find him. . . ."

"That fellow must be crazy," an indignant voice said. "Came in stark naked and started pulling switches!"

"Let's search over this way, then if we don't find him we'll get the police down here with tear gas and floodlights. . . . Talking about a nigger in a wood pile! Whew!"

"Tear gas will flush him! . . . Say . . ."

"What is it—?"

"That door there!"

Shoes scraped upon the concrete floor, turning. "Where?"

"Over there. Maybe he went in there. . . ."

"For Christ's sake—can't you see that it's just leaning there, that it isn't hung?"

"Sure, it's leaning against the wall."

"Can't you see it?"

"I do now. Let's go."

They left, their voices receding, seeming to move before them with the lights.

What should I do? They'd return soon with the police and tear gas. Standing, I could see the dappling lights continuing for about twenty feet to my right, then fading off. I was in a tight place and now in attempting to turn between the couch and something, the floor had tilted. I stumbled, falling against the door, feeling it swing inward, almost throwing me into space. It was not dismantled at all, only deceptively hung. Fascinated, I pushed it gently, hearing the men again, but this time they seemed on the other side of some sort of partition, drawing closer. The door sighed. I looked into sheer blackness. A narrow rectangle of blackness set into the dark grey of the basement. Where did it lead? To escape or danger, to dismemberment, insanity or death? It was not a finished doorway, my hands told me, but a kind of improvisation, crude, like a tunnel in a mine, something cut in haste, used furtively and left unexpectedly. . . .

I seemed to feel the light before I saw it stabbing, slanting at the ceiling above me. And for an instant I felt an impulse to walk out into its circular beam with my hands above my head, but the machine loomed in my mind and I stepped into the blackness and pulled the door softly closed. Silence. The passage moved straight ahead, then rose abruptly. Moving with outstretched arms I felt my fingers flickering the narrow sides, touching marks left in the sheer earth, wooden post, and then another. Suddenly something rolled beneath my foot and I lurched forward, hearing the clatter of glass. I felt about, finding bottles, bundles of paper. I kneeled, listening for sound behind me, then pulling up I limped cautiously ahead. It became warm. An image of three huge ovens built themselves up in my mind. Somewhere back there in the past I had been inside a bakery, had seen the hot loaves lined in heated tins, and rows of gingerbread-boys cooling brown upon the well-scrubbed boards. . . . Had I been running even then?

At first it sounded like an engine pounding, then the rasping insinuations of trumpets and saxophones cut through and I realized that it was music. I stood still, breathing in the fumes of stale alcohol. Was the sound coming from straight ahead or from above? I moved forward—until my toes were striking against a wall that seemed to move away. I drew back. The air had suddenly changed, the sound booming out. I swung my foot, encountering void. It was another basement! Another damn basement! And the music came from above. The beery air grew stronger. Cautiously, I moved forward again. Behind there would be tear gas, ahead at least there was music. . . . What had I blundered into? Why should it be connected with the hospital? Was it a bar, a restaurant, some kind of clubroom located in another wing of the building? I hesitated, for minutes it seemed, wishing they'd come and end my indecision. For a moment the music stopped, then boomed out again. I moved, keeping close to the wall. The smell of beer became heavy, I had come to a row of barrels. I could feel their squat shapes following one after another as I felt my way. "I'm under a bar," I thought. That's the jukebox playing. Who would believe that, underneath, the hospital was connected with a bar? There was relief in the idea and I stopped moving and tried to figure my next move. If it was a bar then I could wait until closing time and then go up after they had left and escape—I was tired now. Perhaps Mary's medicine was wearing off. What on earth was the bitter stuff anyway? I had to wait, to sit down, but the floor was covered with sharp pieces of coal. I moved a step, coming upon a wooden structure, a series of rails, a fence, and stopped lest I upset something and give myself away. . . . I leaned against a post, my body seeming still to move. Overhead the jukebox boomed again, a familiar number. A blues. Where had I heard it, what did it mean? Some muted instrument sounded all the world like a muffled voice. Or was it a voice that sounded like a muted horn? What was the voice in the jukebox saying? Another instrument, like a bear growling, took up the refrain. It sounds like Jack-the-Bear, I thought for no reason at all. . . . If only I dare lie down and rest. . . . How long, baby, tell me how long? . . . When would they close up above? What if they were open twenty-four hours? Never closed? The mere idea of time repulsed me. I tried to think of other things. I dozed. . . .

At first I thought it was the jukebox. I was sitting on the floor beside a coal bin blinking my eyes in disbelief, a man stood atop the stairs.

"What the hell!" he yelled. "Hey you! Hey you!"

My vision sharpened. He held a crate of bottles against his white apron, a fat brown man whose large head caught the light upon its baldness. I rolled over and crawled behind the partition and dived behind into the coal bin, lumps of pea coal cutting sharply into my unprotected knees. Now behind me a new voice, "He's over yonder!"

"Where? Just you show me where!"

"He was standing right back yonder!"

"Yonder *where*?"

"Behind them boards!"

"And naked?"

"As ever he come into this world."

"You sure he wasn't painted green, ain't you?"

"Hell, Pritchett, don't be trying to make no fool out of me. I know what I saw."

"You saw him all right, but he ain't there. It was your whiskey that showed him to you."

"So I guess I'm lying?"

"Naw, you ain't lying, you drunk. How the hell's anybody going to get down here behind the bar and past me?"

"I don't know, Pritchett, but I damn sho saw a man down here. I damn sho did! . . . Hey, mister," he called out plaintively. "Mister, if you down there, please will you come out or we'll have to call the cops and the boss don't want no cops fooling round down there. . . ."

"Oh shut up, man, and let's get back to work. . . ."

"You see there, mister, if you don't come up I'll never hear the end of it," the first voice said. "They'll swear I'm drunk and dock me a day's pay. . . ."

I held my breath, amazed at the sincerity in the voice. For a moment it was silent. Then: "You hear me, man?"

I wanted to laugh.

"You speak to him, Pritchett."

"I tell you, man, you drunk. Sloppy drunk!"

"Go on, Pritchett, I swear he's down there."

"Hell! All right. . . . Hey you, down there, if you *is* down there, if you don't come the hell on outa there, we'll know you trying to steal something and we have ta be hard on you," he called, sounding as though he had become convinced, as though by addressing me I *had* to exist. And again I felt an impulse to surrender, fighting it down. I had gone too far to give up now.

"See there," I heard. "Ain't a damn soul down there."

"He's down there all right," the voice said. "He just don't want to do the right thing. I ought to go down there with a baseball bat—he's trying to mess up a whole day's pay for me! Go get the pistol."

Pistol? I burrowed further into the pile of coal, moving slowly lest it slide, or smother me. Behind me they argued heatedly as I worked my way. The coal had spilled into the shape of a pyramid several feet high and I bored between the pile and the wall . . . hearing them coming across the floor.

"Well, you ain't supposed to drink on the job."

"You just come on, you'll see."

I saw them now, two men peering over the partition near where I had dozed off, looking over into the coal toward where I lay afraid to breathe.

"Now where's he?" one of them said.

"He must be here somewhere. He gotta be, 'cause I seen him."

"All right, you find him. He didn't come up by me, so he's got to still be down here."

They moved slowly now, focusing the feeble rays of a flashlight into the darkness.

"Maybe he's got a gun. . . ."

"Gun?"

"Yeah. Let's get out of here."

"Hell, he didn't have nothing. His hands was empty."

"You cain't tell."

"But he's naked. . . ."

"Maybe he's got a knife. . . ."

They moved away. What if they discovered the passage to the hospital? I heard them breathing tensely now, coming toward me from the other side of the coal bin. Pressing closely to the wall, I froze, hearing someone yell, "There he is!"

"Where?"

"Back over there."

"You mean that noise?"

"Yeah, it was him."

"Hell, man, I knowed you was drunk. That was somebody walking across that manhole in the sidewalk. You git drunk just one more time on this job and it'll be the last."

A trickle of coal slid over me, sounding like a crash.

"Hey, Roscoe!" a voice called from the stairs. "What's going on down there?"

"Nothing, we're coming right up."

"Nothing, and the house full of customers?"

"Okey, it was just a big rat."

"A rat?"

"That's right."

"Hell, they're *our* rats ain't they? Leave 'em alone and get the hell on up here, will you?"

"Come on, before that bastard gets mad. We don't get paid for chasing nobody out of the basement anyway."

I watch them wobble in arm-swinging haste back to the stairs, the first shaking his head in puzzlement. Going up, their distorted shadows flowed swiftly against a circular banquet table top and disappeared. The lights snapped off, the jukebox muffled down. What now? I tried to stand, reaching out for support and feeling my hand contact a piece of metal. It was set in the wall, I reached upward finding three more at regular intervals. And before my mind could build the image of a ladder, I was climbing, peering upward. Just as a scraping sound began, then the dull clang of metal and something showering into my face, eyes. I ducked, thinking, "It's the sidewalk," as by some chain reaction the sound of barking came from the stairs. Looking past the vague pyramid of coal I saw several men with flashlights coming down. At first I thought they were from the hospital, then I heard, "I bet twenty to one he'll kill any rat living in three seconds by the clock!"

"Let's find him first."

"Put up your money!"

The dog barked tentatively, searching, sniffing, whining; its nails scratching crisply across the floor. Quietly, I climbed another rung, feeling the bars cold against my body.

"Where I live they got rats that don't give a damn about *no* cats, and only but a few geat big dogs! Weigh fifteen, twenty pounds, man."

"Get him, Little Brother! Sick him, boy!"

The dog barked. I climbed, expecting any moment to hear him scramble into the bin. I was above the pale now, and reaching upward I felt a circular, steel-ringed hole, and above that the dome of a manhole cover that showered down another tuft of dirt. Suddenly the dog grew hysterical.

"He's smelled the rat," a voice yelled.

"Where'd he go?"

"Over there in the coal."

"He better leave that rat get out of that corner!"

"He's over there in the bin!"

"He'll cut a dog's throat in a corner, man!"

I could feel the fury of the dog's malicious bark as they urged him on. I climbed until the steel ring stopped me and clung with my back pressed against the curved mouth of the hole, my knees drawn up to my chin like a boy rolling down a hill in an auto tire.

"Hey, why's he barking up that ladder?"

"He's after the rat!"

"Shine some light up there."

"What the hell! Hey, give me the light, somebody! You see what I see?"

"Saaay—it's a man's leg!"

I went weak inside, hearing, "Bring the other light!"

"Good God!"

"Somebody done stuffed a dead body down that hole!"

I clung like a treed coon, hearing them climbing over the partition, scattering the coal.

"That's all I need to lose my license, to have a dead man found in my basement!"

"I *bet* it's that labor leader."

There was nothing to do but break out and face whatever dangers lay above the surface. Holding with one hand I pushed firmly against the cover, feeling a heavy weight upon my shoulders. Dry dirt showered down. "There's been no rain," I thought distantly. "Outside it's dry. . . ." Then my knee slipped from the ring. For a second it was quiet. Then: "Hey! He moved! That ain't no dead man, that guy's alive!"

"I didn't see anything. . . ."

"Maybe something jarred the walk. . . ."

"Hell no, he *moved!*"

"I tole you, Pritchett! I know damn well I seen somebody down here!"

"Hey!"

I could cling no longer. I felt myself slipping and kicked out, getting one foot on the top ring, then the other, crouching like a monkey on a limb, and pushing upward with one arm. The cover gave, settled back. Something struck the wall beneath me.

"Come down from there, you bastard!"

"Watch him, he might have a gun!"

A blow struck my foot. "Come down!"

I pushed, feeling a hand close around my ankle, pulling down. I kicked, stubbing my toe against something hard, feeling the hand go away.

"Get him!"

"I'm getting the cops!"

"No cops! Hell, no! You want to put me out of business?"

"Watch out the way, you all, I'll get this sonofabitch!"

I looked down. A man's face, half-illuminated from below, started steadily upward. If only I had on shoes, I thought. I could see his eyes. My lips puckered but when I tried to spit my mouth was dry.

"You better watch him, now, Talmadge!"

I pushed again, thrusting my head into the steel cover, muck and all.

"All right now, buddy," the man said, gripping my ankle. Holding on with my hands, I gave him my heel swiftly, three times, feeling his grip tighten. Steadying myself, I measured the next kick, hearing him slip away, yelling, "Get the club from behind the bar," as now, crouching on the topmost rung, I pushed upward from the hips. The weight pressing into my skull, neck, shoulders, then a rush of outside air. For a second the cap tittered upon my head, making a wavering crack through which I could see the glint of street lights. Then it clanged to the side and I pushed it away and seemed to shoot through the hole, moving so furiously that I stumbled and sprawled on the walk, my head striking the pavement, dazing me. Then from above there came a sound like thunder and a woman yelled, "Lord, God, what in the world is this!"

I rolled, looking into the faces of two women dressed in white.

"Police! A naked man, a naked . . . !" the woman screamed. "Police!"

"Oh no! No!" called a woman who crouched against a building front. "Not *naked!* Is he, Sis Spencer? Let's us be sure 'fore we call the cops. Wait'll I change my glasses."

"As ever he was born in the world! Police! Out here on the street like that. . . ."

I got to my knees, breathing hard. I saw a bar with the neon signs in the window behind me. Below the walk men called me names. Then it thundered again and I stood up, feeling the first drops of rain.

"Lawd, God, have mercy, Jesus!" the woman moaned, leaving the building and taking the other's arm. "Come on, Sis Spencer! Come on away from that sinful man!"

"Call the police," I called to them. "They're murdering a man in the basement."

There was a movement at my feet. A hand showed on the ring of the hole and I bent and pushed the manhole cover into place, hearing a curse and a second tremendous clash of thunder. Seeing the women dash scurrying down the street, I ran in the opposite direction, entering a side street of old brownstones. The rain poured. Keeping to the dark side of the street and searching in vain for an alley and remembering that none existed. What sort of people would build a city without alleys? Where did the honey-dipper carts travel? But this was Harlem, I remembered, and I must make my way to old Mary's house.

Rounding the corner in the huge drops of rain, I saw the men looming ahead. They turned and stared.

"Hey, Jack!" one of them called to the others who stood in a doorway passing a bottle between them. "Dig this here game stud!"

I turned and started across the street but a line of cars drove me back. They staggered after me catching my arm before I could cross, bringing the sickening odor of cheap sweet wine. I was surrounded. They stared in drunken amusement.

"Now here's a stud that's naked as a jaybird."

"He had to leave in a hurry, maybe."

"Look, fellows," I said, "he's after me. Let me go."

"Who's this that's after you, old man?"

"Yeah, daddy-o, who's this that's making you cut out? Her husband?"

"Yeah, that's right—"

"Well, no better for you," one of them said. "I'm a husband myself."

"Looks like he had hold to you already, Jack. Your leg is bleeding." I looked, realizing that I had scratched myself emerging from the manhole.

"I got away," I said, "but if he catches me he's liable to kill me!"

"Yeah, but if the cops see you running round like that, they liable to put you under the jail."

"Aw, let the man go."

Another came up and tried to pry his fingers from my arm. "Let him alone."

"Hell, Bridgewater, I'm fixing to help the man."

"Well help him then, and let him go. I once had to grab me a armful of window myself."

"Sure, Bridgewater, who hasn't?" Then to me he said, "Come on upstairs with us, daddy-o, I'll see if I got something you can wear."

I looked at him, then at the others; they were all about my own age, slightly high from the wine and amused at what they thought had been my adventure.

"Okey!" I said and followed them up the steps. We climbed three flights of narrow stairs that reeked with urine, stale cabbage. Then kidding loudly, they steered me down a hall so narrow that it was impossible to walk two abreast until we came to a door, which Bridgewater opened and we pushed inside.

A single dim bulb burned in the ceiling. It was a small room, painted a milky blue gloss. I saw a bed, two old upholstered chairs, a dresser and a beautifully made radio-phonograph.

"Sit down, Tyrone," the owner said, addressing me. "You must be tired!"

"Tyrone? That man's name ain't no Tyrone. How come you call him Tyrone?" one of them asked, laughing.

"Hell, 'cause he's a lover, that's why."

Then turning to me he grinned. "Don't pay me no mind, ole man. I'm just kidding. You want a drink?"

"No thanks."

"You got some gage? Bridgewater, give the man some gage."

"You know I don't fool with that stuff," Bridgewater said, producing a bottle and several glasses from a cabinet. He gravely poured a round of drinks. "Here you go, lover, drink this while I find you a pair of pants and a shirt. They won't be no hell, but good enough for you to get home in."

"That'll be good enough," I said. I drank it down.

"Here's one to hold it down," he said refilling the glass before I could refuse. "You all better drink up too," he said. " 'Cause my gal's due here pretty soon and I don't want her to have to look at all you half-high squares eyeballing her and all that mess."

Soon he quit rummaging in a closet and produced a brown and blue-sleeved sweater and a pair of grey slacks.

"Slip these on, man," he said.

He showed me into a small bedroom where I pulled into the slacks and sweater. The shoes were tight. When I entered the room two girls had come who looked me over as they drank. I took Bridgewater's address, promising to return his clothes, and left.

Outside the rain had begun to pour. I headed for old Mary's.

I hobbled along, keeping to side streets as much as possible, entering the avenues only when necessary and taking only a block at a time, then cutting back into a side street. The side streets were free of policemen and I saw only two on the avenues, each standing whitefaced and grim in a doorway, avoiding the rain.

I had reached the forking of three streets and started across when the man bumped against me.

"Pardon me," the voice said.

"Sure," I said, stepping into the street over the water streaming and gurgling in the gutter, only a passing stream of trucks keeping me from bolting.

"This is a dangerous crossing," the man said, his voice crotchety yet gentle.

"Thanks," I mumbled, disguising my voice. The lights were

red, I had forgotten about such things. Cars shot past, their tires singing on the road. I silently repeated old Mary's address. If I were lucky, I'd soon be there.

"Would you give me a hand, please?" the old man said.

I turned, seeing him for the first time: An old man standing stiffly erect with his head held back at an angle, holding a gleaming white cane, and beneath his broad-brimmed hat, eyes, focused not at me, but out past the falling rain to some point of infinity above the gleaming street and the cars. "He's blind," I thought with relief. "He can't see me."

"All right," I said, reluctant to bother with him even for the short time it would take to cross the street. For not only was there the possibility that I was being searched for at that very moment, but the need to know something definite about myself now filled me with frantic urgency. Indeed, only the presence of a couple that had come up waiting for the lights to change kept me from insulting the old man and going off in another direction. I had to get to old Mary's. Already I had stopped thinking about the old man and taking his arm automatically without waiting for the lights to change, started across.

"How light he is," flashed through my mind as I guided him along. "It's like floating a body buoyed up by water. . . ."

I failed to see the car. It seemed to roll out of nowhere, its brakes screeching as I snatched the old man aside, causing him to stumble on the wet asphalt as the car careened around us and ahead, with the driver's curses bursting upon my ears like acid through the rain. He breathed tensely beside me as I looked up and down the street. A car approached, passed, its horn blowing. Taking his arm, I started off, my nerves screaming with tension. I was furious, both with the driver and myself. It was as though I had deliberately tried to guide this stranger, whom I'd barely seen, into the path of a car.

"Are you all right?" the couple called behind us.

"Yes, everything's all right," the old man called, his head cocked to the side. Then to me, "That was pretty close. I felt the air from his wings as he passed. . . ."

"I'd like to take a shot at him," I said impulsively, "but it was really my fault."

"It's all right," he said.

"I was in too much of a hurry to get to an appointment. I'm sorry."

"Don't worry about it, they almost hit me at least once a day." Our feet made soft steady splashings through the swift water. Cars threw spray that slapped from fenders and humming tires.

"It's like a second flood," he said. "Such rain should purify the world."

We had reached the other side now and I slowed so that he could step upon the curb. What was he jabbering about?

"Well, here you are," I said.

"Thank you, I hope I didn't make you late."

"No, no," I said, suddenly irritated again. "I was in too much of a hurry. . . ." I started away.

"Well, a young fellow has to keep moving. . . ."

I spun in my tracks, as though I had been hit with a club, grasping his arms, there in the middle of the walk, staring into his face as his words beat in my head like the rain.

"Say it again!" I shouted.

"What?" he said. "Whaat?"

"Say it!"

"But what?"

"Goddamit, repeat it! Say the word!"

"Say what, young man?" his voice came patiently.

I cursed him seeing his sightless eyes full upon me, his expression puzzled like one struck suddenly deaf. I shook furiously. "Repeat it!"

"But I don't know—"

"Say what you said about keeping moving!" I managed.

"I don't . . . Oh yes, I said, 'I guess they keep a young fellow like you moving. . . .' "

I searched his face as his words spattered through my mind, seeing the rain dripping and lacing from his hat brim onto my arm. Why was his face so familiar? I mumbled his words like some magic formula, the key word of which I had forgotten. . . .

"Is there something wrong?" he asked.

"No . . ." I said, bewildered. "I guess not. I misunderstood you."

I stared into his eyes, smelling the aura of a strong old pipe about him as he stood quietly in my grasp.

"I don't know," I repeated. "You sound like someone I know."

"Oh, like whom?"

"I can't remember," I said, continuing to stare and hold him.

"Where is your home?" he asked. "Down South?"

"Yes, but I can't remember where. Do you believe me?"

"Yes, I do," he said quietly. "Such things happen—but you'll be late, won't you, son?"

"Late? Late for what?"

"Your appointment. What is it, a party? You've been drinking sweet wine."

Suddenly I laughed; so he was a blind detective. "No, it's not that kind of an appointment. But I'd better be getting there."

And though suddenly atremble with agitation I mumbled an apology and released his arms. He didn't seem at all alarmed by my strange behavior.

"Good night," he said softly, tapping the sidewalk three times with his cane, then after a few cautious steps, moved smoothly away through the rain. I watched him going with a sense of turmoil. There was the weight of a name on my tongue, but I couldn't pronounce it. Watching him I tried vainly to shake the feeling away. The rain was driving now. I was in an awful state, knowing that I should be on my way, yet riveted to the spot. I wiped rain streaming from my face, listening to the tapping cane. Was I going crazy? I repeated the words. Was it his face or his voice that caused this feeling? Or was it both his face *and* his words? Suddenly his face glowed luminously before my eyes as though projected against the falling rain, and it was as though my whole life depended upon my seeing his face once more.

I whirled, to run after him. It was dark. A wide, empty street of apartment buildings on my right and on the left a broad concrete playground fenced with heavy wire. Except for a woman entering one of the dark buildings, the street was empty. My eyes swept along the bleak stoops of the buildings. Where had he gone? Had I dreamed him, had I bumped my head too hard when emerging from the manhole? But that was impossible, I could still feel the lightness of him in my hands, smell the strong tobacco.

Slowing to a walk I could now hear the faint tapping of the cane once more and plunged forward. If only I hadn't been so annoyed with him for having interrupted me I would have seen him back there at the crossing. . . .

"Hey, you. Blind man! Hey! You, Mr. ——" I called and stopped dead in my tracks. I had called him by a name—my grandfather's name! I looked about me, seized with a guilty uneasiness. Where had he gone? I listened, expecting a laugh or a curse. Gone. There was no sound except the racing rain. I ran again, moving painfully in my borrowed shoes, a movement part hobble, part limp, part skip and part crawl; until forced to stop of tiredness. It was a long block and I had not come to its end, but no sign of him. I was sure now that the face in which his sightless eyes were set was a face that haunted my dream. Although more patient and refined, it was the face of my grandfather.

Stopping, I found myself leaning against a stoop guarded by two weather-beaten stone lions when I seemed to hear the taps again. But oddly, this time from above a window in an upper apartment, a hollow sound in the night. Up there, several stories above, I watched a man's extended arm knocking his pipe against the sill, the ash glowing up, then dying in the rain. Then as I heard him clear his throat and start lowering the window, someone began a poorly executed flourish upon a tinny trumpet. Cursing, I plunged ahead. He must have gone into one of the buildings, I thought. He couldn't have been grandfather. Forget about him, he's been dead and you saw him die. There's too much to be done now for you to go chasing off after a ghost. . . . But still I strained my eyes and ears for a glimpse or sound of him. The street was empty, not even a car.

Turning, I started back, searching the dark for a sign. Across the street beneath the floodlighted playground the grey ground glistened with rain and there inexplicitly played one small boy who alone in the great grey square bounced a ball and sang, oblivious to the rain or hour, his voice so small and distant.

For a moment I watched him in bewilderment, then retraced my steps. Where were his parents? I was tired and hungry, too much had burst upon me at once. That which should have been the past had become mixed with the present again, clashing with it, and memory beat upon me like the rain. And though I tried not to think about it, it all came back: the illness in the street, the letters to the trustees; my room at the Young Men's House (retreat), my interrupted career at the college, Bledsoe—everything. How long had it been? I had to get to my room immediately. No, I must have time to think about it. I resolved there and then that every move I made must be weighed carefully before I put it into action. I could take no chances. They might have policemen and attendants stationed at the Men's House to return me to the hospital. How long had it been since I was carried away in the ambulance? Perhaps the best course was to find old Mary's and hide there until I could fill in the blank part of my experience. I would get there as swiftly as possible.

Pauli Murray

Miss Pauli Murray was born in Baltimore, Maryland. Her grandfather on her maternal side fought with the Union armies in the Civil War and later helped to establish the first school system for the free Negroes of Virginia and North Carolina under the authority of the Freedmen's Bureau. Her maternal grandmother was a slave.

Miss Murray is a member of the Bar in California and New York and served as a Deputy Attorney General in California and was on the staff of the Commission on Law and Social Action of the American Jewish Congress. In 1946, she received the *Mademoiselle* magazine award for distinguished achievement in the practice of law.

She attended public schools in Durham, North Carolina, and New York City and graduated from Hunter College with an A.B. degree. She was graduated from the Harvard University School of Law, *cum laude*, with the LL.B degree, was a Rosenwald Foundation Fellow, and received from the University of California School of Jurisprudence the LL.M. degree in 1945.

Miss Murray compiled and edited the book *States' Laws on Race and Color*, and her articles and poems have appeared in various magazines. She received a Eugene F. Saxton Fellowship and was

P A U L I   M U R R A Y292

on two occasions a resident fellow at the MacDowell Colony in
Peterboro, New Hampshire.

Proud Shoes, the Story of an American Family was published
in 1956. This extraordinary memoir is important both as literature
and as social history, and is based upon a record of fact.

From *Proud Shoes*

B Y   P A U L I   M U R R A Y

If Grandfather had not volunteered for the Union in 1863 and
come south three years later as a missionary among the Negro
freedmen, our family might not have walked in such proud shoes
and felt so assured of its place in history. We might have fought
our battles with poverty and color troubles, thinking of ourselves
as nobodies or not thinking of ourselves at all, dying out with nothing to remember of us except a few census figures. Grandfather's
struggle made the difference, although Grandmother Cornelia
supplied her share of pride. What he attempted—far more than
what he finally achieved—made him our colossus and beacon
light. Because of him we felt that we belonged, that we had a stake
in our country's future, and we clung to that no matter how often
it was snatched away from us.

As a child growing up, I was never allowed to forget that Grandfather had been a soldier and that I was a soldier's granddaughter.
This knowledge carried a heavy burden of responsibility and permitted no betrayal of mortal weaknesses. A soldier's granddaughter
must have courage, honor and discipline. I must stand tall and
never indulge in the fears of other children. When Aunt Pauline
wanted me to do something odious or frightening—like swallowing
a dose of castor oil or facing the tombstones after dark to bring in
the slop jar somebody left by the cemetery fence—she never
threatened or offered reward.

"Now, you must be a brave little soldier just like your grandfather. He's not afraid of anything. He'd walk right up to danger
and shake it by the hand," she'd remind me.

At such moments, my shrinking spirit might wrestle with Grandfather's stalwart one and I might wish I were anybody but a Fitzgerald grandchild, but I was honor bound to set my chattering teeth, stiffen my spine and walk in Grandfather's shoes. To hesitate or show fear after this injunction was a disgrace too shameful to endure.

Nor could one admit defeat around Grandfather. His struggle with blindness was a constant challenge to us. It had caused him many setbacks and heartaches and had snatched success from him time and again, but he had never given up. He and Grandmother started married life together in a two-room house. He could see then, and he had great dreams. As his eyesight faded he followed one trade after another as teacher, tanner, farmer, carpenter, contractor and brickmaker, until finally he could not see at all. Through all of this he and Grandmother had managed to bring up six children, give them some education and finally own their own home. To them there was a world of difference between those who paid taxes and those who paid rent.

"Always have your own little patch of ground and your own house if it's nothing but a shack," I was taught.

It took Grandfather twenty years to achieve it. He lost his brick business and most of his land but he held on to one acre and built his house on it. He and Grandmother often went without food to pay for it and keep up the taxes. To his family it was more than a home; it was a monument to Grandfather's courage and tenacity.

There was something solid and indestructible about Grandfather's house. It wasn't very large—it had only six rooms—and it wasn't nearly so fine as his brother Richard's house, but it was free and clear of debt and Grandfather had supervised the laying of each board and brick and shingle although he could see the work only through his fingers. It was as if he had built himself into the structure, for it had his stubborn character. It was sparingly constructed and unpretentious like himself. It wasn't even a two-story house. He called it a story-and-a-jump because the two bedrooms upstairs were part of the steeply slanting roof and had only half windows and low slanting ceilings. Downstairs the small parlor and another bedroom were divided by the narrow hallway which joined the dining room and kitchen at the back of the house.

The wall plaster had cracked from many settlings; the furniture was sparse and very plain; the rooms were small; but each room had a fireplace and in cold weather a fire blazed cheerfully on a hearth somewhere in the house.

It reminded me of Noah's Ark perched on a little slope, its back hugging the ground, its front high on latticed brick underpinnings, and at each end a tall brick chimney built from the ground outside and towering above the roof. The place had a ragged beauty. Honeysuckle and morning-glory vines flowed over the sagging fences and covered the old latticed wellhouse. A trellis of red and white rambler roses sheltered our back door from the cemetery. Rosebushes, jonquils, irises and violets grew along the walks, and at the foot of each elm tree was a round bed of pansies. Apple and pear trees rimmed the garden and blackberry vines fought with the weeds near the garden fence. When I was a small child Grandmother planted a young orchard of plums, peaches, cherries and pears just below the wellhouse. As I watched her setting out the slender twigs she told me, "I won't be here when these bear fruit, child, but they're for your time."

Grandfather's homeplace was about a mile from the center of Durham in the Maplewood Cemetery section of town. When he had it built back in the 1890's, he was so proud of it he called it Homestead on the Hillside, for it sat on a broad shelf of land between two hills. But like much that had changed since Grandfather lost his sight, the hillside behind it had become a cemetery and the forest rising in front of it had given way to the Bottoms.

In fifty years, Durham had spread rapidly from a village to a bustling factory center, sucking in the rolling pine country around it. Shacks for factory workers mushroomed in the lowlands between the graded streets. These little communities, which clung precariously to the banks of streams or sat crazily on washed-out gullies and were held together by cowpaths or rutted wagon tracks, were called the Bottoms. It was as if the town had swallowed more than it could hold and had regurgitated, for the Bottoms was an odorous conglomeration of trash piles, garbage dumps, cow stalls, pigpens and crowded humanity. You could tell it at night by the straggling lights from oil lamps glimmering along the hollows and the smell of putrefaction, pig swill, cow dung and frying foods. Even if you lived on a hill just above the Bottoms, it seemed lower and danker than the meanest hut on a graded street.

Of course, my family would never admit we lived in the Bottoms. They always said we lived "behind Maplewood Cemetery," but either choice was a gloomy one. The cemetery was so close that only a chicken-wire fence separated us. We used to say we would hit a grave if we sneezed hard. It overshadowed our lives. To the west as far as I could see up the hill were rows of turfed mounds, stone crosses, marble figures, tombstones and vaults. The oppressive nearness of this silent white world of stony angels, doves, lambs, tree trunks and columns gave me the feeling that death was always waiting just outside our back door to grasp me. I was never free from the presence of eternity, the somber symbols of the unknown.

The steep hill so dwarfed our house that when one stood on the cemetery side and looked down our house seemed to shrink into the earth. It was like living under a mountain of tombstones that would break loose someday and come tumbling down upon us. There was also something sinister about the Confederate gun at the top of the hill—mounted on a square base and decorated by a pile of black cannon balls at each corner—which pointed downhill directly at our back door.

At times the cemetery was like a powerful enemy advancing relentlessly upon us, pushing us slowly downward into the Bottoms. Indeed, some of its death and decay had already encroached upon us. Grandfather's crib and stable, which hugged the cemetery fence, had sunk into a marsh of standing water. The wellshed had rotted and I could look through a gaping hole in the latticework and see the oily green scum of water below the crumbling floor boards. That well was a childhood terror. I was always afraid I'd stumble and fall through the hole into the water.

The cemetery was looked upon as an intruder by our family, and Grandfather had battled against it for years before it got the upper hand. When he and his brother Richard first came to Durham in 1869, the place was a small village of three hundred people and Main Street was a muddy roadway lined with wooden shacks, warehouses and livery stables. A mile west of the village on the Chapel Hill Road was a tiny graveyard called Maplewood. East of

Chapel Hill Road a forest sloped downward to a wide meadow containing a vein of clay. Back in Pennsylvania, Uncle Richard Fitzgerald had been a brickmaker and Durham seemed the right spot to start in business. The village was earning a reputation for "Durham Bull" smoking tobacco which later assumed the famous trade name "Bull Durham." The future tobacco kings, Washington Duke and his sons, were still relatively poor tobacco farmers and had not yet set up their factory in Durham, but the town was growing and needed bricks for more stores and factories.

Within the next fifteen years Uncle Richard became Durham's leading brickmaker. By 1884, he had a large brickyard on Chapel Hill Road and orders on hand for two million bricks. During the same period Grandfather had a smaller brickyard and made bricks by hand. My family could remember the time when the hillside behind our house was a meadow and wheat fields skirted by a forest of oaks, pines, cedars and sassafrass bushes. Grandfather had an option from the city to dig clay from part of the land and farm the rest.

The trouble started when the city decided to extend Maplewood Cemetery east of Chapel Hill Road and canceled Grandfather's option. Grandfather suddenly found himself facing a neighbor without heart or feelings. Before that time he had had difficulty protecting his own land from the underground springs which bubbled up on the city's side of the line, but he had handled the problem by digging a four-foot ditch on his side to drain the water northward to a stream and putting up a wooden fence between himself and the city to protect his ditch.

Now the city's workmen began making a roadway on the city's side of the line and knocked down Grandfather's fence. They threw wagonloads of dirt over the line and filled his ditch. Water poured down the hill into our yard. Grandfather had his ditch reopened at his own expense and warned the city, but the careless workmen ignored him and kept right on refilling the ditch. Grandfather was furious. He went from one city official to another and got nothing but shrugs and stares. He then hired a lawyer and sued the city for damages.

Nothing came of it. A local newspaper reported derisively that a blind old colored man on the outskirts of town was stubbornly trying to prevent the city's development but had little chance of success. Grandfather was so humiliated and so feeble by now that he dropped the suit, but Grandmother refused to be silenced. She walked the fence line all day long and railed at the workmen. She told them nobody would put a stopper on her mouth as long as she could breathe. She warned that the graveyard would be so full of mean white folks there'd be no place left to bury them. Her prophecy came true sooner than anyone expected, for the town was hit hard by a flu epidemic not very long after that. Tombstones and fresh graves began to appear at the top of the hill. The forest was cut down and the tombstones began to march down the hill toward our back door.

As the graves crept closer and the water from decomposed bodies drained over our property, our well was condemned. For a long time the family had to carry water by hand from a great distance until money could be scraped together to install city water. In a few years Grandfather's Homestead on the Hillside was isolated on its ledge, a basin for drainage from the cemetery hill. During bad weather we were mired in from constant floodings which settled under the house and rotted the foundations of the stable and wellshed. We had to slosh about in boots most of the time. Our house sank lower and lower and the walls began to crack. Late at night you could hear the old place shifting and groaning as it settled like a restless sleeper. We were seldom free from the sickening odor of standing water and rotting weeds. Our yard was crisscrossed with tiny ditches to get rid of it but we never entirely succeeded. Of course, the city never paid Grandfather a cent for any of the damage.

The cemetery had won but there was something stubborn about Grandfather and his land which refused to knuckle under. True, the graveyard was now at our back door, but Grandfather would not sell out and it could not drive him an inch farther. He walled it out by planting trees and rosebushes along our side of the fence. He developed his longest grape arbor parallel to the fence along our garden walk. In late summer ripe clusters of blue grapes hung in bright defiance of the canopies of death just beyond.

I sometimes thought the family never acknowledged they had lost the use of the cemetery land but continued to treat it as an extension of our property. In summertime it was far more my playground than our front yard. My folks were polite but not overfriendly neighbors. Our front field was a kind of moat which kept everybody off unless someone had special business with us. Life flowed gustily through the Bottoms and there was a continual uproar of shouting children, barking dogs, bellowing cows and people hollering back and forth across the low ground, but we were never a part of it. I used to watch the stream of neighborhood activity enviously from my perch on the porch step, but I seldom got a chance to join it unless I was sent on an errand which took me along the dirt road.

The dead behind us were closer and seemed more friendly at times than the living neighbors in front of us. In fact, Grandmother used to say dead neighbors made good neighbors; they kept their mouths shut and weren't always meddling into other folks' business. I think she said this so often just to reassure herself that she didn't really mind living there. She knew how dead set Grandfather was against pulling up stakes again.

The cemetery haunted family conversations. There was constant talk about selling out and getting away from there. Aunt Sallie complained most about it. She said she didn't see the need of people dying before their time and living in the sight of death forever. But Grandfather was settled under his own vine and fig tree at last and nothing but death would dislodge him. This place was his own; he had built and shaped it and he knew almost every furrow in the earth about it. Blindness spared him from the daily spectacle of sorrow the rest of us endured. The thought of change unnerved him, for a new home would bring new neighbors and new quarrels with Grandmother. I also suspect he would not have anyone believe his family was afraid to stay so near a graveyard. It was a living denial of superstition to remain there.

I'm afraid Grandfather would have disowned me if he had known the strange dual life I led—the suppressed terror by night and the macabre fascination by day which the cemetery held for me. As soon as darkness closed down upon us and we were shut in with it, our house became a fortress against imaginary ghostly legions. No matter what my head told me, I was never free from them. Even inside the house with the doors securely locked and bolted and the lamps lighted, I jumped at every noise and shadow. The walls faded and I could see the ever-present formless gray and white shapes just beyond the door. I dreaded to go outside when there was no moon to distinguish the trees and tombstones. Our own trees were whitewashed every spring and looked as ghostly as the stone figures. Sometimes fingers of light from a street lamp swaying in the wind on the opposite hill would probe the darkness. The cemetery would come to life. Dancing ghoulish arms and legs and indefinable shapes made of wind and shadow would move slowly across the faces of the tombstones. The mournful hoot of a stray owl would send fingers of ice down my spine. In cold weather a few frozen leaves left on the trees would clatter like bones. The worst fright of all was when some prankster prowled the graveyard after dark and pushed one of the cannon balls off its pile. The cannon balls would thunder down a bricked alleyway and crash into the cement base of the wire fence with a terrifying impact that shook the house.

Morning transformed the cemetery into a beautiful park of birds, rabbits, squirrels and, in summer, flowers blooming everywhere. But daytime also brought funerals, and the solemn burial preparations were an inescapable part of our lives. Gravediggers would appear with picks and shovels early in the morning, rope off a plot and put up a canopy. Then they'd take turns digging the grave. The digger's head would get lower and lower in the earth until it disappeared entirely and all one could see was the end of a shovel rhythmically throwing little piles of red dirt onto a steep mound of fresh soil.

My folks pointedly ignored the tradition that Maplewood Cemetery belonged to white people and that colored people were not supposed to enter it at all. We used it for our goings and comings to our relatives' homes on Chapel Hill Road. I spent many hours running errands back and forth along its many paths and roadways. Emboldened by daylight and the living creatures which inhabited it in daytime, I would loiter along the flowered paths searching for new graves. I'd make a little detour to visit a plot whenever I found one. A new grave, bright and poignant under its blanket of fresh flowers, always seemed so lonely to me. In a few days the gravediggers would come along and remove the faded wreaths, leaving a new scar on the green hillside. The recent dead seemed closer to the living than to the turfed mounds. I thought it might be comforting to them that someone stopped to wish them well in their unfamiliar home. Strange, now that I think of it, but I was on better speaking terms with and knew more about the *dead* white people of Durham that I did about the *living* ones. There were no barriers between me and the silent mounds.

Death could lower the barriers but never really wipe them out for the living. People whose kin were buried close to our house often came to the fence to borrow scissors, a jar or a hoe to fix up their graves. We never refused them and often they would stand at the fence for a while talking of their dead as if it eased them to have a listener so close by the grave.

Then one day a woman came down to the back fence and called to Grandmother, who was hanging up clothes in the back yard.

"Aint-ee," she said, "kin you lin me a hoe?"

Grandmother didn't answer or turn her head although she wasn't ten feet away from the woman.

"Aint-ee over there, I say kin you lin me a hoe?"

Grandmother walked to the back door and picked up the hoe leaning against the house. She turned around and I saw that her eyes were blazing.

"Don't you 'aint-ee' me, you pore white trash. I'm none of your kinfolks!" she snapped as she went inside and slammed the door shut in the woman's face.

One couldn't be around Grandmother for very long without hearing all about the Chapel Hill Smiths and the University of North Carolina. It was an obsession with her. If a stranger stopped in the yard long enough to pass the time of day, pretty soon I'd hear Grandmother telling him who she was, who the Smiths were and how they endowed the University. Out of her own vivid memories and the tales she heard from her mother and the older Smith slaves, she literally breathed their history.

"Child, you listen to your grandmother," she told me. "Hold your head high and don't take a back seat to nobody. You got good blood in you—folks that counted for something—doctors, lawyers, judges, legislators. Aristocrats, that's what they were, going back seven generations right in this state."

"Mama, don't fill that child's head with all that old stuff," Aunt Pauline complained. "We'd all be better off if we'd never heard it. It never did any of us any good."

"Mind your business," Grandmother retorted. "The truth's the light and the truth never hurt nobody. I'm proud of my kinfolks. Besides, I'm telling this child pure history."

"That's what's wrong with this family now," Aunt Pauline said. "Too much pride and not enough money to back it up."

But Grandmother would have her say although nobody else at home wanted to hear about the Smith philanthropy. She talked of the University as if she were one of its chief benefactors. She never forgot that a great-uncle of the Smiths on their mother's side, the younger Tignal Jones, had offered five hundred acres of his estate in 1792 to get the school located in Chatham County. His offer was rejected in favor of a better location in Chapel Hill, but eventually most of the Smith land passed to the institution.

Grandmother related this fact half proudly, half resentfully, and her proprietary attitude toward the University arose out of her feeling that it had received her inheritance. Mere mention of it aroused only bitter anger in Grandfather and my aunts. Education was a household god at home, yet none of us could attend the University or share the benefits bestowed upon it by Miss Mary Ruffin Smith. When Grandmother began harping on the subject, Grandfather got up disgustedly and stormed out of the room. My aunts started humming and banging things around so they wouldn't hear her. So she made me her wide-eyed audience.

Many a night she sat by the fireplace chewing on her snuff brush and conjuring up the old days at Hillsboro and Chapel Hill before the Civil War. She would trace the Smiths' ancestry back to their maternal great-grandfather, old Tignal Jones, who descended from English settlers in Chatham County during colonial days. Old Tignal's two sons, the younger Tignal and Francis Jones, the Smiths' grandfather, owned thousands of acres of fine timber land and a good many slaves. Francis Jones was something of a local hero around both counties because he had served as a lieutenant in Sharpe's Company during the Revolutionary War.

When he died in 1844—the year Grandmother was born—his lands passed to his grandson, Dr. Francis Jones Smith.

Years later when I looked up the records I found Grandmother's family history to be remarkably accurate. But there was one haunting story she told me about the Smiths and Great-grandmother Harriet which did not appear in the records. I don't think she realized it but she repeated this story again and again with such passionate single-mindedness it was like the recounting of a long-buried wrong which had refused to die and which she expected me to right somehow. I did not hear it all at once. Some of it I found out on my own, but most of it I pieced together from what I heard her say and the stories she had told her own daughters when they were very young.

When Grandmother spoke of Great-grandmother Harriet her face saddened and she shook her head sorrowfully. Sometimes she would break off in the middle of her tale and sigh as if to say what that poor woman went through was too painful to put into words. She would forget I was there and sit nodding her head and rocking back and forth, her eyes fixed on the red embers, as if she were caught up in some strange ritual of memory.

After a long while she would say, "My mother was a good woman and did the best she could, but she couldn't help herself." And then, as if summing up the whole thing, she would quote the Bible: " 'The fathers have eaten a sour grape and the children's teeth are set on edge,' " and add, "How true! How true!"

But it was a different story when she talked of her father. Remembered joy shone in her eyes and her whole being changed and quickened with excitement. An uncontrollable pride in blood welled up in her as she described the ruddy-faced, sharp-eyed, wiry little man with a long bullet-shaped head and quick catlike movements.

"My father walked like he was strung on electric wires and he had a voice that could hold you spellbound for hours. He could make a judge break right down and cry in the courtroom when he was pleading a case." Remembering how Grandmother's own voice rang over the hillside and held the neighbors, I could believe her.

Grandmother referred to the three Smiths of her story as "Miss

Mary Ruffin," "Dr. Frank" and "my father, Lawyer Sidney Smith." They belonged to a leading Orange County family which lived first in Hillsboro and later near Chapel Hill. Their mother, the former Delia Jones, came from an old landholding, slave-owning family of Chatham County. Their father, Dr. James S. Smith, a descendant of Scotch-Irish Protestants who settled in Orange County, was one of North Carolina's most distinguished citizens. During Monroe's administration he served as a Democratic Congressman for two terms and later as a member of North Carolina's House of Commons.

The three Smith children were born and reared in Hillsboro. Later the family moved to Price's Creek, a fourteen-hundred-acre plantation three miles from Chapel Hill on the old Pittsboro Road. By 1850 their land stretched for miles and they owned thirty slaves. Few Orange County families owned more than that. The large white, Doric-columned Smith house sat off the road beyond a great iron gate in a grove of giant oak trees. Grandmother said that when she was a little girl one of her duties in the fall was to rake the oak leaves into great piles and burn them. Dr. Smith was a trustee of the University of North Carolina for many years and his home was a center of political and cultural activity.

Mary Ruffin Smith, the oldest child, was a remarkably intelligent girl and, after the fashion of southern young ladies, was trained by a thorough-going governess, Miss Maria Spear, from New York. In another era, Miss Mary might have had a professional career like her brothers, since she had great ability, was a good manager, read widely on political affairs and maintained a deep interest in medical botany throughout her life. But in her time southern young ladies were not expected to earn a living or have a career. They were trained to become the mistresses of large slave plantations. So she learned music, art, literature and needle-work and spent much of her youth painting with water colors and composing songs and ballads. Miss Maria Spear, the governess, was a warm, gentle, compassionate soul whose Yankee heart was opposed to slavery. Mary Ruffin admired and loved her and kept her in the family until her death around 1881, but she never absorbed her gentle ways. She grew into a proud, stern, inflexible woman.

Her two brothers, Francis Jones and Sidney, attended the University of North Carolina. Francis followed his father's profession and studied medicine while Sidney, the younger boy, was attracted to law and politics. He was a fiery orator and developed into one of the county's most effective stumpers. His father turned Whig in 1841 and was defeated for Congress, but Sidney became a leading local Democrat and went to Raleigh in 1846 as a member of the General Assembly.

Folks thought it was a shame that none of the three Smiths married, considering their talents and the fine family they came from. It was taken for granted that Miss Mary Ruffin would make one of the best catches in the state and that the boys would marry well and have distinguished careers like their father. Everything pointed that way. But as years passed and the Smith men were still bachelors, people hinted darkly that Frank and Sid had wild blood in them. They said their devilment just about wrecked their own lives and drove Miss Mary into a lonely spinsterhood.

Of course some folks said that Harriet was at the bottom of all the trouble, as if she were to blame, although she was the one person who never had any choice at all. Folks claimed that if she just hadn't come to the Smith home, Frank and Sid might have settled down to solid respectable married lives. Nobody would have condemned them too harshly for doing what many southern men of high standing had done—bred two lines of children simultaneously and on the same place, one by their lawful white wives and the other by a slave concubine.

It happened in the best families all the time. It was a sickness of the times which everybody talked about but nobody stopped. The southern lawmakers spent their energies arguing that there was an impassable social gulf between blacks and whites and slavery was therefore the natural condition of the blacks. Yet while they argued, their wives at home secretly hated slavery for the oldest of human reasons. The southern woman was never sure of her husband's fidelity or her sons' morals as long as there was a slave woman in the household. The slave woman's presence threatened her sovereignty, insulted her womanhood and often humiliated her before her friends. She was confronted with a rival by compulsion, whose helplessness she could not fight. Nor could she hide the mulatto children always underfoot who resembled her own children so strongly that no one could doubt their parentage.

It was to Dr. James Smith's credit that he had kept free of this sort of thing. Until he bought Harriet, the slaves he owned were listed as Blacks and there were no mulatto children on his place. In 1834, when Mary Ruffin Smith turned eighteen, she had her coming-out party. The family lived in Hillsboro at the time and kept only a few household slaves on their place. The boys were away in school at Chapel Hill. Dr. Smith was deep in a political campaign to win election as a delegate from Orange County to the state constitutional convention. The Smiths entertained frequently and now that Miss Mary Ruffin was of an age to go about in society, it seemed fitting that she have her own personal maid to accompany her and to serve her at home when she received guests. So that fall Dr. Smith bought Harriet, a fifteen-year-old beauty, paid $450 for her—a tidy sum in those days—and congratulated himself on getting an unusually good bargain.

Even then Harriet was known to be one of the most beautiful girls in the county, white or black. She was small and shapely, had richly colored skin like the warm inner bark of a white birch, delicate features, flashing dark eyes and luxuriant wavy black hair which fell below her knees. She was shy and reticent but her eyes talked. I never knew whether she had any colored blood. Grandmother always said she was three-fourths white and one-fourth Cherokee Indian. It was not uncommon to find Indian mixtures among the slaves. Indian girls were frequently kidnaped and forced into slavery as concubines during colonial days when white women were scarce and the white settlers raided the Indians. There were many skirmishes between the settlers and the Cherokees of western North Carolina before the Cherokee tribe was driven out and made its sorrowful pilgrimage over the Trail of Tears into Oklahoma. The Indian women lost their identity, were listed as mulattoes and were often used as breeders. Their children brought high prices in the slave market. This may have happened to Harriet's Cherokee grandmother.

At the time, Mary Ruffin Smith considered herself most fortunate to have such a handsome young slave girl. She showed off her new maid to her women friends as one displays fine furs or jewelry. She was not beautiful herself—she was a tall, angular, dark-haired, sallow-skinned young woman, inclined to be stiff and awkward—but she commanded another's grace, which was the next best thing to being beautiful. Harriet was a well-mannered, reserved, devoted servant who apparently accepted her lot without question and was unconscious of the striking contrast between them. She waited on Miss Mary hand and foot, and for the first few years of her service she slept on a straw pallet just outside Miss Mary's door where she could waken at her mistress's slightest call. She went with her almost everywhere and was an unobtrusive figure in the background to attend Miss Mary's needs in public.

As Harriet grew older she grew more lovely, and her striking looks drew attention to her wherever she went. Miss Mary noticed that in public her slave girl far more than herself was the object of quick admiring glances from strangers. It was the same way at home when the Smiths entertained. Their guests could scarcely conceal their open-eyed admiration. The women were frankly envious while the men, young and old, stared at Harriet without restraint when she came into the room. They'd leave the most weighty conversation hanging in mid-air to appraise her from head to foot. No one could deny that they knew a good thing when they saw it. After all, these experienced plantation owners were accustomed to judging good horseflesh or sizing up prize cattle at a glance. They did the same with slaves. Dr. Smith's associates tried to outbid one another with handsome offers to buy Harriet, but while he enjoyed all the fanfare he did not need the money and told his friends she was not for sale. Not to be outdone, some of them tried to hire her out for breeding, but Dr. Smith only chuckled and said his daughter could not spare her.

Harriet was around twenty when she expressed the desire to marry young Reuben Day, a free-born mulatto who lived and worked around Hillsboro. Dr. Smith readily gave his permission. It was a good match. He cared nothing for free Negroes generally —he had helped to change the state constitution in 1835 to take away their vote and bar them from education—but he had no objection if one of them wanted to marry his slave girl. It was good business. He had no obligation to the husband, and every child by the marriage would be his slave and worth several hundred dollars at birth.

Grandmother thought mighty well of the Orange County Days. They were a near-white family who had been free for several generations. The older ones had purchased themselves or been emancipated by their white kinsfolk and most of the younger ones were "free issue," or born free. They were hard-working, thrifty and proud as tom turkeys. They had good reason to be proud, because they owned a little land and kept themselves afloat in spite of the hard times which faced all free Negroes in a slave state. The slaveowners were so afraid their slaves would revolt if they saw the free Negroes get ahead that they made the laws especially oppressive against free colored people.

Grandmother never knew her mother's husband, Reuben Day, but she used to talk a lot about his brother, Tom Day, who was well known in ante-bellum North Carolina. Tom was a fine cabinet-maker who had his own business. Wealthy white people came to him from all over the state to have their furniture made to order. By 1860 he was so prosperous he owned three slaves himself whom he used in his business. Grandmother said that when his wife died many years later he made her a rosewood coffin with his own hands.

Reuben Day was not so fortunate. He was a farm worker with no special trade. Reuben and Harriet could not even live together. They had to share brief visits in a little cabin on the Smith lot when Reuben was given permission to see her. When their son Julius was born around 1842, he was a Smith slave like his mother. Reuben did not like this arrangement, of course, and often talked of buying freedom for Harriet and her child, but they were high-priced slaves and it would take many years to save up the purchase money.

That was the way things stood when Francis and Sid came home from school and began practicing their professions around Hillsboro. They had not seen much of Harriet during their school days, but now they found a mature woman just a little younger than themselves and good to look at. Each had the same thought when he saw her and each read the look in the other's eyes.

Sidney had always been a hot-blooded, impetuous little fellow who hurled himself with single-minded fury into whatever caught his interest. Francis was by nature more cautious and restrained. Sidney exploded and spent himself, but Frank knew how to wait and bide his time. He was a tall, dark, brooding man who seemed withdrawn much of the time. While he said little and seemed calm and self-possessed at all times, he had a terrible temper beneath his quiet exterior.

Before long everybody in the house knew that a storm was brewing between the brothers and that Harriet was the cause of it. Francis watched her furtively from a distance, but Sidney was open with it. From the moment he returned home he could not leave her alone. His eyes followed her everywhere when she was in the room. He seemed to be always just behind her when she went out the door or standing in the shadows when she went to her cabin at night after her work was done. He would confront her suddenly on the stairs or in a hallway, block her passage and try to talk to her. She began to dread the sight of him and evenings when she finished her duties at the Smith house, she fled to her cabin, nailed the door from the inside, put sticks across the window and lay trembling for hours.

One day Sidney cornered her in the study and tried to kiss her. She fought him off and ran screaming from the house. Francis heard the fuss and that night the brothers quarreled about it after supper.

"Why don't you leave the girl alone, Sid?" Francis asked.

"That's my business," said Sid.

"Listen, you bullheaded fool," roared Frank. "If I ever catch you on that woman, I'll beat the hell out of you. You won't live to tell the tale."

There was an uneasy truce for a while after that, but Harriet felt like a hunted creature. When Sidney wasn't following her around, Francis' eyes were on her with an unmistakable look in them. Each brother was biding his time. She grew thin and haggard and Miss Mary frequently caught her weeping. Miss Mary was nobody's fool. She had watched her brothers and seen what was coming. Her mother was a meek, delicate little woman who had never taken a strong hand in her sons' affairs and only wrung her hands about it. She spoke to her father, but Dr. Smith seemed strangely unconcerned. He said the boys had to sow a few wild oats and they'd get over it. Miss Mary hoped desperately Frank and Sid would get interested in some of the eligible young women in their social set, but neither of them showed the slightest inclination to take a wife. They had eyes for no woman but Harriet.

Then one evening Sidney walked up to Harriet's cabin as she was saying good night to Reuben.

"Say, boy, what're you doing on this place after nine o'clock? You're not one of our slaves," he said.

"You know me, Marse Sidney," said the astounded Reuben. "I'm Reuben Day, Harriet's husband."

"Husband!" Sidney exclaimed as if it were the first time he had heard such a thing.

"Yes sir. Me and Harriet got married more'n two years ago."

"Somebody's been fooling you, boy. Don't you know slave marriages aren't recognized in this state?"

"Oh, but you see Dr. Smith fixed it up for us. He gave us permission and the preacher said words over us. We're married all right."

"Can't help what the preacher said. You're up against the slave law."

"But Marse Sid, I'm free born and—"

"Then it's too bad you married a slave woman. You'll have to get yourself another wife."

Reuben was stunned. Harriet clung to him wordlessly. Fury and frustration boiled in him but he was helpless. Behind the evil little man who leered at him in the darkness was the oppressive weight of southern law and custom.

"And beside," Sidney was saying, "we don't want you on this place. You're a trespasser and if you come back, I'll have you whipped and thrown in jail."

Reuben started to say something, but Harriet clapped her hand over his mouth and pushed him through the door.

"Do like he says, Reuben," she pleaded. "Don't say no more. It'd only make it worse. Just go now."

Reuben had to leave without a word to Harriet. That was the last she ever saw of him. He tried to slip back to see her once more, but Sidney caught him on the lot before he reached her

cabin. Frank was into it too. The brothers beat Reuben with the
butt end of a carriage whip and when they finally let him go they
told him if he ever came back on the Smith lot they'd shoot him
on sight. He disappeared from the county and nothing was heard
of him again.

Harriet had no one to turn to now. The other slaves on the
place had watched this little drama and knew how it would end,
but they kept their distance. They had learned that a slave was a
marked woman when she got mixed up with the men in the Big
House. Her own men were afraid to have anything to do with her
and it wasn't safe for her to have a husband of her own. Look at
what had happened to Reuben Day, a free man. The women felt
sorry for Harriet, of course, but it was an ill wind that didn't blow
somebody some good. If Marse Frank and Marse Sid wanted
Harriet and got used to her, it might save their own skins for a
while.

It was inevitable that Sidney should be the first to break the
truce. It happened right after Reuben was run off the place.
Harriet had nailed up the door as usual and put barricades against
it one night. Later, after everyone had gone to bed, the other slaves
heard Marse Sid break open Harriet's door. Ear-splitting shrieks
tore the night, although he stuffed rags in the door and window
cracks to muffle Harriet's cries. They heard litle Julius screaming
and Harriet's violent struggle before Sidney had his way with her.
Nobody interfered, of course.

That was only the beginning. After that first night, Harriet
went into fits of hysterical screaming whenever Sidney came near
her. The more she reviled him, the better he seemed to like it. He
raped her again and again in the weeks that followed. Night after
night he would force open her cabin door and nail it up again on
the inside so that she could not get out. Then he would beat her
into submission. She would cry out sharply, moan like a wounded
animal and beg for mercy. The other slaves, hearing her cries,
trembled in their beds and prayed silently for her deliverance.

It came one night when Francis laid for Sidney and caught him
just as he was coming out of Harriet's cabin. The brothers had it
out once and for all, and there was a terrible fight. Early the next
morning one of the slaves found Marse Sid lying unconscious in

the yard, his clothes soaked with blood and an ugly hole in his head. He got over it but it was a long time before he was up and about again. The Smiths never talked about what happened that night; they hushed it up and told some cock-and-bull story about Marse Sid falling off his horse. The slaves knew, however, that Marse Frank had carried out his threat.

Sidney was only twenty-four at the time and had a bright political future ahead of him, but he was never quite the same after that beating. He took to drinking and brooded his life away. He went down to Raleigh for one term in the legislature and there were flashes of brilliant success here and there when he was sober, but in the end he turned out to be one of the worst drunkards in the county.

He learned his lesson. He never touched Harriet again after that night. She was at last free to come and go unmolested, but for months afterward there was a wild look in her eyes as she carried Sidney's child and she went about with a silent smoldering hatred against him to the end of her days.

Everybody around Hillsboro had heard how Frank and Sid Smith had run Harriet's mulatto husband out of the county and fought over her themselves. The family tried to laugh it off as ignorant slave gossip, but it was no laughing matter when Grandmother was born on the Smith lot in early February 1844. Here was the proof of the pudding. She was indistinguishable from a white child and she had Sidney's features. What was more, he was gleeful over her birth. He refused to keep quiet about it and went around boasting to his friends about his fine little daughter.

Dr. Smith was frankly ashamed of his son but had long since ceased to have any influence over him. Luckily he had retired from politics after his defeat a few years earlier or this might have been used against him publicly. Mrs. Smith was heartbroken over the whole thing and some folks thought the shock of it hastened her to her grave. Francis, of course, had already gotten his revenge and said little about it except that he'd kill Sidney and hang for it if it ever happened again.

Mary Ruffin Smith was mortified. She had a strong conscience and deep family pride. She felt Sidney had disgraced them all. Not that she had ever seriously questioned slavery as a way of life or the foundation of her family's wealth and privilege. Nor had she ever disputed a master's absolute right over his slave's person even when it included assault and rape. She had heard her father and Judge Thomas Ruffin expound these views too often to believe otherwise.

The whole thing fell on her shoulders because Harriet was her servant. She was too valuable to get rid of and, besides, the damage was already done. What was to be done with her little bastard? Put it in the slave quarters, of course, and try to live it down. Here was the rub. It was not so easy to act according to fixed ideas when something happened in one's own family. Try as she might to avoid the truth, it struck her with shattering clarity that this was Sidney's child, a *Smith!* She couldn't get around it. Slavery had produced its own monstrosity in Miss Mary's home as it had done elsewhere. Smith progeny had been born into slavery. It could be bought and sold like any other property and in time this girl child of Smith blood could be bred to other men no better or worse than her own father. Miss Mary Ruffin realized with horror that this bastard slave child was also her own flesh and blood—in fact, her niece.

Thus she warred with herself. There were no heirs in the house to soften the blow or conceal her dilemma. The very family pride which made her feel so disgraced by Gandmother's birth also made it impossible for her to let her own kin grow up like a slave. As Grandmother said, blood was thicker than water. Grudgingly, Miss Mary Ruffin brought the baby into the Smith house and kept a private nurse for her until she was six years old. It was the first of many such battles in her soul in which Miss Mary would be torn between conscience and pride. The decision set her on a course of action from which she could not retreat for the remainder of her life. Like Harriet, she was drawn deeper and deeper into a quagmire. She was to experience a common bondage with Harriet which transcended the opposite poles of their existence as mistress and slave.

Not long after Grandmother was born Francis Smith came to Harriet's cabin. She did not cry out; she had been expecting it.

Perhaps she was resigned. Or perhaps in her wretched loneliness she was grateful to him and even flattered by his attention. She had been cast adrift between two irreconcilable worlds. No colored man in the vicinity would dare show interest in her as long as she belonged to the Smiths. She was a mere pawn in her masters' world, desired but not recognized, safe from the predatory Sidney only so long as Francis remained her protector. And while Francis was kinder and more patient than his brother, he was no less determined to possess her exclusively.

It soon became known around the place that Harriet was Frank's woman—and that was that. Theirs was a distant relationship, barren of all communication save that of the flesh. In the Smith house Francis was the silent, remote master who scarcely noticed Harriet's presence. And she waited upon him with the same impartial deference she showed the other Smiths, giving no sign that she was his mistress. Yet, over the years Harriet was silently devoted to him and no one ever heard of his having another woman.

Within five years after Grandmother's birth, Harriet had borne Frank Smith three daughters—Grandmother's half sisters, Emma, Annette and Laura. Shortly after Emma was born, the Smiths moved to Price's Creek. It almost seemed that Dr. Smith pulled up stakes to get away from the glare of Hillsboro society and clacking tongues. First Sid, then Frank laying up with a slave wench and refusing to marry their own kind like decent people. And the Smiths were upholding them in their dirt, bringing their little bastards right into the home and raising them up as if they were part of the family.

If Dr. Smith had sold Harriet and her children the talk would have been worse. Then folks would have said the Smiths sold their own blood into slavery. Conscience is a ruthless master and the Smiths were driven into an enslavement no less wasteful than Harriet's. They were doomed to live with blunted emotions and unnatural restraints, to keep up appearances by acting out a farce which fooled nobody and brought them little comfort.

It was a life of baffling contradictions and ambivalences, of snarls and threats and bitter recriminations. Everybody blamed everybody else for what had happened. It was dog eat dog with Sidney and Frank. They quarreled all the time and the family never knew when one of them might murder the other. Yet neither would give ground and move out. Harriet never spoke to Sidney or came near him unless compelled to do so in the course of her duties. Her sullen anger expressed itself in every gesture when he was anywhere around.

She was now the mother of five children by three different fathers, all growing up on the same plantation but treated according to their fathers' positions. Julius, the oldest, was almost ignored by the Big House. Like any other slave he came up willy-nilly in the quarters. His mother was almost a stranger to him. She was absorbed by the Smiths and had little identity of her own. She must serve them at the Smith home all day and at night she must hurry Julius off to one of the other cabins so he would not be around when Marse Frank came. He was a sweet, lovable boy, but ill luck overtook him. When he was around thirteen, he got lost in the woods during a heavy snowstorm. They found him almost frozen to death. He was severely crippled for the rest of his life.

The four Smith daughters were brought up in the Smith house. They were aware of Harriet as their mother, but their loyalties divided according to their fathers and they looked up to Miss Mary Ruffin for everything. Harriet hovered anxiously in the background, completely overshadowed by the superior authority of her mistress. Miss Mary decided what the girls should wear, where they should go, whom they should play with, how they should be trained and what duties they should perform. She meted out their punishments and their privileges. Until Miss Mary's death Grandmother looked upon her as one looks upon a parent and she seemed to have more pity than daughterly affection for Great-grandmother Harriet. Indeed, the two elder women had shared a strange motherhood in which neither could fully express her maternal feelings. The same overpowering forces which had robbed the slave mother of all natural rights had thrust them unwanted upon the childless spinster.

The Smiths were as incapable of treating the little girls wholly as servants as they were of recognizing them openly as kin. At times the Smiths' involuntary gestures of kinship were so pronounced the children could not help thinking of themselves as

Smith grandchildren. At other times their innocent overtures of affection were rebuffed without explanation and they were driven away with cruel epithets.

The family carefully preserved a thin veneer of master-servant relationship for the unbelieving public but the children's very presence betrayed them. They were so white-skinned and looked so much like the Smiths nobody was taken in by such pretenses. Sidney would go out of his way to mortify his family. He'd call Grandmother when company was around.

"Come here, Cornelia. This one's *my* daughter. She's smart as a whip, too," he'd say, partly out of fatherly pride and partly out of revenge against Frank. The implication was clear that the other three girls were his brother's children.

Naturally, the girls grew up feeling themselves more Smith heirs than Smith servants. Emma, Laura and Annette were more subdued about it than Grandmother. Frank shrugged them off and treated them as part of the surroundings. They kept a respectful distance from him and addressed him as "Marse Frank." Their daughterly feelings were reserved for their own private conversations among themselves.

There was nothing subdued about Grandmother. She blurted out exactly what she thought and was afraid of no one. She never called anyone "Marse." She had the Smith pride and refused to regard herself as a slave.

"We were free. We were just born in slavery, that's all," she always said. And to her, there was a difference.

Gwendolyn Brooks

GWENDOLYN BROOKS was born in Topeka, Kansas, but she has lived most of her life in Chicago.

In 1950, she received the Pulitzer Prize for her second volume of poetry, *Annie Allen*. She was the recipient of four Poetry Workshop awards given by the Midwestern Writers Conference before the publication of her first volume of poetry, A *Street in Bronzeville*, in 1945. She also received two Guggenheim Fellowships and an American Academy of Arts and Letters Grant in Literature for poetry, in 1946. In addition to her four volumes of poetry, Miss Brooks has published a novel, Maud Martha.

"The Life of Lincoln West" is an original short story published here for the first time. "Helen" is from Maud Martha.

Gwendolyn Brooks states that her "admirations" are Chekhov, Emily Dickinson, John Crowe Ransom, Langston Hughes, and the Joyce of *Dubliners*.

Miss Brooks teaches, lectures, and gives poetry readings. She is married and is the mother of two children.

THE LIFE OF LINCOLN WEST

BY GWENDOLYN BROOKS

The ugliest little boy that everyone ever saw. That is what everyone said.

Even to his mother it was apparent—when the blue-aproned nurse came into the northeast end of the maternity ward bearing his squeals and plump bottom looped up in a scant receiving blanket, bending, to pass the bundle carefully into the waiting mother-hands—that this was no cute little ugliness, no sly baby waywardness that was going to inch away as would baby fat, baby curl and baby spot-rash. The pendulous lip, the branching ears, the eyes so wide and wild, the vague unvibrant brown of the skin, and, most disturbing, the great head: these components of That Look bespoke the sure fiber. The deep grain.

His father could not bear the sight of him. His mother high-piled her pretty, dyed hair and put him among her hairpins and sweethearts, dance slippers, torn paper roses. Although he was not less than these, he was not more.

As the little Lincoln grew, uglily upward and out, he began to understand that something was wrong. His little ways of trying to please his father, the bringing of matches, the jumping aside at warning sound of oh-so-large and rushing stride, the smile that gave and gave and gave—unsuccessful!

Even Christmases and Easters were spoiled. He would be sitting at the family feasting table, really delighting in the displays of mashed potatoes and the rich golden fat-crust of the ham or the festive fowl, when he would look up and find somebody feeling indignant about him.

What a pity what a pity. No love for one so loving. The little Lincoln loved Everybody. Ants. The changing caterpillar. His much-missing mother. His kindergarten teacher.

His kindergarten teacher—whose concern for him was composed of one part sympathy and two parts repulsion. The others ran up with their little drawings. He ran up with his. She tried to be as pleasant with him as with others, but it was difficult. For she was all beauty, all daintiness, all tiny vanilla, with blue eyes and fluffy sun-hair. One afternoon she saw him in the hall looking very bleak against the wall. It was strange because the bell had long since rung and no other child was in sight. Pity flooded her. She buttoned her gloves and suggested cheerfully that she walk him home. She started out bravely, holding him by the hand. But she had not walked far before she regretted it. The little monkey. *Must* everyone look? And clutching her hand like that. . . . Literally pinching it. . . .

At seven, the little Lincoln loved the brother and sister who moved next door. Handsome. Well dressed. Charitable, often, to him. They enjoyed him because he was resourceful, made up games, told stories. But when their more acceptable friends came, were around, they turned their handsome backs on him. He hated himself for responding gratefully to their later "Hi, Linc!"—hated himself for his feeling of well-being when with them, despite—everything.

He spent much time looking at himself in mirrors. What could be done? But there was no shrinking his head. There was no binding his ears.

"Don't touch me!" cried the little fairylike being in the playground.

Her name was Nerissa. The many children were playing tag, but when he caught her, she recoiled, jerked free and ran. It was like all the rainbow that ever was, going off forever, all, all the sparklings in the sunset west.

One day, while he was yet seven, a thing happened. In the downtown movies with his mother, a white man in the seat beside him whispered loudly to a companion, and pointed at the little Linc.

"There! That's the kind I've been wanting to show you! One of the best examples of the species. Not like those diluted Negroes you see so much of on the streets these days, but the real thing. Black, ugly and odd. You can see the savagery. The blunt blankness. That is the real thing."

His mother—her dyed hair had never looked so red around the

dark brown velvet of her face—jumped up, shrieked, "Go to—
go—" She did not finish. She yanked to his feet the little Lincoln,
who was sitting there staring in fascination at his assessors. At the
author of his new idea.

All the way home he was happy. Of course, he had not liked
the word "ugly," but after all, should he not be used to that by
now? What had struck him, among words and meanings he could
little understand, was the phrase "the real thing." He didn't
know quite why, but he liked that. He liked that very much.

When he was hurt, too much stared at—too much left alone—
he thought about that. He told himself, "After all, I'm the real
thing."

It comforted him. For almost four years it meant a lot to him.

HELEN

From *Maud Martha*

BY GWENDOLYN BROOKS

What she remembered was Emmanuel; laughing, glinting in the sun; kneeing his wagon toward them, as they walked tardily home from school. Six years ago.

"How about a ride?" Emmanuel had hailed.

She had, daringly—it was not her way, not her native way—made a quip. A "sophisticated" quip. "Hi, handsome!" Instantly he had scowled, his dark face darkening.

"I don't mean you, you old black gal," little Emmanuel had exclaimed. "I mean Helen."

He had meant Helen, and Helen on the reissue of the invitation had climbed, without a word, into the wagon and was off and away.

Even now, at seventeen—high school graduate, mistress of her fate, and a ten-dollar-a-week file clerk in the very Forty-seventh Street lawyer's office where Helen was a fifteen-dollar-a-week typist —as she sat on Helen's bed and watched Helen primp for a party, the memory hurt. There was no consolation in the thought that not now and not then would she have *had* Emmanuel "off a Christmas tree." For the basic situation had never changed. Helen was still the one they wanted in the wagon, still "the pretty one," "the dainty one." The lovely one.

She did not know what it was. She had tried to find the something that must be there to imitate, that she might imitate it. But she did not know what it was. I wash as much as Helen does, she thought. My hair is longer and thicker, she thought. I'm much smarter. I read books and newspapers and old folks like to talk with me, she thought.

But the kernel of the matter was that, in spite of these things, she was poor, and Helen was still the ranking queen, not only with the Emmanuels of the world, but even with their father—their mother—their brother. She did not blame the family. It was not their fault. She understood. They could not help it. They were enslaved, were fascinated, and they were not at all to blame.

Her noble understanding of their blamelessness did not make any easier to bear such a circumstance as Harry's springing to open a door so that Helen's soft little hands might not have to cope with the sullyings of a doorknob, or running her errands, to save the sweet and fine little feet, or shouldering Helen's part against Maud Martha. Especially could these items burn when Maud Martha recalled her comradely rompings with Harry, watched by the gentle Helen from the clean and gentle harbor of the porch: take the day, for example, when Harry had been chased by those five big boys from Forty-first and Wabash, cursing, smelling, beast-like boys! with bats and rocks, and little stones that were more worrying than rocks; on that occasion out Maud Martha had dashed, when she saw from the front-room window Harry, panting and torn, racing for home; out she had dashed and down into the street with one of the smaller porch chairs held high over her head, and while Harry gained first the porch and next the safety side of the front door she had swung left, swung right, clouting a head here, a head there, and screaming at the top of her lungs, "Y' leave my brother alone! Y' leave my brother alone!" And who had washed those bloody wounds, and afterward vaselined them down? Really—in spite of everything she could not understand why Harry had to hold open doors for Helen, and calmly let them slam in her, Maud Martha's, his friend's, face.

It did not please her either, at the breakfast table, to watch her father drink his coffee and contentedly think (oh, she knew it!), as Helen started on her grapefruit, how daintily she ate, how gracefully she sat in her chair, how pure was her robe and unwrinkled, how neatly she had arranged her hair. Their father preferred Helen's hair to Maud Martha's (Maud Martha knew), which impressed him, not with its length and body, but simply with its apparent untamableness; for he would never get over that zeal of his for order in all things, in character, in housekeeping, in his own labor, in grooming, in human relationships. Always he had worried about Helen's homework, Helen's health. And now that boys were taking her out, he believed not one of them worthy of her, not one of them good enough to receive a note of her sweet voice: he insisted that she be returned before midnight. Yet who was it who sympathized with him in his decision to remain, for the rest of his days, the simple janitor! when everyone else was urging him to get out, get prestige, make more money? Who was it who sympathized with him in his almost desperate love for this old house? Who followed him about, emotionally speaking, loving this, doting on that? The kitchen, for instance, that was not beautiful in any way! The walls and ceilings, that were cracked. The chairs, which cried when people sat in them. The tables, that grieved audibly if anyone rested more than two fingers upon them. The huge cabinets, old and tired (when you shut their doors or drawers there was a sick, bickering little sound). The radiators, high and hideous. And underneath the low sink coiled unlovely pipes, that Helen said made her think of a careless woman's underwear, peeping out. In fact, often had Helen given her opinion, unasked, of the whole house, of the whole "hulk of rotten wood." Often had her cool and gentle eyes sneered, gently and coolly, at her father's determination to hold his poor estate. But take that kitchen, for instance! Maud Martha, taking it, saw herself there, up and down her seventeen years, eating apples after school; making sweet potato tarts; drawing, on the pathetic table, the horse that won her the sixth grade prize; getting her hair curled for her first party, at that stove; washing dishes by summer twilight, with the back door wide open; making cheese and peanut butter sandwiches for a picnic. And even crying, crying in that pantry, when no one knew. The old sorrows brought there!—now dried, flattened out, breaking into interesting dust at the merest look. . . .

"You'll never get a boy friend," said Helen, fluffing on her Golden Peacock powder, "if you don't stop reading those books."

LeRoi Jones

Mr. Jones comments on "The Christians" and "The Rape" which are published for the first time in this collection, as follows: "These two pieces are taken from a larger work called *The System of Dante's Hell*, and as such, they might seem in some ways incomplete, though I do not think this is the case.

"In the complete work I have tried to provide some parallels, i.e., emotional analogies, between my own life and Dante's Hell. The work is modeled after the Hell, and I go into each bolgia (ditch) of each circle of the Hell and drag out some corresponding horror in my own soul.

" 'The Christians' is taken from the eighth circle, bolgia 9, The Makers of Discord. Dante made these the Mohammedans, but I alter this to my own purpose, and cite these as Christians. "The Rape" is taken from the ninth circle, bolgia 1, where those who have committed treachery to their kindred are interned.

"I do not mean for these *connections* to be strictly literary, and if that is the case, I have failed. Rather I have attempted to draw each of these holes of hell out of a strange empathy of symbols connecting my own life with the personal mythology of a medieval Christian poet—and these are supposed to be stories."

LeRoi Jones was born and reared in Newark, New Jersey, studied at Howard University, and pursued graduate studies at Columbia

University and the New School for Social Research. His published works include a volume of poetry, *Preface to a Twenty Volume Suicide Note* (1961), and a non-fiction work, *Blues: Black and White America* (1963).

He is a frequent contributor to many magazines, including the *Evergreen Review, Downbeat, Poetry, Metronome,* and *The Nation,* and is the poetry editor of Corinth Books.

From *The System of Dante's Hell*

BY LeROI JONES

THE CHRISTIANS

Next to nothing. Next to the street, from a window, under all the noise from radios, 9 Cliftons, slickheads in bunches wanting to beat punks up, cops whistling, my uncle coming in the room, changing his collars, putting on checkered coat & 3 pens in breast pocket. I'd be there shining one shoe, taking out the bellbottom "hip" suit (some girl at the Y, a Duke chick, first called it that). And my friends ridiculed it not realizing that I was moved away. Spirit hovered over the big king, the polaks, and Springfield Ave. I knew already how to dance, & hit Beacon St. a couple of times, late, when it was nice, and rubbed sweaty against unknown Negroes.

My sister wd be somewhere in shadows pouting, looking down 4 stories at the chinese restaurant, & hump hatted cool daddies idling past in the cold. Snow already past our window quiet on the street. Friday, cool snow, for everyone cd run out new swag coats & slouch towards their breathing lives. And I'd be getting ready, folding my handkerchief, turning around towards the mirror, getting out the green tyrolean with the peacock band. Cool. I knew I'd be alone, or someone cd be picking me up in a car. (Later, or earlier, we'd crowd in Earl's cadillac & he'd squirm thinking years later how to be an engineer, and confront me at my bohemian lady (who'd turned by now to elevator operator for a church. It shows what happens. I never got to fuck her either, just slick stammerings abt the world & Dylan Thomas & never got the Baudelaire book back either. But that's over & not yet come to. A horizon to look both ways, when you stand straddling it.

Belmont wd be jammed. And even in the winter sound trucks slashed thru the snow yowling blues. The world had opened and stood in it smelling masturbation fingers. Slower, faster, than my time.

The hill slanted & blind men came up cold, coming out of the valentine store pushing snuff under their lips. Guitars blistering the three kegs liquor store sides pushed out, and red whores dangled out the windows.

The bus came finally. 9 Clifton (Becky, her friend, sometimes Garmoney . . . and all the loud drooping sock romeos from Central).

Friday, it was mine tho. White people fleeing the ward (from where?) Parties I didn't care about, old slick haired cats from the south with thin mustaches.

The bus stopped & I looked out the window, or counted buicks, or wondered about the sky sitting so heavy on the Krueger (pronounced Kreeger) factory. Down W. Kinney St., I knew I'd gotten out. Left all that. The Physical world. Under jews, for quarters, or whatever light got in. What talk I gave. My own ego, expanded like the street, ran under a bridge, to the river. But after, loot against my leg, I'd move up the hill, thru Douglass, & finally up on the hill (unless I was late, taking meat out of Steve's window . . . then I'd pack into the Kinney).

It was contrast, doing things both ways . . . & then thinking about it all shoved in my head, grinning at my lips, & hunting echoes of my thot.

Central Ave., near my old neighborhood. (The Secret Seven, Nwk. St., The Boose Bros., Staring Johnny, "Board," &c., yng pussies.)

From there, get out, rush across the street, the 24 or 44 wd come/wild flashes then

with the frontier coming up. East Orange. Talk to anybody, but
not now, this was like Oregon. Or at least an airport now showing
up loaded.

I barely drank tho, &
it was the sharp air turned me on. Moving out, already. The
project. But, again, alone.

No. Nwk. was where the party was. Cookie's place.
(They were hip mostly because they were foreign, for that matter,
myself too. No one knew who I was in the ward. A hero maybe,
with foreign friends. Pretty cool. Some kind of athlete. So when I
came to places like that (in time) I'd show up loose, rangy, very
nice. Some days wind swept thru my eyes and I'd stare off whistling.
This Was An ATTRIBUTE.

Al came down from there to go to
Barringer, also Carl Hargraves, Jonesy, most of Nat's band & a
lot of freckle faced Negroes in Nwk.)

A balance could form then, could rear up &
set itself so soon before you. The snow increased. Made drifts and
the wind was colder, slammed snow against the street lights.

The party was downstairs
in a basement, impressive for me because of Warren & my father's
middleclass spectres. Straight haired lightskinned girls I met only
at picnics. There were some here, & some reputations got to me
peeling tenderness from my fingers.

Slanted lights, Ivory Joe Hunter at Yvette's earlier. But
her people naturally I guess wd move in. Shadows were fascinating
and I might have danced w/ some anonymous american sweating
when I missed her feet. Stronger than I was. More sophisticated in
that world, that dungeon of ignorance. Snow veiled the windows
and the tin music squealed.

Barringer
people. No. Nwk. hoods (there were such, & I was, like the
reputations, amazed. I loved the middleclass & they wd thrust
pikes at me thru my shadows. Everybody rubbed stomachs & I
stood around and wished everyone knew my name.

The Dukes were killing people then. They were talked about
like the State. Like flame against wood. They swooped in Attila
& his huns. They made everything & had brown army jackets &

humped hats like homburgs pulled down on their ears. One knew
Garmoney well, one got killed, I heard last month, one, a guy
named Rabbit who was lightweight golden gloves, loved my sister
& turned up at my house for my father to scream at. We were rich I
insist. (As Kenny or any of the Hillside people cd tell you.)
No Cavaliers made these
things, only, as I sd, occasionally Earl. All that had ended and I
still didn't know. They envied me my interests and slunk outside
the windows weeping.
So it was the end. Formal as a season.
Nine Hester Ave. Mahomet. The sick
tribes of Aegina. Black skies of christendom (the 44 pulled up near
his house & I ran thru the snow right to the door. A blue light
leaned up from the basement & high laughter & The Orioles). A
world, we made then. Dead Columbus "its first victim." Spread out
the world, split open our heads with what rattles in the cold. All
sinners, placed against mute perfection.
They, the Dukes, came in like they did. Slow, with hands shoved
deep in pockets. Laughing, respectable (like gunfighters of the
west. When air stirred years later, and we rode out to the sea).
Now they spread out among
us, & girls' eyes shifted from their men to the hulks sucking up the
shadows. The Orioles were lovely anyway, & the snow increased
whining against the glass.
SURE I WAS FRIGHTENED BUT MAN THERE WAS
NOT A GODDAMNED THING TO DO. IN THIS CONCEP-
TION OF THE ENTIRE WORLD OF TECHNOLOGY WE
TRACE EVERYTHING BACK TO MAN AND FINALLY
DEMAND AN ETHICS SUITABLE TO THE WORLD OF
TECHNOLOGY, IF, INDEED, WE WISH TO CARRY
THINGS THAT FAR.
They had taken up the practice
of wearing berets. Along with the army jackets (& bellbottom
pants which was natural for people in that strange twist of our-
selves, that civil strife our bodies screamed for . . . Now, too, you
readers!).
So everyone, the others, knew
them right away. Girls wdn't dance with them & that cd start it.

Somebody trying to make a point or something. Or if they were really salty they'd just claim you stepped on their shoes. (Murray warned me once that I'd better cool it or I was gonna get my hat blocked. I was grateful, in a way, on W. Market St.: that orange restaurant where they had quarter sets.)

                                                              To-
night someone said something about the records. Whose property or the music wasn't right or some idea came up to spread themselves. Like Jefferson wanting Louisiana, or Bertram deBorn given dignity in Hell. There was a scuffle & the Dukes won.

      (That big fat clown, slick, the husky sinister person, bigeyed evil bastard . . . the one that didn't like me had a weird name I can't think of and well tailored "bells." Rabbit, Oscar (a camp follower) and some other cowboys). They pushed the guy's face in and the light, hung on a chain, swung crazy back and forth and the girls shot up the stairs. He, the No. Nwk. cat, got out tho, up the stairs & split cursing in the snow. Things settled down & the new learning had come in. A New Order, & Cookie clicked his tongue still cool under it, & I sat down talking to a girl I knew was too ugly to attract attention.

                                     This wd be the second phase in our lives. Totalitarianism. Sheep performing in silence.

                                     He came back with six guys and a meat cleaver. Rushed down the wooden stairs & made the whole place no man's land. Dukes took off the tams & tried to shove back in the darkness. Ladies pushed back on the walls. Orioles still grinding for the snow. "Where's that muthafucka?" Lovely Dante at night under his flame taking heaven. A place, a system, where all is dealt with . . . as is proper. "I'm gonna kill that muthafucka." Waved the cleaver and I crept backwards while his mob shuffled faces. "I'm gonna kill somebody." Still I had my coat & edged away from the centre (as I always came on. There. In your ditch, bleeding with you. Christians).

                                  Now the blood turned & he licked his lips seeing their faces suffering. "Kill anybody," his axe slid thru the place throwing people on their stomachs, it grazed my face sending my green hat up against the record player. I wanted it back, but war broke out & I rushed around the bar. They tried

to get up the stairs, the light girls & No. Nwk. people. All the cool
men bolted. I crouched with my mouth against the floor, till
Cookie came hurdling over the bar & crushed my back.

The Dukes fought the others. And were outnumbered (we wd
suffer next week . . .). Nixon punched them (& got his later in
Baxter with a baseball bat). And they finally disappeared up the
stairs, all the fighters.

When we came out &
went slow upstairs the fat guy was spread out in the snow & Nicks
was slapping him in his face with the side of the cleaver. He bled
under the light on the grey snow & his men had left him there to
die.

THE RAPE

A

I'd moved outside to sit. And sitting brought the others out.
(The NEW GROUP, I thought about them with that name
then.) The New Group. What had been my distance. Looking
across the crowd at the motion and smoke they raised. Jackie's
listless band, exciting, in it. Junkies humped over their borrowed
horns and sending beams of cock up niggers' clothes.

Now I'd move past. They had come too. Too see me. Or see
what the great "sharp" world could do. Their white teeth and
mulatto brains to face the ofay houses of history. THE BEAUTI-
FUL MIDDLECLASS HAD FORMED AND I WAS TO BE
A GREAT FIGURE, A GIANT AMONG THEM. THEY
FOLLOWED WITH THEIR EYES, OR LISTENED TO
SOFT MOUTHS SPILL MY STORY OUT TO GIVE THEIR
WIVES.

The fabric
split. Silk patterns run in the rain. What thoughts, the God had
for us, I trampled, lost my way. Ran on what I was, to kill the
arc, the lovely pattern of our lives.

Summers, during college, we all
were celebrities. East Orange parties; people gave us lifts and
said our names to their friends. (What was left of the Golden

Boys, Los Ruedos, splinter groups, and only me from the Cavaliers.)
We'd made our move. They had on suits, and in my suit, names
had run me down. Stymied me with pure voids of heat, moon,
placing fingers on books.

Now, the party moved for us. And we
made all kinds. This one was hippest for our time. East Orange,
lightskinned girls, cars pulling in, smart clothes our fathers'
masters wore. But this was the way. The movement. Our heads
turned open for it. And light, pure warm light, flowed in.

I sat on a stoop. One of the white stoops of the rich (the negro
rich were lovely in their non-importance in the world). Still, I sat
and thought why they moved past me, the ladies, or why questions seemed to ride me down. The world itself, so easy to solve . . .
and get rid of. Why did they want it? What pulled them in, that
passed me by. I could have wept each night of my life.

A muggy dust sat on us. And they made jokes and looked at me
crooked, feasting on my eyes. Wondering why they liked me.

San-
chez, one of Leon's men, came out, whistled at the crowd of Lords,
got his drink, and listened to a funny lie I told. He got in easy.

School came up, my own stupid trials they took as axioms for
their lives. Any awkwardness, what they loved, and told their
mothers of my intelligence. Still it sprung on them, from sitting
in the trees. Silent with the silence; delighted in itself for thinking
brutal concrete moves.

They Could Not Come To Me. It would
be a thrust, or leave it home! Move the bastards out! A New
Order (?) what came later returning to New York, to see Art,
outside my head for the first time, and 200 year old symphonies
I'd written only a few months earlier.

A drunken girl, woman, slut, moved thru the trees. Weaving. I
folded my arms and watched the trees, green almost under the
porch lamp, paste her in. They turned to me to see what noises I
was making. Stupid things I'd thought I heard.

Foot slid down
steps: up. Marking time. Pulling at my tie, I watched and none
of our girls was out. The party pushed noise into the dark. Only

the cellar lights in the house spread out, light brown parents pushed their faces into pillows and hoped the party made their son popular.

She was skinny, dark and drunk. Nothing I'd want, without what pushed inside. They said that to themselves, and to each other. What a desperate sick creature she was, and what she wanted here in their paradise.

And it took hold of me then. Who she was. Why I moved myself. Who she was, and what would be the weight her face would make. So I looked at them and crossed my eyes so they would think, for an instant, what I thought.

The chick was drunk. And probably some dumb whore slept to the end of the Kinney line. From the 3rd ward, she found herself with us. Trees. And the grey homes of the city, the other city, starting to fade on the hill.

She came to me. Direct. Even slit eyes gave me away. She moved straight. And paused to pat her coat. (Sanchez gave her a Lucky Strike.) She asked me with the fire making a shadow on her forehead where was Jones St.

We all knew that was Newark. And I had got the thing stirring.

But how long till the logic of our lives runs us down? Destroys the face the wind sees. The long beautiful fingers numbed in slow summer wave of darkness?

Never. Never. The waves run in. Blue (Our citizens are languid as music. And their hearts are slow motion lives. Dead histories I drag thru the streets of another time. Never.

Five, with me. And the women. Huge red lips, like they were turned inside out. Heavy breath, almost with veins. Her life bleeding slow in the soft summer. And not passion pushed her to me. Not any I could sit with magazines in the white toilet wishing love was some gruesome sunday thing still alive and fishy in my clothes. Still, smelling, that single tone, registered in our heads, as dirt paths where we lay the other ladies naked, and naked bulbs shown squarely on their different flesh.

I said, "Jones

St.," and that held over the street like drums of insects. Like some new morning with weird weather swam into our faces. The meanings, we gave. I gave. (Because it sat alone with me . . . and I raised it. Made it some purely bodily suck. The way my voice would not go down. A tone, to set fire in dry wood. An inferno. Where flame is words, or lives, or the simple elegance of death.)

Sanchez showed his teeth (I think, he stood sideways looking at the car. Jingling the keys at the tone of my words). The others moved. "We'll take you there." I almost fell, so moved that what I could drag into the world would stay. That others could see its shape and make it something in their brittle lives. "I'll take you there."

Calvin, Donald, Sanchez, Leon, Joe & Me.
The Woman.

They made to laugh. They made to get into the car. They made not to be responsible. All with me. (Tho this is new, I tell you now because, somehow, it all is right, whatever. For what sin you find me here. It's mine. My own irreconcilable life. My blood. My footsteps towards the black car smeared softly in the slow shadows of leaves.) The houses shone like naked bulbs. Thin laughter from the party trailed us up the street.

Sanchez threw the car in the wrong gear, nervous. It made that noise, and Donald (the dumb but handsome almost athlete jumped 10 feet . . . the others laughed and I chewed skin quickly off my thumb . . .) the woman talked directions at the floor.

Donald was at the woman's left, I at her right. The others packed in the front. Looking at us, across the seat. (Sanchez thru the mirror.) The whole night tightened, and it seemed our car rumbled on a cliff knocking huge rocks down a thousand feet. The thunderous tires roared. And roared.

B

The laugh got thinner. And the woman had trouble with her head. It flopped against her chest. Or her short brittle hair wd jam against my face, pushing that monstrous smell of old wood

into my life. Old wood and wine. What there is of slum. Of dead
minds, dead fingers flapping empty in inhuman cold.

I winced (be-
cause I thot myself elegant. A fop, I'd become, and made a sign
to Calvin in the mirror that the woman smelled. He grinned and
rubbed his hands to steady them.

Hideous magician! The car rolled
its banging stones against the dark. Ugly fiend screaming in the
fire boiling your bones. Your cock, cunt, whatever in your head you
think to be, is burning. Tied against a rock, straw packed tight into
your eyes. POUR GASOLINE. SPREAD IT ON HIS TONGUE.
NOW LIGHT THE STINKING MESS.

Shadow of a man. (Tied in a ditch, my own flesh burning in
my nostrils. My body goes, simple death, but what of my mind?
Who created me to this pain?)

Oh, the barns of lead are gold. You
have abandoned God.

Now, he abandons you! Your brain runs like
liquid in the grass.

I began to act. First hands dropped on the wino's knee. And she
flopped her head spreading that rancid breath. So I pulled her
head back against the seat, and moved my fingers hard against
her flesh. Tugged at the wool skirt and pushed my hand between
the stocking and the bumps on her skin. Her mouth opened and
she sounded like humming. Also, a shiver, like winter, went thru
her/ and I almost took my hands away.

Donald saw me, and when
I looked across at him he felt her too. The others in front gabbled
& kept informed by craning in their seats.

I moved my fingers harder, pushing the cloth up high until I
saw what I thot were her underwear. Some other color than pink,
with dark stains around the part that fit against her crotch.

Her
head slumped forward but the eyes had opened, and there was
a look in them made me look out the window. But I never
moved my hands. (Someone giggled up front.)

The car moved at a steady rate. The dim lights on. Up out of East Orange and into dark Montclair. With larger whiter homes. Some dirt along the way, which meant to us, who knew only cement, some kind of tortured wealth. We would all live up here some way. Big dogs barked at the car from driveways and Sanchez looked over his shoulder at me to get his signals straight.

Donald said something to me across the woman and she raised her head, glaring at Calvin's back.

"What the hells goin on?" Calvin laughed. I moved my fingers swifter straining for the top of the pants. Donald simply rolled her stockings down. And the woman grabbed his hand, quietly at first. But when she sensed that we would pile on her in the car shoving our tender unwashed selves in her eyes and mouth, she squeezed Donald's hand so hard it hurt.

"Bitch!"

"What're you boys tryina do?" No answer from us. The front riders sat tight in their seats, watching the big houses, and wishing probably, it was now, when they are sitting prying the dark with staler eyes.

(In those same houses, waiting until I die when they can tell all these things with proper reverence to my widow.)

The woman changed her mind. (She saw what was happening and stared at me for seconds before she spoke again. She braced herself against the seat and made a weeping sound.)

"Oh my life is so fucked up. So wasted and shitty. You boys don't know. How life is. How it takes you down. You don't know . . . Those ties and shirts . . . Shit . . . how hard a woman's life can be"

Her voice got softer or she thot she'd make it tender. It came out almost bleaker than a whine . . .

"I'm sick too. A long time. The kind of thing makes men hate you. Those sores on my self."

(She meant her vagina.)

This was news to everyone. "I'm sick," she moaned again,

making her voice almost loud. "And you boys can ketch it . . . everyone'a you, get it, and scratch these bleeding sores."

Donald moved his hand away. The woman screeched now, not loud, but dragging in her breath.

Apprehension now. As if the wall was almost down but the enemy's hero arrived to pour boiling oil in my warriors' eyes. I wdn't have that easy cop out. Fuck that . . . goddamit, no pleas.

I made Donald put his hands back. I scowled the way I can with one side of my mouth, the other pushing the woman back. "Shit, I don't believe that bullshit! Prove it, baby, lemme see! I wanna see the sores . . . see what they look like!"

New life now. Reinforced, the others laughed. I pushed again. "O.K., mama, run out them sores . . . lemme suck'em till they get well." Another score: but how long, we were deep in Montclair, and some car full of negroes up there wd be spotted by the police . . . that swung thru my mind and I looked up quickly thru my window. Even rolled it down to hear.

"I'm sick . . . and you boys ketch what I got you'll never have no kids. Nobody'll marry you. That's why I'ma drunk whore fallin in the streets."

Marriage. Children. What else could she burn? Donald fell away again. The rest swallowed, or moved their hands. Only Calvin ran to my aid. He grabbed a huge hunting knife still in its scabbard and twisted suddenly in his seat waving it in the woman's face. But the absurdity of it killed the move completely and we broke running down the slope:

"Shutup bitch" (Calvin). "Shutup . . . I'm a goddam policemen (sic) and we're lookin for people like you to lock'umup!"

He waved the knife and Leon even laughed at him. It was over. The woman probably knew but took it further. She screamed as loud as she could. She screamed, and screamed, her voice almost shearing off our tender heads. The scream of an actual damned soul. The actual prisoner of the world.

"SHEEEEEET, YOU BASTARDS LEMME GO. SHE-
EEET. HAALP. AGGGHEEE."
Donald reached across the whore and pushed the door open.
The car still moving about 20 miles an hour and the sudden air
opened my eyes in the smoke. The bitch screamed and we all knew
Montclair was like a beautifully furnished room and someone
would hear and we would die in jail, dead niggers who couldn't
be invited to parties.

Calvin reached across the seat, and shouted
in my face. "Kick the bitch out!" I couldn't move. My fingers were
still on her knee. The plan still fixed in my mind. But the physical
world rushed thru like dirty thundering water thru a dam. They
ran on me.

"Throw this dumb bitch out." Calvin grabbed her by
the arm and Donald heaved against her ass. The woman tumbled
over my knees and rolled, I thought, slow motion out the car. She
smashed against the pavement and wobbled on her stomach hard
against the curb.

The door still swung open and I moved almost
without knowing thru it to bring the woman back. The smoke had
blown away. I saw her body like on a white porcelain table dead
with eyes rolled back. I had to get her.

I dove for the door, even as
Sanchez made the car speed up, and slammed right into the flop-
ping steel. It hit me in the head and Leon wrenched me back
against the seat. Calvin closed the door.

I could see the woman
squatting in the street, under the fake gasoline lamp as we turned
the corner, everybody screaming in the car, some insane allegiance
to me.

Owen Dodson

OWEN DODSON, who has written plays, poems, and novels, is professor of drama at Howard University and head of the Drama Department. His plays have been performed by little-theater groups throughout the United States and England as well as in off-Broadway theaters in New York City.

As director of the Howard Players, Mr. Dodson toured with his theatrical group in Norway, Denmark, Sweden, and Germany under the auspices of the United States Department of State and the Government of Norway. He has conducted drama classes at Atlanta University, Spelman College, and Hampton Institute and has frequently lectured on literature and the theater.

Owen Dodson was born in Brooklyn and educated at Bates College and Yale University. He has received Rosenwald and General Education Board fellowships. His published works include a book of poems, *Powerful Long Ladder*, and a novel, *Boy at the Window*. Recently he won the *Paris Review* prize for a short story, "The Summer Fire." While on a Guggenheim Fellowship he completed a second novel, *A Bent House*, to be published in 1964, and a second book of poems, *Cages*. Several of his poems and plays have won prizes and awards, among them the Maxwell Anderson verse play contest.

His libretto for the opera *A Christmas Miracle*, written with

Mark Fax, of the Howard University faculty, received high praise from critics.

"Come Home Early, Chile" makes its first appearance in this collection.

COME HOME EARLY, CHILE

BY OWEN DODSON

What in the world was Deaconess Quick doing perching on a bar stool. Coin was startled and delighted to see all her great fat way up on high. A pillar of the church, no less, was on that artificial leather stool tasting, with relish, her beer. Well, bless her soul. As he watched her from his distance, she seemed perfectly at home taking small sips and giggling into her glass. She didn't look to left or right but worked her head to the mirror in front of her with secret smilings and panting joy. Maybe he should go out before she recognized him. As he started toward the door, the familiar voice hit his back like a syphon spraying him. He turned.

"Coin Foreman, well now you know. You mean you weren't going to say the word to me . . . I'm ashamed, honey. Yes, I'm ashamed, you know, that you wouldn't press my heart after all these years. Come here, honey, now you know, and say a word." Coin stood at attention. "I ain't ashamed, honey, I learned long ago about the eat, drink and be merry, which is in the *Bible*, Lord."

The people in the room looked first at Coin and then at her and held their laughter in. She was ridiculous as an Easter hat fashioned of paper roses and colored eggs. That's what she had on too. And a violet dress flowered with poppies. She looked like a field held on high. And laughed with fat joy. Her bosoms bloomed toward the bar and settled in satisfaction when Coin walked to her. Getting down from the stool she was a parade of flirtation and arthritis. Now she held him in her arms kissing beer into his cheeks and onto his newly pressed uniform. "Home again, home again," she said. He breathed into her old softness. She patted him into childhood and sobbed the past into his chest. "Here he come, a grown man into my arms. Now you know, that's nice. A old lady is blessed to see you, to see thee. Coin, he has returned to me."

Coin tried to break the embrace gently but Mrs. Quick clung to him like a log in her drowning. "Don't go away, my honey, my dear. Stay with your Deaconess for the second, for my time. Now you realize meeting come but the once or the twice. Stay with me. Do you reckon we could get a table? I can't climb that stool the second time. Coin, get a table and let sit us down and talk now you a grown man and *capable*. Now you do that."

Coin got the table and they sat down with the precious past between them suspended and waiting for the belch of her news. He ordered new drinks as Deaconess Quick grinned at him foolishly and he grinned back at her. There would be other times to hurt people but not now. So he prepared to stay a while.

"Thanks for this here beer, Coin. These old bones needs cooling in this heat. Ain't it something though. I just comes here regular and spends a little change. Not much, mind you. But beer nearly as cheap as coffee or tea. I ain't worried about getting fat. Too late for that. Sometimes when I see the young like you, I just want to wind back my time, honey. Set my clock at eighteen years old. You how old?"

"Just about nineteen, Mrs. Quick."

"Then eighteen is my number. The woman she should always be a step behind the man." She threw back her head in laughter. Coin had to laugh with her. She was enjoying herself so much.

"First let me tell you this. Chile, they tried to put me out of the church. A year ago almost to this hour. Called a meeting of the righteous; they tried to hand my letter back and throw me out like suet, now you know. After all I done nursing the sick and bereaved, working to put my share into them collection plates. Deaconess Redmond, I am surprised at that woman, pointed her finger at me and declared that I had been drinking beer, not only in my home but *also* in a bar. Now, Coin, I never took a drink on the Lord's day, not that every day ain't the Lord's day but on Sundays, I mean. I stop my beers on Saturday sharp at twelve midnight and don't commence again till after twelve midnight Sunday night. Now you know there ain't nothing wrong with that!"

Coin had beckoned the waiter for two more beers.

"I told the Deacon and Deaconess Boards that even our Lord turned the water to wine. And you know, now don't you, that wine is stronger than beer? Yes it is!"

Coin nodded. "Uh, huh."

"And I ain't never disgraced myself in public. That's what I told Deaconess Redmond, and you know what that old fool shouted? 'Don't you, Mrs. Quick'—not even my title of Deaconess did she use—'don't you ever use any word with *grace* in it because you done fell from grace and all the King's horses nor all of God's men can ever glue back together again.'"

Mrs. Quick was leaning across the table and got confidential, whispering: "Well, after she stomped out, I told them Boards a thing or two, not only about Deaconess Redmond but about a few of themselves. And they shut like clams and called that meeting to a close. The upshot is and was that I'm still a Deaconess and"— with this she shook a finger at Coin, reached for her beer and pronounced: "and, I emphasizes, in good standing. That's the truth, just as I'm sitting here, now that's that, please my precious savior. Thank you for this drink, boy." She drained her glass. Without any warning to Coin tears began down the channels of her cheeks.

"O Lord, here I am, a old lady, crying in the public eye."

"Mrs. Quick, would you like to go out for some fresh air?"

She snuffed in the tears, saying, "No, Coin Foreman, when you get as old as me, you crying one minute and laughing the next, or jest set looking at the past, now you know. Take the years you been away, why things happened so fast, you would've thought you was in some of the moving pictures, they went so croweded and so fast. Lord, I been talking so much. Let me hear your adventures. The picture you sent of that island was pretty as your soul, oh it was! Speaking about events going on. You know that old Italian woman, Mrs. Renaldo, who was always wearing black. Just dropped dead in the streets. Didn't even wait for the coma! They say she had liquor on her breath too. But that ain't so much to holler about. The police went up into that apartment, now you know what they found? Guess, son."

"Can't think."

"Well, I can tell you it were no sugar and spice. Tombstone

Catalogues, thousands of them, chile. She'd been collecting for years. Some were large as Montgomery Ward and the Sears and Roebuck's catalogues. Yellow and peeling. And a little doll, a girl doll she must've thought was real, 'cause they found changes of clothes for every description."

Coin had missed Mrs. Renaldo as much as he had missed Mrs. Quick and in the air he smelled the memory of peppermints and Chianti wine and black-dye bosom perspiration. In his mind he saw Mrs. Renaldo's black veils flapping against the doors of all the dead in his past, and her past. He was glad that she had dropped dead suddenly, not rotting away while living.

"Let me tell you about dolls, chile. When I was a girl, now you realize that was many years ago, although many a Deacon wink at me even now. (Men has got filthy minds, sewer places.) When I was a girl in Mississippi my white folks gave me two wax dolls. In them days there were no hard and permanent dolls like they got now. I got to loving those children so much, I talked to them like I'm talking to you about just everything. One summer those folks who give me them dolls decided to travel, in the heat now, to New Orleans. So naturally when we was packing, I didn't pack no dolls. I was bent and determined that I would carry them personal. My Mama said that there was no room for such foolishness, but I kicked up such a storm they let me take *one*. They promised to send the other, crated and in tar paper against the sun. So we traveled on. Of course I was in the Jim Crow car with the windows open and the hot air blowing in and not a fan going. The hottest day of that July I fell asleep by a window cradling that wax in my arms. I woke up in a hot dark sweat. The child's eyes had crossed each other and melted into the cheeks, the pretty pink dress was all wax and my fat doll had done grown skinny. Blond hair matted and lips smeared. I was fit to be tied in my own hair ribbons. Now you know, I wept like Jesus in the chapter. I kicked and I fussed. I cried at the foot of the cross. Let me tell you what I did when we arrived in New Orleans, immediately I asked if the twin doll had arrived and it had. It had! The white folks' houseman uncrated the body at once and delivered it to me. I was quiet as Eastertide when I went to the kitchen, frisking my black self and asked for a knife to cut something or other, I don't remember what lie I told.

Went back to the room, now you recognize I did, and took up the second doll and slashed away at her in New Orleans to make sure the same thing wouldn't happen to my second that happened to my first. Couldn't bear to go through the second grief. Ain't that strange?"

"Deaconess Quick, would you like another glass of beer?"

"Honey, I ain't gonna hop around here like a grasshopper, but I accept your offer. Doesn't come too once in a while, this offer, pain come twice or in all numbers but not a treat!" Coin signaled and presently the beer was brought.

"What brand of beer is this?"

"Draft," she echoed. "One of the best brands there is!"

"Deaconess Quick, is everything O.K.?"

"O.K. as the world, and you know how that is?" A calm settled down. For a moment they were silent together. She finished up the last taste of her glass and with arms outstretched and her head bowed on the table as if it were the altar in the New Corinthian Baptist Church, Mrs. Quick slumped.

"Mrs. Quick, Mrs. Quick!"

"I am," she said as she raised her head, "a Deaconess, not Mrs. Please, Coin, wash Mrs. Redmond and her vicious wart from your mind. Who's gonna wash me white as snow? Wash me in the grace? Nobody. Whilst you were away I attended Miss Lucy Horwitz. Who, now you reckon, is laying in the undertaker's, Branton's Morticians, in her deeds? She's laying there and ain't provided a cent for my nurse's care or the laundry of my uniforms, and I was always neat. That shows just how much you can get attached to nothings out of the goodness of your very heart. Now you know, I never loved that woman. She were distressed and I had to help, naturally, as you'd help anybody in distress. . . ."

"What in the world are you saying, Mrs. Quick."

"Do I have to tell you again, I'm Deaconess . . ."

"Who"—and he held his breath—"who did you say was dead?"

"I want my proper title, do you hear me; I'm a servant of the Lord and I want to be called by my proper title and I ain't gonna say another word till you do." And she sat up righteously and called for another beer. Coin just looked at her while juices of his past life rose in him.

"Deaconess . . ."

"That's better," she shot back, "now where was I . . ."

"Somebody just died. . . ."

"*Miss* Lucy Horwitz refused the help of the doctors till the last minute, she refused the help of Jesus *and* His Father and *my* help at the end. She went to her death without the mercy of a coma, screaming inside a straightened jacket and her teeth turned black. . . . The funeral's tomorrow from the Branton's parlor but that's one funeral I need not attend with my smelling salts and ointments because there won't be nobody there to fall out." She drank the rest of her beer in one long gulp and began to straighten her hat and brush her bosom. She lurched to Coin's side.

"Oh my, Coin Foreman, the world has changed, since my day. I ain't got no day no more. Hypocritics and worry is about the whole story, the only thing I can tell my Jesus." The tears started again. "Boy, this beer is something. What the brand again? Draft, Drafts." Her behind pulled her down and Coin only heard her faintly as she called out: "Waiter. Bring me some drafts. And bring one for my son, I got my son now . . ." Coin was walking toward the door as she smiled at his empty chair saying something that sounded like a drunken prayer. "Death happen only the once to everybody, Coin; ain't that good!" He headed for the bar at Sumner and Quincy to think the news out by himself.

Once in the bar he threw his head on an empty, compassionate table, forced himself to sleep and dreamed.

So he rested on the table and half awake and asleep he tired himself in the dream. Soon he was whipped awake. When he first heard that Miss Lucy Horwitz was dead from Mrs. Quick, he refused to believe it. He had always thought that she would never die, she'd just funk away. At least that's what he had hoped for her. There would be that general decay and finally the smell of the odors of evil: like bat's shit and camel piss, polluted waters, the underground flush of sewers, the halitosis of worms, of snakes, asthmatic dogs, toe jam, uninspected prostitutes, the devil's armpits, the breath of lice and mayonnaise curdled with maggots; seedy diseases feeding on the garbage and marrow left in human bones. The agony she had made his family to suffer grew monumental in his alcoholic brain, and would give him no peace. He fidgeted. She had tried to destroy all of them each in a different way but now she was dead in an undertaker's parlor still bugging him into drink and that might bug him too.

Determination began to grow in Coin as he recovered and drank his beers at the bar on Sumner and Quincy. He had a half pint of blended Green River whiskey in his sock and every once in a while he would go to the room marked GENTS for another taste. Then all the disrupted bowels of his life began to tell on him before he rushed again to GENTS. From upstairs the music made a horror of blanketed noise, a jukebox singer whispered a cozy, noisy song. The urinal flushed in a noisy sound. Coin rushed from the room. He had rejected everything and wished he were swimming where fish were small and the water was clean in the island, water was moving with a clear colored sound of the blue of his dreams and his mothers' laugh: the cozy blessedness of his childhood. Lord have mercy, I'm drunk near my own street and lonely as a hill cat. . . . Astonished at himself, he left some bills on the bar and rushed out for the funeral parlor at a fast clip. He had had so much to drink, so, to keep from reeling and rocking, he hugged his toes in and began to march to a tune the sailors used to sing to keep in step:

> You had a good home but you left,
> You left. You had a good home but you left,
> Left . . .

He leaned against the nearest lamppost and doubled over in ironic laughter. He couldn't stop laughing; his stomach screwed up in a hard ball. Chile, you're on the streets, pull yourself together. "You left!" he shouted into the light overhead. "You left, like shit, you were put out, dispossessed, thrown into the tangles of the world at seventeen." The lines of his mind grew taut; the ball in his stomach began to bounce and he hugged the lamppost like Mary, in those Italian pictures, folding Jesus in her arms. His world had seemed so wide and open before his sister died. Now he had seen the world, some of it leastaways, and he recognized what life could be and was. But he was only in his first semester of hope and grief and here he was marching back to the last death. He wished that he had something to fold in his arms except this iron post with light at the top to search out evil in the streets.

You had a good home but you left,
You left. . . .

He began tramping out the song, still hugging the iron searchlight
with might; around him night was flapping a black-blue flag of
truce. He knew that there was no place for him to go but to the
dead enemy of his youth, dead and vulnerable to the agony of the
unheard taunts, threats, accusations. Ha, ha, death always happened to somebody else, not the dead. He loosed himself free and
proceeded down the street with nothing in his arms to hold. He
felt free now silently walking to the end that had bugged him. But
there was no fear in his staggering.

You had a good home but you left,
You left, left . . .

The dirty old bitch, dilapidated hag. Home! Shit no. It was a
house. A bent house. He never wanted to lay eyes on it again.
Tipping his sailor's cap at a rakish angle, he entered the funeral
home. Home! (It sure is her home now. The final horizontal
home. . . .)

Amber bulbs, shaped like flame, lit the entranceway. The smell
of death hit him. From some unseen source a record was playing
"Nearer my God to Thee." The record was cracked and at each
turn the music bumped and hissed and scratched its way on
through the dust of hundreds of weeping wakes held in this damp,
leaky room where it seemed no sun ever came, where the spirit of
God had never dwelt. Whoever was buried from this place was
bound for someplace just as dilapidated, funky and hot as hell
must be. The thought cheered him up a little. He sure smelled his
beer, as if he had been washed in it. Beer and death on the breath.
He laughed. "Nearer my God to Thee (click, hiss, scratch), nearer
to Thee." There was a stand near the door with a sign over it
asking VISITORS PLEASE SIGN HERE. He didn't hesitate but whipped
out his pen and obliged. He wrote in large, clean letters: COIN
FOREMAN WAS HERE. Let her put that in her pipe and smoke it.
Those words preached a sermon to the wicked. He winked to himself. There were hardly any other names in the book. "Few have
come to call," he whispered to himself as he approached the cheap
oak coffin.

The grain was large and vulgar, the stain was cheap and still smelled, the lining was low-grade rayon sewn in gathers making it appear that the body was lying in whipped cream. The light on the upturned lid sent out rays the color of forty-nine-cent sherry. She had given orders to save on her burial. Death wouldn't get any more of her hard-earned money than necessary. She might need it in the sweet bye and bye. He tilted his hat forward and hiked his pants. He noticed a wreath on the lower part of the casket, of pink and white gladioli. (Pink and white: the colors of spring, the colors of virgins, colors of innocence, affection, love, soft colors of ladies in gardens, colors of houses in southern Italy, where children were abundant and laughter was ready.) There were secondhand flowers from a Negro florist who bought the last and the least and sold them to secondhand people: the last and the least. A real joy shot through him as he moved closer. He would not take his hat off. Not to her. In a way he was shocked that she had never loved him but had used him and his inheritance; had got rid of him to fulfill a perverted affection for his sister which, he was sure, was never consummated. Perhaps that was why she was so bitter, was determined to destroy as much joy for others as possible since joy or even crumbs of happiness would never come to her. Agnes' great simplicity, like his mother's, led her to trust the vultures and the bright snakes of this world—thinking that because they were God's creatures they couldn't be truly treacherous. Miss Lucy Horwitz had never known the geography of natural love or cared for it. No one had ever charted the courses of her body. She was a vagabond to love who tasted where she was tolerated but had never sat down to a full meal. Didn't dare to. For all her hardness, she had been a coward. She had been a destroyer. On his ship last year in hours off he had read the *Inferno*, but Dante's hell was a literary one and truly real; the hell Lucy had created was not to be believed by anyone but him. All her victims were dead.

No. He would not take his hat off. He had learned that much: not to bow to the destroyer, even in death. Death was not so much. Anyway it had its own immaculateness beyond all his potential courtesy. So he moved closer still with his racked hat. The beer came riding up in him like love and destruction. He was in a sudden panic and turned around swiftly to find a hiding place; instead he reached into his sock for his half pint. There were faint noises overhead and smells seemed to ride about the room in waves: bacon frying, chitlin's, greens. A sudden crash of dishes brought him to. They're probably drunk up there too. Who wouldn't be, living with the dead forever in your parlor? There was a frantic rolling overhead and a dog began to howl. And then the barking of human voices, fighting, stoning each other with words. Well, at least Miss Horwitz was in her usual environment. Death couldn't steal her away from that. As he looked down into the sliced mouth of her death he saw that she was really dead in the virgin green of her shroud. Shriveled up in whipped cream. She was as gone as a snuffed-out cigar and the color of one. She looked chewed up, cancerous, utterly finished. She looked hard as pavement. He whispered to it: *Mene, Mene Tekel Upharsin.* She was dead after all. He took another big swig, and standing ten feet tall, in a porous of joy, he spat the whole drink in her dead face. What was left in the bottle he poured over that mouth, on those hands that had commanded him as a child, at puberty, in adolescence. Then he tossed the bottle in her stingy coffin; without staggering he left the foul funeral parlor, like a man.

Frank London Brown

FRANK LONDON BROWN was born in Kansas City, Missouri, and attended Wilberforce University, Roosevelt University, and the Chicago Kent College of Law.

Mr. Brown's novel, *Trumbull Park*, was published in 1959. His numerous articles and stories have appeared in the Chicago *Tribune*, *Downbeat*, the Chicago *Sun-Times*, *Southwest Review*, *The Negro Digest*, the Chicago *Review*, and other publications. He was the winner of the John Hay Whitney Foundation Award for creative writing and a University of Chicago Fellowship.

Frank London Brown worked as a machinist, union organizer, bartender, government employee, and was an associate editor of *Ebony* magazine. He also appeared as a jazz singer and musician with several well-known modern jazz ensembles.

Mr. Brown died in 1962 at the age of thirty-four. At the time of his untimely death he was director of the Union Leadership Program of the University of Chicago and was finishing a revised draft of his second novel, while completing his work for a doctorate in political science at the University of Chicago.

"Singing Dinah's Song" appears here for the first time.

SINGING DINAH'S SONG

BY FRANK LONDON BROWN

A Gypsy woman once told me. She said: "Son, beware of the song
that will not leave you."

But then I've never liked Gypsy women no way, which is why I
was so shook when my buddy Daddy-o did his number the other
day. I mean his natural number.

You see, I work at Electronic Masters, Incorporated, and well,
we don't make much at this joint although if you know how to
talk to the man you might work up to a dollar and a half an hour.

Me, I work on a punch press. This thing cuts steel sheets and
molds them into shells for radio and television speakers. Sometimes
when I'm in some juice joint listening to Dinah Washington and
trying to get myself together, I get to thinking about all that noise
that that big ugly punch press makes, and me sweating and
scuffing, trying to make my rates, and man I get *eee*vil!

This buddy of mine though, he really went for Dinah Washington; and even though his machine would bang and scream all over
the place and all those high-speed drills would whine and cry like
a bunch of sanctified soprano church-singers, this fool would be in
the middle of all that commotion just singing Dinah Washington's
songs to beat the band. One day I went up and asked this fool what
in the world was he singing about; and he looked at me and tucked
his thumbs behind his shirt collar and said: "Baby, I'm singing
Dinah's songs. Ain't that broad mellow?"

Well, I. Really, all I could say was: "Uh, why yes."

And *I* went back to *my* ma*chine*.

It was one of those real hot days when it happened: about ten-
thirty in the morning. I was sweating already. Me and that big
ugly scoundrel punch press. Tussling. Lord, I was *so* beat. I felt
like singing Dinah's songs myself. I had even started thinking in
rhythm with those presses banging down on that steel: sh-bang

boom bop! Sh, bang boom bop, sh'bang boom bop. Then all of a sudden:

In walks Daddy-o!

My good buddy. Sharp? You'd better believe it: dark blue single breast, a white on white shirt, and a black and yellow rep tie! Shoes shining like new money. And that pearl gray hat kinda pulled down over one eye. I mean to tell you, that Negro was sharp.

I was way behind on my quota because, you see, fooling around with those machines is *not* no play thing. You just get tired sometimes and fall behind. But I just *had* to slow down to look at my boy.

James, that was his real name. We call him Daddy-o because he's so. I don't know; there just ain't no other name would fit him. Daddy-o's a long, tall, dark cat with hard eyes and a chin that looks like the back end of a brick. Got great big arms and a voice like ten lions. Actually, sometimes Daddy-o scares you.

He walked straight to his machine. Didn't punch his time card or nothing. I called him: "Hey, Daddy-o, you must have had a good one last night. What's happening?"

Do you know that Negro didn't open his mouth?

"Hey, Daddy-o, how come you come strolling in here at ten-thirty? We start at seven-thirty around this place!"

Still no answer.

So this cat walks over to his machine and looks it up and down and turns around and heads straight for the big boss's office. Well, naturally I think Daddy-o's getting ready to quit, so I kind of peeps around my machine so that I can see him better.

He walked to the big boss's office and stopped in front of the door and lit a cigarette smack-dab underneath the "No Smoking" sign. Then he turned around like he had changed his mind about quitting and headed back to his machine. Well, I just started back to work. After all it's none of my business if a man wants to work in his dark blue suit and a white on white shirt with his hat on.

By this time Charlie walked up just as Daddy-o started to stick his hand into the back of the machine.

Charlie liked to busted a blood vessel. "Hey, what the hell are you doing? You want to 'lectrocute yourself?"

Now I don't blame Charlie for hollering. Daddy-o knows that

you can get killed sticking your hand in the back of a machine. Everybody in the plant knows that.

Daddy-o acted like he didn't hear Charlie, and he kept right on reaching into the hole. Charlie ran up and snatched Daddy-o's hand back. Daddy-o straightened up, reared back and filled his chest with a thousand pounds of air: one foot behind him and both of those oversized fists doubled up. Charlie cleared his throat and started feeling around in his smock like he was looking for something, which I don't think he was.

Pretty soon Mr. Grobber, the big boss, walked up. One of the other foremen came up and then a couple of set-up men from another department. They all stood around Daddy-o and he just stood there cool, smoking one of those long filter-tips. He started to smile, like he was bashful. But whenever anyone went near the machine, he filled up with more air and got those big ham-fists ready.

Well after all, Daddy-o was my buddy and I couldn't just let all those folks surround him without doing *some*thing, so I turned my machine off and walked over to where they were crowding around him.

"Daddy-o, what's the matter, huh? You mad at somebody, Daddy-o?"

Mr. Grobber said: "James, if you don't feel well, why don't you just go home and come in tomorrow?"

All Daddy-o did was to look slowly around the plant. He looked at each one of us. A lot of the people in the shop stopped working and were looking back at him. Others just kept on working. But he looked at them, kind of smiling, like he had a feeling for each and every one of them.

Then quick like a minute, he spread his legs out, and stretched his arms in front of the machine like it was all he had in this world.

I tried once again to talk to him.

"Aww come on, Daddy-o. Don't be that way."

That Negro's nose started twitching. Then he tried to talk but his breath was short like he had been running or something.

"Ain't nobody getting this machine. I own this machine, baby. This is mine. Ten years! On this machine. Baby, this belongs to me."

"I know it do, Daddy-o. I *know* it do."

Charlie Wicowycz got mad hearing him say that, so he said, "Damn," and started into Daddy-o. Daddy-o's eyes got big and he drew his arm back and kind of stood on his toes and let out a holler like, like I don't know what.

"Doonnnn't you *touch* this machiiinnneeeee!"

Naturally Charlie stopped, then he started to snicker and play like he was tickled except his face was as white as a fish belly. I thought I would try, so I touched Daddy-o's arm. It was hard like brick. I let his arm go.

"Daddy-o man, I know how you feel. Let me call your wife so she can come and get you. You'll be all right tomorrow. What's your phone number, Daddy-o? I'll call your wife for you, hear?"

His eyes started twitching and he started blinking like he was trying to keep from crying. Still he was smiling that little baby-faced smile.

"Daddy-o, listen to me. Man, I ain't trying to do nothing to you. Give me your number and your wife will know what to do."

His lips started trembling. Big grown man, standing there with his lips trembling. He opened his mouth. His whole chin started trembling as he started to speak: "Drexel."

I said: "Okay, Drexel. Now Drexel what?"

"*Drexel.*"

"Drexel what else, Daddy-o?"

"Drexel seven-two-three."

"Seven-two-three. What else Daddy-o? Man, I'm trying to help you. I'm going to call your wife. She'll be here in a few minutes. Drexel seven-two-three-what else? What is the rest of your phone number. Daddy-o! I'm talkin' to you!"

"Eight-eight-eight-eight-nine."

"Drexel seven-two-three-eight-nine? That it, Daddy-o?"

Mr. Grobber started walking around scratching his stomach. He stopped in front of Charlie Wicowycz. "Call the police, Charlie."

Charles left.

The other foremen went back to their departments. The setup men followed them. Mr. Grobber, seeing that he was being left alone with Daddy-o, went back to his office.

Daddy-o just stood there smiling.

I ran to the office and called the number he had given me.
Daddy-o's wife wasn't home, but a little girl who said that she
was Daddy-o's "Babygirl" answered and said that she would tell
her mother as soon as she came home from work.

When I walked out of the office, the police were there. I thought
about the time I had to wait three hours for the police to get to
my house the time somebody broke in and took every stitch I had.
One of the cops, a big mean-looking something with ice-water
eyes, moved in on Daddy-o with his club out and Daddy-o just
shuffled his feet, doubled up his fists and waited for him.

I started talking up for my boy.

"Officer, please don't hurt him. He's just sick. He won't do no
harm."

"Who are you? Stay outa."

I tried to explain to him. "Look, Officer, just let me talk to him.
I . . . I'm his friend."

"All right. Talk to him. Tell him to get into the wagon."

I touched Daddy-o's arm again. He moved it away, still smiling.
I said: "Man, Daddy-o, come on now. Come on go with me. I
know how it is. I *know* how it is."

He still had that smile. I swear I could have cried.

I started walking, pulling his arm a bit.

"Come on, Daddy-o."

He came along easy, still smiling, and walking with a kind of
strut. Looking at each and every one of us like we were his best
friends. When we got to the door, he stopped and looked back at
his machine. Still smiling. When we got outside, I led him right
up to the wagon. The back door was open and it was *dark* in there.
Some dusty light scooted through a little window at the back of
the wagon that had a wire grating in it. It didn't look very nice in
there. I turned to Daddy-o.

"Come on, Daddy-o. The man said you should get in. Ain't
nothing going to git you, Daddy-o. Come on, man. Get in."

I felt like anybody's stoolie.

"Come on, get in."

He started moving with me, then he stopped and looked back at
the plant. One of the officers touched his arm. And that's when
he did his natural number.

He braced his arms against the door. And started to scream to bust his lungs: "That *is* my machine. I *own*. Me and *this* machine is *blood* kin. Don't *none* of you somitches touch it. You *heah*? You, you *heah*?"

The water-eyed policeman started to agree with Daddy-o.

"Sure kid. You *know* it. Lotsa machines. You got lots of 'em."

Daddy-o turned to look at him at the same time his partner gave him a shove. The water-eyed policeman shoved him too. Daddy-o swung at him and missed. When he did that, the water-eyed policeman chunked him right behind the ear and Daddy-o fell back into the wagon. Both policemen grabbed his feet and pushed him past the door and the water-eye slammed it.

They jumped in and started to drive away. Daddy-o was up again and at the window. He was hollering, and his voice got mixed up with the trucks and cars that went by. I watched the wagon huff out of sight and I went back into the plant.

Inside, I got to thinking about how sharp Daddy-o was. I was real proud of that. I caught sight of Daddy-o's machine. You know that thing didn't look right without Daddy-o working on it?

I got to thinking about my machine and how I know that big ugly thing better than I know most live people. Seemed funny to think that it wasn't really mine. It sure *seemed* like mine.

Ol' Daddy-o was sure crazy about Dinah Washington. Last few days that's all he sang: her songs. Like he was singing in place of crying; like being in the plant *made* him sing those songs and like finally the good buddy couldn't sing hard enough to keep up the dues on his machine and then . . . Really.

You know what? Looking around there thinking about Daddy-o and all, I caught myself singing a song that had been floating around in my head.

It goes: "I got bad news, baby, and you're the first to know."

That's one of Dinah Washington's songs.

Katherine Dunham

KATHERINE DUNHAM is the internationally known dancer, choreographer, and anthropologist. She studied at the University of Chicago and received special field training for West Indies research at Northwestern University. *Journey to Accompong*, published in 1946, was the result of her anthropological field trip to the West Indies undertaken on Rosenwald Foundation Fellowships.

Miss Dunham was with the Chicago Opera Company in 1935 and 1946, and then supervised the City Theatre writers project on cult studies. She later appeared in *Cabin in the Sky* and other Broadway shows. In 1945 the Katherine Dunham School of Cultural Arts was established in New York, and later she organized the Katherine Dunham Dance Company, which has performed in major cities throughout the world.

A Touch of Innocence, which was published in 1959, is an autobiographical memoir that is a genuine work of literature.

In addition to her two books, Miss Dunham has contributed to *Mademoiselle, Esquire,* and other publications.

THE CREEK

From A *Touch of Innocence*

BY KATHERINE DUNHAM

In spring the creek running alongside the wooded park that separated Rowena Avenue and Elmwood Avenue stayed continuously swollen—in early spring because of melting snow, in late spring because of heavy rains. Now it was late spring, and the creek was at its most turbulent. Both snows and rains had been unusually heavy that year, and the muddy water rushed down its path carrying read tree branches, pieces of shingle torn off in lightning storms, lumps of limestone marl, and even boulders. This rubble would butt against the time-worn retaining walls with such force as to crumble sections of the concrete or congest to form dams that forced the overflow onto the paths, byways, wagon roads, fields, and woodlands that followed the creek from the source of the Illinois River to a tributary of the Desplaines River just beyond the town.

One evening in late spring, full of stormy resentment against her father, the young girl left the Rowena Street tramway and descended the stone steps leading from the street down into the park. It had become his practice to make her wait night after night in the shop until he could drive her home himself in the truck, partly to forestall the innocent conversations she might have with the youth who was the current delivery boy, partly to have occasion for his own increasing demonstrations of intimacy, which bewildered, terrified, and sickened her.

The strain of her confusions and of her coming final examinations was beginning to tell on her, but she was left with one bright hope—that of escape. She wanted to apply herself more earnestly to her studies and to devote consecutive hours, rather than stolen ones, to classes in eurythmics and interpretive dancing. And especially in the spring it became harder than ever to force herself to turn off Desplaines Street and into Bluff Street and go to her father's shop. The odor of gasoline, the confusion of bits of paper with scrawled orders and numbers left for her to enter in the ledger, the pile of fume-filled woolens and silks and satins to be sorted, gave her a feeling of utmost despondency. The sewing woman hired after the split in the Dunham household came early and left early, so that the girl scarcely ever saw her, and only Mr. Crusoe was left working in the shop: he would shut off the steam-pressing machine shortly after her arrival and depart, leaving the more expert hand finishing for her father. Then, outside or upstairs in the carpet room behind the disordered flat where her father lived alone now, there might still be Old Man Ferguson, mumbling, bending over the hand-cranked auxiliary tubs, skimming the murky sediment from almost clear gasoline and sorting it into tin drums, to gratify that endless, hopeless, pathetically optimistic belief of her father's that waste could be done away with, that if one treated dirty gasoline with care, it would become virgin again. So tubs and pails and keys sat in the tumbler room upstairs and out in back, and her father and Old Man Ferguson drained and skimmed and mixed and strained, losing more in the transfer and in clogged and choked pipes and pistons, and eventually in dissatisfied customers, than if they had thrown the used fluid out.

But, fired by an almost naïve confidence in his inventive and rational capacities, Albert Dunham continued in his own way, dreaming of becoming affluent enough to transport his daughter to a warm climate (California became more prominent in conversation as the winters of the Town grew colder) and there establish her permanently, in a bungalow that he would design himself, as a sort of hostess and loving daughter and willing mistress combined. It is doubtful that he understood the full significance of his desires. He must have felt only the drabness, the treadmill inescapability of his life as it seemed cut out for him; and as she grew in likeness to the woman who had first meant love, security, social prestige, and hope in life to him, his frustrations became focused upon his daughter.

On this particular spring night, her work finished, Katherine Dunham had refused to wait longer for her father. Keyed to hypersensitivity, she had begun seeing in every gesture or overture, whether from her father or the delivery boy or even a friendly customer, a possible aggression. Her uneasiness became especially acute now, as the warm spring sun dropped outof sight, and the delivery boy said a goodbye that seemed too intimate, and children stopped playing, and Bluff Street quietened into the hush that meant dinner hour. She went once or twice to the door and looked toward Western Avenue, from which the delivery truck should turn into Bluff Street if her father was on his regular route. The palms of her hands were moist and cold, and she wiped them across the canvas-covered ironing board. She picked up Mrs. McFarland's black pleated skirt with its Paris label and put it down again. Then on impulse she hurried to the rear of the shop and slid the bolt of the back door, felt her way between the pressing machines and out of the front office, and stepped into the strangely deserted street.

Books in hand, she ran the length of Bluff Street. Passing the bottling factory, she glanced aside into the cheerful kitchen-dining room of the Byfields: Helen sat at the table with the books, and her mother stirred something at the gas plate by the sink. Crossing Jefferson Street with a quick look left and right for cars, she almost collided with Art Simon on his new bicycle. They "Hi-ed" at each other, and she went on to the car stop on the far side of the street by the bridge and leaned against the lamp-post in front of Adler's fish market, trying not to show that she was out of breath.

Her old feeling of fearlessness, of being able to run or fight her way out of any harm as a boy would do, came back to her. This was a feeling rarely experienced since the shame of her first blood flow and since the alternate tension and hopelessness that had come over her with a full understanding of her father's attentions: the wanting her to sit close to him in the truck or kiss him goodbye, or the touch and fondling that made everything about her in life seem smudgy and unclean and waiting. (For what? She still didn't know. It was something implied, its very vagueness making it worse, shattering any hope for the love or affection she saw other fathers show their children—comradeship, games together, playful chiding, a check now and then to go shopping with for anything you wanted. The terrible *unknown*, the unclean thing smirked at, was in some way associated *unnaturally* with her own father. Had she done something wrong? Did the closed upstairs room and the gray sweater of her childhood have anything to do with this?)

The Jefferson Street car came, and at Chicago Street she transferred to the smaller, more rural Rowena Avenue streetcar.

The spring evening remained balmy despite the increasing dusk, and she leaned her head wearily against the iron window bars, giving way to the seductive promise of warm weather; smelling the rain over and the rain to come; almost hearing the pushing of buds on trees that leaned toward the open windows; feeling the swell and thrust of small things in the earth under the quiet touch of approaching night. As the streetcar neared the park, she roused herself to decide which path to follow home— the one through the park or the one down the tree-darkened lane past the fretful chained police dog. She chose the former, though she had agreed with her mother not to take this route, even at early dusk. Now the street lights were coming on one by one, pale against the rich red and purple glow of the sky. She stood, swaying in the nearly empty streetcar as she adjusted her middy blouse, and pulled the cord overhead. She waved to the conductor and walked across the bridge, pausing to look down into the littered muddy water, and then descended the wide stone steps to the park.

She felt excited and sure of herself and utterly, independently brave as she stepped from the third step onto the creek wall and started her walk. The narrow path was muddy and full of pockets of water, so she walked along the top of the wall, as she and her brother had done when the whole family had lived so long ago in Rebecca Brown's cottage, or as she did sometimes even now on mornings when she walked all the way to school. There was a certain amount of danger attached to her daring because at this time of year the cement might give way, leaving the rubble interior of the wall to crumble into the water that lapped and swirled against it.

She saw a weak spot ahead, chose a reasonably dry spot in the path, and jumped down. Carefully watching her steps, she had kept her head lowered; and it was only as her feet touched ground that she became aware of a quite different and more immediate danger.

Just ahead of her there was a man, blond, not too young, unshaven, unwashed—the kind of tramp that her mother always hurried her past when they walked home late at night, or scornfully turned away from the back door when one begged food or yard work at the Elmwood Avenue house. There was another kind of tramp—old, ill, used hard by time and circumstance, bleary of eye and shaky of hand—to whom her mother would willingly allot a small amount of yard clearing now and then as payment for a cup of coffee or some left-over scraps of food. But this man was the shunned kind, and curiosity about him distracted the greater part of her fear; she stood in the path, frankly examining the man, holding her ground, with the crumbling wall and rising water on one side, the dark woods on the other. In the gray cast from the sky and a pale flicker from a hanging lamp on the bridge, she could see pale eyes close set on either side of a high, thin-bridged, narrow nose. A small line of mustache detached itself from the unkempt stubble, but it in no way concealed the pathetic weakness of a mouth that kept working, saying things, mouthing things, exposing stained, cracked teeth and a tongue that continuously licked back saliva between muttered words, whose meaning passed completely over her head.

Her first flash of reaction was that he was ill or hungry and that he would take food or the means to procure it in any way that he could. They were *thieves* then, these shifty-eyed others, and for that reason to be feared. She felt safe in having nothing —only two books, a transfer stub, and the three cents left from the ten she had given the Jefferson Street conductor. And he wouldn't want the books, so he could have the rest. Her relief must have made her smile, because the man relaxed a little from a tense watchfulness and moved a step closer. She felt suddenly chilled and retreated a step. Here it was again, that feeling of unknown danger, coupled with revulsion and a kind of fear that gripped all of her hollow parts and made her want to pray out loud for some relief, some passer-by, even a child or a dog.

She noticed the agitation of one hand which had remained in his pocket and of the other which reached toward her as she drew back, ready to grip her, to stop her flight, to do—what? She called on memories of her brother. What would he have done? He would have smiled and told her in so many words not to panic, not to quake—above all, never to show what was going on inside. *Don't cry out, don't give in to fear, don't give the gods the cheap satisfaction of seeing you weaken.* She had been trying to live by that through the bewildering labyrinth of this past year. And so now it was not hard, in spite of deep disquiet, to stare with what she believed to be regal command at this abject person.

"Please," she said politely, trying to step to one side and eying the crumbling line of embankment to her left.

The man moved into a vantage point that crowded her against the wall. He stood at an angle, prepared to block her escape either forward along the path or sideways into the already dark woods. And backward? Up the stone steps and across the wooden bridge? Suppose he grabbed her in the second that she turned to run on the slippery path, in the concealment of the hollowed-out bowl of woods? Who would know, who would see what might have happened, and what would it be? Murder? But why? For three pennies and a used transfer stub?

Her hand moved to the pocket of the middy blouse to extract the proof of her insolvency. But she stopped because the man was saying words directed at her; and garbled as they were, panted, incoherent, she learned that he wanted her to look, to look at him and at what he was going to do. And whatever he was going to do required an accomplice—not an active one, but a spectator. She pieced together words for which Jimmy McGuire had had his mouth washed out with soap, but this man was using them not in anger, not at a playmate who had worsted him in a fistfight.

"Son of a bitch," he said. His words became clearer, steadier, surer as she stood rooted in combined fear and fascination. Here was a person in great and deep and mysterious infinite pain, and still there was no mistaking the mounting need, the concupiscence behind those small burning eyes as they fixed far into hers.

"Son of a bitch." He was beginning to pant now, and, unable either to understand fully or fully reject the meaning in his eyes and voice, she dropped her own eyes and found that while talking he had unfastened his loose-fitting, soiled trousers and inserted one hand into the opening.

She wanted to look away, because what was happening was too intimate, too naked for her to be watching. She knew that by participating even this far she had taken a step from which there was no recall. She would never be able to look again with innocence at men of this kind or even at her school friends or at her brother or her father. Inactively active by being there, by not raising her eyes or closing them, she lost the crystal-clear virginity that had until now carried her, untouched, past a knowledge too long held off. Not a part of the act, she neverthless knew that she was sharing herself with, losing herself to this tramp, not only because she was afraid, but because in a moment she would know what had a moment before been unknown and would breathe easier for having been given some answer to her own dark questioning.

Then distaste arose within her, and she wanted to escape, to save herself any further knowledge of intimacy. She looked behind her, measuring the distance; she looked at the tramp. He read her movement, but then all along he had been reading her thoughts—aware, in spite of preoccupation with self, of her fascination, of her acceptance of his tutelage, of the chain of revelations that were leaving her no longer young. The slit beneath the mustache widened, and the tongue and lips worked faster, accelerating the single monotonous theme. "Son of a bitch. Son of a bitch. Son of a bitch." His breathing became a continuous groan, and, unable to carry the weight of his excitement, he backed up to the tree and leaned against it, rolling his head from side to side against the rough bark, his body striking the trunk convulsively, so that the branches rattled an accompaniment to his ritual.

"Jesus Christ," he said, adding to his vocabulary. "Jesus Christ. Son of a bitch." The obscenities became a single long cry whining up into the tree and descending into a low, helpless, grief-filled moan.

She closed her eyes and leaned trembling against the wall. Then she looked at the man and, loathing him and herself, too, she began to run. Water and mud splashed over her ankles, and her eyes stung with tears of anger and shame. At the other end of the park she stumbled on the top step and fell on knees and palms into the road above. She picked up the Virgil and the Greek mythology and wiped them off with her sleeve. She drew her arm across her eyes and held her trembling body to a slow walk, under the street light, past the Stevens' house, around to the back door of Rebecca Brown's, and into the warm safe glow of her mother's kitchen.

In the dining room Annette Dunham was bent over the sewing machine. She looked up as her daughter entered.

"Katherine, you're late. And you shouldn't have left before your father got back. He phoned twice already and is pretty much annoyed that you would go away and leave the shop like that. Why"—drawing the thread out long, breaking it between her teeth—"just look at you! What on *earth* happened to your dress? And your *shoes!*"

"It's muddy, Mother, I—"

"Did you come by the park, Katherine?"—stopping dead, garment half withdrawn from the machine pedal.

"Yes, Mother, I did"—trying to get as far as the bathroom.

"But, Katherine! Haven't I told you never to—"

"Yes, Mother. I'm sorry. It was such a nice evening, and I wanted to see the creek. It's right up to the top and running over in places. I fell on the steps and skinned my knee a little"—looking down: maybe she could get away now.

Her mother released her, turning again to the sewing machine, inserting a different part of the dress.

"You shouldn't have left without your father," she said.

(*Carefully guarded, so well protected from anything unclean or suggestive. Why, a boy couldn't even have a dance with her at the Christmas charity ball without first asking Mr. Dunham! And then not always getting his consent, because Mr. Dunham loved to dance with his graceful, growing daughter and over and over he would say that he was sorry but she already had this dance with her father, and she would look down and blush with embarrassment at the embarrassment of the boy. And what would she think now when her mother would say to some visitor in the next room:*

"*Oh, that's all right. You just speak right out. Going to have a baby! You don't say! With that horrible old man!*"

Hushed voice from the visitor again, then Annette Dunham again, sure of herself and her faultless upbringing and her upright, sturdy pioneer forebears:

"*Oh, no, Katherine wouldn't even know what we're talking*

about. Why, she doesn't know a thing about such things! And never asks questions. Just as innocent as she was at six!")

She passed her mother and went into the bathroom; she clung to the water cabinet above the toilet seat and hung her head down over the bowl, but was able to render only clear mucus and saliva. She gagged once or twice, and Annette Dunham, pausing between seams, heard the sound.

"Are you all right, Katherine?" She called anxiously, all mother, all concern, all curious.

"Yes, Mother. I'll be right there." She bathed her face in cold water and closed her eyes for a moment. Then she went into the dining room.

"We have veal with green peppers and noodles for dinner," her mother said. "The noodles have been in so long they might be too soft. Just light the fire again and set the table. I have to finish this alteration—Mrs. Hardy will be coming first thing in the morning. She's going to Springfield for her daugher's wedding. My! How time flies! You don't remember her, do you, Katherine?"

No answer needed because the sewing machine whirred on, and Annette Dunham, foot busy on pedal, didn't look up.

"They tell me her husband's one of the richest men in Springfield. Don't see how they managed it. She's a nice girl, but certainly not *pretty*. But he's a widower. Over fifty, Bessie says. Money or no money, I don't see it!"

At the table set in the combination dining and sewing room, mother and daughter sat facing each other while Annette Dunham said grace. Short and to the point.

"Dear Lord, we thank thee for what we are about to receive. Amen."

Before, on Bluff Street, grace had been chiefly a special acknowledgment for Sunday dinner. Now in her self-imposed widowhood the mother seemed to feel that this courtesy not only added a certain dignity to her martyrdom, but emphasized the decorum she was instilling in her daughter. The steaming platter remained in front of the girl.

"No, thank you, Mother. I'm not hungry. I—I just can't eat. And I have a lot of work to do tonight." Head down, she toyed with a piece of bread. Her mother did not like food to be refused or rejected; and growing girls should eat; and food was expensive and shouldn't be wasted.

"Are you sick, Katherine?" In spite of pique, the anxiety was real. "Is it your . . . No, it's not time for that. You'd better eat something anyway. Noodles aren't good the second day."

The daughter shook her head, and the mother decided to say no more. She enjoyed her meal, musing over the strange ways that beset girls during adolescence and particularly wondering at this girl who became daily more enigmatic, more closed, more a stranger.

After dinner there was again the hum of the sewing machine in the dining room and the sound of order being established in the kitchen. That night the daughter sat late over her Virgil. Heavy with exhaustion, she still knew that she would not sleep. Whether she kept her eyes open, fixed on words, or held them tightly closed, the quick, treacherous camera of her mind had developed its print, and before her she saw her last glimpse of the tramp—stolen as she recovered from her fall and picked up her books. He was hardly distinguishable in the darkness and distance, but what she had seen was vivid: one hand still gripping closely, as when she had fled; the other straining at the branch above so that it bent low, its dry ends over the creek wall; Promethean, the white face moving from side to side—chained to the tree, but with enough leeway to keep moving, just so far, left and right, talking, talking.

Through summer and fall and the following winter the West Side Cleaners lost more and more customers and had fewer dresses to alter, and need was growing acute everywhere. Letters from Katherine Dunham's brother thanked her for the stamps or the twenty-five-cent piece or the mangled cigar that she had filched from pockets of incoming suits and sent to him, but thanked her in a way that revealed how important these small tokens were, so that she felt deeply uneasy for his well-being.

One evening after school she had looked for a long time at the drawer where petty cash was kept, waiting for her father to leave the front part of the shop. Each time he had gone out, though, he had returned immediately, as if he had sensed some uneasiness in the air. During one interval, her heart pounding, she had at last managed to extract from the drawer its only one-dollar bill; but her sense of guilt had been so great that at the first opportunity she returned it. She went on trying, however, to be first to go through the soiled clothes as they came in from the delivery wagon, turning pockets inside out, feeling in seams, securing nickels and dimes and pennies to exchange for a larger coin for mailing.

Her brother had received his first fellowship by now, but the two years since he had left home had begun to take their toll, and he wrote of ill health and chest examinations and a possible stay in a state sanatorium: not a great deal of information, but enough so that her heart beat fast with anxiety and her mother's brow furrowed when she read the pages, and she repeated over and over, "He ought to come home. No sense in carrying a thing too far. Not eating enough and working all night to be able to study all day!" And sometimes Annette Dunham's voice quavered, and emotions she seldom displayed rose to the surface: bewilderment at the turn that her marriage had taken, and a conflict in loyalties. The father's rage had been wrong, but then the boy should not have struck his father, should not have left home: he should have continued in the business and not gone on with this nonsense of philosophy, no matter how brilliant he was or how many scholarships he won. Her worry for him always ended intermingled with indignation. But suppose that he *was* ill, that it *was* that dreaded illness that often attacks young people, especially if they don't eat enough. But surely not *her* son, Surely not *Albert*! She would read a page again, trying to see it differently, trying to push off the gnawing fear between each line.

"*It may only be for a year. Don't worry. They aren't sure yet.*"

Once her mother had spoken to her father, on one of those rare occasions when he had stayed to dinner.

"Al, I'm worried about Albert. He wrote Katherine a letter about a chest examination. Do you think it could mean . . . ? Don't you think you could send some money?" (She herself did whenever she could, always secretly in fear that her husband would find out and fly into one of his black jealous rages. But there would not be much left after she had paid the rent and coal and light and a part of the food, because Albert Dunham, accepting the separation from his wife as final and voluntary, contributed less and less to the upkeep of the house on Elmwood Avenue; and as business became worse, he lapsed frequently even in this respect.) "Or ask him to come back? You know, after all, he *is* your son!"

But his son's rebellion was still a sore subject with the father. He pushed his chair back from the table and prepared to leave.

"He is no son of mine," he said, "and if he thinks he's big enough to strike his father, he is certainly big enough to make his own way. And furthermore, Nett, I've told you not to bring that subject up again."

Angry, headstrong, still too young, Albert Dunham flung himself out of the cottage and down the snowy steps to the delivery truck. Mother and daughter sat close in misery, staring at unfinished food, thinking each in her own way, each with her consuming love, of the son, the brother, who might be at that very moment without warm clothing, without shelter, without food. What the scholarship would pay they could not know, but imagined that it would be not much more than enough for the University tuition, perhaps not even enough for the precious and necessary books, for which he would gladly go without food.

At her father's denial of paternity a brief wild hope had arisen in the girl. Suppose it were so? Suppose they had belonged first only to that dim and distant mother of the past and now to Annette alone? But her mirror had belied this a thousand times during the past three years, when she had turned to it looking for some trace of that dead mother, some definite feature to wash out the stamp of *Dunham*. There they were unmistakably—her father's eyes and mouth and nose, her father's round face. *Aren't you Albert Dunham's little girl? She certainly does resemble her father, doesn't she! Just look at that smile! Just like her father!*

And her brother, too, despite the high-bridged aristocratic nose of Fanny June Guillaume, was unmistakably the son of his father.

Wild hope, born to die quickly in the light of reason: she looked into her plate and ate without tasting the food.

Business worries increasingly beset Albert Dunham in these months. New establishments were springing up left and right, but all other things being equal, they would not have worried him.

They came and they went, and few remained, and some even called him in for consultation. What did worry him was the increasing difficulty of finding and keeping responsible help that he could afford to pay, and the rising cost and declining quality of gasoline. The competing plants seemed untroubled by the introduction of lead, ruinous to fine silks and ultimately to machinery. But despite all the straining and skimming that he and Old Man Ferguson did, there never seemed to be enough clear gasoline.

With things as they were now, the big tank of solvent was seldom full, often empty. To do justice to a fragile or fine or special garment, he sometimes had to drive to the filling station at the corner of Raynor and Western avenues with a gallon or a two-gallon can and have it filled for this job alone. Bitterly, as he drove through the winter night on deliveries after hours, he thought of his dreams, his thwarted ambitions, the storms a few years back when he had tried to persuade Annette Dunham to invest in more up-to-date machinery, or to sell out to new companies—then anxious to acquire the clientele of the West Side Cleaners and Dyers—and move the entire family to California. But to the mother further investment in a business already established had seemed a useless luxury, and the idea of such a move had been unthinkable.

So Albert Dunham, Sr., turned his dreams inward. "Asleep in the Deep," "The Wedding of the Winds," "Melody in F," "Dear One," "The World Is Waiting for the Sunrise," had not left the piano-bench drawer since the family separation. In the freezing, dust-covered living room above the shop, the fire was never lighted, and one by one the strings of the guitar strained and snapped in the bitter cold. Sometimes at night as he lay awake in the room where once he and his second wife had slept, he could hear the tension rising under ghostly fingers, the taut wires giving, the squeak of ivory pegs, and then the twang as the fractured ends snapped back and struck the polished satinwood body which had once been his pride and joy; that had, during the best days of Bluff Street and family life, still been a tie to the past, to a life too remote even to dream of any more. . . .

The famous *salons* and musical soirees at the Potter Palmer mansion on Lake Shore Drive; carriages and gaiety and polished floors and shimmering candelabra advanced and recede before his eyes as he lay sleepless in the black room above the shop. In an alcove where four mahogany-colored musicians were tuning their instruments, he, Albert Dunham—young, not long from Memphis, full of a kind of rural charm and wonderment, brimming with hope and ambition—fingered lovingly the strings of his guitar, the polished surface of which reflected candlelight, cut glass, sparkling jewelry, white shoulders, fire glow, and then his own dark face as he leaned closely over it.

His pride was all the greater because he had bought the guitar by the true sweat of his brow: by cuttings and fittings and careful pressings of seams under a twenty-pound hand iron heated on a gas jet in the back of a German tailor shop on the fifteenth floor of the Fair Building in the heart of the fifth largest city in the whole world. At the end of a long day he gratefully inhaled the clear lake air; shoulders aching from hours over the basting needle took new life in this glittering fairyland, where often the musicians were the last to leave, in the hours just before dawn. Albert Dunham was anxious to stay in the midst of such beauty and refinement, but eager, too, to finish, to be away without even touching the table in the servants' dining room, because already he had wooed the glamorous divorcée, and already she had accepted him. . . .

Perhaps as he lay in the arctic isolation of the room above the shop, he would move on to other, later scenes with this same guitar—to Sunday nights in Glen Ellyn before the illness had lined the pale sad face with pain, before the door of the upstairs room stayed shut: lamplight on a gilded harp, a small boy watching the tuning of the instrument, and a smaller child, a daughter, perhaps in his arms as he carefully turned the ivory pegs of the instrument on his knee and plucked the strings, ear bent close, shifting the child in order to lean over and tune to a note on the piano. He could not know then about the glass-topped coffin or the gray sweater or the canal or the creek or the boy who would turn from his father and take the love of his sister with him; nor could he know that the girl would one day grow in likeness to her mother, even though she had inherited none of her actual features, but only their inner meaning. He could not know how disturbing the resemblance would be when the child had grown into a young

girl and the young girl had reached the threshold of womanhood.
. . . At night, when he could hear the busy working of the mice
and the creaking of the giant wheel groaning even in rest under
its own weight in the dust-thick back room, and the reverberant
yield of a broken guitar string—then, unable to sleep, he would take
stock of the frenetic pattern of his life, of the velocity with which
change after change in the wrong direction was taking place, and
—lonely, rebellious, hungry of soul, and bewildered of spirit—
he would conjure up the ideal existence in a California known
only from newspaper travel advertisements or the bragging description of an occasional customer or a rare motion-picture travelogue.
When finally he fell asleep to dream, it would be of this: that
there, in his own house, with her, he would recapture his lost love
and lost youth.

Two years earlier, on a bright Saturday morning in spring, a girl
hired to clean the Bluff Street flat above the shop had splintered
the pane of one of the front windows and, in her hurry to finish
her half-day on schedule, placed the fragmented glass on top of her
scrub bucket in front of the window. Katherine Dunham, eager
to be off to a track meet, had pulled herself inside the frame from
where she had been polishing the outside of the window, swung
down from the sill, and felt stocking and skin sever in one stroke
and seen warm blood ooze from the wide-open, laid-back flesh,
before she realized what had happened. Cloth in hand, she stood
looking at the incision and watching with curiosity the increased
flow of blood, while the servant girl ran for her mother.

Annette Dunham abandoned her sewing machine, called a taxi,
and hurried her daughter to Dr. Williams, who shook his head
gravely, applied antiseptics, and sewed the wound together. She
must be careful, he warned, to move as little as possible, to come
to him for redressing at least twice weekly, to abstain from all unnecessary movement until he should declare her fit.

At that time physical activity was particularly important to the
girl, and though she nodded docilely, she avoided a direct promise.
The wound healed slowly because of stolen moments of exercise,
and as soon as the stitches were out, there was no holding her
back. One day when she was at basketball practice the scar re-

opened, and the flesh exposed beneath was not clean; the treatment had to be started over. But, despite all Dr. Williams' resources, the wound continued to suppurate, and one morning while dressing the girl noticed, inches above the wound on the soft skin behind her knee, a small round blister, sensitive to the touch and filled with the same yellowish matter that oozed constantly through the gauze bandage below.

Without question Annette Dunham threw aside loyalty to Dr. Williams and his wife and made an appointment with a German specialist newly established in the Town. With him the girl proved to be a more co-operative patient than she had been with Dr. Williams: she was subdued by discussions at dinner about the exorbitant charge for each visit to the specialist and by his reluctance to take the case at all in such an advanced condition. And in the end he saved her leg.

At first the wound seemed to have healed level with the rest of the skin surface; but even now, two years later, the surrounding area would grow numb in cold weather and the lesion itself would form a tight mound, not painful but disagreeable enough to prompt a new consultation with the specialist. His advice was daily massage, and for a time the girl would herself engage in this treatment while waiting by the stove in the back room of the shop; but the watching eyes of her father soon discouraged her, and she returned to her open books and her brooding impatience.

One night Albert Dunham began the courtship of his daughter, as he had so many times before, naïvely and almost childishly.

"I don't see why anyone would want to stay in a town like this and in this kind of weather when they could be in a place like California."

No response: just a tightening of throat and stomach muscles and that sick feeling which couldn't be controlled and which she prayed would soon pass if she kept her head buried in her books.

"If your mother had lived, I bet we would have been out of here and settled in some place like Los Angeles or Hollywood a long time ago."

The girl knew that these were only romantic names to him, and, although she might have been able to support this woolgathering in anyone else, in her father she found it absurd, and the references to her dead mother seemed indecorous. Feelings of loyalty toward Annette Dunham made her turn from her father at every allusion to Fanny June Dunham, though at heart she hungered to know more of this by now mythical creature whom, according to her father, she daily grew to resemble more closely and who, according to his reminiscences, must have been possessed of infinite beauty and all the graces combined.

When these overtures evoked no response, the father turned the gas out in the steam iron and began the adjustments of stove, pressing apparatus, and back door that normally announced departure. This night, however, as she closed her book and started to rise from the chair before the stove, he emerged from the front office with the desk chair and placed it near hers and as directly in front as possible. Caught off guard, she must have shown her alarm, because his gaze fell and the rehearsed lines were indistinct and unsure.

"The doctor said that your leg should be massaged." He reached for her ankle and extended her leg across his knee. To keep from touching the stove she had to shift her chair so that she was facing him. "I notice that you haven't been doing it lately," he went on, gaining confidence from her helplessness. "You'd better let me do it every night."

The suggestion had become an order; there seemed to be no retreat without admission of panic. She felt blood drain from her entire body, and she clamped her tongue between her teeth to keep them from chattering. Then, as he reached out to unroll the top of the woolen stocking held in place by elastic below the knee, anger and shame replaced fright and she felt a rush of blood that brought her back into equilibrium. Ignoring his touch, she exchanged her Virgil for a French grammar and began poring over declensions of verbs.

From the corners of her eyes she watched her father's hands. She had forgotten how they felt to the three-year-old child; touched by them now, she felt vague stirrings of memory. As they made persistent, regular strokes, working above the numb spot and to her knee, she pictured them as she had known them since: lifting the pressing iron, tuning the guitar, pointed in anger at her or her brother or her mother; an open palm drawn back to strike

again an already smarting cheek; competent hands on reins guiding
Lady Fern over the asphalt of Black Road. These same hands now
stroked the flesh above her knee which led to the tender exposure
of inner thigh, seeking farther: hands of a lover in first caress.

She had seen mounting desire before, had witnessed its culmina-
tion. Instinctively she began to connect the tramp with this man
who was her father. The cold room became stifling; her hunger
was now distant. Distant, too, the snow-bound cottage, the sewing
machine, her mother. Only the lute strings of the sirens and a
swimming sea, with the hum of the winter wind in the chimney
of the dying stove, and the waning of sounds in the pressing
machine as steam turned to water and murmured comfortably,
settling into the pipes for the night.

As she swung dizzily on the edge of an abyss, an image saved
her. The image of the rabbit at the end of a Sunday hunting trip
years before. A rabbit hanging limp and blood-spattered. Slate sky,
white snow, a child waiting for a man and a boy to return across
ice-bound fields with the kill. A child shrinking from flannel
underwear moist with urine, wiping a nose raw from dripping on
the back of a woolen mitten . . . stinging eyes holding back tears
of defeat . . . helplessness in the bitter cold . . . long ride home.
Then the kitchen, and her father's hand forcing its way into the
rabbit's enlarged anal opening, emerging with viscera bulging
between blood-shiny fingers; again and again, the same hand that
lifted the twenty-pound iron, the same efficient fingers caressing
guitar strings, the same fingers massaging, intruding, insinuating
toward secret places still scarcely known to her.

Nausea drew her violently from the brink of some terror that
she defied to take form. Blindly, with deep breaths, she fought her
way back to safety, nearly succumbed, nearly drowned finding air
again. But life rose triumphant over death wish; over a drawing-
back to womb and even farther, to the swirling engulfing plas-
modium before conception. Her relaxed muscles contracted into
resistance, and from somewhere her own voice sounded—from
across the room or an outer door or an outer space.

"That isn't where it hurts," she said calmly, and surprised herself with this control which seemed to have come from beyond
herself. "I don't need that any more anyway. If I do, I can do it

myself." She added, without bothering to notice the reaction of the man before her, his progressive motion arrested, "I'm hungry. I don't like to wait so long before going home after school. If I'm going to have to wait so long, I would rather walk."

She used her new-found freedom from guilt like an avenging weapon. Now she could hate with reason and not blindly. She could give all of the justifications to her mother and to him if he demanded them—but, most importantly, to herself. She did not know where intimacy would have ended, but by putting together knowledges and glimpses gathered since that spring evening when the tramp had revealed himself to her, she knew it would have been in a place where father and daughter could never meet again in daily life with other people—in some dank, dark, forbidden fen, desolate, stark, lost, never to be returned from. The protective, instinctive mechanism of revulsion gave strength to her limbs and sureness to her conviction.

She talked with malice, pleased to watch the man before her pass from transport to realization to shame. Spitefully, feeling power, she said as she stood up to replace the stocking, rolling it carefully over the elastic, "And about California. If you have that much money, I need a pair of shoes. And Albert needs food. And mother needs money to pay the rent." She said the words carefully, someone else speaking for her. "And I don't want you to touch me again, ever. Not touch me or kiss me or ever get near me, and if you will give me the money, I will go home by myself every night. I don't want anything from you. Anything at all. Because now I know that I hate you!"

Years later, when she understood more about the complex nature of men, when she had been host to loneliness, she would have taken back the words and left only the action. On this night, however, she fastened well the protective mantle of aversion into which she had been retreating farther and farther since childhood; and for many years, until greater wisdom and tolerance and understanding allowed the slow unfolding into mature love, this was all that Albert Dunham was to know of his daughter. As she spoke she saw the beginning of his disintegration, and she knew that she had for the first time consciously exercised the law of self-preservation; to save herself, it couldn't have been otherwise. He would have to place his illusions—his dreams of recapture of things lost, his blind belief in a giving back of something to substitute for things taken away—somewhere else. But the things and places had narrowed down to the Town, and the Town was not generous enough to provide compensation.

Having now accomplished the total estrangement of both his children, Albert Dunham drove his daughter silently through the night, refused his wife's invitation to dinner, and, avoiding the eyes of both mother and daughter, returned to the truck, to the drive through frozen deserted streets, to the room above the West Side Cleaners where he would lie in the darkness and lock into his innermost being his dreams of love and warmth and escape.

Left alone with her mother, the girl lost touch with the Voice, the Thing, the Prompting Angel that had been with her a few minutes before: she felt on her own again, uncertain, miserable, bewildered. What proof had she? What act to point out that could not be construed, if one needed to avoid truth, as fatherly attention and affection? How could she expect her mother to listen with sympathy to the most damning of accusations? Would not she be the one finally blamed? But she knew the truth and reassured herself by reliving situation after situation until no doubt was left.

She decided to speak to her mother after they were in bed, where the shame in her own face and the distress in her mother's would be hidden by darkness. But she waited too long, and when she did summon enough courage to speak, it was with many hesitations, frequent repetitions, a voice sometimes almost inaudible. She began with the seemingly innocent familiarities that might have been mistaken for paternal solicitude—his insistence on her proximity in the delivery wagon, her endless waiting at night after everyone else had gone home, the nightly offers of the house in California.

At one point Annette Dunham rose up on her elbow and stared through the dark at her daughter. Her voice expressed the astonishment that her face must have shown. "Why Katherine! Of course your father should bring you home at night! Why, what are you trying to say? Are you trying to find something wrong with that?"

The stress on the word "wrong" completely discouraged the girl and made her feel suddenly the offender, unspeakably cheap and unclean; made her feel almost in league with the object of her attack. How foolish she had been to hope for some glimmer of understanding, some motherly denouncement of the outrage. She lay in the darkness, scarcely breathing for fear of being called upon for further explanations, and she knew now that there was nothing to say and never would be.

Receiving no reply, Annette Dunham concluded that the matter was dismissed; she turned her back on her daughter and slept.

The subject was never again brought up, and out of it all, the mother was the only survivor not in some way defeated, not in some way loser of a dream.

The girl moved on toward young womanhood; the household remained split; the brother was hospitalized while his mother and sister stayed helpless and grieving. What Albert Dunham felt about his son at this time he kept well within himself, but bitterness was there, and blackness, because both showed plainly on the face that not so long before had been still open, still seeking. Business did not improve, and the nation moved steadily toward the last days before the landslide into deep depression.

The mother stayed bent for more hours over her sewing machine, with less to show for her work at the end of the month. In his fanatical search for some magic solvent that would render clean gasoline from soiled, the father spent restless nights in the tumbler room, alone now because Old Man Ferguson had died and he could not afford a replacement, and Mr. Crusoe had gone to seek more profitable employment in the steel mills. The daughter continued to work at the shop after school, but the battle against stains and rips and tears in increasingly poor material was a losing one; and the pockets of incoming garments yielded few stamps and coins to be secreted for mailing to the hospital outside the City.

At the end of the term, when photographs were taken for the class annual, the girl looked at hers and knew that she was as old then as she would ever be in her life. She would know more, much more, but she could never later be older in the true sense. The sadness in her eyes frightened her, and she begged the mother to let her have new pictures taken, because the secrets captured by the lens belonged to her. But there was no money, and the picture printed in the school annual was a permanent witness not only to her own suffering, but to all of the hidden things in families that one shouldn't tell or be let known: her mother living in one house and her father in another; cardboard neatly folded into shoe soles, but not very useful in rain or snow; her father and brother tossing, locked together on the dining-room floor, with murderous intent; her secret knowledge of the experience shared with the tramp, long ago but still there; and now, for her brother, the sanatorium, because he had gone without food while he studied and lived in winter where there was no heat except a kerosene stove, and because—not being the kind to turn outward, bearing his privations—he had turned inward, and somewhere something had given way.

Ted Poston

Mr. Poston comments that " 'Rat Joiner Routs the Klan' is one of about six short stories I have written around almost forgotten incidents of my childhood in Hopkinsville, Kentucky.

"While I wrote these stories mainly for my own amusement, I felt that given recent civil rights achievements, someone should try to put down the not-always-depressing experiences of a segregated society like the one I grew up in.

"Someday I may add another half dozen such stories to the original and seek to have them published as a thin volume."

"Rat Joiner Routs the Klan" is published here for the first time.

Theodore R. Poston was born in Hopkinsville, Kentucky, and graduated with an A.B. degree from Tennessee Agricultural and Industrial State University in Nashville, Tennessee.

Since 1937 he has been a reporter and feature writer for the New York *Post*, and his articles and short stories have appeared in *The New Republic, Saturday Review, The Nation, Survey, Ebony, The Negro Digest* and other publications.

During the Second World War, Mr. Poston served as Deputy Director of the Office of War Information and held other posts under Presidents Roosevelt and Truman.

RAT JOINER ROUTS THE KLAN

BY TED POSTON

There had never been a Ku Klux Kan in Hopkinsville, Kentucky. So it was sort of surprising how our leading colored citizens got all worked up when they heard that *The Birth of a Nation* was coming to the Rex Theatre down on Ninth Street.

It was we young ones who brought them the news—although it didn't mean anything to us. And it was we young ones who got them out of it when the situation finally reached a stalemate.

The whole thing started one Saturday morning when Bronco Billy Anderson was being featured at the Rex in *The Revenge of the Ranger*. And, of course, not a one of us could afford to miss that.

Natually, the Booker T. Washinton Colored Grammar School was not open on Saturdays, but that meant only one extra hour's sleep. For all of us had to be at the Rex at 9 A.M. to be sure that we could get front row seats in the peanut gallery which was reserved for all of our colored citizens.

It was absolutely essential that we be there when the doors first opened or else the bigger boys would get there first and take the choice seats.

We always thought the big boys were unfair, but there was nothing we could do about it. No self-respecting young colored citizen would dream of squealing to the white folks about it. And furthermore, if we did, we knew the big boys would bop us for doing it.

But this was our problem: The Rex Theater charged only five cents admission for all of our colored citizens under ten years of age. But since Miss Lucy, the white ticket lady who took our nickels, was nearsighted, and saw us only through a peephole as we stood in line in the alley, there was a rumor around the colored community that none of us grew any older after we were nine years old until we suddenly reached twenty-one or more. For all you had to do was bend your knees, look up innocently, and slip your nickel through the slot, and she'd pass you right up the gallery stairs.

There was a story—which I never believed—that Jelly Roll Benson never paid more than a nickel to get into the Rex until he was thirty-five years old.

"That's why he walks with a stoop in his shoulders and a bend in his knees to this day," Rat Joiner always insisted. "He got that way from fooling Miss Lucy. He'd still be doin it now, but he forgot to shave one morning. And she suspected for the first time that he was over ten."

But all this happened before that historic Saturday when we all rushed to see Bronco Billy Anderson in *The Revenge of the Ranger*. All of us were crazy about Bronco Billy, but there was also another reason for going to see him. For in every picture, Bronco Billy's main side-kick was a cowboy named Buffalo Pete. And, believe it or not, Buffalo Pete was as highly visible and 100 per cent colored as any citizen up on Billy Goat Hill.

He was the only colored cowboy or colored anything we ever saw in the movies in those days, and we wouldn't think of missing him. Our enthusiasm was not even dimmed by the cynicism of Rat Joiner, who observed one day: "They don't never let him kill none of them white mens, no matter how evil they is. Oh yeah, they let him knock off a Indian every now and then. But only Bronco Billy kills them white bad mens."

There was an unconfirmed rumor around town that another movie actor, named Noble Johnson, had Negro blood. But we didn't pay that no mind. We figured that the high-yallers in our colored community had dreamed up that story for prestige purposes. And anyway, Noble Johnson played in those silly love stories they showed at the Rex on weekday nights. And who would pay five cents to see one of them?

But *The Revenge of the Ranger* that Saturday was a real knockdown picture and we saw it eight times before they put us out at 5 P.M. in order to let the grownups in for the evening, at fifteen cents a head.

We got downstairs and out of the alley at just about the same time that the little white boys were being put out also, and we noticed that they were all carrying handbills in their fists. Nobody had passed out any handbills upstairs, but we had no difficulty getting some when we found out that Tack Haired Baker had been paid twenty-five cents to stand by the front door in the lobby and pass them out.

We were a little disappointed when we read them, because it didn't mean anything to us then. Bronco Billy and Buffalo Pete weren't even mentioned anywhere on the handbills. They read:

Special   *Special*   *Special*

THE SOUTH RISES AGAIN

Come see D. W. Griffith's:

"THE BIRTH OF A NATION"

(Based on "The Clansman")

Every night——Tuesday Through Friday.   Admission 25 cents.

Most of us threw the handbills away before we got home, and I don't remember how I happened to hold on to mine.

But I still had it in my hand when I climbed up our front steps and tried to make my way through the usual Saturday crowd of elders and sporting men who were holding their weekly session with Papa. Papa was Professor E. Poston, dean of men at Kentucky State Industrial College for Negroes in Frankfort and the official arbiter of all bets and disputes which piled up during his two-weekly absences from home.

My sister Lillian, who is only three years older than I, was showing off by sitting next to Papa while he explained that a Negro jockey named Isaac Murphy was the first man to ride three winners in the Kentucky Derby, in 1884, 1890, and 1891. So as I stepped around Smoky Smith, our leading colored gambling man, who had raised the question, I handed Lillian the handbill. This *Birth of a Nation* thing sounded like one of those silly love-story movies she was always going to, so I thought I was doing her a favor.

But I was absolutely unprepared for the commotion that was raised when Mr. Freddie Williams, the first deacon of our Virginia Street Baptist Church, happened to glance at the handbill and let out a screech.

"Don't that say *The Birth of a Nation?*" he yelled as he snatched it out of Lillian's hands. "And coming to the Rex Theatre here?"

He thrust the crumpled handbill in Papa's face and said: "Professor Poston, you've got to do something about this right away."

I still had no idea what had caused the commotion, but Mr. J. B. Petty, our local insurance man—historian, very soon put me right.

It seemed that this novel, *The Clansman,* and the moving picture *The Birth of a Nation* were something about a bunch of peckerwoods who dressed up in sheets and went around whipping the heads of unsuspecting colored citizens and yelling about white supremacy. And there was one place in both things about some Negro—"played by a white man," Mr. J. B. Petty explained— who chased some poor white woman off the top of a rock quarry, with her yelling "Death before dishonor."

Mr. Freddie Williams was putting it right up to Papa.

"You know what it will mean to show this sort of thing to these hillbillies and peckerwoods around here, Professor Poston," he kept saying. "And I'm sure that the quality white folks will agree with you if you put it up to them right. I'm surprised that Mr. Max Kaplan even thought of letting this happen."

Now even I knew that Mr. Max Kaplan, who owned the Rex, was not exactly quality white folks in the eyes of Hopkinsville, Kentucky, even if he was a very popular white citizen in the colored community.

And neither was Judge Hezekiah Witherspoon, our veteran Republican leader, quality either. But he ran Hopkinsville, Kentucky, and it was to him that the group decided that Papa should make his first appeal.

Papa went right down to see him that Saturday night, but the meeting wasn't altogether successful. As I heard Papa explaining it to Mama when he finally got home, Judge Witherspoon started talking about private enterprise and what were the Negroes excited about anyhow? But Papa had one more weapon up his sleeve, he explained to Mama.

"So I finally said to him," Papa recalled, " 'I don't know if you read the book, Judge Witherspoon, but the whole thing is about the terrible things the scalawags and carpetbaggers did to the people of the South during Reconstruction. And although I didn't want to mention the subject, Judge, you must remember that all of those scalawags and carpetbaggers were Republicans, so I wonder if you want people reminded of that?' "

Papa chuckled as he recalled Judge Witherspoon's reaction.

" 'Eph, you damn Democrat,' he yelled at me," Papa said. "You keep your politics out of this.' But I could see that he was shaken, and I just let him rave for a few minutes.

"But finally he said: 'I'm not gonna get mixed up in this thing. But you go and see Max Kaplan and tell him how the colored people feel about this thing. And tell him I'll back him up if he feels he's got to do something about it.' "

Papa was very set up about the meeting. "I'm going out to see Mr. Max Kaplan tomorrow morning. After all, Sunday is not his Sabbath and he won't be averse to talking a little business."

I still didn't quite understand what the shouting was all about. But I had no doubt that Mr. Max Kaplan would side with our colored citizens if Papa asked him to. For Mr. Max Kaplan was quite an unusual citizen even in Hopkinsville, Kentucky. He had come there years before I was born and had got into hot water the minute he built the Rex Theatre, because he had planned only ground-floor seats for white and colored citizens alike.

Of course, the white folks, including the quality ones, had beaten him down on that, and he had been forced to spend extra money to fix the peanut gallery up for us.

Reaching Pete Washington, a classmate of mine in the Booker T. Washington Colored Grammar School, once said he was glad Mr. Max Kaplan lost that fight. Reaching Pete didn't have a nickel one Saturday when The Clutching Hand serial was playing the Rex, so he kept on up the alley and slipped through the fire-escape door on the ground floor where the white folks sat.

It was dark, of course, and nobody noticed that Reaching Pete had slipped in. But everybody knew it a few minutes later. For when Pete looked up, he was right under the screen and the pictures were twenty feet tall. And just at that moment, the Clutching Hand, a very mean crook who had a claw in place of his right hand, was reaching out for his next victim, and Pete thought he was reaching for him.

Pete closed his eyes and screamed so loud that they had to turn on the lights in the whole theatre to find out what was going on. The cops wanted to lock Reaching Pete up, but Mr. Max Kaplan wouldn't let them. He even let Reaching Pete go upstairs free of charge.

But that wasn't the only thing that endeared Mr. Max Kaplan to our colored community. There was the matter of Tapper Johnson, our motion-picture projectionist. When the white folks balked Mr. Max Kaplan and made him build a whole peanut gallery (after starting a whispering campaign that he was trying to bring his New York City ideas to Hopkinsville), he made up his mind to get even. So he decided to make his most highly paid employee one of our colored citizens. That was when he hired Tapper and trained him to be the only moving-picture-machine operator in all of Hopkinsville. And he paid Tapper thirty-five dollars each and every week.

And Tapper paid Mr. Max Kaplan back real nice too. He became the best moving-picture operator for his size and age in all of Kentucky, and there were rumors that he could have gotten five dollars more a week in Clarksville, Tennessee, if Mr. Kaplan had ever given him a vacation or a day off to go see about it.

But Tapper didn't want a day off. He had only two loves in his life—his motion-picture machine and little Cecelia Penrod with whom he had been in love long before he quit the fourth grade in the Booker T. Washington Colored Grammar School.

His love affair with the Rex Theatre moving-picture machine went along smoothly. But not his love affair with little Cecelia. For Cecelia was one of the nieces of Mrs. Nixola Green, our high-yaller social leader. And she felt that Tapper was too dark to become a member of her family.

In fact, my sister Lillian was always saying that Mrs. Nixola was trying to marry Cecelia off to Pat Slaker (who naturally was yaller), but that Pat and Cecelia weren't paying each other any mind. Cecelia was in love with Tapper, Lillian said, although there wasn't much she could do about it. She never got to go to the Rex Theatre alone. Mrs. Nixola always insisted on accompanying her.

Papa probably had all this in mind that Sunday morning when he hopefully set out for Mr. Max Kaplan's home. But Papa was in for a disappointment. Mr. Kaplan wasn't in town. He'd left three weeks ago for California and he wasn't expected home until Wednesday.

Now *The Birth of a Nation* was due to start running Tuesday night. Time was running out as the elders of Freeman Methodist Chapel and the Virginia Street Baptist Church met that afternoon to receive Papa's report.

"Professor Poston," Mr. Freddie Williams finally said after the discussion had gone on for hours, "I know how you feel about poor white trash. But with Mr. Max Kaplan out of town, there's nothing we can do but appeal to S. J. Bolton."

It took some talking on the part of the elders, but Papa was finally persuaded to lay the matter before Mr. S. J. Bolton, Mr. Kaplan's manager of the Rex, and the results were disastrous, as he reported it to Mama later.

"This clay-eating cracker," Papa said later, in as near an approach to profanity as he ever permitted himself, "had the nerve to call me Eph. He said to me: 'Eph, what are you Nigras upset about? Why, my grandfather was one of the founders of the Klan. No Nigra who knows his place has anything to worry about in this glorious story of the re-rise of the South.'

"And then he added," Papa said, " 'Why, Eph, you must know what my initials, S. J., stand for. Stonewall Jackson Bolton, of course.' "

Papa's indignation at the outcome of his conference was far exceeded by the reaction of the elders who met on our lawn that Sunday afternoon to hear his report.

But none of us young ones felt personally involved until Mr. Freddie Williams summed up the feelings of our elders.

"All right," he said, "if that is the way the white folks feel about it, let them. But I move that if *The Birth of a Nation* opens at the Rex Tuesday evening, then 'The Death of the Rex' should set in that very night. Because if we don't patronize that peanut gallery Mr. Max Kaplan has for us, then they ain't gonna make enough money each week to pay even Tapper's salary. And that means not only us staying away, but our kids as well—Bronco Billy and Buffalo Pete notwithstanding."

Now this created a very desperate situation indeed, as I explained to my classmates at the Booker T. Washington Colored Grammar School the next morning.

But what could we do about it? We were all pretty downcast until Rat Joiner said: "I think I got an idea." And then he explained.

And as soon as school was out that day, we all went to work to raise the fifteen cents Rat said was necessary for the success of his plan. Coca-Cola bottles, scrap wire, everything, went into the pot until we had the fifteen cents.

There was no picket line at the Rex the next night, but some of our most responsible colored citizens were loitering around the alley from the minute the evening tickets went on sale. And most of them were very upset when Rat Joiner, the pride of Billy Goat Hill, showed up as the only colored customer that night who plunked down fifteen cents and requested a peanut-gallery ticket from Miss Lucy.

In fact, there was talk about mentioning the fact to Reverend Timberlake, and having him read Roosevelt Alonzo Taylor Joiner out of the congregation of the Dirt's Avenue Methodist Church.

But that was before they found out the nature of Rat's mission.

For Rat entered the Rex just thirty minutes before the main feature was to go on, just when Tapper was preparing to rewind the film for Hopkinsville's first showing of *The Birth of a Nation*.

Rat knocked on the door of the prejection room, then came right to the matter at hand.

"Tapper," he said, "Mrs. Nixola Green has finally persuaded Cecelia to run off and marry Pat Slaker. They're up at Mrs. Nixola's house on First Street and they're going to head for Clarksville any minute. I know it ain't none of my business, but you always been fair to us and—"

Tapper waited to hear no more. He dashed out of the projection room and headed first for Mrs. Nixola's house on First Street.

Of course, Cecelia wasn't there; the whole family was over in Earlington, Kentucky, attending a family reunion.

But Tapper didn't know this. He rushed down to Irving's Livery Stable and rented the fastest horse and rig for an emergency dash to Clarksville, Tennessee, where he hoped to head off the nuptials.

Well, the downstairs section of the Rex Theatre was crowded

(with only Rat in the peanut gallery) before Mr. S. J. Bolton learned that Hopkinsville's only movie projectionist was no longer in the Rex Theatre. He tried to stall the showing for a half hour, but when Tapper didn't show up then, Mr. S. J. Bolton tried to run the machine himself.

Rat, who had decided to stay inside since he had paid an un-heard-of fifteen cents to be there anyway, explained to us later what happened.

"Tapper had started rewinding the film backward to get to the front," he said, "but Mr. S. J. Bolton didn't know that. So he picked up the first film roll he saw and started running it on that picture thing.

"Well, it turned out that it was the middle of the picture and backwards besides. So, instead of that colored gentleman (played by some white man) chasing that white lady off the top of the quarry, it started with the white lady at the bottom of the quarry. And she was leaping to the top of the quarry so that the colored gentleman (who was really a white man) could grab her.

"The white folks didn't see much of the picture, because Mr. S. J. Bolton yanked that part off so fast that he tore up the whole thing. I waited around another half hour and nothing else came on, so all of us went home."

So Hopkinsville, Kentucky, never got to see The Birth of a Nation. Mr. Max Kaplan came back the next day and substituted an-other film for The Birth of a Nation. There were always two schools of thought in the colored community after that—and even Papa couldn't settle the dispute.

One school held that Mr. Max Kaplan would never have let The Birth of a Nation be booked for the Rex if he had known anything about it and if he hadn't been in Los Angeles. And the other school contended that Mr. S. J. Bolton had so messed up the original print in trying to run it without Tapper that it couldn't have been shown anyway.

In any case, Mr. Max Kaplan took steps to see that a certain situation never obtained again. He had little Cecelia Penrod smuggled out of her house while Mrs. Nixola wasn't watching. And he took her and Tapper down to Judge Hezekiah Wither-spoon, who married both of them on the spot. Mrs. Nixola Green

collapsed at the news and went over to Clarksville, Tennessee, to
recuperate at the home of some of her high-yaller relatives.

When she came back she boasted that she had passed for
white and had seen *The Birth of a Nation* at the Princess Theatre
there.

"And it was a very good picture," she said, "I don't know what
all the fuss over here was about."

Willard Motley

WILLARD MOTLEY's *Knock on Any Door* was a best-selling novel in 1947 and later was made into a successful motion picture. This work, which brought acclaim to Mr. Motley, caused *The New York Times* to comment: "An extraordinary and powerful new naturalistic talent herewith makes its debut in American letters."

In his second and third novels, *We Fished All Night* (1951) and *Let No Man Write My Epitaph* (1958), Mr. Motley continued to write in the "environmentalist" tradition of Richard Wright, although his characters were not Negroes but Italian immigrants living and dying in the slums of Chicago. In these works there is protest but without considerations of race and racial conflict.

"The Almost White Boy" appears for the first time in this collection.

Willard Motley was born in Chicago but lived for a number of years in California, where he was a farm worker, waiter, shipping clerk, cook, and "coal hiker." Upon his return to Chicago he wrote articles for *The Commonweal* and other magazines and worked for the Federal Writers Project, studying living conditions in the Chicago Negro community.

Mr. Motley now makes his home in Mexico.

THE ALMOST WHITE BOY

BY WILLARD MOTLEY

By birth he was half Negro and half white. Socially he was all
Negro. That is when people knew that his mother was a brown-
skin woman with straightened hair and legs that didn't respect
the color line when it came to making men turn around to look at
them. His eyes were gray. His skin was as white as Slim Peterson's;
his blond hair didn't have any curl to it at all. His nose was big
and his lips were big—the only tip-off. Aunt Beulah-May said he
looked just like "poor white trash." Other people, black and white,
said all kinds of things about his parents behind their backs,
even if they were married. And these people, when it came to discussing him, shook their heads, made sucking sounds with their
tongues and said, "Too bad! Too bad!" And one straggly-haired
Irish woman who had taken quite a liking to him had even gone so
far as to tell him, blissfully unmindful of his desires in the matter,
"I'd have you marry my daughter if you was white."

One thing he remembered. When he was small his dad had
taken him up in his arms and carried him to the big oval mirror
in the parlor. "Come here, Lucy," his father had said, calling
Jimmy's mother. His mother came, smiling at the picture her two
men made hugged close together; one so little and dependent, the
other so tall and serious-eyed. She stood beside him straightening
Jimmy's collar and pushing his hair out of his eyes. Dad held him
in between them. "Look in the mirror, son," he said. And they all
looked. Their eyes were serious, not smiling, not staring, just
gloom-colored with seriousness in the mirror. "Look at your
mother . . . Look at me." His dad gave the directions gravely.
"Look at your mother's skin." He looked. That was the dear sweet
mother he loved. "Look at the color of my skin." He looked. That
was his daddy, the best daddy in the world. "We all love each
other, son, all three of us," his dad said, and his mother's eyes
in the mirror caught and held his father's with something shining

and proud through the seriousness; and his mother's arm stole up around him and around his daddy. "People are just people. Some are good and some are bad," his father said. "People are just people. Look—and remember." He had remembered. He would never forget.

Somehow, something of that day had passed into his life. And he carried it with him back and forth across the color line. The colored fellows he palled with called him "the white nigger," and his white pals would sometimes look at him kind of funny but they never said anything. Only when they went out on dates together; then they'd tell him don't let on you're colored. And sometimes when he was around they'd let something slip about "niggers" without meaning to. Then they'd look sheepish. Jim didn't see much difference. All the guys were swell if you liked them; all the girls flirted and necked and went on crying jags now and then. People were just people.

There were other things Jim remembered.

. . . On Fifty-eighth and Prairie. Lorenzo with white eyes in a black face. With his kinky hair screwed down tight on his bald-looking head like flies on flypaper. Ruby with her face all shiny brown and her hair in stiff-standing braids and her pipy brown legs Mom called raxor-legs. Lorenzo saying, "You're black just like us." Ruby singing out, "Yeah! Yeah! You're a white nigger—white nigger—white nigger!" Lorenzo taunting, "You ain't no different. My ma says so. You're just a nigger!" Lorenzo and Ruby pushing up close to him with threatening gestures, making faces at him, pulling his straight blond hair with mean fists, both yelling at the same time, "White nigger! White nigger!"

The name stuck.

. . . Women on the sidewalk in little groups. Their lips moving when he walked past with his schoolbooks under his arm. Their eyes lowered but looking at him. "Too bad! Too bad!" He could see them. He knew they were talking about him. "Too bad! Too bad!"

. . . Mom crying on the third floor of the kitchenette flat on Thirty-ninth Street. Mom saying to Dad, "We've got to move from here, Jim. We can't go on the street together without everybody staring at us. You'd think we'd killed somebody."

"What do we care how much they stare or what they say?"

"Even when I go out alone they stare. They never invite me to their houses. They say—they say that I think I'm better than they are—that I had to marry out of my race—that my own color wasn't good enough for me."

Dad saying, "Why can't people mind their own business? The hell with them." Mom crying. No friends. No company. Just the three of them.

. . . Then moving to the slums near Halstead and Maxwell, where all nationalities lived bundled up next door to each other and even in the same buildings. Jews. Mexicans. Poles. Negroes. Italians. Greeks. It was swell there. People changed races there. They went out on the streets together. No more staring. No more name-calling.

He grew up there.

. . . Getting older. And a lot of the white fellows not inviting him to parties at their houses when there were girls from the neighborhood. But they'd still go out of the neighborhood together and pick up girls or go on blind dates or to parties somewhere else. He didn't like to think of the neighborhood parties with the girls and the music and everything, and the door closed to him.

. . . Only once he denied it. He had been going around with Tony for a couple of weeks over on Racine Avenue. They played pool together, drank beer together on West Madison Street, drove around in Tony's old rattling Chevy. One day Tony looked at him funny and said, point-blank, "Say, what *are* you anyway?"

Jim got red; he could feel his face burn. "I'm Polish," he said.

He was sorry afterwards. He didn't know why he said it. He felt ashamed.

. . . Then he was finished with school and he had to go to work. He got a job in a downtown hotel because nobody knew what he really was and Aunt Beulah-May said it was all right to "pass for white" when it came to making money but he'd better never get any ideas in his head about turning his back on his people. To him it was cheating. It was denying half himself. It wasn't a straight front. He knew how hard it was for colored fellows to find decent jobs. It wasn't saying I'm a Negro and taking the same chances they took when it came to getting a job. But he did it.

Jim remembered many of these things; they were tied inside of him in hard knots. But the color line didn't exist for him and he came and went pretty much as he chose. He took the girls in stride. He went to parties on the South Side, on Thirty-fifth and Michigan, on South Park. He went dancing at the Savoy Ballroom—and the Trianon. He went to Polish hops and Italian *fiestas* and Irish weddings. And he had a hell of a swell time. People were just people.

He had fun with the colored girls. But some of them held off from him, not knowing what he was. These were his people. No—he didn't feel natural around them. And with white people he wasn't all himself either. He didn't have any people.

Then all of a sudden he was madly in love with Cora. This had never happened before. He had sometimes wondered if, when it came, it would be a white girl or a colored girl. Now it was here. There was nothing he could do about it. And he was scared. He began to worry, and to wonder. And he began to wish, although ashamed to admit it to himself, that he didn't have any colored blood in him.

He met Cora at a dance at the Trianon. Cora's hair wasn't as blond as his but it curled all over her head. Her skin was pink and soft. Her breasts stood erect and her red lips were parted in a queer little loose way. They were always like that. And they were always moist-looking.

Leo introduced them. Then he let them alone and they danced every dance together; and when it was time to go home Leo had disappeared. Jim asked her if he could take her home.

"I think that would be awfully sweet of you," she said. Her eyes opened wide in a baby-blue smile.

She leaned back against him a little when he helped her into her coat. He flushed with the pleasure of that brief touching of their bodies. They walked through the unwinding ballroom crowd together, not having anything to say to each other, and out onto Cottage Grove, still not having anything to say. As they passed the lighted-up plate-glass window of Walgreen's drugstore Jim asked her, "Wouldn't you like a malted milk?" She didn't answer but just smiled up at him over her shoulder and he felt the softness of her arm in the doorway.

She sipped her malted milk. He sat stirring his straw around in his glass. Once in a while she'd look up over her glass and wrinkle her lips or her eyes at him, friendly-like. Neither of them said anything. Then, when Cora had finished, he held the match for her cigarette and their eyes came together and stayed that way longer than they needed to. And her lips were really parted now with the cigarette smoke curling up into her hair.

In front of her house they stood close together, neither of them wanting to go.

"It was a nice dance," Cora said; and her fingers played in the hedge-top.

"Yes, especially after I met you."

"I'm going to see you again, aren't I?" Cora asked, looking up at him a little.

Jim looked down at the sidewalk. He hoped he could keep the red out of his cheeks. "I might as well tell you before someone else does—I'm a Negro," he said.

There was a catch in her voice, just a little noise not made of words.

"Oh, you're fooling!" she said with a small, irritated laugh.

"No I'm not. I told you because I like you."

She had stepped back from him. Her eyes were searching for the windows of the house to see that there was no light behind the shades.

"Please, let me see you again," Jim said.

Her eyes, satisfied, came away from the windows. They looked at the sidewalk where he had looked. Her body was still withdrawn. Her lips weren't parted now. There were hard little lines at the corners of her mouth.

"Let me meet you somewhere," Jim said.

Another furtive glance at the house; then she looked at him, unbelievingly. "You didn't mean that—about being colored?"

"It doesn't matter, does it?"

"No—only—"

"Let me meet you somewhere," Jim begged.

Her lips were parted a little. She looked at him strangely, deep into him in a way that made him tremble, then down his body and back up into his eyes. She tossed her head a little. "Well—call me up tomorrow afternoon." She gave him the number.

He watched her go into the house. Then he walked to the corner to wait for his streetcar; and he kicked at the sidewalk and clenched his fists.

Jim went to meet her in Jackson Park. They walked around. She was beautiful in her pink dress. Her lips were pouted a little bit, and her eyes were averted, and she was everything he had ever wanted. They sat on a bench far away from anybody. "You know," she said, "I never liked nig— Negroes. You're not like a Negro at all." They walked to the other end of the park. "Why do you *tell* people?" she asked.

"People are just people," he told her, but the words didn't sound real any more.

Twice again he met her in the park. Once they just sat talking and once they went to a movie. Both times he walked her to the car line and left her there. That was the way she wanted it.

After that it was sneaking around to meet her. She didn't like to go on dates with him when he had his white friends along. She'd never tell him why. And yet she put her body up close to him when they were alone. It was all right too when she invited some of her friends who didn't know what he was.

They saw a lot of each other. And pretty soon he thought from the long, probing looks she gave him that she must like him; from the way she'd grab his hand, tight, sometimes; from the way she danced with him. She even had him take her home now and they'd stand on her porch pressed close together. "Cora, I want you to come over to my house," he told her. "My mother and father are swell. You'll like them." He could see all four of them together. "It isn't a nice neighborhood. I mean it doesn't look good, but the people are nicer than—in other places. Gee, you'll like my mother and father."

"All right, I'll go, Jimmy. I don't care. I don't care."

Dad kidded him about his new flame, saying it must be serious, that he had never brought a girl home before. Mom made fried chicken and hot biscuits. And when he went to get Cora he saw Dad and Mom both with dust rags, shining up everything in the parlor for the tenth time; he heard Dad and Mom laughing quietly together and talking about their first date.

He hadn't told them she was a white girl. But they never batted an eye.

"Mom, this is Cora."

"How do you do, dear. Jimmy has told us so much about you." Dear, sweet Mom. Always gracious and friendly.

"Dad, this is Cora." Dad grinning, looking straight at her with eyes as blue as hers, going into some crazy story about "Jimmy at the age of three." Good old Dad. "People are just people."

Dad and Mom were at ease. Only Cora seemed embarrassed. And she was nervous, not meeting Dad's eyes, not meeting Mom's eyes, looking to him for support. She sat on the edge of her chair. "Y-y-yes sir . . . No, Mrs. Warner." She only picked at the good food Mom had spent all afternoon getting ready. And Jim, watching her, watching Dad and Mom, hoping they wouldn't notice, got ill at ease himself and he was glad when he got her outside. Then they were themselves again.

"Mom and Dad are really swell. You'll have to get to know them," he said, looking at her appealingly, asking for approval. She smiled with expressionless eyes. She said nothing.

On Fourteenth and Halstead they met Slick Harper. Slick was as black as they come. It was sometimes hard, because of his southern dialect and his Chicago black-belt expressions, to know just what he meant in English. He practiced jitterbug steps on street corners and had a whole string of girls—black, brown-skin, high-yellow. Everybody called him Slick because he handed his bevy of girls a smooth line and because he wore all the latest fashions in men's clothes—high-waisted trousers, big-brimmed hats, bright sports coats, Cuban heels and coconut straws with gaudy bands. Slick hailed Jim; his eyes gave Cora the once-over.

"Whatcha say, man!" he shouted. "Ah know they all goes when the wagon comes but where you been stuck away? And no jive! Man, ah been lookin' for you. We're throwing a party next Saturday and we want you to come."

Jim stood locked to the sidewalk, working his hands in his

pockets and afraid to look at Cora. He watched Slick's big purple lips move up and down as they showed the slices of white teeth. Now Slick had stopped talking and was staring at Cora with a black-faced smirk.

"Cora, this is Slick Harper."

"How do you do." Her voice came down as from the top of a building.

"Ah'm glad to meetcha," Slick said. "You sho' got good taste, Jim." His eyes took in her whole figure. "Why don't you bring her to the party?"

"Maybe I will. Well, we've got to go." He walked fast then to keep up with Cora.

Cora never came over again.

Cora had him come over to her house. But first she prepared him a lot. "Don't ever—*ever*—tell my folks you're colored. Please, Jimmy. Promise me. . . . Father doesn't like colored people. . . . They aren't broad-minded like me. . . . And don't mind Father, Jimmy," she warned.

He went. There was a cream-colored car outside the house. In the parlor were smoking stands, and knickknack brackets, and a grand piano nobody played. Cora's father smoked cigars, owned a few pieces of stock, went to Florida two weeks every winter, told stories about the "Florida niggers." Cora's mother had the same parted lips Cora had, but she breathed through them heavily as if she were always trying to catch up with herself. She was fat and overdressed. And admonished her husband when he told his southern stories through the smoke of big cigars: "Now, Harry, you mustn't talk like that. What will this nice young man think of you? There are plenty of fine upright Negroes—I'm sure. Of course I don't know any personally. . . . Now, Harry, don't be so harsh. Don't forget, you took milk from a colored mammy's breast. . . . Oh, Harry, tell them about the little darky who wanted to watch your car—'Two cents a awah, Mistah No'then'ah!' "

Cora sat with her hands in her lap and her fingers laced tightly together. Jim smiled at Mr. Hartley's jokes and had a miserable time. And Jim discovered that it was best not to go to anybody's house. Just the two of them.

Jim and Cora went together for four months. And they had an awful time of it. But they were unhappy apart. Yet when they were together their eyes were always accusing each other. Sometimes they seemed to enjoy hurting each other. Jim wouldn't call her up; and he'd be miserable. She wouldn't write to him or would stand him up on a date for Chuck Nelson or Fred Schultz; then she'd be miserable. Something held them apart. And something pulled them together.

Jim did a lot of thinking. It had to go four revolutions. Four times a part-Negro had to marry a white person before legally you were white. The blood had to take four revolutions. Mulatto —that's what he was—quadroon—octaroon—then it was all gone. Then you were white. His great-grandchildren maybe. Four times the blood had to let in the other blood.

Then one night they were driving out to the forest preserves in Tony's Chevy. "What are you thinking, Jimmy?"

"Oh, nothing. Just thinking."

"Do you like my new dress? How do I look in it?"

"Isn't that a keen moon, Cora?" The car slid along the dark, deserted highway. They came to a gravel road and Jim eased the car over the crushed stone in second gear. Cora put her cheek against the sleeve of his coat. The branches of trees made scraping sounds against the sides of the car. Cora was closer to him now. He could smell the perfume in her hair and yellow strands tickled the end of his nose. He stopped the motor and switched the lights off. Cora lifted his arm up over her head and around her, putting his hand in close to her waist with her hand over his, stroking his. "Let's sit here like this—close and warm," she whispered. Then her voice lost itself in the breast of his coat.

For a long time they sat like that. Then Jim said, "Let's take a walk." He opened the door and, half supporting her, he lifted her out. While she was still in his arms she bit his ear gently.

"Don't do that," he said, and she giggled.

Panting, they walked through the low scrub into the woods. The bushes scratched their arms. Twigs caught in Cora's hair. Their feet sank in the earth. Cora kept putting her fingers in Jim's hair and mussing it. "Don't. Don't," he said. And finally he caught her fingers and held them tight in his. They walked on like this. The moon made silhouettes of them, silhouettes climbing up the slow incline of hill.

Jim found a little rise of land, treeless, grassy. Far to the northeast Chicago sprawled, row on row of dim lights growing more numerous but gentler.

The night was over them.

They sat on the little hillock, shoulder to shoulder; and Cora moved her body close to him. It was warm there against his shirt, open at the neck. They didn't talk. They didn't move. And when Cora breathed he could feel the movement of her body against him. It was almost as if they were one. He looked up at the splash of stars, and the moon clouding over. His arm went around her, shieldingly. He closed his eyes and put his face into her hair. "Cora! Cora!" The only answer she gave was the slight movement of her body.

"Cora, I love you."

"Do you, Jimmy?" she said, snuggling up so close to him that he could feel her heart beat against him.

He didn't move. But after a while she was slowly leaning back until the weight of her carried him back too and they lay full length. They lay like this a long time. He looked at her. Her eyes were closed. She was breathing hard. Her lips were parted and moist.

"Jimmy."

"What?"

"Nothing."

She hooked one of her feet over his. A slow quiver started in his shoulders, worked its way down the length of him. He sat up. Cora sat up.

"There's nobody here but us," she said. Her fingers unbuttoned the first button on his shirt, the second. Her fingers crept in on his chest, playing with the little hairs there.

"There's nobody here but us," she said, and she ran her fingers inside his shirt, over his shoulders and the back of his neck.

"We can't do this, Cora. We can't."

"Do you mean about you being colored? It doesn't matter to me, Jimmy. Honest it doesn't."

"No. Not that. It's because I love you. That's why I can't. That's why I want—"

He sat up straight then. His fingers pulled up some grass. He held it up to the light and looked at it. She had her head in his lap and lay there perfectly still. He could hear her breathing, and her breath was warm and moist on the back of his other hand where it lay on his leg. He threw the grass away, watched how the wind took it and lowered it down to the ground. He lifted her up by the shoulders, gently, until they were close together, looking into each other's eyes.

"I want it to be right for us, Cora," he said. "Will you marry me?"

The sting of red in her cheeks looked as if a blow had left it there; even the moonlight showed that. She sat up without the support of his hands. Her arms were straight and tense under her. Her eyes met his, burning angrily at the softness in his eyes. "You damn dirty nigger!" she said, and jumped up and walked away from him as fast as she could.

When she was gone he lay on his face where he had been sitting. He lay full length. The grass he had pulled stuck to his lips. "People are just people." He said it aloud. "People are just people." And he laughed, hoarsely, hollowly. "People are just people." Then it was only a half-laugh with a sob cutting into it. And he was crying, with his arms flung up wildly above his head, with his face pushed into the grass trying to stop the sound of his crying. Off across the far grass Cora was running away from him. The moon, bright now, lacquered the whiteness of his hands lying helplessly above his head; it touched the blondness of his hair.

James Baldwin

JAMES BALDWIN was born in New York in 1924, the eldest of nine children; his father was a clergyman in Harlem.

The narrative that follows is from Mr. Baldwin's first novel, *Go Tell It on the Mountain*, published in 1953. His other novels are *Giovanni's Room* (1956) and *Another Country* (1962).

Go Tell It on the Mountain, the intense story of family and religious experience in Harlem, was hailed by critics as "beautiful, fierce, extraordinary, powerful." Lionel Trilling wrote that *Go Tell It on the Mountain* "was autobiographical, and this story of a family emigrated from the South to Harlem certainly had its sense of a public issue in its due awareness of the bitterness of Negro life. Yet what made the book notable in its time was its bold assertion that it existed as a literary entity, as something more than a 'social document.' . . . by his concern with style, by his commitment to delicacy of perception, he insisted that his novel was not validated by its subject—to which every ordinarily moral reader was required to respond because it adumbrated a great national injustice—but by the writer's particular treatment of his subject. In making this insistence Mr. Baldwin laid claim not merely to some decent minimum of social rationality, but to all the possible fullness of life, to whatever in art and culture was vivacious, beautiful, and interesting."

In 1946, James Baldwin left the United States to live in Europe. Commenting on this, he stated: "I doubted my ability to survive the fury of the color problem here. (Sometimes I still do.) I wanted to prevent myself from becoming merely a Negro, or even, merely a Negro writer!"

After more than a decade in Europe he returned to the United States. Mr. Baldwin observed: "One day it begins to be borne in on the writer, and with great force, that he is living in Europe as an American. It may be the day someone asks him to explain Little Rock and he begins to feel that it would be simpler—and, corny as the words may sound, more honorable—to go to Little Rock than sit in Europe, on an American passport, trying to explain it. . . . It is the day he realizes that if he has been preparing himself for anything in Europe, he has been preparing himself— for America."

THE SEVENTH DAY

From *Go Tell It on the Mountain*

BY JAMES BALDWIN

> *I looked down the line,*
> *And I wondered.*

Everyone had always said that John would be a preacher when he grew up, just like his father. It had been said so often that John, without ever thinking about it, had come to believe it himself. Not until the morning of his fourteenth birthday did he really begin to think about it, and by then it was already too late.

His earliest memories—which were, in a way, his only memories —were of the hurry and brightness of Sunday mornings. They all rose together on that day; his father, who did not have to go to work, and led them in prayer before breakfast; his mother, who dressed up on that day, and looked almost young, with her hair straightened, and on her head the close-fitting white cap that was the uniform of holy women; his younger brother, Roy, who was silent that day because his father was home. Sarah, who wore a red ribbon in her hair that day, and was fondled by her father. And the baby, Ruth, who was dressed in pink and white, and rode in her mother's arms to church.

The church was not very far away, four blocks up Lenox Avenue, on a corner not far from the hospital. It was to this hospital that his mother had gone when Roy, and Sarah, and Ruth were born. John did not remember very clearly the first time she had gone, to have Roy; folks said that he had cried and carried on the whole time his mother was away; he remembered only enough to be afraid every time her belly began to swell, knowing that each time the swelling began it would not end until she was taken from him, to come back with a stranger. Each time this happened she became a little more of a stranger herself. She would soon be going away again, Roy said—he knew much more about such things than John. John had observed his mother closely, seeing no swelling yet, but his father had prayed one morning for the "little voyager soon to be among them," and so John knew that Roy spoke the truth.

Every Sunday morning, then, since John could remember, they had taken to the streets, the Grimes family on their way to church. Sinners along the avenue watched them—men still wearing their Saturday-night clothes, wrinkled and dusty now, muddy-eyed and muddy-faced; and women with harsh voices and tight, bright dresses, cigarettes between their fingers or held tightly in the corners of their mouths. They talked, and laughed, and fought together, and the women fought like the men. John and Roy, passing these men and women, looked at one another briefly, John embarrassed and Roy amused. Roy would be like them when he grew up, if the Lord did not change his heart. These men and women they passed on Sunday mornings had spent the night in bars, or in cat houses, or on the streets, or on rooftops, or under the stairs. They had been drinking. They had gone from cursing to laughter, to anger, to lust. Once he and Roy had watched a man and woman in the basement of a condemned house. They did it standing up. The woman had wanted fifty cents, and the man had flashed a razor.

John had never watched again; he had been afraid. But Roy

had watched them many times, and he told John he had done it with some girls down the block.

And his mother and father, who went to church on Sundays, they did it too, and sometimes John heard them in the bedroom behind him, over the sound of rats' feet, and rat screams, and the music and cursing from the harlot's house downstairs.

Their church was called the *Temple of the Fire Baptized*. It was not the biggest church in Harlem, nor yet the smallest, but John had been brought up to believe it was the holiest and best. His father was head deacon in this church—there were only two, the other a round, black man named Deacon Braithwaite—and he took up the collection, and sometimes he preached. The pastor, Father James, was a genial, well-fed man with a face like a darker moon. It was he who preached on Pentecost Sundays, and led revivals in the summertime, and anointed and healed the sick.

On Sunday mornings and Sunday nights the church was always full; on special Sundays it was full all day. The Grimes family arrived in a body, always a little late, usually in the middle of Sunday school, which began at nine o'clock. This lateness was always their mother's fault—at least in the eyes of their father; she could not seem to get herself and the children ready on time, ever, and sometimes she actually remained behind, not to appear until the morning service. When they all arrived together, they separated upon entering the doors, father and mother going to sit in the Adult Class, which was taught by Sister McCandless, Sarah going to the Infant's Class, John and Roy sitting in the Intermediate, which was taught by Brother Elisha.

When he was young, John had paid no attention in Sunday school, and always forgot the golden text, which earned him the wrath of his father. Around the time of his fourteenth birthday, with all the pressures of church and home uniting to drive him to the altar, he strove to appear more serious and therefore less conspicuous. But he was distracted by his new teacher, Elisha, who was the pastor's nephew and who had but lately arrived from Georgia. He was not much older than John, only seventeen, and he was already saved and was a preacher. John stared at Elisha all during the lesson, admiring the timbre of Elisha's voice, much deeper and manlier than his own, admiring the leanness, and grace, and strength, and darkness of Elisha in his Sunday suit, wondering if he would ever be holy as Elisha was holy. But he did not follow the lesson, and when, sometimes, Elisha paused to ask John a question, John was ashamed and confused, feeling the palms of his hands become wet and his heart pound like a hammer. Elisha would smile and reprimand him gently, and the lesson would go on.

Roy never knew his Sunday school lesson either, but it was different with Roy—no one really expected of Roy what was expected of John. Everyone was always praying that the Lord would change Roy's heart, but it was John who was expected to be good, to be a good example.

When Sunday school service ended there was a short pause before morning service began. In this pause, if it was good weather, the old folks might step outside a moment to talk among themselves. The sisters would almost always be dressed in white from crown to toe. The small children, on this day, in this place, and oppressed by their elders, tried hard to play without seeming to be disrespectful of God's house. But sometimes, nervous or perverse, they shouted, or threw hymn-books, or began to cry, putting their parents, men or women of God, under the necessity of proving— by harsh means or tender—who, in a sanctified household, ruled. The older children, like John or Roy, might wander down the avenue, but not too far. Their father never let John and Roy out of his sight, for Roy had often disappeared between Sunday school and morning service and had not come back all day.

The Sunday morning service began when Brother Elisha sat down at the piano and raised a song. This moment and this music had been with John, so it seemed, since he had first drawn breath. It seemed that there had never been a time when he had not known this moment of waiting while the packed church paused— the sisters in white, heads raised, the brothers in blue, heads back; the white caps of the women seeming to glow in the charged air like crowns, the kinky, gleaming heads of the men seeming to be lifted up—and the rustling and the whispering ceased and the children were quiet; perhaps someone coughed, or the sound of a car horn, or a curse from the streets came in; then Elisha hit the keys, beginning at once to sing, and everybody joined him, clapping their hands, and rising, and beating the tambourines.

The song might be: *Down at the cross where my Saviour died!*

Or: *Jesus, I'll never forget how you set me free!*

Or: *Lord, hold my hand while I run this race!*

They sang with all the strength that was in them, and clapped their hands for joy. There had never been a time when John had not sat watching the saints rejoice with terror in his heart, and wonder. Their singing caused him to believe in the presence of the Lord; indeed, it was no longer a question of belief, because they made that presence real. He did not feel it himself, the joy they felt, yet he could not doubt that it was, for them, the very bread of life—could not doubt it, that is, until it was too late to doubt. Something happened to their faces and their voices, the rhythm of their bodies, and to the air they breathed; it was as though wherever they might be became the upper room, and the Holy Ghost were riding on the air. His father's face, always awful, became more awful now; his father's daily anger was transformed into prophetic wrath. His mother, her eyes raised to heaven, hands arched before her, moving, made real for John that patience, that endurance, that long-suffering, which he had read of in the Bible and found so hard to imagine.

On Sunday mornings the women all seemed patient, all the men seemed mighty. While John watched, the Power struck someone, a man or woman; they cried out, a long, wordless crying, and, arms outstretched like wings, they began the Shout. Someone moved a chair a little to give them room, the rhythm paused, the singing stopped, only the pounding of feet and the clapping hands were heard; then another cry, another dancer; then the tambourines began again, and the voices rose again, and the music swept on again, like fire, or flood, or judgment. Then the church seemed to swell with the Power it held, and, like a planet rocking in space, the temple rocked with the Power of God. John watched, watched the faces, and the weightless bodies, and listened to the timeless cries. One day, so everyone said, this Power would possess him; he would sing and cry as they did now, and dance before his King. He watched young Ella Mae Washington, the seventeen-year-old granddaughter of Praying Mother Washington, as she began to dance. And then Elisha danced.

At one moment, head thrown back, eyes closed, sweat standing on his brow, he sat at the piano, singing and playing; and then, like a great, black cat in trouble in the jungle, he stiffened and trembled, and cried out. *Jesus, Jesus, oh Lord Jesus!* He struck on the piano one last, wild note, and threw up his hands, palms upward, stretched wide apart. The tambourines raced to fill the vacuum left by his silent piano, and his cry drew answering cries. Then he was on his feet, turning, blind, his face congested, contorted with this rage, and the muscles leaping and swelling in his long, dark neck. It seemed that he could not breathe, that his body could not contain this passion, that he would be, before their eyes, dispersed into the waiting air. His hands, rigid to the very fingertips, moved outward and back against his hips, his sightless eyes looked upward, and he began to dance. Then his hands closed into fists, and his head snapped downward, his sweat loosening the grease that slicked down his hair; and the rhythm of all the others quickened to match Elisha's rhythm; his thighs moved terribly against the cloth of his suit, his heels beat on the floor, and his fists moved beside his body as though he were beating his own drum. And so, for a while, in the center of the dancers, head down, fists beating, on, on, unbearably, until it seemed the walls of the church would fall for very sound; and then, in a moment, with a cry, head up, arms high in the air, sweat pouring from his forehead, and all his body dancing as though it would never stop. Sometimes he did not stop until he fell—until he dropped like some animal felled by a hammer—moaning, on his face. And then a great moaning filled the church.

There was sin among them. One Sunday, when regular service was over, Father James had uncovered sin in the congregation of the righteous. He had uncovered Elisha and Ella Mae. They had been "walking disorderly"; they were in danger of straying from the truth. And as Father James spoke of the sin that he knew they had not committed yet, of the unripe fig plucked too early from the tree—to set the children's teeth on edge—John felt himself grow dizzy in his seat and could not look at Elisha where he stood, beside Ella Mae, before the altar. Elisha hung his head as Father James spoke, and the congregation murmured. And Ella Mae was not so beautiful now as she was when she was singing and testifying, but looked like a sullen, ordinary girl. Her full lips were loose and her eyes were black—with shame, or rage, or both. Her grandmother, who had raised her, sat watching quietly, with folded hands. She was one of the pillars of the church, a powerful evangelist and very widely known. She said nothing in Ella Mae's defense, for she must have felt, as the congregation felt, that Father James was only exercising his clear and painful duty; he was responsible, after all, for Elisha, as Praying Mother Washington was responsible for Ella Mae. It was not an easy thing, said Father James, to be the pastor of a flock. It might look easy to just sit up there in the pulpit night after night, year in, year out, but let them remember the awful responsibility placed on his shoulders by almighty God—let them remember that God would ask an accounting of him one day for every soul in his flock. Let them remember this when they thought he was hard, let them remember that the Word was hard, that the way of holiness was a hard way. There was no room in God's army for the coward heart, no crown awaiting him who put mother, or father, sister, or brother, sweetheart, or friend above God's will. Let the church cry amen to this! And they cried: "Amen! Amen!"

The Lord had led him, said Father James, looking down on the boy and girl before him, to give them a public warning before it was too late. For he knew them to be sincere young people, dedicated to the service of the Lord—it was only that, since they were young, they did not know the pitfalls Satan laid for the unwary. He knew that sin was not in their minds—not yet; yet sin was in the flesh; and should they continue with their walking out alone together, their secrets and laughter, and touching of hands, they would surely sin a sin beyond all forgiveness. And John wondered what Elisha was thinking—Elisha, who was tall and handsome, who played basketball, and who had been saved at the age of eleven in the improbable fields down South. *Had* he sinned? Had he been tempted? And the girl beside him, whose white robes now seemed the merest, thinnest covering for the nakedness of breasts and insistent thighs—what was her face like when she was alone with Elisha, with no singing, when they were not surrounded by the saints? He was afraid to think of it, yet he could think of nothing else; and the fever of which they stood accused began also to rage in him.

After this Sunday, Elisha and Ella Mae no longer met each other each day after school, no longer spent Saturday afternoons wandering through Central Park, or lying on the beach. All that was over for them. If they came together again it would be in wedlock. They would have children and raise them in the church.

This was what was meant by a holy life, this was what the way of the cross demanded. It was somehow on that Sunday, a Sunday shortly before his birthday, that John first realized that this was the life awaiting him—realized it consciously, as something no longer far off, but imminent, coming closer day by day.

John's birthday fell on a Saturday in March, in 1935. He awoke on this birthday morning with the feeling that there was menace in the air around him—that something irrevocable had occurred in him. He stared at a yellow stain on the ceiling just above his head. Roy was still smothered in the bedclothes, and his breath came and went with a small, whistling sound. There was no other sound anywhere; no one in the house was up. The neighbors' radios were all silent, and his mother hadn't yet risen to fix his father's breakfast. John wondered at his panic, then wondered about the time; and then (while the yellow stain on the ceiling slowly transformed itself into a woman's nakedness) he remembered that it was his fourteenth birthday and that he had sinned.

His first thought, nevertheless, was: "Will anyone remember?" For it had happened, once or twice, that his birthday had passed entirely unnoticed, and no one had said "Happy birthday, Johnny," or given him anything—not even his mother.

Roy stirred again and John pushed him away, listening to the silence. On other mornings he awoke hearing his mother singing in the kitchen, hearing his father in the bedroom behind him grunting and muttering prayers to himself as he put on his clothes; hearing, perhaps, the chatter of Sarah and the squalling of Ruth, and the radios, the clatter of pots and pans, and the voices of all the folk near by. This morning not even the cry of a bedspring disturbed the silence, and John seemed, therefore, to be listening to his own unspeaking doom. He could believe, almost, that he had awakened late on that great getting-up morning; that all the saved had been transformed in the twinkling of an eye, and had risen to meet Jesus in the clouds, and that he was left, with his sinful body, to be bound in hell a thousand years.

He had sinned. In spite of the saints, his mother and his father, the warnings he had heard from his earliest beginnings, he had sinned with his hands a sin that was hard to forgive. In the school lavatory, alone, thinking of the boys, older, bigger, braver, who made bets with each other as to whose urine could arch higher, he had watched in himself a transformation of which he would never dare to speak.

And the darkness of John's sin was like the darkness of the church on Saturday evenings; like the silence of the church while he was there alone, sweeping, and running water into the great bucket, and overturning chairs, long before the saints arrived. It was like his thoughts as he moved about the tabernacle in which his life had been spent; the tabernacle that he hated, yet loved and feared. It was like Roy's curses, like the echoes these curses raised in John: he remembered Roy, on some rare Saturday when he had come to help John clean the church, cursing in the house of God, and making obscene gestures before the eyes of Jesus. It was like all this, and it was like the walls that witnessed and the placards on the walls which testified that the wages of sin was death. The darkness of his sin was in the hardheartedness with which he resisted God's power; in the scorn that was often his while he listened to the crying, breaking voices, and watched the black skin glisten while they lifted up their arms and fell on their faces before the Lord. For he had made his decision. He would not be like his father, or his father's fathers. He would have another life.

For John excelled in school, though not, like Elisha, in mathematics or basketball, and it was said that he had a Great Future. He might become a Great Leader of His People. John was not much interested in his people and still less in leading them anywhere, but the phrase so often repeated rose in his mind like a great brass gate, opening outward for him on a world where people did not live in the darkness of his father's house, did not pray to Jesus in the darkness of his father's church, where he would eat good food, and wear fine clothes, and go to the movies as often as he wished. In this world John, who was, his father said, ugly, who was always the smallest boy in his class, and who had no friends, became immediately beautiful, tall, and popular. People fell all over themselves to meet John Grimes. He was a poet, or a college president, or a movie star; he drank expensive whisky, and he smoked Lucky Strike cigarettes in the green package.

It was not only colored people who praised John, since they could not, John felt, in any case really know; but white people also said it, in fact had said it first and said it still. It was when John was five years old and in the first grade that he was first noticed; and since he was noticed by an eye altogether alien and impersonal, he began to perceive, in wild uneasiness, his individual existence.

They were learning the alphabet that day, and six children at a time were sent to the blackboard to write the letters they had memorized. Six had finished and were waiting for the teacher's judgment when the back door opened and the school principal, of whom everyone was terrified, entered the room. No one spoke or moved. In the silence the principal's voice said:

"Which child is that?"

She was pointing at the blackboard, at John's letters. The possibility of being distinguished by her notice did not enter John's mind, and so he simply stared at her. Then he realized, by the immobility of the other children and by the way they avoided looking at him, that it was he who was selected for punishment.

"Speak up, John," said the teacher, gently.

On the edge of tears, he mumbled his name and waited. The principal, a woman with white hair and an iron face, looked down at him.

"You're a very bright boy, John Grimes," she said. "Keep up the good work."

Then she walked out of the room.

That moment gave him, from that time on, if not a weapon at least a shield; he apprehended totally, without belief or understanding, that he had in himself a power that other people lacked; that he could use this to save himself, to raise himself; and that, perhaps, with this power he might one day win that love which he so longed for. This was not, in John, a faith subject to death or alteration, nor yet a hope subject to destruction; it was his identity, and part, therefore of that wickedness for which his father

beat him and to which he clung in order to withstand his
father. His fathers' arm, rising and falling, might make him cry,
and that voice might cause him to tremble; yet his father could
never be entirely the victor, for John cherished something that his
father could not reach. It was his hatred and his intelligence that
he cherished, the one feeding the other. He lived for the day
when his father would be dying and he, John, would curse him on
his deathbed. And this was why, though he had been born in
the faith and had been surrounded all his life by the saints and by
their prayers and their rejoicing, and though the tabernacle in
which they worshipped was more completely real to him than the
several precarious homes in which he and his family had lived,
John's heart was hardened against the Lord. His father was God's
minister, the ambassador of the King of Heaven, and John could
not bow before the throne of grace without first kneeling to his
father. On his refusal to do this had his life depended, and John's
secret heart had flourished in its wickedness until the day his sin
first overtook him.

In the midst of all his wonderings he fell asleep again, and when
he woke up this time and got out of bed his father had gone to
the factory, where he would work for half a day. Roy was sitting
in the kitchen, quarreling with their mother. The baby, Ruth, sat
in her high chair banging on the tray with an oatmeal-covered
spoon. This meant that she was in a good mood; she would not
spend the day howling, for reasons known only to herself, allowing
no one but her mother to touch her. Sarah was quiet, not chattering today, or at any rate not yet, and stood near the stove, arms
folded, staring at Roy with the flat black eyes, her father's eyes,
that made her look so old.

Their mother, her head tied up in an old rag, sipped black
coffee and watched Roy. The pale end-of-winter sunlight filled
the room and yellowed all their faces; and John, drugged and
morbid and wondering how it was that he had slept again and had
been allowed to sleep so long, saw them for a moment like figures
on a screen, an effect that the yellow light intensified. The room
was narrow and dirty; nothing could alter its dimensions, no labor
could ever make it clean. Dirt was in the walls and the floorboards,

and triumphed beneath the sink where roaches spawned; was in the fine ridges of the pots and pans, scoured daily, burnt black on the bottom, hanging above the stove; was in the wall against which they hung, and revealed itself where the paint had cracked and leaned outward in stiff squares and fragments, the paper-thin underside webbed with black. Dirt was in every corner, angle, crevice of the monstrous stove, and lived behind it in delirious communion with the corrupted wall. Dirt was in the baseboard that John scrubbed every Saturday, and roughened the cupboard shelves that held the cracked and gleaming dishes. Under this dark weight the walls leaned, under it the ceiling, with a great crack like lightning in its center, sagged. The windows gleamed like beaten gold or silver, but now John saw, in the yellow light, how fine dust veiled their doubtful glory. Dirt crawled in the gray mop hung out of the windows to dry. John thought with shame and horror, yet in angry hardness of heart: *He who is filthy, let him be filthy still.* Then he looked at his mother, seeing, as though she were someone else, the dark, hard lines running downward from her eyes, and the deep, perpetual scowl in her forehead, and the downturned, tightened mouth, and the strong, thin, brown, and bony hands; and the phrase turned against him like a two-edged sword, for was it not he, in his false pride and his evil imagination, who was filthy? Through a storm of tears that did not reach his eyes, he stared at the yellow room; and the room shifted, the light of the sun darkened, and his mother's face changed. Her face became the face that he gave her in his dreams, the face that had been hers in a photograph he had seen once, long ago, a photograph taken before he was born. This face was young and proud, uplifted, with a smile that made the wide mouth beautiful and glowed in the enormous eyes. It was the face of a girl who knew that no evil could undo her, and who could laugh, surely, as his mother did not laugh now. Between the two faces there stretched a darkness and a mystery that John feared, and that sometimes caused him to hate her.

Now she saw him and she asked, breaking off her conversation with Roy: "You hungry, little sleepyhead?"

"Well! About time you was getting up," said Sarah.

He moved to the table and sat down, feeling the most bewilder-

ing panic of his life, a need to touch things, the table and chairs
and the walls of the room, to make certain that the room existed
and that he was in the room. He did not look at his mother, who
stood up and went to the stove to heat his breakfast. But he asked,
in order to say something to her, and to hear his own voice:

"What we got for breakfast?"

He realized, with some shame, that he was hoping she had prepared a special breakfast for him on his birthday.

"What you *think* we got for breakfast?" Roy asked scornfully.
"You got a special craving for something?"

John looked at him. Roy was not in a good mood.

"I ain't said nothing to you," he said.

"Oh, I *beg* your pardon," said Roy, in the shrill, little-girl tone
he knew John hated.

"What's the *matter* with you today?" John asked, angry, and
trying at the same time to lend his voice as husky a pitch as possible.

"Don't you let Roy bother you," said their mother. "He cross as
two sticks this morning."

"Yeah," said John, "I reckon." He and Roy watched each other.
Then his plate was put before him: hominy grits and a scrap of
bacon. He wanted to cry, like a child: "But, Mama, it's my birthday!" He kept his eyes on his plate and began to eat.

"You can *talk* about your daddy all you want to," said his
mother, picking up her battle with Roy, "but *one* thing you can't
say—you can't say he ain't always done his best to be a father to
you and to see to it that you ain't never gone hungry."

"I been hungry plenty of times," Roy said, proud to be able to
score this point against his mother.

"Wasn't *his* fault, then. Wasn't because he wasn't *trying* to feed
you. That man shoveled snow in zero weather when he ought've
been in bed just to put food in your belly."

"Wasn't just *my* belly," said Roy indignantly. "He got a belly,
too, I *know*—it's a *shame* the way that man eats. I sure ain't asked
him to shovel no snow for me." But he dropped his eyes, suspecting
a flaw in his argument. "I just don't want him beating on me all
the time," he said at last. "I ain't no dog."

She sighed, and turned slightly away, looking out of the window. "Your daddy beats you," she said, "because he loves you."

Roy laughed. "That ain't the kind of love I understand, old lady. What you reckon he'd do if he didn't love me?"

"He'd let you go right on," she flashed, "right on down to hell where it looks like you is just determined to go anyhow! Right on, Mister Man, till somebody puts a knife in you, or takes you off to jail!"

"Mama," John asked suddenly, "is Daddy a good man?"

He had not known that he was going to ask the question, and he watched in astonishment as her mouth tightened and her eyes grew dark.

"That ain't no kind of question," she said mildly. "You don't know no better men, do you?"

"Looks to me like he's a mighty good man," said Sarah. "He sure is praying all the time."

"You children is young," their mother said, ignoring Sarah and sitting down again at the table, "and you don't know how lucky you is to have a father what worries about you and tries to see to it that you come up right."

"Yeah," said Roy, "we don't know how lucky we *is* to have a father what don't want you to go to movies, and don't want you to play in the streets, and don't want you to have no friends, and he don't want this and he don't want that, and he don't want you to do *nothing*. We so *lucky* to have a father who just wants us to go to church and read the Bible and beller like a fool in front of the altar and stay home all nice and quiet, like a little mouse. Boy, we sure is lucky, all right. Don't know what I done to be so lucky."

She laughed. "You going to find out one day," she said, "you mark my words."

Yeah," said Roy.

"But it'll be too late, then," she said. "It'll be too late when you come to be . . . sorry." Her voice had changed. For a moment her eyes met John's eyes, and John was frightened. He felt that her words, after the strange fashion God sometimes chose to speak to men, were dictated by Heaven and were meant for him. He was fourteen—was it too late? And this uneasiness was reinforced by the impression, which at that moment he realized had been his all along, that his mother was not saying everything she meant. What, he wondered, did she say to Aunt Florence when they talked together? Or to his father? What were her thoughts? Her face would never tell. And yet, looking down at him in a moment that was like a secret, passing sign, her face did tell him. Her thoughts were bitter.

"I don't care," Roy said, rising. "When *I* have children I ain't going to treat them like this." John watched his mother; she watched Roy. "I'm *sure* this ain't no way to be. Ain't got no right to have a houseful of children if you don't know how to treat them."

"You mighty grown up this morning," his mother said. "You be careful."

"And tell me something else," Roy said, suddenly leaning over his mother, "tell me how come he don't never let me talk to him like I talk to you? He's my father, ain't he? But he don't never listen to me—no, I all the time got to listen to him."

"Your father," she said, watching him, "knows best. You listen to your father, I guarantee you you won't end up in no jail."

Roy sucked his teeth in fury. "I ain't looking to go to no *jail*. You think that's all that's in the world is jails and churches? You ought to know better than that, Ma."

"I know," she said, "there ain't no safety except you walk humble before the Lord. You going to find it out, too, one day. You go on, hardhead. You going to come to grief."

And suddenly Roy grinned. "But you be there, won't you, Ma—when I'm in trouble?"

"You don't know," she said, trying not to smile, "how long the Lord's going to let me stay with you."

Roy turned and did a dance step. "That's all right," he said. "I know the Lord ain't as hard as Daddy. Is he, boy?" he demanded of John, and struck him lightly on the forehead.

"Boy, let me eat my breakfast," John muttered—though his plate had long been empty, and he was pleased that Roy had turned to him.

"That sure is a crazy boy," ventured Sarah, soberly.

"Just listen," cried Roy, "to the little saint! Daddy ain't never going to have no trouble with her—*that* one, she was born holy. I bet the first words she ever said was: 'Thank you, Jesus.' Ain't that so, Ma?"

"You stop this foolishness," she said, laughing, "and go on about your work. Can't nobody play the fool with you all morning."

"Oh, is you got work for me to do this morning? Well, I declare," said Roy, "what you got for me to do?"

"I got the woodwork in the dining-room for you to do. And you going to do it, too, before you set foot out of *this* house."

"Now, why you want to talk like that, Ma? Is I said I wouldn't do it? You know I'm a right good worker when I got a mind. After I do it, can I go?"

"You go ahead and do it, and we'll see. You better do it right."

"I *always* do it right," said Roy. "You won't know your old woodwork when *I* get through."

"John," said his mother, "you sweep the front room for me like a good boy, and dust the furniture. I'm going to clean up in here."

"Yes'm," he said, and rose. She *had* forgotten about his birthday. He swore he would not mention it. He would not think about it any more.

To sweep the front room meant, principally, to sweep the heavy red and green and purple Oriental-style carpet that had once been that room's glory, but was now so faded that it was all one swimming color, and so frayed in places that it tangled with the broom. John hated sweeping this carpet, for dust rose, clogging his nose and sticking to his sweaty skin, and he felt that should he sweep it forever, the clouds of dust would not diminish, the rug would not be clean. It became in his imagination his impossible, lifelong task, his hard trial, like that of a man he had read about somewhere, whose curse it was to push a boulder up a steep hill, only to have the giant who guarded the hill roll the boulder down again—and so on, forever, throughout eternity; he was still out there, that hapless man, somewhere at the other end of the earth, pushing his boulder up the hill. He had John's entire sympathy, for the longest and hardest part of his Saturday mornings was his voyage with the broom across this endless rug; and, coming to the French doors that ended the living-room and stopped the rug, he felt like an indescribably weary traveler who sees his home at last. Yet for each

dustpan he so laboriously filled at the doorsill demons added to the
rug twenty more; he saw in the expanse behind him the dust that
he had raised settling again into the carpet; and he gritted his
teeth, already on edge because of the dust that filled his mouth,
and nearly wept to think that so much labor brought so little reward.

Nor was this the end of John's labor; for, having put away the
broom and the dustpan, he took from the small bucket under the
sink the dustrag and the furniture oil and a damp cloth, and returned to the living-room to excavate, as it were, from the dust that
threatened to bury them, his family's goods and gear. Thinking
bitterly of his birthday, he attacked the mirror with the cloth,
watching his face appear as out of a cloud. With a shock he saw
that his face had not changed, that the hand of Satan was as yet
invisible. His father had always said that his face was the face of
Satan—and was there not something—in the lift of the eyebrow, in
the way his rough hair formed a V on his brow—that bore witness to his father's words? In the eye there was a light that was
not the light of Heaven, and the mouth trembled, lusful and
lewd, to drink deep of the wines of Hell. He stared at his face
as though it were, as indeed it soon appeared to be, the face
of a stranger, a stranger who held secrets that John could never
know. And, having thought of it as the face of a stranger, he tried
to look at it as a stranger might, and tried to discover what other
people saw. But he saw only details: two great eyes, and a broad,
low forehead, and the triangle of his nose, and his enormous
mouth, and the barely perceptible cleft in his chin, which was,
his father said, the mark of the devil's little finger. These details
did not help him, for the principle of their unity was undiscover-
able, and he could not tell what he most passionately desired to
know: whether his face was ugly or not.

And he dropped his eyes to the mantelpiece, lifting one by one
the objects that adorned it. The mantelpiece held, in brave confusion, photographs, greeting cards, flowered mottoes, two silver
candlesticks that held no candles, and a green metal serpent,
poised to strike. Today in his apathy John stared at them, not
seeing; he began to dust them with the exaggerated care of the
profoundly preoccupied. One of the mottoes was pink and blue,

and proclaimed in raised letters, which made the work of dusting harder:

> Come in the evening, or come in the morning,
> Come when you're looked for, or come without warning,
> A thousand welcomes you'll find here before you,
> And the oftener you come here, the more we'll adore you.

And the other, in letters of fire against a background of gold, stated:

For God so loved the world, that He gave His only begotten Son, that whosoever should believe in Him should not perish, but have everlasting life.

JOHN III, 16

These somewhat unrelated sentiments decorated either side of the mantelpiece, obscured a little by the silver candlesticks. Between these two extremes, the greeting cards, received year after year, on Christmas, or Easter, or birthdays, trumpeted their glad tidings; while the green metal serpent, perpetually malevolent, raised its head proudly in the midst of these trophies, biding the time to strike. Against the mirror, like a procession, the photographs were arranged.

These photographs were the true antiques of the family, which seemed to feel that a photograph should commemorate only the most distant past. The photographs of John and Roy, and of the two girls, which seemed to violate this unspoken law, served only in fact to prove it most iron-hard: they had all been taken in infancy, a time and a condition that the children could not remember. John in his photograph lay naked on a white counterpane, and people laughed and said that it was cunning. But John could never look at it without feeling shame and anger that his nakedness should be here so unkindly revealed. None of the other children was naked; no, Roy lay in his crib in a white gown and grinned toothlessly into the camera, and Sarah, somber at the age of six months, wore a white bonnet, and Ruth was held in her mother's arms. When people looked at these photographs and laughed, their laughter differed from the laughter with which they greeted the naked John. For this reason, when visitors tried to make advances to John he was sullen, and they, feeling that for some reason he disliked them, retaliated by deciding that he was a "funny" child.

Among the other photographs there was one of Aunt Florence, his father's sister, in which her hair, in the old-fashioned way, was worn high and tied with a ribbon; she had been very young when this photograph was taken, and had just come North. Sometimes, when she came to visit, she called the photograph to witness that she had indeed been beautiful in her youth. There was a photograph of his mother, not the one John liked and had seen only once, but one taken immediately after her marriage. And there was a photograph of his father, dressed in black, sitting on a country porch with his hands folded heavily in his lap. The photograph had been taken on a sunny day, and the sunlight brutally exaggerated the planes of his father's face. He stared into the sun, head raised, unbearable, and though it had been taken when he was young, it was not the face of a young man; only something archaic in the dress indicated that this photograph had been taken long ago. At the time this picture was taken, Aunt Florence said, he was already a preacher, and had a wife who was now in Heaven. That he had been a preacher at that time was not astonishing, for it was impossible to imagine that he had ever been anything else; but that he had had a wife in the so distant past who was now dead filled John with a wonder by no means pleasant. If she had lived, John thought, then he would never have been born; his father would never have come North and met his mother. And this shadowy woman, dead so many years, whose name he knew had been Deborah, held in the fastness of her tomb, it seemed to John, the key to all those mysteries he so longed to unlock. It was she who had known his father in a life where John was not, and in a country John had never seen. When he was nothing, nowhere, dust, cloud, air, and sun, and falling rain, *not even thought of*, said his mother, *in Heaven with the angels*, said his aunt, she had known his father, and shared his father's house. She had loved his father. She had known his father when lightning flashed and thunder rolled through Heaven, and his father said: "Listen. God is talking." She had known him in the mornings of that far-off country when his father turned on his bed and opened his eyes, and she had looked into those eyes, seeing what they held, and she had not been afraid. She had seen him baptized, *kicking like a mule and howling,* and she had seen him weep when his mother died; *he was a right young man then,* Florence said. Because she had looked into those eyes before they had looked on John, she knew what John would never know —the purity of his father's eyes when John was not reflected in their depths. She could have told him—had he but been able from his hiding-place to ask!—how to make his father love him. But now it was too late. She would not speak before the judgment day. And among those many voices, and stammering with his own, John would care no longer for her testimony.

When he had finished and the room was ready for Sunday, John felt dusty and weary and sat down beside the window in his father's easy chair. A glacial sun filled the streets, and a high wind filled the air with scraps of paper and frosty dust, and banged the hanging signs of stores and storefront churches. It was the end of winter, and the garbage-filled snow that had been banked along the edges of sidewalks was melting now and filling the gutters. Boys were playing stickball in the damp, cold streets; dressed in heavy woolen sweaters and heavy pants, they danced and shouted, and the ball went *crack!* as the stick struck it and sent it speeding through the air. One of them wore a bright-red stocking cap with a great ball of wool hanging down behind that bounced as he jumped, like a bright omen above his head. The cold sun made their faces like copper and brass, and through the closed window John heard their coarse, irreverent voices. And he wanted to be one of them, playing in the streets, unfrightened, moving with such grace and power, but he knew this could not be. Yet, if he could not play their games, he could do something they could not do; he was able, as one of his teachers said, to think. But this brought him little in the way of consolation, for today he was terrified of his thoughts. He wanted to be with these boys in the street, heedless and thoughtless, wearing out his treacherous and bewildering body.

But now it was eleven o'clock, and in two hours his father would be home. And then they might eat, and then his father would lead them in prayer, and then he would give them a Bible lesson. By and by it would be evening and he would go to clean the church, and remain for tarry service. Suddenly, sitting at the window, and with a violence unprecedented, there arose in John a flood of fury and tears, and he bowed his head, fists clenched against the windowpane, crying, with teeth on edge: "What shall I do? What shall I do?"

Then his mother called him; and he remembered that she was in the kitchen washing clothes and probably had something for him to do. He rose sullenly and walked into the kitchen. She stood over the washtub, her arms wet and soapy to the elbows and sweat standing on her brow. Her apron, improvised from an old sheet, was wet where she had been leaning over the scrubbing-board. As he came in, she straightened, drying her hands on the edge of the apron.

"You finish your work, John?" she asked.

He said: "Yes'm," and thought how oddly she looked at him; as though she were looking at someone else's child.

"That's a good boy," she said. She smiled a shy, strained smile. "You know you your mother's right-hand man?"

He said nothing, and he did not smile, but watched her, wondering to what task this preamble led.

She turned away, passing one damp hand across her forehead, and went to the cupboard. Her back was to him, and he watched her while she took down a bright, figured vase, filled with flowers only on the most special occasions, and emptied the contents into her palm. He heard the chink of money, which meant that she was going to send him to the store. She put the vase back and turned to face him, her palm loosely folded before her.

"I didn't never ask you," she said, "what you wanted for your birthday. But you take this, son, and go out and get yourself something you think you want."

And she opened his palm and put the money into it, warm and wet from her hand. In the moment that he felt the warm, smooth coins and her hand on his, John stared blindly at her face, so far above him. His heart broke and he wanted to put his head on her belly where the wet spot was, and cry. But he dropped his eyes and looked at his palm, at the small pile of coins.

"It ain't much there," she said.

"That's all right." Then he looked up, and she bent down and kissed him on the forehead.

"You getting to be," she said, putting her hand beneath his chin and holding his face away from her, "a right big boy. You going to be a mighty fine man, you know that? Your mama's counting on you."

And he knew again that she was not saying everything she meant; in a kind of secret language she was telling him today something that he must remember and understand tomorrow. He watched her face, his heart swollen with love for her and with an anguish, not yet his own, that he did not understand and that frightened him.

"Yes, Ma," he said, hoping that she would realize, despite his stammering tongue, the depth of his passion to please her.

"I know," she said, with a smile, releasing him and rising, "there's a whole lot of things you don't understand. But don't you fret. The Lord'll reveal to you in His own good time everything He wants you to know. You put your faith in the Lord, Johnny, and He'll surely bring you out. Everything works together for good for them that love the Lord."

He had heard her say this before—it was her text, as *Set thine house in order* was his father's—but he knew that today she was saying it to him especially; she was trying to help him because she knew he was in trouble. And this trouble was also her own, which she would never tell to John. And even though he was certain that they could not be speaking of the same things—for then, surely, she would be angry and no longer proud of him—this perception on her part and this avowal of her love for him lent to John's bewilderment a reality that terrified and a dignity that consoled him. Dimly, he felt that he ought to console her, and he listened, astounded, at the words that now fell from his lips:

"Yes, Mama. I'm going to try to love the Lord."

At this there sprang into his mother's face something startling, beautiful, unspeakably sad—as though she were looking far beyond him at a long, dark road, and seeing on that road a traveler in perpetual danger. Was it he, the traveler? or herself? or was she thinking of the cross of Jesus? She turned back to the washtub, still with this strange sadness on her face.

"You better go on now," she said, "before your daddy gets home."

In Central Park the snow had not yet melted on his favorite hill. This hill was in the center of the park, after he had left the circle of the reservoir, where he always found, outside the high wall of crossed wire, ladies, white, in fur coats, walking their great dogs, or old, white gentlemen with canes. At a point that he knew by instinct and by the shape of the buildings surrounding the park, he struck out on a steep path overgrown with trees, and climbed a short distance until he reached the clearing that led to the hill. Before him, then, the slope stretched upward, and above it the brilliant sky, and beyond it, cloudy, and far away, he saw the skyline of New York. He did not know why, but there arose in him an exultation and a sense of power, and he ran up the hill like an engine, or a madman, willing to throw himself headlong into the city that glowed before him.

But when he reached the summit he paused; he stood on the crest of the hill, hands clasped beneath his chin, looking down. Then he, John, felt like a giant who might crumble this city with his anger; he felt like a tyrant who might crush this city beneath his heel; he felt like a long-awaited conqueror at whose feet flowers would be strewn, and before whom multitudes cried, Hosanna! He would be, of all, the mightiest, the most beloved, the Lord's anointed; and he would live in this shining city which his ancestors had seen with longing from far away. For it was his; the inhabitants of the city had told him it was his; he had but to run down, crying, and they would take him to their hearts and show him wonders his eyes had never seen.

And still, on the summit of that hill he paused. He remembered the people he had seen in that city, whose eyes held no love for him. And he thought of their feet so swift and brutal, and the drak gray clothes they wore, and how when they passed they did not see him, or, if they saw him, they smirked. And how their lights, unceasing, crashed on and off above him, and how he was a stranger there. Then he remembered his father and his mother, and all the arms stretched out to hold him back, to save him from this city where, they said, his soul would find perdition.

And certainly perdition sucked at the feet of the people who walked there; and cried in the lights, in the gigantic towers; the marks of Satan could be found in the faces of the people who waited at the doors of movie houses; his words were printed on the great movie posters that invited people to sin. It was the roar of the damned that filled Broadway, where motor cars and buses and the hurrying people disputed every inch with death. *Broadway:* the way that led to death *was* broad, and many could be found thereon; but narrow was the way that led to life eternal, and few there were who found it. But he did not long for the narrow way, where all his people walked; where the houses did not rise, piercing, as it seemed, the unchanging clouds, but huddled, flat, ignoble, close to the filthy ground, where the streets and the hallways and the rooms were dark, and where the unconquerable odor was of dust, and sweat, and urine, and homemade gin. In the narrow way, the way of the cross, there awaited him only humiliation forever; there awaited him, one day, a house like his father's house, and a church like his father's, and a job like his father's, where he would grow old and black with hunger and toil. The way of the cross had given him a belly filled with wind and had bent his mother's back; they had never worn fine clothes, but here, where the buildings contested God's power and where the men and women did not fear God, here he might eat and drink to his heart's content and clothe his body with wondrous fabrics, rich to the eye and pleasing to the touch. And then what of his soul, which would one day come to die and stand naked before the judgment bar? What would his conquest of the city profit him on that day? To hurl away, for a moment of ease, the glories of eternity!

These glories were unimaginable—but the city was real. He stood for a moment on the melting snow, distracted, and then began to run down the hill, feeling himself fly as the descent became more rapid, and thinking: "I can climb back up. If it's wrong, I can always climb back up." At the bottom of the hill, where the ground abruptly leveled off onto a gravel path, he nearly knocked down an old white man with a white beard, who was walking very slowly and leaning on his cane. They both stopped, astonished, and looked at one another. John struggled to catch his breath and apologize, but the old man smiled. John smiled back. It was as though he and the old man had between them a great secret; and the old man moved on. The snow glittered in patches all over the park. Ice, under the pale, strong sun, melted slowly on the branches and the trunks of trees.

He came out of the park at Fifth Avenue where, as always, the old-fashioned horse-carriages were lined along the curb, their drivers sitting on the high seats with rugs around their knees, or standing in twos and threes near the horses, stamping their feet and smoking pipes and talking. In summer he had seen people riding in these carriages, looking like people out of books, or out of movies in which everyone wore old-fashioned clothes and rushed at nightfall over frozen roads, hotly pursued by their enemies who wanted to carry them back to death. *"Look back, look back,"* had cried a beautiful woman with long blonde curls, *"and see if we are pursued!"*—and she had come, as John remembered, to a terrible end. Now he stared at the horses, enormous and brown and patient, stamping every now and again a polished hoof, and he thought of what it would be like to have one day a horse of his own. He would call it Rider, and mount it at morning when the grass was wet, and from the horse's back look out over great, sun-filled fields, his own. Behind him stood his house, great and rambling and very new, and in the kitchen his wife, a beautiful woman, made breakfast, and the smoke rose out of the chimney, melting into the morning air. They had children, who called him Papa and for whom at Christmas he bought electric trains. And he had turkeys and cows and chickens and geese, and other horses besides Rider. They had a closet full of whisky and wine; they had cars—but what church did they go to and what would he teach his children when they gathered around him in the evening? He looked straight ahead, down Fifth Avenue, where graceful women in fur coats walked, looking into the windows that held silk dresses, and watches, and rings. What church did they go to? And what were their houses like when in the evening they took off these coats, and these silk dresses, and put their jewerly in a box, and leaned back in soft beds to think for a moment before they slept of the day gone by? Did they read a verse from the Bible every night and fall on their knees to pray? But no, for their thoughts were not of God, and their way was not God's way. They were in the world, and of the world, and their feet laid hold on Hell.

Yet in school some of them had been nice to him, and it was hard to think of them burning in Hell forever, they who were so gracious and beautiful now. Once, one winter when he had been very sick with a heavy cold that would not leave him, one of his teachers had bought him a bottle of cod liver oil, especially prepared with heavy syrup so that it did not taste so bad: this was surely a Christian act. His mother had said that God would bless that woman; and he had got better. They were kind—he was sure that they were kind—and on the day that he would bring himself to their attention they would surely love and honor him. This was not his father's opinion. His father said that all white people were wicked, and that God was going to bring them low. He said that white people were never to be trusted, and that they told nothing but lies, and that not one of them had ever loved a nigger. He, John, was a nigger, and he would find out, as soon as he got a little older, how evil white people could be. John had read about the things white people did to colored people; how, in the South, where his parents came from, white people cheated them of their wages, and burned them, and shot them—and did worse things, said his father, which the tongue could not endure to utter. He had read about colored men being burned in the electric chair for things they had not done; how in riots they were beaten with clubs; how they were tortured in prisons; how they were the last to be hired and the first to be fired. Niggers did not live on these streets where John now walked; it was forbidden; and yet he walked here, and no one raised a hand against him. But did he dare to enter this shop out of which a woman now casually walked, carrying a great round box? Or this apartment before which a white man stood, dressed in a brilliant uniform? John knew he did not dare, not today, and he heard his father's laugh: *"No, nor tomorrow neither!"* For him there was the back door, and the dark stairs, and the kitchen or the basement. This world was not for him. If he refused to believe, and wanted to break his neck trying, then he could try until the sun refused to shine; they would never let him enter. In John's mind then, the people and the avenue underwent a change, and he feared them and knew that one day he could hate them if God did not change his heart.

He left Fifth Avenue and walked west towards the movie houses. Here on 42nd Street it was less elegant but no less strange. He loved this street, not for the people or the shops but for the stone lions that guarded the great main building of the Public Library, a building filled with books and unimaginably vast, and which he had never yet dared to enter. He might, he knew, for he was a member of the branch in Harlem and was entitled to take books from any library in the city. But he had never gone in because the building was so big that it must be full of corridors and marble steps, in the maze of which he would be lost and never find the book he wanted. And then everyone, all the white people inside, would know that he was not used to great buildings, or to many books, and they would look at him with pity. He would enter on another day, when he had read all the books uptown, an achievement that would, he felt, lend him the poise to enter any building in the world. People, mostly men, leaned over the stone parapets of the raised park that surrounded the library, or walked up and down and bent to drink water from the public drinking-fountains. Silver pigeons lighted briefly on the heads of the lions or the rims of fountains, and strutted along the walks. John loitered in front of Woolworth's, staring at the candy display, trying to decide what candy to buy—and buying none, for the store was crowded and he was certain that the salesgirl would never notice him—and before a vender of artificial flowers, and crossed Sixth Avenue where the Automat was, and the parked taxis, and the shops, which he would not look at today, that displayed in their windows dirty postcards and practical jokes. Beyond Sixth Avenue the movie houses began, and now he studied the stills carefully, trying to decide which of all these theaters he should enter. He stopped at last before a gigantic, colored poster that represented a wicked woman, half undressed, leaning in a doorway, apparently quarreling with a blond man who stared wretchedly into the street. The legend above their heads was: "There's a fool like him in every family—and a woman next door to take him over!" He decided to see this, for he felt identified with the blond young man, the fool of his family, and he wished to know more about his so blatantly unkind fate.

And so he stared at the price above the ticket-seller's window

and, showing her his coins, received the piece of paper that was
charged with the power to open doors. Having once decided to
enter, he did not look back at the street again for fear that one
of the saints might be passing and, seeing him, might cry out his
name and lay hands on him to drag him back. He walked very
quickly across the carpeted lobby, looking at nothing, and pausing only to see his ticket torn, half of it thrown into a silver box
and half returned to him. And then the usherette opened the
doors of this dark palace and with a flashlight held behind her
took him to his seat. Not even then, having pushed past a wilderness of knees and feet to reach his designated seat, did he dare
to breathe; nor, out of a last, sick hope for forgiveness, did he
look at the screen. He stared at the darkness around him, and at
the profiles that gradually emerged from this gloom, which was
so like the gloom of Hell. He waited for this darkness to be
shattered by the light of the second coming, for the ceiling to
crack upward, revealing, for every eye to see, the chariots of fire
on which descended a wrathful God and all the host of Heaven.
He sank far down in his seat, as though his crouching might make
him invisible and deny his presence there. But then he thought:
"Not yet. The day of judgment is not yet," and voices reached
him, the voices no doubt of the hapless man and the evil woman,
and he raised his eyes helplessly and watched the screen.

The woman was most evil. She was blonde and pasty white,
and she had lived in London, which was in England, quite some
time ago, judging from her clothes, and she coughed. She had a
terrible disease, tuberculosis, which he had heard about. Someone
in his mother's family had died of it. She had a great many boy
friends, and she smoked cigarettes and drank. When she met the
young man, who was a student and who loved her very much, she
was very cruel to him. She laughed at him because he was a
cripple. She took his money and she went out with other men,
and she lied to the student—who was certainly a fool. He limped
about, looking soft and sad, and soon all John's sympathy was
given to this violent and unhappy woman. He understood her
when she raged and shook her hips and threw back her head in
laughter so furious that it seemed the veins of her neck would
burst. She walked the cold, foggy streets, a little woman and not

pretty, with a lewd, brutal swagger, saying to the whole world: "You can kiss my ass." Nothing tamed or broke her, nothing touched her, neither kindness, nor scorn, nor hatred, nor love. She had never thought of prayer. It was unimaginable that she would ever bend her knees and came crawling along a dusty floor to anybody's altar, weeping for forgiveness. Perhaps her sin was so extreme that it could not be forgiven; perhaps her pride was so great that she did not need forgiveness. She had fallen from that high estate which God had intended for men and women, and she made her fall glorious because it was so complete. John could not have found in his heart, had he dared to search it, any wish for her redemption. He wanted to be like her, only more powerful, more thorough, and more cruel; to make those around him, all who hurt him, suffer as she made the student suffer, and laugh in their faces when they asked pity for their pain. *He* would have asked no pity, and his pain was greater than theirs. Go on, girl, he whispered, as the student, facing her implacable ill will, sighed and wept. Go on, girl. One day he would talk like that, he would face them and tell them how much he hated them, how they had made him suffer, how he would pay them back!

Nevertheless, when she came to die, which she did eventually, looking more grotesque than ever, as she deserved, his thoughts were abruptly arrested, and he was chilled by the expression on her face. She seemed to stare endlessly outward and down, in the face of a wind more piercing than any she had felt on earth, feeling herself propelled with speed into a kingdom where nothing could help her, neither her pride, nor her courage, nor her glorious wickedness. In the place where she was going, it was not these things that mattered but something else, for which she had no name, only a cold intimation, something that she could not alter in any degree, and that she had never thought of. She began to cry, her depraved face breaking into an infant's grimace; and they moved away from her, leaving her dirty in a dirty room, alone to face her Maker. The scene faded out and she was gone; and though the movie went on, allowing the student to marry another girl, darker, and very sweet, but by no means so arresting, John thought of this woman and her dreadful end. Again, had the thought not been blasphemous, he would have thought that it

was the Lord who had led him into this theater to show him an
example of the wages of sin. The movie ended and people stirred
around him; the newsreel came on, and white girls in bathing suits
paraded before him and boxers growled and fought, and baseball
players ran home safe and presidents and kings of countries that
were only names to him moved briefly across the flickering square
of light John thought of Hell, of his soul's redemption, and
struggled to find a compromise between the way that led to life
everlasting and the way that ended in the pit. But there was
none, for he had been raised in the truth. He could not claim, as
African savages might be able to claim, that no one had brought
him the gospel. His father and mother and all the saints had
taught him from his earliest childhood what was the will of
God. Either he arose from this theater, never to return, putting
behind him the world and its pleasures, its honors, and its glories,
or he remained here with the wicked and partook of their certain
punishment. Yes, it was a narrow way—and John stirred in his
seat, not daring to feel it God's injustice that he must make so
cruel a choice.

As John approached his home again in the late afternoon, he
saw little Sarah, her coat unbuttoned, come flying out of the house
and run the length of the street away from him into the far drugstore. Instantly, he was frightened; he stopped a moment, staring
blankly down the street, wondering what could justify such
hysterical haste. It was true that Sarah was full of self-importance,
and made any errand she ran seem a matter of life or death; nevertheless, she had been sent on an errand, and with such speed that
her mother had not had time to make her button up her coat.
    Then he felt weary; if something had really happened it would
be very unpleasant upstairs now, and he did not want to face it.
But perhaps it was simply that his mother had a headache and
had sent Sarah to the store for some aspirin. But if this were
true, it meant that he would have to prepare supper, and take
care of the children, and be naked under his father's eyes all the
evening long. And he began to walk more slowly.
    There were some boys standing on the stoop. They watched
him as he approached, and he tried not to look at them and to

approximate the swagger with which they walked. One of them said, as he mounted the short, stone steps and started into the hall: "Boy, your brother was hurt real bad today."

He looked at them in a kind of dread, not daring to ask for details; and he observed that they, too, looked as though they had been in a battle; something hangdog in their looks suggested that they had been put to flight. Then he looked down, and saw that there was blood at the threshold, and blood spattered on the tile floor of the vestibule. He looked again at the boys, who had not ceased to watch him, and hurried up the stairs.

The door was half open—for Sarah's return, no doubt—and he walked in, making no sound, feeling a confused impulse to flee. There was no one in the kitchen, though the light was burning— the lights were on all through the house. On the kitchen table stood a shopping-bag filled with groceries, and he knew that his Aunt Florence had arrived. The washtub, where his mother had been washing earlier, was open still, and filled the kitchen with a sour smell.

There were drops of blood on the floor here too, and there had been small, smudged coins of blood on the stairs as he walked up.

All this frightened him terribly. He stood in the middle of the kitchen, trying to imagine what had happened, and preparing himself to walk into the living-room, where all the family seemed to be. Roy had been in trouble before, but this new trouble seemed to be the beginning of the fulfillment of a prophecy. He took off his coat, dropping it on a chair, and was about to start into the living-room when he heard Sarah running up the steps.

He waited, and she burst through the door, carrying a clumsy parcel.

"What happened?" he whispered.

She stared at him in astonishment, and a certain wild joy. He thought again that he really did not like his sister. Catching her breath, she blurted out, triumphantly: "Roy got stabbed with a knife!" and rushed into the living-room.

Roy got stabbed with a knife. Whatever this meant, it was sure that his father would be at his worst tonight. John walked slowly into the living-room.

His father and mother, a small basin of water between them,

knelt by the sofa where Roy lay, and his father was washing the blood from Roy's forehead. It seemed that his mother, whose touch was so much more gentle, had been thrust aside by his father, who could not bear to have anyone else touch his wounded son. And now she watched, one hand in the water, the other, in a kind of anguish, at her waist, which was circled still by the improvised apron of the morning. Her face, as she watched, was full of pain and fear, of tension barely supported, and of pity that could scarcely have been expressed had she filled all the world with her weeping. His father muttered sweet, delirious things to Roy, and his hands, when he dipped them again in the basin and wrung out the cloth, were trembling. Aunt Florence, still wearing her hat and carrying her handbag, stood a little removed, looking down at them with a troubled, terrible face.

Then Sarah bounded into the room before him, and his mother looked up, reached out for the package, and saw him. She said nothing, but she looked at him with a strange, quick intentness, almost as though there were a warning on her tongue which at the moment she did not dare to utter. His Aunt Florence looked up, and said: "We been wondering where you was, boy. This bad brother of yours done gone out and got hisself hurt."

But John understood from her tone that the fuss was, possibly a little gerater than the danger—Roy was not, after all, going to die. And his heart lifted a little. Then his father turned and looked at him.

"Where you been, boy," he shouted, "all this time? Don't you know you's needed here at home?"

More than his words, his face caused John to stiffen instantly with malice and fear. His father's face was terrible in anger, but now there was more than anger in it. John saw now what he had never seen there before, except in his own vindictive fantasies: a kind of wild, weeping terror that made the face seem younger, and yet at the same time unutterably older and more cruel. And John knew, in the moment his father's eye swept over him, that he hated John because John was not lying on the sofa where Roy lay. John could scarcely meet his father's eyes, and yet, briefly, he did, saying nothing, feeling in his heart an odd sensation of triumph, and hoping in his heart that Roy, to bring his father low, would die.

His mother had unwrapped the package and was opening a bottle of peroxide. "Here," she said, "you better wash it with this now." Her voice was calm and dry; she looked at his father briefly, her face unreadable, as she handed him the bottle and the cotton.

"This going to hurt," his father said—in such a different voice, so sad and tender!—turning again to the sofa. "But you just be a little man and hold still; it ain't going to take long."

John watched and listened, hating him. Roy began to moan. Aunt Florence moved to the mantelpiece and put her handbag down near the metal serpent. From the room behind him, John heard the baby begin to whimper.

"John," said his mother, "go and pick her up like a good boy." Her hands, which were not trembling, were still busy: she had opened the bottle of iodine and was cutting up strips of bandage.

John walked into his parents' bedroom and picked up the squalling baby, who was wet. The moment Ruth felt him lift her up she stopped crying and stared at him with a wide-eyed, pathetic stare, as though she knew that there was trouble in the house. John laughed at her so ancient-seeming distress—he was very fond of his baby sister—and whispered in her ear as he started back to the living-room: "Now, you let your big brother tell you something, baby. Just as soon as you's able to stand on your feet, you run away from *this* house, run far away." He did not quite know why he said this, or where he wanted her to run, but it made him feel instantly better.

His father was saying, as John came back into the room: "I'm sure going to be having some questions to ask you in a minute, old lady. I'm going to be wanting to know just how come you let this boy go out and get half killed."

"Oh, no, you ain't," said Aunt Florence. "You ain't going to be starting none of that mess this evening. You know right doggone well that Roy don't never ask *nobody* if he can do *nothing* —he just go right ahead and do like he pleases. Elizabeth sure can't put no ball and chain on him. She got her hands full right here in this house, and it ain't her fault if Roy got a head just as hard as his father's."

"You got a awful lot to say, look like for once you could keep from putting your mouth in my business." He said this without looking at her.

"It ain't my fault," she said, "that you was born a fool, and always done been a fool, and ain't never going to change. I swear to my father you'd try the patience of Job."

"I done told you before," he said—he had not ceased working over the moaning Roy, and was preparing now to dab the wound with iodine—"that I didn't want you coming in here and using that gutter language in front of my children."

"Don't you worry about my language, brother," she said with spirit, "you better start worrying about your *life*. What these children hear ain't going to do them near as much harm as what they *see*."

"What they *see*," his father muttered, "is a poor man trying to serve the Lord. *That's* my life."

"Then I guarantee *you*," she said, "that they going to do their best to keep it from being *their* life. *You* mark my words."

He turned and looked at her, and intercepted the look that passed between the two women. John's mother, for reasons that were not at all his father's reasons, wanted Aunt Florence to keep still. He looked away, ironically. John watched his mother's mouth tighten bitterly as she dropped her eyes. His father, in silence, began bandaging Roy's forehead.

"It's just the mercy of God," he said at last, "that this boy didn't lose his eye. Look here."

His mother leaned over and looked into Roy's face with a sad, sympathetic murmur. Yet, John felt, she had seen instantly the extent of the danger to Roy's eye and to his life, and was beyond that worry now. Now she was merely marking time, as it were, and preparing herself against the moment when her husband's anger would turn, full force, against her.

His father now turned to John, who was standing near the French doors with Ruth in his arms.

"You come here, boy," he said, "and see what them white folks done done to your brother."

John walked over to the sofa, holding himself as proudly beneath his father's furious eyes as a prince approaching the scaffold.

"Look here," said his father, grasping him roughly by one arm, "look at your brother."

John looked down at Roy, who gazed at him with almost no expression in his dark eyes. But John knew by the weary, impatient set of Roy's young mouth that his brother was asking that none of this be held against him. It wasn't his fault, or John's, Roy's eyes said, that they had such a crazy father.

His father, with the air of one forcing the sinner to look down into the pit that is to be his portion, moved away slightly so that John could see Roy's wound.

Roy had been gashed by a knife, luckily not very sharp, from the center of his forehead where his hair began, downward to the bone just above his left eye: the wound described a kind of crazy half-moon and ended in a violent, fuzzy tail that was the ruin of Roy's eyebrow. Time would darken the half-moon wound into Roy's dark skin, but nothing would bring together again the so violently divided eyebrow. This crazy lift, this question, would remain with him forever, and emphasize forever something mocking and sinister in Roy's face. John felt a sudden impulse to smile, but his father's eyes were on him and he fought the impulse back. Certainly the wound was now very ugly, and very red, and must, John felt, with a quickened sympathy towards Roy, who had not cried out, have been very painful. He could imagine the sensation caused when Roy staggered into the house, blinded by his blood; but just the same, he wasn't dead, he wasn't changed, he would be in the streets again the moment he was better.

"You see?" came now from his father. "It was white folks, some of them white folks *you* like so much that tried to cut your brother's throat."

John thought, with immediate anger and with a curious contempt for his father's inexactness, that only a blind man, however white, could possibly have been aiming at Roy's throat; and his mother said with a calm insistence:

"And he was trying to cut theirs. Him and them bad boys."

"Yes," said Aunt Florence, "I ain't heard you ask that boy nary a question about how all this happened. Look like you just

determined to rise Cain any*how* and make everybody in this
house suffer because something done happened to the apple of
your eye."

"I done asked you," cried his father in a fearful exasperation,
"to stop running your *mouth*. Don't none of this concern you.
This is *my* family and this is my house. You want me to slap
you side of the head?"

"You slap me," she said, with a placidity equally fearful, "and I
do guarantee you you won't do no more slapping in a hurry."

"Hush now," said his mother, rising, "ain't no need for all this.
What's done is done. We ought to be on our knees, thanking the
Lord it weren't no worse."

"Amen to that," said Aunt Florence, "*tell* that foolish nigger
something."

"You can tell that foolish *son* of yours something," he said to
his wife with venom, having decided, it seemed, to ignore his
sister, "him standing there with them big buckeyes. You can tell
him to take this like a warning from the Lord. *This* is what
white folks does to niggers. I been telling you, now you see."

"*He* better take it like a warning?" shrieked Aunt Florence. "*He*
better take it? Why, Gabriel, it ain't *him* went halfway across
this city to get in a fight with white boys. This boy on the sofa
went *deliberately*, with a whole lot of other boys, all the way to
the west side, just *looking* for a fight. I declare, I do wonder
what goes on in your head."

"You know right well," his mother said, looking directly at
his father, "that Johnny don't travel with the same class of boys
as Roy goes with. You done beat Roy too many times, here, in
this very room for going out with them bad boys. Roy got hisself
hurt this afternoon because he was out doing something he didn't
have no business doing, and that's the end of it. You ought to be
thanking your Redeemer he ain't dead."

"And for all the care you take of him," he said, "he might as
well be dead. Don't look like you much care whether he lives,
or dies."

"*Lord*, have mercy," said Aunt Florence.

"He's my son, too," his mother said, with heat. "I carried him
in my belly for nine months and I know him just like I know

his daddy, and they's just *exactly* alike. Now. You ain't got no *right* in the world to talk to me like that."

"I reckon you *know*," he said, choked, and breathing hard, "all about a mother's love. I sure reckon on you telling me how a woman can sit in the house all day and let her own flesh and blood go out and get half butchered. Don't you tell me you don't know no way to stop him, because I remember *my* mother, God rest her soul, and *she'd* have found a way."

"She was my mother, too," said Aunt Florence, "and I recollect, if you don't, you being brought home many a time more dead than alive. She didn't find no way to stop *you*. She wore herself out beating on you, just like you been wearing yourself out beating on this boy here."

"My, my, *my*," he said, "you got a lot to say."

"I ain't doing a thing," she said, "But trying to talk some sense into your big, black, hard head. You better stop trying to blame everything on Elizabeth and look to your own wrongdoings."

"Never mind, Florence," his mother said, "it's all over and done with now."

"I'm out of this house," he shouted, "every day the Lord sends, working to put the food in these children's mouths. Don't you think I got a right to ask the mother of these children to look after them and see that they don't break their necks before I get back home?"

"You ain't got but one child," she said, "that's liable to go out and break his neck, and that's Roy, and you know it. And I don't know how in the world you expect me to run this house, and look after these children, and keep running around the block after Roy. No, I can't stop him, I done told you that, and you can't stop him neither. You don't know *what* to do with this boy, and that's why you all the time trying to fix the blame on somebody. Ain't nobody to *blame*, Gabriel. You just better pray God to stop him before somebody puts another knife in him and puts him in his grave."

They stared at each other a moment in an awful pause, she with a startled, pleading question in her eyes. Then, with all his might, he reached out and slapped her across the face. She crumpled at once, hiding her face with one thin hand, and Aunt

Florence moved to hold her up. Sarah watched all this with greedy eyes. Then Roy sat up, and said in a shaking voice:

"Don't you slap my mother. That's my *mother*. You slap her again, you black bastard, and I swear to God I'll kill you."

In the moment that these words filled the room, and hung in the room like the infinitesimal moment of hanging, jagged light that precedes an explosion, John and his father were staring into each other's eyes. John thought for that moment that his father believed the words had come from him, his eyes were so wild and depthlessly malevolent, and his mouth was twisted into such a snarl of pain. Then, in the absolute silence that followed Roy's words, John saw that his father was not seeing him, was not seeing anything unless it were a vision. John wanted to turn and flee, as though he had encountered in the jungle some evil beast, croaching and ravenous, with eyes like Hell unclosed; and exactly as though, on a road's turning, he found himself staring at certain destruction, he found that he could not move. Then his father turned and looked down at Roy.

"What did you say?" his father asked.

"I told you," said Roy, "not to touch my mother."

"You cursed me," said his father.

Roy said nothing; neither did he drop his eyes.

"Gabriel," said his mother, "Gabriel. Let us pray. . . ."

His father's hands were at his waist, and he took off his belt. Tears were in his eyes.

"Gabriel," cried Aunt Florence, "ain't you done playing the fool for tonight?"

Then his father raised his belt, and it fell with a whistling sound on Roy, who shivered, and fell back, his face to the wall. But he did not cry out. And the belt was raised again, and again. The air rang with the whistling, and the *crack!* against Roy's flesh. And the baby, Ruth, began to scream.

"*My Lord, my Lord,*" his father whispered, "*my Lord, my Lord.*"

He raised the belt again, but Aunt Florence caught it from behind, and held it. His mother rushed over to the sofa and caught Roy in her arms, crying as John had never seen a woman, or anybody, cry before. Roy caught his mother around the neck and held on to her as though he were drowning.

His Aunt Florence and his father faced each other.

"Yes, Lord," Aunt Florence said, "you was born wild, and you's going to die wild. But ain't no use to try to take the whole world with you. You can't change nothing, Gabriel. You ought to know that by now."

John opened the church door with his father's key at six o'clock. Tarry service officially began at eight, but it could begin at any time, whenever the Lord moved one of the saints to enter the church and pray. It was seldom, however, that anyone arrived before eight-thirty, the Spirit of the Lord being sufficiently tolerant to allow the saints time to do their Saturday-night shopping, clean their houses, and put their children to bed.

John closed the door behind him and stood in the narrow church aisle, hearing behind him the voices of children playing, and ruder voices, the voices of their elders, cursing and crying in the streets. It was dark in the church; street lights had been snapping on all around him on the populous avenue; the light of the day was gone. His feet seemed planted on this wooden floor; they did not wish to carry him one step further. The darkness and silence of the church pressed on him, cold as judgment, and the voices crying from the window might have been crying from another world. John moved forward, hearing his feet crack against the sagging wood, to where the golden cross on the red field of the altar cloth glowed like smothered fire, and switched on one weak light.

In the air of the church hung, perpetually, the odor of dust and sweat; for, like the carpet in his mother's living-room, the dust of this church was invincible; and when the saints were praying or rejoicing, their bodies gave off an acrid, steamy smell, a marriage of the odors of dripping bodies and soaking, starched white linen. It was a storefront church and had stood, for John's lifetime, on the corner of this sinful avenue, facing the hospital to which criminal wounded and dying were carried almost every night. The saints, arriving, had rented this abandoned store and taken out the fixtures; had painted the walls and built a pulpit, moved in a piano and camp chairs, and bought the biggest Bible they could find. They put white curtains in the show window, and painted across this window TEMPLE OF THE FIRE BAPTIZED. Then they were ready to do the Lord's work.

And the Lord, as He had promised to the two or three first gathered together, sent others; and these brought others and created a church. From this parent branch, if the Lord blessed, other branches might grow and a mighty work be begun throughout the city and throughout the land. In the history of the Temple the Lord had raised up evangelists and teachers and prophets, and called them out into the field to do His work; to go up and down the land carrying the gospel, or to raise other temples—in Philadelphia, Georgia, Boston, or Brooklyn. Wherever the Lord led, they followed. Every now and again one of them came home to testify of the wonders the Lord had worked through him, or her. And sometimes on a special Sunday they all visited one of the nearer churches of the Brotherhood.

There had been a time, before John was born, when his father had also been in the field; but now, having to earn for his family their daily bread, it was seldom that he was able to travel further away than Philadelphia, and then only for a very short time. His father no longer, as he had once done, led great revival meetings, his name printed large on placards that advertised the coming of a man of God. His father had once had a mighty reputation; but all this, it seemed, had changed since he had left the South. Perhaps he ought now to have a church of his own— John wondered if his father wanted that; he ought, perhaps, to be leading, as Father James now led, a great flock to the Kingdom. But his father was only a caretaker in the house of God. He was responsible for the replacement of burnt-out light bulbs, and for the cleanliness of the church, and the care of the Bibles, and the hymn-books, and the placards on the walls. On Friday night he conducted the Young Ministers' Service and preached with them. Rarely did he bring the message on a Sunday morning; only if there was no one else to speak was his father called upon. He was a kind of fill-in speaker, a holy handyman.

Yet he was treated, so far as John could see, with great respect. No one, none of the saints in any case, had ever reproached or rebuked his father, or suggested that his life was anything but spotless. Nevertheless, this man, God's minister, had struck John's

mother, and John had wanted to kill him—and wanted to kill
him still.

John had swept one side of the church and the chairs were
still piled in the space before the altar when there was a knocking
at the door. When he opened the door he saw that it was Elisha,
come to help him.

"Praise the Lord," said Elisha, standing on the doorstep, grinning.

"Praise the Lord," said John. This was the greeting always
used among the saints.

Brother Elisha came in, slamming the door behind him and
stamping his feet. He had probably just come from a basketball
court; his forehead was polished with recent sweat and his hair
stood up. He was wearing his green woolen sweater, on which
was stamped the letter of his high school, and his shirt was open
at the throat.

"You ain't cold like that?" John asked, staring at him.

"No, little brother, I ain't cold. You reckon everybody's frail
like you?"

"It ain't only the little ones gets carried to the graveyard,"
John said. He felt unaccustomedly bold and lighthearted; the
arrival of Elisha had caused his mood to change.

Elisha, who had started down the aisle toward the back room,
turned to star at John with astonishment and menace. "Ah," he
said, "I see you fixing to be sassy with Brother Elisha tonight—
I'm going to have to give you a little correction. You just wait
till I wash my hands."

"Ain't no need to wash your hands if you come here to work.
Just take hold of that mop and put some soap and water in the
bucket."

"Lord," said Elisha, running water into the sink, and talking, it
seemed, to the water, "that sure is a sassy nigger out there. I sure
hope he don't get hisself hurt one of these days, running his
mouth thataway. Look like he just *won't* stop till somebody
busts him in the eye." He sighed deeply, and began to lather his
hands. "Here I come running all the way so he wouldn't bust a
gut lifting one of them chairs, and all he got to say is 'put some
water in the bucket.' Can't do nothing with a nigger nohow." He

stopped and turned to face John. "Ain't you got no manners, boy? You better learn how to talk to old folks."

"You better get out here with that mop and pail. We ain't got all night."

"Keep on," said Elisha. "I see I'm going to have to give you your lumps tonight."

He disappeared. John heard him in the toilet, and then over the thunderous water he heard him knocking things over in the back room.

"*Now* what you doing?"

"Boy, leave me alone. I'm fixing to work."

"It sure sounds like it." John dropped his broom and walked into the back. Elisha had knocked over a pile of camp chairs, folded in the corner, and stood over them angrily, holding the mop in his hand.

"I keep telling you not to hide that mop back there. Can't nobody get at it."

"I always get at it. Ain't everybody as clumsy as you."

Elisha let fall the stiff gray mop and rushed at John, catching him off balance and lifting him from the floor. With both arms tightening around John's waist he tried to cut John's breath, watching him meanwhile with a smile that, as John struggled and squirmed, became a set, ferocious grimace. With both hands John pushed and pounded against the shoulders and biceps of Elisha, and tried to thrust with his knees against Elisha's belly. Usually such a battle was soon over, since Elisha was so much bigger and stronger and as a wrestler so much more skilled; but tonight John was filled with a determination not to be conquered, or at least to make the conquest dear. With all the strength that was in him he fought against Elisha, and he was filled with a strength that was almost hatred. He kicked, pounded, twisted, pushed, using his lack of size to confound and exasperate Elisha, whose damp fists, joined at the small of John's back, soon slipped. It was a deadlock; he could not tighten his hold, John could not break it. And so they turned, battling in the narrow room, and the odor of Elisha's sweat was heavy in John's nostrils. He saw the veins rise on Elisha's forehead and in his neck; his breath became jagged and harsh, and the grimace on his face became more cruel; and John watching these manifestations of his power, was filled with a wild delight. They stumbled against the folding-chairs, and Elisha's foot slipped and his hold broke. They stared at each other, half grinning. John slumped to the floor, holding his head between his hands.

"I didn't hurt you none, did I?" Elisha asked.

John looked up. "*Me?* No, I just want to catch my breath."

Elisha went to the sink, and splashed cold water on his face and neck. "I reckon you going to let me work now," he said.

"It wasn't *me* that stopped you in the first place." He stood up. He found that his legs were trembling. He looked at Elisha, who was drying himself on the towel. "You teach me wrestling one time, okay?"

"No, boy," Elisha said, laughing, "I don't want to wrestle with *you*. You too strong for me." And he began to run hot water into the great pail.

John walked past him to the front and picked up his broom. In a moment Elisha followed and began mopping near the door. John had finished sweeping, and he now mounted to the pulpit to dust the three thronelike chairs, purple, with white linen squares for the headpieces and for the massive arms. It dominated all, the pulpit: a wooden platform raised above the congregation, with a high stand in the center for the Bible, before which the preacher stood. There faced the congregation, flowing downward from this height, the scarlet altar cloth that bore the golden cross and the legend: *Jesus Saves*. The pulpit was holy. None could stand so high unless God's seal was on him.

He dusted the piano and sat down on the piano stool to wait until Elisha had finished mopping one side of the church and he could replace the chairs. Suddenly Elisha said, without looking at him:

"Boy, ain't it time you was thinking about your soul?"

"I guess so," John said with a quietness that terrified him.

"I know it looks hard," said Elisha, "from the outside, especially when you young. But you believe me, boy, you can't find no greater joy than you find in the service of the Lord."

John said nothing. He touched a black key on the piano and it made a dull sound, like a distant drum.

"You got to remember," Elisha said, turning now to look at him, "that you think about it with a carnal mind. You still got Adam's mind, boy, and you keep thinking about your friends, you want to do what they do, and you want to go to the movies, and I bet you think about girls, don't you, Johnny? Sure you do," he said, half smiling, finding his answer in John's face, "and you don't want to give up all that. But when the Lord saves you He burns out all that old Adam, He gives you a new mind and a new heart, and then you don't find no pleasure in the world, you get all your joy in walking and talking with Jesus every day."

He stared in a dull paralysis of terror at the body of Elisha. He saw him standing—had Elisha forgotten?—beside Ella Mae before the altar while Father James rebuked him for the evil that lived in the flesh. He looked into Elisha's face, full of questions he would never ask. And Elisha's face told him nothing.

"People say it's hard," said Elisha, bending again to his mop, "but, let me tell you, it ain't as hard as living in this wicked world and all the sadness of the world where there ain't no pleasure nohow, and then dying and going to Hell. Ain't nothing as hard as that." And he looked back at John. "You see how the Devil tricks people into losing their souls?"

"Yes," said John at last, sounding almost angry, unable to bear his thoughts, unable to bear the silence in which Elisha looked at him.

Elisha grinned. "They got girls in the school I go to"—he was finished with one side of the church and he motioned to John to replace the chairs—"and they nice girls, but their minds ain't on the Lord, and I try to tell them the time to repent ain't tomorrow, it's today. They think ain't no sense to worrying now, they can sneak into Heaven on their deathbed. But I tell them, honey, ain't everybody lies down to die—people going all the time, just like that, today you see them and tomorrow you don't. Boy, they don't know what to make of old Elisha because he don't go to movies, and he don't dance, and he don't play cards, and he don't go with them behind the stairs." He paused and stared at John, who watched him helplessly, not knowing what to say. "And, boy, some of them is real nice girls, I mean *beautiful* girls, and when you got so much power that *they* don't tempt you then you know you saved sure enough. I just look at them and I tell them Jesus saved me one day, and I'm going to go all the way with *Him*. Ain't no woman, no, nor no man neither going to make me change my mind." He paused again, and smiled and dropped his eyes. "That Sunday," he said, "that Sunday, you remember?—when Father got up in the pulpit and called me and Ella Mae down because he thought we was about to commit sin —well, boy, I don't want to tell no lie, I was mighty hot against the old man that Sunday. But I thought about it, and the Lord made me to see that he was right. Me and Ella Mae, we didn't have nothing on our minds at all, but look like the devil is just everywhere—sometime the devil he put his hand on you and look like you just can't breathe. Look like you just a-burning up, and you got to do something, and you can't do nothing; I been on my knees many a time, weeping and wrestling before the Lord—*crying*, Johnny—and calling on Jesus' name. That's the only name that's got power over Satan. That's the way it's been with *me* sometime, and I'm *saved*. What you think it's going to be like for you, boy?" He looked at John, who, head down, was putting the chairs in order. "Do you want to be saved, Johnny?"

"I don't know," John said.

"Will you try him? Just fall on your knees one day and ask him to help you to pray?"

John turned away, and looked out over the church, which now seemed like a vast, high field, ready for the harvest. He thought of a First Sunday, a Communion Sunday not long ago when the saints, dressed all in white, ate flat, unsalted Jewish bread, which was the body of the Lord, and drank red grape juice, which was His blood. And when they rose from the table, prepared especially for this day, they separated, the men on the one side, and the women on the other, and two basins were filled with water so that they could wash each other's feet, as Christ had commanded His disciples to do. They knelt before each other, woman before woman, and man before man, and washed and dried each other's feet. Brother Elisha had knelt before John's father. When the service was over they had kissed each other with a holy kiss. John turned again and looked at Elisha.

Elisha looked at him and smiled. "You think about what I said, boy."

When they were finished Elisha sat down at the piano and played to himself. John sat on a chair in the front row and watched him.

"Don't look like nobody's coming tonight," he said after a long while. Elisha did not arrest his playing of a mournful song: "Oh, Lord, have mercy on me."

"They'll be here," said Elisha.

And as he spoke there was a knocking on the door. Elisha stopped playing. John went to the door, where two sisters stood, Sister McCandless and Sister Price.

"Praise the Lord, son," they said.

"Praise the Lord," said John.

They entered, heads bowed and hands folded before them around their Bibles. They wore the black cloth coats that they wore all week and they had old felt hats on their heads. John felt a chill as they passed him, and he closed the door.

Elisha stood up, and they cried again: "Praise the Lord!" Then the two women knelt for a moment before their seats to pray. This was also passionate ritual. Each entering saint, before he could take part in the service, must commune for a moment alone with the Lord. John watched the praying women. Elisha sat again at the piano and picked up his mournful song. The women rose, Sister Price first, and then Sister McCandless, and looked around the church.

"Is we the first?" asked Sister Price. Her voice was mild, her skin was copper. She was younger than Sister McCandless by several years, a single woman who had never, as she testified, known a man.

"No, Sister Price," smiled Brother Elisha, "Brother Johnny here was the first. Him and me cleaned up this evening."

"Brother Johnny is mighty faithful," said Sister McCandless. "The Lord's going to work with him in a mighty way, you mark my words."

There were times—whenever, in fact, the Lord had shown His favor by working through her—when whatever Sister McCandless said sounded like a threat. Tonight she was still very much under the influence of the sermon she had preached the night before. She was an enormous woman, one of the biggest and blackest God had ever made, and He had blessed her with a mighty voice with which to sing and preach, and she was going out soon into the field. For many years the Lord had pressed Sister McCandless to get up, as she said, and move; but she had been of timid disposition and feared to set herself above others. Not until He laid her low, before this very altar, had she dared to rise and preach the gospel. But now she had buckled on her traveling shoes. She would cry aloud and spare not, and lift up her voice like a trumpet in Zion.

"Yes," said Sister Price, with her gentle smile, "He says that he that is faithful in little things shall be made chief over many."

John smiled back at her, a smile that, despite the shy gratitude it was meant to convey, did not escape being ironic, or even malicious. But Sister Price did not see this, which deepened John's hidden scorn.

"Ain't but you two who cleaned the church?" asked Sister McCandles with an unnerving smile—the smile of the prophet who sees the secrets hidden in the hearts of men.

"Lord, Sister McCandless," said Elisha, "look like it ain't never but us two. I don't know what the other young folks does on Saturday nights, but they don't come nowhere near here."

Neither did Elisha usually come anywhere near the church on Saturday evenings; but as the pastor's nephew he was entitled to certain freedoms; in him it was a virtue that he came at all.

"It sure is time we had a revival among our young folks," said Sister McCandless. "They cooling off something terrible. The Lord ain't going to bless no church what lets its young people get so lax, no sir. He said, because you ain't neither hot or cold I'm going to spit you outen my mouth. That's the Word." And she looked around sternly, and Sister Price nodded.

"And Brother Johnny here ain't even saved yet," said Elisha. "Look like the saved young people would be ashamed to let him be more faithful in the house of God than they are."

"He said that the first shall be last and the last shall be first," said Sister Price with a triumphant smile.

"Indeed, He did," agreed Sister McCandless. "This boy going

to make it to the Kingdom before any of them, you wait and see.

"Amen," said Brother Elisha, and he smiled at John.

"Is Father going to come and be with us tonight?" asked Sister McCandless after a moment.

Elisha frowned and thrust out his lower lip. "I don't reckon so, Sister," he said. "I believe he going to try to stay home tonight and preserve his strength for the morning service. The Lord's been speaking to him in visions and dreams and he ain't got much sleep lately."

"Yes," said Sister McCandless, "that sure is a praying man. I tell you, it ain't every shepherd tarries before the Lord for his flock like Father James does."

"Indeed, that is the truth," said Sister Price, with animation. "The Lord sure done blessed us with a good shepherd."

"He mighty hard sometimes," said Sister McCandless, "but the Word is hard. The way of holiness ain't no joke."

"He done made me to know that," said Brother Elisha with a smile.

Sister McCandless stared at him. Then she laughed. "Lord," she cried, "I *bet* you can say so!"

"And I loved him for that," said Sister Price. "It ain't every pastor going to set down his own nephew—in front of the whole church, too. And Elisha hadn't committed no big fault."

"Ain't no such thing," said Sister McCandless, "as a little fault or a big fault. Satan get his foot in the door, he ain't going to rest till he's in the room. You is in the Word or you *ain't*—ain't no halfway with God."

"You reckon we ought to start?" aswed Sister Price doubtfully, after a pause. "Don't look to me like nobody else is coming."

"Now, don't you sit there," laughed Sister McCandless, "and be of little faith like that. I just believe the Lord's going to give us a great service tonight." She turned to John. "Ain't your daddy coming out tonight?"

"Yes'm," John replied, "he said he was coming."

"There!" said Sister McCandless. "And your mama—is she coming out, too?"

"I don't know," John said. 'She mighty tired."

"She ain't so tired she can't come out and pray a *little* while,"
said Sister McCandless.

For a moment John hated her, and stared at her fat, black
profile in anger. Sister Price said:

"But I declare, it's a wonder how that woman works like she
does, and keeps those children looking so neat and clean and all,
and gets out to the house of God almost every night. Can't be
nothing but the Lord that bears her up."

"I reckon we might have a little song," said Sister McCandless,
"just to warm things up. I sure hate to walk in a chcurch where
folks is just sitting and talking. Look like it takes all my spirit
away."

"Amen," said Sister Price.

Elisha began a song: "This may be my last time," and they
began to sing:

> *"This may be the last time I pray with you,*
> *This may be my last time, I don't know."*

As they sang, they clapped their hands, and John saw that Sister
McCandless looked about her for a tambourine. He rose and
mounted the pulpit steps, and took from the small opening at
the bottom of the pulpit three tambourines. He gave one to
Sister McCandless, who nodded and smiled, not breaking her
rhythm, and he put the rest on a chair near Sister Price.

> *"This may be the last time I sing with you*
> *This may be my last time, I don't know."*

He watched them, singing with them—because otherwise they
would force him to sing—and trying not to hear the words that
he forced outward from his throat. And he thought to clap his
hands, but he could not; they remained tightly folded in his lap.
If he did not sing they would be upon him, but his heart told
him that he had no right to sing or to rejoice.

> *"Oh, this*
> *May be my last time*
> *This*
> *May be my last time*
> *Oh, this*
> *May be my last time . . ."*

And he watched Elisha, who was a young man in the Lord; who, a priest after the order of Melchizedek, had been given power over death and Hell. The Lord had lifted him up, and turned him around, and set his feet on the shining way. What were the thoughts of Elisha when night came, and he was alone where no eye could see, and no tongue bear witness, save only the trumpetlike tongue of God? Were his thoughts, his bed, his body foul? What were his dreams?

> *"This may be my last time,*
> *I don't know."*

Behind him the door opened and the wintry air rushed in. He turned to see, entering the door, his father, his mother, and his aunt. It was only the presence of his aunt that shocked him, for she had never entered this church before: she seemed to have been summoned to witness a bloody act. It was in all her aspect, quiet with a dreadful quietness, as she moved down the aisle behind his mother and knelt for a moment beside his mother and father to pray. John knew that it was the hand of the Lord that had led her to this place, and his heart grew cold. The Lord was riding on the wind tonight. What might that wind have spoken before the morning came?

William Demby

WILLIAM DEMBY, who now lives in Rome and writes screen plays for the Italian film industry, was born in the coal-mining town of Clarksburg, West Virginia, and attended West Virginia State College for Negroes, Fisk University, and the University of Rome, where he studied art after service with the American Army in Italy.

While he was in the Army, Mr. Demby wrote for *Stars & Stripes*, and upon his return to Fisk University his work appeared in the Fisk *Herald* and other publications.

Beetlecreek, Mr. Demby's only published novel, received little notice when published in 1950 although it is worthy of serious critical attention. *Beetlecreek* is a highly imaginative work, rich with symbolic meaning and suggestion and concerned with questions of good and evil that go beyond race.

In this novel the complex relationship between individual white persons and colored persons is treated with an unusual sensitivity and the life of the Negro world is harshly and honestly depicted. In *Beetlecreek*, Negroes are as much the victims of one another as they are of white society.

From *Beetlecreek*

BY WILLIAM DEMBY

Always when he looked in the mirror his eyes were different. Sometimes they peered from out of the broken glass asking an unanswerable question, sometimes they were angry and damning, sometimes they were sullen and brooding—too often they were the eyes of a dead man, jellied and blank. This ritual of looking at himself went on every day as soon as he got out of bed. His thick, blunt fingers would clutch at each other, moving back and forth slowly like the antennae of insects. His long, fleshy nose with its countless red pin pricks would expand and contract in time to his breathing and the gray-striped lips that refused to open over the severe outward slant of the front teeth would strain themselves into the subtlest kind of smile. There were deep vertical wrinkles along his cheek and at the corners of his eyes which gave an impression of kindliness. These wrinkles moved up and down, restlessly recording the changing climates of his emotions. Thus he would stand, sometimes for over an hour, a silent ugly man who could no longer tell whether he was inside the mirror or inside himself.

Bill Trapp had not long been at the mirror that afternoon when he heard a rustling in the bushes near the stone wall. Quickly he ran his hand through his matted hair and put on a huge felt hat. He walked very slowly, half on tiptoes, until he arrived at a bush. There, he kneeled down on the cold mud and parted the branches. He waited until he heard the rustling again and then rose high enough to see the intruders. His heart beat fast as it always did. Always when they came he would look into their faces. He would be filled with uncontrollable excitement knowing that he was seeing them while they couldn't see him. Faster and faster his heart would beat until filled with shame and rage, he would rush out at them waving his arms wildly, shouting, almost screaming, long after they had disappeared down the road.

In fifteen years he had had only one visitor, a tramp who came to his door to beg because he was too proud to beg from the Negroes down by the bridge. He gave coffee and sandwiches to this tramp, who, as soon as he had finished eating, went away. Once some colored ladies started to come into the yard and he chased them away with his shotgun. Sometimes, out of a furious impulse to break the clammy silence, he would begin singing songs he had heard in the towns along the river. Once a week, when he went to town to fetch the provisions he needed to live on or to sell the fruits and vegetables he grew, he found himself still talking in whispers, and people who spoke with him then would whisper too.

This time there were four boy Negroes under the tree. Three of them, wild-eyed and grinning, were signaling frantically to the boy in the tree to hurry and throw down to them some of the waxy, red apples.

The face of the boy in the tree held Bill Trapp's attention. He had never seen this boy before although the faces of the others were all familiar. All the boys were between the ages of thirteen and fifteen but the face of this boy seemed at once younger and older. It was a gentle, pear-shaped face; the eyes were clever and slanted and there was a serious monkey expression on it as the boy tried to concentrate on reaching for the apples.

For almost ten minutes the white man watched. Soon he felt the familiar itchy nervousness coming. But instead of rage this time, he was filled with curiosity. Very careful not to rustle the leaves, he rose to his feet; then, slowly and silently, he walked toward where the boys were crouching.

As soon as they saw him, the boys on the ground fled shrieking, but he paid no attention to them. His eyes were on the boy in the tree and toward him he walked. Even as he came nearer and nearer the tree and saw that the boy made no move to escape, he felt that it was he himself who should be fleeing. Closer and closer he came to the tree and slower and slower became his footsteps. Then, as he realized there was no backing away, that he would have to speak to the boy, he was filled with complete panic. His sweaty fingers deep through the holes in his pocket pulled at the long hairs of his thigh.

The boy's eyes swept back and forth like the eyes of a movable valentine. His pouting lips were parted and he breathed with difficulty.

"Come down," Bill Trapp said, and while the words were still forming on his lips, he realized that by an act of his own will he was ending his fifteen years of silence and solitude.

He bade the boy Negro sit down on the porch while he went into the shack, mumbling incoherently that he had something to do. The moment he was inside, he peeped out the window and was surprised that the boy seemed not to be frightened but was relaxed against the two-by-four support of the roof. Realizing that the boy was not going to run away as he had at first hoped and feared, he experienced a strange feeling—a feeling of tenderness toward the boy and indeed, to all people. With no more preparation than that—in one instant—the fifteen-year-old desire to be alone was wiped away.

He ran to the mirror and looked at himself. He tried to smile. For years and years he hadn't washed his teeth. He found a broken piece of comb and tried to do something with his hair. He found two cracked cups and filled them with cider he had bought recently from the A & P. These he carried out to the boy on the porch, who turned with wide-eyed surprise to face him. Still trembling, he offered one of the cups to the boy. They drank nervously and silently. Neither would look at the other.

"I didn' mean nothing by it," the boy said finally, holding the empty cup close to his ear as if he were listening to a seashell.

The sound of the boy's voice came as a shock to him, came as a clap of thunder, and he didn't know what he should say.

"You kids should ask for the fruit . . . all you had to do was ask and you coulda had all you wanted."

The cider was all gone—they each had had three cups—and there was no longer any excuse for the boy to stay. Once the boy turned toward him and looked straight into his eyes. Bill Trapp blushed and tried desperately to pry his mouth open in some kind of smile. He felt dizzy, tingling all over with thoughts that appeared and disappeared in his consciousnes like so many fireflies. He kept saying to himself: Chase the kid away, give him a bawling out and chase him away. Instead, he asked the boy his name. And then asked him where he lived, realizing after a few moments that he was having a conversation with him. The boys' name was Johnny Johnson. He was from Pittsburgh and had come to stay with his aunt and uncle while his mother was in the hospital. He wanted to look at the boy's face again to see if he was scared. He found himself rooting in his nostril, wiping his thick finger on his pants. But the boy didn't see this and he was relieved. He coughed and began to fidget.

"I could tell you something, Johnny, about being here all by yourself. I never would of chased nobody away 'cept they don't ask. I come from respectable folks and I respect people's property." But he saw that the boy wasn't listening.

When he looked toward where the boy was looking, he saw the gate burst open and a tall, distracted-looking Negro run into the yard. He looked questioning at Johnny and even moved closer to the boy as if to protect himself.

"That's my uncle," Johnny said.

"What's he want?" Bill Trapp asked. "I've got my rights and I respect people's property. . . ."

"What're you doing with that boy?" the man demanded, grasping hold of Johnny's hand as if to pull him away.

Bill Trapp couldn't open his mouth to speak. He was deaf. There was too much sound about him. He could hear the clock on the table inside the house. What did it mean, having these people on his porch? He was afraid, but he had gone this far, there was no turning back.

"He wasn't hurting me, Uncle David," the boy said. "We was just talking."

"I respect people's property, Mister. I'm a law-abidin' citizen. I'm an old man now. But I don't hurt nobody. See all this place here. I built it up. We come from respectable folks." He got up and went into the house. When he came out he brought a bottle of dandelion wine. The Negro man and boy became very quiet.

They drank; their breaths and sighs were in unison. They stole looks at each other from out of the corner of their eyes. And then the Negro man laughed.

"So you're Mister Bill Trapp?" he said. "Well, sir, it's a pleasure to be here with you. A real pleasure."

"I don't have many visitors," Bill Trapp said. "I'm what you call a retired man. I've done my share. But I could tell you a thing or two about being here all alone, no one to talk to. Gets so you forget a lot of things. But we come from respectable folks. I don't mean nobody no harm."

The light faded to near darkness and the three of them were still sitting there. To Bill Trapp it was like something out of his fantastic dreams to have the Negro man and boy on his porch. There was a lot of talk. The Negro man talked continuously with a nervous, jerky flow of words that Bill Trapp finally gave up trying to follow. He had been too long alone. He remembered a warning feeling which came to him, a feeling which as soon as it came he hastened to brush away. He felt vaguely that he was in danger. But dominating all that he was feeling was the tremendous resolution not to go back to the lonely ways of before. He was conscious of a change of life in him, a change that seemed to have come suddenly but which he knew was prepared for years before.

Before his visitors left, he recklessly promised to meet the man that night, promised to go with him to Telrico's Café.

Alone once more, still trembling, he went to the mirror and looked at his eyes. They were milky damp. His eyelids were sweating. This time he stayed at the mirror until it was so dark he could see only the slightest reflection on the whites of his eyes. What kind of mad thing had he let himself in for? He stayed up just long enough to warm himself a can of beans. By six o'clock he was undressed and in bed speculating on whether or not he would get up to meet the Negro man. He was hot and sweating. He kept the lamp lit so that he could watch the clock. Slowly and meticulously, his clumsy fingers pulled hairs from his thighs.

Johnny Johnson, completely undressed except for his underwear, lay across the bed. A *Doctor Zorro and the Dope Smugglers* lay unopened across his stomach. He had wanted to go outside where he knew the boys were waiting to hear what happened at Bill Trapp's, but, because he had been caught, his Aunt Mary had been very strict with him. He could hear them whooping and laughing and every once in a while he could hear the Leader calling his dog.

He looked around at the pink-rosed wallpaper. Everything was strange here, he decided. From the time when his cousin put him on the bus and he'd been left alone, sitting all by himself in the back of the bus watching the smooth West Virginia mountains already tinted by patches of red and brown gold, he had had the feeling he sometimes had when walking on a strange street in a strange neighborhood, a feeling like walking up the aisle of a full movie house when the lights were on, seeing all the faces, yet not seeing—feeling. A feeling of vague, itchy fear.

And that afternoon sitting with the old white man on his porch at the May Farm, drinking cider and feeling the man's terrible eyes on him, seeing the shack and the funny-shaped trees and the big flowers like nothing he had ever seen before, he had had the same feeling.

He wished he were back in his room at home in Pittsburgh. He rose and sat on the edge of the bed and turned on another light. He stared toward the closed door as if he expected the source of his fears to come in.

From downstairs, as he held his breath waiting, came the sound of his aunt's sobbing. Now with the fear was the conflicting desire to go to her, to put his arms around her waist as he remembered he used to do many years ago to his mother. He jumped up. His book fell to the floor and the sound startled him so that he couldn't close his mouth.

Quickly he slipped into his trousers and shoes and went to the living room, where she sat crumpled in the rocker.

"Aunt Mary," he began, and the sound of the words seemed to crystallize and echo and echo through the room, mixing finally with the hoarse sound of her crying. She became rigid and their eyes met. A look, first of shame and afterwards of anger, darted across her eyes in quick succession.

"Well, I'll be! What are you doing up and sneaking around the house for?" she snarled.

The savagery of her tone chilled him. He stuttered, "Can-n-n I ... can I do something for you?"

"You can get right upstairs to your room, that's what you can do. We don't have to put up with any of that Pittsburgh smart-aleckness out of you!"

He ran up the stairs and slammed his door. He was ashamed now to have gone downstairs to his aunt. He fell across the bed and lay there shaking until he felt sleep coming—sleep and the dreaming.

He knew how it would be, even to the soft, billowy feeling of the bed being pushed upward from underneath. He faced toward the corner from which it would come, always the same:

First, the silverness that was like a cloud of mercury that formed from nothing. Then a hot, electric feeling as if the room had been filled with electricity. Then a feeling of movement as if everything in the room were vibrating from a streetcar running overhead. Then the rain which wasn't exactly like rain but rather a feeling of millions and trillions of things falling. And then, the procession:

That night there was his mother dressed in a white nightgown from the hospital that was stained green and brown with blood that dripped from her neck. She was smiling but was convulsed by silent coughing. Very slowly she walked toward him. He squinched his eyes so he wouldn't see her. Closer and closer she walked until she had passed over his stomach. When he looked up, there was blood dripping on him and he could see that she was still smiling and nodding her head and coughing.

Then there was the old white man, Bill Trapp. There was a flock of sheep with him and he had a staff like a Bible shepherd. And the sheep were all afraid and kept prancing up and down like nervous horses in a lightning storm—like the horses did that time at the county fair when he went with his father. Bill Trapp would raise his hand and smile and the sheep would be even more frightened, prancing higher and higher. And when they came too close, he ducked his head so their hoofs wouldn't hurt him, but they passed over him so lightly, he didn't feel anything. Then the old man glided to him. His face was so close he could look right into his deep, strange eyes, and the eyes were green and there were long, green hairs growing out of the corners of them. It didn't look like Bill Trapp though. The face was sly and young, a combination of the Leader's face and the old man's, a shiny, hazy face that could be identified only by the hat. . . .

The dream would have gone on except that he was awakened

by the creaking of the door. His sleep muscles tightened as he tried to hold on to the warmth and color of the dream.

He knew his Aunt Mary was there, a ghostlike figure in her nightgown—the odor of her bedclothing more than the sight of her indicating her presence.

"Johnny! Johnny! You 'wake?" She touched him lightly under the chin and her cool hand felt pleasant in the hot, sweaty grove at his neck.

He kept very still, holding his breath, waiting until she would call again.

"You 'wake, Johnny?"

He could smell her unpleasant night breath as she bent her head close to his.

Yawning elaborately, he turned over as if he were just awakening. "Yeah, I'm awake," he said.

"Your uncle ain't come home and it's after one o'clock . . . don't ever stay out this late . . . might have been a raid like they had last spring. I think you better go on up there and see about him coming home. . . ."

She switched on the light and Johnny saw that she was dressed in a pink-ribboned nightgown. Her hair was down and in the soft light of the bedroom she looked very young, like a little girl, Johnny thought. One of her breasts was showing and Johnny felt a rush of hot blood rise to the top of his head.

As soon as she left him, he began to dress.

Out on the street, he breathed deeply of the cool night air. He was filled with a sense of adventure and was awed by the expansiveness of the darkness. The street was completely quiet and deserted and in none of the houses was there light. Despite the urgency he felt, he walked slowly, relishing the sound of his footsteps echoing between the sides of the houses. Before many minutes had passed, he turned the corner at the creek road and could see Telrico's red neon sign.

As he opened the doors, the smell of stale smoke and beer rushed out to engulf him. Right away he saw that no one was at the bar. Telrico was sitting by the stove reading a newspaper and didn't even bother to look up. Young Telrico, a thick-faced youth with pimples, was sweeping the floor. He looked up as Johnny entered, and just when Johnny was about to ask him, nodded toward the back of the café.

"If you're lookin' for somebody, they're all in the back."

Johnny walked toward the back room, carefully avoiding the pile of trash and sawdust heaped in the middle of the floor. The whole scene seemed part of the crazy things that were happening to him. Bill Trapp was sitting very close to his uncle with his head resting on his shoulder.

"Hello, Uncle David," Johnny said, and then, pretending he had just noticed the old white man, he said very stiffly, "And how are you, Mr. Bill?"

The two men were both very drunk. On the table before them were many empty beer bottles. The white man had unbuttoned his shirt and had one hand inside, restlessly rubbing it back and forth. His eyes, instead of being closed with drunkenness, were opened wide beyond the limits of the whites and were glazed, covered with an opaque film. His face was covered by a gratework of wrinkles. He ignored Johnny's greeting but sat with his head down, grinning, leaning all the time on Uncle David.

As Johnny stood over the dimly lit booth, his uncle rose. He smiled, swallowed the remainder of his beer, and motioned for Johnny to sit down beside him.

"He won't give me any more beer. It's after midnight he says. . . . Hell, Sam, it ain't after midnight, I've got a visitor. It ain't after midnight, Sam, it ain't after midnight yet. . . ." His voice died into a child's pleading.

Johnny held his breath wondering what Sam Telrico would say. Bill Trapp looked as if he were sleeping.

Without looking up from his newspaper, Telrico said, "We're closing up now, Diggs, and that's final. It's after midnight and we've got to close."

Young Telrico had stopped sweeping and was leaning on his broom, watching with frank amusement all that was going on. The way he was looking at Bill Trapp made Johnny angry and ashamed. (Look at that fart, he said to himself, I bet with all those pimples he plays with himself.)

"I guess we better be goin'," Bill Trapp said, rising. "It's a nice place you have here, sir," he said, bowing from the waist to Telrico, who was wrapping a scarf around his neck.

David began coughing. "All right, Johnny boy," he said when he got his breath, "we'll go home . . . go home to our little rest." Then after a moment of looking intently at Johnny's face, he said, "You sure look like her all right—you're Sis's boy all right you are. Nice boy . . . good kid. . . ."

". . . a very nice place," Bill Trapp continued, "reminds me a lot of Sid Carr's saloon in Cincinnati. Maybe they tore it down. Don't know now. Eighteen years . . . let's see . . ."

"Look, Diggs, you've got to go," Telrico shouted from behind the bar. In his dark blue overcoat he looked strangely smaller and insignificant, more like a bank clerk than a bartender now. The yellow business smile had disappeared and he seemed really irritated. "They've been makin' raids," he complained, "and I ain't takin' no chances on losin' my license."

Bill Trapp began helping David into his coat.

"I wouldn't want them tin cops from the county to pull your license," David said, making an elegant sweeping gesture with both hands. "We're going home to our little nest, aren't we, boy? By the way, Sam, you haven't met my little nephew, have you? This is my sister's boy, Johnny, and he's staying with us while his mother's in the hospital. He's from Pittsburgh."

Sam bowed and shook hands with Johnny. "Well, sir, you're some young man now, ain't you?" he said. "Can't say he looks like you though. Lot better lookin' than you are."

Johnny was pleased. He hurried to the door and held it open for Bill Trapp. He noticed how young Telrico stepped aside out of the old man's way as if he were afraid of him. Johnny fixed his eyes on the festering pimples on the youth's face; at least I don't have those, he thought to himself.

The old man leaned on Johnny for support. Johnny was surprised that he was so light. That afternoon, out on the May Farm, the old man had seemed tall and heavy, almost a giant. Now he was a weak old man and Johnny felt sorry for him.

They followed the creek road, walking in single file without speaking; sometimes the moon rode out from behind a cloud to light up the black lace pattern of bare trees that lined the bank of the creek. Sometimes the moon reflected on the top of the water shot out a single ray of light into the darkness at the bottom of the bushes.

They left Bill Trapp at the swinging bridge. "I'm much obliged to you for inviting me to the beer," he said earnestly, "much obliged." He held David by the shoulders and looked him straight in the eyes. He tweaked Johnny on the cheek and then disappeared among the blackest shadows of the bushes along the water.

"Come out and see me, come out and visit me, both of you come and see me . . ." his voice trailed away and the sound of his irregular drunken steps became fainter and fainter.

Back on their street again, they saw a light in an upstairs window of Mrs. Johnson's house.

"Must be worse, old lady Johnson," David said, stopping in front of the house. "Been saying down at the barbershop that she was in really bad shape this time."

They stood close together on the sidewalk looking up toward the window where shadows moved behind the lowered shade. Johnny felt his uncle become tense. There was something forbidding about the darkened house. One side of the roof caught the reflection of the moonlight and there was piece of loose roofing paper that flapped with the breeze.

Johnny didn't like being on the deserted street now, especially not in front of the sick woman's house. Nor did he feel safe and secure with his uncle.

"Let's go, Uncle David," he whined, "I'm getting sleepy."

Just as they were about to enter their own door, David whispered to Johnny, "Don't bother saying anything to your Aunt Mary about Bill Trapp being there tonight."

They pretended they didn't see him when he walked over to the railing of the bridge. They were standing slouched and posed with their hands in their pockets, smoking in rotation a short, wet cigarette butt.

"Hiya, Pittsburgh Kid!" Baby Boy was the first one to speak. He put his arm around Johnny's shoulder and steered him toward the rest of the boys. Johnny was grateful for Baby Boy's attention.

The Leader had his back toward Johnny and was busy chipping hunks of wood from the railing.

"Hello, fellows," Johnny said. He tried to make himself sound casual, but he realized right away that his voice was quivering. He took a tennis ball from his pocket and began bouncing it as if it were a basketball.

No one answered his greeting although all of them except the Leader grunted or hunched their shoulders in way of response. But, in spite of all this, Johnny could tell by the way the other two boys stole looks at him from the corners of their lowered eyes, that he had won new respect from them because of what had happened at Bill Trapp's.

"I saw you and yo uncle last night," the Leader said, a wry smile barely concealing the nervousness revealed in his sleepy eyes. "That fart of yours sure was drunk, must of been nursed on a bottle."

The Leader hoisted up his trousers and pulled on the frayed red suspender that was hanging from his shoulder. As if this were a signal, a titter circled the group and crescendoed into uncontrolled laughter. Only Baby Boy and Johnny didn't laugh.

Johnny felt the very same stabbing fears and embarrassments he had felt almost two weeks before, when he first encountered the gang. He could think of nothing to say that would belittle them. He hated and at the same time envied the Leader for his way of leaning back rocking on his heels with his thumb in the red suspenders. Even the thought that they were down-home boys and he was from the big city didn't comfort him.

The Leader was standing so close Johnny could feel the rise and fall of his stomach against his own. There was a sickening, sour milk smell about him.

Finally, Baby Boy asked, "What about it, Johnny? What'd he do to you?"

"Oh, it wasn't nothing. . . ."

There was a hole in the bottom plank of the bridge and in it was a waxy beetle struggling to get off its back. He took the beetle, and turning so they couldn't see him, he placed it carefully on the leaf of a bush.

"If you wouldn't of been so slow, you could of got away easy," the Leader said, looking from one boy's face to the other as if seeking confirmation in their expressions.

"He didn't do nothing," Johnny said. "Took me to the house and gave me cider, that's all."

He was angry with himself. This wasn't what he wanted to say at all. He had planned an entirely different story, a more exciting story that would give him more heroic importance.

The Leader sat on the railing and the other boys followed his example until there was only Johnny standing in the middle of the bridge.

"At first I was scared . . . he sure is a fearsome guy . . . looked at me with those funny eyes . . . I didn't know what he was going to do."

Johnny couldn't continue. Everything he had planned to say escaped his memory just like the time he had a Christmas recitation to say and he hadn't been able to remember whether he was supposed to say Hail the newborn King, or Hail, the King is born.

He took the tennis ball and threw it high in the air and clapped his hands once before catching it.

"What do you say we go to the shanty," Baby Boy said.

"D'you want to go to the shanty?" the Leader asked Johnny.

"Sure," Johnny said. They had never invited him before and he felt a little nervous.

They walked to the end of the bridge on the same side of the railroad tracks and climbed down through a path under a small trestle where the creek had backed up to form a small pond. On the side of the pond nearest the pillars of the trestle, in fact, nailed to the trestle, was a small shanty with a sloping, tarpaper roof partly hidden by low-hanging branches of a wild cherry tree.

"Hotdiggedy!" Johnny exclaimed.

The boys, all smiling proudly, made room for him while he pushed through the bushes in front of the doorway. He was about to open the door when the Leader stopped him.

"Wait a minute, boy! Don't just anybody go in there. This here's a secret place. You only go in there if you're a member or a guest."

"What is it, a club?"

The only club to which Johnny had even belonged was the Civics Club in school.

"S'a secret society," Baby Boy whispered.

"We's the Nightriders," one of the other two boys who up to now had remained silent, said. He had a long, red scaly neck.

"Well, how about it?" insisted the Leader. "You want to join or don't you?"

Johnny didn't know what to say. This was more than he had hoped for. They were really asking him to join their club!

"Sure, I'll join," Johnny stammered rather too eagerly, "what do I have to do?"

"You'll be initiated," Baby Boy whispered to him excitedly.

It was too dark to see anything at first, but the Leader struck a match and lit a lantern that swung from the ceiling. The room was larger than it appeared from outside. Johnny liked the fetid, closed-in smell of the room, a smell like that of a moldy, damp pocketbook he had once found under his back porch.

When his eyes became accustomed to the dark, he saw that the walls were covered with pictures torn from magazines. Some of the pictures were of baseball players and orchestra leaders, but most of them were photographs of movie actresses in bathing suits.

"C'mere. Look at this," the Leader said. And he steered Johnny to a corner where there was what appeared to be a kind of curtain tacked to the wall. The other four boys gathered around.

He pulled the curtain aside. "Look at these farts," he said. And there, pasted to the walls, were pictures cut from a pornographic cartoon book.

Johnny felt a wave of heat tear at his stomach muscles. He wanted to turn his head away in disgust, at the same time wanted very much to look and look at the wonderful pictures of things he had never seen before. He was afraid that if he tried to say anything, he would be unable to make a sound.

Baby Boy, who was standing behind him, was hopping up and down in a kind of dance, his hands between his legs. "Woo, woo!" he shouted, all the while giggling.

The red-necked boy had his hands in his pockets and was rubbing them back and forth nervously, at the same time he shimmied up and down the floor.

"I bet you can't even dog-water," said one of the other boys who was seated in a dark corner.

Johnny turned his head and saw what the boy was doing. He wanted to run away from the terrible shack and the terrible boys. Their fingernails will fall out and their teeth, he mumbled to himself. But he remembered his own sins and this made him even more ashamed. Quickly he turned his head so that he wouldn't have to look at them or say anything—most of all he feared their laughter and ridicule. Only this fear kept him from running out the door.

He turned his back toward them and began leafing through a sport magazine, hoping in this way to calm himself. He could hear their heavy breathing and occasional gasps of high-pitched laughter. He fought an almost overwhelming desire to go to the corner to look at the pictures again. He kept seeing one picture in particular, Little Orphan Annie in the embrace of Punjab.

After a while, the boys pulled out cigarette butts and began to pass them around.

"You want to smoke?" Baby Boy asked Johnny.

Johnny had never smoked before; once he had started to smoke a cornsilk cigarette but the odor had made him sick.

"Well . . . I don't know . . . maybe I better not. I got a sore throat."

But when he saw the amused looks the others were giving him, he accepted the brown-stained butt the boy was handing him and gingerly put it in his mouth. He kept his lips as dry as possible because he knew Baby Boy hadn't washed his hands after what he had just done.

They were all sitting on the floor with their backs to the wall. Baby Boy was half leaning on Johnny's shoulder while the Leader told them a dirty joke:

". . . and when the fart jumped in with her, he found out hers was bigger than his!"

Johnny joined in the laughter but he didn't see anything funny in the joke. He was panic-stricken when Baby Boy asked him to tell one. The only joke he knew had to do with a school teacher who found out that her pupil had put catsup in the inkwell, but it wasn't a dirty joke at all.

A frightened baby pigeon flew into the room through the small window and zipped back and forth over their heads and against the floor and ceiling.

Johnny reached out his hand and tried to catch it. So did the other boys, but the crazy bird was not to be caught. They ran back and forth through the narrow space, stumbling over each other, screaming with excitement.

"Whoo-whoo! Little fart . . . h'ya is . . . whoo-whoo! Now I's got ya. . . ."

Until finally Johnny caught the bird, trapped him in the corner where the ceiling was low, and cupped his hands over the soft, trembling wings and held it firm. Birds reminded Johnny of feeling sorry for animals and he caressed the warm, pulsating softness. He was about to set the bird free, when the Leader snatched it from his hands.

"Don't! You'll hurt it," Johnny exclaimed. He saw the red, glassy eyes of the bird and how strangely they contrasted with the purple head.

The Leader took the bleating bird by the neck and began to swing it over his head in an ever increasing arc. Johnny watched horrified as drops of blood sprinkled the floor. Suddenly the body was torn from the head and smashed against the wall with a loud thud.

The Leader's eyes were shining and his mouth was open in a toothy, insane grin. For a moment he kept looking at the spot where the bird's body had struck the wall, then, realizing that he still held the bloody fragment of the bird's head in his hand, he burst out laughing and all the boys began to laugh—all except Johnny.

Johnny felt sick in the stomach and was afraid he would vomit. Suddenly, the Leader ran at Johnny, thrusting the bloody bird head in Johnny's face. Johnny became pale—frozen with fright. He couldn't get his breath.

With all the strength that remained, he kept himself from breaking out in tears. "I'll see you guys," he said, and he walked out the door.

No one said anything. Johnny wouldn't look at them but when he was out on the railroad tracks, he heard a single voice laughing.

There was a purple and gray feather on his shirt. He took the feather and rubbed it between his fingers and then put it up to his nose to smell, but there was no odor.

Johnny was afraid and he was very sad. He crossed the swinging bridge and began walking aimlessly along the creek road away from the village. He didn't want to go home, it was still too early for lunch, besides he wanted to be alone.

Once his mother had appeared suddenly in the bathroom while he was taking a bath and had warned him against doing the devil's work. She had shown him a picture, in a large leather-covered doctor's book, of a boy with a huge head and popping eyes, one of which was blind. The boy was bald and his face covered with hideous sores. "This is what will happen to you," she said. And this, he had never forgotten, and always afterward he would pray fervently for God to forgive him, and he couldn't face anyone, and every day he would check his face for signs of change.

He was sorry to have seen what he had seen, sorry to have felt what he had felt. Because, before, it had been a secret sin. He was alone, the only sinner, and as such, could bear his sin. But to see it in others—to have seen what the boys were doing—was like telling the world of his own sin.

The baby pigeon that had flown into the room was a soft little bird and he had felt sorry for it. His instinct had been to protect it, but the Leader had swung it round and round over his head until the body was separated from the head, till blood dropped to the floor, till purple and gray feathers drifted gently as in a dream through the air, until the bleating had stopped. And he knew that, behind the terror and the feeling sorry for the bird, the dead creature, was also a new feeling: a new feeling of envy for the power the Leader had over things and creatures and the other boys, power and contempt, a certain hardness that he, Johnny, had never had but which he recognized now as an important thing. And Johnny, walking along the creek road, puzzled and pondered over these thoughts, all the while rubbing the piece of feather between his fingers.

Now the days were long; time moved slowly for Bill Trapp. Every morning found him up and about long before dawn. He was restless and spent his time doing unnecessary things; he mended traps and pruned trees, working always near the road, hoping to see the colored boy, hoping to see any human walking toward his place. One day, a colored lady pushing a wheelbarrow of ashes passed on the road. He stopped working to watch her broad behind disappear around the bend of the road. Every evening as soon as the sun had set he would begin drinking. This he did to hasten the passing of night. His sleep then would be heavy; only toward morning, just before dawn, would he dream. Once he dreamed of a gigantic circus tent that stretched as far as the eye could see. Dressed in the fancy military uniform, holding the torches, he stood in the very middle of the circular stage; all around him were thousands and thousands of children who applauded and screamed as he waved the torches in the air.

Sometimes in the morning, feeling safe in the sweaty warmth of the blankets, he would try to think back to the days when he was with Harry Simcoe's Continental Show. Almost always then his thoughts would cluster about a certain smell, a feeling connected with the carnival. Most of the time he would think of the place behind Mr. Stein's tent where everyone went to pass their water.

He used to stand there in the darkness behind that tent resigned and happy to be there, straddling the puddle of his own steaming urine. No matter where they were—Martinsville, Harperstown, Mansfield, Braddock, Cleveland—the puddle was always the same, a tiny lake of steaming lava in the sand or sawdust. The patched piece of canvas on the back wall of the tent, as well as the frayed piece of rope looped three times around the tent peg, were always there to fix the gaze upon. In a time when his life was made up of moving about through strange town landscapes, this place behind Mr. Stein's tent where everyone came to do it remained fixed and unchangeable. Dogs sniffed happily around this place.

As soon as he finished unpacking the prizes on nights he didn't have anything else to do, he would rush there to stand quietly while thoughts of the past would rise up out of the steam.

He would try to think of being a child; he would try to re-create the picture of him and Hilda saying their prayers together while Mrs. Haines stood there behind them, her heavy asthmatic breathing filling in the spaces between the rushed syllables of "Now I laymee . . ." Then, just thinking of the name Mrs. Haines made him remember the shame he used to feel of being an adopted child, made him remember how sorry he felt for her having an ugly child like him on her hands, though, when some of the children at school told him she got money from the county for taking care of them, he felt better.

As a child, almost every thought he had was conditioned by his ugliness, and even as an adult, long after Mrs. Haines was dead and Hilda and he had no one but themselves, he would blush with terrible embarrassment for his sister whenever anyone would remark how much they resembled one another. He expected very little from people. He was rather ashamed to be in the world and claimed few rights for himself. Outside of him was Hilda, upon whose love he could count, though even this love he accepted gingerly, hardly daring to believe it real.

When Mrs. Haines died, they both left school to take jobs, he in a blacksmith shop which later became a garage, and Hilda as a maid in a ladies' boardinghouse. Every Saturday night he would take half of his pay to her, stopping first to buy two pints of ice cream and a fifteen-cent cake which gravely they would eat sitting on the back steps. Then, when they had finished and washed their hands, she would tell him that they must save their money so that someday they could live as respectable people should. Twenty years passed before they knew it. Twice during that time the price of ice cream changed.

The garage where he worked closed down one winter and he took a job as handyman with a carnival that happened to be passing through. Hilda left the town that same winter to take up residence in a ladies' boardinghouse in a nearby town. There she did needlework and lived from the money she had saved.

Now he could only visit his sister twice a year, once in the winter and once in the late spring. He still took presents with him when he went to visit her, usually a souvenir basket of fruit from California wrapped in real silk ribbons. She would place the gift down on the table, pretending to ignore it, and immediately start giving him a tongue lashing. "Why you want to waste away your life running around the country with a carnival is more than I can see," she would say, her long nose twitching and her hands imploring the air. "We're respectable folks but *you* don't seem to care anything about my reputation." He would sit there on the stiff-backed chair trying to keep from touching with his back the doily she'd stitched herself. When she would finish and he'd finished the tea she always served him in tiny fragile cups, he would leave filled with the conviction that she was right and that he must do something about his life.

It was after one of these visits that he decided to take up the Retirement Plan Insurance. All the week before, he kept seeing the picture of the Happy Man and Cottage in the back pages of the western magazine they used for toilet paper in the portable latrine. At first he tried to ignore the picture but always, thinking of what his sister had told him, the picture would come back to his mind. Once, unable to ignore the call any longer, he went into the toilet and took the magazine to his tent and filled out the coupon. When the important-looking envelope filled with pink forms arrived, he felt very excited, almost as if he was taking his first communion.

Carefully he filled out the forms and when they were safely in the mail, he wrote a long letter to his sister telling her in the same words of the advertisement just what the Retirement Insurance Plan was. She thought it was a splendid idea and told him again of how they came from respectable folks, and that he owed it to the memory of their folks to try to better himself. He was past forty then, but the insurance made him feel much younger.

Hilda died of pneumonia soon after he began the Retirement Insurance. Mr. Stein gave him two days off to go to the funeral. He didn't know any of the ladies dressed in black and navy blue who cried at the funeral and was ashamed to make himself known to them. As soon as it was over, he slipped away unnoticed and decided to go to Niagara Falls, where he had never been before.

He waited until the guide took the group back down for the trip under the falls and stood all alone there at the railing, while the roar of the water blasted away his identity. Then, with the perfumed memory of the pretty funeral and flowers Hilda had had combined in his mind with the feeling of being on a kind of vacation, his first, he began to cry out for joy. For the first time in his life he almost understood something. He wasn't ashamed. On his way back to the bus stop he stopped in a road-house to have a beer. For once he felt like respectable folks and even put money in the music box.

He didn't take up with the Italian at once; a year of gray-passing time went by and he no longer sent money to the Retirement Plan. The envelopes which kept coming he placed in a neat pile on his washstand box where the wind blowing through the tent kept them free from dust. Hair began growing on his soul. Never before in his life had he been without someone who could confirm his own existence, into whose life he could sometime look.

But one rainy night he was standing behind the money-counting tent watching the slow, cheap bracelet swinging of the Ferris wheel when the Italian appeared there behind him. "You've been standing there a long time," the Italian said.

He should have been ashamed but he wasn't. He stood aside for the Italian, but instead the Italian accompanied him back to the street. "My dog's sick," he said, "it's the rain and this food. . . ." Bill Trapp was glad that it was dark and misty and that he couldn't see the Italian's face; it sounded as if he were crying.

Although he had seen the Italian many times, he had never spoken one word to him. The Italian was a performer, though a shabby one in ill repute with the flashier performers, and he was only a handyman; but it wasn't that that kept them apart. The Italian drank constantly and this as much as his own shyness kept him from ever doing more than to nod in passing. But this time he went with him to look at the dog, an aged hound with long shiny hair and a face like an old complaining woman. From that day on, he and the Italian became friends.

The Italian gave him a costume, the uniform of an old Corsican cavalier, and allowed him to participate in the dog act. All Bill Trapp had to do was to hold a flaming torch that changed colors as different powders burned throughout the entire act, while the dogs "talked," rolled over, counted, and played dead. They don't understand theater, these American audiences, the Italian would complain after every act.

Bill Trapp knew that their friendship obviously depended on the fact that he was the only one who would listen to the Italian's drunken conversations, but just as when he was a child he used to accept the other children's taunts willingly if it meant some kind of recognition for himself, he now accepted the Italian's abuse. Every time they came to a new town, as soon as he had tied up the last loop around headquarters tent, he would hurry uptown to buy a bottle of cheap liquor to give the Italian. He would hurry through his supper then (the Italian insisted on eating alone in his tent with the dogs) and afterwards, cleanly shaven, would make his call on the Italian.

During those years, he was almost happy. There was a kind of order to his life that hadn't been before, and every evening he could count on listening to the Italian complain about the world. His soul became alive again and the possibility of a future became real to him. He told the Italian about the Retirement Insurance Plan but the Italian only laughed at him, saying that the only true investment was the investment of the mind. Soon afterwards they sent away for a set of books, *The Facts of Life Series:* "A Compilation of all the World's Knowledge with Particular Emphasis on the Wonderful Mysteries of the Human Machine." Though it was mostly his money that was sent, he didn't mind, because he spent little money for himself and had never touched the money he'd begun saving when he first began working.

First the Italian's dog died and then the Italian himself. When the dog died, the Italian took the body to a taxidermist and left it there to be stuffed. He didn't go to get the dog till a week later when they'd already moved to another town. He disappeared for almost a week and everyone had given him up for good. ("Good riddance," said Mr. Stein, who'd kept the Italian and the dog act just because the Italian had once been such a famous trapeze artist.) Bill Trapp held tight inside himself and wouldn't let himself feel anything. He took to standing a long time at the urine puddle again. Then one night, standing there thinking soft fuzzy balls of thoughts, he saw the Italian enter the tent. He was covered with mud and his eyes were pus-filled but he carried the oily stuffed dog in his arms. He wouldn't speak to Bill Trapp when he went into the tent; he just lay there looking a hole through the ceiling. The new books were covered with toothpaste and spoiled food and they sometimes used them to sit on. A bottle of sour

milk stunk up the close atmosphere inside the tent. That same
night the Italian died.

No one knew what to do with the stuffed dog. Bill Trapp didn't
want it. He wouldn't accept anything that had belonged to the
Italian except the uniform, some of the fire powder that he used
in the torches, and the books. The only real regret he had was that
he could no longer dress up and participate in the dog act. Standing there before the people, especially the children, he had felt
important, belonging to the world, worthwhile and unashamed.
Now that would be no more. As far as the Italian's death, he had
become used to the necessity of death, and now decided to wait
peaceably for his own. He suddenly felt like an old man. He had
been a child once, now he was an old man. There had been no
middle period of youth.

The county took the body away and that was the end for Bill
Trapp and the carnival. They were in Ridgeville then and when
he saw the farm known as the May Place there between the Negro
part of town and the white business section, he made up his mind
to buy it and live there the rest of his life. Way in the back of his
mind was the picture of the Happy Man and Cottage of the Retirement Plan.

One more night, for the last time, he straddled the puddle of
his own steaming urine, and, just as at Niagara Falls that day, he
came close to understanding something, he came close to understanding why it was that he had never lived, why it was that his
life had been incomplete, only half tasted; he understood (though
vaguely, without the thoughts taking the form of words or ideas)
the necessity of giving himself the right and power to reach out
and touch people, to love. He blamed no one for the shriveled
paleness of his soul. But now it was too late. All these years he
had waited for the touch, the gesture, from others, fearing to make
the gesture, the touch, himself for fear of being rebuffed. He
kicked a pile of sawdust into the puddle then and left the carnival.
Ten years had gone by.

Negroes passed back and forth to see him move into the May
Place. All that week, while he cut grass and made the shanty liv-
able, they moved back and forth restlessly on the road.

Mr. Stein had never hired Negroes for the carnival, but they were always the first to begin hanging around whenever the big tents went up. In the afternoon, in the dust and direct heat, whenever the white people were all indoors, there would still be Negroes shuffling through the sawdust picking up bits of paper to look at, kicking at tent pegs. Sometimes they would sit in the shade and he would hear them talking softly like church whispering. From the slit in the corner of his tent, he would watch them. Even from that distance, he felt close to them. Watching them secretly as he did, he could see that they were always dodging something, were ashamed of something just as he was; they were the same breed as he. Still, whenever they would stand behind him while he hammered down the stakes and he would feel their cue-ball eyes measuring his back, his hands would sweat with something akin to fear. Sometimes he would miss a stroke and wonder if they were winking at each other, making their secret jokes there behind his back.

He began to think about that colored boy, Johnny, and the boy's uncle. Why didn't they come back to visit him? Sitting there in the café that night, listening to the rush of talk the colored man made reminded him of the times he would listen to the Italian. He had been so excited and touched to be there with the man that he hardly understood what was being said. And it didn't matter. With his sister and with the Italian he had developed the habit of nodding his head in time to the cadence of people's talk and this was better than listening.

Now he was anxious to test his new sociability. He felt reckless. After all the years of silence, he had talked to the colored boy and to the man in the café, now he wanted to talk to other people. He made a plan: he would go uptown to the store where he bought his provisions and sold his produce. To all the children he passed, he would smile and in this way they would know that there had come a change over him.

Usually, walking through the streets of Beetlecreek, he walked fast, his head bent low as if in anticipation of the stones children sometimes threw at him. Now, however, he walked slowly and boldly in the very middle of the street, his head thrown back and swinging as if inside himself he was singing a song.

All the children were indoors or in school; the streets were deserted. He was very disappointed about this and hurried on to the store.

Up until the moment he entered the store, he didn't know what it was he would buy. Except for the clerk sitting on a barrel reading a newspaper, the store was deserted. "What'll you have?" asked the clerk without looking up. Bill Trapp looked about him. What should he buy? In front of the counter was a high pyramid of Naughton's Toilet Tissues. He pointed to the stack. The clerk seemed astonished and handed him the roll without wrapping it or saying a word. Going out the door, Bill Trapp smiled and called out a squeaking "Good morning," but the clerk went back to reading the newspaper and didn't return the smile. Outside on the curb, Bill Trapp was so flustered he stumbled and almost fell. He looked around to see if anyone was watching but because of the cold, there were few people on the street.

By the time he was back in Beetlecreek, the colored grade school had let out. Hordes of children ran shireking up and down the street. He tucked in his belt, straightened his hat, and boldly began to walk past them. A determined stiff smile cracked his dry lips. Passing very close to a group of small children—there were three girls and a little boy—he reached out his hand to touch their heads. Up to that moment he may have been unnoticed, but then, it seemed as if every child on the block had seen. They became very quiet. It was as if they had all stopped breathing. One of the little girls made a low moan; the other children began to scream. The smallest girl began to cry. They formed a line on either side of him. One boy spit at him. Some of them began yelling hysterically: "Peckerwood, peckerwood! Ya-aa-a, ya-a-a!" He still smiled stiffly. His hands, still gripping the toilet paper, were dripping sweat. He felt the whizz of a stone pass close to his head and saw the tiny splash it made in a puddle a few yards ahead of him. His steps became faster and faster so that by the time he had passed the last house on the street, he was almost running. Though, walking down the creek road, he felt a danger warning in all that had happened, he refused to let any such thoughts come to his mind. It is all my fault, he kept telling himself. Somehow, what he had done was not right. He was determined not to let himself go back through the tunnel of the years already passed. He was determined to hold on to all he had gained since the day the boy sat on his porch.

Then a strange thing happened. Arriving at his farm, his head bent low, the toilet paper clutched tight as if from it alone could he hope to get relief from the fears that persistently lit up the back of his head, he heard the sound of children laughing. At first he wouldn't look up. Somehow he thought it was some of the children come to follow him. But no! When he looked to see, he saw two little white girls swinging on his gate. Very seldom did white children venture this far down toward the Negro village and he looked upon this scene as a kind of omen. The knowledge that they would know nothing of him gave him courage and once again he tucked in his belt and straightened his hat. He set his lips in a smile and nervously, walking almost sideways, he approached them.

"You all want to go in?" he croaked.

"Why? You live here?" one of the girls asked suspiciously. They were hardly more than eleven years old; both were very blonde with brown eyes. He could tell that they were sisters.

His heart began to beat faster. "Won't you come in?" he asked, his voice shaded in such a way that he might have been making an invitation to a formal dinner party.

Just as he had done the afternoon when Johnny and his uncle were there, he invited the little girls to drink some of the cider. He stuck the battered roll of toilet paper in a drawer and once again looked at himself in the mirror. He was smiling broadly and his yellowed teeth were completely revealed.

He spit into a tin can two yards from the porch and this amused the little girls. One of them tried to spit into the can too, but succeeded only in wetting the front of her coat. This made them all laugh and he spit again to show them how.

Later, he climbed the ladder leaning against one of the apple trees and chose four big apples to give them. Their big brown eyes twinkled to see such fruit and when he saw that it was getting late in the afternoon, he told them that they better be going home. He said this very gently; he didn't want them to get in trouble with their families by coming home late and thus be prevented from coming back the next week to visit him as they had promised.

Already he was so happy he had forgotten completely what had happened while he was on his way back from the store. He walked with the girls to the gate and stood there nibbling at an apple while watching them disappear around the bend in the road.

That night, as a celebration, he drank much dandelion wine. He put on the uniform. He became drunk and took a large quantity of the powder he had used in the Italian's act to burn in the very center of the yard. It made a weird green and red light that silvered up each leaf of the tree and swelled up the pumpkins with a squeezing flicker of shadow. He leaped around through the smoke like a primitive witch doctor, laughing, almost shrieking, until he fell exhausted on the steps.

The next morning when he awoke, he was ashamed and took one of the dusty books to look at. He wiped the dust away with an old pair of overalls and sat himself by the window. But reading was impossible; he couldn't keep his eyes away from the road.

Thinking about the little girls, he decided that one of the things he would do, would be to go downtown to the Western Clothing Store to buy a flannel work shirt, maybe a new handkerchief to wear around his neck.

He went to the wall and began raking through the weeds and fallen leaves that grew near the mossy stones. There were vines there that seemed to move and catch themselves to his feet as he walked. Often he put down his rake to look longingly toward the village. He kept hoping that he would see the boy Johnny heading his way.

Finally, he climbed one of the apple trees and spent the rest of the morning like some kind of vulture bird perched on the highest, thinnest limb of the tree, rocked back and forth by the wind, picking his nose in quiet serene anticipation.

Dorothy West

DOROTHY WEST's *The Living Is Easy* (1948) provides an unusual revelation and insight into the social material of Negro life. This novel is a scathing and bitter attack upon the values and destructive behavior of the Negro middle class.

The Living Is Easy describes the emotional consequences of the obsession with respectability, success, and money among the black petty bourgeoisie and is distinguished by a sharp and effective delineation of personality and character.

Miss West is a native of Boston and was educated at Boston University and the Columbia School of Journalism. Her earliest work appeared in the late 1920's in the Boston *Post, Opportunity,* and the *Saturday Evening Quill,* published by a group of Negro intellectuals living in and around Boston. Later, Miss West was the editor of *Challenge* and *New Challenge,* periodicals devoted to Negro life and art, and a relief investigator in Harlem during the depression years; then she worked for a time on the Federal Writers Project. Miss West continues to write short stories and articles for various publications.

From *The Living Is Easy*

BY DOROTHY WEST

Cleo sailed up Northampton Street with Judy in tow. Dark, unshaven faces split in wide grins, and low, lewd whistles issued from between thick lips. This was her daily cross to bear in this rapidly deteriorating section of Boston. The once fine houses of the rich were fast emptying of middle-class whites and filling up with lower-class blacks. The street was becoming another big road, with rough-looking loungers leaning in the doorways of decaying houses and dingy stores. Coarse conversations balanced like balls in mouths stretched wide to catch the dirty pellets and toss them to other agile word jugglers all along the way.

They kept on the lookout for Cleo because she walked proud with her eyes on a point above their bullet heads. They had sworn to a man to make her smile.

"Look away, look away," moaned an ogling admirer. "The yeller sun has took up walking like a natchal woman."

Roars of appreciative guffaws greeted this attempt at wit. As the laughter subsided, a falsetto voice implored, "Lawd, take me to heaven while I'm happy. You done open my eyes and I done see a host of angels coming at me. She look like fire, and she ack like ice. I'm hot, I'm cold. Oh, Lawd, have mercy on my soul."

Twin spots glowed in Cleo's cheeks. A stream of white-hot words erupted inside her, but did not pass the thin line of her lips. She swallowed them down and felt the spleen spread to the pit of her stomach. Men were her enemies because they were male.

The trolley wires began to hum. "Here comes the trolley," said Cleo, with an expelled breath of profound relief. "Pick up your feet and don't you dare fall down. If you get yourself dirty before we get to Brookline, I'll give you to a Chinaman to eat."

The trolley halted, and she boosted Judy aboard. She dropped a single fare in the slot—Judy was small for going on six—asked for a transfer, guided Judy down the aisle of the swaying car, and shuttled her into a window seat. She sank down beside her and fanned herself elegantly with one gloved hand, stirring no air whatever.

She looked herself now, gay and earth-rooted and intensely alive. Her gray eyes sparkled at Judy, at the slyly staring passengers, at the streets that grew cleaner and wider as the trolley left the Negro neighborhood, at the growing preponderance of white faces.

Judy's nose was pressed against the glass. Cleo nudged her and whispered, "Judy, what do I tell you about making your nose flat?"

Judy sighed and straightened up. The exciting street scene was a whole inch farther away. She withdrew into an injured silence and studied her reflection in the glass. It was not very clear, but she knew what she looked like. She looked like Papa.

The people on the streetcar didn't know that. They regarded her in a way that she was quite used to. They were wondering where Cleo got her. They carefully scrutinized Cleo, then they carefully scrutinized her, and raised their eyebrows a little.

She was dark. She had Papa's cocoa-brown skin, his soft dark eyes, and his generous nose in miniature. Cleo worked hard on her nose. She had tried clothespins, but Judy had not known what to do about breathing. Now Cleo was teaching her to keep the bridge pinched, but Judy pinched too hard, and the rush of dark blood made her nose look larger than ever.

A little white dog with a lively face and a joyful tail trotted down the street. Judy grinned and screwed around to follow him with her eyes.

Cleo hissed in her ear: "Don't show your gums when you smile, and stop squirming. You've seen dogs before. Sit like a little Boston lady. Straighten your spine."

The trolley rattled across Huntington Avenue, past the fine granite face of Symphony Hall, and continued up Massachusetts Avenue, where a cross-street gave a fair and fleeting glimpse of the Back Bay Fens, and another cross-street showed the huge dome of the magnificent mother church of Christian Science. At the corner of Boylston Street, within sight of Harvard Bridge and the highway to Cambridge, Cleo and Judy alighted to wait for the Brookline Village trolley.

Cleo saw with satisfaction that she was already in another world, though a scant fifteen-minute ride away from the mean streets of the Negro neighborhood. There were white people everywhere with sallow-skinned, thin, austere Yankee faces. They had the look that Cleo coveted for her dimpled daughter. She was dismayed by Judy's tendency to be a happy-faced child, and hoped it was merely a phase of growth. A proper Bostonian never showed any emotion but hauteur. Though Cleo herself had no desire to resemble a fish, she wanted to be able to point with the pride of ownership to someone who did.

The Village trolley came clanging up Boylston Street, and Judy clambered up the steps, pushed by her mother and pulled by the motorman. Cleo was pleased to see that there were no other colored passengers aboard. The occupants of the half-filled car were mostly matrons, whose clothes were unmodish and expensive. All of them had a look of distinction. They were neither Cabots nor Lowells, but they were old stock, and their self-assurance sat well on their angular shoulders.

They did not stare at Cleo and Judy, but they were discreetly aware of the pair, and appreciative of their neat appearance. Boston whites of the better classes were never upset or dismayed by the sight of one or two Negroes exercising equal rights. They cheerfully stomached three or four when they carried themselves inconspicuously. To them the minor phenomenon of a colored face was a reminder of the proud rôle their forebears had played in the freeing of the human spirit for aspirations beyond the badge of house slave.

The motorman steered his rocking craft down a wide avenue and settled back for the first straight stretch of his roundabout run. Cleo looked at the street signs, and her heart began to pound with excitement. This was Brookline. There wasn't another colored family she knew who had beaten her to it. She would be the first to say, "You must come to see us at our new address. We've taken a house in Brookline."

She began to peer hard at house numbers. A row of red-brick houses began, and Cleo suddenly pulled the bell cord.

"We get off here," she said to Judy, and shooed her down the aisle.

Cleo walked slowly toward the number she sought, taking in her surroundings. Shade trees stood in squares of earth along the brick-paved sidewalk. Each house had a trim plot of grass enclosed by a wrought-iron fence. The half-dozen houses in this short block were the only brick houses within immediate sight except for a trio of new apartment houses across the way, looking flat-faced and ugly as they squatted in their new cement sidewalk.

In the adjoining block was a row of four or five weathered frame houses with wide front porches, big bay windows, and great stone chimneys for the spiraling smoke of logs on blackened hearths. The area beyond was a fenced-in field, where the sleek and beautiful firehorses nibbled the purple clover and frisked among the wild flowers. Near by was the firehouse with a few Irish heads in the open windows, and a spotted dog asleep in a splash of sun.

Directly opposite from where Cleo walked was a great gabled mansion on a velvet rise, with a carriage house at the end of a graveled drive. The house was occupied, but there was an air of suspended life about it, as if all movement inside it was slow. Its columned porch and long French windows and lovely eminence gave the house grandeur.

A stone's throw away was the winding ribbon of the Riverway Drive, over which the hooves of carriage horses clip-clopped and shiny automobiles choked and chugged. Beyond were the wooded Fens, at the outset of their wild wanderings over the city to Charlesgate.

Cleo was completely satisfied with everything she saw. There were no stoop-sitters anywhere, nor women idling at windows, nor loose-lipped loiterers passing remarks. Her friend who lived in Dorchester, or Cambridge, or Everett had nice addresses, of course. But Brookline was a private world.

She stopped and glanced down at her daughter to see if her ribbed white stockings were still smooth over her knees, and if the bright ribbons on the ends of her bobbing braids were as stiff and stand-out as they had been when she tied them. She scanned the small upturned face, and a rush of protective tenderness flooded her heart. For a moment she thought she had never seen anything as lovely as the deep rich color that warmed Judy's cheeks. She herself had hated being bright-skinned when she was a child. Mama had made her wash her face all day long, and in unfriendly moments her playmates had called her yaller punkins. Now her northern friends had taught her to feel defensive because Judy was the color of her father.

"Don't speak unless you're spoken to," Cleo warned Judy, and mounted the steps of the house before which they stood.

In a moment or two a colored maid responded to her ring. She looked at Cleo with open-mouthed surprise, then her look became sly and secret. "Y'all come see about the house?" she asked in a conspiratorial whisper.

"I beg your pardon," Cleo said coolly. "I've come to see Mr. Van Ryper."

The maid's face froze. She knew these stuck-up northern niggers. Thought they were better than southern niggers. Well, all of them looked alike to the white man. Let this high-yaller woman do down South and she'd find out.

"Step inside," she said surlily. "You're letting in flies."

"I'm sorry," Cleo said sweetly. "I see a big black fly got in already." With a dazzling smile she entered the house, and instantly drew a little breath at sight of the spacious hall with its beautiful winding stairway.

"What's the name?" the maid asked briefly. If this woman wanted to be treated like white folks, at least she wasn't going to be treated like quality white folks.

"The name is Mrs. Judson," Cleo said readily. She had been asked a proper question, however rudely, and she was perfectly willing to answer it. This peevish incivility was much less insulting than the earlier intimacy. If she had wanted to gossip with the servant before seeing the master, she would have used the back door.

"Wait here," the woman said, and began a snail-pace ascent of the stairs, with her rocking buttocks expressive of her scorn.

"Always remember," said Cleo loudly and sweetly to Judy, "that good manners put you in the parlor and poor manners keep you in the kitchen." The maid's broad back seemed to swell the seams of her uniform. "That's what I'm paying good money to your governess for," Cleo added impressively. "So you won't have to wear an apron."

Judy stared down at her shoes, feeling very uncomfortable because Cleo's voice was carrying to the woman on the stairs. Miss Binney always said that a lady must keep her voice low, and never boast, and never, never say anything that might hurt somebody's feelings.

"She heard you," said Judy in a stricken voice.

Cleo gave her a look of amiable impatience. "Well, I expected her to hear. Who did you think I was talking to? I certainly wasn't talking to you."

Her eyes grew lively with amusement as she studied her daughter's distress. Sometimes she wondered where she had got Judy. Judy had no funny bone. Thea was probably responsible. She had no funny bone either. Their diversions were so watery. What was the sense in Judy's taking delight in a dog's wagging tail if she was going to miss the greater eloquence of that woman's wagging rear, and then look shocked when her mother talked back at it? You really had to love Bostonians to like them. And the part of Cleo that did love them was continually at war with the part of her that preferred the salt flavor of lusty laughter.

Her eyes clouded with wistfulness. The more the years increased between the now and the long ago, the more the broad A's hemmed her in, the more her child grew alien to all that had made her own childhood an enchanted summer, so in like degree did her secret heart yearn for her sisters. She longed for the eager audience they would have provided, the boisterous mirth she would have evoked when she flatfooted up an imaginary flight of stairs, agitating her bottom. Who did she know in the length and breadth of Boston who wouldn't have cleared an embarrassed throat before she got going good on her imitation?

Sometimes you felt like cutting the fool for the hell of it. Sometimes you hankered to pick a bone and talk with your mouth full. To Cleo culture was a garment that she had learned to get into quickly and out of just as fast.

She put on her parlor airs now, for Mr. Van Ryper was descending the stairs. Her eyebrows arched delicately, her luscious mouth pursed primly, and a faint stage smile ruffled her smooth cheeks.

These artifices had no effect on Mr. Van Ryper, who was elderly.

He reached the bottom step and peered at her. "Carrie should have shown you in here," he said fussily, piloting Cleo and Judy into the parlor.

He waved at a chair. "Sit down, Mrs.—uh—Jenkins, and you, young lady. What's your name, Bright Eyes or Candy Kid? Let's see if it's Candy Kid. Look in that box on the table, and mind you don't stick up yourself or the furniture."

Judy murmured her thanks and retired. She had learned to dissolve when grown-ups were talking. They forgot you and said very interesting things.

"Now, then, Mrs.—uh—Jordan," said Mr. Van Ryper. "I expect you've come about the house."

Cleo looked about the gracious room. The lacquered floors were of fine hardwood, the marble above the great hearth was massive and beautiful. The magnificent sliding doors leading into the dining room were rich mahogany, the wallpaper was exquisitely patterned. From the center of the high ceiling the gas chandelier spun its crystal tears.

"It's a beautiful house," said Cleo with awe.

"Best house on the block. Sorry to leave it, but I'm too old to temper my prejudices."

Cleo looked startled and felt humiliated. Were there colored people next door? Was that why Mr. Van Ryper was moving away? Should her pride make her rise and exit with dignity, or should she take the insult in exchange for this lovely house? Who were the people next door? If they were anybody, Miss Binney would have known them. They must be old second-class niggers from way down South, whom she wouldn't want to live next door to herself.

"Do you happen to know what part of the South the family came from?" she asked delicately.

Mr. Van Ryper looked startled now. "What family?" he asked testily, peering hard at Cleo with the intent of reading her foolish feminine mind.

"The colored family you're prejudiced at," Cleo said belligerently.

Mr. Van Ryper rose to his feet. His face purpled with anger.

"Madam, my father was a leader in the Underground Movement. I was brought up in an Abolitionist household. Your accusation of color prejudice is grossly impertinent. I believe in man's inalienable right to liberty. Let me lecture you a bit for the enlightenment of your long-eared child, who is probably being brought up in cotton batting because she's a little colored Bostonian who must never give a backward look at her beginnings.

"We who are white enslaved you who are—to use a broad term, madam—black. We reduced your forebears to the status of cattle. It must be our solemn task to return their descendants to man's estate. I have been instrumental in placing a good many Southern Negroes in the service of my friends. My maid Carrie is lately arrived from the South. She is saving her wages to send for her family. They will learn here. They will go to night school. Their children will go to day school. Their grandchildren will go to high school, and some of them will go to college.

"Negroes are swarming out of the South. The wheat and the chaff are mixed. But time is a sifting agent. True, the chaff will forever be our cross to bear, but one fine day the wheat will no longer be part of the Negro problem."

Cleo looked unimpressed. She had lent an unwilling ear to this long speech, and had stubbornly closed her mind every time Mr. Van Ryper used the word "Negro," because colored Bostonians were supposed to feel scandalized whenever they heard this indecent appellation. This fancy talk was just to cover up his saying he didn't like niggers.

"Well, it's nice when people aren't prejudiced," Cleo said politely.

"Madam, I am distinctly prejudiced against the Irish," Mr. Van Ryper said wearily, thinking that colored women, for all they had to endure, were as addlepated as their fairer-skinned sisters. "The Irish present a threat to us entrenched Bostonians. They did not come here in chains or by special invitation. So I disclaim any responsibility for them, and reserve the right to reject them. I do reject them, and refuse to live in a neighborhood they are rapidly overrunning. I have decided to rent my house to colored. Do you or don't you want it?"

"I do," said Cleo faintly, thinking this was the oddest white man she had ever met. It would take an educated person like Miss Binney to understand how his mind worked.

"And is the rent within your means? Thirty-five dollars, but it struck me as a fair sum. There are ten rooms. I hope you won't mind if I don't show them to you now. The parish priest is waiting upstairs in the sitting room. Seems some neighbors have complained about my attitude. He's a man of taste and intelligence. Pity he has to be Irish, but I understand that some of his blood is English."

Cleo rose, with a little nod at Judy, who came as obediently as a puppy trained to heel. There was a ring of chocolate around her mouth that made her look comical, and a smudge of it on one of her gloves. Cleo sighed a little. Children made a mess with chocolate candy. Any fool ought to know that. What did this old man think lollipops were invented for?

"About the rent, Mr. Van Ryper," she said, wiping Judy's mouth with the cotton handkerchief and taking this opportunity to glare in her eye, thirty dollars would suit me better. And you wouldn't have to wait for it. You'd have it every month on the dot. My husband told me to tell you that."

Mr. Van Ryper gestured toward the dining-room doors. His voice was patient and instructive. "Madam, each one of those doors cost two hundred dollars. The staircase cost a small fortune. There is a marble bowl in the master bedroom. The bathtub is porcelain, and so is the—ah—box. But if thirty dollars is all you can afford, I hope you will make up the difference in appreciation."

"Indeed I will," Cleo promised fervently. "It's been my dream to live in Brookline."

"This isn't Brookline," Mr. Van Ryper said crossly. "The other side of the street is Brookline. This side is Roxbury, which that thundering herd of Irish immigrants have overrun. They have finally pushed their boundary to here. Time was when Roxbury was the meeting place of great men. Now its fine houses are being cut up into flats for insurrectionists. I'm moving to Brookline within a few days. Brookline is the last stronghold of my generation."

Cleo swallowed her disappointment. Several colored families were already living in Roxbury. They didn't talk about the Irish the way Mr. Van Ryper did. They called them nice white people. They said they lived next door to such nice white people, and made you feel out of fashion because your neighbors were colored.

She opened her purse, taking great care that its contents were not wholly revealed to Mr. Van Ryper.

"Just one other thing first," he said. "Your reference. That is to say, your husband's employer."

"My husband's in business," Cleo explained. "He has a wholesale place in the Market. All kinds of fruit, but mostly bananas."

Mr. Van Ryper's eyes filled with interest. "Bart Judson? The Black Banana King? Never met him, but I hear he's pretty amazing. Well, well. I'm happy to rent my house to him. I like to do business with a businessman. Tell you what. We'll settle on a rental of twenty-five dollars. Ah, that pleases you, doesn't it? But there's a condition to it. I'd want your husband to take care of minor repairs. You see, I'm a tired old man, quite unused to being a landlord. I'd hate to be called out of bed in the middle of the night to see about a frozen water pipe.'

The matter was settled at once and Cleo handed over the money. Mr. Van Ryper found a scrap of paper and a stub of pencil in his pockets, and paused in the writing of the receipt to make an inquiry. Did Mrs. Judson want it in ink? Cleo answered hastily and heartily that pencil was fine.

Simeon Binney bent over his desk. Behind him, in the dingy back room, the two small presses were noisily clattering. But his ear was turned inward. He was writing his father's obituary. The doctor had said that his father would die before morning. He had felt no shock or sorrow, and he had come away as soon as Thea returned to relieve him. She would give their father her tears, as he could not.

Simeon had been born in this house when the neighborhood was wholly Caucasian, except for the Binneys, who, according to their neighbors' praise, represented the best in the colored race. They behaved as if they were white. Simeon played with the neighborhood children and sat beside them in Sunday school. But

his brownness made him seem different to them, just as Thea's fair
skin made her seem the same.

He was darker than either parent, a throwback to a paternal
grandfather. He was not an undesirable shade by the standards
of his parents' set. Indeed, he was considered the handsomest
colored child in Boston. In the usual way, most people made the
unamusing witticism that it was a pity that a boy should be prettier
than his sister. He was tan, with fine features, great black eyes,
and black curls. He was tall for his age and strongly built, in
every way giving a manly appearance. Nobody guessed the extent
of his sensitiveness, his insecurity in what was considered his safe
and happy world.

He felt that he lived in two worlds. There was the world outside, peopled with whites, whites everywhere. He couldn't understand why his parents were proud that he and Thea were always
the only colored children in school, in church, in their block. Didn't
they know that made him feel lonely? It was good to come into
the other world, the narrow nursery world, and play with Thea,
and pretend that this was the whole, that he and she alone existed.

He hadn't had any inherent dislike of white children. He hadn't
known there was anything special about them at first. For Thea
and his father were fair, his mother was very light. He had never
noticed that he was darker. Nor had he known that their skin
shades were preferable to darker ones.

The five-year-old boy, big enough now to play outside without
his Irish nurse's supervision, approached the children on the block
with vulnerable innocence. He had never head any discussions
about the difference in man. All that he knew was that there was
a favored race of people called Bostonians, and that he was fortunate enough to be one of them.

The group of children he approached stared at him open-
mouthed. They were also five-year-olds, and their world had been as
prescribed as his. They, too, knew they were little Bostonians, and
they thought all little Bostonians looked alike. They were unprepared for the exotic appearance of this brown boy. He might have
stepped out of one of their picture books of strange boys in strange
lands.

"Hello," Simeon said.

"Hello," they said soberly, somewhat surprised that he spoke their tongue.

"I'm Simeon Binney," he offered cheerfully.

They were silent. They did not know whether they wanted to tell this odd boy their names or not.

Simeon stuck out his hand. He had been taught to do that. And he was used to hearing delighted murmurs at this charming display of grown-up manners.

The boys backed away. They had never seen a brown hand extended. Then one asked shyly, "Will it come off?"

"What?" asked Simeon blankly.

"The brown on your hand," the boy explained.

"It isn't dirt," he said indignantly. Then he felt surprised. What was it?

"Where do you come from?" a pink-cheeked boy asked.

"Over there." He pointed to his house, the corner house, the finest in the block of brownstone dwellings.

"No," the pink-cheeked child said patiently, "I mean, what country?"

"Boston," Simeon answered in a shocked tone, for he had supposed that all Bostonians recognized Bostonians. Certainly he had known without question that these children, whose dress, whose accent, whose houses were identical with his, were his fellow countrymen.

One of the boys drew a sputtering breath. "I think you're a colored boy," he said. It frightened him a little to make this pronouncement, for he didn't know whether it was good or bad.

"I'm a Boston boy," Simeon said with a sob. "Same as you."

Plainly this didn't make sense to them. They looked at each other, shifted self-consciously, and began to sidle away. This was something they wanted explained by a grown-up as soon as they could reach one. They chorused Good-bye, for, after all, he was a small person like themselves, and the inherent humanity of children evoked this gesture of brotherhood.

Simeon played by himself. He could not go in to his mother. He felt ashamed, though he could not explain his feeling. When a reasonable time had passed, he mounted the stone steps quietly and scooted up the back stairs. In the bathroom he scrubbed his hands vigorously, but it was just as he had known it would be, there was no whiteness under the brown. He was not like the other boys. He was not a Bostonian.

He waited for his father to come home and explain to him what a colored boy was. He was reluctant to ask his mother. He knew that she was modest, and did not speak of unseemly things. His father failed him. He was prepared for this moment, and said deftly: "Everybody is colored, Simeon. Some skins are colored lighter than others. Like Thea's. Some look as if they were not colored at all. Like those boys. But put them beside a sheet of white paper, and you will see that they look pale gray. Those boys had never seen a brown boy. Had you been red-haired, they would have asked you if your hair was on fire." Simeon was supposed to smile at this, but his face stayed solemn. For he knew that a red-haired boy wouldn't have smiled either. "You're the color of an Indian, Simeon, and the Indians are the oldest Americans. If any boy ever asks you again why you're brown, you may say it's because your grandfather was a full-blooded Indian."

Simeon accepted this half-truth without enthusiasm. No matter how long the Indians had lived in America, they hadn't lived in Boston. No wonder those boys had asked him what country he came from. He couldn't understand why his father had let the doctor leave a boy who looked like an Indian instead of a boy who looked like a Bostonian.

The next day, when Simeon unwillingly went out to play, the little boys rushed to greet him and vigorously pumped his hand. They, too, had had instructions in correct demeanor from their fathers, who had been preparing for their questions as soon as they saw that the Binney boy looked old enough to come out to play. Their fathers had explained to them that you did not speak of color to colored persons. It hurts their feelings. You must always act as if they had no color at all. God made everybody, and in His infinite wisdom He had made some people brown. It was as rude to ask a colored boy why he was brown as it was to ask a lame boy why he limped. The way for a well-bred Boston boy to behave was with generosity toward those with fewer blessings.

Through the long afternoon Simeon waited to return to the subject of race. He had decided not to say he was an Indian. He was going to stand pat on being a Bostonian. He was going to fight about it if he had to. But the subject was never reopened.

The boys had set out to be bountiful. From that day on, he was never left out of anything. To all outward appearances he was the most popular boy in the block. Yet no boy ever fought him, though they fought each other, no boy called him by a nickname, though they were Fatty and Skinny and Shorty as soon as they left their stoops, and no boy ever contradicted him, though they shouted each other down with "You did!" "I didn't!"

He was never their equal. He was their charge, whom they were honor-bound to treat with charity. They never knew whether they liked him or not. They only knew it was something of a bother to be with him, for the feelings of a colored boy had to be coddled.

When Thea was old enough to go out alone to play, these boys and their sisters treated her as one of themselves, for her pink cheeks and chestnut hair were close enough in color to theirs not to distract them. Their easy acceptance established a loyalty in her that made her unable to understand Simeon's distrust. With Thea, as with Simeon, the first ten years of her life left a profound impression. She was never quite at ease with her own group. Her very fair skin and chestnut hair singled her out, accorded her a special treatment that she was unused to, that pointed out to her how preferable was the status of whites, since even a near-white was made an idol.

When Simeon was twelve and Thea nine, the poorer streets surrounding theirs began to be populated by the black newcomers to the North. They soon learned of the rich colored family living right alongside rich white folks on a near-by street. They took to strolling down this street to see if they could espy their own kind and color riding fat and sassy behind a bang-up coachman. They would stand and gape at the windows, their voices loud and approving and proud. Some would even go so far as to start a conversation with Thea and Simeon.

Thea would toss her chestnut hair and skip away. She was a little bit scared. These people smelled, they wore queer clothes, they spoke a strange tongue, and their blood was black, while hers was blue.

But Simeon sensed that their blood was the same, and he was

ashamed. Because he was ashamed, he could not run away like Thea. He had to face them for his own pride. He had to believe that he could stand in the company of these people and still feel confident of the wall of culture between them.

Mr. Binney was completely outraged by the ever-increasing concourse of dark faces within the sacred precincts of his street. He didn't feel at all like a king with worshipping subjects. He felt like a criminal who had been found and tracked down. In his wildest nightmare he had never imagined that his house would be a mecca for lower-class Negroes. They were ruining the character of the street. They were making it a big road. The worst thing of all was that Simeon, who was being so carefully brought up, who scarcely knew the difference between white and colored, whose closest friends had always been white, was making friends with the little black urchins who boldly hung around the back door in the hope of enticing him away from his playmates on the front stoop.

The day Mr. Binney made up his mind to move was the un-forgettable Sunday that he heard sounds of battle, rushed to the back window to find Simeon in his new suit engaged in strife. Simeon, who had never fought in his life, was rolling all over the alley with a ruffian who had never worn shoes until he came North. It was spring. Windows were open. Neighbors were witnessing this unholy spectacle of young Binney so demeaning himself as to fight with a boy beneath his station. It put them both in the same class.

Mr. Binney so far forgot himself as to bellow for his son. Simeon disentangled himself, shook his opponent's hand, and bounded into the house. He felt wonderfully elated, and he was scared but happy that his father had witnessed the fight. His father had never seen him fight in his life.

"Come in, sir!" his father commanded, leading him into his den. He turned and faced Simeon. "I have never been so ashamed in my life. My son behaving like an alley rat. I've never known you to raise your hand to one of the boys in the block. You've had the reputation of being a perfect young gentleman. Then the whole street sees you and that dirty black imp sprawled all over the alley. Do you know what they said to themselves?" Mr. Binney

took a deep breath. He was going to say the worst thing he had
ever said to Simeon. But Simeon had to be roundly shocked into
full realization of his unpardonable breach of conduct. "They
said, 'Isn't that just like niggers?'"

The word had never been used in Simeon's household. Its effect
was not explosive. As a matter of fact, Mr. Binney had the uncomfortable feeling that Simeon accepted the ugly word as if he
supposed it was part of his father's vocabulary.

"I know," said Simeon quietly. "I suppose they said 'colored'
instead of 'nigger,' but that doesn't matter. I've always known
they've never seen me as like themselves. They fight with each
other, Father. Not in the alley, and not on Sunday. But I have to
fight when I can. It mayn't make sense to you, Father, but Scipio
Johnson"—Mr. Binney visibly winced—"is the first boy who ever
fought me man to man."

It didn't make sense to Mr. Binney. "It is time you learned a
hard-and-fast rule, Simeon. A colored man can never afford to
forget himself, no matter what the provocation. He must always
be superior to a white man if he wants to be that white man's
equal. We are better fixed financially than any family on this
street. You and Thea attend private schools. The other children
go to public school. Your manners are superior. Your mother has
more help. We set a finer table. If our manner of living was
exactly like theirs, we would not be considered good enough to
live on this street."

Simeon thought that he and his father had met on common
ground. He, too, had something to say that was better said now.
"I don't like white people, Father. I think I hate them."

His father was shocked and disturbed. "Never say such an
unreasonable thing again. You get that from those wretched black
boys. Do you know why they hate white people? Because they're
lazy and shiftless and poor. They hate them because they envy
them. You are Simeon Binney. You will never have to envy anyone. You are being raised like a white man's son. Pay me the
courtesy, sir, of thinking like one."

The Binney's moved to Cambridge. They were the first family
on their street to move away because of the rapid encroachment
of Negroes. They began the general exodus. Mr. Binney could say

with pride, right up to the day of his death, that he had never lived on a street where other colored people resided.

Simeon went to Harvard. He ranked among the top ten in all his classes, because colored men must be among the first in any field if they are not to be forever lost among the mediocre millions.

He took the classical courses. Mr. Binney was disappointed that Simeon didn't want to specialize in law or medicine or dentistry. All of the sons of his friends were aspiring to the professions. They were the gentlemen that meant to be titled. Their fathers were gentlemen without higher education. They had learned their manners and mode of living in service to the rich. They were ambitious for their sons and instilled in them the Boston tradition that knowledge has no equal. That there would be a surfeit of professional men in a city where the majority of Negroes were too poor and ignorant to seek professional services did not deter them. In his heart each hopeful student supposed that he would be the one to establish a practice among whites. This was Boston, where a man was appraised for his worth, and paid in New England currency accordingly. What they did not know was that the whites, whom they dreamed of doctoring and advising, were confidently expecting them to attend their own, thereby effecting a painless segregation.

Mr. Binney was somewhat mollified when Simeon explained that he intended to work for a doctorate. At least Simeon would have a title even if he would never be able to hang out a shingle on which to display it. Still, he was worried about the boy. He hoped he did not think he could be a rich man's idle son. He had the elegance for it, but now there was not going to be the money. He, Mr. Binney, could not hold on to his business another year. The ten-thousand-dollar rent alone was far in excess of last year's profits. He was already drawing heavily on his capital. There was just enough left to see Thea through finishing school and Simeon through college.

Simeon would have to work for his living. Perhaps he would elect to teach. Perhaps it was not too fantastic to imagine he might even teach at Harvard. They thought the world and all of him there. The faculty had the highest praise for him. His class respected him. He was even putting away a fair sum tutoring undergraduates. If Simeon would just make up his mind to teach, a position at Harvard should be his for the asking.

Simeon elected to edit a Negro newspaper. It was a sudden decision arrived at a few weeks before he received his doctorate. Thea was just home from school. She and Simeon were out for an evening's stroll in the vicinity of the Yard. She was holding his arm, and her face, full of lively affection, was upturned to his. A group of young men, in freshman caps, approached them. They were not very steady. They did not know Simeon, nor he them. They stopped in front of him and Thea and would not let them pass.

"Watch your step, nigger. Let go that white girl," one of them said.

"Move out of our way," said Simeon quietly.

"Who's going to make us?"

Simeon said quickly to Thea, "Run home and don't look back." Then he hunched his shoulders and gave a little prancing step. "Put up your dukes," he said.

It was not a fair fight. There were three of them, and they attacked from all sides. But it didn't matter to Simeon. It was what he'd been wanting since he was five. A fight with white men. That there were three of them, that his fists could smash three faces, that his wild, tortured curses could befoul three pairs of ears, that he could smell the hated blood that flowed in three hot streams, made it the moment in his life that satisfied the long waiting.

He was found unconscious a few minutes later by a passing patrolman. His watch, his wallet were on him. He was carted off to jail as a drunk and thrown into a cell to sleep it off.

When he roused he didn't mind being where he was. His head was throbbing, there were bruises on his face, and blood in his mouth. But it wasn't important. This would wake these sleeping colored Bostonians. They would see they were not a privileged group, that no Negro was immune from a white man's anger when he did not watch his step. These self-styled better Negroes were standing still, sticking their heads in the sand, pretending that liberalism was still alive in Boston. They were using the transplanted Southerner for their scapegoat. It was he, they insisted, who was causing the changed attitude, if one existed, not the changing times. The colored problem began with their coming. It was no wonder. They were coming in such droves. These upper-class Negroes, Simeon argued to himself, didn't have the sense to see that a minority group was never a problem until its numerical strength threatened the dominant race at the polls. What power had the Old Colored Families, sparsely scattered by preference in the many suburbs of Boston? They had none, and they did not know it was desirable. To them the Irish were pushing, and they were proud that they were not. They would have been out-raged and astounded if they had been told that they knew their place, and kept it.

All of these things Simeon expected to say in a rousing speech to the press when it was discovered that a Harvard graduate had been beaten by brother Harvardites for no other crime than walk-ing with his sister in the neighborhood of his own house.

Toward midnight he was summoned to the sergeant's desk. His father was there, looking distressed. There was somebody from the dean's office, looking uncomfortable. There were three bloodied freshmen, looking sober and sheepish. The policeman who had made the arrest, looking red-faced. And the sergeant and two re-porters, looking bored.

A solution had been arrived at by everyone concerned except Simeon. The unfortunate happening was to be considered a freshman prank, prompted by an overindulgence in strong drink. The freshmen were to apologize, which they did easily and ear-nestly, thrusting out their well-kept hands, which Simeon ignored until he heard his father's embarrassed plea, "Simeon, remember you are as much a gentleman as these young men," and felt that he would look foolish and childish if he continued to stand on what his father and the others did not recognize as his dignity. The Irish policeman apologized next. He did it gruffly, because he was upset by all the formality and fine English. It made him feel inferior to everbody present and that was ridiculous since two of them were niggers.

In a few brief minutes it was over. There was general hand-shaking, with Simeon's hand feeling cold as a clam to whoever touched it. The young men and the dean's representative bowed themselves out, not with obsequiousness, but with the graciousness befitting those who have transgressed against the rule of *noblesse oblige*.

Simeon turned to his father. "I thought you would bring your lawyer," he said.

Mr. Binney looked scandalized. "Fineberg's crudity would have been out of place in a delicate situation like this. He would have made a race issue out of it, and taken it to court."

"It was a race issue," said Simeon stolidly. "They said, 'Nigger, let go that white woman.'"

His father looked racked. Everybody had been carefully avoiding any reference to those unhappy words. "They were drunk, Simeon. They forgot themselves. As soon as they sobered, they were Harvard gentlemen."

"And when they get drunk again, they'll insult some other couple whose juxtaposition doesn't suit them."

"Simeon, be reasonable. You and your sister have walked together through the streets of Cambridge half your lives. Have you ever been insulted before? It isn't likely that you'll be insulted again. They made a very natural mistake. Thea is fair enough to appear white. You must face facts, Simeon. Since that riffraff has come up from the South, their men have run after white women. You see them all over the South End, the worst elements of colored men walking with low-type white women."

"Thea and I are hardly comparable," said Simeon stiffly. He disliked having to say that. It weakened the point of the argument. But his pride could not let that observation pass.

"Of course, you're not," said his father soothingly. "Those young men were the first to say so when they sobered." He patted Simeon's shoulder. "Lets's go home now. Your face needs attention. You need rest. You will get your degree in a few weeks. It will be a wonderful occasion for me. Don't spoil it by making a mountain out of a molehill. I want you to look and feel your best."

"I'll be ready in a moment," said Simeon wearily. "I want a word with the reporters. Will you wait for me outside?"

His father's patience broke. "They're not going to print anything, Simeon. They promised. They know how the better class of colored people feel about any story that is derogatory to the race. You're young and headstrong. I won't let you do anything tonight that you'll regret tomorrow. Rest assured that your name will appear in every paper in Boston when you receive your Ph.D. That will be a proud day. Don't do anything to take away from its glory. Give me your promise."

Simeon promised. He supposed he owed his father that much for his education. They walked toward home. Simeon was silent. He knew what he meant to do. He would publish a newspaper for colored people and make them face the facts of their second-class citizenship. He had enough savings to make a down payment on a printing press. His father would not deny him the use of the unoccupied South End house when he convinced him that he would either edit a paper for Negroes or harangue on Boston Common before audiences largely composed of whites.

For two years now Simeon had struggled to keep the paper in circulation. The people who read it were not the people who could pay for subscriptions. There were only occasional ads for church socials and rooms for rent. His bills were mounting. His single helper was underpaid. He himself never had a decent meal unless he ran over to Cleo's. Cambridge was too far away, and there was the carfare, and poor Thea was a rotten cook, with little enough to cook anyway.

If he could not keep the six-page sheet alive, at least he had established the need for a Negro newspaper. It passed around from hand to hand in the South End. On the day of its appearance there were little clusters of shabby people with nickels in their hand's, waiting for the shabby newsboy to appear.

Thea did the social column. It was the only thing that kept the better Bostonians even mildly interested. It satisfied their curiosity as to who might have had a party to which they had not been invited, or what person of social prominence from New York, Philadelphia, or Washington was visiting what socially prominent Bostonian at his beautiful home in the suburbs.

Nothing else in the paper met with their approval. Every other word was "colored." That this was Simeon's concession to their sensibilities did not make it any more palatable. Had he used the word "Negro," they would have refused to read the paper altogether.

There was far too much, they complained, about the happenings below the Mason-Dixon line. They could be resolved quite easily. The nice colored people should come North. They needn't all come to Boston. There were many other large cities among which they could disperse themselves without dispossessing the already established families. As for the other elements, their extermination was the best thing possible. Every locality had its thieves and cut-throats. In the South they happened to be black. That Simeon should waste his time and talent writing long editorials protesting their punishments, urging the improvement of their conditions, was the folly of hotheaded youth. It was thoughtless cruelty to call attention to the dregs of the colored race.

Simeon, they concluded, was much too race-conscious for a young man who had been brought up exactly as if he were white. His persistence in identifying himself with anybody and everybody who happened to be black just showed what lasting effect those few months of contact with common colored children had had on a growing boy.

Simeon picked up his pencil. "Carter Burrows Binney was born in Boston in the year this once abolitionist city sent its son to liberate the enslaved black souls of the South . . ."

Across the sea England was writing the obit of a Kaiser. The world was at war.

Benjamin A. Brown

BENJAMIN A. BROWN was born in Wichita Falls, Texas, and attended Morehouse College in Atlanta, Georgia.

Mr. Brown was the editor of the *Harlem Quarterly*, a literary
journal that developed out of the Harlem Writers Workshop in
1945, and his short stories have appeared in various publications.

The following story is from Mr. Brown's unpublished novel
Thunder at Dawn and appears in print here for the first time.

From *Thunder at Dawn*

BY BENJAMIN A. BROWN

Johnny followed Mr. Simpson and Louis through the revolving
door into the lobby of the Winslow Arms Hotel. The small room
was quiet at midday. There were three or four red-leather lounge
chairs placed in a semicircle around a white pillar situated in the
center of the floor. In the rear was the hotel clerk's desk, behind
which sat a red-headed middle-aged white woman. She looked up
and frowned when she saw the new boy. Her mouth was opened
to speak but she said nothing. The bell captain went over to

her. "Sadie, ring up Mrs. Winslow and tell her I'm bringing up a new boy for her to see, will you?" he said.

Sadie grunted her assent without relaxing her frown, glanced again at Johnny somewhat apprehensively, then rung up Mrs. Winslow and relayed the message. "Mrs. Winslow says you can come up, Charley," she said; then, softening, she asked, "Is that the new boy over there?"

"Yeah," replied Charley; then, turning to Louis, he said, "Louis, you better go on back to the den."

"Yeah, I'd better. See you in the bellhops' den later," he said to Johnny, smiling.

"Okay, Louis," answered Johnny, smiling.

As Louis ran up the circular staircase ahead of them, Charley turned to Johnny. "I think she'll like you," he said, grinning. "As white folks go, she's a very nice lady." Johnny nodded his head.

Charley knocked gently on Mrs. Winslow's door. She said, "Come in," and they entered. The hotel manager looked up from her desk. She was a handsome chestnut-haired woman of middle age. She removed her reading glasses and studied Johnny from her seated position. Her eyes scrutinzed him from foot to head. She smiled faintly. "He looks like a nice clean boy, Charles," she said, "but kinda young for the job. How old are you boy?"

"Eighteen, Mrs. Winslow," replied Johnny, blushing in spite of himself.

Charley interjected, "He's just graduated from high school, Mrs. Winslow." He stepped back and studied Johnny, then looked approvingly at Mrs. Winslow, nodding his head with a slight grin. "He's smart," Charley added. "I know we can make a good bellhop outa him."

"Did you tell him about the work and the rules of the hotel?"

"Oh, yes ma'am, Mrs. Winslow."

"What's your name, boy?" she asked.

"Oh, Johnny Morgan, ma'am."

"Turn around." Johnny followed her instructions. Mrs. Winslow smiled broadly. Turning to Charley, she said, "Yes, Charley, I think you've found me a good boy. Now take him to the den and fit him up with a uniform. He ought to look right smart as tall and slender as he is." She turned seriously to Johnny. "You be courteous, polite and quick on the trigger in answering your bells, boy, and I'm sure you'll get along here. Now the pay is ten dollars a week." She paused and eyed Johnny, who had frowned slightly.

"Ten dollars?" Johnny repeated, as though thinking out loud, but he didn't have time to question the salary figure.

Mrs. Winslow put on her glasses and stood up, her false smile gone, an impatient expression clouding her face. "That's the salary, boy, ten dollars a week and tips. Do you want the job?"

"Oh, yes ma'am," Johnny replied anxiously. He forced a reassuring smile.

Charley, who had been frowning at Johnny's reactions along with Mrs. Winslow, now smiled approvingly. "The pay ain't much, son, but if you're a hustler, why you'll make out fine. Shucks, some of us more'n double our salary in tips."

"Yes, sir." Johnny forcefully smiled again. Then to Mrs. Winslow, who had put on her false smile, he said, "I'll take the job and make a good bellboy for you, Mrs. Winslow."

Mrs. Winslow sat down and returned to the work on her desk, saying, "All right, Charley, take the boy to the den and fit him up with a uniform."

On the way down the hall to the bellhops' den Charley said, "I'm glad you didn't dispute her on the pay, boy, 'cause she was ready to send you off."

"Yeah, I observed that," Johnny replied, "but the pay is mighty small."

"That's why she uses colored help; that's the main reason anyhow. If she had white boys she'd have to pay them almost twice that much. But as white folks go, she's a mighty fine woman to work for."

Johnny was tempted to say, "Sure, because it suits her purpose!" but instead he swallowed his pride and said, "Yeah, she seems very nice."

Johnny entered the small cluttered den after Charley. Two bellmen sat on their stools reading magazines. "Boys, meet our new bellhop, Johnny Morgan," Charley said. Smiling, the two men got to their feet. "This is Jim Wakefield." Jim was a tall and lanky coffee-brown fellow with a hawk face like an Indian. "And this is Eddie Jones." Eddie was a short cocoa-brown chap with narrow penetrating eyes. Johnny shook their hands and the men exchanged greetings. Johnny sat on the edge of the old bathtub as Charley looked through the departed bellhop's locker for a clean uniform. The walls were filled with clippings of pinup girls in all angles and poses. A lone small window gave ventilation to the musty room. Four tiny lockers joined together occupied one corner, four small stools another.

"Here's a clean suit," Charley said, handing it to Johnny. "Harry only wore it once, so it's still kinda clean."

Johnny said, "Oh, thanks, Mr. Simpson," and hanging it up, took off his trousers and put on the blue uniform with gold trimmings. He looked himself over and smiled proudly.

"You look right nice, boy," Charley said, and the others agreed.

"He's about the same size as Harry," Jim added.

The door opened and Louis came in. "Hey there, kid. Say, that suit really fits you." Louis turned to Charley. "The old lady liked my kid buddy, huh?"

"Yeah, she found him a nice smart boy," Charley replied. He hesitated an instant. "Of course, the kid winced at ten bucks a week, and when she saw it I thought maybe she wouldn't take him." Charley chuckled to make light of the incident. "Johnny sensed it, I guess." He looked at Johnny.

Johnny grinned. "Yeah, I did, so right away I said I'd take the job." He shrugged his shoulders.

"She's a nice peckerwood but she's cheap," Louis said, "but I'm glad you took the job anyway."

"It ain't bad," Eddie said, as one of his bells rang. He got up. "The salary ain't nothing; it's the hustle that gets the real money."

"Don't mind Eddie," Jim cut in. "Whatever the white folks say is awright with him. Don't think she's got us here 'cause she likes us."

"Hell naw," Louis agreed. "Ofay boys would cost her a hell of a lot more."

"Awright, awright, cut the gab," Charley ordered. He pointed to the bell chart. "Eddie and Jim go hop them bells." The two men hustled to their feet and went out. Charley got up. "This bell chart has five rows, son," he explained. "Each one of us has a floor to cover. Now, for example, your floor is the top one, the sixth. When one of your guests wants service they'll ring and the room number will show up just like these two did." He pointed to the two rooms being covered by Eddie and Jim. "Now they should have thumped up these two before they went out, so they'd know these rooms had been covered. Ah, now there goes one of yours. . . ." Johnny put on his uniform cap. "Take this order pad with you," Charley added, handing him the notebook.

"Thanks, Mr. Simpson." Johnny started out the door and Louis followed. "Thanks again for getting me on, Louis," Johnny said, as they went down the hall together.

"Glad you came along at the right time, kid. Like the other fellows said, the pay ain't much on this job, but if you hustle like mad you can do pretty good. Now don't let these men peckerwoods' cracks bother you, but if they do bother you, just don't show it. If you do show it, then they'll like that and continue to meddle; if you ignore it then most of the time they'll leave you alone. Now some of these peckerwood women will sure try to entice you, but they're goddamned tricky, so leave them strictly alone."

"I surely will," Johnny replied, feeling uneasy at the prospect of such an encounter.

"Let me give you an example. Now if you were working around a colored girl, and she kept showing you her legs, you'd know she wanted to be layed by you, right?"

"Well, yeah," Johnny answered.

"What you mean, 'Well, yeah'? Man you *know* she'd want you real bad. Ain't you ever got any stuff?"

To this question Johnny blushed in hesitation. He had never had any stuff, although he surely had wanted some, but he couldn't admit it to his older, experienced buddy. "Oh, sure, I've had it."

Louis looked at him and grinned doubtfully. "Well, anyway, that ain't the way it is with these Southern white women. They know damned well your hands are tied, and they get a big thrill outa teasing a Negro."

"Oh," Johnny said, betraying his innocence.

They had reached the fifth floor. "See you later, kid buddy," Louis said, dashing down the hall.

"Okay, Louis!"

Johnny paused in reflection for an instant, then hurried down the hall to Room 616. As he knocked on the door he felt like he was walking on a tightrope. From within there was a shuffling of feet but no reply. He waited for a sew seconds then knocked again. The door was opened by a freckle-faced redheaded soldier, who was bare from the waist up. "C'mon in, bellboy . . ." he said, scratching his head. Near the bed stood a blushing pale brunette girl of nineteen or twenty; over a white skirt she was wearing the soldier's khaki shirt, which had corporal's stripes on the sleeves. The soldier turned to his companion. "Well, whatcha wanna eat, honey girl?" His voice was a deep Southern drawl. "Fried chicken? Pork chops? Barbeque? *Anything* you want! . . ."

"I want some juicy lean beef barbeque," the girl said, putting an arm around the soldier. "Think you can find some lean beef barbeque, boy"

"Yes, miss," Johnny said, readying pad and pencil. "Old Pop Brady makes fine beef barbeque."

"Awrighty, then get me some with a lotta hot, juicy sauce." She smacked her lips girlishly, giggled at her own folly, and continued, "And some cole slaw . . . and—" She looked questioningly at the corporal.

"G'wan, go ahead and order anything, everything else you want," he urged with a grandiose air while drawing her closer to him.

"Thanks, soldier boy," she grinned, "and I want some sweet-potatoe pie, ice cream and . . . and I reckon that's all for me. . . ."

"Awright, boy, bring me the same thing." He put his hairy tattooed arms around the girl and hugged her tightly, then slipped a hand into his pocket and brought out a five-dollar bill. "Oh, yeah, and brang us 'bout six Budweiser beers, some Camels and . . ." He let the girl go and walked with Johnny to the door. "And brang me some thin rubbers," he whispered. "Know where to find 'em?"

"Er—yes, sir, I'll find them for you—"

"Awright, boy, here's five bucks. I think that's enough, ain't it?"

"Oh yes, sir!" Johnny quickly rechecked the orders to make sure that he had everything jotted down. "Okay, I have everything." He turned and started towards the door.

"Hurrup, bellboy, make it snappy!" called the corporal, sitting down on the bed with the girl. "But be sure to knock before you come in!"

"Oh, yes, I will."

Johnny closed the door and hurried down the hall as fast as his legs would carry him. He bounded down the stairs two at a time. He was a bellhop and he was happy. How exciting. Momentarily he forgot about the low salary. He had a nice clean job with a a smart trim uniform. A job with a certain dignity about it. And the first white people he had met were nice people. Well, anyway, they were not antagonistic towards him. The soldier had picked himself up a cute little chick, and they were going to have a little party. They had probably been undressed when he had knocked, and hurriedly slipped into something before admitting him. He chuckled to himself, picturing the scuffle that went on before they opened the door.

On the last flight of stairs Johnny passed the bell captain. He paused a second, "Oh, hello, Mr. Simpson!" he panted.

"Oh, hello, son. Running your first errand?"

"Yes, sir."

"Well, that's the stuff, boy," he grinned. "Hustle, hustle!"

"Yes, sir!"

The early June sun had reached its midday height and it was very hot, but johnny did not feel the heat of it. Now it was a bright cheerful spring day. The workmen had finished putting up a huge banner announcing the coming "Annual Seneca Falls Rodeo." Noonday pedestrians clustered under the banner and read and talked about the forthcoming cowboy show. How different the city, the people, the world, looked to him now. An hour before, he had felt dejected and frustrated in his search for a decent job; now he was proud and happy. The job didn't pay very much, but he would hustle, doggone it, be snappy, efficient, and earn good tips. Rubbers, he had to find them first. He had heard older fellows say that they bought them in cigar stores. Wolff Brothers, that was the name of the store often mentioned. It was up the street a couple of blocks on the corner of Cactus Avenue and Main Street. That's where some fellows had bought those dirty funny books that went the rounds in school. Wolff Brothers sold them from under the counter. He remembered looking at one that

Dooley had brought to school. It was one about white folks doing it all kinds of ways. There was a real funny one about Hitler, too, but he didn't ever get a chance to see it. He entered the cigar store and inhaled the rich aroma of tobacco.

"I'd like a package of rubbers, thin rubbers, please," he told the short fat man behind the counter.

"*Thin* rubbers?" The man grinned sarcastically.

Johnny blushed and looked down. "Yes, sir, thin ones." He didn't want to engage the man in conversation. He put the money on the counter.

The man threw the package on the counter. "Jest watch out who you use them things on, boy," he said, an air of hostility in his voice.

Johnny picked up the package and started out. Feeling the hostile eyes on him, he turned and said sarcastically, "They're not for me!" and went out. "Nosy bastard!" he uttered under his breath, as he turned the corner. The nerve of him sticking his big snout into my personal business.

Old Pop Brady's Café was crowded with the noon-hour rush. Frequently he had come here to get hamburgers and soda to take into the nearby Gem Theater; also his mother stopped in from work occasionally and got orders of barbeque to take home. While waiting his turn to be served he breathed deeply of the rich spicy flavors of chili sauces and grew hungry himself, but he couldn't stop to eat now. He had to hurry and get back with the orders. At last the counterman turned to him. "Whatcha want there, bell-boy?" the big, red-faced, affable man asked.

Johnny handed him the order. While waiting he turned to listen to the record that was playing on the jukebox. Lena Horne was singing "St. Louis Blues," and a lone soldier stood leaning on the jukebox, a bottle of beer in one hand, listening to the song with a deep faraway expression on his sunburned face. As soon as the record ended the soldier put another nickel in the machine, and taking a long drink from the bottle, fell again into that deep reflective mood. It seemed strange that a man could be so preoccupied in the middle of a noisy café. What memories did "St. Louis Blues" bring back to him? Was it of his girl that he had left back home? His gray eyes were transfixed in space; he was oblivious of his surroundings; he pushed his cap back on his head and smiled blankly, his dark brown hair falling partly over his lean studious face. A shapely blonde girl sauntered over to him and hesitated, to attract his attention. She wore a tight-fitting white cotton skirt, white high-heeled shoes, and a candy-striped blouse. It seemed to Johnny that she was the only one of the crowd who had noticed this forlorn soldier. The soldier ignored her, and obviously flustered, the girl turned away from him in a huff. Damn, his mind is really far off, Johnny said to himself. He grinned as the soldier put still another nickel in the jukebox.

"Awright, boy, your orders are ready," said the counterman. Johnny paid the bill, and taking a final look at the strange soldier, hurriedly picked up the tray and went back to the hotel.

Ascending the six flights of stairs wasn't nearly as rapid as the descending of them had been, especially with a full tray of food and beer. When Johnny reached his floor he was completely out of breath. No wonder none of the other bellmen took this floor, he thought, as he walked down the hall to 616. Shucks, though, he was young and strong; he'd soon be running up and down those old stairs like a jack rabbit! In front of the room he quickly checked his orders again, then knocked. He grinned when he heard the familiar shuffle take place inside. "Is that you, bellboy?" called the soldier.

"Yes, sir."

"Awright, jest a minute, now, jest . . . a . . . minute." The shuffling ceased. "Awright, awright, c'mon in."

Johnny entered. The soldier zipped up his pants and looked around for a place to put the tray. The girl lay across the bed covered over by a sheet, her bare feet and smiling face projecting from underneath. The corporal took a chair and placed it beside the bed. "Jest put the tray down there, boy," he said.

As Johnny set the tray on the chair, the girl raised up on her elbows and looked hungrily at the food, saying, "It sure smells good."

"Lay down!" the soldier snapped, and then shot a menacing glance at Johnny. Johnny had turned his head away from the bared breasts. Seeing his eyes averted, the soldier sighed audibly, and forcing a grin, went over to the girl and patted her hair. "Sorry for snapping atcha, honey girl," he said, "but I thought . . ."

"Uh-huh, you thought he was looking," she giggled, kicking up her legs mischievously.

Johnny laughed imperceptibly. When the soldier turned back to Johnny, Johnny gave him the rubbers. The corporal smiled. "Mighty fine service, bellboy, mighty fine," he said, as he drew a half dollar from his pocket and gave it to Johnny.

"Oh, thanks a lot, corporal."

"Awrighty, that's all, boy," the soldier said, dismissing him. As Johnny went out he heard the soldier slap the girl on the rump playfully, saying. "Don' be mad now, honey girl . . . git up and let's eat."

Johnny skipped gaily down the hall towards the stairs. A whole half dollar for his first tip! Gee, if all of his guests were that generous he'd really do all right. He ran down the stairs hoping he had another call waiting for him. He stopped for a drink on the second floor, where the den was, and came up from the fountain laughing at the incident of the soldier and his girl. The frisky moves of the girl and the exasperation of the soldier! Damn, it's sure good that I turned my head away from that white girl before that jealous white soldier shot his eyes at me!

Louis stood at the open window looking out over the city, a cigarette puffing from his lips. He was alone and preoccupied with his thoughts, but he turned and grinned when Johnny entered the den. "Hiya doing, kid buddy?"

"Okay, Louis, just made my first tip—fifty cents!" Smiling proudly, Johnny took out the half dollar and flipped it up in the air and caught it.

"Fifty cents? Good, boy, good. Who gave it to you?" Louis asked, propping a foot on the bathtub and resting an elbow on his knee.

"Oh, that soldier in Room 616."

Louis pointed to a stool, musing at Johnny's excitement. "Sit down and rest a minute, kid." He offered a cigarette to Johnny.

"Oh, no thanks, don't smoke."

Louis lighted another cigarette for himself. "Soldiers are pretty good tippers, kid, especially when they got a girl."

"Man, he had himself a pretty little gal, a real pretty thing."

Louis waved his hand knowingly. "Shucks, boy, you're gonna see a lot of that. But all your guests ain't gonna tip like soldiers."

"He bought up a lot of food and beer, and when I came back with the stuff . . ." He paused, blushing and mopping sweat from his face.

Louis laughed and choked on his cigarette smoke. "What were they doin'—screwing?" He sat on the edge of the bathtub, crossed his legs, and listened to Johnny recount the incident.

Johnny got up and paced the tiny den in describing the scene. It was nothing new to Louis, but he got a big kick out of Johnny's boyish excitement. Johnny repeated the motion of putting the tray of food and beer on the chair. "The saucy barbeque smelled so good that the naked girl raised up to sniff it," Johnny said, his eyes wide with excitement, "and—and—"

Louis jumped to his feet. "And so you saw her white nipples?" he said, doubling over in laughter.

Johnny was ruffled by Louis's laughter. He stood up. The incident hadn't been that funny to him. He had wanted to make a point, but now the point had been lost in the laughter. He put on his cap and went over to the window.

Louis raised up from his laughter, and sensing that something was wrong, went over to Johnny. He put his hand on Johnny's shoulder. Johnny tightened his lip. "Aw, I'm sorry I riled you, kid buddy," Louis said, now serious.

"Oh, that's awright," Johnny replied. He bit his lip and smothered an angry outburst.

"You'll see a lot of white whores showing off like that, kid; course you did right by looking off, because that paddy woulda got so mad—"

The bell rang. They turned and looked at the bell chart. "Oh, another bell, 609," Johnny said, starting for the door.

Jim came in. "Hey, Jim, is old Hot-Rod Dan still in 609?" Louis asked.

"Huh? Oh, yeah," Jim answered, sitting down and fanning himself with his cap. He looked up at Johnny. "He's a damn big bullshitter, boy. Don' let 'em keep you up there all day!"

"Okay, Jim, I'm off."

"Hop to it, boy!" Louis grinned, as Johnny went out.

Johnny knocked on Room 609 and a hoarse voice called out: "C'mon in, boy!" He opened the door. A short gray-haired old man looked at him with surprise. His pale-blue eyes frowned. "Where's the other bellboy?" he growled, taking a cigar stub from his tobacco-stained mouth. "I rung for Harry."

"Oh, Harry, he was drafted into the Army." Johnny took out his order pad and pencil. "I'm taking his place."

Hot-Rod Dan put his cigar stub back in his mouth, ran his chubby fingers up and down his suspenders, and studied Johnny with a malevolent half grin. He was plainly disappointed that Harry was gone. Suddenly he jerked his hands out of his suspenders, and clapping them together, said spiritedly: "Well, c'mon there, boy, and do me a buck dance!"

Johnny's mouth fell open. "Buck dance?"

"Yeah, buck dance," grinned Hot-Rod Dan in anticipation.

Johnny shook his head. "I don't buck dance, mister. I'm a bellhop, and I'm here to—"

"Here, here's a quarter," Hot-Rod Dan interrupted, throwing the coin on the floor. "Now c'mon there, black boy, and *strut yo' stuff!*"

Johnny got angry. He had heard of white men throwing Negro boys coins and saying "Strut yo' stuff" in the streets of the town, but it had never happened to him. Some danced to amuse the peckerwoods, but not him! "No thanks, I'm no buffoon! I came up here to—"

"G'wan, git outta here, nigger," shouted Hot-Rod Dan, picking up an old shoe, "before I—"

Johnny whirled around and hurried out of the room. When he reached the stairs he heard the old white man's voice shout from behind him: "Come back here, you black bastard!" Johnny paused and looked back at the outraged peckerwood. Several doors opened and guests looked out to see what was the matter. If it weren't for the other guests, he would have ignored the old bastard, but now he didn't know what to do. "Goddammit, I said come on back here!" The soldier and his girl opened their door at the second outburst. The soldier stood in the doorway in his shorts, looking first at Johnny, then at the old man. The girl peered out from behind him.

"What's all this fuss about?" asked the soldier, frowning.

Old Hot-Rod Dan snapped, "Are you gonna run my errand, or aintcha!" with a scowl on his red face and a threat in his voice. Amidst accusing stares Johnny averted his eyes and returned to the old man's door. He took out his order pad. Johnny was again outwardly composed. No frown betrayed his buried anger. He had to go back. His job was to service the guests. To *please the guests!* He looked at the old peckerwood standing in the doorway rolling his cigar around in his mouth. He stared hard at Johnny, and when he found no defiance evident in his face, he lit his cold cigar, fetched a bill from his pocket, and shoved it at Johnny. "Hurrup downstairs and git me a quart of London Dry gin," he snapped.

Johnny took the five-dollar bill, and starting out, asked, "Anything else you want . . . ?"

"What? Yeah, I want you to hurry yo' ass up and get back up here with it!" Ignoring the remark, Johnny left the room.

On his way down the hall he saw that the soldier and his girl had finished with their tray and had set it outside. He picked it up and took it with him. What else could I have done but go back to the old short peckerwood? he asked himself. If he hadn't, the old geeser would've called the manager, and, hell, he wasn't gonna lose his job because of that old bastard. Yet it was hard going back, walking back with his head down to that old peck. And then there was that old Uncle Tom nigger who was buck dancing and buffooning and disgracing the race. No wonder these pecks expect Negroes to act the fool clown. But he wasn't gonna disgrace himself by cutting the fool for these pecks! Wonder if all the others think the same way he does?

He returned the tray of empty dishes and bottles to the café, where, to his surprise, he received the money back for the bottle deposits. Pocketing the thirty cents, he asked himself whether he should give the change back to the soldier. Yes, he would, he decided immediately. The soldier was a nice fellow, and anyhow the money belonged to him. He shifted the deposit money to his other front pocket so he wouldn't forget it, then hurried towards the liquor store.

"Hey, Johnny!" someone called from across the street.

Johnny turned and recognized Jack Spinner.

"Aw, hello there, man."

Jack came across the street grinning. The short, stocky light-brown fellow looked Johnny over. "Boy, what you doing in that monkey suit?"

"Man, I'm a bellhop. You find a job yet?"

"Naw, I been looking though. When you start?"

"Just today, this morning."

"They got any more jobs at the Winslow?" Jack's voice was anxiously hopeful.

Johnny shook his head. "Naw, man. I was just lucky. The other fellow went to the Army yesterday, and I just happened to bump into Louis Jackson this morning, and he helped me to get it."

"Damn, you sure was lucky, man." Jack mopped perspiration from his face. "Sounds like a good job."

"Well, it ain't bad." Johnny motioned for Jack to walk with him. "It doesn't pay much, but it's clean work, and if you hustle they say you can make good in tips."

"There ain't much for us here, Johnny, you know that? You graduate from high school and what're you offered?"

"Porter and dishwashing jobs mostly. You're right. A diploma doesn't mean a damn thing down here, and that's why I'm clearing out."

Jack looked at Johnny with surprise and interest. "Where you going, man?"

"Soon as I get enough money saved up I'm going North."

"Oh, yeah?" The venture clearly impressed Jack.

"Yeah, only way I see it to get away before I get stuck down here. Look at Louis. He graduated several years ago, planned to go away to school to become a dentist, messed around with Ophelia and knocked her up, and now he's stuck down here."

Jack shook his head. "Goddamn, that's a bitch of a situation to get in, ain't it?"

"It sure is. And I ain't gonna get stuck. Ain't no future down here for a newspaperman, not a colored one! Comes the last of August I'm heading for New York."

Jack had followed Johnny's words thinking about himself, and after a second of contemplation, he extended his hand. "Boy, if you head North in August I'll go with you."

It was a challenge and a vow. Johnny shook his hand vigorously, and surprised and glad, said: "Boy it's a deal!"

Johnny stopped in front of the liquor store, where he suddenly remembered the urgency of his errand. "I gotta run, Chucky," he said anxiously.

"Awright, Lanky, see you Saturday night?"

"Yeah, I'll be there."

Johnny bought the bottle of gin and hurried back to the hotel. On his way up the stairs he met Eddie. "Man, 609 has been ringing your bell like crazy," he told Johnny.

"Oh, thanks, Eddie, I'm on my way up there now." Johnny ran up the stairs without an instant's pause, and came huffing and puffing upon the half-opened door of old Dan. He rapped nervously.

"C'mon in, goddammit!" growled the old man. He stood with doubled fists on his hips in the middle of the floor. He stepped forward and snatched the bottle from Johnny's hands. Ignoring this, Johnny handed him the change. "Goddamn! What you have to do—distill this gin!"

"No, sir, I had to return some dishes—" Johnny began.

"Aw horseshit! Horseshit! Damn slow nig—" He interrupted himself and rammed his hand into his pocket. He took out a dime and flipped it at Johnny. "G'wan, git!" Johnny started out the door. "That's what you black boys call a 'peckerwood's tip,' " old Dan grinned maliciously. "Now g'wan and git outa here!"

Louis and Eddie were sitting reading magazines when Johnny came into the den. Louis looked up. "Well, how'd you and old Hot-Rod Dan get along, kid?" he asked, grinning.

"Oh, he's a real character," Johnny said, sitting down on the edge of the bathtub. He related to Louis what had happened.

"You did right, kid," Louis said. "Don't pay him any mind. He's a grouchy old cheap sonofabitch."

"How'd he get the name Hot-Rod Dan?" Johnny asked.

"He's a brakeman on the railroad . . ." Louis began, but Eddie interrupted.

"How much did he ask you to dance for?" Eddie asked.

"A quarter, but that's not the point—"

"Shit, I would've danced for a quarter," said Eddie.

"Don't pay this Negro any mind, kid," Louis said sharply, "he's an Uncle Tom anyhow—"

"Who's a Uncle Tom!" snapped Eddie, turning to Louis.

"*You* are, Negro, always acting the fool for the white folks for a tip," Louis said.

"Not me—I get along with 'em better'n any of you!"

"Sure, because you're always kissing their asses!"

Louis stood up, anticipating a move by Eddie, but Eddie just waved his hand with indifference, and went back to looking at his magazine. "Just don't do any fool things he does—I'll tell you about him sometime—or you'll find yourself in trouble."

Johnny felt that he should change the subject because he didn't want to get mixed up in their private argument. Moreover, he had remembered Louis as a football star on the high-school team, and at that time he had been his idol. Now he studied him casually and organized a probe into this once popular and promising local hero. "Louis, you don't look any different from your football days," Johnny ventured.

Louis brightened with a reflective smile. "Man, that was a great team we had back in thirty-eight and thirty-nine." He lighted a cigarette, shifted to a more comfortable position, and continued in an animated voice. "We had Buck "Streak of Lightning" playing quarterback, Boots at halfback, Nelson at left tackle, and long-legged Graham at right end—"

"And you at fullback," Johnny interjected. "Man, you were great!"

"Yeah, man I—" Louis continued, but was cut off by Eddie, who had looked up with a frown.

"Goddamn, ole Louis still boasting 'bout his football!"

Louis stared hard at Eddie, as though he had hit upon sacred ground. "Listen, jackass! If you don't wanna listen, then go sit in the shithouse!" Eddie got up and went out.

"I was down in the grades but I remember that team," Johnny said. "We won the state championship when?"

"In thirty-eight." Louis crushed his cigarette and lighted another one. "Man, we were most hell that year. After we took the Negro state championship, we came home with our chests stuck way out, and there was the white boys with theirs stuck out too, 'cause they'd won the white championship, and there we were! Well, everybody, colored and white, got to talking 'bout which was the best team—ours or the whites. Naturally the Negroes said ours was and the whites said, naturally, the white team was! Well, they decided to pit us together, 'cause that was the only way to settle it —so they did!"

Jim came in and caught the substance of the conversation. He sighed with expressive boredom, and shrugging his shoulders as though he too had heard Louis's stories too much, sat down and buried his face in a magazine.

"Man, that was some game—the first and the last time colored and white played together—and we trucked all over them ofay boys! We beat 'em 14 to 7, but god–damn, what a game it was! Graham got his arm broke, I got a rib cracked, and Boots got his face stepped on, but goddamnit, we won!"

Room 621 signalled. Johnny jumped up and went out to hop the bell. Poor Louis. It seemed that his rising star had already set, that his dreams were all in the past, that his future had passed. But then he could be wrong. He would look more into sad Louis.

Johnny knocked at Room 621 and a female voice from within called: "C'mon in, bellboy," in a fine Southern drawl. He opened the door and saw a surprised redheaded plump white woman sitting on the edge of the bed. On seeing him she pulled the white robe more closely around her neck. She frowned. "I rung for Harry. Where's Harry!" She stood up.

Johnny backed away. "Oh, Harry the other bellhop, he went to the Army." Johnny sounded apologetic. "I'm—I'm taking his place." Nervously he fumbled with the order pad and pencil, as she looked him over with cold gray eyes. He felt uneasy under her stare. "Can I get something for you, miss?"

"Naw! Idea of that nigger going to the Army!" she grumbled, lighting a cigarette.

The casual ease with which the white woman flung out the word "nigger" shocked and surprised Johnny. She showed no hostility; it was a common household word with her! And what did she think—that he went to the army of his own will! "He didn't volunteer, miss, he was drafted!"

"Aw, yeah? Too bad." She grinned sympathetically. "I used that boy to massage my rheumatism . . ." Her voice trailed off. Johnny waited. At length she turned to Johnny and said, "G'wan, boy, I can't use you!"

"Yes, ma'am," he said, and started for the door.

"Wait a minute," she said, stroking the calf of her right leg. "Boy, you know how to rub?"

Johnny turned around, surprised. "Ma'am? Oh, no, ma'am!"

"Well, you gonna learn, goddamnit!" she said sharply. "These pains in my legs are killing me." She went to the dresser and took a bottle of liniment out of the top drawer. "Now, c'mon over here." She beckoned towards the bed. Johnny held back, shaking his head politely but firmly. She turned to find him near the door. "Did you hear me, boy?"

"Yes, ma'am, I heard you, but I can't do that. . . ." He put his hand on the doorknob. "I wish I could help you, but I gotta get back—"

"If you don' come back here"—she flushed red with a threat— "I'm gonna *call the manager* on you!"

Johnny dropped his hand from the knob of the door and stood frozen in his place. What did this fool white woman want of him? What kind of Negro had that Harry been? Had he really rubbed this white woman, or was she plotting to trap him?

"C'mon, I'll show you how Harry used to do it." She opened the bottle and handed it to him, then she slipped off her robe. Again Johnny stepped back, as she revealed herself in her underslip. He looked away. She lay down on the bed, unaware of his averted eyes, and said, "You the scariest black boy I ever saw!" Then turning towards him, she continued, "I thought any black boy'd be glad to rub a white woman—"

Johnny shook his head, "No, ma'am, not me!" It defied everything he had been taught about morals.

"C'mon, boy, I'm ready!" the woman said irritably. Johnny approached the bed on tiptoe. God, what would happen now if her husband came in! Goddamn, if *any* white man came in! "Rub my legs—massage my calves first." Rub the hell outa her and get it over with, Johnny ordered himself. He filled his palms with liniment, and spreading it generously over one of her legs, began massaging vigorously with both hands. As the yellowish-white flesh turned red under the pressure of his hands, the woman sighed with relief.

"Ah-h . . . ah, that's better . . . harder, harder, yeah, keep it up. . . . Now up higher, harder. . . . Damn rheumatism! Now the other leg . . . down below . . . that's it, harder . . . !" Johnny performed his work with mechanical efficiency and indifference. He felt nothing. Over and over again he applied linament and rubbed, rubbed, and rubbed, the upper parts of her legs, the lower parts of her legs, exerting all of his strength, until, exhausted and relieved, the woman cried out, "Ah, ah, that's it, now—now that's enough, enough!"

Johnny straightened up and wiped perspiration from his face. The white woman turned over on her back, then sat up in the bed, breathing hard but grinning. "Damn, boy! You'd rub the white off of me if I letcha!" She got up and Johnny turned his back as she put on her robe. Again he became momentarily apprehensive of the woman's motives, but his fear proved groundless when the woman made no untoward act or outcry. She found her handbag, took out a half dollar, and handed it to him. "Now, I didn't hurtcha, did I, boy?" she grinned.

"No, ma'am, and thank you very much, miss." Johnny started out.

At the door the woman said, "Next time you won't be scared?"

"Next time? Oh, no, ma'am, just ring me and I'm at your service, miss."

Johnny left Room 621 in a daze. My God, what an experience, what an unpredictable job, this bellhopping. You never know from one room to the next what you're gonna run into. That white woman had scared the crap out of him at first, but then slowly he began to realize that she really had rheumatism, that *all she wanted was for him to rub her!* The hardest part was touching her the first time. She didn't jump up and holler like the white women in the many stories he had heard and read who screamed when Negro men touched them, either by accident or through the women's own foolishness! The whole episode was queer. How could he explain it to the other bellhops, or his buddies, or his mother! He couldn't; the fool situation was so strange that he wouldn't know how to try to describe it or explain it. It was one of those things that you just forgot about. And so he did.

On the second day at the Winslow Arms, Johnny was assigned to work in the lobby. He was stationed there by the bell captain to handle all incoming and outgoing baggage, and to run short errands for the guests who were seated in leather armchairs in a semicircle around the single white pillar in the center of the room. A young woman sat in the center chair knitting with army wool material; a dark-haired, swarthy, short man worked at business figures in a chair to the right of the woman. A tall, slender, sandy-haired man in his late thirties held an open newspaper before him; He was the most restless of the trio. Although he held the paper in a pretense of reading it, he was observing the young woman. He looked at her slim but shapely crossed legs, then moved his gray eyes upwards to her waist, her breasts, then her face. She kept her soft brown eyes steadily on her fingers, which worked feverishly at the knitting, and her face was a mask of abstraction. He dropped his paper into his lap, lit a cigar, and studied her openly, his eyes centering on her legs. She did not look up. He sighed and looked at the dark-haired middle-aged man. "Well, what do you think of the war, Mr.—er—Mr. Sophos—or Sophocles?" he asked.

The little man looked up and frowned. "Not Sophocles, Mr. Throckmorton," he said indignantly. "Sophocles Dimitros." And with this curt correction the Greek businessman returned to his figures, showing no interest in continuing the conversation.

"Well, I'm sorry, sir," Throckmorton replied sarcastically in a slow drawl. "Always get these foreign names mixed up. In your case I didn't know the hind name from the front."

The young woman had looked up from her work to observe briefly the exchange between Throckmorton and Dimitros, and Throckmorton had caught her eye. He smiled, but she did not return his smile. Instead, she returned to her feverish pace of knitting. "Making a sweater, Mrs. Rogers?" he asked.

She looked up with surprise. "What? Oh, yes, yes, it's to be a sweater," she explained, with a trace of annoyance in her voice. She felt his eyes on her legs and uncrossed them.

He relighted his cigar. "Of course, it doesn't get cold enough down here for it, now does it?"

"I don't know," Mrs. Rogers sighed, vexed, as a reflective frown clouded her face, "one never knows where a soldier will be sent next." After an instant's pause she lifted her needles to resume her work, but failing to steady her hands, she got up abruptly and ran up the stairs.

Throckmorton followed the shapely legs all the way up the stairs until they were out of view. Then, as he turned his head away, his eyes fell on Dimitros with a hostile stare. He took his cigar out of his mouth, cleared his throat, and spat contemptuously at the spittoon that lay between them.

Johnny had observed and overhead all that had transpired from his position near the stairway. However, he had pretended to be oblivious of everything. He had heard of the arrogant and mean Throckmorton, and was determined to avoid him if possible. But now Throckmorton, who was reputed to be a rich cattle buyer, turned his attention to Johnny. Johnny caught his gaze and looked away from him. Throckmorton got up, stretched, tossed his newspaper on the armchair and walked over to Johnny. "Boy, what's your name?" he asked, digging his fingers under his belt and puffing smoke into Johnny's face.

"My name's Johnny Morgan, sir," Johnny answered, looking up into the man's cunning eyes.

"You new here, aintcha?"

"Yes, sir, I started to work here yesterday."

Throckmorton rested his weight on one foot, grinned mischievously, and dug a coin out of his pocket. He flipped the coin into the air, caught it, then said, "Lookahere, boy, I've been having some bad luck lately, know that?"

Johnny shook his head and averted his eyes. "No, sir, I didn't know."

Throckmorton puffed hard on his cigar. "Well, I have, and you can help me change it. Know how?"

Johnny coughed a little from the smoke. "Well, what can I do for you, sir?" he asked, taking out his order pad in a facetious gesture.

Throckmorton frowned. "Boy, how's about my rubbing your head for good luck?"

"Sir . . . !" Johnny stepped back indignantly, as Throckmorton raised his hand.

"C'mon, nigger, let me rub your head!" snapped Throckmorton, stepping forward, holding the coin up. "Here's a quarter. . . ."

"No, sir, don't touch my head!" Johnny said, waving the coin away.

"Don't get smart with me, you uppity nigger!" Throckmorton pointed a finger at Johnny menacingly. Johnny sulked but did not reply. "Why won't you let me rub your head for good luck, boy?"

Johnny stiffened and looked straight into the white man's eyes. "You wouldn't want me to rub your head, would you?"

Throckmorton's mouth fell open and his face turned a deep red, and his eyes widened with an incredulous stare. "Rub *my* head!" He doubled up his fists and rushed at Johnny. "G'wan, nigger— rub my head!" He charged with his blond head bent forward. Johnny shook his head, with fright in his dark-brown eyes, and moved out of arms reach. "Touch me so I can stomp the goddamn shit outa you!"

"What's the matter down there?" called Mrs. Winslow from the second-floor bannister.

Throckmorton had grabbed Johnny by the coat lapel and drawn back his fist to hit him, but now he dropped his hands to his side. "Oh, Mrs. Winslow . . ." Mrs. Winslow descended the stairs hurriedly. "It's your smart little nigger boy—" Throckmorton began.

"I did nothing to him," Johnny interrupted.

Throckmorton whirled at Johnny and scowled.

"Go up to my room, boy!" Mrs. Winslow said firmly. Johnny nodded his head, and saying, "Yes, ma'am," started up the stairs. Mrs. Winslow folded her arms, and motioning with her head for the desk clerk to sit down, turned to her irate guest. "Now, what did my boy do wrong, Mrs. Throckmorton?"

Johnny paused out of sight on the second floor to listen. Charley and Louis came up from behind him to listen. "What happened, boy?" Charley asked irritably.

"He wanted to rub my head *for good luck!*"

Louis laughed softly. "That peckerwood is always trying something like that."

Charley frowned. "What did you say to him?"

"I said, 'You wouldn't want me to rub *your* head!' "

Charley gasped. "What!" Louis laughed out loud. "You shouldn't have done that!" Charley snapped at Johnny.

"Yeah, but—" Johnny began, but Charley cut him off.

"What did she tell you to do, boy?"

"To go to her room . . ."

"Well, g'wan then!" ordered the bell captain. "I'll speak to her."

Johnny walked down the hall towards Mrs. Winslow's room. In his mind he re-enacted the episode with Throckmorton. Could he have avoided it? Looking back, it seemed impossible. That old peckerwood had no business trying to "rub his head for good luck." He, Johnny, wasn't an Uncle Tom and he wasn't gonna act like one, no sir! He reached Room 212 and entered it. Immediately he felt uneasy in that richly furnished and slightly perfumed suite. He didn't know whether to sit or stand, so he stood. Above Mrs. Winslow's desk hung an imposing painting of an army officer. Probably her husband who was killed in the First World War, he thought. The other bellhops had told him that Major Winslow had been killed in Germany. He sat stern-faced, with his hands holding a crop in his lap, and his blue eyes staring directly out of his rugged pink face. Soon the sharp, accusing eyes of Mrs. Winslow would be staring at him. What should he say for himself? He knew that that peckerwood Throckmorton would have depicted him as a *sassy, uppity nigger*, and twisted the whole incident to favor him. Would she listen to *his* side of the story? Or would she storm right in and say he was fired? He would tell the whole straight truth if he got a chance to. . . .

The door opened and Mrs. Winslow entered. Charley followed her and closed the door. She put her hands on her hips and walked swiftly up to Johnny. She frowned, "Boy, why did you get smart and uppity with Mr. Throckmorton?"

"I didn't get smart with him, Mrs. Winslow—" Johnny began, but was interrupted.

"What happened to start the fuss—*tell me the truth*, boy!" As she spoke she shook her finger in his face. Johnny got jittery and couldn't talk.

Charley spoke up. "Speak up, boy, and tell Mrs. Winslow what happened downstairs!"

Johnny composed himself and related precisely what had transpired between him and Throckmorton. "And that's the honest truth, Mrs. Winslow," he said, looking her straight in the face.

Mrs. Winslow looked at Charley, then at Johnny, then at the floor, performing all of these gestures in an instant; then she rubbed her chin. "Boy, I thought I was gonna fire you," she said, looking at him with deliberation. "If you weren't so obviously in the right, I'd still fire you, but Mr. Throckmorton had no right trying to rub your head, *for good luck*, as he put it, so I'm gonna let you off this time." She relaxed her face and forced a grin. Then sternly she continued, "But next time don't try to be so smart. Come and tell me if you have any more trouble."

Johnny nodded his head. "Yes, ma'am." He sighed inwardly.

"All right, boy, go on back to the lobby, but behave yourself," Mrs. Winslow said firmly. "I'll speak to Mr. Throckmorton and ask him to leave you alone."

Charley walked down the hall with Johnny. "You were lucky you didn't get fired, boy!" he said harshly. "You can't go around talking up to these peckerwoods like that."

Johnny was tempted to argue with him, but he restrained himself. Charley was the old-type Negro with antiquated ideas, and there was not point in trying to change him. All he said was "Charley, would you have let that white man rub your head?"

"Naw, I wouldn't have let him, but I wouldn't have said 'Let me rub yourn!' to that rich white man. He's a big bad sonofabitch, and it don't pay to fuck with him. He's big enough to buy jest 'bout anything he wants, and you'd better remember that, boy!"

Johnny did not reply, and Charley looked at him for his concurrence. "I'm not gonna start anything with him, Mr. Simpson," he reassured Charley as they parted at the bellhops' den. As he continued down the hall to the lobby, Johnny said to himself that he was glad that Throckmorton wasn't a guest on his floor, because sooner or later they surely would have a clash.

He returned to the lobby with a cautious and timid feeling, anxious as to what Throckmorton's reactions would be on seeing him. He looked around the room with a casual but eager eye. The lobby was deserted. He looked at the clock and found the reason why. It was noontime. He sighed. He felt relieved, but he knew that it was only a temporary relief. Throckmorton would be

back with his hostile cold gray eyes; he would always come back
as an image of white supremacy. As he took his position at the foot
of the stairway, he re-enacted the scene with Throckmorton again.
What arrogance, what contempt that bastard showed wanting to
rub his head. He pondered the significance of the act and the attitude. There seemed more to it even than he had felt before. What
was it? Was it a feeling of assurance of being able to do it? No, it
was something else; it was more of an expression of a right. That
was it—that peckerwood acted from a feeling of right, his right
to abuse and to degrade a Negro! This is what had angered him.
A Negro in his bigoted eyes was an object of fun-making, buffoonery, and ridicule, and he had the right to treat him as such! The
rational conclusion was disturbing and frightening, opening his
eyes for the first time to the psychology of peckerwoods. Up to
now he had never really given any thought to why they acted as
they did: why they kept to themselves in schools, churches, play-
grounds, everywhere. He had assumed that the races were kept
separate for peace and harmony, and that all this separation business was a sort of mutual arrangement. But now the sky opened
up and revealed the raw truth. He was not considered equal! Had
he been a white bellhop that peckerwood wouldn't have dared try
to rub his head, nor would he have felt he had a right to do so
against the boy's will! The impact of the implication struck him
like a bolt of lightning, and he sat down on the steps and cupped
his face in trembling hands. He sat there for several minutes
engulfed in fear and anger, oblivious of his surroundings, and
limp with despair.

"What's wrong with you, boy," Charley called, descending the
stairs rapidly, with an expression of exasperation on his face.

Johnny jumped to his feet dazed and surprised. "Oh, nothing's
wrong, Mr. Simpson," he said.

"Did Mr. Throckmorton bother you again?" Charley put his
hand on Johnny's shoulder solicitously.

"No, sir." Johnny wiped his eyes and tried to pull himself together. For the first time he saw Eddie standing above Charley,
looking on with wide-open eyes.

Charley flushed with anger. "Well, what the hell you sitting
down and crying for?"

"I wasn't crying, Mr. Simpson . . ."

"Well, what the hell was you doing?"

"I was . . . I was just . . . just thinking . . ."

"Thinking! What the hell is wrong with you, boy? Huh!" Charley exclaimed, waving his hands furiously.

Sadie got up from the clerk's desk and hurried over to them with an anxious expression on her face, asking, "What's the matter with him, Charley?" looking first at him and then at Johnny.

"Huh? Oh, this don't concern you, Sadie."

"You want me to call Mrs. Winslow?" she asked, frowning at Johnny suspiciously.

"Naw, I'll take care of it, Sadie," Charley said, waving her back to her desk. Turning to Eddie, he said, "Eddie, you take over down here," then to Johnny, "Boy, you come with me!"

Sadie lingered near Eddie, and when Charley and Johnny were midway up the stairs, she whispered, "What's it all about, boy?"

Eddie shook his head. "Huh? I don't know," he said, and shrugged his shoulders.

"Thinking!" Charley repeated disparagingly when his foot touched the second floor. Johnny dropped his head. "Boy, you ain't paid to sit on your black ass and think, know that? You paid to service these white folks, and you damn well better remember that! Thinking! What the fuck could you be sitting there thinking 'bout anyhow?" He looked at Johnny incredulously.

Johnny shook his head as one does after a deep cry. It was too much, too complex to try to explain to old Charley. Doubtless he would say that he was queer or crazy or something, sitting on his ass in this white hotel and thinking about the psychology of peckerwoods!

"You hear me!" snapped Charley, grabbing him by the sleeve. "What was you doing sitting there and thinking?" Such audacity demanded an explanation for the bell captain.

"I was thinking," sighed Johnny, fumbling with his hands, "about the psychology of peckerwoods. . . ."

Charley gasped. "What! 'Bout the psy—psy—" He paused and looked cautiously around. "Nigger, you must be crazy! You acting goddamn strange and you better watch yo' step. Any more of this foolishness with these peck—these white folks and that queer thinking shit and you'll find yo'self out on the street, you hear!"

"Yes, sir."

They looked up and saw Mrs. Winslow coming out of her room. "Goddam Sadie!" Charley said in a mumble. He gave Johnny a shove towards the den.

"What's the trouble, Charley?" she asked, looking first at Johnny and then at him.

Charley forced a grin. "Aw, nothing much, Mrs. Winslow. The boy just got a stomach ache. . . ."

Cyrus Colter

Mr. Colter states in a note written April 29, 1962: "I live in Chicago and am a lawyer and state official. I have served for thirteen years now as a member of the Illinois Commerce Commission, concerned with the regulation of public utilities. I was born in Noblesville, Indiana, January 8, 1910, and began writing fiction only two years ago, as a weekend hobby. It's still a hobby—I have no illusions at fifty-two. I've had only four stories published, all in 'little' magazines. 'The Beach Umbrella' will be my fifth publication of fiction. My first story appeared about eighteen months ago in an Irish quarterly, *Threshold*, published in Belfast. Then followed stories in the Fall 1961 issue of *Epoch* (Cornell University), in the Winter 1961 issue of the *University of Kansas City Review*, and, the last one, in the Winter 1962 issue of *Epoch*.

" 'The Beach Umbrella' came about in this way: One Saturday evening last August—it was just twilight—my wife and I were driving past the thirty-first Street beach in Chicago. We saw a little man (later Elijah) in swimming trunks leaving the beach. He carried his clothes and shoes in one hand and a huge, folded red-and-white beach umbrella in the other. He walked slowly with his head down, as if despondent, perplexed. I said to my wife, 'That fellow's got problems'—and promptly forgot the whole incident. But intermittently for days Elijah would reappear in my mind—

with his problems. I mentioned it to my wife, a woman of uncommon intuition, and she said, 'Write about him, and you'll get rid of him.' So I did (both)."

"The Beach Umbrella" appears here for the first time.

THE BEACH UMBRELLA

BY CYRUS COLTER

The Thirty-first Street beach lay dazzling under a sky so blue that Lake Michigan ran to the horizon like a sheet of sapphire silk, studded with little barbed white sequins for sails; and the heavy surface of the water lapped gently at the boulder "sea wall" which had been cut into, graded, and sanded to make the beach. Saturday afternoons were always frenzied: three black lifeguards, giants in sunglasses, preened in their towers and chaperoned the bathers— adults, teen-agers, and children—who were going through every physical gyration of which the human body is capable. Some dove, swam, some hollered, rode inner tubes, or merely stood waist-deep and pummeled the water; others—on the beach—sprinted, did handsprings and somersaults, sucked Eskimo pies, or just buried their children in the sand. Then there were the lollers—extended in their languor under a garish variety of beach umbrellas.

Elijah lolled too—on his stomach in the white sand, his chin cupped in his palm; but under no umbrella. He had none. By habit, though, he stared in awe at those who did, and sometimes meddled in their conversation: "It's gonna be gettin' *hot* pretty soon—if it ain't careful," he said to a Bantu-looking fellow and his girl sitting near by with an older woman. The temperature was then in the nineties. The fellow managed a negligent smile. "Yeah," he said, and persisted in listening to the women. Buoyant still, Elijah watched them. But soon his gaze wavered, and then moved on to other lollers of interest. Finally he got up, stretched, brushed sand from his swimming trunks, and scanned the beach for a new spot. He started walking.

He was not tall. And he appeared to walk on his toes—his walnut-colored legs were bowed and skinny and made him hobble like a jerky little spider. Next he plopped down near two men and two girls—they were hilarious about something—sitting beneath a big purple-and-white umbrella. The girls, chocolate brown and shapely, emitted squeals of laughter at the wisecracks of the men. Elijah was enchanted. All summer long the rambunctious gaiety of the beach had fastened on him a curious charm, a hex, that brought him gawking and twiddling to the lake each Saturday. The rest of the week, save Sunday, he worked. But Myrtle, his wife, detested the sport and stayed away. Randall, the boy, had been only twice and then without little Susan, who during the summer was her mother's own midget reflection. But Elijah came regularly, especially whenever Myrtle was being evil, which he felt now was almost always. She was getting worse, too—if that was possible. The Woman was money-*crazy*.

"You gotta sharp-lookin' umbrella there!" he cut in on the two laughing couples. They studied him—the abruptly silent way. Then the big-shouldered fellow smiled and lifted his eyes to their spangled roof. "Yeah? . . . Thanks," he said. Elijah carried on: "I see a lot of 'em out here this summer—much more'n last year." The fellow meditated on this, but was noncommittal. The others went on gabbing, mostly with their hands. Elijah, squinting in the hot sun, watched them. He didn't see how they could be married; they cut the fool too much, acted like they'd itched to get together for weeks and just now made it. He pondered going back in the water, but he'd already had an hour of that. His eyes traveled the sweltering beach. Funny about his folks; they were every shape and color a God-made human could be. Here was a real sample of variety—pink white to jetty black. Could you any longer call that a *race* of people? It was a complicated complication—for some real educated guy to figure out. Then another thought slowly bore in on him: the beach umbrellas blooming across the sand attracted people—slews of friends, buddies; and gals, too. Wherever the loudest racket tore the air, a big red, or green, or yellowish umbrella—bordered with white fringe maybe —flowered in the middle of it all and gave shade to the happy good-timers.

Take, for instance, that tropical-looking pea-green umbrella over there, with the Bikini-ed brown chicks under it, and the portable radio jumping. A real beach party! He got up, stole over, and eased down in the sand at the fringe of the jubilation—two big thermos jugs sat in the shade and everybody had a paper cup in hand as the explosions of buffoonery carried out to the water. Chief provoker of mirth was a bulging-eyed old gal in a white bathing suit who, encumbered by big flabby overripe thighs, cavorted and pranced in the sand. When, perspiring from the heat, she finally fagged out, she flopped down almost on top of him. So far, he had gone unnoticed. But now, as he craned in at closer range, she brought him up: "Whatta *you* want, Pops?" She grinned, but with a touch of hostility.

Pops! Where'd she get that stuff? He was only forty-one, not a day older than that boozy bag. But he smiled. "Nothin'," he said brightly, "but you sure got one goin' here." He turned and viewed the noise-makers.

"An' you wanta get in on it!" she wrangled.

"Oh, I was just lookin'—"

"—You was just lookin'. Yeah, you was just lookin' at them young chicks there!" She roared a laugh and pointed at the sexy-looking girls under the umbrella.

Elijah grinned weakly.

"Beat it!" she catcalled, and turned back to the party.

He sat like a rock—the hell with her. But soon he relented, and wandered down to the water's edge—remote now from all inhospitality—to sit in the sand and hug his raised knees. Far out, the sailboats were pinned to the horizon and, despite all the close-in fuss, the wide miles of lake lay impassive under a blazing calm; far south and east down the long-curving lake shore, miles in the distance, the smoky haze of the Whiting plant of the Youngstown Sheet and Tube Company hung ominously in an otherwise bright sky. And so it was that he turned back and viewed the beach again—and suddenly caught his craving. Weren't they something —the umbrellas! The flashy colors of them! And the swank! No wonder folks ganged round them. Yes . . . yes, he too must have one. The thought came slow and final, and scared him. For there stood Myrtle in his mind. She nagged him now night and day, and it was always money that got her started; there was never enough—for Susan's shoes, Randy's overcoat, for new kitchen linoleum, Venetian blinds, for a better car than the old Chevy. "I just don't understand you!" she had said only night before last. "Have you got any plans at all for your family? You got a family, you know. If you could only bear to pull yourself away from that deaf old tightwad out at that warehouse, and go get yourself a *real* job . . . But no! Not *you!*"

She was talking about old man Schroeder, who owned the warehouse where he worked. Yes, the pay could be better, but it still wasn't as bad as she made out. Myrtle could be such a fool sometimes. He had been with the old man nine years now; had started out as a freight handler, but worked up to doing inventories and a a little paper work. True, the business had been going down recently, for the old man's sight and hearing were failing and his key people had left him. Now he depended on *him*, Elijah—who of late wore a necktie on the job, and made his inventory rounds with a ball-point pen and clipboard. The old man was friendlier, too—almost "hat in hand" to him. He liked everything about the job now—except the pay. And that was only because of Myrtle. She just wanted so much; even talked of moving out of their rented apartment and buying out in the Chatham area. But one thing had to be said for her: she never griped about anything for herself; only for the family, the kids. Every payday he endorsed his check and handed it over to her, and got back in return only gasoline and cigarette money. And this could get pretty tiresome. About six weeks ago he'd gotten a ten-dollar-a-month raise out of the old man, but that had only made her madder than ever. He'd thought about looking for another job all right; but where would he go to get another white-collar job? There weren't many of them for him. *She* wouldn't care if he went back to the steel mills, back to pouring that white-hot ore out at Youngstown Sheet and Tube. It would be okay with *her*—so long as his pay check was fat. But that kind of work was no good, undignified; coming home on the bus you were always so tired you went to sleep in your seat, with your lunch pail in your lap.

Just then two wet boys, chasing each other across the sand, raced by him into the water. The cold spray on his skin made him jump, jolting him out of his thoughts. He turned and slowly scanned the beach again. The umbrellas were brighter, gayer, bolder than ever—each a hiving center of playful people. He stood up finally, took a long last look, and then started back to the spot where he had parked the Chevy.

The following Monday evening was hot and humid as Elijah sat at home in their plain living room and pretended to read the newspaper; the windows were up, but not the slightest breeze came through the screens to stir Myrtle's fluffy curtains. At the moment she and nine-year-old Susan were in the kitchen finishing the dinner dishes. For twenty minutes now he had sat waiting for the furtive chance to speak to Randall. Randall, at twelve, was a serious, industrious boy, and did deliveries and odd jobs for the neighborhood grocer. Soon he came through—intent, absorbed— on his way back to the grocery for another hour's work.

"Gotta go back, eh, Randy?" Elijah said.

"Yes, sir." He was tall for his age, and wore glasses. He paused with his hand on the doorknob.

Elijah hesitated. Better wait, he thought—wait till he comes back. But Myrtle might be around then. Better ask him now. But Randall had opened the door. "See you later, Dad," he said— and left.

Elijah, shaken, again raised the newspaper and tried to read. He should have called him back, he knew, but he had lost his nerve—because he couldn't tell how Randy would take it. Fifteen dollars was nothing though, really—Randy probably had fifty or sixty stashed away somewhere in his room. Then he thought of Myrtle, and waves of fright went over him—to be even thinking about a beach umbrella was bad enough; and to buy one, especially now, would be to her some kind of crime; but to borrow even a part of the money for it from Randy . . . well, Myrtle would go out of her mind. He had never lied to his family before. This would be the first time. And he had thought about it all day long. During the morning, at the warehouse, he had gotten out the two big mail-order catalogues, to look at the beach umbrellas; but the ones shown were all so small and dinky-looking he was contemptuous. So at noon he drove the Chevy out to a sporting-goods store on West Sixty-Third Street. There he found a gorgeous assortment of yard and beach umbrellas. And there he found his prize. A beauty, a big beauty, with wide red and white stripes, and a white fringe. But oh the price! Twenty-three dollars! And he with nine.

"What's the matter with you?" Myrtle had walked in the room. She was thin, and medium brown-skinned with a saddle of freckles across her nose, and looked harried in her sleeveless house dress with her hair unkempt.

Startled, he lowered the newspaper. "Nothing," he said.

"How can you read looking *over* the paper?"

"Was I?"

Not bothering to answer, she sank in a chair. "Susie," she called back into the kitchen, "bring my cigarettes in here, will you, baby?"

Soon Susan, chubby and solemn, with the mist of perspiration on her forehead, came in with the cigarettes. "Only three left, Mama," she said, peering into the pack.

"Okay," Myrtle sighed, taking the cigarettes. Susan started out. "Now, scour the sink good, honey—and then go take your bath. You'll feel cooler."

Before looking at him again, Myrtle lit a cigarette. "School starts in three weeks," she said, with a forlorn shake of her head. "Do you realize that?"

"Yeah? . . . Jesus, time flies." He could not look at her.

"Susie needs dresses, and a couple of pairs of *good* shoes—and she'll need a coat before it gets cold."

"Yeah, I know." He patted the arm of the chair.

"Randy—bless his heart—has already made enough to get most of *his* things. That boy's something; he's all business—I've never seen anything like it." She took a drag on her cigarette. "And old man Schroeder giving you a ten-dollar raise! What was you thinkin' about? What'd you *say* to him?"

He did not answer at first. Finally he said, "Ten dollars is ten dollars, Myrtle. You know business is slow."

"*I'll* say it is! And there won't be any business before long—and then where'll you be? I tell you over and over again, you better start looking for something *now*! I been preachin' it to you for a year."

He said nothing.

"Ford and International Harvester are hiring every man they can lay their hands on! And the mills out in Gary and Whiting are going full blast—you see the red sky every night. The men make *good* money."

"They earn every nickel of it, too," he said in gloom.

"But they *get* it! Bring it home! It spends! Does that mean anything to you? Do you know what some of them make? Well, ask Hawthorne—or ask Sonny Milton. Sonny's wife says his checks some weeks run as high as a hundred twenty, hundred thirty, dollars. One week! Take-home pay!"

"Yeah? . . . And Sonny told me he wished he had a job like mine."

Myrtle threw back her head with a bitter gasp. "Oh-h-h, God! Did you tell him what you made? Did you tell him that?"

Suddenly Susan came back into the muggy living room. She went straight to her mother and stood as if expecting an award. Myrtle absently patted her on the side of the head. "Now, go and run your bath water, honey," she said.

Elijah smiled at Susan. "Susie," he said, "d'you know your tummy is stickin' way out—you didn't eat too much, did you?" He laughed.

Susan turned and observed him; then looked at her mother. "No," she finally said.

"Go on, now, baby," Myrtle said. Susan left the room.

Myrtle resumed. "Well, there's no use going through all this again. It's plain as the nose on your face. You got a family—a good family, I think. The only question is, do you wanta get off your hind end and do somethin' for it. It's just that simple."

Elijah looked at her. "You can talk real crazy sometimes, Myrtle."

"I think it's that old man!" she cried, her freckles contorted. "He's got you answering the phone, and taking inventory—wearing a necktie and all that. You wearing a necktie and your son mopping in a grocery store, so he can buy his own clothes." She snatched up her cigarettes, and walked out of the room.

His eyes did not follow her, but remained off in space. Finally he got up and went into the kitchen. Over the stove the plaster was thinly cracked, and, in spots, the linoleum had worn through the

pattern; but everything was immaculate. He opened the refrigerator, poured a glass of cold water, and sat down at the kitchen
table. He felt strange and weak, and sat for a long time sipping the
water.

Then after a while he heard Randall's key in the front door,
sending tremors of dread through him. When Randall came into
the kitchen, he seemed to him as tall as himself; his glasses were
steamy from the humidity outside, and his hands were dirty.

"Hi, Dad," he said gravely without looking at him, and opened
the refrigerator door.

Elijah chuckled. "Your mother'll get after you about going in
there without washing your hands."

But Randall took out the water pitcher and closed the door.

Elijah watched him. Now was the time to ask him. His heart
was hammering. Go on—now! But instead he heard his husky
voice saying, "What'd they have you doing over at the grocery
tonight?"

Randall was drinking the glass of water. When he finished, he
said, "Refilling shelves."

"Pretty hot job tonight, eh?"

"It wasn't so bad." Randall was matter-of-fact as he set the
empty glass over the sink, and paused before leaving.

"Well . . . you're doing fine, son. Fine. Your mother sure
is proud of you . . ." Purpose had lodged in his throat.

The praise embarrassed Randall. "Okay, Dad," he said, and
edged from the kitchen.

Elijah slumped back in his chair, near prostration. He tried to
clear his mind of every particle of thought, but the images became
only more jumbled, oppressive to the point of panic.

Then before long Myrtle came into the kitchen—ignoring him.
But she seemed not so hostile now as coldly impassive, exhibiting
a bravado he had not seen before. He got up and went back into
the living room and turned on the television. As the TV-screen
lawmen galloped before him, he sat oblivious, admitting the failure
of his will. If only he could have gotten Randall to himself long
enough—but everything had been so sudden, abrupt; he couldn't
just ask him out of the clear blue. Besides, around him, Randall
always seemed so busy, too busy to talk. He couldn't understand

that; he had never mistreated the boy, never whipped him in his life; had shaken him a time or two, but that was long ago, when he was little.

He sat and watched the finish of the half-hour TV show. Myrtle was in the bedroom now. He slouched in his chair, lacking the resolve to get up and turn off the television.

Suddenly he was on his feet.

Leaving the television on, he went back to Randall's room in the rear. The door was open and Randall was asleep, lying on his back on the bed, perspiring, still dressed except for his shoes and glasses. He stood over the bed and looked at him. He was a good boy; his own son. But how strange—he thought for the first time—there was no resemblance between them. None whatsoever. Randy had a few of his mother's freckles on his thin brown face, but he could see none of himself in the boy. Then his musings were scattered by the return of his fear. He dreaded waking him. And he might be cross. If he didn't hurry, though, Myrtle or Susie might come strolling out any minute. His bones seemed rubbery from the strain. Finally he bent down and touched Randall's shoulder. The boy did not move a muscle, except to open his eyes. Elijah smiled at him. And he slowly sat up.

"Sorry, Randy—to wake you up like this."

"What's the matter?" Randall rubbed his eyes.

Elijah bent down again, but did not whisper. "Say, can you let me have fifteen bucks—till I get my check? . . . I need to get some things—and I'm a little short this time." He could hardly bring the words up.

Randall gave him a slow, queer look.

"I'll get my check a week from Friday," Elijah said, ". . . and I'll give it back to you then—sure."

Now instinctively Randall glanced toward the door, and Elijah knew Myrtle had crossed his thoughts. "You don't have to mention anything to your mother," he said with casual suddenness.

Randall got up slowly off the bed, and, in his socks, walked to the little table where he did his homework. He pulled the drawer out, fished far in the back a moment, and brought out a white business envelope secured by a rubber band. Holding the envelope close to his stomach, he took out first a ten-dollar bill, and then a five, and, sighing, handed them over.

"Thanks, old man," Elijah quivered, folding the money. "You'll get this back the day I get my check. . . . That's for sure."

"Okay," Randall finally said.

Elijah started out. Then he could see Myrtle on payday—her hand extended for his check. He hesitated, and looked at Randall, as if to speak. But he slipped the money in his trousers pocket and hurried from the room.

The following Saturday at the beach did not begin bright and sunny. By noon it was hot, but the sky was overcast and angry, the air heavy. There was no certainty whatever of a crowd, raucous or otherwise, and this was Elijah's chief concern as, shortly before twelve o'clock, he drove up in the Chevy and parked in the bumpy, graveled stretch of high ground that looked down eastward over the lake and was used for a parking lot. He climbed out of the car, glancing at the lake and clouds, and prayed in his heart it would not rain—the water was murky and restless, and only a handful of bathers had showed. But it was early yet. He stood beside the car and watched a bulbous, brown-skinned woman, in bathing suit and enormous straw hat, lugging a lunch basket down toward the beach, followed by her brood of children. And a fellow in swimming trunks, apparently the father, took a towel and sandals from his new Buick and called petulantly to his family to "just wait a minute, please." In another car, two women sat waiting, as yet fully clothed and undecided about going swimming. While down at the water's edge there was the usual cluster of dripping boys who, brash and boisterous, swarmed to the beach every day in fair weather or foul.

Elijah took off his shirt, peeled his trousers from over his swiming trunks, and started collecting the paraphernalia from the back seat of the car: a frayed pink rug filched from the house, a towel, sunglasses, cigarettes, a thermos jug filled with cold lemonade he had made himself, and a dozen paper cups. All this he stacked on the front fender. Then he went around to the rear and opened the trunk. Ah, there it lay—encased in a long, slim package trussed with heavy twine, and barely fitting athwart the spare tire. He felt prickles of excitment as he took the knife from the tool bag, cut the twine, and pulled the wrapping paper away. Red and white stripes sprang at him. It was even more gorgeous than when it had first seduced him in the store. The white fringe gave it style; the wide red fillets were cardinal and stark, and the white stripes glared. Now he opened it over his head, for the full thrill of its colors, and looked around to see if anyone else agreed. Finally after a while he gathered up all his equipment and headed down for the beach, his short, nubby legs seeming more bowed than ever under the weight of their cargo.

When he reached the sand, a choice of location became a pressing matter. That was why he had come early. From past observation it was clear that the center of gaiety shifted from day to day; last Saturday it might have been nearer the water, this Saturday, well back; or up, or down, the beach a ways. He must pick the site with care, for he could not move about the way he did when he had no umbrella; it was too noticeable. He finally took a spot as near the center of the beach as he could estimate, and dropped his gear in the sand. He knelt down and spread the pink rug, then moved the thermos jug over onto it, and folded the towel and placed it with the paper cups, sunglasses, and cigarettes down beside the jug. Now he went to find a heavy stone or brick to drive down the spike for the hollow umbrella stem to fit over. So it was not until the umbrella was finally up that he again had time for anxiety about the weather. His whole morning's effort had been an act of faith, for, as yet, there was no sun, although now and then a few azure breaks appeared in the thinning cloud mass. But before very long this brighter texture of the sky began to grow and spread by slow degrees, and his hopes quickened. Finally he sat down under the umbrella, lit a cigarette, and waited.

It was not long before two small boys came by—on their way to the water. He grinned, and called to them, "Hey, fellas, been in yet?"—their bathing suits were dry.

They stopped, and observed him. Then one of them smiled, and shook his head.

Elijah laughed. "Well, whatta you waitin' for? Go on in there and get them suits wet!" Both boys gave him silent smiles. And they lingered. He thought this a good omen—it had been different the Saturday before.

Once or twice the sun burst through the weakening clouds. He forgot the boys now in watching the skies, and soon they moved on. His anxiety was not detectable from his lazy posture under the umbrella, with his dwarfish, gnarled legs extended and his bare heels on the little rug. But then soon the clouds began to fade in earnest, seeming not to move away laterally, but slowly to recede into a lucent haze, until at last the sun came through hot and bright. He squinted at the sky and felt delivered. They would come, the folks would come!—were coming now; the beach would soon be swarming. Two other umbrellas were up already, and the diving board thronged with wet, acrobatic boys. The lifeguards were in their towers now, and still another launched his yellow rowboat. And up on the Outer Drive, the cars, one by one, were turning into the parking lot. The sun was bringing them out all right; soon he'd be in the middle of a field day. He felt a low-key, welling excitement, for the water was blue, and far out the sails were starched and white.

Soon he saw the two little boys coming back. They were soaked. Their mother—a thin, brown girl in a yellow bathing suit—was with them now, and the boys were pointing to his umbrella. She seemed dignified for her youth, as she gave him a shy glance and then smiled at the boys.

"Ah, ha!" he cried to the boys." You've been in *now* all right!" And then laughing to her, "I was kiddin' them awhile ago about their dry bathing suits."

She smiled at the boys again. "They like for me to be with them when they go in," she said.

"I got some lemonade here," he said abruptly, slapping the thermos jug. "Why don't you have some?" His voice was anxious.

She hesitated.

He jumped up. "Come on, sit down." He smiled at her and stepped aside.

Still she hesitated. But her eager boys pressed close behind her. Finally she smiled and sat down under the umbrella.

"You fellas can sit down under there too—in the shade," he said to the boys, and pointed under the umbrella. The boys flopped down quickly in the shady sand. He started at once serving them cold lemonade in the paper cups.

"Whew! I thought it was goin' to rain there for a while," he said, making conversation after passing out the lemonade. He had squatted on the sand and lit another cigarette. "Then there wouldn't a been much goin' on. But it turned out fine after all—there'll be a mob here before long."

She sipped the lemonade, but said little. He felt she had sat down only because of the boys, for she merely smiled and gave short answers to his questions. He learned the boys' names, Melvin and James; their ages, seven and nine; and that they were still frightened by the water. But he wanted to ask *her* name, and inquire about her husband. But he could not capture the courage.

Now the sun was hot and the sand was hot. And an orange-and-white umbrella was going up right beside them—two fellows and a girl. When the fellow who had been kneeling to drive the umbrella spike in the sand stood up, he was stringbean tall, and black, with his glistening hair freshly processed. The girl was a lighter brown, and wore a lilac bathing suit, and, although her legs were thin, she was pleasant enough to look at. The second fellow was medium, really, in height, but short beside his tall, black friend. He was yellow-skinned, and fast getting bald, although still in his early thirties. Both men sported little shoestring mustaches.

Elijah watched them in silence as long as he could. "You picked the right spot all right!" he laughed at last, putting on his sunglasses.

"How come, man?" The tall, black fellow grinned, showing his mouthful of gold teeth.

"You see *every*body here!" happily rejoined Elijah. "They all come here!"

"Man, I been coming here for years," the fellow reproved, and sat down in his khaki swimming trunks to take off his shoes. Then he stood up. "But right now, in the water I goes." He looked down at the girl. "How 'bout you, Lois, baby?"

"No, Caesar," she smiled, "not yet; I'm gonna sit here awhile and relax."

"Okay, then—you just sit right there and relax. And Little Joe" —he turned and grinned to his shorter friend—"you sit there an' relax right along with her. You all can talk with this gentleman here"—he nodded at Elijah—"an' his nice wife." Then, pleased with himself, he trotted off toward the water.

The young mother looked at Elijah, as if he should have hastened to correct him. But somehow he had not wanted to. Yet too,
Caesar's remark seemed to amuse her, for she soon smiled. Elijah
felt the pain of relief—he did not want her to go; he glanced at
her with a furtive laugh, and then they both laughed. The boys had
finished their lemonade now, and were digging in the sand. Lois
and Little Joe were busy talking.

Elijah was not quite sure what he should say to the mother. He
did not understand her, was afraid of boring her, was desperate
to keep her interested. As she sat looking out over the lake, he
watched her. She was not pretty; and she was too thin. But he
thought she had poise; he liked the way she treated her boys—
tender, but casual; how different from Myrtle's frantic herding.

Soon she turned to the boys. "Want to go back in the water?"
she laughed.

The boys looked at each other, and then at her. "Okay," James
said finally, in resignation.

"Here, have some more lemonade," Elijah cut in.

The boys, rescued for the moment, quickly extended their cups.
He poured them more lemonade, as she looked on smiling.

Now he turned to Lois and Little Joe sitting under their orange-
and-white umbrella. "How 'bout some good ole cold lemonade?"
he asked with a mushy smile. "I got plenty of cups." He felt he
must get something going.

Lois smiled back. "No, thanks," she said, fluttering her long
eyelashes, "not right now."

He looked anxiously at Little Joe.

"*I'll* take a cup!" said Little Joe, and turned and laughed to
Lois: "Hand me that bag there, will you?" He pointed to her
beach bag in the sand. She passed it to him, and he reached in and
pulled out a pint of gin. "We'll have some *real* lemonade," he
vowed, with a daredevilish grin.

Lois squealed with pretended embarrassment. "Oh, *Joe!*"

Elijah's eyes were big now; he was thinking of the police. But he
handed Little Joe a cup and poured the lemonade, to which Joe
added gin. Then Joe, grinning, thrust the bottle at Elijah. "How
'bout yourself, chief?" he said.

Elijah, shaking his head, leaned forward and whispered, "You ain't supposed to drink on the beach, y'know."

"*This* ain't a drink, man—it's a taste!" said Little Joe, laughing and waving the bottle around toward the young mother. "How 'bout a little taste for your wife here?" he said to Elijah.

The mother laughed and threw up both hands. "No, not for me!"

Little Joe gave her a rakish grin. "What'sa matter? You *'fraid* of that guy?" He jerked his thumb toward Elijah. "You 'fraid of gettin' a whippin', eh?"

"No, not exactly," she laughed.

Elijah was so elated with her his relief burst up in hysterical laughter. His laugh became strident and hoarse and he could not stop. The boys gaped at him, and then at their mother. When finally he recovered, Little Joe asked him, "Whut's so funny 'bout *that?*" Then Little Joe grinned at the mother. "You beat *him* up sometimes, eh?"

This started Elijah's hysterics all over again. The mother looked concerned now, and embarrassed; her laugh was nervous and shadowed. Little Joe glanced at Lois, laughed, and shrugged his shoulders. When Elijah finally got control of himself again he looked spent and demoralized.

Lois now tried to divert attention by starting a conversation with the boys. But the mother showed signs of restlessness and seemed ready to go. At this moment Caesar returned. Glistening beads of water ran off his long, black body; and his hair was unprocessed now. He surveyed the group and then flashed a wide, gold-toothed grin. "One big, happy family, like I said." Then he spied the paper cup in Little Joe's hand. "Whut you got there, man?"

Little Joe looked down into his cup with a playful smirk. "Lemonade, lover boy, lemonade."

"Don't hand me that jive, Joey. "You ain't never had any straight lemonade in your life."

This again brought uproarious laughter from Elijah. "I got the straight lemonade *here!*" He beat the thermos jug with his hand. "Come on—have some!" He reached for a paper cup.

"Why, sure," said poised Caesar. He held out the cup and

received the lemonade. "Now, gimme that gin," he said to Little Joe. Joe handed over the gin, and Caesar poured three fingers into the lemonade and sat down in the sand with his legs crossed under him. Soon he turned to the two boys, as their mother watched him with amusement. "Say, ain't you boys goin' in any more? Why don't you tell your daddy there to take you in?" He nodded toward Elijah.

Little Melvin frowned at him. "My daddy's workin'," he said.

Caesar's eyebrows shot up. "Ooooh, la, la!" he crooned. "Hey, now!" And he turned and looked at the mother and then at Elijah, and gave a clownish little snigger.

Lois tittered before feigning exasperation at him. "There you go again," she said, "talkin' when you shoulda been listening."

Elijah laughed along with the rest. But he felt deflated. Then he glanced at the mother, who was laughing too. He could detect in her no sign of dismay. Why then had she gone along with the gag in the first place, he thought—if now she didn't hate to see it punctured?

"*Hold the phone!*" softly exclaimed Little Joe. "Whut is *this?*" He was staring over his shoulder. Three women, young, brown, and worldly-looking, wandered toward them, carrying an assortment of beach paraphernalia and looking for a likely spot. They wore scant bathing suits, and were followed, but slowly, by an older woman with big, unsightly thighs. Elijah recognized her at once. She was the old gal who, the Saturday before, had chased him away from her beach party. She wore the same white bathing suit, and one of her girls carried the pea-green umbrella.

Caesar forgot his whereabouts ogling the girls. The older woman, observing this, paused to survey the situation. "How 'bout along in here?" she finally said to one of the girls. The girl carrying the thermos jug set it in the sand so close to Caesar it nearly touched him. He was rapturous. The girl with the umbrella had no chance to put it up, for Caesar and Little Joe instantly encumbered her with help. Another girl turned on a portable radio, and grinning, feverish Little Joe started snapping his fingers to the music's beat.

Within a half hour, a boisterous party was in progress. The little radio, perched on a hump of sand, blared out hot jazz, as the older woman—whose name turned out to be Hattie—passed around some cold, rum-spiked punch; and before long she went into her dancing-prancing act—to the riotous delight of all, especially Elijah. Hattie did not remember him from the Saturday past, and he was glad, for everything was so different today! As different as milk and ink. He knew no one realized it, but this was *his* party really—the wildest, craziest, funniest, and best he had ever seen or heard of. Nobody had been near the water—except Caesar, and the mother and boys much earlier. It appeared Lois was Caesar's girl friend, and she was hence more capable of reserve in face of the come-on antics of Opal, Billie, and Quanita—Hattie's girls. But Little Joe, to Caesar's tortured envy, was both free and aggressive. Even the young mother, who now volunteered her name to be Mrs. Green, got frolicsome, and twice jabbed Little Joe in the ribs.

Finally Caesar proposed they all go in the water. This met with instant, tipsy acclaim; and Little Joe, his yellow face contorted from laughing, jumped up, grabbed Billie's hand, and made off with her across the sand. But Hattie would not budge. Full of rum, and stubborn, she sat sprawled with her flaccide thighs spread in an obscene V, and her eyes half shut. Now she yelled at her departing girls: "You all watch out, now! Dont'cha go in too far. . . . Just wade! None o' you can swim a lick!"

Elijah now was beyond happiness. He felt a floating, manic glee. He sprang up and jerked Mrs. Green splashing into the water, followed by her somewhat less ecstatic boys. Caesar had to paddle about with Lois and leave Little Joe unassisted to caper with Billie, Opal, and Quanita. Billie was the prettiest of the three, and, despite Hattie's contrary statement, she could swim; and Little Joe, after taking her out in deeper water, waved back to Caesar in triumph. The sun was brazen now, and the beach and lake thronged with a variegated humanity. Elijah, a strong, but awkward, country-style swimmer, gave Mrs. Green a lesson in floating on her back, and, though she too could swim, he often felt obligated to place both his arms under her young body and buoy her up.

And sometimes he would purposely let her sink to her chin, whereupon she would feign a happy fright and utter faint simian screeches. Opal and Quanita sat in the shallows and kicked up their heels at Caesar, who, fully occupied with Lois, was a grinning, water-threshing study in frustration.

Thus the party went—on and on—till nearly four o'clock. Elijah had not known the world afforded such joy; his homely face was a wet festoon of beams and smiles. He went from girl to girl, insisting she learn to float on his outstretched arms. Once begrudging Caesar admonished him, "Man, you gonna *drown* one o' them pretty chicks." And Little Joe bestowed his highest accolade by calling him "lover boy," as Elijah nearly strangled from laughter.

At last, they looked up to see old Hattie as she reeled down to the water's edge, coming to fetch her girls. Both Caesar and Little Joe ran out of the water to meet her, seized her by the wrists, and, despite her struggles and curses, dragged her in. "Turn me loose! You big galoots!" she yelled and gasped as the water hit her. She was in knee-deep before she wriggled and fought herself free and lurched out of the water. Her breath reeked of rum. Little Joe ran and caught her again, but she lunged backwards, and free, with such force she sat down in the wet sand with a thud. She roared a laugh now, and spread her arms for help, as her girls came sprinting and splashing out of the water and tugged her to her feet. Her eyes narrowed to vengeful, grinning slits as she turned on Caesar and Little Joe: "I know whut you two're up to!" She flashed a glance around toward her girls. "I been watchin' both o' you studs! Yeah, yeah, but your eyes may shine, an' your teeth may grit . . ." She went limp in a sneering, raucous laugh. Everybody laughed now—except Lois and Mrs. Green.

They had all come out of the water now, and soon the whole group returned to their three beach umbrellas. Hattie's girls immediately prepared to break camp. They took down their pea-green umbrella, folded some wet towels, and donned their beach sandals, as Hattie still bantered Caesar and Little Joe.

"Well, you sure had *your*self a ball today," she said to Little Joe, who was sitting in the sand.

"Comin' back next Saturday?" asked grinning Little Joe.

"I jus' might at that," surmised Hattie. "We wuz here last Saturday."

"Good! Good!" Elijah broke in. "Let's *all* come back—next Saturday!" He searched every face.

"*I'll* be here," chimed Little Joe, grinning to Caesar. Captive Caesar glanced at Lois, and said nothing.

Lois and Mrs. Green were silent. Hattie, insulted, looked at them and started swelling up. "Never mind," she said pointedly to Elijah, "you jus' come on anyhow. You'll run into a slew o' folks lookin' for a good time. You don't need no *certain* people." But a little later, she and her girls all said friendly goodbyes and walked off across the sand.

The party now took a sudden downturn. All Elijah's efforts at resuscitation seemed unavailing. The westering sun was dipping toward the distant buildings of the city, and many of the bathers were leaving. Caesar and Little Joe had become bored; and Mrs. Green's boys, whining to go, kept a reproachful eye on their mother.

"Here, you boys, take some more lemonade," Elijah said quickly, reaching for the thermos jug. "Only got a little left—better get while gettin's good!" He laughed. The boys shook their heads.

On Lois he tried cajolery. Smiling, and pointing to her wet, but trim bathing suit, he asked, "What color would you say that is?"

"Lilac," said Lois, now standing.

"It sure is pretty! Prettiest on the beach!" he whispered.

Lois gave him a weak smile. Then she reached down for her beach bag, and looked at Caesar.

Caesar stood up. "Let's cut," he turned and said to Little Joe, and began taking down their orange-and-white umbrella.

Elijah was desolate. "Whatta you goin' for? It's gettin' cooler! Now's the time to *enjoy* the beach!"

"I've got to go home," Lois said.

Mrs. Green got up now; her boys had started off already. "Just a minute, Melvin," she called, frowning. Then, smiling, she turned and thanked Elijah.

He whirled around to them all. "Are we comin' back next Saturday? Come on—let's all come back! Wasn't it great! It was *great*! Don't you think? Whatta you say?" He looked now at Lois and Mrs. Green.

"We'll see," Lois said, smiling, "Maybe."

"Can *you* come?" He turned to Mrs. Green.

"I'm not sure," she said. "I'll try."

"Fine! Oh, that's fine!" He turned on Caesar and Little Joe. "I'll be lookin' for you guys, hear?"

"Okay, chief," grinned Little Joe." An' put somethin' in that lemonade, will ya?"

Everybody laughed . . . and soon they were gone.

Elijah slowly crawled back under his umbrella, although the sun's heat was almost spent. He looked about him. There was only one umbrella on the spot now, his own; where before there had been three. Cigarette butts and paper cups lay strewn where Hattie's girls had sat, and the sandy imprint of Caesar's enormous street shoes marked his site. Mrs. Green had dropped a bobby pin. He too was caught up now by a sudden urge to go. It was hard to bear much longer—the lonesomeness. And most of the people were leaving anyway. He stirred and fidgeted in the sand, and finally started an inventory of his belongings. . . . Then his thoughts flew home, and he reconsidered. Funny—he hadn't thought of home all afternoon. Where had the time gone anyhow? . . . It seemed he'd just pulled up in the Chevy and unloaded his gear; now it was time to go home again. Then the image of solemn Randy suddenly formed in his mind, sending waves of guilt through him. He forgot where he was as the duties of his existence leapt on his back—where would he ever get Randy's fifteen dollars? He felt squarely confronted by a great blank void. It was an awful thing he had done—all for a day at the beach . . . with some sporting girls. He thought of his family and felt tiny—and him itching to come back next Saturday! Maybe Myrtle was right about him after all. Lord, if she knew what he had done. . . .

He sat there for a long time. Most of the people were gone now. The lake was quiet save for a few boys still in the water. And the sun, red like blood, had settled on the dark silhouettes of the housetops across the city. He sat beneath the umbrella just as he had at one o'clock . . . and the thought smote him. He was jolted. Then dubious. But there it was—quivering, vital, swelling inside his skull like an unwanted fetus. So this was it! He mutinied inside. So he must sell it . . . his *umbrella*. Sell it for anything—only as long as it was enough to pay back Randy. For fifteen dollars even, if necessary. He was dogged; he couldn't do it; that wasn't the answer anyway. But the thought clawed and clung to him, rebuking and coaxing him by turns, until it finally became conviction. He must do it; it was the right thing to do; the only thing to do.

Maybe then the awful weight would lift, the dull commotion in his stomach cease. He got up and started collecting his belongings; placed the thermos jug, sunglasses, towel, cigarettes, and little rug together in a neat pile, to be carried to the Chevy later. Then he turned to face his umbrella. Its red and white stripes stood defiant against the wide, churned-up sand. He stood for a moment mooning at it. Then he carefully let it down and, carrying it in his right hand, went off across the sand.

The sun now had gone down behind the vast city in a shower of crimson-golden glints, and on the beach only a few stragglers remained. For his first prospects, he approached two teen-age boys, but suddenly realizing they had no money, he turned away and went over to an old woman, squat and black, in street clothes—a spectator—who stood gazing eastward out across the lake. She held in her hand a little black book, with red-edged pages, which looked like the New Testament. He smiled at her. "Wanna buy a nice new beach umbrella?" He held out the collapsed umbrella toward her.

She gave him a beatific smile, but shook her head. "No, son," she said, "that ain't what *I* want." And she turned to gaze out on the lake again.

For a moment he still held the umbrella out, with a question mark on his face. "Okay, then," he finally said, and went on.

Next he hurried down to the water's edge, where he saw a man and two women preparing to leave. "Wanna buy a nice new beach umbrella?" His voice sounded high-pitched, as he opened the umbrella over his head. "It's brand-new. I'll sell it for fifteen dollars— it cost a lot more'n that."

The man was hostile, and glared. Finally he said, "Whatta you take me for—a fool?"

Elijah looked bewildered, and made no answer. He observed the man for a moment. Finally he let the umbrella down. As he moved away, he heard the man say to the women, "It's hot—he stole it somewhere."

Close by, another man sat alone in the sand. Elijah started toward him. The man wore trousers, but was stripped to the waist, and bent over intent on some task in his lap. When Elijah reached him, he looked up from half a hatful of cigarette butts he was breaking open for the tobacco he collected in a little paper bag. He grinned at Elijah, who meant now to pass on.

"No, I ain't interested either, buddy," the man insisted as Elijah passed him. "Not me. I jus' got *outa* jail las' week—an' ain't goin' back for no umbrella." He laughed, as Elijah kept on.

Now he saw three women, still in their bathing suits, sitting together near the diving board. They were the only people he had not yet tried—except the one lifeguard left. As he approached them, he saw that all three wore glasses and were sedate. Some schoolteachers maybe, he thought, or office workers. They were talking—until they saw him coming; then they stopped. One of them was plump, but a smooth dark brown, and sat with a towel around her shoulders. Elijah addressed them through her: "Wanna buy a nice beach umbrella?" And again he opened the umbrella over his head.

"Gee! It's beautiful," the plump woman said to the others. "But where'd you get it?" she suddenly asked Elijah, polite mistrust entering her voice.

"I bought it—just this week."

The three women looked at each other. "Why do you want to sell it so soon, then?" a second woman said.   .

Elijah grinned. "I need the money."

"Well!" The plump woman was exasperated. "No, we don't want it." And they turned from him. He stood for a while, watching them; finally he let the umbrella down and moved on.

Only the lifeguard was left. He was a huge youngster, not over twenty, and brawny and black, as he bent over cleaning out his beached rowboat. Elijah approached him so suddenly he looked up startled.

"Would you be interested in this umbrella?" Elijah said, and proffered the umbrella. "It's brand-new—I just bought it Tuesday. I'll sell it cheap." There was urgency in his voice.

The lifeguard gave him a queer stare; and then peered off toward the Outer Drive, as if looking for help. "You're lucky as hell," he finally said. "The cops just now cruised by—up on the Drive. I'd have turned you in so quick it'd made your head swim. Now you get the hell outa here." He was menacing.

Elijah was angry. "Whatta you mean? I *bought* this umbrella —it's mine."

The lifeguard took a step toward him. "I said you better get the hell outa here! An' I mean it! *You thievin' bastard, you!*"

Elijah, frightened now, gave ground. He turned and walked away a few steps; and then slowed up, as if an adequate answer had hit him. He stood for a moment. But finally he walked on, the umbrella drooping in his hand.

He walked up the gravelly slope now toward the Chevy, forgetting his little pile of belongings left in the sand. When he reached the car, and opened the trunk, he remembered; and went back down and gathered them up. He returned, threw them in the trunk and, without dressing, went around and climbed under the steering wheel. He was scared, shaken; and before starting the motor sat looking out on the lake. It was seven o'clock; the sky was waning pale, the beach forsaken, leaving a sense of perfect stillness and approaching night; the only sound was a gentle lapping of the water against the sand—one moderate *hallo-o-o-o* would have carried across to Michigan. He looked down at the beach. Where were they all now—the funny, proud, laughing people? Eating their dinners, he supposed, in a variety of homes. And all the beautiful umbrellas—where were they? Without their colors the beach was so deserted. Ah, the beach . . . after pouring hot ore all week out at Youngstown Sheet and Tube, he would probably be too fagged out for the beach. But maybe he wouldn't —who knew? It was great while it lasted . . . great. And his umbrella . . . he didn't know what he'd do with that . . . he might never need it again. He'd keep it, though—and see. Ha! . . . hadn't he sweat to get it! . . . and they thought he had stolen it . . . stolen it . . . ah . . . and maybe they were right. He sat for a few moments longer. Finally he started the motor, and took the old Chevy out onto the Drive in the pink-hued twilight. But down on the beach the sun was still shining.

SECTION III

POEMS

Gwendolyn Brooks

For a note on Gwendolyn Brooks, see page 316

Four poems from A *Street in Bronzeville*

BY GWENDOLYN BROOKS

THE MOTHER

Abortions will not let you forget.
You remember the children you got that you did not get,
The damp small pulps with a little or with no hair,
The singers and workers that never handled the air.
You will never neglect or beat
Them, or silence or buy with a sweet.
You will never wind up the sucking-thumb
Or scuttle off ghosts that come.
You will never leave them, controlling your luscious sigh,
Return for a snack of them, with gobbling mother-eye.

I have heard in the voices of the wind the vocies of my dim killed
        children.
I have contracted. I have eased
My dim dears at the breasts they could never suck.

I have said, Sweets, if I sinned, if I seized
Your luck
And your lives from your unfinished reach,
If I stole your births and your names,
Your straight baby tears and your games,
Your stilted or lovely loves, your tumults, your marriages, aches,
      and your deaths,
If I poisoned the beginnings of your breaths,
Believe that even in my deliberateness I was not deliberate.
Though why should I whine,
Whine that the crime was other than mine?—
Since anyhow you are dead.
Or rather, or instead,
You were never made.
But that too, I am afraid,
Is faulty: oh, what shall I say, how is the truth to be said?
You were born, you had body, you died.
It is just that you never giggled or planned or cried.

Believe me, I loved you all.
Believe me, I knew you, though faintly, and I loved, I loved you
All.

A SONG IN THE FRONT YARD

I've stayed in the front yard all my life.
I want a peek at the back
Where it's rough and untended and hungry weed grows.
A girl gets sick of a rose.

I want to go in the back yard now
And maybe down the alley,
To where the charity children play.
I want a good time today.

They do some wonderful things.
They have some wonderful fun.

My mother sneers, but I say it's fine
How they don't have to go in at quarter to nine.
My mother, she tells me that Johnnie Mae
Will grow up to be a bad woman.
That George'll be taken to Jail soon or late
(On account of last winter he sold our back gate).

But I say it's fine. Honest, I do.
And I'd like to be a bad woman, too,
And wear the brave stockings of night-black lace
And strut down the streets with paint on my face.

WHEN YOU HAVE FORGOTTEN
SUNDAY: THE LOVE STORY

——And when you have forgotten the bright bedclothes on a
　　　Wednesday and a Saturday,
And most especially when you have forgotten Sunday—
When you have forgotten Sunday halves in bed,
Or me sitting on the front-room radiator in the limping afternoon
Looking off down the long street
To nowhere,
Hugged by my plain old wrapper of no-expectation
And nothing-I-have-to-do and I'm-happy-why?
And if-Monday-never-had-to-come—
When you have forgotten that, I say,
And how you swore, if somebody beeped the bell,
And how my heart played hopscotch if the telephone rang;
And how we finally went in to Sunday dinner,
That is to say, went across the front room floor to the ink-spotted
　　　table in the southwest corner
To Sunday dinner, which was always chicken and noodles
Or chicken and rice
And salad and rye bread and tea
And chocolate chip cookies—
I say, when you have forgotten that,
When you have forgotten my little presentiment

That the war would be over before they got to you;
And how we finally undressed and whipped out the light and flowed
    into bed,
And lay loose-limbed for a moment in the week-end
Bright bedclothes,
Then gently folded into each other—
When you have, I say, forgotten all that,
Then you may tell,
Then I may believe
You have forgotten me well.

THE SUNDAYS
OF SATIN-LEGS SMITH

Inamorata, with an approbation,
Bestowed his title. Blessed his inclination.)

He wakes, unwinds, elaborately: a cat
Tawny, reluctant, royal. He is fat
And fine this morning. Definite. Reimbursed.

He waits a moment, he designs his reign,
That no performance may be plain or vain.
Then rises in a clear delirium.

He sheds, with his pajamas, shabby days.
And his desertedness, his intricate fear, the
Postponed resentments and the prim precautions.

Now, at his bath, would you deny him lavender
Or take away the power of his pine?
What smelly substitute, heady as wine,
Would you provide? life must be aromatic.
There must be scent, somehow there must be some.
Would you have flowers in his life? suggest
Asters? a Really Good geranium?
A white carnation? would you prescribe a Show
With the cold lilies, formal chrysanthemum

Magnificence, poinsettias, and emphatic
Red of prize roses? might his happiest
Alternative (you muse) be, after all,
A bit of gentle garden in the best
Of taste and straight tradition? Maybe so.
But you forget, or did you ever know,
His heritage of cabbage and pigtails,
Old intimacy with alleys, garbage pails,
Down in the deep (but always beautiful) South
Where roses blush their blithest (it is said)
And sweet magnolias put Chanel to shame.

No! He has not a flower to his name.
Except a feather one, for his lapel.
Apart from that, if he should think of flowers
It is in terms of dandelions or death.
Ah, there is little hope. You might as well—
Unless you care to set the world a-boil
And do a lot of equalizing things,
Remove a little ermine, say, from kings,
Shake hands with paupers and appoint them men,
For instance—certainly you might as well
Leave him his lotion, lavender and oil.

Let us proceed. Let us inspect, together
With his meticulous and serious love,
The innards of this closet. Which is a vault
Whose glory is not diamonds, not pearls,
Not silver plate with just enough dull shine.
But wonder-suits in yellow and in wine,
Sarcastic green and zebra-striped cobalt.
All drapes. With shoulder padding that is wide
And cocky and determined as his pride;
Ballooning pants that taper off to ends
Scheduled to choke precisely.

                  Here are hats
Like bright umbrellas; and hysterical ties
Like narrow banners for some gathering war.

People are so in need, in need of help.
People want so much that they do not know.

Below the tinkling trade of little coins
The gold impulse not possible to show
Or spend. Promise piled over and betrayed.

These kneaded limbs receive the kiss of silk.
Then they receive the brave and beautiful
Embrace of some of that equivocal wool.
He looks into his mirror, loves himself—
The neat curve here; the angularity
That is appropriate at just its place;
The technique of a variegated grace.

Here is all his sculpture and his art
And all his architectural design.
Perhaps you would prefer to this a fine
Value of marble, complicated stone.
Would have him think with horror of baroque,
Rococo. You forget and you forget.

He dances down the hotel steps that keep
Remnants of last night's high life and distress.
As spat-out purchased kisses and spilled beer.
He swallows sunshine with a secret yelp.
Passes to coffee and a roll or two.
Has breakfasted.
                              Out. Sounds about him smear,
Become a unit. He hears and does not hear
The alarm clock meddling in somebody's sleep;
Children's governed Sunday happiness;
The dry tone of a plane; a woman's oath;
Consumption's spiritless expectoration;
An indignant robin's resolute donation
Pinching a track through apathy and din;
Restaurant vendors weeping; and the L
That comes on like a slightly horrible thought.

Pictures, too, as usual, are blurred.
He sees and does not see the broken windows
Hiding their shame with newsprint; little girl
With ribbons decking wornness, little boy
Wearing the trousers with the decentest patch,
To honor Sunday; women on their way
From "service," temperate holiness arranged
Ably on asking faces; men estranged
From music and from wonder and from joy
But far familiar with the guiding awe
Of foodlessness.
            He loiters.
                      Restaurant vendors
Weep, or out of them rolls a restless glee.
The Lonesome Blues, the Long-lost Blues, I Want A
Big Fat Mama. Down these sore avenues
Comes no Saint-Saëns, no piquant elusive Grieg,
And not Tchaikovsky's wayward eloquence
And not the shapely tender drift of Brahms.
But could he love them? Since a man must bring
To music what his mother spanked him for
When he was two: bits of forgotten hate,
Devotion: whether or not his mattress hurts:
The little dream his father humored: the thing
His sister did for money: what he ate
For breakfast—and for dinner twenty years
Ago last autumn: all his skipped desserts.

The pasts of his ancestors lean against
Him. Crowd him. Fog out his identity.
Hundreds of hungers mingle with his own,
Hundreds of voices advise so dexterously
He quite considers his reactions his,
Judges he walks most powerfully alone,
That everything is—simply what it is.

But movie-time approaches, time to boo
The hero's kiss, and boo the heroine

Whose ivory and yellow it is sin
For his eye to eat of. The Mickey Mouse,
However, is for everyone in the house.

Squires his lady to dinner at Joe's Eats.
His lady alters as to leg and eye,
Thickness and height, such minor points as these,
From Sunday to Sunday. But no matter what
Her name or body positively she's
In Queen Lace stockings with ambitious heels
That strain to kiss the calves, and vivid shoes
Frontless and backless, Chinese fingernails,
Earrings, three layers of lipstick, intense hat
Dripping with the most voluble of veils.
Her affable extremes are like sweet bombs
About him, whom no middle grace or good
Could gratify. He had no education.
In quiet arts of compromise. He would
Not understand your counsels on control, nor
Thank you for your late trouble.

                              At Joe's Eats
You get your fish or chicken on meat platters.
With coleslaw, macaroni, candied sweets,
Coffee and apple pie. You go out full.
(The end is—isn't it?—all that really matters.)

                    And even and intrepid come
                    The tender boots of night to home.

                    Her body is like new brown bread
                    Under the Woolworth mignonette.
                    Her body is a honey bowl
                    Whose waiting honey is deep and hot.
                    Her body is like summer earth,
                    Receptive, soft, and absolute . . .

Five poems from *Annie Allen*

BY GWENDOLYN BROOKS

INTERMISSION

1

(deep summer)

By all things planetary, sweet, I swear
Those hands may not possess these hands again
Until I get me gloves of ice to wear.
Because you are the headiest of men!
Your speech is whiskey, and your grin is gin.
I am well drunken. Is there water near?
I've need of wintry air to crisp me in.
—But come here—let me put this in your ear:
I would not want them now! You gave me this
Wildness to gulp. Now water is too pale.
And now I know deep summer is a bliss
I have no wish for weathering the gale.
So when I beg for gloves of ice to wear,
Laugh at me. I am lying, sweet, I swear!

2

High up he hoisted me, and cruel rock
Was lovely for a love seat. Then our talk
Came, making sweet-mouth waves ridiculous,
Who could not hope to honey it with us.

High up he hoisted me, after the year.
And rock was silly business for a chair.
We tried to make the waves ridiculous.
But sweet-mouth waves got very square with us.

3

Stand off, daughter of the dusk,
And do not wince when the bronzy lads
Hurry to cream-yellow shining.
It is plausible. The sun is a lode.

True, there is silver under
The veils of the darkness.
But few care to dig in the night
For the possible treasure of stars.

4

People protest in sprawling lightless ways
Against their deceivers, they are never meek—
Conceive their furies, and abort them early;
Are hurt, and shout, weep without form, are surly;
Or laugh, but save their censures and their damns.

And ever complex, ever taut, intense,
You hear man crying up to Any one—
"Be my reviver; be my influence,
My reinstated stimulus, my loyal.
Enable me to give my golds goldly.
To win.
To
Take out a skulk, to put a fortitude in.
Give me my life again, whose right is quite
The charm of porcelain, the vigor of stone."

And he will follow many a cloven foot.

5

Men of careful turns, haters of forks in the road,
The strain at the eye, that puzzlement, that awe—
Grant me that I am human, that I hurt,
That I can cry.

Not that I now ask alms, in shame gone hollow,
Nor cringe outside the loud and sumptuous gate.
Admit me to our mutual estate.

Open my rooms, let in the light and air.
Reserve my service at the human feast.
And let the joy continue. Do not hoard silence
For the moment when I enter, tardily,
To enjoy my height among you. And to love you
No more as a woman loves a drunken mate,
Restraining full caress and good My Dear,
Even pity for the heaviness and the need—
Fearing sudden fire out of the uncaring mouth,
Boiling in the slack eyes, and the traditional blow.
Next, the indifference formal, deep and slow.

Comes in your graceful glider and benign,
To smile upon me bigly; now desires
Me easy, easy; claims the days are softer
Than they were; murmurs reflectively "Remember
When cruelty, metal, public, uncomplex,
Trampled you obviously and every hour. . . ."
(Now cruelty flaunts diplomas, is elite,
Delicate, has polish, knows how to be discreet):
        Requests my patience, wills me to be calm,
        Brings me a chair, but the one with broken straw,
        Whispers "My friend, no thing is without flaw.
        If prejudice is native—and it is—you
        Will find it ineradicable—not to
        Be juggled, not to be altered at all,

But left unvexed at its place in the properness
Of things, even to be given (with grudging) honor.
    What
We are to hope is that intelligence
Can sugar up our prejudice with politeness.
Politeness will take care of what needs caring.
For the line is there.
And has a meaning. So our fathers said—
And they were wise—we think—At any rate,
They were older than ourselves. And the report is
What's old is wise. At any rate, the line is
Long and electric. Lean beyond and nod.
Be sprightly. Wave. Extend your hand and teeth.
But never forget it stretches there beneath."
The toys are all grotesque
And not for lovely hands; are dangerous,
Serrate in open and artful places. Rise.
Let us combine. There are no magics or elves
Or timely godmothers to guide us. We are lost, must
Wizard a track through our own screaming weed.

M. B. Tolson

BORN IN Moberly, Missouri, Melvin B. Tolson was educated at Fisk, Lincoln, and Columbia universities. He is the author of several plays, including *The Moses of Beale Street, Southern Front,* and a dramatization of George Schuyler's novel *Black No More.* Of his verse drama, *Libretto for the Republic of Liberia,* published in 1953, Allen Tate in his preface stated: "For the first time, it seems to me, a Negro poet has assimilated completely the full poetic language of his time and, by implication, the language of the Anglo-American poetic tradition."

Mr. Tolson was the recipient of the Bess Hokin Award of the Modern Poetry Association (1952) and other honors. His poetry has appeared in *The Atlantic, Poetry, The Prairie Schooner,* and in several collections, including *The Negro Caravan* (1941). He is currently Professor of creative literature and director of the Dust Bowl Theatre at Langston University, Langston, Oklahoma.

"Abraham Lincoln of Rock Hill Farm" is published here for the first time.

ABRAHAM LINCOLN OF
ROCK SPRING FARM

by M. B. TOLSON

I

Along the Wilderness Road, through Cumberland Gap,
The black ox hours limped toward Sunday's sun,
Across a buff clay belt with scrawls of stone,
Where bird and beast quailed in the bosom brush
From February's fang and claw; the stars,
Blue white, like sheer icicles, spired aglow
As if the three wise men barged in the East
Or priests in sackcloth balked the Scourge of God.

Foursquare by the rite of arm and heart and law,
The scrubby log cabin dared the compass points
Of Rock Spring farm, man's world, God's universe,
The babel of the circumstance and era.
The frozen socket of its window stared
Beyond the spayed crabapple trees, to where
The skulls of hills, the skeletons of barrens,
Lay quiet as time without the watch's tick.

Not knowing muck and star would vie for him,
The man Tom sank upon an ax-split stool,
Hands fisted, feet set wide to brace the spirit,
Big shoulders shoved, dark hazel eyes glazed by
Grotesqueries of flame that yawled and danced
Up, up, the stick-clay chimney. While fire imps combed
The black and bristling hair, the acids of thoughts
Made of the orby face an etching-plate.

II

Near pyrotechnic logs, the purling kettle,
Aunt Peggy puffed her pipe on God's rich time:
A granny at a childbed on the border,
Where head and backbone answered the tomahawk.
Her wise old eyes had seen a hundred Nancys
In travail tread the dark winepress alone;
Her wise old hands had plucked a stubborn breed
Into the outer world of pitch and toss.

The cabin that her myth and mission entered
Became a castle in which Aunt Peggy throned
A dynasty of grunts and nods and glances.
The nest, the barn, the hovel had schooled her in
The ABC of motherhood, and somehow
She'd lost her ego in the commonweal:
She sensed so accurately a coming child
That rakes dubbed her the St. Bernard of Sex!

And now her keyhole look explored Tom Lincoln
Beneath the patched homespun, the hue and cry
Of malice, until she touched his loneliness,
The taproot that his fiber gave no tongue.
Then, lulling the wife, troubled in flesh and mind,
She eased the sack quilts higher and mused the while:
There's but one way of coming into the world,
And seven times seventy ways of leaving it!

III

The woman Nancy, like a voyager sucked
Into the sea's whale belly by a wreck,
Buoyed to the surface air of consciousness
And clutched the solace of her corn-husk bed.
Her dark face, sharped in forehead, cheekbone, chin,

Cuddled in dark brown hair; her eyes waxed grayer
With wonder of the interlude: her beauty
And courage choked Aunt Peggy's hyperbole!

Out of the fog of pain, the bog of bygones,
The bag of cabin cant and tavern tattle,
She picked the squares to piece tomorrow's quilt:
She puzzled now, as then, about her father
Who let wild Lucy Hanks bundle and carry
Flesh of his flesh beyond the Cumberland Gap:
A strange roof is no roof when imps of fear
Pilfer the fatherless in blossom time.

Year in, year out, the daughter tinkered with
The riddle of her birth; the mother chided
The woman Nancy as she had the child,
"Hush thee, hush thee, thy father's a gentleman."
The butt of bawd, grand jury, Sunday bonnet,
Lucy, driven, taught her daughter the Word,
And Nancy, driven, taught her son the Word,
And Abraham, driven, taught his people the Word!

IV

The man Tom bit his fingernails, then rammed
His pockets with the hector hands that gave
Raw timber the shape of cabinet and coffin,
And in his lame speech said: "Aunt Peggy, listen.
Now that our Nancy's time is come, I'm haunted
By my own nothingness. Why breed nobodies?"
He tapped the dirt floor with the iron-capped boot
That aided fist and skull in border fights.

Aunt Peggy counseled: "Tom, you say the say
Poor Joseph probably said in that low stable
Ere Jesus came into this mishmash world."
She paused, then boxed the ears of cynicism:

"It's true, down in the barnyard, blood speaks loud,
Among the hogs, the chickens, the cows, the horses;
But, when it comes to Man, who knows, who knows
What greatness feeds down in the lowliest mother?"

The man Tom turned and spat: his naked surmise
Ranged out and out. Aunt Peggy's innermost said:
"Your father Abraham, bred like Daniel Boone,
Conquered a land with gun and ax and plow,
Baptized it in his blood! I say, I've said,
What's in a baby is God Almighty's business;
How the elders wring it out is worry enough!
The best, the worst—it's all, all human nature."

V

The tavern, Tom remembered, the New Year's Eve,
The clubfoot scholar bagged in Old World clothes,
With arrowy eyes and a hoary mushroom beard.
An Oxford don, he hymned the Bastille's fall
In spite of the hair-hung sword; his betters set
Him free to hail new truths in new lands, where
He seined with slave and master, knave and priest,
And out of all fished up the rights of man:

"As Citizen Lincoln asks, 'What's human nature?'
His full mug says a clear mind puts the question
Which ties the fogey scholar in a knot!
My new idea fed to his new baby
Would fetch the New World and the New Year peace!
The sum of anything unriddles the riddle:
The child whose wet nurse is the mother-of-all
Grows like a pine unmarked by rock or wind.

"To make a New World and a New Year, Plato
And Jesus begged the boon of little children!
Now Citizen Lincoln asks, 'What's human nature?'

It's what we elders have: no baby has it.
It's what our good and bad graft on the neutral.
It's what our rulers feed the boy and girl.
It's what society garbs nature in.
It's a misnomer: call it *human nurture!*"

VI

Aunt Peggy hovered closer, with flawless rites
Grown lyrical from habit: muffled pain sounds
Dragged from the bed of cleated poles; she hawed
Tom Lincoln, as one turns a nag aside,
Then swooped her way, even as a setting hen
Carves a dictatorship from yard to nest.
And Tom again was squeezed into a cell
Whose inmates were the ghosts of unsuccess.

Later his memories climbed a gala peak,
His Nancy's infare that ran riotous:
The bear meat, venison, wild turkey, duck,
The maple sugar hanging for the whiskey,
The red ham, gourds of syrup, bowls of honey,
The wood coal pit with brown and juicy sheep,
The guzzling, fiddling, guttling, monkeyshining:
A continent sprawled between that day and this!

A havenot on the frontier is no havenot;
A Crusoe without Friday has no conscience:
Yet Tom's grub living gnawed him like the teeth
Of slavery, land titles, melancholy.
He, like his forebears, visioned a Promised Land
And tidied ways and means to fly the barrens
That doomed the flesh to peck, to patch, to pinch,
And wrung the soul of joy and beauty dry.

VII

The black ox hours limped by, and day crawled after.
White prongs of ice, like dinosaur fangs, gleamed in
The cavernous mouth of Rock Spring; snowbirds shivered
And chirped rebellion; a cow with jags and gaps
Chewed emptily; hogs squealed in hunger fits;
And scrags of dogs huddled against the chimney,
Which shoveled smoke dust into the throats and noses
Of ragged winds kicking up snow in the desert.

Nancy lay white, serene, like virgin milk
After the udder's fury in the pail.
Beneath the sack quilts and the bearskin robe,
In yellow petticoat and linsey shirt,
The baby snuggled at her breast and gurgled—
An anonymity of soft red wrinkles.
Aunt Peggy, hovering, grinned, "He's Sabbath-born.
Remember . . . Sunday—it's red-letter day!"

Like ax and helve, like scythe and snath, the bond
Held Tom and Nancy: she smiled at his halt smile,
His titan's muss in picking up the baby.
Tom frowned and spat, then gulped, "He's legs! All legs!"
Aunt Peggy beamed, "Long legs can eat up miles."
Tom gloomed, "The hands—look at the axman's hands!"
And Nancy mused, "The Hankses' dream, the Lincolns',
Needs such a man to hew and blaze the way."

Robert Hayden

ROBERT HAYDEN is associate professor of English at Fisk University, Nashville, Tennessee. He has received the University of Michigan Hopwood Award for Poetry (1942), a Rosenwald Fellowship (1947), and a Ford Foundation grant (1954). Mr. Hayden's poems have appeared in *The Atlantic, Poetry, Phylon, Mid-West Journal,* and other publications. His work is included in several collections, among them *Poetry of the Negro* (selected by Langston Hughes and Arna Bontemps), *Cross Section* (1945 and 1947), *The Negro Caravan* (1941), and several Swedish, German, and Italian anthologies.

Two volumes of Mr. Hayden's poetry have been published—*Heartshape in the Dust* (1940) and *A Ballad of Remembrance* (1962).

VERACRUZ

BY ROBERT HAYDEN

I

Sunday afternoon,
and couples walk the breakwater
heedless of the bickering spray.
Near the shoreward end,
Indian boys idle and fish.
A shawled brown woman
Squinting against
the ricocheting brilliance
of sun and water
shades her eyes and gazes
toward the fort,
fossil of Spanish power,
looming in the harbor.

At the seaward end,
a pharos like a temple rises.
From here the shore
seen across marbling waves
is arabesque ornately green
that hides the inward-falling slum,
the stains and dirty tools of struggle;
appears a destination dreamed of,
never to be reached.
Here only the sea is real—
the barbarous multifoliate sea
with its rustlings of leaves,
fire, graments, wind;
its clashing of phantasmal jewels,
its lunar thunder,
animal and human sighing.

Leap now,
and cease from error.
Escape. Or shoreward turn,
accepting all—
the losses and farewells,
the long warfare with self,
with God.

The waves roar in and break
roar in and break
with granite spreeing hiss
on bronzegreen rocks below
and glistering upfling of spray.

II

Thus reality
    bedizened in the warring colors
        of a dream
parades through these
    arcades ornate with music and
        the sea.

Thus reality
    become unbearably a dream
        beckons
out of reach in flyblown streets
    of lapsing rose and purple, dying
        blue.

Thus marimba'd night
    and multifoliate sea become
        phantasmal
space, and there,
    light-years away, one farewell image
        burns and fades and burns.

FULL MOON

BY ROBERT HAYDEN

No longer throne of a goddess to whom we pray,
no longer the bubble house of childhood's
tumbling Mother Goose man,

The emphatic moon ascends—
the brillant challenger of rocket experts,
the white hope of communications men.

Some I love who are dead
were watchers of the moon and knew its lore;
planted seeds, trimmed their hair,

Pierced their ears for gold hoop earrings
as the moon advised.
It shines tonight upon their graves.

And burned in the garden of Gethsemane,
its light made holy by the dazzling tears
with which it mingled.

And spread its radiance on the exile's path
of Him who was The Glorious One,
its light made holy by His holiness.

Already a coveted goal and tomorrow perhaps
an arms base, a livid sector,
the full moon dominates the anxious dark.

M. Carl Holman

Mr. Holman is professor of English at Clark College, Atlanta, and editor of a weekly newspaper, *The Atlanta Inquirer*. He holds graduates degrees from the University of Chicago and Yale University. In 1944 he was the recipient of the University of Chicago's John Billings Fiske Poetry Prize. His prose and poetry have appeared in *Phylon*, *Verse*, and other publications and in several collections, including *Poetry of the Negro* (selected by Langston Hughes and Arna Bontemps).

"Picnic," "Three Brown Girls Singing," and "Mr. Z" are published here for the first time.

PICNIC: THE LIBERATED

BY M. CARL HOLMAN

En route to the picnic they drive through
    their history,
Telling jokes and watching the road, but
    averting their eyes
From the rows of sun-flayed faces barely
    darker than theirs

Through which they pass like foreigners
      or spies.

The children play word games, count cows,
      inspect
Their armament of softballs, glasses, rods
      and hooks,
Survey the molten prairies overhead for
      signs of rain,
Retreat like crayfish to their comic books.

Grown-up laughter dwindles; they enter the
      wool-hat town
Like a gangster funeral, under the
      chastening eye
Of Confederate cannon, depot, First
      Baptist Church,
The white frame hospital that would let
      them die.

But out of sight is as safe as out of mind:
Dust lifts a protective screen half a mile
      down a winding road
Opening into a grove of pines, the green
      lake beyond
And the smoky pungence of barbecue as the
      cars unload.

So the long day blossoms in the
      sumptuous shade
Where the velvet-limbed girls parade their
      peacock beauty
In slacks and shorts, ignoring, excited by
      the clashing glances
Of waspish wives who lose track of
      matronly duty

And the men rotating their drinks in
      dixie cups,

Absently talking of civil rights, money
       and goods
But stirred by audacious dreams of rendezvous,
Boar-ramping conquests deep in the
       secret woods.

The tadpole hunters soak their shoes at the
       scummy edge
Of the lake where a boat capsizes but
       nobody drowns,
The badminton birds veer off course toward
      the tables
Where the gold-toothed winner grins, the
       loser frowns.

The sky contracts, the country dark
       creeps in,
Flicking a chilly tongue across the grass.
Uneasily the motors cough, headlights
       blink on,
Goodbys go flat, and tempers turn to glass.

Their tags are passports as they straggle home
To sprinklered lawns on Circles, Lanes
       and Drives,
Claiming once more the preferential signs
With which the Southern city stamps their lives.

Deep in the night the wind walks past the
       lake,
Leaps the pinewoods, lays an impartial
       hand
On cannon, croppers' shacks, touches at last
The handsome mortgaged houses where they sleep—
Mounting their private myths of freedom
       and command,
Privileged prisoners in a haunted land.

THREE BROWN GIRLS SINGING

BY M. CARL HOLMAN

In the ribs of an ugly school building
Three rapt faces
Fuse one pure sound in a shaft of April light:
Three girls, choir robes over their arms, in a
       stairwell singing
Compose the irrelevancies of a halting
       typewriter,
Chalk dust and orange peel,
A French class drilling,
Into a shimmering column of flawed perfection;
Lasting as long
As their fresh, self-wondering voices climb
       to security;
Outlasting
The childbed death of one,
The alto's divorce,
The disease-raddled face of the third
Whose honey brown skin
Glows now in a nimbus of dust motes,
But will be as estranged
As that faceless and voiceless typist
Who, unknown and unknowing, enters the
       limpid column,
Joins chalk, French verbs, the acrid perfume of oranges,
To mark the periphery
Of what shall be saved from calendars and decay.

MR. Z

BY M. CARL HOLMAN

Taught early that his mother's skin was the sign
    of error,
He dressed and spoke the perfect part of honor;
Won scholarships, attended the best schools,
Disclaimed kinship with jazz and spirituals;
Chose prudent, raceless views for each situation,
Or when he could not cleanly skirt dissension,
Faced up to the dilemma, firmly seized
Whatever ground was Anglo-Saxonized.

In diet, too, his practice was exemplary:
Of pork in its profane forms he was wary;
Expert in vintage wines, sauces and salads,
His palate shrank from cornbread, yams and collards.

He was as careful whom he chose to kiss:
His bride had somewhere lost her Jewishness,
But kept her blue eyes; an Episcopalian
Prelate proclaimed them matched chameleon.
Choosing the right addresses, here, abroad,
They shunned those places where they might be barred;
Even less anxious to be asked to dine
Where hosts catered to kosher accent or exotic skin.

And so he climbed, unclogged by ethnic weights,
An airborne plant, flourishing without roots.
Not one false note was struck—until he died:
His subtly grieving widow could have flayed
The obit writers, ringing crude changes on a clumsy phrase:
"One of the most distinguished members of his race."

Langston Hughes

For a note on Langston Hughes, see page 106.

Three poems from *Ask Your Mama:
12 Moods for Jazz*

BY LANGSTON HUGHES

BLUES IN STEREO

YOUR NUMBERS COMING OUT!   TACIT
BOUQUETS I'LL SEND YOU
AND DREAMS I'LL SEND YOU
AND HORSES SHOD WITH GOLD
ON WHICH TO RIDE IF MOTORCARS
WOULD BE TOO TAME—
TRIUMPHAL ENTRY SEND YOU—
SHOUTS FROM THE EARTH ITSELF
BARE FEET TO BEAT THE GREAT DRUMBEAT
OF GLORY TO YOUR NAME AND MINE

ONE AND THE SAME:
YOU BAREFOOT, TOO,
IN THE QUARTER OF THE NEGROES
WHERE AN ANCIENT RIVER FLOWS

PAST HUTS THAT HOUSE A MILLION BLACKS
AND THE WHITE GOD NEVER GOES
FOR THE MOON WOULD WHITE HIS WHITENESS
BEYOND ITS MASK OF WHITENESS
AND THE NIGHT MIGHT BE ASTONISHED
AND SO LOSE ITS REPOSE.

IN A TOWN NAMED AFTER STANLEY
NIGHT EACH NIGHT COMES NIGHTLY   *drum-*
AND THE MUSIC OF OLD MUSIC'S   *African*
BORROWED FOR THE HORNS   *beats*
THAT DON'T KNOW HOW TO PLAY   *over*
ON LPs THAT WONDER   *blues*
HOW THEY EVER GOT THAT WAY.   *that*
                                            gradually
      WHAT TIME IS IT, MAMA?   *mount*
      WHAT TIME IS IT NOW?   *in*
      MAKES NO DIFFERENCE TO ME—   *intensity*
      BUT I'M ASKING ANYHOW.   *to*
      WHAT TIME IS IT, MAMA?   *end*
      WHAT TIME NOW?   *in*
                                            climax.

DOWN THE LONG HARD ROW THAT
    I BEEN HOEING   TACIT
I THOUGHT I HEARD THE HORN OF PLENTY BLOW-
    ING.
BUT I GOT TO GET A NEW ANTENNA, LORD—
MY TV KEEPS ON SNOWING.

ASK YOUR MAMA

FROM THE SHADOWS OF THE QUARTER
SHOUTS ARE WHISPERS CARRYING
TO THE FARTHEREST CORNERS
OF THE NOW KNOWN WORLD:
5th AND MOUND IN CINCI, 63rd IN CHI,
23rd AND CENTRAL, 18th STREET AND VINE.
I'VE WRITTEN, CALLED REPEATEDLY,
EVEN RUNG THIS BELL ON SUNDAY, YET
YOUR THIRD-FLOOR TENANT'S NEVER HOME.
DID YOU TELL HER THAT OUR CREDIT OFFICE
HAS NO RECOURSE NOW BUT TO THE LAW?

YES, SIR, I TOLD HER.
WHAT DID SHE SAY?
SAID, TELL YOUR MA.   *Figurine.*

17 SORROWS
AND THE NUMBER
6–0–2.
HIGH BALLS, LOW BALLS:
THE 8-BALL
IS YOU.
7–11!
COME 7!
PORGY AND BESS
AT THE PICTURE SHOW.
I NEVER SEEN IT.
BUT I WILL,
YOU KNOW,
IF I HAVE

THE MONEY
TO GO.   *Delicate*
FILLMORE OUT IN FRISCO, 7th ACROSS   *post-bop*
    THE BAY   *suggests*
18th AND VINE IN K. C., 63rd IN CHI,   *pleasant*
ON THE CORNER PICKING SPLINTERS   *evenings and*
OUT OF THE MIDNIGHT SKY   *flirtatious*
IN THE QUARTER OF THE NEGROES   *youth*
AS LEOLA PASSES BY   *as it*
THE MEN CAN ONLY MURMUR   *gradually*
MY! . . . MY! MY!   *weaves*
                                              into its
LUMUMBA LOUIS ARMSTRONG   *pattern*
PATRICE AND PATTI PAGE   *a*
HAMBURGERS PEPSI-COLA   *musical*
KING COLE JUKEBOX PAYOLA   *echo of*
IN THE QUARTER OF THE NEGROES   *Paris*
GOD WILLING DROP A SHILLING   *which*
FORT DE FRANCE, PLACE PIGALLE   *continues*
VINGT FRANCS NICKEL DIME   *until*
BAHIA LAGOS DAKAR LENOX   *very*
KINGSTON TOO GOD WILLING   *softly*
A QUARTER OR A SHILLING. PARIS—   *the*
AT THE DOME VINGT FRANCS WILL DO   *silver*
ROTONDE SELECT DUPONT FLORE   *call*
TALL BLACK STUDENT   *of a*
IN HORN-RIM GLASSES,   *hunting*
WHO AT THE SORBONNE HAS   *horn*
    SIX CLASSES   *is*
IN THE SHADOW OF THE CLUNY   *heard*
CONJURES UNICORN,   *far away.*
SPEAKS ENGLISH FRENCH SWAHILI   *African*
HAS ALMOST FORGOTTEN MEALIE.   *drums*
BUT WHY RIDE ON MULE OR DONKEY   *begin*
WHEN THERE'S A UNICORN?   *a softly*
                                              mounting
NIGHT IN A SÉKOU TOURÉ CAP   *rumble*
DRESSED LIKE A TEDDY BOY   *soon*

BLOTS COLORS OFF THE MAP.   *to fade*
PERHAPS IF IT BE GOD'S WILL   *into a*
AZIKIWE'S SON, AMEKA,   *steady*
SHAKES HANDS WITH EMMETT TILL.   *beat*
BRICKBATS BURST LIKE BUBBLES   *like*
STONES BURST LIKE BALLOONS   *the*
BUT HEARTS KEEP DOGGED BEATING   *heart.*
        SELDOM BURSTING
        UNLIKE BUBBLES
        UNLIKE BRICKBATS   TACIT
        FAR FROM STONE.
IN THE QUARTER OF THE NEGROES
WHERE NO SHADOW WALKS ALONE
LITTLE MULES AND DONKEYS SHARE
THEIR GRASS WITH UNICORNS.   *Repeat high*
                                     flute call
                                     to segue into
                                     up-tempo blues
                                     that continue
                                     behind the
                                     next sequence. . . .

JAZZTET MUTED

IN THE NEGROES OF THE QUARTER
PRESSURE OF THE BLOOD IS SLIGHTLY
   HIGHER
IN THE QUARTER OF THE NEGROES
WHERE BLACK SHADOWS MOVE LIKE
   SHADOWS
CUT FROM SHADOWS CUT FROM SHADE
IN THE QUARTER OF THE NEGROES
SUDDENLY CATCHING FIRE
FROM THE WING TIP OF A MATCH TIP
ON THE BREATH OF ORNETTE COLEMAN.

IN NEON TOMBS THE MUSIC
FROM JUKEBOX JOINTS IS LAID
AND FREE-DELIVERY TV SETS
ON GRAVESTONES DATES ARE PLAYED.
EXTRA-LARGE THE *KINGS* AND *QUEENS*
AT EITHER SIDE ARRAYED
HAVE DOORS THAT OPEN OUTWARD
TO THE QUARTER OF THE NEGROES
WHERE THE PRESSURE OF THE BLOOD
IS SLIGHTLY HIGHER—
DUE TO SMOLDERING SHADOWS
THAT SOMETIMES TURN TO FIRE.

     HELP ME, YARDBIRD!
     HELP ME!

*Bop
blues
into
very
modern
jazz
burning
the
air
eerie
like
a neon
swamp-
fire
cooled
by
dry
ice
until
suddenly
there is
a single
ear-
piercing
flute
call. . . .*

Six poems from *Montage of a Dream Deferred*

BY LANGSTON HUGHES

DREAM BOOGIE

Good morning daddy!
Ain't you heard
The boogie-woogie rumble
Of a dream deferred?

Listen closely:
You'll hear their feet
Beating out and beating out a—

>   *You think*
>   *It's a happy beat?*

Listen to it closely:
Ain't you heard
something underneath
like a—

>   *What did I say?*

Sure,
I'm happy!
Take it away!

>   *Hey, pop!*
>   *Re-bop!*
>   *Mop*

>   *Y-e-a-h!*

PARADE

Seven ladies
and seventeen gentlemen
at the Elks Club Lounge
planning planning a parade:
Grand Marshal in his white suit
will lead it.
Cadillacs with dignitaries
will precede it.
And behind will come
with band and drum
on foot . . . on foot . . .
on foot . . .

Motorcycle cops,
white,
will speed it
out of sight
if they can:
Solid black,
can't be right.

marching . . . marching . . .
marching . . .
noon till night . . .

I never knew
that many Negroes
were on earth,
did you?

I never knew!

PARADE!

A chance to let

PARADE!

the whole world see

PARADE!

old black me!

CHILDREN'S RHYMES

When I was a chile we used to play,
"One—two—buckle my shoe!"
and things like that. But now, Lord,
listen at them little varmits!

> *By what sends*
> *the white kids*
> *I ain't sent:*
> *I know I can't*
> *be President.*

There is two thousand children
in this block, I do believe!

> *What don't bug*
> *them white kids*
> *sure bugs me:*
> *We knows everybody*
> *ain't free!*

Some of these young ones is cert'ly bad—
One batted a hard ball right through my window
and my gold fish et the glass.

> *What's written down*
> *for white folks*
> *ain't for us a-tall:*
> *"Liberty and Justice—*
> *Huh—For All."*

Oop-pop-a-da!
Skee! Daddle-de-do!
Be-bop!
Salt'peanuts!
De-dop!

NIGHT FUNERAL IN HARLEM

Night funeral
in Harlem:

*Where did they get
Them two fine cars?*

Insurance man, he did not pay—
His insurance lapsed the other day—
Yet they got a satin box
For his head to lay.

Night funeral
in Harlem:

*Who was it sent
That wreath of flowers?*

Them flowers came
from that poor boy's friends—
They'll want flowers, too,
When they meet their ends.

Night funeral
in Harlem:

*Who preached that
Black boy to his grave?*

Old preacher-man
Preacher that boy away—

Charged Five Dollars
His girl friend had to pay.

Night funeral
in Harlem:

When it was all over
And the lid shut on his head
and the organ had done played
and the last prayers been said
and six pallbearers
Carried him out for dead
And off down Lenox Avenue
That long black hearse sped,
   The street light
   At his corner
   Shined just like a tear—
That boy that they was mournin'
Was so dear, so dear
To them folks that brought the flowers,
To that girl who paid the preacher-man—
It was all their tears that made
   That poor boy's
   Funeral grand.

Night funeral
in Harlem.

HARLEM

What happens to a dream deferred?

Does it dry up
like a raisin in the sun?
Or fester like a sore—
And then run?
Does it stink like rotten meat?
Or crust and sugar over—
like a syrupy sweet?

Maybe it just sags
like a heavy load.
Or does it explode?

SAME IN BLUES

I said to my baby,
Baby, take it slow.
I can't, she said, I can't!
I got to go!

> *There's a certain*
> *amount of traveling*
> *in a dream deferred.*

Lulu said to Leonard,
I want a diamond ring.
Leonard said to Lulu,
You won't get a goddam thing!

> *A certain*
> *amount of nothing*
> *in a dream deferred.*

Daddy, daddy, daddy,
All I want is you.
You can have me, baby—
but my lovin' days is through.

> *A certain*
> *amount of impotence*
> *in a dream deferred.*

Three parties
On my party line—
But that third party,
Lord, ain't mine!

There's liable
to be confusion
in a dream deferred.

From river to river
Uptown and down,
There's liable to be confusion
when a dream gets kicked around.

Three translations from the French by Langston Hughes

EPIGRAM

BY ARMAND LANUSSE
(Louisiana Creole, U.S.A.)

"Do you not wish to renounce the Devil?"
Asked a good priest of a woman of evil
Who had so many sins that every year
They cost her endless remorse and fear.
"I wish to renounce him forever," she said,
"But that I may lose every urge to be bad,
Before pure grace takes me in hand,
Shouldn't I show my daughter how to get a man?"

SHE LEFT HERSELF ONE EVENING

BY LÉON DAMAS
(French Guiana)

SHE LEFT HERSELF ONE EVENING
to prowl around
my misery
like a mad dog
like a naked dog
like a doggish dog
quite mad
quite naked
quite doggishly
dog

thus simply
the drama began

FLUTE PLAYERS

BY JEAN JOSEPH RABÉARIVELO
(Madagascar)

Your flute,
    you carved from the shin bone of a strong bull,
    and you polished it on barren hills beaten by sun.
His flute,
    he carved from a reed trembling in the breeze
    and cut its little holes beside a flowing brook
    drunk on dreams of moonlight.
Together
    you made music in the late afternoon
    as if to hold back the round boat
    sinking on the shores of the sky,
    as if to save it from its fate:
    but are your plaintive incantations
    heard by the gods of the wind,
    and of the earth, and of the forest,
    and of the sand?
Your flute
    throws out a beat like the march of an angry bull
    toward the desert
    but who comes back running,
    burned by thirst and hunger
    and defeated by weariness
    at the foot of a shadeless tree
    with neither leaves nor fruit.
His flute
    is like a reed that bends
    beneath the weight of a bird in flight—
    but not a bird captured by a child

whose feathers are stroked
but a bird lost from other birds
who looked at his own shadow for company
in the flowing water.
Your flute
and his—
regret their beginnings
in the sorrows of your songs.

Ossie Davis

Ossie Davis is the author of the successful Broadway stage play *Purlie Victorious,* in which he played the lead, and he has performed in television and motion pictures as well as in the theater. He was born in a small town near Waycross, Georgia, attended Howard University, and writes short stories and poetry in addition to his work as a playwright.

"To a Brown Girl" is published here for the first time.

TO A BROWN GIRL

BY OSSIE DAVIS

Since I care naught for what is pale and cold,
My heart must hunger when the snows are down
For dearer climates, where the sun, of old,
Taught us that love is something warm and brown.

Here, like a stranger, stranded in the north,
I dream the scarlet dream of purple skies,

And strain for glimpses, as I hurry forth,
Of shy reports: rich-black, and passion-wise.

And laugh to plumb the deep-remembered flood
of tropic heats, where winter cannot come.
And feel within the pulses of my blood
The white-eyed throbbings of some ancient drum.

And I can treasure this: to catch a trace,
Still burning hot and bright beneath the chill—
Beneath the bosom of your brown embrace
Hot suns of Africa are burning still!

LeRoi Jones

For a note on LeRoi Jones, see pages 323–4

CHARLIE PARKER: THE HUMAN CONDITION

BY LeROI JONES

(bridge

Pressures. The voids, and threads
of nature's brain. The skies
of her failure, the deep colorless
past. The invasion of the meat. Violence
as an invention. Our lives. (Our
lives. The precious light
from the sun. Each ray perfect. Each
life, it goes into, as perfect.

You can find what the hands need. (What
rhythms
conspire.

Find,
the delicate stutter
of life
just beneath
your skin. Beneath
your words. (Where
the soul
stews. Makes
its proportions
known.

All this, as a singer,
in an ancient tradition.

We talked of Pressures. Singer. We talked
of the abstract world
of ourselves.
        The pull.
           play.
              the distance

gives. Love
is, as precious.
        (Where
the heart
breaks. As
laughter,
or,
    a mere thin smile
of departure

Three poems from *Preface to a Twenty Volume Suicide Note*

BY LeROI JONES

THE INSIDIOUS DR. FU MAN CHU

If I think myself
strong, then I am
not true to the misery
in my life. The uncertainty.
(of what I am saying, who
I have chose to become, the
very air pressing my skin
held gently away, this woman
and the one I taste continually
in my nebular pallet tongue face
mouth feet, standing in piles
of numbers, hills, lovers.
                                        If
I think myself ugly
& go to the mirror, smiling,
at the inaccuracy, or now
the rain pounds dead grass
in the stone yard, I think
how very wise I am. How very
very wise.

THE NEW SHERIFF

There is something
in me so cruel, so
silent. It hesitates
to sit on the grass
with the young white
                    virgins
of my time. The blood-
letter, clothed in what
it is. Elemental essence,
animal grace, not that, but
a rude stink of color
huger, more vast, than
this city suffocating. Red
street. Waters noise
in the ear, inside
the hard bone
of the brain. Inside
the soft white meat
of the feelings. Inside
your flat white stomach
I move my tongue

THE TURNCOAT

The steel fibrous slant & ribboned glint
of water. The Sea. Even my secret speech is moist
with it. When I am alone & brooding, locked in
with dull memories & self hate, & the terrible disorder
of a young man.

I move slowly. My cape spread stiff & pressing cautiously
in the first night wind off the Hudson. I glide down
onto my own roof, peering in at the pitiful shadow of myself.

How can it mean anything? The stop & spout, the
wind's dumb shift. Creak of the house & wet smells
coming in. Night forms on my left. The blind still
up to admit a sun that no longer exists. Sea move.

I dream long bays & towers . . . & soft steps on moist sand.
I become them, sometimes. Pure flight. Pure fantasy. Lean.

Paul Vesey

Samuel W. Allen, who writes poetry under the name of Paul Vesey, graduated from Fisk University and holds an LL.B. degree from Harvard University Law School. He pursued additional studies at the Sorbonne and the New School for Social Research, and is Assistant General Counsel, United States Information Agency, Washington, D.C.

A volume of poetry by Paul Vesey entitled *Ivory Tusks* was published in a bilingual edition in Germany in 1956, and he was the editor of the book *Pan Africanism Reconsidered*. Mr. Allen translated Jean-Paul Sartre's *Black Orpheus* into English for *Présence Africaine*; his published essays include "Tendencies in African Poetry," "Negritude and Its Relevance for American Negro Writers," and "Negritude, Agreement and Disagreement."

"To Satch (or American Gothic)" is published here for the first time.

TO SATCH
(OR AMERICAN GOTHIC)

BY PAUL VESEY

Sometimes I feel like I will *never* stop
Just go on forever
Till one fine mornin
I'm gonna reach up and grab me a handfulla stars
Swing out my long lean leg
And whip three hot strikes burnin down the heavens
And look over at God and say
How about that!

NOTE: *The legendary Satchell Paige was a star pitcher in Negro baseball in the days of Ruth and Gehrig—whom he frequently struck out in exhibition games. After several successful years in the American League, Satch is still somewhere in professional baseball, practicing his trade, at an age at least, admittedly, in the fifties.*

From *Ivory Tusks*

BY PAUL VESEY

A MOMENT PLEASE

When I gaze at the sun
  I walked to the subway booth
  for change for a dime.
and know that this great earth
  Two adolescent girls stood there
  alive with eagerness to know
is but a fragment from it thrown
  all in their new found world
  there was for them to know
in heat and flame a billion years ago,
  they looked at me and brightly asked
  "Are you Arabian?"
that then this world was lifeless
  I smiled and cautiously
  —for one grows cautious—
  shook my head.
as, a billion hence
  "Egyptian?"
it shall again be,
  Again I smiled and shook my head
  and walked away.
what moment is it that I am betrayed,
  I've gone but seven paces now
oppressed, cast down,
  and from behind comes swift the sneer
or warm with love or triumph?
  "Or Nigger?"

  A moment, please

What is it that to fury I am roused?
      for still it takes a moment
What meaning for me
      and now
in this homeless clan
      I'll turn
the dupe of space
      and smile
the toy of time?
      and nod my head.

A Note about the Editor

HERBERT HILL has lectured extensively on race and culture at schools and universities in the United States, England, and Europe. He has made many studies relating to a variety of social and economic issues and is co-author of *The Citizen's Guide to Desegregation: A Study of Social and Legal Change in American Life* (1955). His articles have appeared in *Commentary, New Statesman and Nation, The Journal of Negro Education, The New Leader, Phylon, Midstream, Dissent,* and other publications. Mr. Hill is on the staff of the National Association for the Advancement of Colored People.

A Note on the Type

THIS BOOK is set in ELECTRA, a Linotype face designed by W. A. Dwiggins (1880-1956). This face cannot be classified as either modern or old-style. It is not based on any historical model, nor does it echo any particular period or style. It avoids the extreme contrasts between thick and thin elements that mark most modern faces, and attempts to give a feeling of fluidity, power, and speed.

Composed, printed, and bound by
The Haddon Craftsmen, Inc., Scranton, Pa.
Typography and binding design by

VINCENT TORRE